Hockey Scouting Report 1997-1998

SHERRY ROSS

GREY**S**TONE
BOOKS

Douglas & McIntyre
Vancouver/Toronto

To the little devil, Tyler Heath Ross.

Greystone Books
A division of Douglas & McIntyre Ltd.
1615 Venables Street
Vancouver, British Columbia V5L 2H1

Editing by Anne Rose and Kerry Banks
Cover design by Peter Cocking
Cover photograph of Paul Kariya by Bruce Bennett/Bruce Bennett Studios
Typesetting by MicroMega Designs
Printed and bound in Canada

The publisher gratefully acknowledges the assistance of the Canada Council for the Arts and of the British Columbia Ministry of Tourism, Small Business and Culture.

SHERRY ROSS

Yrs. of NHL service: 19
Born: Randolph, NJ
Position: in press box
Height: no way
Weight: you gotta be kidding
Uniform no.: DKNJ
Shoots: from the lip

LAST SEASON
Worked for *The New York Daily News* as a beat reporter, covering the New Jersey Devils.

THE FINESSE GAME
The versatile Ross began her career in 1978-79, covering the New York Rangers as they reached the Stanley Cup finals. In addition to working as a sportswriter for 16 years for various newspapers such as the *Bergen (N.J.) Record*, *Newsday* and *The National*, she became the NHL's first female team sportscaster in 1992 when she was hired as a colour commentator for the Devils' radio broadcasts on WABC-AM. In 1994, she was the first woman to call a major professional men's championship when she was the colour analyst for the NHL radio network in the Stanley Cup finals.

As a freelance writer, Ross has also contributed to *Sports Illustrated*, the *Hockey News*, and *Beckett Hockey Monthly*. She is the on-line correspondent for *The Sporting News*, and serves as the secretary-treasurer for the Professional Hockey Writers Association.

THE PHYSICAL GAME
Ross has demonstrated the endurance necessary to travel the full 82-game schedule, but she charges her batteries with trail rides on her horse, Cody, and frequent trips to Walt Disney World. She is a terrible skater.

THE INTANGIBLES
Although her hand-eye coordination may have diminished in recent years, her passion for the game keeps Ross from unplugging her laptop computer. She is rooting for an NHL franchise in Orlando.

ACKNOWLEDGEMENTS
Sunny days in June and July are spent talking, analyzing men who will be filling our winters in hockey rinks from San Jose to Ottawa, from Greensboro (welcome to the NHL, y'all) to Vancouver. Without the help of people to whom hockey is a year-round sport, this book would not be possible. These gentlemen — scouts, GMs, coaches, assistant coaches, and former and current players — are anonymous to the reader but never cease to amaze the author with their generosity and insight. Without them, the *Hockey Scouting Report* would cease to exist.

We hope you will like some of the changes in this year's edition, which for pool players includes a new "Projection" section that should let you know if a player is on his up or down swing. We hope we can help. We have continued to focus on young players who will be making an impact, as we did last year with players such as Jarome Iginla. That means a lot of old faithfuls, like Dale Hawerchuk and Jamie Macoun, had to be dropped from this year's edition to make way for the new.

On that note, there were three deletions that were painful to make. Mario Lemieux and Joe Mullen, two of the game's greats, will not be returning next season (Mullen's retirement was unofficial at press time) and they will be missed. And in the week after winning the Stanley Cup, Detroit defenseman Vladimir Konstantinov was seriously injured in an automobile accident. We join the rest of the hockey world in hoping for his complete recovery.

Thanks to my *Daily News* colleague Frank Brown for his help with this book and for his friendship, which manages to survive more crises than the N.Y. Islanders ownership. Andy McGowan of the NHL provided invaluable assistance all season, as have many of the NHL teams, but especially Mike Gilbert and Mike Levine of the New Jersey Devils, Ken Arnold and Roger Ross (no relation) of the San Jose Sharks, Ginger Killian of the N.Y. Islanders, John Rosasco and staff of the N.Y. Rangers, Mark Piazza of the Philadelphia Flyers and Donald Beauchamp of the Montreal Canadiens.

Thanks also to my computer guru Kelly Dresser, who has taught me the value of "pkzip," among other obscure (to this technophobe) minutiae, and to editors Kerry Banks and Anne Rose, who catch my many errors and who are true character players.

Thanks most of all to you readers, who have responded so favourably to the work all of the above have put into this series.

CONTENTS

Top 100 NHL Scorers 1

Anaheim Mighty Ducks 3

Boston Bruins....................................20

Buffalo Sabres 37

Calgary Flames 54

Carolina Hurricanes....................................71

Chicago Blackhawks....................................88

Colorado Avalanche 107

Dallas Stars....................................126

Detroit Red Wings 143

Edmonton Oilers 161

Florida Panthers....................................175

Los Angeles Kings 194

Montreal Canadiens....................................213

New Jersey Devils 231

New York Islanders 247

New York Rangers....................................264

Ottawa Senators....................................282

Philadelphia Flyers 301

Phoenix Coyotes....................................321

Pittsburgh Penguins....................................339

San Jose Sharks 354

St. Louis Blues 370

Tampa Bay Lightning....................................388

Toronto Maple Leafs 402

Vancouver Canucks....................................421

Washington Capitals....................................438

Player Index....................................458

TOP 100

NHL Scoring Statistics 1996-97

RANK	POS.	PLAYER	GP	G	A	PTS	+/-	PP	S	PCT
1.	C	MARIO LEMIEUX	76	50	72	122	27	15	327	15.3
2.	R	TEEMU SELANNE	78	51	58	109	28	11	273	18.7
3.	L	PAUL KARIYA	69	44	55	99	36	15	340	12.9
4.	L	JOHN LECLAIR	82	50	47	97	44	10	324	15.4
5.	C	WAYNE GRETZKY	82	25	72	97	12	6	286	8.7
6.	R	JAROMIR JAGR	63	47	48	95	22	11	234	20.1
7.	C	MATS SUNDIN	82	41	53	94	6	7	281	14.6
8.	R	ZIGMUND PALFFY	80	48	42	90	21	6	292	16.4
9.	C	RON FRANCIS	81	27	63	90	7	10	183	14.8
10.	L	BRENDAN SHANAHAN	81	47	41	88	32	20	336	14.0
11.	L	KEITH TKACHUK	81	52	34	86	-1	9	296	17.6
12.	C	PETER FORSBERG	65	28	58	86	31	5	188	14.9
13.	C	PIERRE TURGEON	78	26	59	85	8	5	216	12.0
14.	C	STEVE YZERMAN	81	22	63	85	22	8	232	9.5
15.	C	MARK MESSIER	71	36	48	84	12	7	227	15.9
16.	C	MIKE MODANO	80	35	48	83	43	9	291	12.0
17.	R	BRETT HULL	77	42	40	82	-9	12	302	13.9
18.	C	ADAM OATES	80	22	60	82	-5	3	160	13.8
19.	C	DOUG GILMOUR	81	22	60	82	2	4	143	15.4
20.	C	DOUG WEIGHT	80	21	61	82	1	4	235	8.9
21.	C	VINCENT DAMPHOUSSE	82	27	54	81	-6	7	244	11.1
22.	R	MARK RECCHI	82	34	46	80	-1	7	202	16.8
23.	C	ERIC LINDROS	52	32	47	79	31	9	198	16.2
24.	D	BRIAN LEETCH	82	20	58	78	31	9	256	7.8
25.	R	PETER BONDRA	77	46	31	77	7	10	314	14.6
26.	R	TONY AMONTE	81	41	36	77	35	9	266	15.4
27.	C	JOZEF STUMPEL	78	21	55	76	-22	6	168	12.5
28.	C	ALEXEI YASHIN	82	35	40	75	-7	10	291	12.0
29.	C	JOE SAKIC	65	22	52	74	-10	10	261	8.4
30.	R	ALEXANDER MOGILNY	76	31	42	73	9	7	174	17.8
31.	C	PETR NEDVED	74	33	38	71	-2	12	189	17.5
32.	R	DANIEL ALFREDSSON	76	24	47	71	5	11	247	9.7
33.	C	JEREMY ROENICK	72	29	40	69	-7	10	228	12.7
34.	L	MARTIN GELINAS	74	35	33	68	6	6	177	19.8
35.	D	SANDIS OZOLINSH	80	23	45	68	4	13	232	9.9
36.	L	GEOFF SANDERSON	82	36	31	67	-9	12	297	12.1
37.	R	THEOREN FLEURY	81	29	38	67	-12	9	336	8.6
38.	C	STEVE RUCCHIN	79	19	48	67	26	6	153	12.4
39.	L	VALERI KAMENSKY	68	28	38	66	5	8	165	17.0
40.	C	ANDREW CASSELS	81	22	44	66	-16	8	142	15.5
41.	C	TRAVIS GREEN	79	23	41	64	-5	10	177	13.0
42.	R	MIKE GARTNER	82	32	31	63	-11	13	271	11.8
43.	R	OWEN NOLAN	72	31	32	63	-19	10	225	13.8
44.	C	SERGEI FEDOROV	74	30	33	63	29	9	273	11.0
45.	C	CHRIS GRATTON	82	30	32	62	-28	9	230	13.0

GP = games played; G = goals; A = assists; PTS = points; +/- = goals-for minus goals-against while player is on ice; PP = power-play goals; S = no. of shots; PCT = percentage of goals to shots; * = rookie

RANK	POS.	PLAYER	GP	G	A	PTS	+/-	PP	S	PCT
46.	C	JEFF FRIESEN	82	28	34	62	-8	6	200	14.0
47.	C	BOBBY HOLIK	82	23	39	62	24	5	192	12.0
48.	C	ROBERT REICHEL	82	21	41	62	5	6	214	9.8
49.	C	ALEXEI ZHAMNOV	74	20	42	62	18	6	208	9.6
50.	L	RYAN SMYTH	82	39	22	61	-7	20	265	14.7
51.	L	ADAM GRAVES	82	33	28	61	10	10	269	12.3
52.	L	DAVE ANDREYCHUK	82	27	34	61	38	4	233	11.6
53.	R	DINO CICCARELLI	77	35	25	60	-11	12	229	15.3
54.	R	ADAM DEADMARSH	78	33	27	60	8	10	198	16.7
55.	R	RAY SHEPPARD	68	29	31	60	4	13	226	12.8
56.	C	DAVE GAGNER	82	27	33	60	2	9	228	11.8
57.	L	BRIAN SAVAGE	81	23	37	60	-14	5	219	10.5
58.	L	ANDREI KOVALENKO	74	32	27	59	-5	14	163	19.6
59.	L	ROD BRIND'AMOUR	82	27	32	59	2	8	205	13.2
60.	L	DEREK KING	82	26	33	59	-6	6	181	14.4
61.	R	MIKAEL RENBERG	77	22	37	59	36	1	249	8.8
62.	C	JASON ARNOTT	67	19	38	57	-21	10	248	7.7
63.	L	GEOFF COURTNALL	82	17	40	57	3	4	203	8.4
64.	D	NICKLAS LIDSTROM	79	15	42	57	11	8	214	7.0
65.	C	BRYAN SMOLINSKI	64	28	28	56	8	9	183	15.3
66.	R	SCOTT MELLANBY	82	27	29	56	7	9	221	12.2
67.	L	DIMITRI KHRISTICH	75	19	37	56	8	3	135	14.1
68.	C	SAKU KOIVU	50	17	39	56	7	5	135	12.6
69.	L	MARTIN RUCINSKY	70	28	27	55	1	6	172	16.3
70.	L	ED OLCZYK	79	25	30	55	-14	5	195	12.8
71.	R	PAVEL BURE	63	23	32	55	-14	4	265	8.7
72.	C	JOHN CULLEN	70	18	37	55	-14	5	116	15.5
73.	D	OLEG TVERDOVSKY	82	10	45	55	-5	3	144	6.9
74.	R	JOHN MACLEAN	80	29	25	54	11	5	254	11.4
75.	D	KEVIN HATCHER	80	15	39	54	11	9	199	7.5
76.	C	IGOR LARIONOV	64	12	42	54	31	2	95	12.6
77.	C	DEREK PLANTE	82	27	26	53	14	5	191	14.1
78.	R	PAT VERBEEK	81	17	36	53	3	5	172	9.9
79.	C	CRAIG JANNEY	77	15	38	53	-1	5	88	17.0
80.	L	NIKLAS SUNDSTROM	82	24	28	52	23	5	132	18.2
81.	L	GERMAN TITOV	79	22	30	52	-12	12	192	11.5
82.	C	MIKE RIDLEY	75	20	32	52	0	3	79	25.3
83.	D	DMITRI MIRONOV	77	13	39	52	16	3	177	7.3
84.	C	JOE NIEUWENDYK	66	30	21	51	-5	8	173	17.3
85.	C	KEITH PRIMEAU	75	26	25	51	-3	6	169	15.4
86.	R	ALEXANDRE DAIGLE	82	26	25	51	-33	4	203	12.8
87.	L	TED DONATO	67	25	26	51	-9	6	172	14.5
88.	C	BRIAN HOLZINGER	81	22	29	51	9	2	142	15.5
89.	C	CLIFF RONNING	69	19	32	51	-9	8	171	11.1
90.	R	DONALD AUDETTE	73	28	22	50	-6	8	182	15.4
91.	R	*JAROME IGINLA	82	21	29	50	-4	8	169	12.4
92.	D	RAY BOURQUE	62	19	31	50	-11	8	230	8.3
93.	L	ROB ZAMUNER	82	17	33	50	3		216	7.9
94.	L	WENDEL CLARK	65	30	19	49	-2	6	212	14.2
95.	L	MARTY MCINNIS	80	23	26	49	-8	5	182	12.6
96.	C	MICHAEL PECA	79	20	29	49	26	5	137	14.6
97.	C	STU BARNES	81	19	30	49	-23	5	176	10.8
98.	R	DARREN MCCARTY	68	19	30	49	14	5	171	11.1
99.	R	KEITH JONES	78	25	23	48	3	14	170	14.7
100.	L	LUC ROBITAILLE	69	24	24	48	16	5	200	12.0

GP = games played; G = goals; A = assists; PTS = points; +/- = goals-for minus goals-against while player is on ice; PP = power-play goals; S = no. of shots; PCT = percentage of goals to shots; * = rookie

ANAHEIM MIGHTY DUCKS

Players' Statistics 1996-97

POS.	NO.	PLAYER	GP	G	A	PTS	+/-	PIM	PP	SH	GW	GT	S	PCT
R	8	TEEMU SELANNE	78	51	58	109	28	34	11	1	8	2	273	18.7
L	9	PAUL KARIYA	69	44	55	99	36	6	15	3	10		340	12.9
C	20	STEVE RUCCHIN	79	19	48	67	26	24	6	1	2	1	153	12.4
D	15	DMITRI MIRONOV	77	13	39	52	16	101	3	1	2		177	7.3
C	17	JARI KURRI	82	13	22	35	-13	12	3		3		109	11.9
L	23	BRIAN BELLOWS	69	16	15	31	-15	22	8		1		168	9.5
C	12	KEVIN TODD	65	9	21	30	-7	44			1		95	9.5
R	14	JOE SACCO	77	12	17	29	1	35	1	1	2		131	9.2
D	36	J.J. DAIGNEAULT	66	5	23	28	0	58			1		62	8.1
D	29	*DARREN VAN IMPE	74	4	19	23	3	90	2				107	3.7
R	46	JEAN-FRANCOIS JOMPHE	64	7	14	21	-9	53		1			81	8.6
C	13	TED DRURY	73	9	9	18	-9	54	1		2	1	114	7.9
D	2	BOBBY DOLLAS	79	4	14	18	17	55	1		1	1	96	4.2
L	16	WARREN RYCHEL	70	10	7	17	6	218	1	1	1		59	16.9
C	54	*SEAN PRONGER	39	7	7	14	6	20	1		1	1	43	16.3
D	33	DAVE KARPA	69	2	11	13	11	210			1		90	2.2
L	22	KEN BAUMGARTNER	67		11	11	0	182					20	
D	28	JASON MARSHALL	73	1	9	10	6	140					34	2.9
C	24	MARK JANSSENS	66	2	6	8	-13	137					39	5.1
D	34	*DANIEL TREBIL	29	3	3	6	5	23					30	10.0
L	27	*MIKE LECLERC	5	1	1	2	2				1		3	33.3
C	32	RICHARD PARK	12	1	1	2	-1	10					10	10.0
R	11	VALERI KARPOV	9	1		1	-2	16					4	25.0
R	52	*PETER LEBOUTILLIER	23	1		1	0	121					5	20.0
D	26	*NIKOLAI TSULYGIN	22		1	1	-5	8					10	
D	5	*RUSLAN SALEI	30		1	1	-8	37					14	
G	31	GUY HEBERT	67		1	1	0	4						
G	1	MICHAEL O'NEILL	1				0							
L	42	BARRY NIECKAR	2				0	5						
R	39	*FRANK BANHAM	3				-2						1	
R	51	*CRAIG REICHERT	3				-2						3	
L	40	*JEREMY STEVENSON	5				-1	14					1	
D	25	ADRIAN PLAVSIC	6				-5	2					3	
L	19	SHAWN ANTOSKI	15				1	51					3	
G	35	M. SHTALENKOV	24				0	4						

GP = games played; G = goals; A = assists; PTS = points; +/- = goals-for minus goals-against while player is on ice; PIM = penalties in minutes; PP = power-play goals; SH = shorthanded goals; GW = game-winning goals; GT = game-tying goals; S = no. of shots; PCT = percentage of goals to shots; * = rookie

BRIAN BELLOWS

Yrs. of NHL service: 15
Born: St. Catharines, Ont.; Sept. 1, 1964
Position: left wing
Height: 5-11
Weight: 210
Uniform no.: 23
Shoots: left

Career statistics:

GP	G	A	TP	PIM
1101	462	515	977	686

1993-94 statistics:

GP	G	A	TP	+/-	PIM	PP	SH	GW	GT	S	PCT
77	33	38	71	+9	36	13	0	2	1	251	13.1

1994-95 statistics:

GP	G	A	TP	+/-	PIM	PP	SH	GW	GT	S	PCT
41	8	8	16	-7	8	1	0	1	0	110	7.3

1995-96 statistics:

GP	G	A	TP	+/-	PIM	PP	SH	GW	GT	S	PCT
79	23	26	49	-14	39	13	0	4	0	190	12.1

1996-97 statistics:

GP	G	A	TP	+/-	PIM	PP	SH	GW	GT	S	PCT
69	16	15	31	-15	22	8	0	1	0	168	9.5

PROJECTION

Bellows's days as a scoring leader are over, but he can chip in 45 to 50 points as a second-line forward and power-play specialist.

LAST SEASON

Acquired from Tampa Bay for 1997 sixth-round draft pick, November 18, 1996. Third on team in power-play goals. Missed five games with strained back.

THE FINESSE GAME

Although you won't notice him much in open ice, Bellows is scary around the net. A power-play specialist, he has great hands and instincts in deep. He is not as big as the prototypical power forward, but he plays that style in driving to the crease. He is nimble in traffic and can handle the puck in a scrum. He has good balance for scrapping in front. He works down low on the first power-play unit.

Bellows moves and shoots the puck quickly — he doesn't like to fool around with it. He has a strong one-timer and powerful wrist shot. Once in awhile he'll score from a drive off the wing, but most of his goals come from in close.

Bellows's five-on-five play improves when he is teamed with the kind of centre who will get the puck to him and who is defensively alert. Unfortunately for Bellows, the Ducks aren't very deep at centre.

THE PHYSICAL GAME

Bellows plays bigger than his size. He will bump and crash and work the boards in the offensive zone, but he is better as a finisher in front of the net. When he has the right linemate, he can focus on scoring.

THE INTANGIBLES

Bellows would be more effective if Anaheim could shore up its weakest position up the middle.

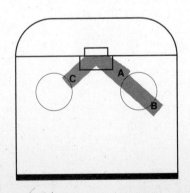

BOBBY DOLLAS

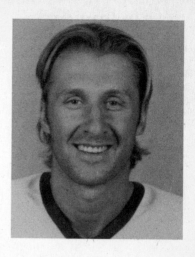

Yrs. of NHL service: 7
Born: Montreal, Que.; Jan. 31, 1965
Position: right defense
Height: 6-2
Weight: 212
Uniform no.: 2
Shoots: left

Career statistics:

GP	G	A	TP	PIM
453	34	74	108	312

1993-94 statistics:

GP	G	A	TP	+/-	PIM	PP	SH	GW	GT	S	PCT
77	9	11	20	+20	55	1	0	1	0	121	7.4

1994-95 statistics:

GP	G	A	TP	+/-	PIM	PP	SH	GW	GT	S	PCT
45	7	13	20	-3	12	3	1	1	0	70	10.0

1995-96 statistics:

GP	G	A	TP	+/-	PIM	PP	SH	GW	GT	S	PCT
82	8	22	30	+9	64	0	1	1	0	117	6.8

1996-97 statistics:

GP	G	A	TP	+/-	PIM	PP	SH	GW	GT	S	PCT
79	4	14	18	+17	55	1	0	1	1	96	4.2

LAST SEASON

Missed three games with chicken pox.

THE FINESSE GAME

Dollas is an excellent skater with speed, mobility and agility, and he's strong on his feet. He doesn't like to get involved too much in the offense, preferring to make a smart, quick pass to start a teammate off. He makes poised plays out of the defensive zone but has become more and more conservative.

Dollas gets a lot of ice time, and can handle it because he doesn't wear himself out racing up and down the ice. He takes the offensive chance when it's a high-percentage play, and he is skilled enough to handle point work on the second unit.

Dollas is being asked to be a number one defenseman, which is not his ideal slot, but until the Mighty Ducks acquire or develop a better defenseman, Dollas will do his best to handle the role. He has a strong shot from the point, but it takes him awhile to release it and more often than not the shot gets blocked.

THE PHYSICAL GAME

Because of his size, Dollas was thrust into the role of an enforcer with three different organizations. But he's not tough, doesn't like to fight, and he got an unfair label as a soft player when the Red Wings (his last club before Anaheim) accused him of shirking while he had a back injury.

The Mighty Ducks knew what they were getting and didn't ask anything more of Dollas than to play steady two-way hockey. That he does. He uses his size to tie up rather than rub out players around the net. He doesn't scare people but he won't be intimidated.

THE INTANGIBLES

Dollas is content in his role, and Anaheim seems happy with a defenseman who is a stabilizing force. The acquisition of Dmitri Mironov has at last given Dollas a strong offensive partner with whom to work.

PROJECTION

One of three original Mighty Ducks (with Guy Hebert and Joe Sacco), Dollas's contribution isn't measured in points.

TED DRURY

Yrs. of NHL service: 4
Born: Boston, Mass.; Sept. 13, 1971
Position: centre
Height: 6-0
Weight: 185
Uniform no.: 13
Shoots: left

Career statistics:

GP	G	A	TP	PIM
199	27	34	61	165

1993-94 statistics:

GP	G	A	TP	+/-	PIM	PP	SH	GW	GT	S	PCT
50	6	12	18	-15	36	0	1	1	1	80	7.5

1994-95 statistics:

GP	G	A	TP	+/-	PIM	PP	SH	GW	GT	S	PCT
34	3	6	9	-3	21	0	0	0	0	31	9.7

1995-96 statistics:

GP	G	A	TP	+/-	PIM	PP	SH	GW	GT	S	PCT
42	9	7	16	-19	54	1	0	1	1	80	11.3

1996-97 statistics:

GP	G	A	TP	+/-	PIM	PP	SH	GW	GT	S	PCT
73	9	9	18	-9	54	1	0	2	1	114	7.9

PROJECTION

Drury is still in the Mighty Ducks' plans as a third-liner, but because his offensive production is minimal, he'll be on the bubble if the team gets deeper.

LAST SEASON

Missed five games with fractured wrist.

THE FINESSE GAME

Drury is a cerebral player who is appreciated by coaches for his adaptability on the penalty kill. He sticks to the game plan. If a strong forecheck is needed, he provides it. If the team has to key on a special opponent, a Brett Hull or a Jaromir Jagr, Drury plays it the way it's drawn on the chalkboard. He can play centre or left wing as needed.

Drury is a shifty skater with decent speed. His forte is his passing ability. He isn't much of a finisher. He is an asset on the power play because of his effort and timing in moving the puck, and can stickhandle through traffic. He's a poor man's Craig Janney, but with better defensive instincts. He has superb hockey sense.

THE PHYSICAL GAME

Drury is underrated by opponents, who see a rather average-sized forward and underestimate his wiry strength. He plays a determined game to stay at the NHL level. Drury delivered the hit on Jeremy Roenick that injured (accidentally) Roenick's knee.

THE INTANGIBLES

Drury underwent a delicate surgical operation on his wrist two years ago that has robbed him of some of his strength and flexibility, but his hands were never his best feature anyway. His legs are, and he still has great wheels.

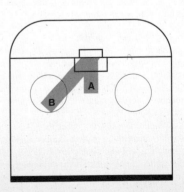

GUY HEBERT

Yrs. of NHL service: 5
Born: Troy, N.Y.; Jan. 7, 1967
Position: goaltender
Height: 5-11
Weight: 185
Uniform no.: 31
Catches: left

Career statistics:

GP	MIN	GA	SO	GAA	A	PIM
254	14220	689	13	2.91	2	16

1993-94 statistics:

GP	MIN	GAA	W	L	T	SO	GA	S	SAPCT	PIM
52	2991	2.83	20	27	3	2	141	1513	.907	2

1994-95 statistics:

GP	MIN	GAA	W	L	T	SO	GA	S	SAPCT	PIM
39	2092	3.13	12	20	4	2	109	1132	.904	2

1995-96 statistics:

GP	MIN	GAA	W	L	T	SO	GA	S	SAPCT	PIM
59	3326	2.83	28	23	5	4	157	1820	.914	6

1996-97 statistics:

GP	MIN	GAA	W	L	T	SO	GA	S	SAPCT	PIM
67	3863	2.67	29	25	12	4	172	2133	.919	4

LAST SEASON

Career high in wins. Career best in goals-against average. Tied for fifth in NHL in save percentage. Missed two games due to concussion. Missed three games due to fatigue.

THE PHYSICAL GAME

Hebert is technically solid. He squares himself to the shooter and combines good angle play with quick reflexes. He stands up well and doesn't get flustered when he sees a lot of shots. He deadens pucks with his pads and doesn't leave big rebounds. Hebert challenges shooters but falls into lapses of staying too deep in his net. When he does, he struggles.

He uses his stick effectively around the net to control rebounds and deflect passes, but he doesn't handle the puck aggressively outside his net. Hebert doesn't have to whip the puck up ice like Ron Hextall, but he should be secure enough to make little passes to avoid pressure and help his defensemen.

Hebert's lateral movement has gotten better. He takes away a lot of the net low and forces shooters to go high. Since he is a small goalie, shooters expect him to go down and scramble, but he stands his ground effectively. He allows very few soft goals.

Hebert wore down physically, starting 42 of 43 games from December 20 to March 28, and had to be benched due to fatigue.

THE MENTAL GAME

One of the best things to happen to Hebert last season was the addition of goalie coach Francois Allaire (Patrick Roy's goalie guru). Allaire helped Hebert sharpen his focus and improve his technique. Hebert is coachable and willing to work to correct his flaws. He's become a much more reliable goalie as a result.

THE INTANGIBLES

Some goalies who establish themselves with bad teams often can't handle the pressure when the team around them starts getting competitive. That isn't the case with Hebert, who has risen to the challenge. Unfortunately, he was hurt in the second round of the playoffs and we couldn't get a good read on him, but the signs were positive.

Hebert was a favourite of departed coach Ron Wilson, and how Hebert relates to his successor will bear watching.

PROJECTION

Assuming Anaheim gives Hebert a more reasonable work schedule next season (remember, he will probably go to Nagano as the number two goalie behind Mike Richter for the U.S. Olympic Team), Hebert will be in better shape down the stretch and into the playoffs.

PAUL KARIYA

Yrs. of NHL service: 3
Born: North Vancouver, B.C.; Oct. 16, 1974
Position: left wing
Height: 5-11
Weight: 175
Uniform no.: 9
Shoots: left

Career statistics:

GP	G	A	TP	PIM
198	112	134	246	30

1994-95 statistics:

GP	G	A	TP	+/-	PIM	PP	SH	GW	GT	S	PCT
47	18	21	39	-17	4	7	1	3	1	134	13.4

1995-96 statistics:

GP	G	A	TP	+/-	PIM	PP	SH	GW	GT	S	PCT
82	50	58	108	+9	20	20	3	9	0	349	14.3

1996-97 statistics:

GP	G	A	TP	+/-	PIM	PP	SH	GW	GT	S	PCT
69	44	55	99	+36	6	15	3	10	0	340	12.9

LAST SEASON

Won 1997 Lady Byng Trophy (second consecutive season). Finalist for Hart Trophy. Named to NHL First All-Star Team. Led NHL in game-winning goals and shots. Led team in shorthanded goals and plus-minus. Second on team in goals, assists and points. Missed 11 games with groin injury. Missed two games with concussion.

THE FINESSE GAME

Kariya may be the best skater in the NHL. He is so smooth and fluid his movements appear effortless. He's also explosive, with a good change of direction, and he can turn a defender inside out on a one-on-one rush. His speed is a weapon, since he forces defenders to play off him for fear of being burnt, and that opens the ice for his playmaking options. He combines his skating with no-look passes that are uncanny.

Teemu Selanne is the perfect linemate for him, because the Finnish Flash breaks as soon as he sees Kariya with control of the puck. Kariya puts on a burst of speed and can lift his pass over the sticks of defenders just ahead of Selanne for him to skate into. He uses his speed defensively, too, and is quick on the backcheck to break up passes. Kariya kills penalties by hounding the point men and pressuring them into bad passes, which he turns into scoring chances.

Kariya is smart; some would say cerebral. He is a magician with the puck and can make a play when it looks as if there are no possible options. He likes to use the net for protection, like his idol Wayne Gretzky, and make passes from behind the goal line. His release on his shot is excellent. Playing with the defensively alert Steve Rucchin gives Kariya and Selanne the freedom to make their breakout dashes, but Kariya never goes for high-risk plays when it might cost his team.

Kariya is a low maintenance superstar. He has worked on his weaknesses, becoming stronger on the puck, less fancy in his passing, and more willing to shoot. He is willing and able to carry a team on his back.

THE PHYSICAL GAME

Kariya added about 10 pounds of muscle coming into last season, and the weight helped him absorb some of the punishment he takes as a member of Anaheim's top (some might say only) line. He has powerful thighs and legs and has improved his upper body. He's gritty in his own way and plays through minor nicks, and major ones, without a whimper.

THE INTANGIBLES

It was tough to argue with Buffalo's Dominik Hasek as the league MVP, but when Kariya missed the first 11 games of the season with his groin injury, the Ducks went 1-8-2. Kariya proved to be as excellent a player in the playoffs as he is during the regular season. As the youngest captain in the NHL, Kariya has accepted the role as team spokesman and understands how he can contribute to promote the game he plays with such passion.

PROJECTION

As we said in last year's *HSR*, 50 goals and 100 points is the norm for Kariya (his prorated totals for last year were 52/117).

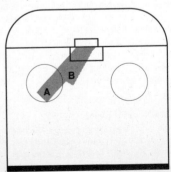

DAVE KARPA

Yrs. of NHL service: 4
Born: Regina, Sask.; May 7, 1971
Position: right defense
Height: 6-1
Weight: 202
Uniform no.: 33
Shoots: right

Career statistics:

GP	G	A	TP	PIM
245	11	45	56	746

1993-94 statistics:

GP	G	A	TP	+/-	PIM	PP	SH	GW	GT	S	PCT
60	5	12	17	0	148	2	0	0	0	48	10.4

1994-95 statistics:

GP	G	A	TP	+/-	PIM	PP	SH	GW	GT	S	PCT
28	1	5	6	-1	91	0	0	0	0	33	3.0

1995-96 statistics:

GP	G	A	TP	+/-	PIM	PP	SH	GW	GT	S	PCT
72	3	16	19	-3	270	0	1	1	0	62	4.8

1996-97 statistics:

GP	G	A	TP	+/-	PIM	PP	SH	GW	GT	S	PCT
69	2	11	13	+11	210	0	0	1	0	90	2.2

PROJECTION

Karpa has become a regular among the Ducks' top four defensemen and should be a sure bet for 200 penalty minutes.

LAST SEASON

Second on team in penalty minutes. Missed 12 games with fractured hand.

THE FINESSE GAME

Karpa's stock rose dramatically last season, as he has improved his skills to become a defensive regular and hasn't lost an iota of his aggravating, annoying, irritating (get the picture?) personality.

When He was toiling in the AHL years ago, Karpa's defensive skills were so lacking that in order to keep his size and aggression in the lineup, he played forward for Cornwall. But Karpa is learning the game and he is much less mistake-prone now.

His skating is adequate for strength and balance, but he's on the slow side. He masks it well with proper positioning. His reputation helps him defensively, too. He plays hard, and anyone skating in on him will play it safe, go outside, and just shoot or dump the puck. They know if they try to drive to the net on him he will make them pay the price with a check or a two-hander.

THE PHYSICAL GAME

Karpa is a physical veteran who plays with a natural snicker on his face. He is highly competitive and aggressive. He will fight anyone and although he doesn't always win his fights, he is game.

THE INTANGIBLES

There are a lot of teams who would love a Karpa on their side, but he is especially valuable to the Mighty Ducks, who have a lot of star finesse players who need bodyguards. He stands up for his teammates.

VALERI KARPOV

Yrs. of NHL service: 3
Born: Chelyabinsk, Russia; Aug. 5, 1971
Position: right wing
Height: 5-10
Weight: 190
Uniform no.: 11
Shoots: left

Career statistics:

GP	G	A	TP	PIM
76	14	15	29	32

1994-95 statistics:

GP	G	A	TP	+/-	PIM	PP	SH	GW	GT	S	PCT
30	4	7	11	-4	6	0	0	0	0	48	8.3

1995-96 statistics:

GP	G	A	TP	+/-	PIM	PP	SH	GW	GT	S	PCT
37	9	8	17	-1	10	0	0	1	0	42	21.4

1996-97 statistics:

GP	G	A	TP	+/-	PIM	PP	SH	GW	GT	S	PCT
9	1	0	1	-2	16	0	0	0	0	4	25.0

LAST SEASON

Scored 18-17 — 35 in 30 games with Long Beach (IHL). Scored 4-8 — 12 in 10 games with Baltimore (AHL). Missed eight games with postconcussion syndrome.

THE FINESSE GAME

Karpov is an above-average skater. He doesn't have outstanding breakaway speed, but he has a nice change of pace and handles the puck well. He has great hands. He goes to the net and gets his shots away quickly, more in the manner of Valeri Zelepukin than Pavel Bure.

Karpov plays with some grit when he has a mind to and creates chances with his quickness. He has the hand skills and clever shots to put his opportunities away. He has not exactly torn up the minor leagues in scoring, which isn't a promising sign.

THE PHYSICAL GAME

Karpov's size may hold him back, but he has gotten stronger since his draft year. He still doesn't have a great knack for handling physical play, and will try to play his game in open ice.

THE INTANGIBLES

Karpov is small and highly skilled, but he needs to try harder every night and needs to get stronger to compete in the NHL.

PROJECTION

Karpov is inconsistent and will probably get his last shot at a full-time job this year. The Mighty Ducks didn't use him in the playoffs.

MIKE LECLERC

Yrs. of NHL service: 0
Born: Winnipeg, Man.; Nov. 10, 1976
Position: left wing
Height: 6-1
Weight: 205
Uniform no.: 27
Shoots: left

Career statistics:

GP	G	A	TP	PIM
5	1	1	2	0

1996-97 statistics:

GP	G	A	TP	+/-	PIM	PP	SH	GW	GT	S	PCT
5	1	1	2	+2	0	0	0	0	0	3	33.3

LAST SEASON

Will be entering first NHL season. Third in scoring for Baltimore (AHL) with 29-27 — 56 in 71 games.

THE FINESSE GAME

Leclerc is a power forward in the making. His idol is Cam Neely, which is not a bad role model for a kid with size, touch and a bit of a temper, as Leclerc appears to have.

Leclerc has a long reach with a lot of power on his shot, which is accurate and quickly released. He is unselfish and will dish the puck off, though his coaches will want him to shoot. He has very good vision and is at his best in tight.

Leclerc is very defensively aware for a young player and works hard in all three zones. Skating is the only thing that might hold him back. He lacks quickness and acceleration, but has a long, strong stride once he gets in gear.

THE PHYSICAL GAME

Leclerc uses his body well. He matches up well against other teams' rugged forwards, because he's not awed by them and he's certainly not afraid to drop his gloves. He fights to get into the quality scoring zones around the net.

THE INTANGIBLES

Leclerc is intense and plays hard every night. He's a quiet kid and coachable, a good team player who will be an asset for years to come.

PROJECTION

Leclerc could be one of the sleepers of the season. A finesse-loaded team like the Mighty Ducks could use some power up front, and Leclerc projects as a number two left wing behind Paul Kariya. He's been a scorer at every level so far, and off what we saw last year, a 20-goal rookie season is in the offing.

DMITRI MIRONOV

Yrs. of NHL service: 5
Born: Moscow, Russia; Dec. 25, 1965
Position: left defense
Height: 6-3
Weight: 214
Uniform no.: 15
Shoots: right

Career statistics:

GP	G	A	TP	PIM
324	38	133	171	335

1993-94 statistics:

GP	G	A	TP	+/-	PIM	PP	SH	GW	GT	S	PCT
76	9	27	36	+5	78	3	0	0	2	147	6.1

1994-95 statistics:

GP	G	A	TP	+/-	PIM	PP	SH	GW	GT	S	PCT
33	5	12	17	+6	28	2	0	0	0	68	7.4

1995-96 statistics:

GP	G	A	TP	+/-	PIM	PP	SH	GW	GT	S	PCT
72	3	31	34	+19	88	1	0	1	1	86	3.5

1996-97 statistics:

GP	G	A	TP	+/-	PIM	PP	SH	GW	GT	S	PCT
77	13	39	52	+16	101	3	1	2	0	177	7.3

LAST SEASON

Acquired from Pittsburgh with Shawn Antoski for Alex Hicks and Fredrik Olausson, November 19, 1996. Led team defensemen in scoring with career high. Career high in goals and assists. Missed three games for personal reasons.

THE FINESSE GAME

The consistency that had been eluding Mironov was finally in evidence last season after his trade to Anaheim. Mironov loves to get involved in the attack, which makes him a natural for playing with the Paul Kariya-Teemu Selanne tandem.

Mironov can do phenomenal things with the puck. He understands the game well. He can shoot bullets, but is often reluctant to let fire. He can work the puck up the ice, handle the point on the power play, sees the ice well and is a good passer.

Mironov can be a bit of a risk factor in his own end. He can be beaten one-on-one and it helps him to play with a defensive defenseman, like Bobby Dollas or J. J. Daigneault.

THE PHYSICAL GAME

Mironov has a long reach and is big, but he plays soft and doesn't use either attribute to his best advantage. He gives up easily on plays in his own end. He likes to step up and challenge in the neutral zone, but doesn't take the body well and often lets the opponent get by him.

THE INTANGIBLES

Mironov was among the league's most surprising players last season. His numbers with Anaheim were an impressive 12-34 — 46 and +20 in 62 games. It's taken five seasons, but Mironov is finally living up to his potential, and we haven't seen his best yet.

PROJECTION

In last year's *HSR* we said, "If Mironov scored 55 or 60 points, a team could live with his flaws." Mironov finally made the step up offensively, and needs to make a similar commitment defensively.

SEAN PRONGER

Yrs. of NHL service: 1
Born: Dryden, Ont.; Nov. 30, 1972
Position: centre
Height: 6-2
Weight: 205
Uniform no.: 34
Shoots: left

Career statistics:

GP	G	A	TP	PIM
46	7	8	15	26

1995-96 statistics:

GP	G	A	TP	+/-	PIM	PP	SH	GW	GT	S	PCT
7	0	1	1	0	6	0	0	0	0	3	0.0

1996-97 statistics:

GP	G	A	TP	+/-	PIM	PP	SH	GW	GT	S	PCT
39	7	7	14	+6	20	1	0	1	1	43	16.3

Ducks this season on the checking line.

LAST SEASON

First NHL season. Missed two games with abdominal pull. Scored 26-17 — 43 in 41 games with Baltimore (AHL).

THE FINESSE GAME

The older brother of St. Louis defenseman Chris, Pronger was a polished "rookie" last season thanks to four full seasons in college and two and a half seasons in the minors. He has paid his dues, and his experience and his bloodline gave him a lot of confidence in his debut season.

Pronger has good size and reach, which helps compensate a little for his skating, which is just barely adequate for the NHL. Anaheim is a quick team, and playing him with slick skaters like Ted Drury and Joe Sacco helps.

He has decent hands for handling the puck or winning face-offs. And he has a hard and accurate shot. He moves the puck and sees the ice well, which helps him get some points, but his focus is still defensive. He also has to have a more consistent intensity level, which is a common defect in younger players and looks correctable.

THE PHYSICAL GAME

Pronger needs to be more physical. He is competitive and plays hard, but he has to use his body as well as his reach and be a bit more abrasive.

THE INTANGIBLES

Pronger is developing into a solid third-line centre. His numbers will never be very impressive. He was unfazed by the playoff pressure and carries himself like a pro.

PROJECTION

Pronger has been able to put up numbers in the minors but his skating will prevent him from doing much offensively at the NHL level. He figures to stick with the

STEVE RUCCHIN

Yrs. of NHL service: 3
Born: London, Ont.; July 4, 1971
Position: centre
Height: 6-3
Weight: 210
Uniform no.: 20
Shoots: left

Career statistics:

GP	G	A	TP	PIM
186	44	84	128	59

1994-95 statistics:

GP	G	A	TP	+/-	PIM	PP	SH	GW	GT	S	PCT
43	6	11	17	+7	23	0	0	1	0	59	10.2

1995-96 statistics:

GP	G	A	TP	+/-	PIM	PP	SH	GW	GT	S	PCT
64	19	25	44	+3	12	8	1	4	0	113	16.8

1996-97 statistics:

GP	G	A	TP	+/-	PIM	PP	SH	GW	GT	S	PCT
79	19	48	67	+26	24	6	1	2	1	153	12.4

LAST SEASON

Third on team in goals, assists, points and plus-minus. Games missed were coach's decision.

THE FINESSE GAME

Rucchin is more than just the safety valve for Paul Kariya and Teemu Selanne, though he certainly serves a valuable service in that capacity. Rucchin is just starting to get the idea that he can do much more, and he continues to improve as he pushes the envelope of his talent.

The role isn't easy for Rucchin, but he makes it look simple. First he has to concentrate on being back defensively. Then he has to rush to get into the play to get the puck to his linemates or give them some room to work. Since Rucchin was strictly a defensive centre in college, this has taken some adjusting over the years.

Rucchin is an intelligent, versatile player who came out of nowhere (OK, the University of Western Ontario) to win a job with the Mighty Ducks three seasons ago. A centre with good size and range, he was a bit in awe of the league at first. He has gotten over that.

Rucchin has good hockey sense that enables him to make the most of his above-average skating, passing and shooting skills. He grinds and digs the puck off the wall, and has the vision and the passing skills to find a breaking Kariya and Selanne. He is patient and protects the puck well.

THE PHYSICAL GAME

Rucchin can become a real force. He's strong and balanced, willing to forecheck hard and fight for the puck along the boards and in the corners. When he wins the puck, he's able to create a smart play with it. He has long arms and a long reach for holding off defenders and working the puck one-handed, or reaching in defensively to knock the puck away from an attacker.

Rucchin often matches up against other teams' big centres, such as Mark Messier. He plays hurt, as he did in the playoffs (separated shoulder).

THE INTANGIBLES

Rucchin was a healthy scratch three times early in the season, which may have had more to do with Paul Kariya's injury than Rucchin's ability. The Ducks are still working on Rucchin psychologically, so he will think of himself as more than a caddy for the big two.

PROJECTION

We said in last year's *HSR* that Rucchin would hit the 60- to 70- point range. Now, like the Ducks, we'll ask more of him. He can score 80 to 85 points and be a Selke Trophy contender.

JOE SACCO

Yrs. of NHL service: 6
Born: Medford, Mass.; Feb. 4, 1969
Position: left/right wing
Height: 6-1
Weight: 195
Uniform no.: 14
Shoots: right

Career statistics:

GP	G	A	TP	PIM
338	65	70	135	173

1993-94 statistics:

GP	G	A	TP	+/-	PIM	PP	SH	GW	GT	S	PCT
84	19	18	37	-11	61	3	1	2	1	206	9.2

1994-95 statistics:

GP	G	A	TP	+/-	PIM	PP	SH	GW	GT	S	PCT
41	10	8	18	-8	23	2	0	0	0	77	13.0

1995-96 statistics:

GP	G	A	TP	+/-	PIM	PP	SH	GW	GT	S	PCT
76	13	14	27	+1	40	1	2	2	1	132	9.8

1996-97 statistics:

GP	G	A	TP	+/-	PIM	PP	SH	GW	GT	S	PCT
77	12	17	29	+1	35	1	1	2	0	131	9.2

PROJECTION

Sacco will never score more than 15 to 20 goals a season, but there isn't a team in the NHL that can't use his wheels.

LAST SEASON

Missed five games with chest muscle strain.

THE FINESSE GAME

Sacco has third-line hands and second-line skating ability. A player can build a 10-year pro career with his speed. A left-handed shot, he plays primarily on his off-wing and scores most of his goals driving to the net from the right side. There is nothing creative or dazzling about his moves. He just goes full-tilt. When he does score, it's highlight material.

Sacco is not a great finisher. He loves to shoot but isn't always in the best spot to do so, and he doesn't have a quick release. If he learned to use his teammates better, such as finding an open man after he has forced the defense back, he would be a more dangerous threat, but he has tunnel vision with the puck. Basically, he's just not a very smart player, though he works very hard. When the game steps up a notch, you notice Sacco getting better.

He has never been a prolific scorer at the pro level (minors or NHL). He is solid defensively, good in his own zone and keeps the game simple.

THE PHYSICAL GAME

Sacco does not play an involved game physically. He has a decent size to at least bang around a bit, but is better with the puck than at trying to obtain it.

THE INTANGIBLES

Sacco's speed is an intimidating weapon that drives the defense back, but he doesn't have the finishing skills to be a more dangerous player.

RUSLAN SALEI

Yrs. of NHL service: 1
Born: Minsk, Belarus; Nov. 2, 1974
Position: left defense
Height: 6-1
Weight: 200
Uniform no.: 5
Shoots: left

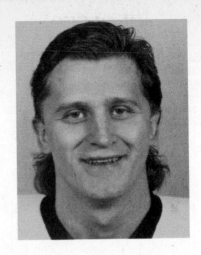

Career statistics:

GP	G	A	TP	PIM
30	0	1	1	37

1996-97 statistics:

GP	G	A	TP	+/-	PIM	PP	SH	GW	GT	S	PCT
30	0	1	1	-8	37	0	0	0	0	14	0.0

LAST SEASON

First NHL season. Scored 1-4 — 5 in 12 games with Baltimore (AHL). Scored 0-2 — 2 in eight games with Las Vegas (IHL).

THE FINESSE GAME

Salei is a fairly agile skater, but doesn't have great breakaway speed. He skates well backwards and is not easy to beat one-on-one.

His defensive reads are very good, and he can kill penalties. There is a possibility he could see time on a second power-play unit, because he moves the puck well and appears to have an NHL-calibre point shot. He shoots well off the pass and it's high velocity.

THE PHYSICAL GAME

Salei is mature and solidly built and he initiates a lot of contact. He is not afraid to hit anyone, and he has a little nasty streak that results in some cheap hits, but he can play it hard and clean, too.

THE INTANGIBLES

Salei has been a disappointment. He was expected to step into the Ducks' top six last year. He is still adjusting to North America and should get one more season's grace for that reason, but there were not many encouraging signs last year.

PROJECTION

The Mighty Ducks gambled in 1996 by taking the older Salei ninth overall out of the IHL instead of taking an 18-year-old prospect, and appear to have lost the gamble. Several other players have started to move past Salei on the depth chart. He will have to show something extra in training camp to win a job.

TEEMU SELANNE

Yrs. of NHL service: 5
Born: Helsinki, Finland; July 3, 1970
Position: right wing
Height: 6-0
Weight: 200
Uniform no.: 8
Shoots: right

Career statistics:

GP	G	A	TP	PIM
337	218	237	451	125

1993-94 statistics:

GP	G	A	TP	+/-	PIM	PP	SH	GW	GT	S	PCT
51	25	29	54	-23	22	11	0	2	0	191	13.1

1994-95 statistics:

GP	G	A	TP	+/-	PIM	PP	SH	GW	GT	S	PCT
45	22	26	48	+1	2	8	2	1	1	167	13.2

1995-96 statistics:

GP	G	A	TP	+/-	PIM	PP	SH	GW	GT	S	PCT
79	40	68	108	+5	22	9	1	5	0	267	15.0

1996-97 statistics:

GP	G	A	TP	+/-	PIM	PP	SH	GW	GT	S	PCT
78	51	58	109	+28	34	11	1	8	2	273	18.7

LAST SEASON

Named to NHL First All-Star Team. Finalist for 1997 Lady Byng Trophy. Second in NHL and led team in points. One of only two NHL players to score more than 100 points. Second in NHL and led team in goals. One of only four players in NHL to score 50 or more goals. Led team in assists and shooting percentage. Second on team in plus-minus, power-play goals, game-winning goals and shots. Missed four games with rib injury.

THE FINESSE GAME

Selanne is a better all-around player now than when he scored 76 goals in his rookie season in Winnipeg. Part of that is due to playing with the speedy, brainy Paul Kariya. But much credit is also due to the veteran Jari Kurri, who went from a sniper to one of the game's most underrated defensive forwards, and who has tutored Selanne.

Selanne has Porsche turbo speed. He gets down low and then simply explodes past defensemen, even when he starts from a standstill. He gets tremendous thrust from his legs and has quick feet. Acceleration, balance, change of gears, it's all there.

Everything you could ask for in a shot is there as well. Selanne employs all varieties of attacks and is equally comfortable on either wing. He plays off Kariya's puck control and exquisite lead passes. So often these two players will simply "alley oop" to the other with perfect timing, so that they receive the puck in full stride.

Selanne is constantly in motion. If his first attempt is stopped, he'll pursue the puck behind the net, make a pass and circle out again for a shot. He is almost impossible to catch and is tough to knock down because of his balance. He will set up on the off-wing on the power play and can score on the backhand. His shot is not especially hard, but it is quick and accurate.

Selanne doesn't just try to overpower with his skating, he also outwits opponents. He has tremendous hockey instincts and vision, and is as good a playmaker as a finisher. Selanne has a reputation for being selfish with the puck, but he is more generous with Kariya and feeds him for one-timers.

THE PHYSICAL GAME

Anaheim is pretty much a one-line team, so Kariya, Selanne and Steve Rucchin have to deal with checking pressure every night. Teams set out to bump and grind Selanne from the first shift, and he has fight his way through the junk. When the referees are slow on the whistle, he takes matters into his own hands, usually with his stick. He is one of the toughest young players in the league, European or otherwise. He is big and uses his strength along the wall.

THE INTANGIBLES

Selanne's career looked in doubt because of a severed Achilles' tendon two years ago, but he has overcome that to become one of the game's premier marksmen.

PROJECTION

Selanne is a consistent 50-goal, 100-point scorer.

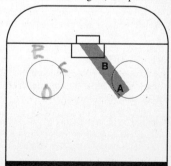

DANIEL TREBIL

Yrs. of NHL service: 1
Born: Edina, Minn.; Apr. 10, 1974
Position: right defense
Height: 6-3
Weight: 185
Uniform no.: 34
Shoots: right

Career statistics:

GP	G	A	TP	PIM
29	3	3	6	23

1996-97 statistics:

GP	G	A	TP	+/-	PIM	PP	SH	GW	GT	S	PCT
29	3	3	6	+5	23	0	0	0	0	30	10.0

LAST SEASON

First NHL season. Second among defensemen in scoring for Baltimore (AHL) with 4-20 — 24 in 49 games.

THE FINESSE GAME

The first thing you notice about Trebil is his poise with the puck. He is extremely calm and never seems to rush his play, always taking the extra half-stride, the extra half-second, to make the safe bank off the boards or to reach the redline to avoid an icing call. He is composed enough to handle defensive duties against other teams' top lines.

Trebil has good hockey sense and plays well positionally, using his tall, rangy frame to take up a lot of space, cut off the route to the net and generally act as a human roadblock. He needs a little more foot speed. He is not quick in his turns and has poor acceleration.

Trebil makes good decisions with and without the puck. He doesn't get involved offensively and won't get a lot of points.

THE PHYSICAL GAME

The trouble with Trebil is that he's not very physical or aggressive. He's not afraid, but he has decent size and he's just not punishing. He prefers to angle off his man and tie him up along the boards, but he could add a little more aggression. He's not afraid and he will play the body to make the play.

Trebil's father is a fitness expert, and his son is a prize pupil. He's strong and can handle a lot of ice time.

THE INTANGIBLES

Trebil moved ahead of first-round draft pick Ruslan Salei on the Mighty Ducks' defense depth chart last season and dressed for nine playoff games.

PROJECTION

Trebil isn't an exciting prospect, but he's a steady, safe defenseman who makes a nice complement to a more offensive-minded partner.

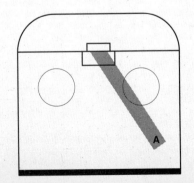

DARREN VAN IMPE

Yrs. of NHL service: 1
Born: Saskatoon, Sask.; May 18, 1973
Position: left defense
Height: 6-0
Weight: 195
Uniform no.: 29
Shoots: left

Career statistics:

GP	G	A	TP	PIM
91	5	22	27	104

1994-95 statistics:

GP	G	A	TP	+/-	PIM	PP	SH	GW	GT	S	PCT
1	0	1	1	-3	0	0	0	0	0	5	0.0

1995-96 statistics:

GP	G	A	TP	+/-	PIM	PP	SH	GW	GT	S	PCT
16	1	2	3	+8	14	0	0	1	0	13	7.7

1996-97 statistics:

GP	G	A	TP	+/-	PIM	PP	SH	GW	GT	S	PCT
74	4	19	23	+3	90	2	0	0	0	107	3.7

LAST SEASON
First NHL season.

THE FINESSE GAME
Van Impe's game needs polish in his decision-making process and reads, but this should come with more experience. Last season was his third year of pro, after spending the bulk of the previous two seasons in the minors. He's in obvious need of defensive coaching help.

Van Impe is a pretty decent stickhandler, but he will sometimes get caught carrying the puck into trouble instead of finding the safe play, and he has to learn to move the puck more quickly (he started doing this better at the end of the season and in the playoffs).

He's a good skater with a change of speed and is solid on his feet. He doesn't get involved much offensively.

THE PHYSICAL GAME
Van Impe isn't going to run you over, but he'll stand his ground and make you go through him. There isn't a mean streak in him, but he won't be intimidated, either. He wants to play in the NHL and he'll make it tough for you in his zone of the ice.

THE INTANGIBLES
Van Impe is an upbeat player who is well-liked by his teammates and coaches for his attitude and effort. He doesn't have much upside but he plays to the best of his abilities. He is the nephew of former NHLer Ed Van Impe.

PROJECTION
Van Impe stepped up last year to become one of Anaheim's starting six, and that's about as high as he'll go. He's not a top four defenseman, but is perfectly situated in a support role where he can produce 20 points a season.

BOSTON BRUINS

Players' Statistics 1996-97

POS.	NO.	PLAYER	GP	G	A	PTS	+/-	PIM	PP	SH	GW	GT	S	PCT
C	16	JOZEF STUMPEL	78	21	55	76	-22	14	6		1		168	12.5
L	21	TED DONATO	67	25	26	51	-9	37	6	2	2		172	14.5
D	77	RAY BOURQUE	62	19	31	50	-11	18	8	1	3	1	230	8.3
R	41	JASON ALLISON	72	8	26	34	-6	34	2		1		99	8.1
R	19	ROB DIMAIO	72	13	15	28	-21	82		3	2		152	8.6
D	32	DON SWEENEY	82	3	23	26	-5	39					113	2.7
R	23	STEVE HEINZE	30	17	8	25	-8	27	4	2	2		96	17.7
R	43	JEAN-YVES ROY	52	10	15	25	-8	22	2		1	1	100	10.0
L	42	TIM SWEENEY	36	10	11	21	0	14	2		2		65	15.4
R	27	*LANDON WILSON	49	8	12	20	-5	72					83	9.6
C	11	*ANSON CARTER	38	11	7	18	-7	9	2	1	2		79	13.9
R	33	SHELDON KENNEDY	56	8	10	18	-17	30		4			65	12.3
D	46	BARRY RICHTER	50	5	13	18	-7	32	1				79	6.3
L	65	BRETT HARKINS	44	4	14	18	-3	8	3		2		52	7.7
L	20	TODD ELIK	31	4	12	16	-12	16	1				72	5.6
R	36	JEFF ODGERS	80	7	8	15	-15	197	1		1		84	8.3
L	29	TROY MALLETTE	68	6	8	14	-8	155		2	1		61	9.8
D	18	KYLE MCLAREN	58	5	9	14	-9	54			1		68	7.4
R	45	SANDY MOGER	34	10	3	13	-12	45	3				54	18.5
D	47	*MATTIAS TIMANDER	41	1	8	9	-9	14				1	62	1.6
D	38	JON ROHLOFF	37	3	5	8	-14	31	1				69	4.3
C	25	TRENT MCCLEARY	59	3	5	8	-16	33			1		41	7.3
D	34	BOB BEERS	27	3	4	7	0	8	1				49	6.1
C	37	CLAYTON BEDDOES	21	1	2	3	-1	13					11	9.1
D	28	DEAN CHYNOWETH	57		3	3	-12	171					30	
D	14	*ANDERS MYRVOLD	9		2	2	-1	4					8	
L	49	*ANDRE ROY	10		2	2	-5	12					12	
D	62	*YEVGENY SHALDYBIN	3	1		1	-2						5	20.0
L	17	*DAVIS PAYNE	15		1	1	-4	7					8	
L	26	CAMERON STEWART	15		1	1	-2	4					21	
C	48	*RANDY ROBITAILLE	1			0								
G	31	TIM CHEVELDAE	2			0								
L	14	*KEVIN SAWYER	2			0								
G	1	*PAXTON SCHAFER	3			0								
L	40	*P.C. DROUIN	3			0	1						1	
C	52	DAVID EMMA	5			0	-1						3	
G	39	*SCOTT BAILEY	8			0								
G	35	*ROBBIE TALLAS	28			0								
D	44	DEAN MALKOC	33				-14	70					7	
G	30	JIM CAREY	59			0		2						

GP = games played; G = goals; A = assists; PTS = points; +/- = goals-for minus goals-against while player is on ice; PIM = penalties in minutes; PP = power-play goals; SH = shorthanded goals; GW = game-winning goals; GT = game-tying goals; S = no. of shots; PCT = percentage of goals to shots; * = rookie

RAY BOURQUE

Yrs. of NHL service: 18
Born: Montreal, Que.; Dec. 28, 1960
Position: right defense
Height: 5-11
Weight: 210
Uniform no.: 77
Shoots: left

Career statistics:

GP	G	A	TP	PIM
1290	362	1001	1363	953

1993-94 statistics:

GP	G	A	TP	+/-	PIM	PP	SH	GW	GT	S	PCT
72	20	71	91	+26	58	10	3	1	1	386	5.2

1994-95 statistics:

GP	G	A	TP	+/-	PIM	PP	SH	GW	GT	S	PCT
46	12	31	43	+3	20	9	0	2	0	210	5.7

1995-96 statistics:

GP	G	A	TP	+/-	PIM	PP	SH	GW	GT	S	PCT
82	20	62	82	+31	58	9	2	2	1	390	5.1

1996-97 statistics:

GP	G	A	TP	+/-	PIM	PP	SH	GW	GT	S	PCT
62	19	31	50	-11	18	8	1	3	1	230	8.3

LAST SEASON

Seventh among NHL defensemen and third on team in scoring. Led team in power-play goals, game-winning goals and shots. Second on team in assists. Missed nine games with shoulder injury. Missed three games with ankle injury. Missed eight games with abdominal injury.

THE FINESSE GAME

Bourque has tremendous defensive instincts, though his offensive skills usually get the headlines. His defensive reads are almost unmatched in the NHL, and he is an excellent transition player. He is not afraid to make the simple play, if it is the right one, instead of making a flashy play. If he is under pressure and his team is getting scrambly, Bourque is not too proud to simply flip the puck over the glass for a face-off.

As a passer, Bourque can go tape-to-tape as well as anybody in the NHL. He has the touch and the vision of a forward, and eagerly makes what for anyone else would be a low-percentage play, because his passes and skating are so sure.

Bourque is adept at keeping the puck in the zone at the point. He is a key performer on special-team units. On the point, he has a low, heavy shot with a crisp release. He is an excellent skater who will also shoot from mid-range with a handy snap shot, or in close with a wrist shot. He does not squander his scoring chances and is a precise shooter down low. Bourque is able to go top shelf to either corner, which few other defensemen, let alone forwards, can match. His impressive point totals would be even higher if he had played with a talented partner on the point, but for the most part it is has been all Bourque all these years.

Willing to lead a rush or jump up into the play, he is a balanced skater, with speed, agility and awesome balance. It takes a bulldozer to knock him off the puck.

THE PHYSICAL GAME

Bourque is single-minded in his approach to fitness. Only twice in his 17 seasons has he failed to play more than 60 games a season (and one of those was an asterisk year, the 1994-95 lockout). He is no perimeter player, either.

He plays a physical game when he has to. It's amazing what kind of punishment he has been able to absorb over the years, and last year's succession of nagging injuries was just the wear and tear catching up with him. He is not very big by today's standards for defensemen (or forwards, for that matter). Other teams try to eliminate him physically, and the Bruins superstar has paid a big price because of it.

THE INTANGIBLES

In last year's *HSR* we made note of Bourque's probable decline and added, "He could go down in league history as the best player never to win the Cup, and this season, he might not even make the playoffs." The Bruins failed to make the playoffs for the first time since 1966-67, and now that Bourque has signed a two-year contract extension to stay in Boston, the rest of the prediction will also come true. Loyalty is one thing, but does Bourque suffer from a fear of success?

PROJECTION

The Bruins should be marginally better under new coach Pat Burns. Bourque, at 38, will rebound slightly from last season, but we don't see more than 55 to 60 points.

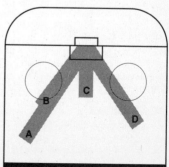

JIM CAREY

Yrs. of NHL service: 3
Born: Dorchester, Mass.; May 31, 1974
Position: goaltender
Height: 6-2
Weight: 205
Uniform no.: 30
Catches: left

Career statistics:

GP	MIN	GA	SO	GAA	A	PIM
158	8970	379	14	2.54	1	8

1994-95 statistics:

GP	MIN	GAA	W	L	T	SO	GA	S	SAPCT	PIM
28	1604	2.13	18	6	3	4	57	654	.913	0

1995-96 statistics:

GP	MIN	GAA	W	L	T	SO	GA	S	SAPCT	PIM
71	4069	2.26	35	24	9	9	153	1631	.906	6

1996-97 statistics:

GP	MIN	GAA	W	L	T	SO	GA	S	SAPCT	PIM
59	3297	3.08	22	31	3	1	169	1480	.886	2

LAST SEASON

Acquired from Washington with Anson Carter, Jason Allison, a 1997 third-round draft pick and a conditional draft pick in 1998 for Adam Oates, Bill Ranford and Rick Tocchet, March 1, 1997.

THE PHYSICAL GAME

We hate to say we told you so . . . no, we don't. We're pleased to say we saw this one coming and hope you were all paying attention last year.

Carey is a tremendous athlete with great reflexes but his game is riddled with flaws, the prominent one being his problem with lateral movement. Teams that play a strong east-west game against him and get him moving from post to post are able to pick him apart.

Carey is great straight on. If you come down the wing and blast he'll stop you. He's great in tight because of his dynamic reflexes. But Carey is a big man and doesn't look as big as he should in the net.

He is also very poor handling the puck, and creates his own problems when he is forced to do too much. Carey solves this by trying to do as little as possible outside his net. He is starting to use his stick better around the goal to break up plays, but he could also improve in this area.

THE MENTAL GAME

Carey will be asked to backstop a pretty weak young team, and his ego had to take a beating after last year, when he had to be pulled four times in 19 appearances with the Bruins.

THE INTANGIBLES

Can this goalie be saved? Only if the Bruins make a top-notch goalie coach an off-season priority. The Bruins have always skimped in this area in the past, but now that they've made a commitment to Pat Burns, he'll convince them of the need for a full-time goalie coach. Carey's flaws are fixable, and the fine-tuning can be done without ruining his strengths.

PROJECTION

We'll have to confess we've never been big Carey fans, and don't consider him among the NHL's top dozen goalies.

ANSON CARTER

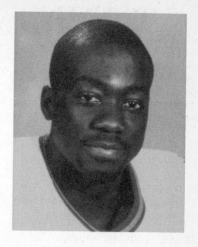

Yrs. of NHL service: 1
Born: Toronto, Ont.; June 6, 1974
Position: centre
Height: 6-1
Weight: 175
Uniform no.: 11
Shoots: right

Career statistics:

GP	G	A	TP	PIM
38	11	7	18	9

1996-97 statistics:

GP	G	A	TP	+/-	PIM	PP	SH	GW	GT	S	PCT
38	11	7	18	-7	9	2	1	2	0	79	13.9

LAST SEASON

Acquired from Washington with Jim Carey, Jason Allison, a third-round draft pick in 1997, and a conditional pick in 1998 for Adam Oates, Bill Ranford and Rick Tocchet, March 1, 1997. First NHL season. Scored 19-19 — 38 in 27 games with Portland (AHL).

THE FINESSE GAME

Carter has the highest upside of any of the young players acquired in the trade — including 1996 Vezina Trophy-winner Carey — and is probably the number two prospect in the entire organization after Joe Thornton.

Carter is a deceptive skater with a long, rangy, loping stride. He moves faster than he appears to be moving because he covers so much ground. But he isn't a bit awkward in turns. What really sets Carter apart is his hockey intelligence. He thinks the game well in all zones. He has very good hands and a good shot.

THE PHYSICAL GAME

A late bloomer physically, Carter still needs to add another 10 pounds, but he is not afraid to hit, not afraid to take a hit, and like Eric Lindros and Peter Forsberg, will make a preemptive hit while he's carrying the puck. He's not dirty or mean, just honestly tough. As one of the few blacks to make it to the NHL, you know he's mentally tough.

Carter played a full four years in college (Michigan State) and a year and a half in the minors before getting the full-time job with the Bruins after the trade. He should be a huge star in Boston.

PROJECTION

On one of the top teams in the league, Carter would be a good, hard, third-line player, but in Boston he will play on the top two lines and he will score. He'll probably be moved to the right wing, 22 to 25 minutes a game, and score 22 to 25 goals. It's a shame he went over the 25-game mark last season, or he would be a

Calder Trophy candidate.

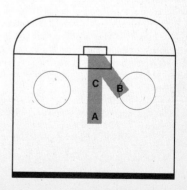

TED DONATO

Yrs. of NHL service: 5
Born: Dedham, Mass.; Apr. 28, 1969
Position: centre
Height: 5-10
Weight: 181
Uniform no.: 21
Shoots: left

Career statistics:

GP	G	A	TP	PIM
372	96	116	212	221

1993-94 statistics:

GP	G	A	TP	+/-	PIM	PP	SH	GW	GT	S	PCT
84	22	32	54	0	59	9	2	1	1	158	13.9

1994-95 statistics:

GP	G	A	TP	+/-	PIM	PP	SH	GW	GT	S	PCT
47	10	10	20	+3	10	1	0	1	0	71	14.1

1995-96 statistics:

GP	G	A	TP	+/-	PIM	PP	SH	GW	GT	S	PCT
82	23	26	49	+6	46	7	0	1	0	152	15.1

1996-97 statistics:

GP	G	A	TP	+/-	PIM	PP	SH	GW	GT	S	PCT
67	25	26	51	-9	37	6	2	2	0	172	14.5

LAST SEASON

Led team in goals with career high. Second on team in points. Tied for second on team in power-play goals. Missed two games with groin strain. Missed 13 games with broken finger.

THE FINESSE GAME

Donato is a small man who is able to survive in a big man's game because of his hockey sense. He is a good power-play man on the second unit. When Donato gets the chance, he can work down low or use a shot from the point.

Donato has always had the knack for scoring big goals at every level he has played. He scored the winning goal in the NCAA Championship game when Harvard beat Minnesota, and he scored the winning goal for his high school to win the championships in Massachusetts.

He is also a strong penalty killer, especially working with Steve Heinze (they were teammates with the U.S. Olympic team in 1992 and began killing penalties together then). He can thrive as a forward on the shorthanded team because opponents are more concerned about getting the puck than hitting, and he is usually in the middle part of the ice. He gets a lot of defensive assignments but creates offense with his anticipation.

Donato is like a quarterback, very aware of what is going on around him and always communicating with his teammates so they know what is going on, too. He has good hands and makes hard or soft passes as the occasion warrants.

THE PHYSICAL GAME

Donato is cunning and doesn't allow himself to get into situations where he's close to the boards and could get taken out. He is a very elusive skater. He can be outmuscled, but he hustles for the puck and often manages to keep it alive along the boards.

THE INTANGIBLES

Donato is a defensive forward thrust into a first-line role because of injuries and trades. He never quits.

PROJECTION

Donato exceeded our expectations for a second straight year. If he continues to get significant power-play time, he may top 20 goals again.

DAVE ELLETT

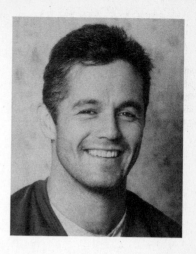

Yrs. of NHL service: 13
Born: Cleveland, Ohio; Mar. 30, 1964
Position: left defense
Height: 6-2
Weight: 205
Uniform no.: 2
Shoots: left

Career statistics:

GP	G	A	TP	PIM
941	148	381	529	881

1993-94 statistics:

GP	G	A	TP	+/-	PIM	PP	SH	GW	GT	S	PCT
68	7	36	43	+6	42	5	0	1	1	146	4.8

1994-95 statistics:

GP	G	A	TP	+/-	PIM	PP	SH	GW	GT	S	PCT
33	5	10	15	-6	26	3	0	1	0	84	6.0

1995-96 statistics:

GP	G	A	TP	+/-	PIM	PP	SH	GW	GT	S	PCT
80	3	19	22	-10	59	1	1	0	0	153	2.0

1996-97 statistics:

GP	G	A	TP	+/-	PIM	PP	SH	GW	GT	S	PCT
76	6	15	21	-6	40	1	0	2	0	105	5.7

LAST SEASON

Signed as free agent, July 1, 1997. Acquired by New Jersey from Toronto with Doug Gilmour for Jason Smith, Steve Sullivan and rights to Alyn McCauley, February 25, 1997. Missed one game with eye injury. Missed one game with bruised thigh.

THE FINESSE GAME

Ellett is a sound player for someone who was labelled as an offensive defenseman early in his career. He is used in all situations: power play, penalty killing, four-on-four, protecting a lead or helping his team come from behind.

His game has always been powered by his skating. He is a graceful mover, but in high tempo games looks dreadfully slow. Playing in the Devils' system at the end of the season protected him, but he will be more exposed on a weaker Bruins team. His lateral mobility is not great, which is why he's not an elite point man on the power play. He sometimes has trouble getting his shot through.

Ellett started using a shorter stick a few seasons ago and his shots were more accurate and more quickly released. His hand skills are fine, too, but instead of using his skills to jump into the offense at every opportunity, he conserves his energy for the defensive part of the ice. He understands the game and is aware of his importance to the team. He is not expected to go end to end, but instead to be steady and move the puck. He is a good passer with a soft touch, and uses his skills to get to the puck, get turned, make the first pass and watch the forwards go.

THE PHYSICAL GAME

Ellett uses his skills to keep himself out of physical situations. By getting to the puck and moving it briskly out of the corner, he can avoid getting crunched. He doesn't have a physical presence and doesn't clear out the front of his net as well as he should for a player of his size. He will tie up players with his long reach.

THE INTANGIBLES

Versatile and a good team player, the classy Ellett has developed into a solid two-way defenseman. He turned his considerable finesse skills to defense first and became a much better all-around defenseman.

PROJECTION

Ellett's 50-point seasons are far in the past, but he will probably get first-unit power-play time in Boston and get back up into the 30-point range.

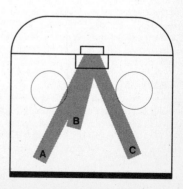

STEVE HEINZE

Yrs. of NHL service: 5
Born: Lawrence, Mass.; Jan. 30, 1970
Position: right wing
Height: 5-11
Weight: 193
Uniform no.: 23
Shoots: right

Career statistics:

GP	G	A	TP	PIM
306	71	57	128	155

1993-94 statistics:

GP	G	A	TP	+/-	PIM	PP	SH	GW	GT	S	PCT
77	10	11	21	-2	32	0	2	1	0	183	5.5

1994-95 statistics:

GP	G	A	TP	+/-	PIM	PP	SH	GW	GT	S	PCT
36	7	9	16	0	23	0	1	0	0	70	10.0

1995-96 statistics:

GP	G	A	TP	+/-	PIM	PP	SH	GW	GT	S	PCT
76	16	12	28	-3	43	0	1	3	0	129	12.4

1996-97 statistics:

GP	G	A	TP	+/-	PIM	PP	SH	GW	GT	S	PCT
30	17	8	25	-8	27	4	2	2	0	96	17.7

LAST SEASON

Missed 52 games with knee, hip, and groin injuries and abdominal surgery.

THE FINESSE GAME

Heinze's injuries were all the result of one collision in mid- December, just as he was well on his way to a career year. He easily had a career half-year.

Heinze is a traditional, grinding Bruins forward who skates up and down his wing. He has surprisingly good hands for a grinder, with a quick snap shot. He gets goals that go in off his legs, arms and elbows from his work in front of the net.

He's smart at trailing plays along the way and digging out loose pucks, which he either takes to the net himself or, more often, passes off.

Heinze has a good first step to the puck, which helps in his penalty killing as he forces the puck carrier. He was a big scorer at Boston College with David Emma and Marty McInnis (the HEM Line), but he succeeded at that level mainly because he was able to overpower people; he doesn't have that same edge in the pros. He plays an intelligent game and is a good playmaker with passing skills on his forehand and backhand.

THE PHYSICAL GAME

Heinze is hampered by his lack of size and strength. His probable future is as a third-line checking winger, but he doesn't have the power to line up against other teams' top power forwards. He is willing to get in the way and force people to go through him. The trouble is, they usually do.

THE INTANGIBLES

Heinze is another one of those moderately priced, moderately talented Bruins who work like a demon and, in Heinze's case, overachieve. His abdominal surgery was in March, so expect a slow first half.

PROJECTION

If Heinze is healthy, he'll get his ice time on the top two lines, even though he is ideally suited for the third.

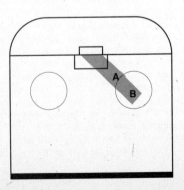

TRENT MCCLEARY

Yrs. of NHL service: 2
Born: Swift Current, Sask.; Oct. 10, 1972
Position: right wing
Height: 6-0
Weight: 180
Uniform no.: 25
Shoots: right

Career statistics:

GP	G	A	TP	PIM
134	7	15	22	101

1995-96 statistics:

GP	G	A	TP	+/-	PIM	PP	SH	GW	GT	S	PCT
75	4	10	14	-15	68	0	1	0	0	58	6.9

1996-97 statistics:

GP	G	A	TP	+/-	PIM	PP	SH	GW	GT	S	PCT
59	3	5	8	-16	33	0	0	1	0	41	7.3

LAST SEASON

Missed 18 games with knee sprain.

THE FINESSE GAME

Rough around the edges, McCleary is a less talented version of Dirk Graham or Mike Keane. He has good foot speed and is very strong along the wall. He needs to get stronger for his one-on-one battles, and he seems willing to work to improve. While he is not good enough to play on a first or second line, he has played with some skilled players, such as Geoff Sanderson in junior, and he complements better players as a safety valve. He doesn't do anything fancy, but if a team plays a dump-and-chase style he will excel.

McCleary is a dependable penalty killer. He is willing to learn and will adapt his style to follow the coaches' tactics.

THE PHYSICAL GAME

McCleary can't fight because of a detached retina, an injury that occurred in the minors, and he has to wear a tinted shield because of it. His vision is not a problem, but it's tough to be a tough guy and not be able to back it up with your fists, which McCleary would be willing to do.

THE INTANGIBLES

McCleary fits the mould of the grinding Bruins forward. He is a serviceable winger on the third or fourth line who can kill penalties because of his speed and hockey sense, but his production will be limited because his hand skills are average and he is not very creative.

PROJECTION

Even on a team as bad as the Bruins, McCleary is on the bubble, and will have to stand out in training camp to earn a role.

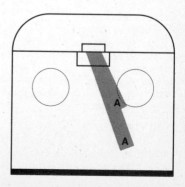

KYLE MCLAREN

Yrs. of NHL service: 2
Born: Humbolt, Sask.; June 18, 1977
Position: left defense
Height: 6-4
Weight: 210
Uniform no.: 18
Shoots: left

Career statistics:

GP	G	A	TP	PIM
132	10	21	31	127

1995-96 statisics:

GP	G	A	TP	+/-	PIM	PP	SH	GW	GT	S	PCT
74	5	12	17	+16	73	0	0	0	0	74	6.8

1996-97 statistics:

GP	G	A	TP	+/-	PIM	PP	SH	GW	GT	S	PCT
58	5	9	14	-9	54	0	0	1	0	68	7.4

LAST SEASON

Second NHL season. Missed 24 games with shoulder, thigh and thumb injuries.

THE FINESSE GAME

McLaren can play either right or left defense, and his advanced defensive reads allow him to adapt, which is very hard to do for a young player.

His puckhandling ability is much better than people give him credit for. He moves the puck out of the zone quickly and without panicking. He can rush with the puck or make the cautious bank off the boards to clear the zone if that is his best option.

McLaren is a very good penalty killer because he is fearless. He blocks shots and takes away passing lanes. He can also play on the power play, and probably will improve in this area because he plays heads-up and has a hard and accurate slap shot with a quick release. As he gains more confidence, he will become more of an offensive factor.

THE PHYSICAL GAME

McLaren has to play through people, but last year he seemed to lose his edge and started to get more free-wheeling and offensive. His shoulder problems last season might have made him a little timid. If he's not going to hit, Boston's defense is going to be worse than it was last year.

McLaren is tough and aggressive, but he doesn't go looking for fights and doesn't take foolish penalties. When he does get into a scrap, he can go toe-to-toe and has already earned some respect around the league as a player you don't want to tick off. He is strong on the puck, strong on the wall and doesn't allow loitering in front of his crease.

THE INTANGIBLES

Don't underestimate the effect that new coach Pat Burns will have in bringing McLaren back from what looked on paper like a step backwards from his rookie year. McLaren is still a kid who worked more on his strengths than his weaknesses, and he needs to be taken in hand to correct his bad on-ice habits.

PROJECTION

McLaren is a budding star; as Ray Bourque's career winds down, he could well step into the role as the Bruins' number one rearguard. After nearly a decade of first-round draft disasters (Dmitri Kvartalnov, anyone?), the Bruins have gotten one right. Expect a bounce-back season in the 30-point range.

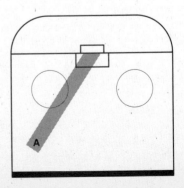

SANDY MOGER

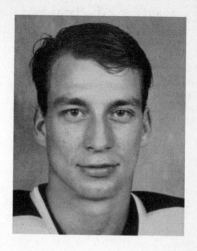

Yrs. of NHL service: 2
Born: Vernon, B.C.; Mar. 21, 1969
Position: left wing
Height: 6-3
Weight: 208
Uniform no.: 45
Shoots: right

Career statistics:

GP	G	A	TP	PIM
132	27	23	50	116

1994-95 statistics:

GP	G	A	TP	+/-	PIM	PP	SH	GW	GT	S	PCT
18	2	6	8	-1	6	2	0	0	0	32	6.3

1995-96 statistics:

GP	G	A	TP	+/-	PIM	PP	SH	GW	GT	S	PCT
80	15	14	29	-9	65	4	0	6	0	103	14.6

1996-97 statistics:

GP	G	A	TP	+/-	PIM	PP	SH	GW	GT	S	PCT
34	10	3	13	-12	45	3	0	0	0	54	18.5

LAST SEASON

Missed 25 games with fractured elbow and surgery. Missed 14 games with broken finger. Appeared in three conditioning games with Providence (AHL), scoring 0-2 — 2 with 19 penalty minutes.

THE FINESSE GAME

Moger has been described by one scout as a "poor man's Tim Kerr." Or maybe the poor Bruins' Cam Neely. The Bruins should be so lucky. Moger has a big body and he thrives on the power play. He has an excellent release on his shot and sharp hand-eye coordination for deflecting pucks.

Moger has good hockey sense and, in addition to his gifts around the net, is very reliable killing penalties in his own end. He knows when to back off and protect the front of the net.

His downside is his foot speed. Moger is a marginal NHL skater but his diligence gets him where he has to go. He is well balanced on his skates for battles in the crease.

THE PHYSICAL GAME

Moger is a fearless, dangerous hitter. Injuries slowed him down last season, but we don't expect any long-term effects. He is not afraid of taking abuse and will compete for any loose puck. He's a bit of a stringbean and he could use some bulking up. He needs to get stronger because he does the dirty work in the trenches.

THE INTANGIBLES

Moger has made himself into an NHL player. Signed as a free agent by the Bruins in 1994, he was targeted as a career minor leaguer but has shown the desire to play in the bigs. He has an excellent work ethic and will probably get plenty of ice time again this season to improve himself.

PROJECTION

The Bruins are weak on the right side, and Moger should get time on the top two lines with a chance at 25 to 30 goals if he can stay intact this season. About a third of his goals will be on the power play.

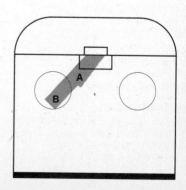

JEFF ODGERS

Yrs. of NHL service: 6
Born: Spy Hill, Sask.; May 31, 1969
Position: right wing
Height: 6-0
Weight: 195
Uniform no.: 36
Shoots: right

Career statistics:

GP	G	A	TP	PIM
414	55	42	97	1198

1993-94 statistics:

GP	G	A	TP	+/-	PIM	PP	SH	GW	GT	S	PCT
81	13	8	21	-13	222	7	0	0	1	73	17.8

1994-95 statistics:

GP	G	A	TP	+/-	PIM	PP	SH	GW	GT	S	PCT
48	4	3	7	-8	117	0	0	1	0	47	8.5

1995-96 statistics:

GP	G	A	TP	+/-	PIM	PP	SH	GW	GT	S	PCT
78	12	4	16	-4	192	0	0	1	1	84	14.3

1996-97 statistics:

GP	G	A	TP	+/-	PIM	PP	SH	GW	GT	S	PCT
80	7	8	15	-15	197	1	0	1	0	84	8.3

PROJECTION

Ideally, Odgers is a third-line winger. He won't score much more than 10 to 15 goals a season.

LAST SEASON

Led Bruins in penalty minutes.

THE FINESSE GAME

Odgers is a meat-and-potatoes skater. He patrols up and down his wing with diligence, if not much style or creativity. Any scoring opportunities he generates come from his hard work off the forecheck.

He lacks the hands skills and the vision to be much of a playmaker, but anyone playing with him is wise to follow in his wake because he churns up a lot of loose pucks. And he's smart enough to play as a safety valve on a line with better offensive talent. He drops back to cover high if the other winger and/or the defensemen move deep into the attacking zone.

Odgers has some good speed and balance, but only if he's travelling in a straight line without the puck. He lacks mobility and agility, though effort can compensate for a lot of finesse shortcomings.

THE PHYSICAL GAME

Odgers takes the body and plays tough. He loves to forecheck and finds it a special challenge to outwit goalies who are strong stickhandlers, getting in on top of them quickly to try to force a bad pass. He takes a lot of aggressive penalties, though he has cut down on the bad penalties that hurt his team.

THE INTANGIBLES

Odgers is one of those lunchpail types the Bruins prize so much. He adds toughness and leadership to the team and tries to fill in at any role.

JON ROHLOFF

Yrs. of NHL service: 3
Born: Mankato, Minn.; Oct. 3, 1969
Position: right defense
Height: 5-11
Weight: 220
Uniform no.: 38
Shoots: right

Career statistics:

GP	G	A	TP	PIM
150	7	25	32	129

1994-95 statistics:

GP	G	A	TP	+/-	PIM	PP	SH	GW	GT	S	PCT
34	3	8	11	+1	39	0	0	1	1	51	5.9

1995-96 statistics:

GP	G	A	TP	+/-	PIM	PP	SH	GW	GT	S	PCT
79	1	12	13	-8	59	1	0	0	0	106	0.9

1996-97 statistics:

GP	G	A	TP	+/-	PIM	PP	SH	GW	GT	S	PCT
37	3	5	8	-14	31	1	0	0	0	69	4.3

PROJECTION

Rohloff's groin injury is a bit of a concern. He's good for 15 to 20 points in a two-way role if healthy.

LAST SEASON

Missed 23 games with groin injury. Missed seven games with ankle injury. Played three conditioning games with Providence (AHL), scoring 1-1 — 2.

THE FINESSE GAME

Rohloff has a mature, polished game. He is good enough to play on his off side, which is something few defensemen can handle. We have probably already seen the best he has to offer, which is a number six defenseman's role with some spot play in offensive situations, like a second-unit power play.

Rohloff has a big shot. He has to develop more confidence in his shooting and scoring ability, though. He is also a smart passer. He can skate or move the puck out of his own end. His finesse skills are good enough that the desperate Bruins moved him up to forward for several games last season.

THE PHYSICAL GAME

Rohloff's groin injury is common to players rehabbing from major knee surgery, since a player tends to favor one leg, and that is what happened to Rohloff last season. He is a fine skater and defends well one-on-one. He eliminates the body effectively and does a great job in his own end taking away space. He competes every night, every shift, but his game has its limitations.

THE INTANGIBLES

Rohloff is not that gifted an offensive defenseman, though the Bruins tried to shoehorn him into that role. He is on his way to becoming a solid two-way defenseman but not one who will be on the ice at critical moments.

JOZEF STUMPEL

Yrs. of NHL service: 4
Born: Nitra, Czechoslavkia; June 20, 1972
Position: centre/right wing
Height: 6-1
Weight: 208
Uniform no.: 16
Shoots: right

Career statistics:

GP	G	A	TP	PIM
274	54	122	176	54

1993-94 statistics:

GP	G	A	TP	+/-	PIM	PP	SH	GW	GT	S	PCT
59	8	15	23	+4	14	0	0	1	0	62	12.9

1994-95 statistics:

GP	G	A	TP	+/-	PIM	PP	SH	GW	GT	S	PCT
44	5	13	18	+4	8	1	0	2	0	46	10.9

1995-96 statistics:

GP	G	A	TP	+/-	PIM	PP	SH	GW	GT	S	PCT
76	18	36	54	-8	14	5	0	2	0	158	11.4

1996-97 statistics:

GP	G	A	TP	+/-	PIM	PP	SH	GW	GT	S	PCT
78	21	55	76	-22	14	6	0	1	0	168	12.5

LAST SEASON

Led team in assists and points with career highs. Second on team in goals with career high. Tied for second on team in power-play goals. Missed four games with injuries.

THE FINESSE GAME

Despite his limited game, Stumpel made the most of the ice time given to him as a number two centre. Asking him to become a number one after the trade of Adam Oates was simply asking too much, and Stumpel could drop back to the second line if number one draft pick Joe Thornton has a halfway decent camp.

On a deeper team, Stumpel's lack of skating speed would drop him down farther on the depth chart. He has good hand skills, which allow him to compensate for his skating up to a point. He also has a deft scoring touch and is a passer with a good short game.

Stumpel has keen hockey sense and is still adjusting to a full-time role. Given more time on the power play he could respond to the responsibility, but he will never be a front-line player, because of his skating.

THE PHYSICAL GAME

Stumpel is not an overly physical player and can be intimidated. He goes into the corners and bumps and protects the puck with his body, but when the action gets really fierce he backs off.

THE INTANGIBLES

If the Bruins can be just a little bit stronger, Stumpel will either lose ice time (not likely — they're not going to improve that fast) or benefit from playing with a slightly better cast (more likely). But he's at about the top of his game now. Don't expect drastic improvement.

PROJECTION

Despite the extra ice time, we don't see him scoring many more than 20 goals, though his assist total should be 40 to 50 again.

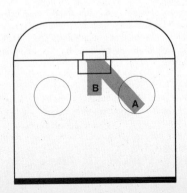

MIKE SULLIVAN

Yrs. of NHL service: 6
Born: Marshfield, Mass.; Feb. 27, 1968
Position: centre
Height: 6-2
Weight: 190
Uniform no.: 32
Shoots: left

Career statistics:

GP	G	A	TP	PIM
376	36	49	85	103

1993-94 statistics:

GP	G	A	TP	+/-	PIM	PP	SH	GW	GT	S	PCT
45	4	5	9	-1	10	0	2	1	0	48	8.3

1994-95 statistics:

GP	G	A	TP	+/-	PIM	PP	SH	GW	GT	S	PCT
38	4	7	11	-2	14	0	0	2	0	31	12.9

1995-96 statistics:

GP	G	A	TP	+/-	PIM	PP	SH	GW	GT	S	PCT
81	9	12	21	-6	24	0	1	1	1	106	8.5

1996-97 statistics:

GP	G	A	TP	+/-	PIM	PP	SH	GW	GT	S	PCT
67	5	6	11	-11	10	0	3	2	0	64	7.8

Don't underestimate the hometown boy factor (he played for Boston University).

LAST SEASON

Acquired by Boston for a sixth-round draft pick, June 21, 1997. Missed two games with back spasms.

THE FINESSE GAME

Speed, speed, speed. Sullivan is one of the flat-out fastest skaters in the league, but doesn't possess the hand skills to do much damage offensively. He is so much faster without the puck than with it.

Sullivan works hard and forechecks energetically. But his decision-making process is slow and he can't do much with the puck even when he forces a turnover. He can be asked to shadow some of the quickest forwards in the league.

He is effective killing penalties because of his speed and effort, and is fairly good on face-offs. He is able to bend low (he is a rather tall player) and tie up the opposing centre's stick.

THE PHYSICAL GAME

Sullivan does not play the body well. Considering his size, he would be much more effective if he got involved. He could just flatten people because of his momentum, but he avoids contact.

THE INTANGIBLES

Sullivan is a blur when he is skimming impressively all over the ice, but he is not the asset he could be because of his bad hands. He's a poor man's Shawn McEachern.

PROJECTION

Sullivan is on the move again, off the ice, that is. He could provide 20 points with regular playing time.

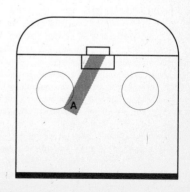

DON SWEENEY

Yrs. of NHL service: 9
Born: St. Stephen, N.B.; Aug. 17, 1966
Position: left defense
Height: 5-10
Weight: 188
Uniform no.: 32
Shoots: left

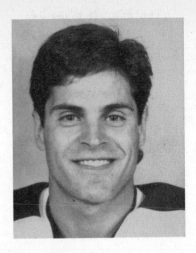

Career statistics:

GP	G	A	TP	PIM
611	40	142	182	442

1993-94 statistics:

GP	G	A	TP	+/-	PIM	PP	SH	GW	GT	S	PCT
75	6	15	21	+29	50	1	2	2	0	136	4.4

1994-95 statistics:

GP	G	A	TP	+/-	PIM	PP	SH	GW	GT	S	PCT
47	3	19	22	+6	24	1	0	2	0	102	2.9

1995-96 statistics:

GP	G	A	TP	+/-	PIM	PP	SH	GW	GT	S	PCT
77	4	24	28	-4	42	2	0	3	0	142	2.8

1996-97 statistics:

GP	G	A	TP	+/-	PIM	PP	SH	GW	GT	S	PCT
82	3	23	26	-5	39	0	0	0	0	113	2.7

LAST SEASON

Only Bruin to appear in all 82 games.

THE FINESSE GAME

Sweeney has found a niche for himself in the NHL. He's mobile, physical and greatly improved in the area of defensive reads. He has good hockey sense for recognizing offensive situations as well.

He mostly stays at home and out of trouble, but he is a good enough skater to get involved in the attack and take advantage of open ice. He is a good passer and has an adequate shot, and he has developed more confidence in his skills. He skates his way out of trouble and moves the puck well.

Sweeney is also an intelligent player who knows his strengths and weaknesses. He didn't get much playing time in his first two seasons in Boston, but, despite being a low draft pick (166th overall), he wouldn't let anyone overlook him.

THE PHYSICAL GAME

Sweeney is built like a little human Coke machine. He is tough to play against, and while wear and tear is a factor, he never hides. He is always in the middle of physical play. He utilizes his lower-body drive and has tremendous leg power. He is also shifty enough to avoid a big hit when he sees it coming, and many a large forechecking forward has sheepishly picked himself up off the ice after Sweeney has scampered away from the boards with the puck.

Sweeney is the ultimate gym rat, devoting a great deal of time to weightlifting and overall conditioning. Pound for pound, he is one of the strongest defensemen in the NHL.

THE INTANGIBLES

Sweeney is highly competitive. Despite his small size, a lot of teams would welcome him on their blueline.

PROJECTION

Sweeney remains one of Boson's top three defensemen, but his point totals won't go much higher than 25.

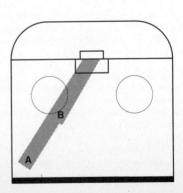

JOE THORNTON

Yrs. of NHL service: 0
Born: London, Ont.; July 2, 1979
Position: centre
Height: 6-4
Weight: 198
Uniform no.: n.a.
Shoots: left

Career junior statistics:

GP	G	A	TP	PIM
125	71	127	198	176

1996-97 junior statistics:

GP	G	A	TP	PIM
59	41	81	122	123

LAST SEASON

Will be entering first NHL season. Drafted first over-all by Boston in 1997 Entry Draft. Second in league and led Sault Ste. Marie (OHL) in scoring with 41-81 — 122 and 123 penalty minutes in 59 games. Scored 11-8 — 19 in 11 OHL playoff games.

THE FINESSE GAME

Imagine a bigger, angrier Wayne Gretzky, and you've got the summation of the scouting reports on Thornton's junior career. Heck, Thornton even played for the same junior team that Gretzky (briefly) did.

The first thing you notice about Thornton is his size, but his key asset will be instantly recognizable in his first game. He has exceptional vision of the ice and the hand skills to make things happen. All the tools, and the toolbox, too.

Thornton is so good at finding holes and passing lanes that teammates will have to be exceptionally alert when playing with him, because he will create something out of nothing. He loves to shoot, as well, and works the boards, corners and front of the net.

Thornton's skating could use some improvement, but it's NHL calibre.

THE PHYSICAL GAME

Like Eric Lindros, another big forward to whom he has been compared, Thornton will find it a rough gauntlet to run in his first NHL season. He has a short fuse and can be goaded off his game. Unless the Bruins can get a dominant physical winger (Landon Wilson, if he gets his act together) to put on a line with Thornton, this prize pick will be spending entirely too much time in the box.

Thornton is still filling out and could add another 10 to 12 pounds by training camp.

THE INTANGIBLES

No one's been labelled this much of a "can't-miss" since Lindros. Thornton appears levelheaded enough to handle the pressure and scrutiny, and he'll have the classy Ray Bourque to guide him.

PROJECTION

The number one centre's job is his in Boston. Might as well give him the Calder Trophy, too. Lindros scored 75 points in his first year, which sounds about right for Thornton to shoot for.

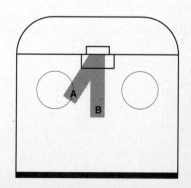

LANDON WILSON

Yrs. of NHL service: 1
Born: St. Louis, Mo; Mar. 13, 1975
Position: right wing
Height: 6-2
Weight: 202
Uniform no.: 27
Shoots: right

Career statistics:

GP	G	A	TP	PIM
56	9	12	21	78

1995-96 statistics:

GP	G	A	TP	+/-	PIM	PP	SH	GW	GT	S	PCT
7	1	0	1	+3	6	0	0	0	0	6	16.7

1996-97 statistics:

GP	G	A	TP	+/-	PIM	PP	SH	GW	GT	S	PCT
49	8	12	20	-5	72	0	0	0	0	83	9.6

LAST SEASON

First NHL season. Acquired from Colorado with Anders Myrvold for 1998 first-round draft pick, November 22, 1996. Missed 22 games with shoulder and thigh injuries. Played two conditioning games with Providence (AHL), scoring 2-1 — 3.

THE FINESSE GAME

A fine all-around athlete with good stamina, Wilson has developed a variety of shots. He can stickhandle around a defender and release a quick snap shot, or he can unload a powerful slap shot from the top of the circles. He has keen offensive instincts, and he's a finisher.

He doesn't have blazing speed, but he has good anticipation that buys him a step in a race. He powers his way to the net with the puck or in pursuit of a rebound. Wilson has decent hands, and on Boston he doesn't have to beat out a lot of people to play with some of the better players on the Bruins.

THE PHYSICAL GAME

The only way Wilson is going to be an NHL player is if he uses his body and finishes his checks. There are some question marks about his intensity, and he doesn't want to be a physical player all the time. Wilson is big, solidly built and strong on his skates. He competes for the puck in the high-traffic areas. He has not been able to dominate games in the pros the way he did as a younger player.

THE INTANGIBLES

Wilson went from a team (Colorado) where he could barely buy a shift, to a team (Boston) that is desperate for his services. He couldn't make up his mind between football and hockey when he was growing up. Now he has to make the decision to be an NHL player. The fact that the Avalanche gave up on this inexpensive young player when they have a lot of fat contracts coming up is a bad sign.

PROJECTION

A job on one of the top two lines is his if Wilson steps up. He needs to score 20 to 25 goals to stick.

BUFFALO SABRES

Players' Statistics 1996-97

POS.	NO.	PLAYER	GP	G	A	PTS	+/-	PIM	PP	SH	GW	GT	S	PCT
C	26	DEREK PLANTE	82	27	26	53	14	24	5		6	1	191	14.1
C	19	BRIAN HOLZINGER	81	22	29	51	9	54	2	2	6		142	15.5
R	28	DONALD AUDETTE	73	28	22	50	-6	48	8		5	1	182	15.4
C	27	MICHAEL PECA	79	20	29	49	26	80	5	6	4		137	14.6
R	17	JASON DAWE	81	22	26	48	14	32	4	1	3		136	16.2
R	15	DIXON WARD	79	13	32	45	17	36	1	2	4		93	14.0
R	36	MATTHEW BARNABY	68	19	24	43	16	249	2		1		121	15.7
L	81	MIROSLAV SATAN	76	25	13	38	-3	26	7		3		119	21.0
D	3	GARRY GALLEY	71	4	34	38	10	102	1	1	1		84	4.8
L	18	MICHAL GROSEK	82	15	21	36	25	71	1		2	1	117	12.8
D	44	ALEXEI ZHITNIK	80	7	28	35	10	95	3	1		1	170	4.1
L	12	RANDY BURRIDGE	55	10	21	31	17	20	1	3			85	11.8
D	42	RICHARD SMEHLIK	62	11	19	30	19	43	2		1		100	11.0
D	8	DARRYL SHANNON	82	4	19	23	23	112	1		1		94	4.3
D	4	MIKE WILSON	77	2	9	11	13	51			1		57	3.5
R	32	ROB RAY	82	7	3	10	3	286			1		45	15.6
D	74	*JAY MCKEE	43	1	9	10	3	35					29	3.4
C	16	PAT LAFONTAINE	13	2	6	8	-8	4	1				38	5.3
D	6	BOB BOUGHNER	77	1	7	8	12	225					34	2.9
C	37	*CURTIS BROWN	28	4	3	7	4	18			1		31	12.9
L	10	BRAD MAY	42	3	4	7	-8	106	1		1		75	4.0
C	93	ANATOLI SEMENOV	25	2	4	6	-3	2	1		1		21	9.5
C	76	*WAYNE PRIMEAU	45	2	4	6	-2	64	1				25	8.0
R	5	ED RONAN	18	1	4	5	4	11					10	10.0
G	39	DOMINIK HASEK	67		3	3	0	30						
D	22	CHARLIE HUDDY	1				-1							
D	40	*RUMUN NDUR	2				1	2						
G	30	ANDREI TREFILOV	3				0							
L	25	*VACLAV VARADA	5				0	2					2	
G	31	*STEVE SHIELDS	13				0	4						

GP = games played; G = goals; A = assists; PTS = points; +/- = goals-for minus goals-against while player is on ice; PIM = penalties in minutes; PP = power-play goals; SH = shorthanded goals; GW = game-winning goals; GT = game-tying goals; S = no. of shots; PCT = percentage of goals to shots; * = rookie

DONALD AUDETTE

Yrs. of NHL service: 6
Born: Laval, Que.; Sept. 23, 1969
Position: right wing
Height: 5-8
Weight: 175
Uniform no.: 28
Shoots: right

Career statistics:

GP	G	A	TP	PIM
334	140	105	245	264

1993-94 statistics:

GP	G	A	TP	+/-	PIM	PP	SH	GW	GT	S	PCT
77	29	30	59	+2	41	16	1	4	0	207	14.0

1994-95 statistics:

GP	G	A	TP	+/-	PIM	PP	SH	GW	GT	S	PCT
46	24	13	37	-3	27	13	0	7	0	124	19.4

1995-96 statistics:

GP	G	A	TP	+/-	PIM	PP	SH	GW	GT	S	PCT
23	12	13	25	0	18	8	0	1	0	92	13.0

1996-97 statistics:

GP	G	A	TP	+/-	PIM	PP	SH	GW	GT	S	PCT
73	28	22	50	-6	48	8	0	5	1	182	15.4

LAST SEASON

Led team in goals and power-play goals. Third on team in points and game-winning goals. Missed five games with groin injury. Missed three games recovering from knee surgery. Missed one game with food poisoning.

THE FINESSE GAME

Audette rebounded well from his reconstructive knee surgery in January 1997. It usually takes a full year for a player to come back from such an operation, which means if all goes well, Audette should hit his best stride in midseason. He is a bustling forward who barrels to the net at every opportunity. He is eager and feisty down low and has good hand skills. He also has keen scoring instincts, along with the quickness to make good things happen. His feet move so fast (with a choppy stride) that he doesn't look graceful, but he can really get moving and he has good balance.

A scorer first, Audette has a great top-shelf shot, which he gets away quickly and accurately. He can also make a play, but he will do this at the start of a rush. Once he is inside the offensive zone and low, he wants the puck. His selfishness can be forgiven, considering his scoring touch.

Audette is at his best on the power play. He is smart enough not to just stand around and take his punishment. He times his jumps into the space between the left post and the bottom of the left circle.

THE PHYSICAL GAME

Opponents hate Audette, which he takes as a great compliment. He runs goalies, yaps and takes dives — then goes out and scores on the power play after the opposition takes a bad penalty.

He will forecheck and scrap for the puck but isn't as diligent coming back. He's not very big, but around the net he plays like he's at least a six-footer. He keeps jabbing and working away until he is bowled over by an angry defender.

THE INTANGIBLES

Audette lacks size but not heart. He loves a challenge, which the rehabilitation of his knee was. He played the first half of last season on adrenaline, wore down at the end of the year with no goals in his last six games, but had a decent playoffs.

PROJECTION

Audette's maximum production is around 60 points.

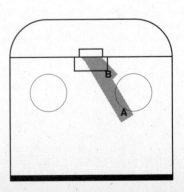

MATTHEW BARNABY

Yrs. of NHL service: 4
Born: Ottawa, Ont.; May 4, 1973
Position: right wing
Height: 6-0
Weight: 170
Uniform no.: 36
Shoots: left

Career statistics:

GP	G	A	TP	PIM
201	38	45	83	816

1993-94 statistics:

GP	G	A	TP	+/-	PIM	PP	SH	GW	GT	S	PCT
35	2	4	6	-7	106	1	0	0	0	13	15.4

1994-95 statistics:

GP	G	A	TP	+/-	PIM	PP	SH	GW	GT	S	PCT
23	1	1	2	-2	116	0	0	0	0	27	3.7

1995-96 statistics:

GP	G	A	TP	+/-	PIM	PP	SH	GW	GT	S	PCT
73	15	16	31	-2	335	0	0	0	0	131	11.5

1996-97 statistics:

GP	G	A	TP	+/-	PIM	PP	SH	GW	GT	S	PCT
68	19	24	43	+16	249	2	0	1	0	121	15.7

LAST SEASON

Second on team in penalty minutes. Career high in points. Missed five games in contract holdout. Missed four games with knee injury.

THE FINESSE GAME

Barnaby's offensive skills are minimal. He gets some room because of his reputation, and that buys him a little time around the net to get a shot away. He is utterly fearless and dives right into the thick of the action going for loose pucks.

But no one hires Barnaby for his scoring touch. His game is marked by his fierce intensity. He hits anyone, but especially loves going after the other team's big names. He is infuriating.

He skates well enough not to look out of place and is strong and balanced on his feet. He will do anything to win. If he could develop a better scoring touch he would start reminding people of Dale Hunter.

THE PHYSICAL GAME

Barnaby brings a lot of energy to the game; considering his size, it's a wonder he survived the season. He has to do some cheap stuff to survive, which makes him an even more irritating opponent. Big guys especially hate it, because it's a no-win when a Bob Probert or Randy McKay takes on the poor underdog Barnaby, but he's so obnoxious they just can't help it.

THE INTANGIBLES

Barnaby is the Sabres' emotional leader, and losing him just before the playoffs hurt Buffalo's chances of accomplishing much in the postseason (of course, Dominik Hasek's injury had a lot to do with it, too).

He has worked hard to step up his skill level and become a more useful everyday player. He can do even more. Not all gunslingers can handle this role, but Barnaby appears to thrive on it. Now he just needs to develop the same confidence in other parts of his game.

PROJECTION

His 200 penalty minutes are a sure thing. We're not so sure about 50 to 55 points, but Barnaby is improving every season, so why not?

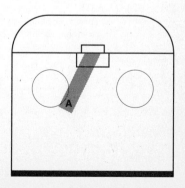

JASON DAWE

Yrs. of NHL service: 4
Born: North York, Ont.; May 29, 1973
Position: left wing
Height: 5-10
Weight: 195
Uniform no.: 17
Shoots: left

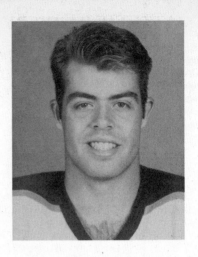

Career statistics:

GP	G	A	TP	PIM
222	60	62	122	96

1993-94 statistics:

GP	G	A	TP	+/-	PIM	PP	SH	GW	GT	S	PCT
32	6	7	13	+1	12	3	0	1	0	35	17.1

1994-95 statistics:

GP	G	A	TP	+/-	PIM	PP	SH	GW	GT	S	PCT
42	7	4	11	-6	19	0	1	2	0	51	13.7

1995-96 statistics:

GP	G	A	TP	+/-	PIM	PP	SH	GW	GT	S	PCT
67	25	25	50	-8	33	8	1	0	2	130	19.2

1996-97 statistics:

GP	G	A	TP	+/-	PIM	PP	SH	GW	GT	S	PCT
81	22	26	48	+14	32	4	1	3	0	136	16.2

LAST SEASON

Fourth on team in points.

THE FINESSE GAME

Dawe missed training camp in a contract dispute and took a long time getting his game untracked, with only nine goals in the first half of the season. He is a skill player with the added element of being an eager forechecker. He is also intelligent enough to trail into the play if he is being used with faster forwards who are less alert defensively.

Dawe has a quick release on his shot, usually from the top of the left circle in. He has the good sense to read the play and knows when to back off and support the defense as the third man high.

Dawe is a good skater with a fluid stride and good balance. He's shifty and handles the puck well at high tempo (though he isn't much of a one-on-one threat) and in traffic. He is very effective on the power play.

THE PHYSICAL GAME

Dawe is willing to do the grunt work for his line. He's not big, but he is stocky and strong and will bang people off the puck. He is a diligent backchecker and has an aggressive streak.

THE INTANGIBLES

Dawe's lack of size is always an issue, and his season was compromised by missing training camp.

PROJECTION

Dawe is just one of the many smallish, 50-point scorers on the Sabres.

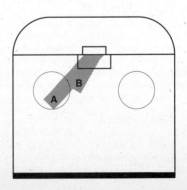

MICHAL GROSEK

Yrs. of NHL service: 3
Born: Vszkov, Czechoslovakia; June 1, 1975
Position: left wing
Height: 6-2
Weight: 296
Uniform no.: 18
Shoots: right

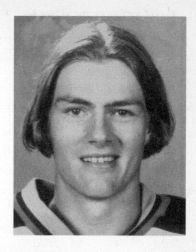

Career statistics:

GP	G	A	TP	PIM
132	24	27	51	123

1993-94 statistics:

GP	G	A	TP	+/-	PIM	PP	SH	GW	GT	S	PCT
3	1	0	1	-1	0	0	0	0	0	4	25.0

1994-95 statistics:

GP	G	A	TP	+/-	PIM	PP	SH	GW	GT	S	PCT
24	2	2	4	-3	21	0	0	1	0	27	7.4

1995-96 statistics:

GP	G	A	TP	+/-	PIM	PP	SH	GW	GT	S	PCT
23	6	4	10	-1	31	2	0	1	1	34	17.6

1996-97 statistics:

GP	G	A	TP	+/-	PIM	PP	SH	GW	GT	S	PCT
82	15	21	36	+25	71	1	0	2	1	117	12.8

LAST SEASON

Second on team in plus-minus. One of four Sabres to appear in all 82 games.

THE FINESSE GAME

Maddeningly inconsistent, Grosek has an array of NHL-calibre skills at his disposal but doesn't always have the inclination to use them. He is still very young and has an eagerness to succeed at the NHL level. He is an excellent stickhandler, and he can be absolutely magical with the puck. He is good enough to play his off-wing (left) as well as the right. He doesn't have a great shot, but he intimidates with his speed and drives to the net. With more confidence, his release may improve.

Grosek is a bundle of talent whose first shot at an NHL job was derailed by two serious injuries. He uses his speed and size to create some room and he is genuinely tough.

Defensively, Grosek's game has improved, largely from getting to play with Mike Peca. If only Peca's work ethic would rub off as well.

THE PHYSICAL GAME

Grosek has gotten bigger and stronger. He can be a little undisciplined, but once he's given a responsible role he plays more intelligently. In the past, he has always had to fight for ice time. Once he started feeling more comfortable, his all-around game improved. He's inconsistent in his gritty play but when he sticks his nose in and plays hard, he is an impact player.

THE INTANGIBLES

Grosek came up empty down the stretch (no goals in the last 12 games) and had a quiet playoffs, neither of which are promising signs.

PROJECTION

Grosek fell well below our expectations of 25 goals for last season. He has the skills to do it. We don't know if he has the desire. Maybe the coaching change in Buffalo will be the key.

DOMINIK HASEK

Yrs. of NHL service: 6
Born: Pardubice, Czech.; Jan. 29, 1965
Position: goaltender
Height: 5-11
Weight: 168
Uniform no.: 39
Catches: left

Career statistics:

GP	MIN	GA	SO	GAA	A	PIM
278	15866	635	20	2.40	7	52

1993-94 statistics:

GP	MIN	GAA	W	L	T	SO	GA	S	SAPCT	PIM
58	3358	1.95	30	20	6	7	109	1552	.930	6

1994-95 statistics:

GP	MIN	GAA	W	L	T	SO	GA	S	SAPCT	PIM
41	2416	2.11	19	14	7	5	85	1221	.930	2

1995-96 statistics:

GP	MIN	GAA	W	L	T	SO	GA	S	SAPCT	PIM
59	3417	2.83	22	30	6	2	161	2011	.920	6

1996-97 statistics:

GP	MIN	GAA	W	L	T	SO	GA	S	SAPCT	PIM
67	4037	2.27	37	20	10	5	153	2177	.930	30

LAST SEASON

Won 1997 Hart Trophy and Vezina Trophy. Named to First NHL All-Star Team. Fourth in NHL in goals-against average. Led NHL in save percentage. Tied for second in NHL in wins with career high. Missed eight games with fractured ribs.

THE PHYSICAL GAME

The Sabres were 2-6-0 when Hasek was out with his rib injury in mid-March, and 4-6 without him when he was sidelined by a knee injury and suspension in the playoffs. MVP? You bet. Without him, the Sabres not only would have failed to win the Northeast Division regular-season title, but would have been in a battle to even make the playoffs.

Nobody has worse technique nor better leg reflexes than Hasek. His foot speed is simply tremendous. He wanders and flops and sprawls. But he stops the puck. Usually what Hasek sees, he stops, and to him the puck seems to be moving more slowly than it does for other goalies. He watches it come off the shooter's stick into his glove or body, and he always seems in control, even while he looks to be flopping like a trout.

He is adept at directing his rebounds away from onrushing attackers. He prefers to hold pucks for face-offs, and the Sabres have a decent corps of centres so that tactic works fine for his team. Hasek instructs his defensemen to get out of the way so he can see the puck, and they follow orders.

Hasek learned to come out of his net a little bit more but he still doesn't cut down his angles well. He also has to work on his puckhandling. He has the sin-gle most bizarre habit of any NHL goalie we've seen in recent years. In scrambles around the net, he abandons his stick entirely and grabs the puck with his blocker hand. His work with the stick is brutal, which may be why he lets go of it so often.

THE MENTAL GAME

On the ice, Hasek is competitive and unflappable. He is always prepared for tough saves early in a game, and has very few lapses of concentration. His excitable style doesn't bother his teammates, who have developed faith in his ability.

THE INTANGIBLES

Now the heat is on. First Hasek assaulted a writer during the playoffs, and his feud with coach-of-the-year Ted Nolan was a factor in the popular coach leaving Buffalo (this after Nolan won his own power struggle with GM John Muckler). Like Brett Hull and Mark Messier before him, Hasek will have to stand and deliver again this year.

PROJECTION

There's not much more Hasek can do other than win games singlehandedly, which he did for most of last season and will continue to try to do behind an unimproved Sabres team this season.

BRIAN HOLZINGER

Yrs. of NHL service: 2
Born: Parma, Ohio; Oct. 10, 1972
Position: centre
Height: 5-11
Weight: 180
Uniform no.: 19
Shoots: right

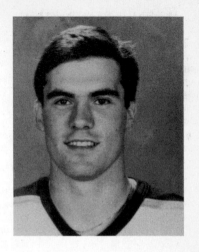

Career statistics:

GP	G	A	TP	PIM
143	32	42	74	91

1994-95 statistics:

GP	G	A	TP	+/-	PIM	PP	SH	GW	GT	S	PCT
4	0	3	3	+2	0	0	0	0	0	3	0.0

1995-96 statistics:

GP	G	A	TP	+/-	PIM	PP	SH	GW	GT	S	PCT
58	10	10	20	-21	37	5	0	1	0	71	14.1

1996-97 statistics:

GP	G	A	TP	+/-	PIM	PP	SH	GW	GT	S	PCT
81	22	29	51	+9	54	2	2	6	0	142	15.5

LAST SEASON

Tied for team lead in game-winning goals. Second on team in points. Tied for second on team in assists.

THE FINESSE GAME

Holzinger has a fine touch down low and patience with the puck to find the open passing lane. He needs to work with a grinder on one wing, because he is too small to do much effective work in the corners. He isn't quite as gritty as teammate Pat LaFontaine, nor does he have the latter's speed. He is more like Neal Broten (a former Hobey Baker winner, like Holzinger), crafty and deceptively quick.

Holzinger is not a natural scorer but he has some speed, which he can learn to use to his advantage.

The key to Holzinger's development will be adding the little things to his game that make a complete player. He has to ask himself how he can contribute if he's not scoring. He can play, but can he win? He has a lot of raw talent, but at the moment he's an open-ice break player. He has a lot of hockey sense and may be adaptable. His defense has improved.

THE PHYSICAL GAME

Holzinger will have to work for his open ice in the NHL. He is not very big, nor very strong. Strength and conditioning work must figure in his summer vacation plans again.

THE INTANGIBLES

LaFontaine's injury opened a door for Holzinger to seize the second-line centre's role, but if LaFontaine comes back, it will be tough finding a spot for him.

PROJECTION

Holzinger's 51 points exceeded expectations, and to match that this season he'll need to earn the ice time.

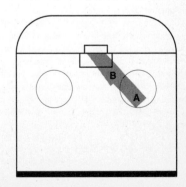

PAT LAFONTAINE

Yrs. of NHL service: 13
Born: St. Louis, Mo.; Feb. 22, 1963
Position: centre
Height: 5-10
Weight: 180
Uniform no.: 16
Shoots: right

Career statistics:

GP	G	A	TP	PIM
798	445	506	951	539

1993-94 statistics:

GP	G	A	TP	+/-	PIM	PP	SH	GW	GT	S	PCT
16	5	13	18	-4	2	1	0	0	0	40	12.5

1994-95 statistics:

GP	G	A	TP	+/-	PIM	PP	SH	GW	GT	S	PCT
22	12	15	27	+2	4	6	1	3	1	54	22.2

1995-96 statistics:

GP	G	A	TP	+/-	PIM	PP	SH	GW	GT	S	PCT
76	40	51	91	-8	36	15	3	7	1	224	17.9

1996-97 statistics:

GP	G	A	TP	+/-	PIM	PP	SH	GW	GT	S	PCT
13	2	6	8	-8	4	1	0	0	0	38	5.3

LAST SEASON
Missed 69 games with postconcussion syndrome.

THE FINESSE GAME
If LaFontaine were a baseball player, he would be like the midget Bill Veeck once sent up to the plate. With LaFontaine's skating crouch, there is no strike zone. He's a ball of fire on the ice, low to the ground and almost impossible to catch or knock off stride. He gears up in the defensive zone and simply explodes.

Inexhaustible, he is double-shifted almost every night and doesn't miss a call. Nor does he float: he's like a shark, always circling and in motion. He has great quickness and acceleration, with deep edges for turns. Few players can get as many dekes into a short stretch of ice at high speed as LaFontaine does when he is bearing down on a goalie. His favourite move is "patented" but still almost unstoppable. He streaks in, moves the puck to his backhand, then strides right with the puck on his forehand. A goalie's only hope is for LaFontaine to lose control. Slim chance.

LaFontaine takes almost all of the Sabres' offensive-zone draws. He has quick hands and after winning the draw will burst past the opposing centre to the net. On the power play, LaFontaine likes to lurk behind the cage, then burst out into the open ice at either side of the net for a pass and a scoring chance.

Opposing teams have to make the percentage play in their defensive zone against LaFontaine because of his anticipation and alertness in picking off passes.

THE PHYSICAL GAME
LaFontaine is much less of a perimeter player than people think. He goes into high-traffic areas and crashes the net. He won't knock people down and he won't run around making useless hits, but he will battle effectively in the neutral zone.

Strong on his skates and on his stick, LaFontaine will push off a defender with one arm and get a shot away one-handed. He is very disciplined and, despite the abuse he takes, spends little time in the penalty box.

THE INTANGIBLES
Obviously, all of the above hinges on whether LaFontaine will be given medical clearance to play again. He had only resumed light skating by the end of last season. It would be unthinkable to have to say goodbye to both Mario Lemieux and LaFontaine in the same year.

PROJECTION
There are too many question marks about LaFontaine's health to determine whether he will regain his position as the team's number one centre.

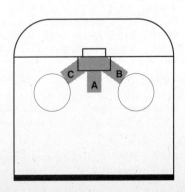

BRAD MAY

Yrs. of NHL service: 6
Born: Toronto, Ont.; Nov. 29, 1971
Position: left wing
Height: 6-1
Weight: 210
Uniform no.: 10
Shoots: left

Career statistics:

GP	G	A	TP	PIM
389	63	82	145	1210

1993-94 statistics:

GP	G	A	TP	+/-	PIM	PP	SH	GW	GT	S	PCT
84	18	27	45	-6	171	3	0	3	0	166	10.8

1994-95 statistics:

GP	G	A	TP	+/-	PIM	PP	SH	GW	GT	S	PCT
33	3	3	6	+5	87	1	0	0	0	42	7.1

1995-96 statistics:

GP	G	A	TP	+/-	PIM	PP	SH	GW	GT	S	PCT
79	15	29	44	+6	295	3	0	4	0	168	8.9

1996-97 statistics:

GP	G	A	TP	+/-	PIM	PP	SH	GW	GT	S	PCT
42	3	4	7	-8	106	1	0	1	0	75	4.0

LAST SEASON

Missed 27 games with shoulder surgery. Missed nine games with broken right hand. Missed four games with broken thumb.

THE FINESSE GAME

May is better off trying to make the safe play instead of the big play, as more often than not, the safe play leads to the big play. He has more than brute strength on his side and possesses nice passing skills, but he's not a very smart player and doesn't think the game well at all.

He is not much of a finisher, and it's starting to look like he never will be, though as he becomes more relaxed and confident (he was neither again last year) this may develop. He is certainly not a natural scorer; his goals come off his hard work around the net.

May does have sound defensive instincts. He is not a very fast or agile skater so he has to be conscious of keeping his position. He won't be able to race back to cover for an error in judgement.

THE PHYSICAL GAME

May is strong along the boards and in front of the net. A well-conditioned athlete, he has good balance and leg drive and is difficult to knock off his feet. He takes a hit to make a play and protects the puck well. He plays through pain.

THE INTANGIBLES

May has been given sufficient time and sufficient ice time to develop into a bona fide power forward. If the Sabres were even modestly stocked on the left wing, May would be on his way out. He looked a lot better and a lot smarter playing with Pat LaFontaine.

PROJECTION

We predicted May's backslide in last year's *HSR*. Injuries were a factor but not an alibi. He won't do much beyond 10 to 15 goals.

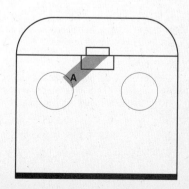

JAY MCKEE

Yrs. of NHL service: 1
Born: Kingston, Ont.; Sept. 8, 1977
Position: left defense
Height: 6-3
Weight: 195
Uniform no.: 74
Shoots: left

Career statistics:

GP	G	A	TP	PIM
44	1	10	11	37

1995-96 statistics:

GP	G	A	TP	+/-	PIM	PP	SH	GW	GT	S	PCT
1	0	1	1	+1	2	0	0	0	0	2	0.0

1996-97 statistics:

GP	G	A	TP	+/-	PIM	PP	SH	GW	GT	S	PCT
43	1	9	10	+3	35	0	0	0	0	29	3.4

LAST SEASON

First NHL season. Scored 2-5 — 7 in 7 games with Rochester (AHL).

THE FINESSE GAME

McKee was able to pile up some pretty impressive numbers in junior, but his future is as a two-way defenseman with most of the emphasis on his defense.

McKee is a very good skater, which powers his open-ice hits. He has good acceleration and quickness to carry the puck out of the zone. He will get involved in the attack because of his skating, but he doesn't have elite hands or playmaking skills.

McKee has good hockey sense and plays an advanced positional game for a young player.

THE PHYSICAL GAME

McKee has good size and is wiry and tough. He exhibited a mean streak in junior but has been a little quieter at the pro level, and could get a little more involved.

THE INTANGIBLES

Even before the departure of Garry Galley, McKee worked his way into the Sabres' top six. His biggest battles last season were with coach Ted Nolan, who had little patience with what he felt were McKee's bad practise habits and benched him from the lineup for nearly a month in midseason. McKee gets a fresh slate with a new GM and coach. The Sabres may need him to step up to be a top three defenseman.

PROJECTION

McKee has a lot of upside, but expect him to concentrate on defense first. The Sabres are a low-scoring team, so 20 to 25 points would be a fine output from McKee.

MIKE PECA

Yrs. of NHL service: 3
Born: Toronto, Ont.; March 26, 1974
Position: centre
Height: 5-11
Weight: 180
Uniform no.: 27
Shoots: right

Career statistics:

GP	G	A	TP	PIM
184	37	55	92	179

1993-94 statistics:

GP	G	A	TP	+/-	PIM	PP	SH	GW	GT	S	PCT
4	0	0	0	-1	2	0	0	0	0	5	0.0

1994-95 statistics:

GP	G	A	TP	+/-	PIM	PP	SH	GW	GT	S	PCT
33	6	6	12	-6	30	2	0	1	1	46	13.0

1995-96 statistics:

GP	G	A	TP	+/-	PIM	PP	SH	GW	GT	S	PCT
68	11	20	31	-1	67	4	3	1	0	109	10.1

1996-97 statistics:

GP	G	A	TP	+/-	PIM	PP	SH	GW	GT	S	PCT
79	20	29	49	+26	80	5	6	4	0	137	14.6

LAST SEASON

Won 1997 Selke Trophy. Led league and team in shorthanded goals. Led team in plus-minus. Tied for second on team in assists. Missed two games with shoulder injury. Missed one game with charley horse.

THE FINESSE GAME

Last year we dubbed him "Peca the checka," and his award as the league's best defensive forward was richly deserved. Peca is a strong, sure skater who plays every shift as if a pink slip will be waiting on the bench if he slacks off. He's good with the puck but not overly creative. He just reads offensive plays well and does a lot of the little things, especially when forechecking, that create turnovers and scoring chances. His goals come from his quickness and his effort. He challenges anyone for the puck.

Although Peca is known for his dogged defensive play, he is intelligent enough to be a useful offensive player. The Sabres used him on their power-play unit (something that wouldn't happen if Pat LaFontaine were around). His hustle and attitude have earned him his NHL job, and league-wide respect. Peca thinks the game well and can be used in all situations.

Peca is at his worst offensively when he has too much time to think. He creates breakaway chances with his reads and anticipation but seldom converts. He is smart about disrupting plays and knows what to do once he gains control of the puck.

THE PHYSICAL GAME

Peca plays much bigger than his size. He's gritty and honest, and is always trying to add more weight. He has a tough time even keeping an extra five pounds

on, and the Sabres have to be cautious about overplaying him. He's among the best open-ice hitters in the league. He will also drop the gloves and go after even the biggest foe. He is fearless.

THE INTANGIBLES

Peca is an ideal third-line player. Although he lacks the size to match up with some of the league's bigger forwards, he is tireless in his pursuit and effort. He adds energy to the lineup. That deal for Alexander Mogilny looked so lopsided in Vancouver's favour in 1995, but the Sabres got a player who cares and shows up every night. Can't say the same for the Canucks.

PROJECTION

Peca surpassed the 40 points we predicted for him last season. He could do the same again and be in the running for a second Selke.

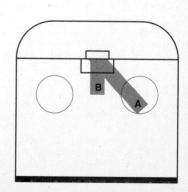

DEREK PLANTE

Yrs. of NHL service: 4
Born: Cloquet, Minn.; Jan. 17, 1971
Position: centre
Height: 5-11
Weight: 180
Uniform no.: 26
Shoots: left

Career statistics:

GP	G	A	TP	PIM
282	74	113	187	88

1993-94 statistics:

GP	G	A	TP	+/-	PIM	PP	SH	GW	GT	S	PCT
77	21	35	56	+4	24	8	1	2	0	147	14.3

1994-95 statistics:

GP	G	A	TP	+/-	PIM	PP	SH	GW	GT	S	PCT
47	3	19	22	-4	12	2	0	0	0	94	3.2

1995-96 statistics:

GP	G	A	TP	+/-	PIM	PP	SH	GW	GT	S	PCT
76	23	33	56	-4	28	4	0	5	0	203	11.3

1996-97 statistics:

GP	G	A	TP	+/-	PIM	PP	SH	GW	GT	S	PCT
82	27	26	53	+14	24	5	0	6	1	191	14.1

LAST SEASON

Led team in points and shots. Tied for team lead in game-winning goals. Second on team in goals. Tied for third on team in power-play goals. One of four Sabres to appear in all 82 games.

THE FINESSE GAME

Plante was probably the least likely number one centre in the NHL this season. He has a frail-looking build, yet didn't miss a game. He compensates for his lack of stature with quickness and hand skills. He does not have blazing speed but he can get the edge on a defender with a quick initial burst. He's very mobile, with a change of gears.

It would obviously help Plante to play with a big winger who could convert his passes, but the Sabres don't have any power forwards fitting that description. He is an excellent passer, with sharp instincts around the net, and works very well with the open ice on the power play. Plante would rather pass than shoot, but overcame that reluctance a bit more successfully last season out of necessity.

Despite his good hand-eye coordination, Plante is average on draws and really loses an edge to bigger centres.

THE PHYSICAL GAME

Plante has a very slender frame and is not strong. He has always had trouble with the length of the pro season, tending to wear down if he gets too much ice time. He pays attention to conditioning, which helps, but he is limited by his physique. He loses a lot of one-on-one battles.

THE INTANGIBLES

No team had a leading scorer with fewer points than Plante, which only points out how fitting it was for goalie Dominik Hasek to win the Hart Trophy. Plante would be an adequate number two centre on a stronger team. If Pat LaFontaine is unable to play again next season, Plante will again be forced to be the top line centre. He deserves credit for an honest effort in the playoffs.

PROJECTION

Without a better supporting cast, 50 to 55 points is really quite an amazing output for Plante.

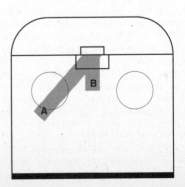

ROB RAY

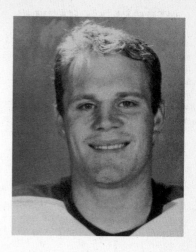

Yrs. of NHL service: 8
Born: Belleville, Ont.; June 8, 1968
Position: left wing
Height: 6-0
Weight: 203
Uniform no.: 32
Shoots: left

Career statistics:

GP	G	A	TP	PIM
506	31	30	61	2032

1993-94 statistics:

GP	G	A	TP	+/-	PIM	PP	SH	GW	GT	S	PCT
82	3	4	7	+2	274	0	0	0	0	34	8.8

1994-95 statistics:

GP	G	A	TP	+/-	PIM	PP	SH	GW	GT	S	PCT
46	0	3	3	-4	173	0	0	0	0	7	0.0

1995-96 statistics:

GP	G	A	TP	+/-	PIM	PP	SH	GW	GT	S	PCT
71	3	6	9	-8	287	0	0	0	1	21	14.3

1996-97 statistics:

GP	G	A	TP	+/-	PIM	PP	SH	GW	GT	S	PCT
82	7	3	10	+3	286	0	0	1	0	45	15.6

LAST SEASON

Led team and fourth in NHL in penalty minutes. One of four Sabres to appear in all 82 games.

THE FINESSE GAME

Ray is a good skater for a big guy, very mobile and surprisingly quick. He is a solid forechecker and is learning to keep his gloves and stick down. There is nothing wrong with taking aggressive penalties, but Ray is big enough to check cleanly and effectively.

Ray has to work hard for his points. He has a nice wrist shot from in close and a hard slap shot. He doesn't do much creatively but patrols up and down his wing. He has good balance and can plant himself in front of the net, but he doesn't have really quick hands for picking up loose pucks, and he remains a fourth-line winger.

THE PHYSICAL GAME

Ray is one of those hitters who can galvanize a bench and a building. A defender with the puck knows Ray is coming and either has to be willing to stand up to the check or bail out — either way, Ray has a good shot at loosening a puck and getting a turnover. The problem is that he can't do much with the puck once he gets it and needs a clever linemate to trail in and pick up the pieces.

A good fighter who doesn't get challenged much anymore, Ray was the player chiefly responsible for a rule change three seasons ago that penalized a player for shucking his jersey before an altercation, and was probably one of the inspirations for the tiedown rule. Of course, Ray circumvented that rule with using an extra-long tiedown. He is very good at making it look like the opponent has pulled off his jersey, which he wears large and loose and with the protective equipment sewn onto it. He's hockey's version of Demi Moore, since he goes topless at every opportunity.

THE INTANGIBLES

There is still a place in the NHL for a Rob Ray, especially on a team that is so small up front.

PROJECTION

Ray was one goal shy of tying his career high last season, a result of sheer will and effort.

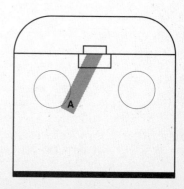

MIROSLAV SATAN

Yrs. of NHL service: 2
Born: Topolcany, Czech.; Oct. 22, 1974
Position: left wing
Height: 6-1
Weight: 185
Uniform no.: 81
Shoots: left

Career statistics:

GP	G	A	TP	PIM
138	43	30	73	48

1995-96 statistics:

GP	G	A	TP	+/-	PIM	PP	SH	GW	GT	S	PCT
62	18	17	35	0	22	6	0	4	0	113	15.9

1996-97 statistics:

GP	G	A	TP	+/-	PIM	PP	SH	GW	GT	S	PCT
76	25	13	38	-3	26	7	0	3	0	119	21.0

consistency could add another 10.

LAST SEASON

Acquired from Edmonton for Barrie Moore and Craig Millar, March 18, 1997. Second NHL season. Led team in shooting percentage. Second on team in power-play goals. Third on team in goals.

THE FINESSE GAME

Satan has terrific breakaway speed, which allows him to pull away from many defenders. He uses his skills in a strictly offensive sense. He developed as a fairly conscientious two-way player but in recent years has become more of a high-risk player.

Satan isn't shy about shooting. He keeps his head up and looks for his shooting holes, and is accurate with a wrist and snap shot. He sees his passing options and will sometimes make the play, but he is the sniper on whatever line he is playing and prefers to take the shot himself.

Satan's biggest drawback is his lack of intensity, and with it, a lack of consistency. When he isn't scoring, he isn't doing much else to help his team win. He was really big when it counted down the stretch, while his teammates were all slumping.

THE PHYSICAL GAME

Satan has added muscle during his first two NHL seasons, but has to get the idea that it's okay to bump people. He's not huge but he's solid.

THE INTANGIBLES

Satan is in a great spot in Buffalo because he doesn't have to beat out much to earn playing time as the number one left-winger. He obviously was happy with the move, scoring 8-2 — 10 in 12 games after the trade. He had a disappointing playoffs but was hampered by an inflamed appendix.

PROJECTION

Goals, goals, goals. Forget playmaking. Satan wants to score. He's a sure bet for 25 goals and with more

RICHARD SMEHLIK

Yrs. of NHL service: 4
Born: Ostrava, Czechoslovakia; Jan. 23, 1970
Position: right defense
Height: 6-3
Weight: 208
Uniform no.: 42
Shoots: left

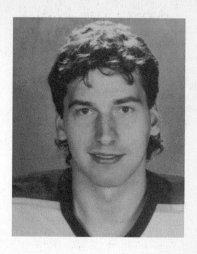

Career statistics:

GP	G	A	TP	PIM
265	33	80	113	217

1993-94 statistics:

GP	G	A	TP	+/-	PIM	PP	SH	GW	GT	S	PCT
84	14	27	41	+22	69	3	3	1	1	106	13.2

1994-95 statistics:

GP	G	A	TP	+/-	PIM	PP	SH	GW	GT	S	PCT
39	4	7	11	+5	46	0	1	1	0	49	8.2

1995-96 statistics:

Did Not Play -- Injured

1996-97 statistics:

GP	G	A	TP	+/-	PIM	PP	SH	GW	GT	S	PCT
62	11	19	30	+19	43	2	0	1	0	100	11.0

PROJECTION

Smehlik's game wasn't bad considering he missed all of the previous season. We saw enough encouraging signs to think he'll be back at a 40- to 45-point level this season.

LAST SEASON

Missed 13 games with rehab complications from reconstructive knee surgery.

THE FINESSE GAME

After missing the entire 1995-96 season and the start of last season after major knee surgery, Smehlik's slow start was understandable. Skating is his strong suit, and for any player — but especially a defenseman — time is needed to develop confidence after surgery. Smehlik is an agile skater with good lateral movement and very solid on his skates. Because his balance is so good, he is tough to knock down.

If Smehlik is given more responsibility offensively, he will respond. He has good passing skills and fair hockey vision, and he can spot and hit the breaking forward. Most of his assists will be traced back to a headman feed out of the defensive zone.

Smehlik is vulnerable to a strong forecheck. Teams are aware of this deficiency and try to work his corner.

THE PHYSICAL GAME

Smehlik can use his body well but has to be more consistent and authoritative. He has to clean up his crease better but he's not a mean hitter. He prefers to use his stick to break up plays, and he does this effectively. He has a long reach and is able to intercept passes, or reach in around a defender to pry the puck loose.

THE INTANGIBLES

If the Sabres lose Garry Galley and fail to sign a veteran defenseman, Smehlik will be asked to step up as one of the top pairing, something he's not capable of without a smart and experienced partner.

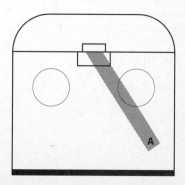

MIKE WILSON

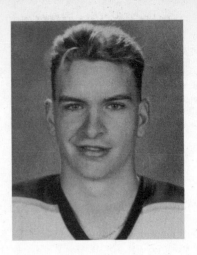

Yrs. of NHL service: 2
Born: Brampton, Ont.; Feb. 26, 1975
Position: left defense
Height: 6-6
Weight: 210
Uniform no.: 4
Shoots: left

Career statistics:

GP	G	A	TP	PIM
135	6	17	23	92

1995-96 statistics:

GP	G	A	TP	+/-	PIM	PP	SH	GW	GT	S	PCT
58	4	8	12	+13	41	1	0	1	0	52	7.7

1996-97 statistics:

GP	G	A	TP	+/-	PIM	PP	SH	GW	GT	S	PCT
77	2	9	11	+13	51	0	0	1	0	57	3.5

LAST SEASON

Second NHL season. Missed one game due to illness.

THE FINESSE GAME

Wilson is a stay-at-home defenseman with raw skills, who needs to take another step up in his reads to become more effective.

He is an average skater, occasionally clumsy, and accordingly plays a very conservative positional game. He is very strong on his feet, and that's a factor along the boards and in the corners. He does not get involved in the attack to much extent, though he will make the rush now and again when space opens up. He has a long stride but is not quick. Wilson does have a capable first pass out of the zone, though, which at this stage is his best asset.

THE PHYSICAL GAME

Wilson is big, but plays stiffly and never drives his body into opponents. Instead of hitting, he just tries to use his wide wingspan to make players take the long way around him, essentially reducing himself to a human pylon.

THE INTANGIBLES

Wilson started losing ice time to Jay McKee late in the season; he needs to learn to use his body to become an effective everyday player in the NHL. A sophomore slump is expected, but his desire was called into question last season.

PROJECTION

Wilson will be in a battle for one of the last two spots on defense. Just showing up won't be enough. His offensive numbers will never amount to much, but physically he could be an impact player.

ALEXEI ZHITNIK

Yrs. of NHL service: 5

Born: Kiev, Ukraine; Oct. 10, 1972

Position: left defense

Height: 5-11

Weight: 204

Uniform no.: 44

Shoots: left

Career statistics:

GP	G	A	TP	PIM
341	41	144	185	395

1993-94 statistics:

GP	G	A	TP	+/-	PIM	PP	SH	GW	GT	S	PCT
81	12	40	52	-11	101	11	0	1	1	227	5.3

1994-95 statistics:

GP	G	A	TP	+/-	PIM	PP	SH	GW	GT	S	PCT
32	4	10	14	-6	61	3	0	0	0	66	6.1

1995-96 statistics:

GP	G	A	TP	+/-	PIM	PP	SH	GW	GT	S	PCT
80	6	30	36	-25	58	5	0	0	0	193	3.1

1996-97 statistics:

GP	G	A	TP	+/-	PIM	PP	SH	GW	GT	S	PCT
80	7	28	35	+10	95	3	1	0	1	170	4.1

LAST SEASON

Second among team defensemen in scoring. Served two-game suspension for high-sticking incident.

THE FINESSE GAME

Zhitnik has a bowlegged skating style that ex-coach, Barry Melrose, once compared to Bobby Orr's. Zhitnik is no Orr, but he was born with skates on. He has speed, acceleration and lateral mobility.

He plays the right point on the power play to open up his forehand for the one-timer. And he likes to rush the puck and shoots well off the fly. He uses all of the blueline well on the power play. He has a good, hard shot, but needs to work on keeping it low for tips and deflections in front.

Zhitnik sees the ice well and is a good playmaker. He can snap a long, strong headman pass or feather a short pass on a give-and-go. He can also grab the puck and skate it out of danger. Consistency continues to elude him, but he has the ingredients to put a great game together.

Defensively, Zhitnik can be a nightmare. He is a high-stakes gambler who thinks offense first, and he frequently leaves his defense partner outnumbered.

THE PHYSICAL GAME

Zhitnik has an undisciplined side to his game. He makes wild, leaping checks that are borderline charges, but for the most part he plays sensibly and doesn't take bad penalties. Teams often target Zhitnik physically and try to take him out of a game early; the tactic will work as he wears out. He has to get stronger and pay more attention to conditioning.

THE INTANGIBLES

Zhitnik plays a better defensive game than he is usually given credit for, but will still have his wild nights when he just throws defense to the wind.

PROJECTION

Zhitnik is the number two defenseman in Buffalo by default, gets prime ice time and will net another 35 to 40 points (more if Pat LaFontaine is able to return).

CALGARY FLAMES

Players' Statistics 1996-97

POS.	NO.	PLAYER	GP	G	A	PTS	+/-	PIM	PP	SH	GW	GT	S	PCT
R	14	THEOREN FLEURY	81	29	38	67	-12	104	9	2	3	3	336	8.6
C	51	DAVE GAGNER	82	27	33	60	2	48	9		4	1	228	11.8
L	13	GERMAN TITOV	79	22	30	52	-12	36	12		4		192	11.5
R	12	*JAROME IGINLA	82	21	29	50	-4	37	8	1	3		169	12.4
L	18	MARTY MCINNIS	80	23	26	49	-8	22	5	1	4	1	182	12.6
L	44	*JONAS HOGLUND	68	19	16	35	-4	12	3		6	1	189	10.1
C	34	COREY MILLEN	61	11	15	26	-19	32	1				82	13.4
C	16	CORY STILLMAN	58	6	20	26	-6	14	2				112	5.4
C	23	AARON GAVEY	57	8	11	19	-12	46	3		1	1	62	12.9
L	20	TODD HLUSHKO	58	7	11	18	-2	49					76	9.2
R	22	RONNIE STERN	79	7	10	17	-4	157		1	1		98	7.1
D	36	YVES RACINE	46	1	15	16	4	24	1				82	1.2
D	5	TOMMY ALBELIN	72	4	11	15	-8	14	2				103	3.9
D	27	*TODD SIMPSON	82	1	13	14	-14	208				1	85	1.2
L	42	ED WARD	40	5	8	13	-3	49			1		33	15.2
L	32	MIKE SULLIVAN	67	5	6	11	-11	10		3	2		64	7.8
D	4	GLEN FEATHERSTONE	54	3	8	11	-1	106					67	4.5
D	19	*CHRIS O'SULLIVAN	27	2	8	10	0	2	1		1		41	4.9
D	6	*JOEL BOUCHARD	76	4	5	9	-23	49	1				61	6.6
R	15	SANDY MCCARTHY	33	3	5	8	-8	113	1		1		38	7.9
D	29	*CALE HULSE	63	1	6	7	-2	91	1				58	1.7
L	17	*HNAT DOMENICHELLI	23	3	3	6	-3	9	1				30	10.0
D	3	JAMES PATRICK	19	3	1	4	2	6	1				22	13.6
C	41	*DALE MCTAVISH	9	1	2	3	-4	2					14	7.1
G	37	TREVOR KIDD	55		2	2	0	16						
D	8	*SAMI HELENIUS	3		1	1	1						1	-
L	38	*SASHA LAKOVIC	19		1	1	-1	54					10	
L	35	*PAXTON SCHULTE	1				1	2					1	
D	33	ZARLEY ZALAPSKI	2				-1						7	
C	28	*MARTY MURRAY	2				0	4					2	
C	45	*MARKO JANTUNEN	3				-1						7	
D	2	*JAMIE ALLISON	20				-4	35					8	
G	30	DWAYNE ROLOSON	31				0	2						

GP = games played; G = goals; A = assists; PTS = points; +/- = goals-for minus goals-against while player is on ice; PIM = penalties in minutes; PP = power-play goals; SH = shorthanded goals; GW = game-winning goals; GT = game-tying goals; S = no. of shots; PCT = percentage of goals to shots; * = rookie.

TOMMY ALBELIN

Yrs. of NHL service: 10
Born: Stockholm, Sweden; May 21, 1964
Position: defense
Height: 6-1
Weight: 190
Uniform no.: 5
Shoots: left

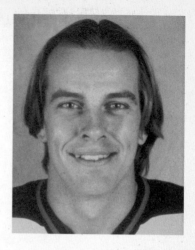

Career statistics:

GP	G	A	TP	PIM
545	33	146	179	327

1993-94 statistics:

GP	G	A	TP	+/-	PIM	PP	SH	GW	GT	S	PCT
62	2	17	19	+20	36	1	0	1	0	62	3.2

1994-95 statistics:

GP	G	A	TP	+/-	PIM	PP	SH	GW	GT	S	PCT
48	5	10	15	+9	20	2	0	0	0	60	8.3

1995-96 statistics:

GP	G	A	TP	+/-	PIM	PP	SH	GW	GT	S	PCT
73	1	13	14	+1	18	0	0	0	0	121	0.8

1996-97 statistics:

GP	G	A	TP	+/-	PIM	PP	SH	GW	GT	S	PCT
72	4	11	15	8-	14	2	0	0	0	103	3.9

LAST SEASON

Missed 10 games with abdominal/groin strain.

THE FINESSE GAME

With Zarley Zalapski and James Patick sidelined most of the season with injuries, Albelin was one of the few veterans left. He helped some of the Flames' baby defensemen along.

Albelin is a strong skater, and agile enough to be used as a checking forward in a real pinch. He is fluid, with a big, loping stride that covers a lot of ground with little wasted motion. He skates backwards well and keeps his body positioned to break up passes. He can quickly turn an interception into a breakout pass, as he sees his options well and doesn't panic with the puck.

Albelin doesn't like to carry the puck; he prefers to use his teammates, but he can lug it if necessary. He has good hand skills for handling the puck if he goes in deep, though he usually stays at the tops of the circle (unless, of course, he is playing forward).

Albelin isn't a great power-play quarterback because his shot is not overpowering, nor does it always get through to the net. He is a smart penalty killer.

THE PHYSICAL GAME

Albelin gets good drive from his powerful legs to take his man out along the boards, but he's not a big open-ice hitter. He won't be intimidated and he's slow to rile, which is unpopular with some coaches who would prefer a bit more emotion.

THE INTANGIBLES

Albelin is like a white shirt; he goes with everything.

He is versatile enough to play forward or defense, or play the right or left side on D. He can complement nearly any kind of player. He is like a utility infielder in baseball. He may not have his own niche, but he can fill a lot of cracks in a team.

PROJECTION

Probably because he has played so long in the Devils' system, Albelin long ago abandoned all hope of getting involved offensively. He should get 20 to 25 points in a regular role.

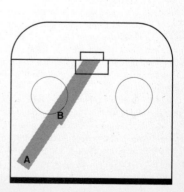

HNAT DOMENICHELLI

Yrs. of NHL service: 0
Born: Edmonton, Alberta; Feb. 17, 1976
Position: centre/left wing
Height: 6-0
Weight: 175
Uniform no.: 17
Shoots: left

Career statistics:

GP	G	A	TP	PIM
23	3	3	6	9

1996-97 statistics:

GP	G	A	TP	+/-	PIM	PP	SH	GW	GT	S	PCT
23	3	3	6	-3	9	1	0	0	0	30	10.0

LAST SEASON

Will be entering first NHL season. Acquired from Hartford with Glen Featherstone, a second-round 1997 draft pick, and a third-round 1998 draft pick for Steve Chiasson and a conditional draft pick. Scored 24-24 — 48 in 39 games with Springfield (AHL). Scored 1-1 — 2 in one game with Saint John (AHL).

THE FINESSE GAME

Domenichelli's size is a big drawback. He's of average height but very, very slender and easy to knock off the puck.

His best asset is his hockey sense. He can play centre or wing, and has good vision, good hands and a decent shot. If Domenichelli can get some power-play time he'll be a factor. He is a creative playmaker but won't pass up a good shot if he has it.

Domenichelli is a good skater with quickness and agility, but doesn't possess real breakaway speed.

THE PHYSICAL GAME

Domenichelli tries, but he's just not going to win one-on-one battles. He will have to dedicate himself to getting much stronger if he is going to succeed in the NHL.

THE INTANGIBLES

The Flames acquired Domenichelli largely because he was Jarome Iginla's linemate in junior, and they would like to recapture some of that old Kamloops magic. While this thinking doesn't always result in great results at the NHL level (See: Pat Falloon-Ray Whitney), the offense-starved Flames can't be blamed for trying.

Domenichelli didn't get much of a look in his stint with the Flames. He went to the minors (Saint John) at the end of the season and scored five goals in five AHL playoff games. He's been a scorer at the junior and minor-league levels. Now it's time to find out if he can do it in the majors.

PROJECTION

Domenichelli doesn't seem to have the skills to be a first-line player to accompany Iginla. He should be more comfortable starting out the season with the Flames and has potential as a second-line player. He obviously wants to score, and if the Flames can get 15 to 20 goals out of him in a regular role, they'd be happy.

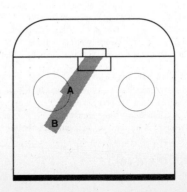

THEOREN FLEURY

Yrs. of NHL service: 9
Born: Oxbow, Sask.; June 29, 1968
Position: right wing/centre
Height: 5-6
Weight: 160
Uniform no.: 14
Shoots: right

Career statistics:

GP	G	A	TP	PIM
649	307	376	683	1207

1993-94 statistics:

GP	G	A	TP	+/-	PIM	PP	SH	GW	GT	S	PCT
83	40	45	85	+30	186	16	1	6	0	278	14.4

1994-95 statistics:

GP	G	A	TP	+/-	PIM	PP	SH	GW	GT	S	PCT
47	29	29	58	+6	112	9	2	5	0	173	16.8

1995-96 statistics:

GP	G	A	TP	+/-	PIM	PP	SH	GW	GT	S	PCT
80	46	50	96	+17	112	17	5	4	0	353	13.0

1996-97 statistics:

GP	G	A	TP	+/-	PIM	PP	SH	GW	GT	S	PCT
81	29	38	67	-12	104	9	2	3	3	336	8.6

LAST SEASON

Led team in goals, points and shots for third consecutive season. Second in NHL in shots. Led team in assists. Career low in points for full season. Tied for second on team in power-play goals.

THE FINESSE GAME

Considering what Fleury was able to accomplish without a quality centre to play with all season, his numbers don't look as bad as they do in black and white. Toss in his fatigue from the World Cup, his battles with (now ex-) coach Pierre Page and a sore knee, and it's downright remarkable the Fleury wasn't ground down to nothing.

Fleury continues to prove that a small man can excel in a big man's game. Possessing great speed and quickness, he often seems to be dancing over the ice with his blades barely touching the frozen surface. He is always on the move, which is as much a tactic as an instinct for survival. You can't catch what you can't hit. He uses his outside speed to burn slower, bigger defensemen, or he can burst up the middle and split two defenders. He uses all of the ice.

A better finisher than playmaker, Fleury is not at his best handling the puck; he's much better at receiving the pass late and then making things happen, which is why he must be paired with a playmaking centre. He always has his legs churning, and he draws penalties by driving to the net. He has a strong wrist shot that he can get away from almost anywhere. He can score even if he is pulled to his knees.

Fleury is an effective penalty killer, blocking shots and getting the puck out along the boards. He is very poised and cool with the puck under attack, holding it until he finds an opening instead of just firing blindly. His defensive play has improved, and he does a good job as a backchecker in holding up opposing forwards so his defensemen have extra time with the puck.

His hand quickness makes him very effective on draws, and he takes offensive-zone draws.

THE PHYSICAL GAME

Fleury can take a hit and not get knocked down because he is so solid and has a low centre of gravity. He uses his stick liberally and will take a lot of penalties sticking up for himself and his teammates.

THE INTANGIBLES

Fleury's name was being dangled in trade talks during the off-season, and we expect him to be in a new uniform. He was already under fire in Calgary when he tossed a match on the Flames by criticizing the team's goaltending (his road roommate is Trevor Kidd. Oops!). After Sheldon Kennedy's disclosure of abuse by his junior coach, Graham James, Fleury (who also played on team coaches by James) had to deal with that issue. And his Crohn's disease. And the team's struggles. He needs a change of scene.

PROJECTION

Only his size prevents Fleury from being among the NHL's elite forwards. He can flirt with the 100-point mark again if he ends up with the right team.

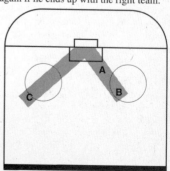

AARON GAVEY

Yrs. of NHL service: 2
Born: Sudbury, Ont; Feb. 22, 1974
Position: centre
Height: 6-1
Weight: 194
Uniform no.: 23
Shoots: left

Career statistics:

GP	G	A	TP	PIM
130	16	15	31	102

1995-96 statistics:

GP	G	A	TP	+/-	PIM	PP	SH	GW	GT	S	PCT
73	8	4	12	-6	56	1	1	2	0	65	12.3

1996-97 statistics:

GP	G	A	TP	+/-	PIM	PP	SH	GW	GT	S	PCT
57	8	11	19	-12	46	3	0	1	1	62	12.9

LAST SEASON

Acquired from Tampa Bay for Rick Tabaracci, November 19, 1996. Second NHL season. Missed games with neck injury.

THE FINESSE GAME

Gavey is being groomed as a two-way centre. The highest hopes are that he will develop into a Ron Francis type who plays intelligent defense but also has terrific offensive ability.

Gavey has a very good shot, a strong wrist or snap. He is also very strong on face-offs. He has met every challenge so far and is ready for more.

He reads plays with exceptional intelligence for a young player, and his defensive game is advanced for a player his age. Gavey is a key first-unit penalty killer and can be put on the ice when his team is two men down.

THE PHYSICAL GAME

Gavey needs to get stronger. He is a weedy six foot one and needs to bulk up a little — not much, or it will throw his overall game off. But he won't succeed at the NHL level without more strength. He is very competitive and plays to the last second of a period.

THE INTANGIBLES

Gavey has performed well in pressure situations, whether it's the Memorial Cup or the World Junior Championships. Depending on what Calgary does with Michael Nylander, he will have a shot at the number two centre's job with the Flames.

PROJECTION

Last season was something of a washout for Gavey because of the trade (the first time being dealt is always a shock) and his neck injury. If he comes into camp healthy and with the proper mental attitude, this could be his breakout year. We'll err on the side of caution and estimate 40 points.

TODD HLUSHKO

Yrs. of NHL service: 2
Born: Toronto, Ont.; Feb. 7, 1970
Position: left wing
Height: 5-11
Weight: 185
Uniform no.: 20
Shoots: left

Career statistics:

GP	G	A	TP	PIM
66	8	12	20	57

1993-94 statistics:

GP	G	A	TP	+/-	PIM	PP	SH	GW	GT	S	PCT
2	1	0	1	+1	0	0	0	0	0	2	50.0

1994-95 statistics:

GP	G	A	TP	+/-	PIM	PP	SH	GW	GT	S	PCT
2	0	1	1	+1	2	0	0	0	0	3	0.0

1995-96 statistics:

GP	G	A	TP	+/-	PIM	PP	SH	GW	GT	S	PCT
4	0	0	0	0	6	0	0	0	0	6	0.0

1996-97 statistics:

GP	G	A	TP	+/-	PIM	PP	SH	GW	GT	S	PCT
58	7	11	18	-2	49	0	0	0	0	76	9.2

of those. The Flames traded a similar player (Mike Sullivan), which is good news for Hlushko.

PROJECTION

Hlushko will play a third- or fourth-line role with the Flames, and isn't likely to score much more than 10 goals.

LAST SEASON

First full NHL season. Missed eight games with concussion.

THE FINESSE GAME

Hlushko is one of those forwards that almost any team can use, but his skills are so nondescript that he has a tough time making the final cut. He brings zip and energy to the ice. He plays a basic game, hustling up and down the wing, doing nothing more creative that dumping the puck in and starting a strong forecheck.

Some nights, that's enough. He can revive and re-juvenate his team, especially after a goal has been scored against and the building needs some life (though Dr. Frankenstein couldn't have brought the Saddledome crowd back into the land of the living last season).

Hlushko's best skill is his skating, and he knows it, so he is always generating speed through the neutral zone. He can't handle the puck at tempo and doesn't have much of a shot, or he could do a lot more dam-age. He is an effective penalty killer.

THE PHYSICAL GAME

Hlushko isn't very big but he's always moving and he's willing to hit people. He can be irritating to play against in a hit-and-run kind of way. He'll even fight when he has to. He's strong for his size.

THE INTANGIBLES

Because he won't pick up many points, Hlushko will always be on the bubble. Coaches will want to insert players who can produce more, but Hlushko has his points as a momentum-shifter; every team can use one

JONAS HOGLUND

Yrs. of NHL service: 1
Born: Hammaro, Sweden; Aug. 29, 1972
Position: left wing
Height: 6-3
Weight: 200
Uniform no.: 44
Shoots: right

Career statistics:

GP	G	A	TP	PIM
68	19	16	35	12

1996-97 statistics:

GP	G	A	TP	+/-	PIM	PP	SH	GW	GT	S	PCT
68	19	16	35	-4	12	3	0	6	1	189	10.1

LAST SEASON

First NHL season. Led team and tied for lead among NHL rookies in game-winning goals. Third among NHL rookies in power-play assists. Led NHL rookies in shots.

THE FINESSE GAME

Hoglund is a natural goal scorer. Every time he gets the puck, he has a chance to score. Like New Jersey's John MacLean, he can shoot from almost any wicked angle and score. The trick is to encourage him to shoot more. When he played with veterans such as Theo Fleury and Dave Gagner, Hoglund was too deferential or unsure of himself and would try to set them up rather than take the shot himself. He has a good, hard slap shot and half-wrister.

Hoglund proved to be a fast learner. By the second half of the season he was much improved with his defensive and positional play. Play along the boards was a new concept to him, but he was unafraid of getting involved.

Hoglund skates well for a big man. He's no speed skater, but his skating is NHL calibre.

THE PHYSICAL GAME

Hoglund is a big guy but doesn't play a physical game. He has a long reach, which he uses instead of his body to try to win control of the puck or slow down an opponent. He's getting used to the idea of hitting but has to get better at it. He started running out of gas around midseason, which is common for Europeans, who are used to a shorter schedule. It's all part of his learning experience.

THE INTANGIBLES

If it hadn't been for Jarome Iginla, Hoglund would have been the star rookie forward for the Flames last season. It's just as well that Calgary was able to keep him a secret for a year while he became acclimatized to the NHL.

PROJECTION

Hoglund is a potential 50-goal scorer down the road if he gets the right personnel to play with, but the Flames will be happy to see him net 35 to 30 next season.

CALE HULSE

Yrs. of NHL service: 1
Born: Edmonton, Alberta; Nov. 10, 1973
Position: right defense
Height: 6-3
Weight: 210
Uniform no.: 29
Shoots: right

Career statistics:

GP	G	A	TP	PIM
74	1	6	7	111

1995-96 statistics:

GP	G	A	TP	+/-	PIM	PP	SH	GW	GT	S	PCT
11	0	0	0	+1	20	0	0	0	0	9	0.0

1996-97 statistics:

GP	G	A	TP	+/-	PIM	PP	SH	GW	GT	S	PCT
63	1	6	7	-2	91	0	1	0	0	58	1.7

LAST SEASON

First NHL season. Missed four games with ankle injury.

THE FINESSE GAME

Hulse is a big guy without a lot of quickness, and the Flames concentrated on speed drills with him last season to improve his puck movement, which was one of his weakest areas. He relies more heavily on his defensive ability and willingness to hit.

Hulse is a better than average skater. He has a long, strong stride with good balance. Like many defensemen schooled in the Devils' system, Hulse is sound in the defensive aspects of the game, but is reluctant to get involved even modestly in the attack.

Hulse has a good shot from the point. Once he comprehends he can actually cross the far blueline once in awhile, he could work on a second power-play unit with more experience. Intelligent and steady, he may also develop into a mainstay on the penalty-killing squad.

THE PHYSICAL GAME

Hulse is tough, an outstanding fighter who doesn't go looking for trouble but won't back down from a challenge, either. He will hit hard along the boards and in the corners. He's not a strong open-ice hitter, but he plays well positionally and makes attackers pay the price for coming into his piece of the ice. He's intense and won't take a night, or a shift, off.

THE INTANGIBLES

Patience is required to develop a big defenseman like Hulse. He was in and out of the lineup at the start of the season, but was steadier in the second half.

PROJECTION

Hulse's numbers may not ever be impressive, but his overall game will be. He could be among Calgary's top four defensemen.

JAROME IGINLA

Yrs. of NHL service: 1
Born: Edmonton, Alberta; July 1, 1977
Position: right wing
Height: 6-1
Weight: 193
Uniform no.: 12
Shoots: right

Career statistics:

GP	G	A	TP	PIM
82	21	29	50	37

1996-97 statistics:

GP	G	A	TP	+/-	PIM	PP	SH	GW	GT	S	PCT
82	21	29	50	-4	37	8	1	3	0	169	12.4

LAST SEASON

Named to NHL All-Rookie Team. Finalist for Calder Trophy. Led all NHL rookies and fourth on team in points. Led NHL rookies in power-play goals. Tied for fifth among NHL rookies in shots. One of three Flames to appear in all 82 games.

THE FINESSE GAME

Iginla is an ideal second-line player who was forced to handle first-line responsibility with talent-starved Calgary; for most of the season he held up well under the circumstances. If he hadn't run into a second-half slump, he would have given Bryan Berard a better run for the Calder.

Iginla doesn't have great speed but he's smart and energetic. What puts Iginla ahead of other 19-year-olds is his defensive play, which he developed first in junior. The scoring touch came later, which is the reverse for most young players and is one of the reasons why he was able to step into the NHL with such success. He has a veteran's understanding of the game, though he may never be a great scorer and will have to work hard for his goals. Throw out Adam Graves's one 50-goal season and you are looking at Iginla's future.

Iginla does his best work in the corners and in front of the net. He is strong, and doesn't mind the trench warfare. In fact, he thrives on it.

THE PHYSICAL GAME

Iginla is gritty, powerful and aggressive. He will take a hit to make a play but, even better, he will initiate the hits. He has a mean streak and will have to control himself at the same time he is proving his mettle around the NHL; a fine line to walk.

THE INTANGIBLES

The key word to describe Iginla is character. He has played on winners in Kamloops (two Memorial Cups) and Team Canada (one World Junior Championship). He was not a bit player in those titles, either. He will pay his share of dues with a rebuilding Calgary team, but he proved last year he was all he was advertised to be when the Flames acquired him from Dallas for Joe Nieuwendyk. Iginla's only flaw was learning how to concentrate on each game, but that will come with experience.

PROJECTION

Iginla's 20 to 25 goals a season will be invaluable, combined as they are with his play in all three zones. He's a power forward who plays both ends of the rink, and there aren't many players with that description in the NHL.

TREVOR KIDD

Yrs. of NHL service: 4
Born: Dugald, Man.; March 29, 1972
Position: goaltender
Height: 6-2
Weight: 190
Uniform no.: 37
Catches: left

Career statistics:

GP	MIN	GA	SO	GAA	A	PIM
178	9746	460	10	2.83	9	26

1993-94 statistics:

GP	MIN	GAA	W	L	T	SO	GA	S	SAPCT	PIM
31	1614	3.16	13	7	6	0	85	752	.887	4

1994-95 statistics:

GP	MIN	GAA	W	L	T	SO	GA	S	SAPCT	PIM
43	2463	2.61	22	14	6	3	107	1170	.909	2

1995-96 statistics:

GP	MIN	GAA	W	L	T	SO	GA	S	SAPCT	PIM
47	2570	2.78	15	21	8	3	119	1130	.895	4

1996-97 statistics:

GP	MIN	GAA	W	L	T	SO	GA	S	SAPCT	PIM
55	2979	2.84	21	23	6	4	141	1416	.900	16

LAST SEASON

Second season with 20 or more wins.

THE PHYSICAL GAME

Kidd is a big goalie who loses his size advantage by going to his knees and staying there. He's a butterfly-style netminder who is good low, but he has an extremely awkward style. There are a lot of times when Kidd gets up so slowly from a skirmish that he looks as if he's been injured. His technique needs a great deal of work.

Kidd is athletic, and is able to make his saves on sheer talent alone. He concentrates well to keep his attention on the puck through screens, but he often plays too deep in his net. At least that helps him on wraparounds. He challenges shooters, but when he does he tends to lunge at them, rather than move out and keep himself square to the shooter.

Kidd is one of the better skating goalies in the league. He's very quick at coming out to stop the hardarounds behind his net. He has adapted well to the seamless glass in his home Saddledome rink. The puck can zip off the glass in a hurry, but Kidd plays it confidently, sometimes overly so.

THE MENTAL GAME

Kidd has won and lost the number one goalie role several times; right now it is his by default. He is competitive, and he has not had the benefit of playing behind a very good team for the past three years. He was stung by his road roommate Theo Fleury's off-season criticism of the team's goaltending.

THE INTANGIBLES

Let's see. The Flames trade goalie Rick Tabaracci in November to make sure Kidd knows the goaltending job is his. He stumbles, so Dwayne Rolson takes a bite out of his starts. And in the off-season, the Flames reacquire the cast-off Tabaracci. We're not quite sure what's going on here, except for Calgary's underwhelming faith in Kidd, who was drafted ahead of both Martin Brodeur and Felix Potvin in 1990.

PROJECTION

Kidd will probably end up with another team this season, and we doubt his ability to be a legitimate number one goalie.

SANDY MCCARTHY

Yrs. of NHL service: 4
Born: Toronto, Ont.; June 15, 1972
Position: right wing
Height: 6-3
Weight: 225
Uniform no.: 15
Shoots: right

Career statistics:

GP	G	A	TP	PIM
224	22	20	42	560

1993-94 statistics:

GP	G	A	TP	+/-	PIM	PP	SH	GW	GT	S	PCT
79	5	5	10	-3	173	0	0	0	0	39	12.8

1994-95 statistics:

GP	G	A	TP	+/-	PIM	PP	SH	GW	GT	S	PCT
37	5	3	8	+1	101	0	0	2	0	29	17.2

1995-96 statistics:

GP	G	A	TP	+/-	PIM	PP	SH	GW	GT	S	PCT
75	9	7	16	-8	173	3	0	1	0	98	9.2

1996-97 statistics:

GP	G	A	TP	+/-	PIM	PP	SH	GW	GT	S	PCT
33	3	5	8	-8	113	1	0	1	0	38	7.9

LAST SEASON

Missed 49 games with ankle injury and surgery.

THE FINESSE GAME

McCarthy's lost season prevented him from continuing the slow but steady progress he had been making over the past few years. McCarthy doesn't have dazzling finesse skills. He does have some scoring instincts, however, enough to earn him a future role on the third line and some power-play shifts on the second unit. He knows his job in the attacking zone is to drive to the net and screen the goalie. He's hard to budge from in front of the net and will take abuse to fight for a loose rebound.

McCarthy has a decent shot but most of his chances come from in close. As he becomes a better skater, he will be able to force the play off the forecheck. He pressures more than a few defensemen into a hurry-up pass if he gets a good head of steam going.

McCarthy has to work more on his defensive game to become a better all-around player.

THE PHYSICAL GAME

McCarthy has taken a mature approach to improving his off-ice conditioning program. Off-season rehab will be a key for him this year. He is massive and he works on his leg strength to get more power out of his stride, and to be more of a force around the net. He doesn't back down from any challenge, and he can throw 'em when the gloves come off.

THE INTANGIBLES

Enormous forwards who can also play are a rare and coveted commodity in the NHL, and especially in Calgary, which had one of the smallest teams in the league last season with McCarthy sidelined.

PROJECTION

With good work habits, McCarthy could score 10 to 15 goals and supply an intimidating physical presence, providing he recovers well from his injury.

MARTY MCINNIS

Yrs. of NHL service: 5
Born: Hingham, Mass.; June 2, 1970
Position: left wing
Height: 5-11
Weight: 183
Uniform no.: 18
Shoots: right

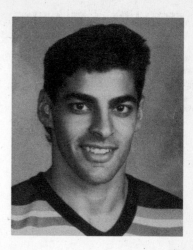

Career statistics:

GP	G	A	TP	PIM
347	82	123	205	117

1993-94 statistics:

GP	G	A	TP	+/-	PIM	PP	SH	GW	GT	S	PCT
81	25	31	56	+31	24	3	5	3	1	136	18.4

1994-95 statistics:

GP	G	A	TP	+/-	PIM	PP	SH	GW	GT	S	PCT
41	9	7	16	-1	8	0	0	1	0	68	13.2

1995-96 statistics:

GP	G	A	TP	+/-	PIM	PP	SH	GW	GT	S	PCT
74	12	34	46	-11	39	2	0	1	0	167	7.2

1996-97 statistics:

GP	G	A	TP	+/-	PIM	PP	SH	GW	GT	S	PCT
80	23	26	49	-8	22	5	1	4	1	182	12.6

LAST SEASON

Acquired from N.Y. Islanders for Tyrone Garner and a sixth-round draft pick for Robert Reichel, March 18, 1997. Third on team in goals. Tied for team lead in game-winning goals.

THE FINESSE GAME

McInnis does a lot of the little things well. He plays positionally, is smart and reliable defensively, and turns his checking work into scoring opportunities with quick passes and his work down low.

McInnis isn't fast but he is deceptive, with a quick first few strides to the puck. He seems to be more aware of where the puck is than his opponents are, so while they're looking for the puck, he's already heading towards it.

McInnis is a good penalty killer because of his tenacity and anticipation. He reads plays well on offense and defense. Playing the off-wing opens up his shot for a quick release. He's always a shorthanded threat.

THE PHYSICAL GAME

McInnis is not very big or tough, but he is sturdy and will use his body to bump and scrap for the puck. He always tries to get in the way, but he loses a lot of battles in tight to larger forwards because he is not that strong.

THE INTANGIBLES

Most Americans dislike a trade to the Great White North, but McInnis not only accepted the move away from the Islanders (where he was disliked by GM Mike Milbury) but happily embraced the expanded role the Flames gave him. McInnis scored 3-4 — 7 in 10 games with the Flames. He's the perfect player for a left-wing lock system, if that's what the new Calgary coach plans to employ.

PROJECTION

McInnis is a suitable third-line checking winger with enough talent to handle some second-line power-play time and score 25 goals a season.

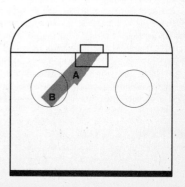

MICHAEL NYLANDER

Yrs. of NHL service: 3
Born: Stockholm, Sweden; Oct. 3, 1972
Position: centre
Height: 5-11
Weight: 190
Uniform no.: 92
Shoots: left

Career statistics:

GP	G	A	TP	PIM
211	41	103	144	88

1993-94 statistics:

GP	G	A	TP	+/-	PIM	PP	SH	GW	GT	S	PCT
73	13	42	55	+8	30	4	0	1	2	95	13.7

1994-95 statistics:

GP	G	A	TP	+/-	PIM	PP	SH	GW	GT	S	PCT
6	0	1	1	+1	2	0	0	0	0	2	0.0

1995-96 statistics:

GP	G	A	TP	+/-	PIM	PP	SH	GW	GT	S	PCT
73	17	38	55	0	20	4	0	6	0	163	10.4

1996-97 statistics:

P	G	A	TP	+/-	PIM	PP	SH	GW	GT	S	PC
						Did not play in NHL					

LAST SEASON

Eighth in the Swiss National League in scoring with 12-43 — 55 in 36 games. Led his team, Lugano, in assists and points.

THE FINESSE GAME

Considered the best player not in the NHL last season, Nylander returns after a season in Europe to a team desperate for his services. They'll take him despite his flaws, which are prominent, because Nylander can make so many good things happen offensively. He's an inconsistent, one-way forward. Some nights he cuts to the net with the puck and fights through checks; some nights he hangs on the perimeter.

An excellent skater with great composure with the puck, Nylander hangs onto the disk and looks at all the options to make a play. This is a gift — not a skill that a coach can teach. He holds the puck until the last split second before making the pass, a skill that has earned him some comparisons to Wayne Gretzky, but Nylander does not resemble the Great One in any other way.

Nylander can do things with the puck that are magical. He knows all about time and space. He is an open-ice player, but still needs to improve his shot. If anything, he is guilty of hanging onto the puck too long and passing up quality scoring chances to force a pass to a teammate who is not in as good a position for the shot.

THE PHYSICAL GAME

Nylander is on the small side and plays even smaller. He uses his body to protect the puck, though he won't fight hard to get it away from the opposition. Word is that Nylander is aware of his deficiencies and worked with a personal trainer during the off-season.

THE INTANGIBLES

Nylander doesn't have the maturity to go with his talent. He battled with (now ex-) coach Pierre Page in 1995-96 (one of the reasons why he refused to play for the Flames last season) and reportedly has a "good behaviour" clause in his contract. If the Flames don't keep him, they'll be able to help themselves with a deal, because Nylander will be fairly marketable.

PROJECTION

If Nylander is all grown up, we could see a new man this season. The Swede has something to prove, to himself and to the NHL. His best NHL season was only 55 points, and we expect him to top that by at least 20.

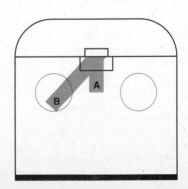

TODD SIMPSON

Yrs. of NHL service: 1
Born: Edmonton, Alta.; May 28, 1973
Position: left defense
Height: 6-3
Weight: 215
Uniform no.: 27
Shoots: left

Career statistics:

GP	G	A	TP	PIM
88	1	13	13	240

1995-96 statistics:

GP	G	A	TP	+/-	PIM	PP	SH	GW	GT	S	PCT
6	0	0	0	0	32	0	0	0	0	3	0.0

1996-97 statistics:

GP	G	A	TP	+/-	PIM	PP	SH	GW	GT	S	PCT
82	1	13	14	-14	208	0	0	1	0	85	1.2

LAST SEASON

First NHL season. Only rookie in NHL to lead team in penalty minutes. One of three Flames to appear in all 82 games.

THE FINESSE GAME

Simpson is known first and foremost for his fighting, but he is capable of doing some other things. For most of the season, he and fellow rookie Joel Bouchard were the ones given the top assignments against other teams' top lines, and they were competitive.

He still has a lot to learn, but Simpson is coachable, and will play intelligent position defense and make attackers pay the price for coming into his area of the ice. His skating, stickhandling and shooting skills are average, but what sets him apart (besides his size) is his determination. He won't give up on a play in any zone. He kills penalties on the first unit and blocks shots. He's smart enough to make some plays offensively, though he doesn't have much confidence in that part of the game. Put it this way: When he decides to go to the net, there aren't too many people who can stop him.

THE PHYSICAL GAME

Simpson is unafraid of big guys and big names. If he has to hit Pavel Bure and Peter Forsberg, he'll hit them. If he has to drop his gloves against a goon, he'll do that, too.

THE INTANGIBLES

Simpson probably earned a spot in the organization back in 1995, when he scrapped with tough guy Sandy McCarthy in a training camp scrimmage. This season, Simpson handled the policeman's role with McCarthy sidelined most of the season by an ankle injury. Simpson doesn't care about winning heavyweight bouts. He only cares how those fights relate to his team's chances of winning. He's a tremendous heart-and-soul character player, who reminds us a lot of a young Mark Tinordi.

PROJECTION

Simpson has had to fight for a role on every team he's played for at every level, and as long as he keeps that motivation, he'll keep improving into a defenseman who might someday score 25 to 30 points.

RON STERN

Yrs. of NHL service: 8
Born: Ste. Agathe, Que.; Jan. 11, 1967
Position: right wing
Height: 6-0
Weight: 195
Uniform no.: 22
Shoots: right

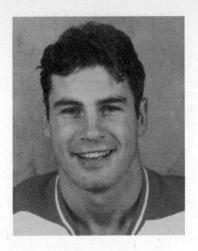

Career statistics:

GP	G	A	TP	PIM
493	64	72	136	1768

1993-94 statistics:

GP	G	A	TP	+/-	PIM	PP	SH	GW	GT	S	PCT
71	9	20	29	+6	243	0	1	3	0	105	8.6

1994-95 statistics:

GP	G	A	TP	+/-	PIM	PP	SH	GW	GT	S	PCT
39	9	4	13	+4	163	1	0	0	0	69	13.0

1995-96 statistics:

GP	G	A	TP	+/-	PIM	PP	SH	GW	GT	S	PCT
52	10	5	15	+2	111	0	0	1	1	64	15.6

1996-97 statistics:

GP	G	A	TP	+/-	PIM	PP	SH	GW	GT	S	PCT
79	7	10	17	-4	157	0	1	1	0	98	7.1

LAST SEASON

Second on team in penalty minutes. Missed three games with back injury.

THE FINESSE GAME

Stern is a rugged, seek-and-destroy missile with modest skills. He is not a pretty skater or a good shooter, but he has the offensive instincts to make some smart plays in the attacking zone; his second effort often catches defenders napping. He has the quickness to get a jump on the defender, and looks for help from his linemates. He will drive to the cage and create his scoring chances off his physical involvement in front of the net.

Stern is not mesmerized by the puck. He doesn't make a lot of pretty plays but instead looks to get rid of the puck quickly with a pass or a shot.

He would be ideally suited as a checking winger but for his lack of skating ability. He also isn't as alert defensively as offensively, but he works hard at whatever task he's given.

THE PHYSICAL GAME

Stern makes his teammates feel a few inches taller and a few pounds heavier. He has no fear of anyone or any situation. He never bails out of a corner — no matter what's coming. He's willing and able to go toe-to-toe with anybody. If he plays on a checking line, he's defensively aware and finishes every check. He can play in the crunch to protect a lead. If he plays on a fourth line, he will act as the catalyst, coming out with a strong shift to lift his bench.

THE INTANGIBLES

Stern's mission is to get momentum on the Flames' side. He is an effective fourth-liner. He plays with a sense of purpose.

PROJECTION

If he can upgrade his production to 15 goals or so, that will be a fine contribution, but 10 is likely his maximum.

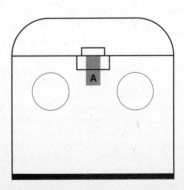

CORY STILLMAN

Yrs. of NHL service: 2
Born: Peterborough, Ont.; Dec. 20, 1970
Position: centre
Height: 6-0
Weight: 180
Uniform no.: 16
Shoots: left

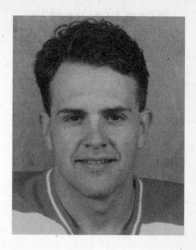

Career statistics:

GP	G	A	TP	PIM
142	22	41	63	57

1994-95 statistics:

GP	G	A	TP	+/-	PIM	PP	SH	GW	GT	S	PCT
10	0	2	2	+1	2	0	0	0	0	7	0.0

1995-96 statistics:

GP	G	A	TP	+/-	PIM	PP	SH	GW	GT	S	PCT
74	16	19	35	-5	41	4	1	3	0	132	12.1

1996-97 statistics:

GP	G	A	TP	+/-	PIM	PP	SH	GW	GT	S	PCT
58	6	20	26	-6	14	2	0	0	0	112	5.4

LAST SEASON

Second NHL season. Missed games with shoulder injury.

THE FINESSE GAME

Stillman complained about spending most of his time as a left- winger last season, which was a defensive role under the Flames' system and prevented him from establishing a forecheck — essential to his offensive game.

Stillman brings a centre's playmaking ability to the wing. He's intelligent and has sound hockey instincts, but may not have that extra notch of speed needed to be a quality player at the NHL level. Since he's not very big (which hampers his odds of playing centre, his preferred position), he needs every advantage he can get.

Stillman has a good enough point shot to be used on the power play. He has good hands and a keen understanding of the game. Dale Hawerchuk isn't a great skater, either, but possesses great patience and puck-handling skills, and is efficient in small areas. Stillman has the potential to be that kind of player, if he is supported by gifted forwards. He needs to play with finishers.

THE PHYSICAL GAME

Stillman is thick and sturdy enough to absorb some hard hits. He is not overly aggressive, but will protect the puck.

THE INTANGIBLES

Stillman played on a number two line with the Flames last season and was one of only two rookies to survive a freshman purge as Calgary went with an older lineup. He is a coachable type. He has some upside but won't be a real impact player.

The Flames were unhappy with his output in his first two seasons and he will be on the bubble in training camp if he isn't moved.

PROJECTION

Stillman will have trouble seeing ice time if he stays in Calgary. He is capable of 35 to 40 points in a modestly expanded role.

GERMAN TITOV

Yrs. of NHL service: 4
Born: Moscow, Russia; Oct. 16, 1965
Position: centre/left wing
Height: 6-1
Weight: 190
Uniform no.: 13
Shoots: left

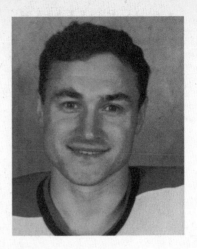

Career statistics:

GP	G	A	TP	PIM
277	89	99	188	104

1993-94 statistics:

GP	G	A	TP	+/-	PIM	PP	SH	GW	GT	S	PCT
76	27	18	45	+20	28	8	3	2	0	153	17.6

1994-95 statistics:

GP	G	A	TP	+/-	PIM	PP	SH	GW	GT	S	PCT
40	12	12	24	+6	16	3	2	3	0	88	13.6

1995-96 statistics:

GP	G	A	TP	+/-	PIM	PP	SH	GW	GT	S	PCT
82	28	39	67	+9	24	13	2	2	2	214	13.1

1996-97 statistics:

GP	G	A	TP	+/-	PIM	PP	SH	GW	GT	S	PCT
79	22	30	52	-12	36	12	0	4	0	192	11.5

LAST SEASON

Led team in power-play goals. Third on team in assists and points. Tied for second on team in game-winning goals. Missed one game with ankle injury.

THE FINESSE GAME

Titiv works hard to get himself in a great scoring position and then . . . he doesn't shoot. He uses a short stick and does a lot of one-handed puckhandling. This gives him good control and makes it harder for the defense to knock the puck loose without knocking him down and taking a penalty. It also gives him a quick release on his underutilized wrister.

Titov was used primarily on the wing again last season, but prefers playing centre and using all of the ice, weaving with his linemates. He will be happy if former linemate Michael Nylander returns to the team. Titov shows great hockey sense in all zones. He is very creative, but is a streaky scorer. He lacks consistency and doesn't step up on a nightly basis. He plays on the first power-play unit.

Titov is an agile skater, if not outstandingly fast. He is very quick coming off the boards and driving to the circle for a shot, and has a good inside-out move and a change of gears. Strong on his skates, he is tough to knock down. He has good hands on the draw. He kills penalties well and blocks shots.

THE PHYSICAL GAME

Titov uses his size well. He takes a hit to make a play, blocks shots and sacrifices his body. He protects the puck in an unusual way, by getting his left leg out to kick away the stick of a defender so that he can't be sweep- or poke-checked. It's a move that requires superb balance.

THE INTANGIBLES

Titov needs to be combined with linemates who play a European style of weaving and puck control rather than dump-and-chase.

PROJECTION

Titov has 75-point potential, but that will be attained only if Calgary upgrades its forwards.

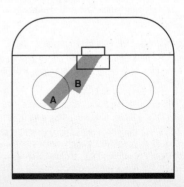

CAROLINA HURRICANES

Players' Statistics 1996-97

POS.	NO.	PLAYER	GP	G	A	PTS	+/-	PIM	PP	SH	GW	GT	S	PCT
L	8	GEOFF SANDERSON	82	36	31	67	-9	29	12	1	4	1	297	12.1
C	21	ANDREW CASSELS	81	22	44	66	-16	46	8		2		142	15.5
L	27	DEREK KING	82	26	33	59	-6	22	6		3		181	14.4
C	55	KEITH PRIMEAU	75	26	25	51	-3	161	6	3	2	2	169	15.4
R	11	KEVIN DINEEN	78	19	29	48	-6	141	8		5	2	185	10.3
R	16	NELSON EMERSON	66	9	29	38	-21	34	2	1	2		194	4.6
R	12	STEVEN RICE	78	21	14	35	-11	59	5		2		159	13.2
D	20	GLEN WESLEY	68	6	26	32	0	40	3	1			126	4.8
C	92	JEFF O'NEILL	72	14	16	30	-24	40	2	1	2		101	13.9
D	3	STEVE CHIASSON	65	8	22	30	-21	39	4	2	1		168	4.8
R	24	SAMI KAPANEN	45	13	12	25	6	2	3		2		82	15.9
R	18	ROBERT KRON	68	10	12	22	-18	10	2		4	1	182	5.5
D	7	CURTIS LESCHYSHYN	77	4	18	22	-18	38	1	1	1		102	3.9
L	28	PAUL RANHEIM	67	10	11	21	-13	18		3	1		96	10.4
D	14	KEVIN HALLER	62	2	11	13	-12	85					77	2.6
D	6	ADAM BURT	71	2	11	13	-13	79					85	2.4
C	44	KENT MANDERVILLE	44	6	5	11	3	18			1		51	11.8
R	17	CHRIS MURRAY	64	5	3	8	-7	124					41	12.2
D	5	ALEXANDER GODYNYUK	55	1	6	7	-10	41			1		34	2.9
D	23	*MAREK MALIK	47	1	5	6	5	50			1		33	3.0
L	32	STU GRIMSON	76	2	2	4	-8	218					17	11.8
R	46	KEVIN BROWN	11		4	4	-6	6					12	
D	41	*NOLAN PRATT	9		2	2	0	6					4	
L	37	JEFF DANIELS	10		2	2	2						6	
G	1	SEAN BURKE	51		2	2	0	14						
D	7	BRIAN GLYNN	1	1		1	2	2					2	50.0
C	26	*STEVE MARTINS	2		1	1	0						2	
G	29	JASON MUZZATTI	31		1	1	0	18						
D	27	JEFF BROWN	1				0							
D	25	*JASON MCBAIN	6				-4						1	
G	47	*J SEBASTIEN GIGUERE	8				0							

GP = games played; G = goals; A = assists; PTS = points; +/- = goals-for minus goals-against while player is on ice; PIM = penalties in minutes; PP = power-play goals; SH = shorthanded goals; GW = game-winning goals; GT = game-tying goals; S = no. of shots; PCT = percentage of goals to shots; * = rookie

JEFF BROWN

Yrs. of NHL service: 11
Born: Ottawa, Ont.; Apr. 30, 1966
Position: right defense
Height: 6-1
Weight: 204
Uniform no.: 27
Shoots: right

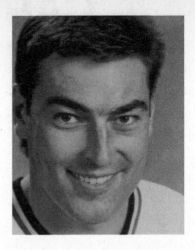

Career statistics:

GP	G	A	TP	PIM
687	153	405	555	466

1993-94 statistics:

GP	G	A	TP	+/-	PIM	PP	SH	GW	GT	S	PCT
74	14	52	66	-11	56	7	0	3	1	237	5.9

1994-95 statistics:

GP	G	A	TP	+/-	PIM	PP	SH	GW	GT	S	PCT
33	8	23	31	-2	16	3	0	0	0	111	7.2

1995-96 statistics:

GP	G	A	TP	+/-	PIM	PP	SH	GW	GT	S	PCT
76	8	47	55	+8	56	5	0	0	0	177	4.5

1996-97 statistics:

GP	G	A	TP	+/-	PIM	PP	SH	GW	GT	S	PCT
1	0	0	0	0	0	0	0	0	0	0	0.0

LAST SEASON

Missed 81 games with back injury and spinal fusion.

THE FINESSE GAME

Brown is a natural quarterback on the power play. He moves to the left side on the point and likes to glide to the top of the circle to step into a one-timer.

Brown's game stems from his skating ability. He has impressive lateral movement and can handle the puck at tempo. He's a very good playmaker for a defenseman, ready to unleash his strong point shot or fake the slap and pass, or headman the pass off a break out of the defensive zone. He sees the ice well and slips perfect passes ahead to speedy wingers like Geoff Sanderson.

Defensively, his game needs improvement. He has too much hockey sense and too much skill not to be a better player.

THE PHYSICAL GAME

Brown is an offensive defenseman, but that doesn't mean he should be fishing for the puck in front of the net when he could be dropping someone onto the seat of his pants. He doesn't finish his checks consistently, and he lacks the mean streak needed to be a more dominating player.

Rehab from his back surgery and conditioning will be a factor, especially in the first half of the season after missing essentially all of last year.

THE INTANGIBLES

Brown is not an elite-class defenseman, but when he elevates his game he is a B version of Ray Bourque. It's going to be another long season for the relocated Whalers and Brown will be counted upon as one of the top offensive defensemen on the team.

PROJECTION

Players have come back successfully from operations like Brown's, but it's better to take a wait-and-see attitude if you're a pool player. If healthy, Brown could bag 55 to 60 points.

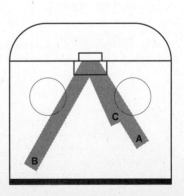

SEAN BURKE

Yrs. of NHL service: 8
Born: Windsor, Ont.; Jan. 29, 1967
Position: goaltender
Height: 6-4
Weight: 208
Uniform no.: 1
Catches: left

Career statistics:

GP	MIN	GA	SO	GAA	A	PIM
418	23541	1305	14	3.33	15	195

1993-94 statistics:

GP	MIN	GAA	W	L	T	SO	GA	S	SAPCT	PIM
47	2750	2.99	17	24	5	2	137	1458	.906	16

1994-95 statistics:

GP	MIN	GAA	W	L	T	SO	GA	S	SAPCT	PIM
42	2418	2.68	17	19	4	0	108	1233	.912	8

1995-96 statistics:

GP	MIN	GAA	W	L	T	SO	GA	S	SAPCT	PIM
66	3669	3.11	28	28	6	4	190	2034	.907	16

1996-97 statistics:

GP	MIN	GAA	W	L	T	SO	GA	S	SAPCT	PIM
51	2985	2.69	22	22	6	4	134	1560	.914	14

LAST SEASON

Missed three games with back spasms. Missed 19 games due to dislocated right thumb. Missed one game with hip flexor.

THE PHYSICAL GAME

Burke was voted the team's MVP by his teammates for the fourth straight season, which makes one wonder if Carolina would have accepted the Whalers if the team hadn't included Burke.

Burke is consistent, seldom beating himself, and he'll steal games his team has no right winning. He challenges the shooter well and comes out to the top of his crease, instead of sitting back, an old habit he appears to have shed.

Burke handles the puck well. He is confident and active on the dump-ins, and with the type of neutral-zone defense Carolina plays, his work out of the net is crucial. He gives his defensemen a chance to handle the puck more easily and break out of the zone with less effort.

Burke fills up the net and is very quick for a net-minder of his size. He may be one of the best big goalies in the league on shots in tight because of his superior reflexes. He has improved his angle play and control of rebounds, though the latter is one area where he could still improve.

Burke has a quick glove hand, but he will often drop it and give the shooter the top corner over his left shoulder. He also holds his blocker hand too low on his stick, which makes him lean over too far and throws him off balance.

THE MENTAL GAME

When a goalie has been playing for as bad a team as the Whalers for as long as Burke has, you wonder about his ability to step up when crunch-time finally does arrive, as it did last year in the failed drive to the playoffs. Burke couldn't be blamed for two losses in the last 11 games when the Whalers were shut out, but a 5-4 loss in Ottawa near the end of the season, followed by a 6-4 loss to the Islanders in which Burke was pulled, helped eliminate the Whalers.

THE INTANGIBLES

A major concern for Burke is his recurring back injuries, which are common for a big goalie. He may be on the trading block. It would be interesting to see him play again for a team whose games count. Burke is the new version of Bill Ranford, who played well all those seasons in obscurity in Edmonton. You wonder how good the guy really is.

PROJECTION

Burke somehow regularly manages to win 20 games with this bunch, which is pretty commendable.

ADAM BURT

Yrs. of NHL service: 8
Born: Detroit, Mich.; Jan. 15, 1969
Position: left defense
Height: 6-2
Weight: 207
Uniform no.: 6
Shoots: left

Career statistics:

GP	G	A	TP	PIM
499	35	92	127	723

1993-94 statistics:

GP	G	A	TP	+/-	PIM	PP	SH	GW	GT	S	PCT
63	1	17	18	-4	75	0	0	0	0	91	1.1

1994-95 statistics:

GP	G	A	TP	+/-	PIM	PP	SH	GW	GT	S	PCT
46	7	11	18	0	65	3	0	1	0	73	9.6

1995-96 statistics:

GP	G	A	TP	+/-	PIM	PP	SH	GW	GT	S	PCT
78	4	9	13	-4	121	0	0	1	0	90	4.4

1996-97 statistics:

GP	G	A	TP	+/-	PIM	PP	SH	GW	GT	S	PCT
71	2	11	13	-13	79	0	0	0	0	85	2.4

LAST SEASON

Missed eight games with groin injury. Missed three games with shoulder injury.

THE FINESSE GAME

Burt is reliable night in and night out. He plays a strong physical game, and brings the puck out of the zone with authority if not great speed.

Burt gets involved in the attack but not to an overwhelming extent. He gets some time on the second power-play unit, but is not a top-flight point man. Once in a great while he'll surprise everyone and sneak into the circle for a shot, but this is rare.

An excellent one-on-one defender on a transition defense, he will strip the puck from a player using a poke-check and stand up to skaters at the blueline.

Burt has evolved into a pretty smart defenseman. He makes much better decisions with the puck and has limited his mental mistakes. He moves the puck smartly without creating opportunities for the opposing team — once one of his greatest weaknesses — and has cut down on his turnovers.

THE PHYSICAL GAME

Big but not strong, Burt works hard off the ice to gain more upper-body and leg strength. He does not consistently control his man along the wall, nor does he drive people off the puck as well as a player of his size should. He is aware that his team needs him to establish a more physical presence, and he combines a willingness to hit with the desire to build himself up so he can be a legitimate thrasher. A more uptempo physical game will give him more room to move and more time to make better plays — an asset, since his hand and foot speed is only average.

Fighting does not come naturally to Burt, but he will do it and hold his own in order to make a point or aid a teammate. He plays hard every night.

THE INTANGIBLES

Burt is a coach's favourite, since no one ever has to worry about whether or not he will show up. His attitude is upbeat and he is quick to learn and improve. If the 'Canes try to break in a young defenseman or two this season, Burt will help them out.

PROJECTION

Burt is never going to accumulate showy point totals — 20 points a season should be his max — but he will be a steady defenseman who contributes in all zones.

ANDREW CASSELS

Yrs. of NHL service: 7
Born: Bramalea, Ont.; July 23, 1969
Position: centre
Height: 6-0
Weight: 192
Uniform no.: 21
Shoots: left

Career statistics:

GP	G	A	TP	PIM
498	105	272	377	242

1993-94 statistics:

GP	G	A	TP	+/-	PIM	PP	SH	GW	GT	S	PCT
79	16	42	58	-21	37	8	1	3	0	126	12.7

1994-95 statistics:

GP	G	A	TP	+/-	PIM	PP	SH	GW	GT	S	PCT
46	7	30	37	-3	18	1	0	1	0	74	9.5

1995-96 statistics:

GP	G	A	TP	+/-	PIM	PP	SH	GW	GT	S	PCT
81	20	43	63	+8	39	6	0	1	2	135	14.8

1996-97 statistics:

GP	G	A	TP	+/-	PIM	PP	SH	GW	GT	S	PCT
81	22	44	66	-16	46	8	0	2	0	142	15.5

LAST SEASON

Led team in assists. Second on team in points and shooting percentage. Tied for second on team in power-play goals. Missed one game with charley horse.

THE FINESSE GAME

The first word most people associate with Cassels is smart. He is an intelligent player with terrific hockey instincts, who knows when to recognize passing situations, when to move the puck and who to move it to. He has a good backhand pass in traffic and is almost as good on his backhand as his forehand. He is a creative passer who is aware of his teammates.

Cassels just hates to shoot. He won't do it much, and although he has spent a great deal of time practising it, his release is just not NHL calibre. He has quick hands, though, and can swipe a shot off a bouncing puck in midair. He doesn't always fight through checks to get the kind of shots he should.

A mainstay on both specialty teams, Cassels has improved on draws. He backchecks and blocks shots. He has good speed but lacks one-step quickness. He has improved his puckhandling at a high tempo.

THE PHYSICAL GAME

To complement his brains, Cassels needs brawn. He is facing a lot of defensive pressure now and has to force his way through strong forechecks and traffic around the net. He tends to get run down late in the season or during a tough stretch in the schedule, and when he gets fatigued he is not nearly as effective.

THE INTANGIBLES

Cassels is a number two centre who is sometimes forced into the number one role. He's smart, but his skill level isn't high.

PROJECTION

Cassels will get 60 to 65 points as long as he stays linemates with Geoff Sanderson.

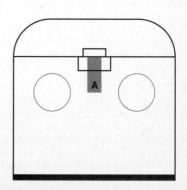

STEVE CHIASSON

Yrs. of NHL service: 11
Born: Barrie, Ont.; Apr. 14, 1967
Position: left defense
Height: 6-1
Weight: 205
Uniform no.: 3
Shoots: left

Career statistics:

GP	G	A	TP	PIM
612	83	247	330	987

1993-94 statistics:

GP	G	A	TP	+/-	PIM	PP	SH	GW	GT	S	PCT
82	13	33	46	+17	122	4	1	2	0	238	5.5

1994-95 statistics:

GP	G	A	TP	+/-	PIM	PP	SH	GW	GT	S	PCT
45	2	23	25	+10	39	1	0	0	0	110	1.8

1995-96 statistics:

GP	G	A	TP	+/-	PIM	PP	SH	GW	GT	S	PCT
76	8	25	33	+3	62	5	0	2	0	175	4.6

1996-97 statistics:

GP	G	A	TP	+/-	PIM	PP	SH	GW	GT	S	PCT
65	8	22	30	-21	39	4	2	1	0	168	4.8

LAST SEASON

Acquired from Calgary with a future conditional draft pick for Hnat Domenichelli, Glen Featherstone, a second-round draft pick in 1997 and a third-round draft pick in 1998. Second among team defensemen in scoring. Missed 19 games with knee injuries.

THE FINESSE GAME

Chiasson's finesse game has improved along with his skating. The two go hand-in-hand (or foot-in-skate), and Chiasson has dedicated himself to improving in this critical area. He still has a bit of a choppy stride, but he's quick and better at getting himself into position offensively. He has a cannon shot. He saw more power-play time last season, frequently on the first unit after his trade to the Whalers.

Chiasson is not afraid to gamble in deep, either, and has good instincts about when to pinch in. He handles the puck well down low and uses a snap or wrist shot. He is poised with the puck on the attack. He one-times a shot well.

Defensively, Chiasson plays a solid positional game and reads rushes well. While not great in any one area (save, perhaps, his shot), he has a nice overall package of skills.

THE PHYSICAL GAME

Chiasson is a competitor. He will play hurt, he will defend his teammates and he is prepared to compete every night. He lacked conditioning early in his career and it hurt him, but he has matured in his approach to his livelihood and it's paying off. He keeps his emotions under wraps and plays a disciplined game.

THE INTANGIBLES

Chiasson has become a solid two-way defenseman and is one of the game's more underrated blueliners. He takes his leadership role to heart. His character and his finesse skills are needed by the Hurricanes.

PROJECTION

Chiasson scored 14 points in 18 games after the trade, after scoring 16 in 47 games with Calgary. He will get quality ice time in Carolina and has a shot at a 50-point season.

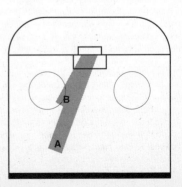

ENRICO CICCONE

Yrs. of NHL service: 5
Born: Montreal, Que.; Apr. 10, 1970
Position: left defense
Height: 6-5
Weight: 220
Uniform no.: 39
Shoots: left

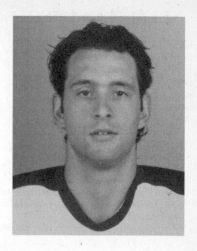

Career statistics:

GP	G	A	TP	PIM
273	7	13	20	1167

1993-94 statistics:

GP	G	A	TP	+/-	PIM	PP	SH	GW	GT	S	PCT
57	1	2	3	-4	226	0	0	0	0	33	3.0

1994-95 statistics:

GP	G	A	TP	+/-	PIM	PP	SH	GW	GT	S	PCT
41	2	4	6	+3	225	0	0	0	0	43	4.7

1995-96 statistics:

GP	G	A	TP	+/-	PIM	PP	SH	GW	GT	S	PCT
66	2	4	6	+1	306	0	0	0	0	60	3.3

1996-97 statistics:

GP	G	A	TP	+/-	PIM	PP	SH	GW	GT	S	PCT
67	2	2	4	-1	233	0	0	1	0	65	3.1

LAST SEASON

Acquired from Chicago for Ryan Rysidore and a draft pick, July 25, 1997. Second on team in penalty minutes. Missed six games with rib injury.

THE FINESSE GAME

Ciccone's overall play is limited because of his skating. He has slow feet, and though he is well-balanced in tight quarters, he's at a disadvantage where any quick turn of foot is needed, even in corners or around the net. Chicago has a top six defense that is tough to crack, and Ciccone will have to add to his repertoire to get ice time. He has worked to improve his puck movement and positioning — two skills that can minimize his slow turn of foot.

Ciccone tends to overhandle the puck, especially in the defensive zone. He does block shots well, but he would be better off using bigger gloves (small ones come off more easily for fights) for defensive purposes. He has some skill and if he keeps working hard he can earn a spot in the lineup.

THE PHYSICAL GAME

Ciccone doesn't back down from any challenge and often goes around issuing them himself. He can fight and he is a punishing checker. Coaches have tried to rein in his enthusiasm a bit, but they don't want to take away his physical presence. You can be tough without being dumb. Ciccone has to learn the difference.

THE INTANGIBLES

Ciccone saw limited ice time in Chicago last season and wasn't exactly an upbeat presence around the team. Carolina is desperate for his size and toughness and he will be utilized more this season.

PROJECTION

Ciccone doesn't play a smart enough game to add much to a lineup, and probably doesn't work as hard as he should for a player with his ability.

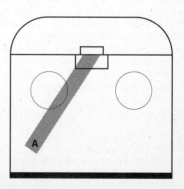

NELSON EMERSON

Yrs. of NHL service: 6
Born: Hamilton, Ont.; Aug. 17, 1967
Position: centre/left wing
Height: 5-11
Weight: 175
Uniform no.: 16
Shoots: right

Career statistics:

GP	G	A	TP	PIM
443	130	212	342	348

1993-94 statistics:

GP	G	A	TP	+/-	PIM	PP	SH	GW	GT	S	PCT
83	33	41	74	-38	80	4	5	6	1	282	11.7

1994-95 statistics:

GP	G	A	TP	+/-	PIM	PP	SH	GW	GT	S	PCT
48	14	23	37	-12	26	4	1	1	0	122	11.5

1995-96 statistics:

GP	G	A	TP	+/-	PIM	PP	SH	GW	GT	S	PCT
81	29	29	58	-7	78	12	2	5	0	247	11.7

1996-97 statistics:

GP	G	A	TP	+/-	PIM	PP	SH	GW	GT	S	PCT
66	9	29	38	-21	34	2	1	2	0	194	4.6

LAST SEASON

Missed 16 games with recurring ankle injury and fracture.

THE FINESSE GAME

Emerson's problematic ankle contributed mightily to his disappointing season. A mainstay on the power play, his mobility on the point was limited.

On the power play, Emerson can either play the point or work down low. He has an excellent point shot, keeping it low, on target and tippable. He is intelligent with the puck and doesn't always fire from the point, but works it to the middle of the blueline and uses screens well. When he carries in one-on-one against a defender, especially on a shorthanded rush, he always manages to use the defenseman to screen the goalie.

Emerson works well down low at even strength. He is mature and creative, with a terrific short game. He has quick hands for passing or snapping off a shot. He likes to work from behind the net, tempting the defense to chase him behind the cage. Speed and puck control are the essence of his game.

He has nice quickness and balance, and he darts in and out of traffic in front of the net. He's too small to do any physical damage, which is why he needs to play with physical linemates. Emerson can use his speed to drive wide on a defenseman, who will think he has Emerson angled off only to watch him blast past.

THE PHYSICAL GAME

Emerson has good skating balance, and that will give him a little edge to knock a bigger player off-stride once in awhile. He works hard defensively but has to play a smart, small man's game to avoid getting pasted. He plays bigger than his size but isn't really feisty.

THE INTANGIBLES

His ankle injury and the departure of Brendan Shanahan spelled disaster for Emerson. His stock plummeted and he was being shopped around during the off-season.

PROJECTION

Emerson can be a 60-point scorer again if he ends up with the right team. He'll be a spare part with the Hurricanes.

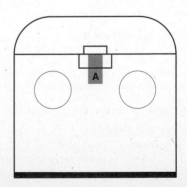

SAMI KAPANEN

Yrs. of NHL service: 2
Born: Vantaa, Finland; June 14, 1973
Position: left wing
Height: 5-10
Weight: 170
Uniform no.: 24
Shoots: left

Career statistics:

GP	G	A	TP	PIM
80	18	16	34	8

1995-96 statistics:

GP	G	A	TP	+/-	PIM	PP	SH	GW	GT	S	PCT
35	5	4	9	0	6	0	0	0	0	46	10.9

1996-97 statistics:

GP	G	A	TP	+/-	PIM	PP	SH	GW	GT	S	PCT
45	13	12	25	+6	2	3	0	2	0	82	15.9

LAST SEASON

Led team in plus-minus and shooting percentage. Missed 35 games with knee injuries. Missed two games with flu.

THE FINESSE GAME

Kapanen is a small, skilled forward who is always moving. He handles the puck well while in motion, although like a lot of European forwards he tends to hold onto the puck too long. He will shoot on the fly, however, and has an NHL shot when he does release it. He has a fine wrist shot, and he can score off the rush, as he proved with his penalty-shot goal last season.

Kapanen has quickness, good balance, good strength and he's smart. He makes few mistakes. He knows where to be on the ice and how to use big players as picks and screens. He sticks to the perimeter until he darts into holes. He takes care of his defensive assignments, and even though he's too small to body check, he is able to harrass opponents by lifting up a stick and swiping the puck.

THE PHYSICAL GAME

Kapanen's size will always be a detriment: he's very lean without much muscle mass. He plays a spunky game and picks up the team on its quieter nights because he sprints to the pucks and tries on every shift.

THE INTANGIBLES

Kapanen established chemistry with big centre Keith Primeau, who loves playing with this small, creative winger. Kapanen has been described as a poor man's Saku Koivu.

PROJECTION

If he stays healthy, Kapanen could score 25 to 30 goals.

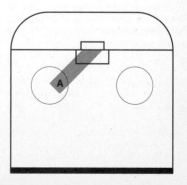

ROBERT KRON

Yrs. of NHL service: 7
Born: Brno, Czechoslovakia; Feb. 27, 1967
Position: left wing
Height: 5-11
Weight: 185
Uniform no.: 18
Shoots: left

Career statistics:

GP	G	A	TP	PIM
416	94	109	203	75

1993-94 statistics:

GP	G	A	TP	+/-	PIM	PP	SH	GW	GT	S	PCT
77	24	26	50	0	8	2	1	3	0	194	12.4

1994-95 statistics:

GP	G	A	TP	+/-	PIM	PP	SH	GW	GT	S	PCT
37	10	8	18	-3	10	3	1	1	0	88	11.4

1995-96 statistics:

GP	G	A	TP	+/-	PIM	PP	SH	GW	GT	S	PCT
77	22	28	50	-1	6	8	1	3	0	203	10.8

1996-97 statistics:

GP	G	A	TP	+/-	PIM	PP	SH	GW	GT	S	PCT
68	10	12	22	-18	10	2	0	4	1	182	5.5

LAST SEASON

Tied for second on team in game-winning goals. Missed 12 games with knee sprain.

THE FINESSE GAME

Kron's inconsistency was his biggest problem last season. The knee injury didn't occur until midseason, and he was slumping before that.

Kron has good speed and can control the puck at high tempo, which gives him the ability to intimidate and drive opposing defensemen back off the blueline. One of the best things to happen to his career was the reinstatement of four-on-four play in the case of coincidental minor penalties. He thrives on the extra open ice. Kron is aware in all three zones. He can kill penalties and work on the power play as well. Defensively reliable, he can be used on the ice at any time in the game. He is a very creative player, more of a playmaker than a shooter, but he needs to shoot more because of his good hands. He tries to be too fine with his shot and misses the net frequently when he is in a prime scoring area. He likes to use a snap shot more than a slapper and will get a quick release away from 15 to 20 feet out.

THE PHYSICAL GAME

Kron is very fit, but he is a small player and doesn't play a physical style. He's not afraid and doesn't bail out of tough situations. He will need to be shored up by big forwards, but linemates with hands, since Kron will create good scoring chances that shouldn't go to waste.

THE INTANGIBLES

Kron plummeted down the team's depth chart (which, frankly, wasn't very deep). Half of his goals were either tied or won games, but he only scored 10 goals.

PROJECTION

Unless he wakes up this season, Kron is on the bubble. He's a skilled guy but he's older now. We don't anticipate much.

CURTIS LESCHYSHYN

Yrs. of NHL service: 9
Born: Thompson, Man.; Sept. 21, 1969
Position: left defense
Height: 6-1
Weight: 205
Uniform no.: 7
Shoots: left

Career statistics:

GP	G	A	TP	PIM
593	37	118	155	541

1993-94 statistics:

GP	G	A	TP	+/-	PIM	PP	SH	GW	GT	S	PCT
77	4	15	19	-7	143	0	2	1	0	66	6.1

1994-95 statistics:

GP	G	A	TP	+/-	PIM	PP	SH	GW	GT	S	PCT
44	2	13	15	+29	20	0	0	0	0	43	4.7

1995-96 statistics:

GP	G	A	TP	+/-	PIM	PP	SH	GW	GT	S	PCT
77	4	15	19	+32	73	0	0	1	0	76	5.3

1996-97 statistics:

GP	G	A	TP	+/-	PIM	PP	SH	GW	GT	S	PCT
77	4	18	22	-18	38	1	1	1	0	102	3.9

LAST SEASON

Acquired from Washington for Andrei Nikolishin, November 9, 1996. Acquired by Washington with Chris Simon for Keith Jones, a 1998 first-round draft pick and a fourth-round pick in 1998, November 2, 1996. Missed five games with abdominal injury.

THE FINESSE GAME

Leschyshyn has excellent skills for a big man, especially his skating, which is strong forwards and backwards. He has great lateral movement and quickness.

Leschyshyn has finely tuned stick skills. His passes are soft, and he will jump into the rush by skating the puck out of the defensive zone, moving it off his forehand or backhand. He is not as effective with his passes out of the zone, as he tends to get flustered, so he will usually lug it out when he gets the chance.

He has a nice point shot. It's low and accurate, and he gets it away quickly, but it's not elite enough for the first-unit power play. He will also make a foray into the circle on occasion and can utilize his quick wrist shot. He knows the importance of getting the shot on target and would rather take a little velocity off the puck to make sure his aim is true.

Leschyshyn is not overly creative, and has become more defense-oriented in the past season. His reads are excellent.

THE PHYSICAL GAME

Leschyshyn is very fit. He made a successful comeback from a potentially career-threatening knee injury, a challenge that is more mental than physical. And he provides consistency and strong defensive-zone coverage.

Leschyshyn has become a more confident hitter, but he is not a big open-ice checker. He does make efficient take-outs to eliminate his man, and doesn't run around the ice trying to pound people.

THE INTANGIBLES

After playing his entire career with one organization (Quebec/Colorado), Leschyshyn was traded twice in a week, which had to be unsettling. He has a Stanley Cup ring, a rarity in his team's room.

PROJECTION

Leschyshyn is a solid two-way defenseman whose point totals will never rise much beyond the 25 to 30 range. He has settled into using his finesse skills defensively.

MAREK MALIK

Yrs. of NHL service: 2
Born: Ostrava, Czechoslovkia; June 24, 1975
Position: left defense
Height: 6-5
Weight: 190
Uniform no.: 23
Shoots: left

Career statistics:

GP	G	A	TP	PIM
55	1	6	7	54

1994-95 statistics:

GP	G	A	TP	+/-	PIM	PP	SH	GW	GT	S	PCT
1	0	1	1	+1	0	0	0	0	0	0	0.0

1995-96 statistics:

GP	G	A	TP	+/-	PIM	PP	SH	GW	GT	S	PCT
7	0	0	0	-3	4	0	0	0	0	2	0.0

1996-97 statistics:

GP	G	A	TP	+/-	PIM	PP	SH	GW	GT	S	PCT
47	1	5	6	+5	50	0	0	1	0	33	3.0

LAST SEASON

First NHL season. Scored 0-3 — 3 in 3 games with Springfield (AHL). Missed three games with flu. Missed two games with shin injury.

THE FINESSE GAME

Malik has very good potential because of his high skill level in all areas. He is a good skater for his size, though he's a straight-legged skater and a bit awkward. He uses his range mostly as a defensive tool and is not much involved in the attack.

Malik is poised with the puck. He is a good passer and playmaker and moves the puck out of his own end quickly. He won't try to do too much himself but will use his teammates well. He's big but does a lot of the little things, which makes him a solid defensive player. He limits his offensive contributions to a shot from the point, however, he may develop better skill as a playmaker.

THE PHYSICAL GAME

Tall but weedy, Malik needs to fill out more to be able to handle some of the NHL's big boys. Like Kjell Samuelsson, he takes up a lot of space with his arms and stick, and is more of an octopus-type defenseman than a solid hitter. He is strong in front of his net. He has some aggressiveness in him but needs to find a consistency level.

THE INTANGIBLES

Malik should be ready physically to win a job this season, but he has to mature in other ways and was frequently a healthy scratch. The Whalers gave him a lot of chances to step up last season due to injuries; he didn't.

PROJECTION

Malik is still young and he should become a regular on the third defense pairing.

JEFF O'NEILL

Yrs. of NHL service: 2
Born: Richmond Hill, Ont.; Feb. 23, 1976
Position: centre
Height: 6-0
Weight: 190
Uniform no.: 92
Shoots: right

Career statistics:

GP	G	A	TP	PIM
137	22	35	57	80

1995-96 statistics:

GP	G	A	TP	+/-	PIM	PP	SH	GW	GT	S	PCT
65	8	19	27	-3	40	1	0	1	0	65	12.3

1996-97 statistics:

GP	G	A	TP	+/-	PIM	PP	SH	GW	GT	S	PCT
72	14	16	30	-24	40	2	1	2	0	101	13.9

lacks emotion) that keep him from being top drawer.

LAST SEASON

Worst plus-minus on team. Missed one game with injury. Played one game for Springfield (AHL) with no points.

THE FINESSE GAME

To be a Pat LaFontaine — to whom O'Neill has often been compared — a player needs all the tools, and except for his skating, O'Neill's skills are not good enough to place him among the top centres. He has a good sense of timing and is patient with his passes. He doesn't have a big-time release but he has a decent one-timer. He is an excellent skater with balance, speed, acceleration and quickness.

O'Neill likes to carry the puck down the left-wing boards to protect the puck, and with his speed he is able to blow by defensemen. He does not follow this move up by driving to the net. Defensively, he has to remind himself not to leave the zone before the puck does. He is often too anxious to get the counterattack going before his team has control.

THE PHYSICAL GAME

O'Neill has to demonstrate a better nose for the net, like his idol, Jeremy Roenick. If he plays a little grittier he would step up his game.

THE INTANGIBLES

O'Neill is not a true number one centre, and by the end of the season he was a number four. He has a lot of growing up to do. Nobody looks better in warmups than O'Neill, whose fancy moves work when nobody is checking him, but not in games. He would be better off just making the play than trying to earn style points. O'Neill was rushed into the NHL and could use a season in the minors.

PROJECTION

O'Neill will never be a 90- to 100-point scorer because of the flaws in his game and his makeup (he

KEITH PRIMEAU

Yrs. of NHL service: 7
Born: Toronto, Ont.; Nov. 24, 1971
Position: centre
Height: 6-4
Weight: 210
Uniform no.: 55
Shoots: left

Career statistics:

GP	G	A	TP	PIM
438	123	160	281	942

1993-94 statistics:

GP	G	A	TP	+/-	PIM	PP	SH	GW	GT	S	PCT
78	31	42	73	+34	173	7	3	4	2	155	20.0

1994-95 statistics:

GP	G	A	TP	+/-	PIM	PP	SH	GW	GT	S	PCT
45	15	27	42	+17	99	1	0	3	0	96	15.6

1995-96 statistics:

GP	G	A	TP	+/-	PIM	PP	SH	GW	GT	S	PCT
74	27	25	52	+19	168	6	2	7	0	150	18.0

1996-97 statistics:

GP	G	A	TP	+/-	PIM	PP	SH	GW	GT	S	PCT
75	26	25	51	-3	161	6	3	2	2	169	15.4

LAST SEASON

Acquired from Detroit with Paul Coffey and a 1997 first-round draft pick for Brendan Shanahan and Brian Glynn, October 9, 1996. Tied for team lead in short-handed goals. Second on team in penalty minutes. Tied for second on team in goals. Third on team in shooting percentage. Missed one game with flu. Missed on game with concussion. Missed one game with asthma. Served two-game suspension for slashing.

THE FINESSE GAME

When a player forces a trade, as Primeau did, he is under the gun to produce. Playing for a lame-duck team in Hartford wasn't the easiest task, but Primeau came through fairly well.

Primeau has improved in two major areas in the past few seasons. First is his skating. With better skating has come more ice time, more confidence and more responsibility. Second is his increasing versatility. He has worked hard at all aspects of his game and can be used in almost any role, including penalty killing and four-on-four play. His face-off work has improved dramatically.

Primeau has a huge stride with a long reach. A left-hand shot, he will steam down the right side, slide the puck to his backhand, get his feet wide apart for balance, shield the puck with his body and use his left arm to fend off the defenseman before shovelling the puck to the front of the net for a linemate.

Primeau is clever enough to accept the puck at top speed and, instead of wondering what to do with the puck, make a move.

THE PHYSICAL GAME

It used to be that if Primeau had contact with someone, he would be the one to fall. Now, he has im-proved his posture and balance, and can knock some pretty big men on their cans. He would rather go through you than around you.

Primeau has a fiery temper and can lose control. Emotion is a desirable quality, but he has become too valuable a player to spend too much time in the penalty box. He might have swung the pendulum back a little too far last season, though, and was too tame on some nights. He needs to wig out once in awhile (like with the slash on Joe Juneau that earned his suspension — though we don't advocate actually hurting people, just scaring them).

THE INTANGIBLES

Because he's a left-handed shot and isn't too adroit with his backhand pass, Primeau didn't play with Hartford's premier sniper, Geoff Sanderson. A skilled right-winger is needed to make the most of Primeau. Sami Kapanen could be the guy, if he can stay healthy.

PROJECTION

Carolina isn't going to be a much deeper team next season, but playing in a new city will at least add some excitement for the players. Primeau should feel more comfortable starting the season with the team and we expect better numbers.

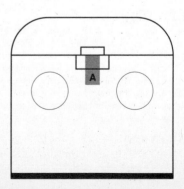

STEVEN RICE

Yrs. of NHL service: 5
Born: Kitchener, Ont.; May 26, 1971
Position: right wing
Height: 6-0
Weight: 217
Uniform no.: 12
Shoots: right

Career statistics:

GP	G	A	TP	PIM
282	62	57	119	237

1993-94 statistics:

GP	G	A	TP	+/-	PIM	PP	SH	GW	GT	S	PCT
63	17	15	32	-10	36	6	0	1	1	129	13.2

1994-95 statistics:

GP	G	A	TP	+/-	PIM	PP	SH	GW	GT	S	PCT
40	11	10	21	+2	61	4	0	1	1	57	19.3

1995-96 statistics:

GP	G	A	TP	+/-	PIM	PP	SH	GW	GT	S	PCT
59	10	12	22	-4	47	1	0	2	0	108	9.3

1996-97 statistics:

GP	G	A	TP	+/-	PIM	PP	SH	GW	GT	S	PCT
78	21	14	35	-11	59	5	0	2	0	159	13.2

LAST SEASON

Career high in goals. Missed two games with back spasms.

THE FINESSE GAME

Rice has to go to the net and shoot. He is less effective when he tries to do too much with the puck because he is not creative and isn't much of a passer. He isn't going to drive around defensemen and rip a shot from the face-off dot. He has decent hands for shots in tight and uses his body well for screens and tips on the power play.

Rice isn't a very good skater for a player of his size. He is solid and has good balance for work around the net, but he lacks quickness and is slow getting back into the play defensively.

THE PHYSICAL GAME

It's disappointing to have the size Rice has and not use it on a consistent basis. He could be much more of a factor every night. He's built along the stocky lines of Trent Klatt but lacks Klatt's speed and willingness to get involved.

THE INTANGIBLES

Players with Rice's size are always valued, and the Hurricans rewarded him with a new contract before this season. Power forwards do take a long time to develop, but, at 26, Rice has shown few indications that he is going to be among the league's elite.

PROJECTION

Rice has shown slight but steady progress in recent years. Still, he probably won't score more than 25 goals.

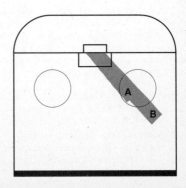

GEOFF SANDERSON

Yrs. of NHL service: 6
Born: Hay River, N.W.T.; Feb. 1, 1972
Position: left wing
Height: 6-0
Weight: 185
Uniform no.: 8
Shoots: left

Career statistics:

GP	G	A	TP	PIM
439	189	163	352	181

1993-94 statistics:

GP	G	A	TP	+/-	PIM	PP	SH	GW	GT	S	PCT
82	41	26	67	-13	42	15	1	6	2	266	15.4

1994-95 statistics:

GP	G	A	TP	+/-	PIM	PP	SH	GW	GT	S	PCT
46	18	14	32	-10	24	4	0	4	0	170	10.6

1995-96 statistics:

GP	G	A	TP	+/-	PIM	PP	SH	GW	GT	S	PCT
81	34	31	65	0	40	6	0	7	0	314	10.8

1996-97 statistics:

GP	G	A	TP	+/-	PIM	PP	SH	GW	GT	S	PCT
82	36	31	67	-9	29	12	1	4	1	297	12.1

LAST SEASON

Led team in goals, points, power-play goals and shots. Tied for second on team in game-winning goals. Third on team in assists. One of two Whalers to appear in all 82 games.

THE FINESSE GAME

Sanderson still doesn't make the best use of his speed, which prevents him from becoming the southpaw version of Mike Gartner. His skating speed gives him a tremendous edge over the majority of NHL players, but it's not as big a weapon as it should be.

Sanderson has to go, go, go, and take lots of shots. When he plays that way, he is far more dangerous. He can drive wide on a defenseman or open up space by forcing the defense to play back off him. He doesn't score often off the rush because he doesn't have a heavy shot. He can create chaos off the rush, though, and finish up by getting open in the slot for a pass from his linemates.

He has a superb one-timer on the power play, where he likes to score on his off-wing in the deep right slot. Sanderson has become a better all-around player. He is more intelligent in his own end and his checking is more consistent. He can also kill penalties. His speed makes him a shorthanded threat.

THE PHYSICAL GAME

Sanderson has to learn and desire to fight his way through checkers. He is wiry but gets outmuscled, and although his speed keeps him clear of a lot of traffic, he has to battle when the room isn't there. He would benefit if the team added a little muscle up front. Keith Primeau was acquired, but Sanderson usually played with Andrew Cassels, a non-physical type.

THE INTANGIBLES

Sanderson wants to be the go-to guy, which is commendable, but he scored only three goals in 13 games down the stretch as the Whalers tried to say farewell to Hartford with a playoff appearance.

PROJECTION

Sanderson has the speed and the trigger to be a 50-goal scorer. The step to that elite class will take some help from his teammates, but a lot more has to come from Sanderson's mental toughness and commitment. The question is whether he wants to work harder to become an elite player, or if he is content being a very good one. He is a more complete player now that his work ethic has improved.

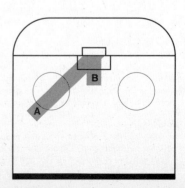

GLEN WESLEY

Yrs. of NHL service: 10
Born: Red Deer, Alta.; Oct. 2, 1968
Position: left defense
Height: 6-1
Weight: 197
Uniform no.: 20
Shoots: left

Career statistics:

GP	G	A	TP	PIM
721	93	286	379	599

1993-94 statistics:

GP	G	A	TP	+/-	PIM	PP	SH	GW	GT	S	PCT
81	14	44	58	+1	64	6	1	1	1	265	5.3

1994-95 statistics:

GP	G	A	TP	+/-	PIM	PP	SH	GW	GT	S	PCT
48	2	14	16	-6	50	1	0	1	0	125	1.6

1995-96 statistics:

GP	G	A	TP	+/-	PIM	PP	SH	GW	GT	S	PCT
68	8	16	24	-9	88	6	0	1	0	129	6.2

1996-97 statistics:

GP	G	A	TP	+/-	PIM	PP	SH	GW	GT	S	PCT
68	6	26	32	0	40	3	1	0	0	126	4.8

LAST SEASON

Led team defensemen in scoring. Second on team in plus-minus. Missed 12 games with broken foot. Missed one game with hip flexor. Missed one game with flu.

THE FINESSE GAME

Wesley simply isn't an offensive force, though he keeps being shoehorned into that role. He is at best a number two defenseman, and is ideally suited as a three or four. But since the Whalers paid a huge price to get him they'll keep trying to get their money's worth. They really don't have much else in their system.

Wesley is solid, but not elite class. He is very good with the puck. He clicks on the power play because he knows when to jump into the holes. He has good but not great offensive instincts, gauging when to pinch, when to rush, when to pass the puck and when to back off. He is a good skater who is not afraid to veer into the play deep; he seldom gets trapped there. He has a good slap shot from the point and snap shot from the circle.

You could count on two hands the number of times Wesley has been beaten one-on-one during his career, and there are very few defensemen you can say that about. He makes defensive plays with confidence and is poised even when outnumbered in the rush. He has to keep his feet moving.

THE PHYSICAL GAME

Wesley is not a bone-crunching defenseman, but neither was Jacques Laperriere, and he's in the Hall of Fame. We're not suggesting that Wesley is in that class, but just that you don't have to shatter glass to be a solid checker, which he is. He's not a mean hitter, but he will execute a take-out check and not let his man get back into the play.

He is also sly about running interference for his defense partner, allowing him time to move the puck and giving him confidence that he won't get hammered by a forechecker.

THE INTANGIBLES

Wesley will never be able to do enough because his price tag (two first-round draft picks, one of which turned out to be Kyle McLaren), was so steep.

PROJECTION

Wesley is, at best, a 40- to 50-point scorer.

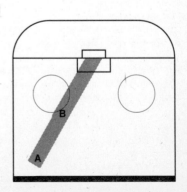

CHICAGO BLACKHAWKS

Players' Statistics 1996-97

POS.	NO.	PLAYER	GP	G	A	PTS	+/-	PIM	PP	SH	GW	GT	S	PCT
R	10	TONY AMONTE	81	41	36	77	35	64	9	2	4	2	266	15.4
C	26	ALEXEI ZHAMNOV	74	20	42	62	18	56	6	1	2		208	9.6
D	7	CHRIS CHELIOS	72	10	38	48	16	112	2		2		194	5.2
L	55	ERIC DAZE	71	22	19	41	-4	16	11		4		176	12.5
C	32	MURRAY CRAVEN	75	8	27	35	0	12	2		1		122	6.6
R	22	ULF DAHLEN	73	14	19	33	-2	18	4		4		131	10.7
D	2	ERIC WEINRICH	81	7	25	32	19	62	1			1	115	6.1
L	19	*ETHAN MOREAU	82	15	16	31	13	123			1	1	114	13.2
R	16	KEVIN MILLER	69	14	17	31	-10	41	5	1	2		139	10.1
C	11	JEFF SHANTZ	69	9	21	30	11	28		1	1		86	10.5
D	20	GARY SUTER	82	7	21	28	-4	70	3			1	225	3.1
C	18	DENIS SAVARD	64	9	18	27	-10	60	2		2		82	11.0
R	25	SERGEI KRIVOKRASOV	67	13	11	24	-1	42	2		3		104	12.5
L	38	JAMES BLACK	64	12	11	23	6	20			3		122	9.8
L	24	BOB PROBERT	82	9	14	23	-3	326	1		3		111	8.1
D	4	KEITH CARNEY	81	3	15	18	26	62			1		77	3.9
D	6	MICHAL SYKORA	63	3	14	17	4	69	1				77	3.9
C	12	BRENT SUTTER	39	7	7	14	10	18			1		62	11.3
R	15	JIM CUMMINS	65	6	6	12	4	199				1	61	9.8
D	39	ENRICO CICCONE	67	2	2	4	-1	233			1		65	3.1
C	22	ADAM CREIGHTON	19	1	2	3	-2	13					20	5.0
D	8	CAM RUSSELL	44	1	1	2	-8	65					19	5.3
L	37	*JEAN-YVES LEROUX	1	1	1	1	5							
D	44	*CHRISTIAN LAFLAMME	4		1	1	3	2					3	
D	46	*TUOMAS GRONMAN	16		1	1	-4	13					9	
G	31	JEFF HACKETT	41		1	1	0	6						
C	17	*SERGEI KLIMOVICH	1				0	2						
G	29	JIM WAITE	2				0							
C	14	STEVE DUBINSKY	5				2						4	
R	23	*MIKE PROKOPEC	6				-1	6					2	
L	54	DAVE CHYZOWSKI	8				1	6					6	
L	17	BASIL MCRAE	8				-2	12					1	
D	5	STEVE SMITH	21				4	29					7	
G	40	CHRIS TERRERI	29				0							

GP = games played; G = goals; A = assists; PTS = points; +/- = goals-for minus goals-against while player is on ice; PIM = penalties in minutes; PP = power-play goals; SH = shorthanded goals; GW = game-winning goals; GT = game-tying goals; S = no. of shots; PCT = percentage of goals to shots; * = rookie

TONY AMONTE

Yrs. of NHL service: 6
Born: Hingham, Mass.; Aug. 2, 1970
Position: right wing
Height: 6-0
Weight: 190
Uniform no.: 10
Shoots: left

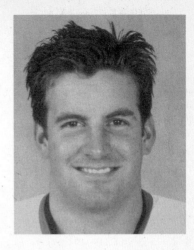

Career statistics:

GP	G	A	TP	PIM
451	172	190	362	308

1993-94 statistics:

GP	G	A	TP	+/-	PIM	PP	SH	GW	GT	S	PCT
79	17	25	42	0	37	4	0	4	0	195	8.7

1994-95 statistics:

GP	G	A	TP	+/-	PIM	PP	SH	GW	GT	S	PCT
48	15	20	35	+7	41	6	1	3	1	105	14.3

1995-96 statistics:

GP	G	A	TP	+/-	PIM	PP	SH	GW	GT	S	PCT
81	31	32	63	+10	62	5	4	5	0	216	14.4

1996-97 statistics:

GP	G	A	TP	+/-	PIM	PP	SH	GW	GT	S	PCT
81	41	36	77	+35	64	9	2	4	2	266	15.4

LAST SEASON

Led team in goals, points, plus-minus, shots and shooting percentage. Tied for team lead in game-winning goals. Second on team in power-play goals. Third on team in assists. Career highs in games, assists and points. Missed one game with bruised knee.

THE FINESSE GAME

What World Cup hangover? Not only did Amonte spur Team USA to the World Cup gold in September, he never stopped competing at a world-class level depsite the debris all around him as the Blackhawks crumbled.

Mr. Longhair is blessed with exceptional speed and acceleration. His timing is accurate and his anticipation keen. He has good balance and can carry the puck at a pretty good clip, though he is more effective when streaking down the wing and getting the puck late. Playing on the left side leaves his forehand open for one-timers, but he is equally secure on the right wing. He's been called a young Yvan Cournoyer for the way he uses his speed to drive wide around the defense to the net.

Amonte has a quick release on his wrist shot. He likes to go top shelf, just under the crossbar, and can also go to the backhand shot or a wrist shot off his back foot, like a fadeaway jumper. Amonte is a top power-play man, since he is always working himself into open ice. His power-play numbers would be higher if the Hawks ever acquire a bona fide power-play quarterback. He is an accurate shooter but is also creative in his playmaking. He passes very well, and is conscious of where his teammates are; he usually makes the best percentage play. He has confidence in his shot now and wants the puck when the game is on the line.

Offensively, Amonte is a smart player away from the puck. He sets picks and creates openings for his teammates. He is an aggressive penalty killer and a shorthanded threat.

THE PHYSICAL GAME

Amonte's speed and movement keep him out of a lot of trouble zones, but he will also drive to the front of the net and take punishment there if that's the correct play. He loves to score, he loves to help his linemates score, and although he is outweighed by a lot of NHL defensemen, he is seldom outworked. He's intense and is not above getting chippy and rubbing his glove in someone's face.

Amonte takes a lot of abuse and plays through the checks. He seldom takes bad retaliatory penalties. He just keeps his legs driving and draws calls with his nonstop skating.

THE INTANGIBLES

Amonte made a full recovery from a knee injury at the end of the 1995-96 season and returned with all of his speed intact, and then some. He has established himself among the NHL's elite now. He became a highly attractive Group 2 free agent during the off-season, and wants to stay in Chicago — but the right offer wouldn't be matched by the el cheapo Hawks.

PROJECTION

Amonte surpassed the 70 points we predicted for him last season, but it will be tough to surpass that number unless the Blackhawks upgrade their overall talent.

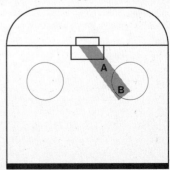

KEITH CARNEY

Yrs. of NHL service: 5
Born: Providence, R.I.; Feb. 3, 1970
Position: left defense
Height: 6-2
Weight: 205
Uniform no.: 4
Shoots: left

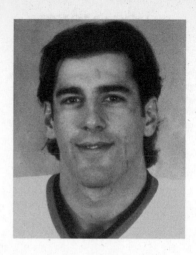

Career statistics:

GP	G	A	TP	PIM
262	16	43	59	279

1993-94 statistics:

GP	G	A	TP	+/-	PIM	PP	SH	GW	GT	S	PCT
37	4	8	12	+14	39	0	0	0	0	37	10.8

1994-95 statistics:

GP	G	A	TP	+/-	PIM	PP	SH	GW	GT	S	PCT
18	0	1	1	-1	11	0	0	1	0	14	7.1

1995-96 statistics:

GP	G	A	TP	+/-	PIM	PP	SH	GW	GT	S	PCT
82	5	14	19	+31	94	1	0	1	0	69	7.2

1996-97 statistics:

GP	G	A	TP	+/-	PIM	PP	SH	GW	GT	S	PCT
81	3	15	18	+26	62	0	0	1	0	77	3.9

PROJECTION

His concentration on defense (and the roles of Chelios and Gary Suter as the offensive defensemen on the Hawks) will limit Carney's point total to around 20 to 25.

LAST SEASON

Led team in plus-minus for second consecutive season.

THE FINESSE GAME

Carney was an offensive defenseman when he first tried to break into the league, but he lacked the elite skills to succeed on that style alone. He has turned his finesse skills to his defensive advantage and is now strictly a stay-at-home type.

Carney is quick and agile, and he positions himself well defensively. He is a smart penalty killer who works on the first unit with Chris Chelios. He might be one of the best penalty killers in the league. He has good hockey sense and great anticipation. He reads the play well and moves the puck smoothly and quickly out of the zone. He's also a fine skater.

THE PHYSICAL GAME

Carney is not a hitter, though he will get in the way of people. He will hit, but he's not punishing. He is a well-conditioned athlete who appreciates the second chance he's been given, and is about the last one off the ice in practice.

THE INTANGIBLES

Carney had been written off by the Sabres and nearly met the same fate in Chicago until the coaches made him a special project. He persevered to redefine his game. He is a capable fifth defenseman, and can even step up to a number four role in the right circumstances.

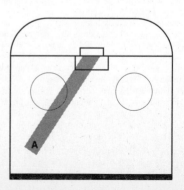

CHRIS CHELIOS

Yrs. of NHL service: 13
Born: Chicago, Ill.; Jan. 25, 1962
Position: right defense
Height: 6-1
Weight: 186
Uniform no.: 7
Shoots: right

Career statistics:

GP	G	A	TP	PIM
920	153	567	720	2038

1993-94 statistics:

GP	G	A	TP	+/-	PIM	PP	SH	GW	GT	S	PCT
76	16	44	60	+12	212	7	1	2	0	219	7.3

1994-95 statistics:

GP	G	A	TP	+/-	PIM	PP	SH	GW	GT	S	PCT
48	5	33	38	+17	72	3	1	0	0	166	3.0

1995-96 statistics:

GP	G	A	TP	+/-	PIM	PP	SH	GW	GT	S	PCT
81	14	58	72	+25	140	7	0	3	0	219	6.4

1996-97 statistics:

GP	G	A	TP	+/-	PIM	PP	SH	GW	GT	S	PCT
72	10	38	48	+16	112	2	0	2	0	194	5.2

LAST SEASON

Led team defensemen in scoring for fourth consecutive season. Second on team in assists. Third on team in points. Tied for eighth among NHL defensemen in scoring. Missed eight games with left knee injury. Missed two games with back injury.

THE FINESSE GAME

Chelios played hurt from the start of last season, with lingering abdominal, shoulder, hip and knee injuries that never allowed him to play at the top of his game. Chicago cut back his ice time from about 35 to 40 minutes per game to 28 to 32, and he will probably average about 28 to 30 minutes per game again this season.

Chelios is among the top two-way defensemen in the league. Whatever the team needs they'll get from him. He can become a top offensive defenseman, pinching boldly at every opportunity. He can create offense off the rush, make a play through the neutral zone or quarterback the power play from the point. He has a good, low, hard slap shot. He is not afraid to skate in deep, where he can handle the puck well and use a snap shot or wrist shot with a quick release. He and Gary Suter may have been the best power-play point duo in the NHL last season.

If defense is needed, Chelios will rule in his own zone. He is extremely confident and poised with the puck and doesn't overhandle it. He wants to get the puck away from his net by the most expedient means possible. He is aggressive in forcing the puck carrier to make a decision by stepping up. Chelios also steps up in the neutral zone to break up plays with his stick.

Chelios is an instinctive player. When he is on his game, he reacts and makes plays few other defensemen can. When he struggles, which is seldom, he is back on his heels. He tries to do other people's jobs and becomes undisciplined.

He has excellent anticipation and is a strong penalty killer when he's not doing time in the box himself. He's a mobile, smooth skater with good lateral movement. He is seldom beaten one-on-one, and he's even tough facing a two-on-one. In his mind, he can do anything. He usually does.

THE PHYSICAL GAME

Chelios has an absurdly high pain threshold. It was revealed after the 1997 playoffs that he had suffered a torn anterior cruciate ligament in his right knee in 1996 and a torn medial collateral ligament in his left knee last season and didn't have surgery either time.

Chelios doesn't seem to tire, no matter how much ice time he gets, and he routinely plays 30 minutes or handles four-minute shifts. He is not that big, but plays like an enormous defenseman. He is tough and physical, strong and solid on his skates, and has a mean streak the size of Lake Michigan. He is fearless.

THE INTANGIBLES

Because Chelios demands so much of himself, he is intolerant of a lesser effort from others — and that includes the Hawks front office. He is underpaid by today's NHL standards, but that bothers him less than emphasizing the bottom line over winning. Chicago now owns the longest Cup drought in the NHL, last winning in 1961; and Chelios desperately wants to end it, but that will take a bigger financial commitment than the Hawks have been inclined to become involved in.

PROJECTION

If Chelios can stay healthy, he should be able to improve his numbers to the 60- to 70-point range.

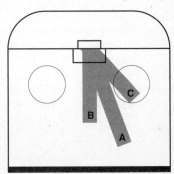

MURRAY CRAVEN

Yrs. of NHL service: 15
Born: Medicine Hat, Alta.; July 20, 1964
Position: left wing/centre
Height: 6-2
Weight: 185
Uniform no.: 32
Shoots: left

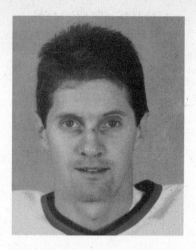

Career statistics:

GP	G	A	TP	PIM
942	250	464	714	477

1993-94 statistics:

GP	G	A	TP	+/-	PIM	PP	SH	GW	GT	S	PCT
78	15	40	55	+5	30	2	1	3	0	115	13.0

1994-95 statistics:

GP	G	A	TP	+/-	PIM	PP	SH	GW	GT	S	PCT
16	4	3	7	+2	2	1	0	2	0	29	13.8

1995-96 statistics:

GP	G	A	TP	+/-	PIM	PP	SH	GW	GT	S	PCT
66	18	29	47	+20	36	5	1	7	0	86	20.9

1996-97 statistics:

GP	G	A	TP	+/-	PIM	PP	SH	GW	GT	S	PCT
75	8	27	35	0	12	2	0	1	0	122	6.6

LAST SEASON

Missed four games with bruised shoulder. Missed three games with shoulder injuries.

THE FINESSE GAME

Craven is the hockey equivalent of a utility infielder. He checks. He scores. He plays first unit on the power play or handles penalty killing. He takes draws. He plays right wing, left wing or centre.

However, Craven has never attained star status because, though he does a lot of things well, he isn't great at any one thing. He's a good skater, but doesn't have the hockey sense to use this skill as well as he should. He isn't a natural scorer. He has to work hard for his 20 or so goals a season and scores most of them from close range. He does have a good slap shot, though, and can be used on the point on the power play in a pinch.

Craven is unselfish and, poised down low, will confidently slide a backhand pass across the goalmouth to a teammate. He goes to the net with determination and has good hands for picking up loose pucks. He has a long reach and can beat a defender one-on-one by using his speed and dangling the puck away from his body but under control. He's no speed demon, but he plays well positionally.

THE PHYSICAL GAME

Craven is wiry but not very big. He loses some one-on-one battles in tight, but he uses his body effectively in the defensive as well as the offensive zone. He digs along the boards and in the corners for the puck.

THE INTANGIBLES

Craven is intelligent and versatile and a coach always knows what he is getting from him. He is a complete hockey player, one who fits nicely into a role as a number two or number three centre, or winger.

PROJECTION

Craven was banged up last year (finishing his season with a broken jaw in the playoffs) and didn't put up the numbers we are used to seeing from him. In a healthy year, he can deliver a reliable 15 to 20 goals and 40 points, but he may be weighting his game more on the defensive side now.

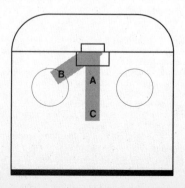

ULF DAHLEN

Yrs. of NHL service: 10
Born: Ostersund, Sweden; Jan. 12, 1967
Position: centre/right wing
Height: 6-2
Weight: 195
Uniform no.: 22
Shoots: left

Career statistics:

GP	G	A	TP	PIM
686	231	249	480	194

1993-94 statistics:

GP	G	A	TP	+/-	PIM	PP	SH	GW	GT	S	PCT
78	25	44	69	-1	10	15	0	5	1	190	13.2

1994-95 statistics:

GP	G	A	TP	+/-	PIM	PP	SH	GW	GT	S	PCT
46	11	23	34	-2	11	4	1	4	0	85	12.9

1995-96 statistics:

GP	G	A	TP	+/-	PIM	PP	SH	GW	GT	S	PCT
59	16	12	28	-21	27	5	0	2	1	103	15.5

1996-97 statistics:

GP	G	A	TP	+/-	PIM	PP	SH	GW	GT	S	PCT
73	14	19	33	-2	18	4	0	4	0	131	10.7

LAST SEASON

Acquired from Chicago with Chris Terreri, Michal Sykora and a conditional pick for Ed Belfour, January 25, 1997. Tied for team lead in game-winning goals (three scored with Chicago, one with San Jose).

THE FINESSE GAME

Dahlen is an intelligent hockey player who sees the ice well. He has great puck skill, though he does not move the puck quickly. He is extremely effective down low on the power play and is a good possession player. He lures defenders to him and opens up ice for his teammates. Dahlen scores goals that are tough to defend against — wraparounds and jam-ins — and those are the kind of goals that frustrate a goaltender. His real gift is puck protection and finding the open man.

Dahlen is an unusual skater, slow but with some deceptive moves. He has good balance and strength and always protects the puck with his body. Along the boards, it's almost impossible to beat him for the puck. It doesn't matter what the size or speed of the opponent is, Dahlen won't surrender the puck. He is one of the best board and corner men in the league as long as the puck is on his blade.

Dahlen has good hands and scores all of his goals from 10 inches to 10 feet away from the net. He slides out once in awhile, but he is usually willing to pay the price to stay in the heavy traffic zone.

THE PHYSICAL GAME

Hitting Dahlen is like hitting a fire hydrant. It takes two or three checks to knock him down. Dahlen doesn't initiate. While he is willing to do just about anything to protect the puck when he has control, he will not win many one-on-one fights to strip the puck away from an opponent. He lacks the aggressiveness to bump his game up a notch.

THE INTANGIBLES

Dahlen got off to a hot start with the Hawks (he was 6-8 — 14 in 30 games with Chicago) but got banged up and was shifted off a line with Alexei Zhamnov. Dahlen has to play a lot to be effective. He is a versatile veteran with a lot of character.

PROJECTION

Dahlen has never been a big point scorer, but if he works with finishers he's capable of doing the grunt work for his more gifted linemates. Depending on how he is used, Dahlen could score from 30 to 50 points.

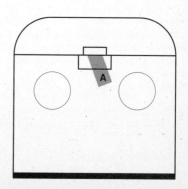

ERIC DAZE

Yrs. of NHL service: 2
Born: Montreal, Que.; July 2, 1975
Position: left wing
Height: 6-4
Weight: 215
Uniform no.: 55
Shoots: left

Career statistics:

GP	G	A	TP	PIM
155	53	43	96	36

1994-95 statistics:

GP	G	A	TP	+/-	PIM	PP	SH	GW	GT	S	PCT
4	1	1	2	+2	2	0	0	0	0	1	100.0

1995-96 statistics:

GP	G	A	TP	+/-	PIM	PP	SH	GW	GT	S	PCT
80	30	23	53	+16	18	2	0	2	0	167	18.0

1996-97 statistics:

GP	G	A	TP	+/-	PIM	PP	SH	GW	GT	S	PCT
71	22	19	41	-4	16	11	0	4	0	176	12.5

LAST SEASON

Second NHL season. Led team in power-play goals. Tied for team lead in game-winning goals. Second on team in assists. Missed eight games with sprained left ankle.

THE FINESSE GAME

Daze struggled through training camp, was hurt in the second game of the season, and took a long time getting his game back on track. The Hawks had hoped that his experience at the World Cup (as an alternate for Team Canada) would be a boost for Daze, but little was accomplished by sending him there to watch and practise. He wasn't ready to start the season.

Although the most impressive thing about Daze is his size, it is his skating ability that sets him apart from other lumbering big men. He isn't a speed demon, but he skates well enough to not look out of place with frequent linemates Tony Amonte and Alexei Zhamnov (although Daze worked even better with Jeff Shantz and Ethan Moreau).

Daze keeps his hands close together on his stick and is able to get a lot on his shot with very little backswing. He has excellent hands for shooting or scoring, and is an adept stickhandler who can draw defenders to him and then slip a pass through to a teammate. He sets screens on the power play. He has good hockey vision and an innate understanding of the game. He's also advanced defensively.

Daze excels when he drives wide, protects the puck and takes it to the net. Very few defensemen can handle him when he does, but he stopped working and stopped moving his feet and seldom showed flashes of his great rookie form.

THE PHYSICAL GAME

Daze doesn't back down, but he doesn't show much

initiative, either. He is very strong, and has a long reach so that he can pass or shoot the puck even when a defenseman thinks he has him all wrapped up and under control. Daze must compete harder on a more consistent basis.

THE INTANGIBLES

One encouraging sign was that Daze finished better than he started last season (the reverse of his rookie year). He had only nine goals by the All-Star break; 13 the rest of the season. He lost some confidence and was benched twice, but he probably understands that it was his own fault.

PROJECTION

Daze needs to play with forwards who will get him the puck. As long as Chicago can provide the passers, Daze will provide the finish. He may not be a 50-goal scorer, but 40 isn't out of the question if he plays on the top line.

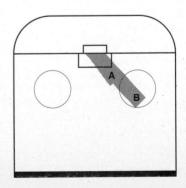

TUOMAS GRONMAN

Yrs. of NHL service: 0
Born: Viitasaari, Finland; Mar, 22, 1974
Position: defense
Height: 6-3
Weight: 198
Uniform no.: 46
Shoots: right

Career statistics:

GP	G	A	TP	PIM
16	0	1	1	13

1996-97 statistics:

GP	G	A	TP	+/-	PIM	PP	SH	GW	GT	S	PCT
16	0	1	1	-4	13	0	0	0	0	9	0.0

Hawks to rest Chris Chelios more.

LAST SEASON

First NHL season. Scored 5-16 — 21 with 89 penalty minutes in 51 games with Indianapolis (IHL).

THE FINESSE GAME

Gronman had a good training camp and looked to have secured a regular spot last year, but his game fell apart early and he was sent back to the minors. Most of his errors are sins of commission rather than omission. Gronman wasn't playing a very smart game, and still has a lot to learn.

Gronman is a defensive defenseman, but he has some nice hand skills to make passes out of his zone and start a rush. His skating is adequate, which is why he is unlikely to join the attack and will largely limit his offense to shots from the point. Gronman is a late-developing (1992 draft) prospect who was brought along slowly in the Quebec/Colorado system before Chicago acquired his rights last year.

THE PHYSICAL GAME

Gronman is aggressive. Sometimes that works against him when he starts running around, looks for the big hit, gets out of position and gets burned. He's built solidly and plays a feisty game; when he settles down and plays with controlled passion he can be effective. Gronman never worked on his strength before and was put on a summer program for this season.

THE INTANGIBLES

Playing for much of the season with Indianapolis helped Gronman learn the game and taught him to pick his spots better. He was a bit in awe in his brief NHL stint but should be more composed this season. Gronman played one year of junior in the WHL, which helps his adjustment to North America.

PROJECTION

Gronman will get a spot in the top six next season if the Blackhawks move a veteran defenseman, as they are expected to do. His development will allow the

JEFF HACKETT

Yrs. of NHL service: 7
Born: London, Ont.; June 1, 1968
Position: goaltender
Height: 6-1
Weight: 180
Uniform no.: 31
Catches: left

Career statistics:

GP	MIN	GA	SO	GAA	A	PIM
226	12369	698	6	3.39	6	32

1993-94 statistics:

GP	MIN	GAA	W	L	T	SO	GA	S	SAPCT	PIM
22	1084	3.43	2	12	3	0	62	566	.890	2

1994-95 statistics:

GP	MIN	GAA	W	L	T	SO	GA	S	SAPCT	PIM
7	328	2.38	1	3	2	0	13	150	.913	0

1995-96 statistics:

GP	MIN	GAA	W	L	T	SO	GA	S	SAPCT	PIM
35	2000	2.40	18	11	4	4	80	948	.916	8

1996-97 statistics:

GP	MIN	GAA	W	L	T	SO	GA	S	SAPCT	PIM
41	2473	2.16	19	18	4	2	89	1212	.927	6

LAST SEASON

Third in NHL with career-best goals-against average. Tied for second in NHL in save percentage. Missed seven games with broken finger.

THE PHYSICAL GAME

Hackett's mechanics are quite good. His positional play is strong. He knows when to challenge a shooter at the top of the crease, and, if anything, has a tendency to be overly aggressive. Hackett plays his angles well.

He has very quick reflexes for bang-bang plays around the net. His glove is a great asset. Hackett will be conservative and hold the puck for a draw to cool off the action.

Hackett's stickhandling has improved slightly over the years, but still remains the weakest aspect of his game. He is sometimes guilty of trying to do too much and he gets in trouble with missed communication with his defensemen, which may have resulted from the team being more used to playing with Ed Belfour.

THE MENTAL GAME

Once Belfour was traded to San Jose, the heat was on Hackett, and he responded. If there were any doubts about how he would deal with the situation, they were eased with Hackett's 36-save performance in a 2-1 win at Madison Square Garden just two days after the trade. He is aware the organization has made the commitment to him, and he is more comfortable with the responsibility than he was as number two, when he knew if he had a bad night he wouldn't get another chance for five or six more games.

THE INTANGIBLES

Hackett is very popular with his teammates, and they love to play for him. He is a student of goaltending and is one of the hardest working players on the team — if anything, he works too hard and has to be urged to conserve himself, since he's an active goalie and isn't the most robust guy in the world. Working with goaltending coach Vladislav Tretiak was a great help to Hackett, who despite his experience is always eager to improve his game. Having Chris Terreri as a backup (if Chicago re-signs him) would also help.

PROJECTION

Hackett has been cursed with playing on some weak defensive teams (Islanders, Sharks) in recent years, and last year was able to show what he can do as a number one with a club that was at least competitive. The Hawks haven't improved much up front, which means that even if Hackett keeps his GAA respectable, it will be a battle to get 20 wins.

SERGEI KRIVOKRASOV

Yrs. of NHL service: 3
Born: Angarsk, Soviet Union; Apr. 15, 1974
Position: right wing
Height: 5-11
Weight: 185
Uniform no.: 25
Shoots: left

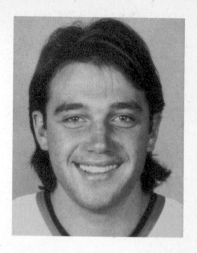

Career statistics:

GP	G	A	TP	PIM
167	32	28	60	113

1993-94 statistics:

GP	G	A	TP	+/-	PIM	PP	SH	GW	GT	S	PCT
9	1	0	1	-2	4	0	0	0	0	7	14.3

1994-95 statistics:

GP	G	A	TP	+/-	PIM	PP	SH	GW	GT	S	PCT
41	12	7	19	+9	33	6	0	2	0	72	16.7

1995-96 statistics:

GP	G	A	TP	+/-	PIM	PP	SH	GW	GT	S	PCT
46	6	10	16	+10	32	0	0	1	0	52	11.5

1996-97 statistics:

GP	G	A	TP	+/-	PIM	PP	SH	GW	GT	S	PCT
67	13	11	24	-1	42	2	0	3	0	104	12.5

LAST SEASON

Career high in goals.

THE FINESSE GAME

Krivokrasov is Russian for "exasperating." Every time the Blackhawks seem ready to give up on him, he comes up with something like an overtime playoff goal (against Colorado, for the second straight spring). Then he turns around and takes a bad penalty in the same playoffs that leads to a demoralizing goal.

Krivokrasov is highly skilled but he's never been consistent, despite getting plenty of chances to earn prime ice time on the top line with Tony Amonte and Alexei Zhamnov. Krivokrasov controls the puck well and reads offensive plays. He will shoot or pass and has good timing in both areas. He draws defenders and opens up ice for a teammate, before dishing off and heading to the net himself for a give-and-go. Sometimes he overhandles the puck, gets too fancy and doesn't shoot when he should. He can score some phenomenal one-on-one goals.

His skating needs to get a hair quicker. He is strong and will drive to the net. Like New Jersey's Valeri Zelepukin, he scores a lot of goals from in tight. He has improved defensively but still has lapses.

THE PHYSICAL GAME

On most nights, Krivokrasov is not a physical player and can be intimidated, but other nights he breathes competitive fire and is a force on the ice.

THE INTANGIBLES

Krivokrasov has the skill to be one of the team's top six forwards. This should be his last chance to prove to the Blackhawks if he has the goods to be a big-time player. He can be a game-breaker or a heartbreaker.

PROJECTION

Every year looks like it is going to be Krivokrasov's year, but he is so inconsistent that no sensible team or poolie should put much stock in him.

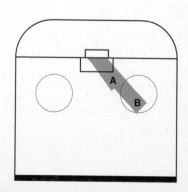

CHRISTIAN LAFLAMME

Yrs. of NHL service: 0
Born: St. Charles, Que.; Nov. 24, 1976
Position: defense
Height: 6-1
Weight: 195
Uniform no.: 44
Shoots: right

Career statistics:

GP	G	A	TP	PIM
4	0	1	1	2

1996-97 statistics:

GP	G	A	TP	+/-	PIM	PP	SH	GW	GT	S	PCT
4	0	1	1	+3	2	0	0	0	0	3	0.0

LAST SEASON

Will be entering first NHL season. Scored 5-15 — 20 with 60 penalty minutes in 62 games for Indianapolis (IHL).

THE FINESSE GAME

Laflamme is a steady defenseman, advanced for his age because of his good hockey sense.

He skates well forwards and backwards. He is a good penalty killer, holding his position well, and he seldom gets suckered into running around and missing his checking assignment.

Laflamme hasn't been shortchanged in any skills department. While he is primarily a defensive defenseman, he can jump up into the play. He will look to pass rather than shoot, though he has an accurate shot from the point. He handles the puck well and finds the open man.

THE PHYSICAL GAME

Laflamme takes pride in his play in his own end and patrols the front of his net with authority. He is a good bodychecker and finishes his checks. He enjoys hitting. Chicago hasn't been a very hard team to play against in recent years. Laflamme will give the Hawks a needed bit of grit, without taking dumb penalties.

THE INTANGIBLES

Laflamme missed two months of the 1995-96 QMJHL season with an injury, which delayed his development, but he came back strong in his first pro season in the IHL. His favourite player is teammate Chris Chelios, and Laflamme is showing signs of developing into a two-way, Chelios-type defenseman. He is bound to concentrate on defense first, but could get second-unit power-play time as the season progresses.

PROJECTION

Laflamme is likely to be used as a number six defenseman until he gets his feet wet. He could be one of the top assist men among rookie defensemen next season if he earns enough playing time.

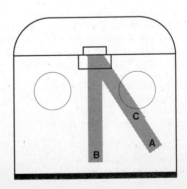

KEVIN MILLER

Yrs. of NHL service: 9
Born: Lansing, Mich.; Sept. 2, 1965
Position: right wing
Height: 5-11
Weight: 190
Uniform no.: 16
Shoots: right

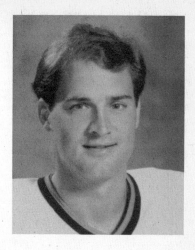

Career statistics:

GP	G	A	TP	PIM
537	142	169	311	406

1993-94 statistics:

GP	G	A	TP	+/-	PIM	PP	SH	GW	GT	S	PCT
75	23	25	48	+6	83	6	3	5	0	154	14.9

1994-95 statistics:

GP	G	A	TP	+/-	PIM	PP	SH	GW	GT	S	PCT
36	8	12	20	+4	13	1	1	2	0	60	13.3

1995-96 statistics:

GP	G	A	TP	+/-	PIM	PP	SH	GW	GT	S	PCT
81	28	25	53	-4	45	3	2	2	2	179	15.6

1996-97 statistics:

GP	G	A	TP	+/-	PIM	PP	SH	GW	GT	S	PCT
69	14	17	31	-10	41	5	1	2	0	139	10.1

LAST SEASON

Signed as free agent on July 17, 1996. Tied for worst plus-minus on team.

THE FINESSE GAME

Miller had one of the most inconsistent years of his career, lacking the one key element, effort, that has always enhanced his game. Miller is a two-way forward, a checker who can create turnovers with his smart, persistent forechecking. He has the finesse skills to produce points as well. His problems start when he thinks he can take the easy route, and that his skills alone will carry him.

Miller is an energetic skater who is all over the ice. A better playmaker than finisher, he's not overly clever and most of his scoring chances come from opportunities from the forecheck. He has fairly quick hands but lacks a soft goal scorer's touch.

He has succeeded at every level he has played — college, Olympic and minor league — and now has stamped himself as an NHL regular. He's small, but he plays much larger.

THE PHYSICAL GAME

The spunky Miller takes the body well, though he doesn't have great size. He is very strong and has a low centre of gravity, which makes it tough to knock him off the puck. He gets overpowered in heavy traffic areas, but that doesn't keep him from trying. Miller will frustrate opponents into taking swings at him and draw penalties.

THE INTANGIBLES

Miller is a good penalty killer and a useful player on the second power-play unit, but he is a third- or fourth-liner who thinks he should be playing on a first or second line.

PROJECTION

If he regains his work ethic, Miller should return to the 20-goal neighbourhood. Last year was the first time in six full NHL seasons that Miller failed to notch 20.

ETHAN MOREAU

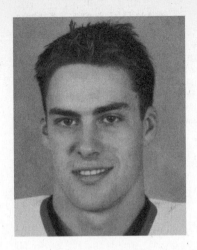

Yrs. of NHL service: 1
Born: Huntsville, Ont.; Sept. 22, 1975
Position: left wing
Height: 6-2
Weight: 205
Uniform no.: 19
Shoots: left

Career statistics:

GP	G	A	TP	PIM
90	15	17	32	127

1995-96 statistics:

GP	G	A	TP	+/-	PIM	PP	SH	GW	GT	S	PCT
8	0	1	1	+1	4	0	0	0	0	1	0.0

1996-97 statistics:

GP	G	A	TP	+/-	PIM	PP	SH	GW	GT	S	PCT
82	15	16	31	+13	123	0	0	1	1	114	13.2

LAST SEASON

First NHL season. One of three Blackhawks to appear in all 82 games. Second on team and fifth among NHL rookies in shooting percentage. Third among NHL rookies in plus-minus.

THE FINESSE GAME

Despite playing all season with a sore shoulder, Moreau was one of the few good things to happen to the Blackhawks. He was very consistent for a young player, took advantage of playing opportunities that opened up through injury, and by the end of the season was a player to rely on.

Moreau is a very intelligent player with good hockey sense. He can also play centre, though his future is clearly at left wing. He is not a natural scorer but has to work for his goals, and with effort, his scoring touch improves. Funny how that works.

Moreau has a long reach and uses a long stick, which allow him to get his strong wrist shots away around a defenseman who may think he has Moreau tied up. Defensively, he's on his way because he has an understanding of positional play.

Moreau's skating was questioned when he was a junior, but a year in the IHL helped him improve and it was never a factor last season. He's a budding power forward who goes to the net hard.

THE PHYSICAL GAME

Moreau has good size and strength and is starting to develop more of a presence. He finishes his checks, especially around the net. He handled himself well in the minors, so there may be a latent aggressive streak that will emerge — especially if that's the difference between making the NHL or another year of riding the bus in the minors. He is strong in the corners and will take a hit to make a play.

THE INTANGIBLES

Size is a desirable commodity in the NHL, and when it's combined with Moreau's drive around the net, that makes for an exciting young prospect. Coach Craig Hartsburg has compared Moreau to a young Bob Gainey, both for his playing style and budding leadership ability.

PROJECTION

Moreau will never be a gifted scorer but he has the potential to score 25 within the next year or two.

BOB PROBERT

Yrs. of NHL service: 11
Born: Windsor, Ont.; June 5, 1965
Position: right wing
Height: 6-3
Weight: 225
Uniform no.: 24
Shoots: left

Career statistics:

GP	G	A	TP	PIM
634	142	180	322	2653

1993-94 statistics:

GP	G	A	TP	+/-	PIM	PP	SH	GW	GT	S	PCT
66	7	10	17	-1	275	1	0	0	0	105	6.7

1994-95 statistics:

P	G	A	TP	+/-	PIM	PP	SH	GW	GT	S	PC
Did not play in NHL											

1995-96 statistics:

GP	G	A	TP	+/-	PIM	PP	SH	GW	GT	S	PCT
78	19	21	40	+15	237	1	0	3	0	97	19.6

1996-97 statistics:

GP	G	A	TP	+/-	PIM	PP	SH	GW	GT	S	PCT
82	9	14	23	-3	326	1	0	3	0	111	8.1

LAST SEASON

Led team and second in NHL in penalty minutes. One of three Blackhawks to appear in all 82 games.

THE FINESSE GAME

Probert came into training camp a little out of shape, but after the first 30 games or so he was as good a forward as the Blackhawks had after Tony Amonte and Alexei Zhamnov.

Probert is a slugger with a nice touch. He needs a little time to get away his shot, but, let's face it, not too many brave souls play him that tight. In traffic, he can stickhandle and even slide a backhand pass down low. His shots aren't heavy, but he is accurate and shoots mostly from close range. He is smart with the puck and doesn't give it away.

He doesn't have open-ice speed, but in tight he has one-step quickness and can even pivot surprisingly well with the puck. He can be used up front on the power play because he parks himself right in front of the net; the goalie looks like a bobble-head doll as he tries to peer around Probert's giant frame for a view of the puck. He gets some second-unit power-play time because of this.

Probert has to play with linemates who get him the puck since he can't help out in pursuing the disk. He plays a low-risk game and doesn't make mistakes that hurt his team.

THE PHYSICAL GAME

Still one of the scariest fighters in the NHL, Probert is strong, quick-fisted and mean, but he is slow to rile on some nights when the other teams decide it is best to let a sleeping dog lie. If he falls asleep on the ice, he's a nonfactor. He steps up for his teammates and is strong along the wall. He works hard every night.

THE INTANGIBLES

After sitting out the entire 1994-95 season and ironing out some of his personal problems, Probert has become a fairly skilled tough guy with a terrific attitude and dedication to the game and his teammates. Chris Chelios has had an enormous impact on helping turn Probert onto the value of conditioning, and Probert was an unsung hero in Chicago.

PROJECTION

Probert is a solid contributor who works hard and knows his role. He will score 25 to 30 points and make everyone around him braver.

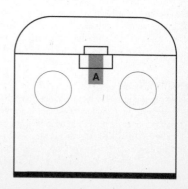

JEFF SHANTZ

Yrs. of NHL service: 4
Born: Duchess, Alta; Oct. 10, 1973
Position: centre
Height: 6-1
Weight: 185
Uniform no.: 11
Shoots: right

Career statistics:

GP	G	A	TP	PIM
244	24	60	84	115

1993-94 statistics:

GP	G	A	TP	+/-	PIM	PP	SH	GW	GT	S	PCT
52	3	13	16	-14	30	0	0	0	0	56	5.4

1994-95 statistics:

GP	G	A	TP	+/-	PIM	PP	SH	GW	GT	S	PCT
45	6	12	18	+11	33	0	2	0	0	58	10.3

1995-96 statistics:

GP	G	A	TP	+/-	PIM	PP	SH	GW	GT	S	PCT
78	6	14	20	+12	24	1	2	0	0	72	8.3

1996-97 statistics:

GP	G	A	TP	+/-	PIM	PP	SH	GW	GT	S	PCT
69	9	21	30	+11	28	0	1	1	0	86	10.5

LAST SEASON

Posted career highs in goals, assists and points. Missed 10 games with sprained knee.

THE FINESSE GAME

Shantz doesn't excel in many technical areas, but he is one of the better Hawks in terms of hockey sense, and he took a major step forward in his development last season. He has good skills, though his game is heavily defense-oriented. Ideally, he is a number three forward (he can play centre or right wing). However, in the playoffs he was forced into the role of a number one centre after Alexei Zhamnov was injured — he performed admirably.

A good skater, Shantz is smooth in his turns with average quickness. He handles the puck well and sees his passing options. He won't be forced into many bad passes, preferring to eat the puck rather than toss it away.

He has a decent touch around the net but doesn't score many highlight goals. He has a heavy shot but doesn't have a quick release. Most of his scoring comes from in tight off his forechecking efforts — perfect for Chicago's dump-and-chase style of attack. Shantz is very good on face-offs.

THE PHYSICAL GAME

The major question mark about Shantz was whether he was big and strong enough to prosper in the NHL, but he checks pretty hard and seems to be acquiring a taste for physical play. He doesn't have much size and will need to keep up his conditioning and strength work. He's gritty, doesn't take bad penalties and plays hard but clean.

THE INTANGIBLES

Shantz is smart defensively, yet he didn't seem up to the wear and tear of a full NHL campaign. Because he was a scorer in junior, he should be able to upgrade his game and become more of a two-way player. He played for a bit on an interesting young line with Ethan Moreau and Eric Daze, which carried the team for a time.

PROJECTION

If Shantz continues to show the improvement he did last season, he should earn a regular role on the third line (inheriting the Brent Sutter job) and register 50 to 60 points. He might get the number two centre job by default.

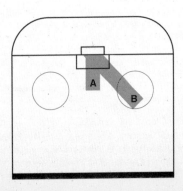

GARY SUTER

Yrs. of NHL service: 12
Born: Madison, Wisc.; June 24, 1964
Position: left defense
Height: 6-0
Weight: 200
Uniform no.: 20
Shoots: left

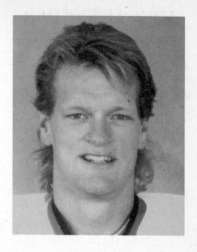

Career statistics:

GP	G	A	TP	PIM
845	167	535	702	1080

1993-94 statistics:

GP	G	A	TP	+/-	PIM	PP	SH	GW	GT	S	PCT
41	6	12	18	-12	38	4	1	0	0	86	7.0

1994-95 statistics:

GP	G	A	TP	+/-	PIM	PP	SH	GW	GT	S	PCT
48	10	27	37	+14	42	5	0	0	0	144	6.9

1995-96 statistics:

GP	G	A	TP	+/-	PIM	PP	SH	GW	GT	S	PCT
82	20	47	67	+3	80	12	2	4	0	242	8.3

1996-97 statistics:

GP	G	A	TP	+/-	PIM	PP	SH	GW	GT	S	PCT
82	7	21	28	-4	70	3	0	0	1	225	3.1

LAST SEASON

One of three Blackhawks to appear in all 82 games. Second on team in shots.

THE FINESSE GAME

Suter has great natural skills, starting with his skating. He's secure on his skates with a wide stance for balance. He has all of the components that make a great skater: acceleration, flat-out speed, quickness and mobility. He skates well backwards and can't be bested one-on-one except by the slickest skaters. He loves to jump into the attack, and he'll key a rush with a smooth outlet pass or carry the puck and lead the parade.

Suter has a superb shot. It's not scary-hard, but he keeps it low. The Hawks changed their power play last season, and he missed Bernie Nicholls's ability to help quarterback a power play.

Not a great playmaker, Suter's creativity comes from his speed and dangerous shot. He can handle some penalty-killing time, though it is not his strong suit.

THE PHYSICAL GAME

Like Chelios, Suter is a marathon man who can handle 30 minutes of ice time a game and not wear down. He has a personal trainer that he, Chelios and several teammates work out with, and as a result Suter is exceptionally fit.

He can be a mean hitter (it was his check in the 1991 Canada Cup that was the start of Wayne Gretzky's back troubles). But he can get carried away with the hitting game and will take himself out of position, even when penalty killing. He doesn't like to be hit; he'll bring his stick up at the last second before contact to protect himself. His defensive reads are average to fair.

THE INTANGIBLES

Suter may be a notch below the league's elite defensemen, but he can handle a lot of responsibility. He has played his best hockey since coming to the Windy City, but the Hawks might be compelled to move him to help beef up their front-line talent.

PROJECTION

In last year's *HSR*, we projected a drop-off in Suter's point totals. His past track performance indicates a "bounce," but he's now 33 and it might be tougher to bounce back into the 60-point range.

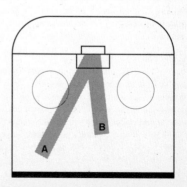

MICHAL SYKORA

Yrs. of NHL service: 3
Born: Pardubice, Czech Republic; July 5, 1973
Position: left defense
Height: 6-5
Weight: 225
Uniform no.: 6
Shoots: left

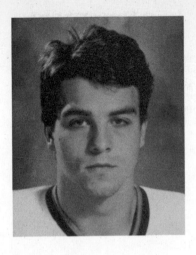

Career statistics:

GP	G	A	TP	PIM
180	8	38	46	147

1993-94 statistics:

GP	G	A	TP	+/-	PIM	PP	SH	GW	GT	S	PCT
22	1	4	5	-4	14	0	0	0	0	22	4.5

1994-95 statistics:

GP	G	A	TP	+/-	PIM	PP	SH	GW	GT	S	PCT
16	0	4	4	+6	10	0	0	0	0	6	0.0

1995-96 statistics:

GP	G	A	TP	+/-	PIM	PP	SH	GW	GT	S	PCT
79	4	16	20	-14	54	1	0	0	0	80	5.0

1996-97 statistics:

GP	G	A	TP	+/-	PIM	PP	SH	GW	GT	S	PCT
63	3	14	17	+4	69	1	0	0	0	77	3.9

LAST SEASON

Acquired from San Jose with Chris Terreri, Ulf Dahlen and a conditional draft pick for Ed Belfour, January 25, 1997.

THE FINESSE GAME

Sykora is a strong skater — forwards or backwards. He has a heavy, hard shot, but hasn't quite adjusted to NHL speed in his offensive decision-making process. He headmans the puck well out of his own zone and doesn't panic under pressure. He's confident in his puckhandling skills in his own end of the ice.

Sykora is an intelligent player who plays a good transition game. He will probably see second-unit power-play time. He has a better offensive upside than he has shown so far in the NHL. Playing on a team with strong defensemen will help his game in all areas.

Sykora has taken some time to learn what to expect from the NHL, and he still has some growing to do, but he has good finesse skills, which he can use offensively or defensively. He is an excellent passer and has a fine shot.

THE PHYSICAL GAME

Because of his size, teams tend to expect Sykora to run people over, but he doesn't play a very physical game. Sykora was a bit weedy at the start of his NHL career and had to pay some dues in the minors to develop better upper-body strength. He has a long reach that he uses to tie up attackers along the boards. He plays well positionally. He needs to compete consistently.

THE INTANGIBLES

Sykora has quietly been developing into a top four defenseman. The Hawks didn't use him much in the last few weeks of the season or in the playoffs, and he's still a project.

PROJECTION

Although he has been concentrating on his defensive play, he was a scorer at the junior level and may have some upside to post better numbers.

ERIC WEINRICH

Yrs. of NHL service: 7
Born: Roanoke, Va.; Dec. 19, 1966
Position: right defense
Height: 6-1
Weight: 210
Uniform no.: 2
Shoots: left

Career statistics:

GP	G	A	TP	PIM
520	39	164	203	385

1993-94 statistics:

GP	G	A	TP	+/-	PIM	PP	SH	GW	GT	S	PCT
62	4	24	28	+1	35	2	0	2	0	115	3.5

1994-95 statistics:

GP	G	A	TP	+/-	PIM	PP	SH	GW	GT	S	PCT
48	3	10	13	+1	33	1	0	2	0	50	6.0

1995-96 statistics:

GP	G	A	TP	+/-	PIM	PP	SH	GW	GT	S	PCT
77	5	10	15	+14	65	0	0	0	0	76	6.6

1996-97 statistics:

GP	G	A	TP	+/-	PIM	PP	SH	GW	GT	S	PCT
81	7	25	32	+19	62	1	0	0	1	115	6.1

LAST SEASON

Second among team defensemen in scoring. Matched career high in goals.

THE FINESSE GAME

Weinrich was probably Chicago's most consistent defenseman last season (factoring in Chris Chelios's injury woes). He's in the shadow of Chris Chelios and Gary Suter in Chicago, but Weinrich is a fine, underrated number three defenseman. His skating is above average. He accelerates quickly and has good straight-away speed, though he doesn't have great balance for pivots or superior leg drive for power. He has improved his skating but needs to get even better. He is not sturdy on his feet.

Weinrich is strong on the puck, shooting and passing hard. He works on the point on the second power-play unit, which doesn't get much ice time because Chris Chelios and Gary Suter play nearly the full two minutes. Weinrich has a low, accurate shot that he gets away quickly. He will not gamble down low, but will sometimes sneak into the top of the circle for a one-timer. His offensive reads are far keener than his defensive reads.

Weinrich plays better with an offensive-minded partner. He is more useful when he is the support player who can move the puck up and move into the play.

THE PHYSICAL GAME

Weinrich is a good one-on-one defender. He always has a high conditioning level and can play a lot of minutes. He is not a soft player (a criticism that dogged him early in his career). He'll fight; it's not in his nature, but he won't get pushed around and will stand up for his teammates. He has gotten stronger over the seasons.

THE INTANGIBLES

Trade rumours always seem to dog Weinrich, but he is well-regarded by the Hawks and it would take a pretty good deal to pry him away. After seeming to settle into a comfort zone a year or two ago, he has taken on more responsibility and become a better player.

PROJECTION

We predict more ice time and better numbers for Weinrich, who last season posted his best point total since 1990-91, when he was named to the All-Rookie Team.

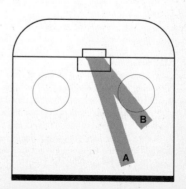

ALEXEI ZHAMNOV

Yrs. of NHL service: 5
Born: Moscow, Russia; Oct. 1, 1970
Position: centre
Height: 6-1
Weight: 195
Uniform no.: 26
Shoots: left

Career statistics:

GP	G	A	TP	PIM
309	123	206	329	261

1993-94 statistics:

GP	G	A	TP	+/-	PIM	PP	SH	GW	GT	S	PCT
61	26	45	71	-20	62	7	0	1	1	196	13.3

1994-95 statistics:

GP	G	A	TP	+/-	PIM	PP	SH	GW	GT	S	PCT
48	30	35	65	+5	20	9	0	4	0	155	19.4

1995-96 statistics:

GP	G	A	TP	+/-	PIM	PP	SH	GW	GT	S	PCT
58	22	37	59	-4	65	5	0	2	0	199	11.1

1996-97 statistics:

GP	G	A	TP	+/-	PIM	PP	SH	GW	GT	S	PCT
74	20	42	62	+18	56	6	1	2	0	208	9.6

LAST SEASON

Acquired from Phoenix with Craig Mills and a 1997 first-round draft pick for Jeremy Roenick, August 16, 1997. Led team in assists. Second on team in points. Third on team in goals, plus-minus and power-play goals.

THE FINESSE GAME

Zhamnov missed the start of the season after a contract holdout, and missing training camp meant a lack of conditioning and a slow start while he was under pressure to be the new Roenick.

Zhamnov is a totally different player from J.R. Zhamnov's game is puck control. He can carry it at top speed or work the give-and-go. The Russian is a crafty playmaker and is not too unselfish. He has an accurate if not overpowering shot. As well, he can blast off the pass, or manoeuvre until he has a screen and then wrist it. On the power play, he works the left point or, if used low, can dart in and out in front of the goalie, using his soft hands for a tip.

Defensively, he is very sound. He is a dedicated backchecker and never leaves the zone too quickly.

THE PHYSICAL GAME

Zhamnov will bump to prevent a scoring chance or go for a loose puck, but body work is not his forte. The knock on Zhamnov is his lack of physical play, but he works hard and competes. He is strong and fights his way through traffic in front of the net to get to a puck. He needs to do a better job of tying up the opposing centre on face-offs, since he wins few draws cleanly.

THE INTANGIBLES

Zhamnov worked well with Tony Amonte, but as the Hawks had only one real scoring line, opponents had an easy time focussing on shutting him down. Acquiring a number two centre would help free up Zhamnov's game. He suffered an ankle injury and subsequent infection in the playoffs, but is expected to be fully recovered for the season.

PROJECTION

Zhamnov can come into this year more relaxed and comfortable, but despite his 100-point skill level, 70 points is his likely output unless the Hawks get drastically better in a hurry.

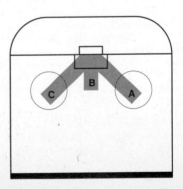

COLORADO AVALANCHE

Players' Statistics 1996-97

POS.	NO.	PLAYER	GP	G	A	PTS	+/-	PIM	PP	SH	GW	GT	S	PCT
C	21	PETER FORSBERG	65	28	58	86	31	73	5	4	4		188	14.9
C	19	JOE SAKIC	65	22	52	74	-10	34	10	2	5		261	8.4
D	8	SANDIS OZOLINSH	80	23	45	68	4	88	13		4	1	232	9.9
L	13	VALERI KAMENSKY	68	28	38	66	5	38	8		4	1	165	17.0
R	18	ADAM DEADMARSH	78	33	27	60	8	136	10	3	4		198	16.7
R	11	KEITH JONES	78	25	23	48	3	118	14	1	7		170	14.7
R	48	SCOTT YOUNG	72	18	19	37	-5	14	7				164	11.0
L	28	ERIC LACROIX	81	18	18	36	16	26	2		4		141	12.8
C	9	MIKE RICCI	63	13	19	32	-3	59	5		3		74	17.6
R	22	CLAUDE LEMIEUX	45	11	17	28	-4	43	5		4		168	6.5
L	20	RENE CORBET	76	12	15	27	14	67	1		3	1	128	9.4
R	25	MIKE KEANE	81	10	17	27	2	63		1	1		91	11.0
C	26	STEPHANE YELLE	79	9	17	26	1	38		1	1		89	10.1
D	24	JON KLEMM	80	9	15	24	12	37	1	2	1		103	8.7
D	4	UWE KRUPP	60	4	17	21	12	48	2		1		107	3.7
D	52	ADAM FOOTE	78	2	19	21	16	135					60	3.3
D	3	*AARON MILLER	56	5	12	17	15	15			3		47	10.6
D	5	ALEXEI GUSAROV	58	2	12	14	4	28					33	6.1
D	2	SYLVAIN LEFEBVRE	71	2	11	13	12	30	1				77	2.6
D	23	BRENT SEVERYN	66	1	4	5	-6	193					55	1.8
L	15	YVES SARAULT	28	2	1	3	0	6					41	4.9
R	27	*CHRISTIAN MATTE	5	1	1	2	1						6	16.7
G	1	CRAIG BILLINGTON	23		2	2	0	2						
C	10	*JOSEF MARHA	6		1	1	0						6	
G	33	PATRICK ROY	62		1	1	0	15					1	
G	30	*MARC DENIS	1				0							
D	32	*RICHARD BRENNAN	2				0							
D	6	*WADE BELAK	5				-1	11					1	
D	29	*ERIC MESSIER	21				7	4					11	

GP = games played; G = goals; A = assists; PTS = points; +/- = goals-for minus goals-against while player is on ice; PIM = penalties in minutes; PP = power-play goals; SH = shorthanded goals; GW = game-winning goals; GT = game-tying goals; S = no. of shots; PCT = percentage of goals to shots; * = rookie

RENE CORBET

Yrs. of NHL service: 2
Born: Victoriaville, Que.; June 25, 1973
Position: left wing
Height: 6-0
Weight: 187
Uniform no.: 20
Shoots: left

Career statistics:

GP	G	A	TP	PIM
126	16	25	41	102

1993-94 statistics:

GP	G	A	TP	+/-	PIM	PP	SH	GW	GT	S	PCT
9	1	1	2	+1	0	0	0	0	0	14	7.1

1994-95 statistics:

GP	G	A	TP	+/-	PIM	PP	SH	GW	GT	S	PCT
8	0	3	3	+3	2	0	0	0	0	4	0.0

1995-96 statistics:

GP	G	A	TP	+/-	PIM	PP	SH	GW	GT	S	PCT
33	3	6	9	+10	33	0	0	0	0	35	8.6

1996-97 statistics:

GP	G	A	TP	+/-	PIM	PP	SH	GW	GT	S	PCT
76	12	15	27	+14	67	1	0	3	1	128	9.4

LAST SEASON

First full NHL season. Career highs in goals, assists and points. Missed three games with concussion.

THE FINESSE GAME

A purely offensive player, Corbet has a tough go of it getting ice time because he isn't in the same elite class as teammates Joe Sakic and Peter Forsberg. Yet Corbet took advantage of injuries to those two players last season to establish a solid NHL game.

He has a terrific shot with a great release. He was a scoring champion in junior (QMJHL) and tore it up pretty good in the AHL, so he has confidence in his ability to find the net.

Corbet's defensive work has improved, as has his skating. As a young player, he hired Olympic speed skater Gaetan Boucher as a coach.

THE PHYSICAL GAME

Corbet is of average height but a little on the light side. He actually looks somewhat fragile, since he tends to work in the high traffic areas and gets bounced around.

THE INTANGIBLES

Corbet has paid his dues for a number of years, as a part-timer and in the minors. He has been labelled as a player with an inconsistent intensity level.

PROJECTION

Corbet's production will be limited to how much he can accomplish getting fourth-line ice time, since we don't see him breaking into the top two lines, not with Colorado, anyway.

ADAM DEADMARSH

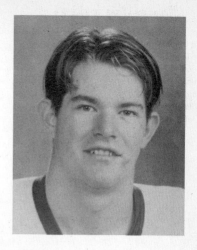

Yrs. of NHL service: 3
Born: Trail, B.C.; May 10, 1975
Position: right wing
Height: 6-0
Weight: 195
Uniform no.: 18
Shoots: right

Career statistics:

GP	G	A	TP	PIM
204	63	62	125	334

1994-95 statistics:

GP	G	A	TP	+/-	PIM	PP	SH	GW	GT	S	PCT
48	9	8	17	+16	56	0	0	0	1	48	18.8

1995-96 statistics:

GP	G	A	TP	+/-	PIM	PP	SH	GW	GT	S	PCT
78	21	27	48	+20	142	3	0	2	0	151	13.9

1996-97 statistics:

GP	G	A	TP	+/-	PIM	PP	SH	GW	GT	S	PCT
78	33	27	60	+8	136	10	3	4	0	198	16.7

LAST SEASON

Led team in goals. Second on team in shorthanded goals and penalty minutes. Tied for third on team in power-play goals. Third on team in shooting percentage. Missed three games with contract holdout.

THE FINESSE GAME

How does a third-line checker lead the skilled Avalanche in goal scoring? By playing the Deadmarsh way: crashing to the net and scattering defensemen like so many bowling pins.

Deadmarsh is a bigger version of Kevin Dineen. He's feisty and tough and can work in a checking role, but he can also score off the chances he creates with his defense and can be moved onto the top two scoring lines and not look out of place. His game is incredibly mature. He is reliable enough to be put out on the ice to protect a lead in the late minutes of a game, because he will do what it takes to win.

Deadmarsh doesn't have to be the glamour guy (Colorado is loaded with those types, anyway), but that doesn't mean he provides unskilled labour. He has dangerous speed and quickness, and a nice scoring touch to convert the chances he creates off his forechecking. He can play centre as well as both wings, so he's versatile. He doesn't play a complex game. He's a basic up-and-down winger, a nice complement to all of the flash and dash on the Avalanche. He excels as a dedicated penalty killer.

THE PHYSICAL GAME

Deadmarsh always finishes his checks. He has a strong work ethic with honest toughness. He never backs down from a challenge and issues some of his own. He isn't a dirty player, but he will fight when challenged or stand up for his teammates. He isn't known for his fitness but handles a lot of ice time and is very durable.

Deadmarsh had two "Gordie Howe hat tricks" last season — a goal, an assist and a fight.

THE INTANGIBLES

Deadmarsh has a huge upside, his only slump — if you can call it that, as it was more of a bump — came because this kid has played a lot of hockey in the past year. The Stanley Cup playoffs, the World Cup, absorbing the ice time of injured stars and playing his gung-ho brand of hockey took its toll. There just aren't enough good things scouts can find to say about Deadmarsh. He is the kind of player who will seldom be one of the three stars of the game, but he'll be one of the guys who found five ways to help win a game.

PROJECTION

We didn't think Deadmarsh could develop into a 100-point scorer, but he is starting to show signs of becoming a Rick Tocchet type who can score 40 goals the hard way. He could join Keith Tkachuk as one of the game's best new power forwards.

ADAM FOOTE

Yrs. of NHL service: 6
Born: Toronto, Ont.; July 10, 1971
Position: right defense
Height: 6-1
Weight: 202
Uniform no.: 52
Shoots: right

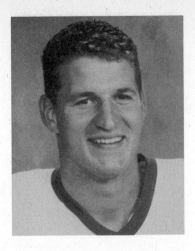

Career statistics:

GP	G	A	TP	PIM
358	15	59	74	554

1993-94 statistics:

GP	G	A	TP	+/-	PIM	PP	SH	GW	GT	S	PCT
45	2	6	8	+3	67	0	0	0	0	42	4.8

1994-95 statistics:

GP	G	A	TP	+/-	PIM	PP	SH	GW	GT	S	PCT
35	0	7	7	+17	52	0	0	0	0	24	0.0

1995-96 statistics:

GP	G	A	TP	+/-	PIM	PP	SH	GW	GT	S	PCT
73	5	11	16	+27	88	1	0	1	0	49	10.2

1996-97 statistics:

GP	G	A	TP	+/-	PIM	PP	SH	GW	GT	S	PCT
78	2	19	21	+16	135	0	0	0	0	60	3.3

LAST SEASON

Tied for second on team in plus-minus. Missed four games with knee injury.

THE FINESSE GAME

Foote has great foot speed and quickness. Defensively, he's strong in his coverage and is a stay-at-home type. He's not creative with the puck, probably his major deficiency, but all of the Avalanche defensemen are encouraged to jump into the attack and Foote eagerly does so when given the chance. He is wise in his pinches and knows when to drive to the slot. He won't take wild chances.

Foote usually skates the puck out of his zone. He is less likely to find the man for an outlet pass. There are few defensemen in the league who can match him in getting the first few strides in and jumping out of the zone. He is an excellent penalty killer.

THE PHYSICAL GAME

Foote is big and solid and uses his body well. He is highly aggressive in his defensive zone; anyone trying to get through Foote to the net will pay a price. He plays it smart and takes few bad penalties. He really stepped up his physical play — possibly a result of gaining confidence after back surgery in 1994 — and dishes out some really powerful checks. He has good lower-body strength and drives his body upwards, resulting in a heavy impact with his unfortunate target.

Foote can fight when provoked and stands up for his teammates.

THE INTANGIBLES

Colorado's defense gets far less credit than its for-wards and goalie, but Foote is an excellent two-way defenseman whose skills are just a notch below elite class.

PROJECTION

Foote plays a defense-heavy game but can still score 25 points.

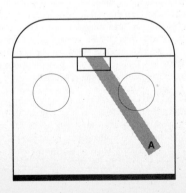

PETER FORSBERG

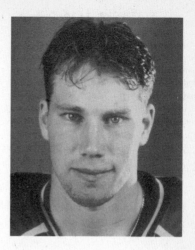

Yrs. of NHL service: 3
Born: Ornskoldsvik, Sweden; July 20, 1973
Position: centre
Height: 6-0
Weight: 190
Uniform no.: 21
Shoots: left

Career statistics:

GP	G	A	TP	PIM
194	73	179	252	136

1994-95 statistics:

GP	G	A	TP	+/-	PIM	PP	SH	GW	GT	S	PCT
47	15	35	50	+17	16	3	0	3	0	86	17.4

1995-96 statistics:

GP	G	A	TP	+/-	PIM	PP	SH	GW	GT	S	PCT
82	30	86	116	+26	47	7	3	3	0	217	13.8

1996-97 statistics:

GP	G	A	TP	+/-	PIM	PP	SH	GW	GT	S	PCT
65	28	58	86	+31	73	5	4	4	0	188	14.9

LAST SEASON

Led team in assists, points, plus-minus and short-handed goals. Tied for second on team in goals. Missed 17 games with thigh injury.

THE FINESSE GAME

There is nothing Forsberg can't do. Since he was traded to Quebec (now Colorado) in the Eric Lindros trade, it is frequently pointed out how much better Forsberg's game is than Lindros's. That's a bit unfair, since, before passing judgement, we would have to see Lindros playing with the same calibre of players that Forsberg does.

Forsberg is used in all game situations: power play, penalty killing and four-on-four. His skill level is world class.

Forsberg protects the puck as well as anybody in the league. He is so strong that he can control the puck with one arm while fending off a checker, and still make an effective pass. His passing is nearly as good as teammate Joe Sakic's. In fact, Colorado now has two of the top four or five playmakers in the league in Sakic and Forsberg, which is joyous news to their wingers but should depress the heck out of the rest of the NHL. Forsberg seems to be thinking a play or two ahead of everyone else on the ice, which was always Wayne Gretzky's great trait.

Forsberg is a smooth skater with explosive speed (think Teemu Selanne) and he can accelerate while carrying the puck. He has excellent vision of the ice and is an outstanding playmaker. One of the few knocks on him is that he doesn't shoot enough. He works best down between the circles with a wrist or backhand shot off the rush.

THE PHYSICAL GAME

Forsberg is better suited for the North American style than most Europeans — or many North Americans, for that matter. He is tough to knock down. He loves the game and dishes out more than he receives. He relishes contact. Just try to knock him off the puck. He has a wide skating base and great balance. He can be cross-checked while he's on his backhand and still not lose control of the puck. Jaromir Jagr may be the only other player in the league who can do that.

Forsberg has a cockiness that many great athletes carry about them like an aura, and he dares people to try to intimidate him. His drive to succeed helps him handle the cheap stuff and keep going. He's got a mean streak, too — just ask Edmonton's Boris Mironov, whose nose was broken by Forsberg's stick in the playoffs. Forsberg plays equally hard on any given inch of the ice.

THE INTANGIBLES

Is there a weakness here? Yes. Just as Sakic learned, shooting is allowed in the NHL. In fact, it's encouraged. Forsberg would be less predictable if he shot more often. He could score 50 goals if he wanted to.

PROJECTION

Forsberg missed our top five scoring prediction due to the injury, which affected his entire second half. Assuming it's healed (it's a similar injury to the one that led to Cam Neely's premature retirement), he will take his place among the league's top four forwards. Over the next few seasons, it will be Forsberg, Eric Lindros, Paul Kariya and Jaromir Jagr dominating All-Star games and trophy balloting.

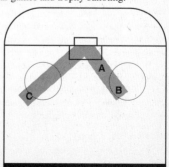

KEITH JONES

Yrs. of NHL service: 5
Born: Brantford, Ont.; Nov. 8, 1968
Position: right wing
Height: 6-2
Weight: 200
Uniform no.: 11
Shoots: left

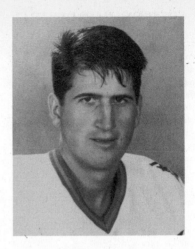

Career statistics:

GP	G	A	TP	PIM
322	85	88	170	559

1993-94 statistics:

GP	G	A	TP	+/-	PIM	PP	SH	GW	GT	S	PCT
68	16	19	35	+4	149	5	0	1	0	97	16.5

1994-95 statistics:

GP	G	A	TP	+/-	PIM	PP	SH	GW	GT	S	PCT
40	14	6	20	-2	65	1	0	4	0	85	16.5

1995-96 statistics:

GP	G	A	TP	+/-	PIM	PP	SH	GW	GT	S	PCT
68	18	23	41	+8	103	5	0	2	0	155	11.6

1996-97 statistics:

GP	G	A	TP	+/-	PIM	PP	SH	GW	GT	S	PCT
78	25	23	48	+3	118	14	1	7	0	170	14.7

LAST SEASON

Acquired from Washington with a first-round and a fourth-round draft pick in 1997 for Chris Simon and Curtis Leschyshyn, November 2, 1996. Led team and tied for fifth in NHL in power- play goals. Led team in game-winning goals. Career highs in goals, assists and points.

THE FINESSE GAME

Must be that clear mountain air in Denver. No sooner did Jones, a grinder by trade, arrive in Colorado than he had a vision of himself as a better hockey player. Without abandoning any of the principles that had helped him establish himself with the offensively uninspired Washington Capitals, Jones discovered the joys of shooting, scoring and playmaking.

Jones doesn't have the greatest hands in the world and he'll never be confused with Peter Forsberg, but he has a good shot. Most of his power-play goals came from within 10 feet of the net. Jones is a spark plug. He likes to make things happen by driving to the front of the net, taking a defenseman with him. His skating is adequate, and he uses quick bursts of speed to power himself to and through the traffic areas.

He is an eager finisher and plays well at both ends of the ice. He keeps the game simple and does his job. He isn't very creative, but his efforts churn up loose pucks for teammates smart enough to trail in his wake. Jones is the antithesis of a natural scorer, because everything he accomplishes is through effort.

THE PHYSICAL GAME

Jones is energetic and uses his size well. He is tough and willing to pay a physical price. The Avalanche could use a couple of more players like him. He isn't the biggest player on the ice, but there are nights when you come away thinking he is.

Jones finishes every check in every zone, and sometimes runs around a bit, but he is becoming more responsible defensively.

THE INTANGIBLES

Jones loves the game and knows what he has to do to stay in the lineup. He's not likely to be spoiled now that people have raised their estimation of him. There's no telling what would have happened if he hadn't gone down with a knee injury in the playoffs.

PROJECTION

No one deserves success more than the hard-working Jones. He may get off to a slow start because of his knee surgery. That's the sole reason why his 25 goals may be tough to match.

VALERI KAMENSKY

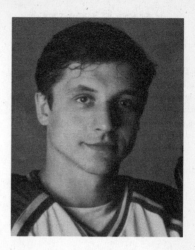

Yrs. of NHL service: 5
Born: Voskresensk, Russia; April 18, 1966
Position: left wing
Height: 6-2
Weight: 198
Uniform no.: 13
Shoots: right

Career statistics:

GP	G	A	TP	PIM
320	126	178	304	215

1993-94 statistics:

GP	G	A	TP	+/-	PIM	PP	SH	GW	GT	S	PCT
76	28	37	65	+12	42	6	0	1	0	170	16.5

1994-95 statistics:

GP	G	A	TP	+/-	PIM	PP	SH	GW	GT	S	PCT
40	10	20	30	+3	22	5	1	5	0	70	14.3

1995-96 statistics:

GP	G	A	TP	+/-	PIM	PP	SH	GW	GT	S	PCT
81	38	47	85	+14	85	18	1	5	0	220	17.3

1996-97 statistics:

GP	G	A	TP	+/-	PIM	PP	SH	GW	GT	S	PCT
68	28	38	66	+5	38	8	0	4	1	165	17.0

range, and should continue to produce.

LAST SEASON

Tied for second on team in goals. Second on team in shooting percentage. Missed five games in contract holdout. Missed nine games with shoulder injuries.

THE FINESSE GAME

Kamensky is primarily a one-way forward. A gifted skater with speed and quickness, he is as dangerous without the puck as with it because of his sense for open ice. He's as effective in four-on-four situations as he is a top transition player. His passes are flat and on the money, with just the right velocity. The recipient does not have to slow down but can collect the puck in stride.

Kamensky has quick hands and a good release on his wrist shot. He gets a lot of power-play time and excels at getting open in the left slot; he just rips his one-timer.

THE PHYSICAL GAME

Kamensky generally tries to avoid contact. He will venture into a spot where he might get hit if he believes he can zip out quickly before any damage is inflicted. Opposing teams generally make a point of hitting Kamensky early to throw him off his game.

THE INTANGIBLES

Kamensky is Peter Forsberg's left-hand man, and Forsberg's injuries caused a decline in Kamensky's production as well.

PROJECTION

Kamensky has to score to be useful, because it's the only thing he does well. He belongs in the 80-point

JON KLEMM

Yrs. of NHL service: 2
Born: Cranbrook, B.C.; Jan. 8, 1970
Position: right defense
Height: 6-3
Weight: 200
Uniform no.: 24
Shoots: right

Career statistics:

GP	G	A	TP	PIM
151	13	28	41	63

1993-94 statistics:

GP	G	A	TP	+/-	PIM	PP	SH	GW	GT	S	PCT
7	0	0	0	-1	4	0	0	0	0	11	0.0

1994-95 statistics:

GP	G	A	TP	+/-	PIM	PP	SH	GW	GT	S	PCT
4	1	0	1	+3	2	0	0	0	0	5	0.0

1995-96 statistics:

GP	G	A	TP	+/-	PIM	PP	SH	GW	GT	S	PCT
56	3	12	15	+12	20	0	1	1	0	61	4.9

1996-97 statistics:

GP	G	A	TP	+/-	PIM	PP	SH	GW	GT	S	PCT
80	9	15	24	+12	37	1	2	1	0	103	8.7

LAST SEASON
Second NHL season.

THE FINESSE GAME
Klemm has enough finesse skills that the Avalanche used him up front due to injuries last season. His defensive skills are good enough that he was assigned the unenviable task of playing the stay-at-home partner to the wayward Sandis Ozolinsh. Let's just say he's had a lot of experience facing two-on-ones.

Klemm is an all-purpose defenseman who does everything the team asks of him. His skating is average, but he plays within his limitations. When he's moved up front he fills the role of a grinding winger, and just plays it safe and smart.

THE PHYSICAL GAME
Klemm doesn't go looking for hits. He eliminates his man but doesn't have the explosive drive from his legs to make powerful highlights hits.

THE INTANGIBLES
Klemm is a sportswriter's nightmare because he's so quiet, yet he's appreciated by his coaches and teammates for his willingness to do anything for the team.

PROJECTION
As long as Klemm is under pressure as Ozolinsh's partner, he will have to concentrate on defense. He can score 20 to 25 points a season.

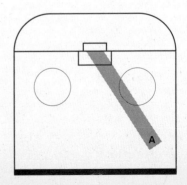

UWE KRUPP

Yrs. of NHL service: 11
Born: Cologne, West Germany; June 24, 1965
Position: right defense
Height: 6-6
Weight: 235
Uniform no.: 4
Shoots: right

Career statistics:

GP	G	A	TP	PIM
617	57	187	244	598

1993-94 statistics:

GP	G	A	TP	+/-	PIM	PP	SH	GW	GT	S	PCT
41	7	14	21	+11	30	3	0	0	0	82	8.5

1994-95 statistics:

GP	G	A	TP	+/-	PIM	PP	SH	GW	GT	S	PCT
44	6	17	23	+14	20	3	0	1	1	102	5.9

1995-96 statistics:

GP	G	A	TP	+/-	PIM	PP	SH	GW	GT	S	PCT
6	0	3	3	+4	4	0	0	0	0	9	0.0

1996-97 statistics:

GP	G	A	TP	+/-	PIM	PP	SH	GW	GT	S	PCT
60	4	17	21	+12	48	2	0	1	0	107	3.7

LAST SEASON

Missed five games with left shoulder injury. Missed eight games with elbow injury. Missed seven games with back injury.

THE FINESSE GAME

The key to Krupp's game is his awareness of his limitations. Not a quick skater even before his knee surgery of two seasons ago, he is now more conservative, yet effective. He reads plays well both offensively and defensively. He positions himself well in his own zone, so he needs only one long stride to cut off the attacker.

Krupp has a hard shot, but it takes him far too long to get his big slapper underway and it's often blocked. Because he is so tall and uses such a long stick, he doesn't one-time the puck well, but instead must stop it and tee it up. He has a good wrist shot that he can use to better purpose, because he can get it away cleanly and with some velocity. He protects the puck well.

Krupp helps his team immeasurably by his ability to move the puck smartly out of the zone. He is a smooth passer and creates a lot of odd-man rushes by spotting the developing play and making the solid first pass.

THE PHYSICAL GAME

Krupp is enormous and takes up a lot of space on the ice, but doesn't use his body as a weapon. It's more of a roadblock, and it's one heck of a detour to get around. Krupp blocks shots willingly and is a very good penalty killer. He plays with restraint and takes few bad penalties. Checkers seem to bounce off him.

On the rare nights when he gets physical he can dominate, but he doesn't often play that way. It's just not his nature.

THE INTANGIBLES

Krupp is reliable and sensible, and he can be used to protect a lead because he never takes unnecessary risks. He has been used with a lot of partners and complements all of them well, especially younger defensemen. He is a steadying influence; now he's a champion as well.

PROJECTION

Krupp's back injury, which prevented him from playing in the playoffs, is a major concern. He's starting to look like an old 32, with his injuries taking awhile to mend.

JARI KURRI

Yrs. of NHL service: 16
Born: Helsinki, Finland; May 18, 1960
Position: right wing
Height: 6-1
Weight: 195
Uniform no.: 17
Shoots: right

Career statistics:

GP	G	A	TP	PIM
1181	596	780	1376	533

1993-94 statistics:

GP	G	A	TP	+/-	PIM	PP	SH	GW	GT	S	PCT
81	31	46	77	-24	48	14	4	3	1	198	15.7

1994-95 statistics:

GP	G	A	TP	+/-	PIM	PP	SH	GW	GT	S	PCT
38	10	19	29	-17	24	2	0	0	1	84	11.9

1995-96 statistics:

GP	G	A	TP	+/-	PIM	PP	SH	GW	GT	S	PCT
71	18	27	45	-16	39	5	1	0	2	158	11.4

1996-97 statistics:

GP	G	A	TP	+/-	PIM	PP	SH	GW	GT	S	PCT
82	13	22	35	-13	12	3	0	3	0	109	11.9

LAST SEASON

Signed as free agent, July 11, 1997. Fifth on Mighty Ducks in scoring. Only Mighty Duck to appear in all 82 games.

THE FINESSE GAME

Kurri has gone from being one of the game's top snipers to one of the most underrated defensive forwards in the NHL. His one-timers no longer terrorize goalies and he has lost a half-step on the outside move that used to burn defenders. Goals are now a bonus instead of his hallmark. His versatility is still a major asset. Kurri can play centre or wing, and still has the finesse skills to step up and play with more talented forwards in a pinch.

Kurri's quickness and anticipation make him a great shorthanded threat when killing penalties. Even so, he is more likely to make a conservative play or pass than try to take the puck to the net himself.

Kurri's knowledge of the game and the way shooters think help him as a checking forward. He has also become quite adept at face-offs, and uses his feet to help control the puck. His skills are still intact enough that he can be useful on a second power-play unit. He makes others around him better players.

THE PHYSICAL GAME

Kurri will get involved in a battle for a loose puck and protects the puck well along the wall. He is not a banger, but Kurri pays the price when it matters.

THE INTANGIBLES

Kurri looked like a kid again last season, especially after a difficult start to the season due to his father's recovery from open heart surgery. He will probably play his last season in Colorado, hoping to go out a winner with a powerful team.

PROJECTION

Kurri's contribution isn't measured in points. He will help compensate for the loss of Mike Keane.

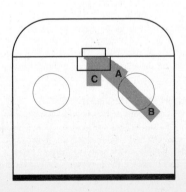

ERIC LACROIX

Yrs. of NHL service: 3
Born: Montreal, Que.; July 15, 1971
Position: left wing
Height: 6-1
Weight: 205
Uniform no.: 28
Shoots: left

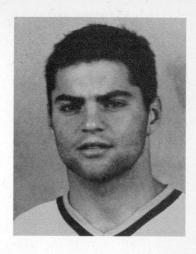

Career statistics:

GP	G	A	TP	PIM
201	43	41	84	192

1993-94 statistics:

GP	G	A	TP	+/-	PIM	PP	SH	GW	GT	S	PCT
3	0	0	0	0	2	0	0	0	0	3	0.0

1994-95 statistics:

GP	G	A	TP	+/-	PIM	PP	SH	GW	GT	S	PCT
45	9	7	16	+2	54	2	1	1	0	64	14.1

1995-96 statistics:

GP	G	A	TP	+/-	PIM	PP	SH	GW	GT	S	PCT
72	16	16	32	-11	110	3	0	1	0	107	15.0

1996-97 statistics:

GP	G	A	TP	+/-	PIM	PP	SH	GW	GT	S	PCT
81	18	18	36	+16	26	2	0	4	0	141	12.8

LAST SEASON

Tied for second on team in plus-minus. Career high in goals, assists and points.

THE FINESSE GAME

Lacroix brings zest and inspiration to every shift. There is nothing fancy to his game. He's not the fastest skater. He doesn't have the biggest shot. He just goes to the net and gets his stick down on the ice.

Lacroix is a bigger, more skilled version of Edmonton's Kirk Maltby. He can certainly complement some finesse players by working the wall and grinding.

If Lacroix has the proper work ethic, he'll become more than a big banger. Hitters and fighters like Rick Tocchet turned themselves into productive scorers first by earning room on the ice, then by practising shooting drills to make use of that extra space. Any improvement will not come easy to Lacroix. He appears willing to work and is a good skater with balance and speed. He forechecks hard and forces turnovers.

THE PHYSICAL GAME

Lacroix hits to hurt, and some of his checks cross the line. He often makes such thunderous contact he gets penalized, because he leaves his feet and sometimes brings his elbows up.

With just a tad more control Lacroix could turn himself into a serious, clean checker who will scare puck carriers into coughing up the rubber, but he is undisciplined at this stage.

THE INTANGIBLES

Lacroix has a lot of upside, and he performed well despite the pressure of being the son of the team's general manager (Pierre Lacroix). Wonder how big a raise dad will give the Group 2 free agent?

PROJECTION

Lacroix's next step should be to become a consistent 20-goal scorer.

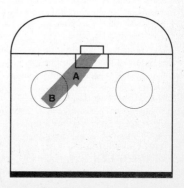

SYLVAIN LEFEBVRE

Yrs. of NHL service: 8
Born: Richmond, Que.; Oct. 14, 1967
Position: right defense
Height: 6-2
Weight: 205
Uniform no.: 2
Shoots: left

Career statistics:

GP	G	A	TP	PIM
559	24	96	120	447

1993-94 statistics:

GP	G	A	TP	+/-	PIM	PP	SH	GW	GT	S	PCT
84	2	9	11	+33	79	0	0	0	1	96	2.1

1994-95 statistics:

GP	G	A	TP	+/-	PIM	PP	SH	GW	GT	S	PCT
48	2	11	13	+13	17	0	0	0	0	81	2.5

1995-96 statistics:

GP	G	A	TP	+/-	PIM	PP	SH	GW	GT	S	PCT
75	5	11	16	+26	49	2	0	0	0	115	4.3

1996-97 statistics:

GP	G	A	TP	+/-	PIM	PP	SH	GW	GT	S	PCT
71	2	11	13	+12	30	1	0	0	0	77	2.6

LAST SEASON

Missed 11 games with fractured wrist.

THE FINESSE GAME

Lefebvre is a good argument for instituting an NHL award for best defensive defensemen (as opposed to the Norris Trophy, which in recent years has gone to offensive defensemen). If there was such a piece of hardware, Lefebvre would be a finalist, if not a winner. He's one of the best at one-on-one coverage. He's always in position and always square with his man. He reads the play well and makes good outlet passes from his own end.

Lefebvre plays his position the way any coach would try to teach it to a youngster. Safe and dependable, Lefebvre makes the first pass and then forgets about the puck. He couldn't be any less interested in the attack. If he has the puck at the offensive blueline and doesn't have a lane, he just throws it into the corner. His game is defense first, and he is very basic and consistent in his limited role. He does it all playing against the other team's top lines on a nightly basis.

Lefebvre actually has below-average skills in speed and puckhandling, but by playing within his limits and within the system he is ultrareliable.

THE PHYSICAL GAME

Tough without being a punishing hitter, Lefebvre patrols and controls the front of his net and plays a hard-nosed style. He plays a containment game.

THE INTANGIBLES

Lefebvre is a rock-solid defensive defenseman. He is a quiet leader, well respected by teammates and opponents.

PROJECTION

Lefebvre prevents points, he doesn't score them.

CLAUDE LEMIEUX

Yrs. of NHL service: 13
Born: Buckingham, Que.; July 16, 1965
Position: right wing
Height: 6-1
Weight: 215
Uniform no.: 22
Shoots: right

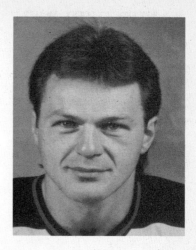

Career statistics:

GP	G	A	TP	PIM
760	272	275	547	1277

1993-94 statistics:

GP	G	A	TP	+/-	PIM	PP	SH	GW	GT	S	PCT
79	18	26	44	+13	86	5	0	5	0	181	9.9

1994-95 statistics:

GP	G	A	TP	+/-	PIM	PP	SH	GW	GT	S	PCT
45	6	13	19	+2	86	1	0	1	0	117	5.1

1995-96 statistics:

GP	G	A	TP	+/-	PIM	PP	SH	GW	GT	S	PCT
79	39	32	71	+14	117	9	2	10	0	315	12.4

1996-97 statistics:

GP	G	A	TP	+/-	PIM	PP	SH	GW	GT	S	PCT
45	11	17	28	-4	43	5	0	4	0	168	6.5

LAST SEASON

Missed 37 games with abdominal injury and surgery.

THE FINESSE GAME

Call him Claude "Le Me." But bear with his selfish behavior and sophomoric humour because Lemieux is a winner.

Lemieux is a shooter, a disturber, a force. He loves the puck, wants the puck, needs the puck and is sometimes obsessed with the puck. When he is struggling, that selfishness hurts the team. But when he gets into his groove everyone is happy to stand back and let him fly, and on the talented Avalanche team, he fits right in.

When Lemieux is on, he can rock the house. He has a hard slap shot and shoots well off the fly. He isn't afraid to jam the front of the net for tips and screens and will battle for loose pucks. He has great hands for close-in shots. Although he wasn't asked to do much defensively for Colorado, he can kill penalties and check top forwards.

THE PHYSICAL GAME

Lemieux was affected all of last season with his November surgery for a recurring abdominal muscle problem. He didn't get rolling until — when else? — the playoffs.

Lemieux is strong, with good skating balance and great upper-body and arm strength. He is very tough along the boards and in traffic in front of the net, outduelling many bigger opponents because of his fierce desire. Because he is always whining and yapping, the abuse Lemieux takes is often ignored, but it's not unusual to find him with welts across his arms and cuts on his face. The satisfaction comes from knowing that his opponent usually looks even worse, but he still takes dumb penalties by jawing at the referees, who have little patience with him after all these years.

Of course, he also infuriates opponents by goading them into dropping their gloves and then turtling. Lemieux will gleefully inform you he's a lover, not a fighter.

THE INTANGIBLES

The Devils won the Stanley Cup, traded Lemieux and then failed to make the playoffs, while Colorado won in his first year in 1996. All along, New Jersey coach Jacques Lemaire insisted he was happier having Steve Thomas in his room instead of Lemieux. You don't get Lemieux for harmony. You get him if you want to win.

PROJECTION

Coaches and pool players alike can ignore Lemieux's shenanigans during the regular season. He is one of the great playoff performers of his generation; he's never played on a team that missed the playoffs.

SANDIS OZOLINSH

Yrs. of NHL service: 5
Born: Riga, Latvia; Aug. 3, 1972
Position: left defense
Height: 6-1
Weight: 195
Uniform no.: 8
Shoots: left

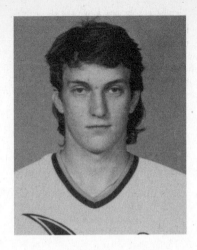

Career statistics:

GP	G	A	TP	PIM
319	79	155	234	236

1993-94 statistics:

GP	G	A	TP	+/-	PIM	PP	SH	GW	GT	S	PCT
81	26	38	64	+16	24	4	0	3	0	157	16.6

1994-95 statistics:

GP	G	A	TP	+/-	PIM	PP	SH	GW	GT	S	PCT
48	9	16	25	-6	30	3	1	2	0	83	10.8

1995-96 statistics:

GP	G	A	TP	+/-	PIM	PP	SH	GW	GT	S	PCT
73	14	40	54	+2	54	8	1	1	1	166	8.4

1996-97 statistics:

GP	G	A	TP	+/-	PIM	PP	SH	GW	GT	S	PCT
80	23	45	68	+4	88	13	0	4	1	232	9.9

LAST SEASON

Norris Trophy finalist. Named to NHL First All-Star Team. Led NHL defensemen in goals. Second in NHL in power-play assists (29). Second among NHL defensemen and third on team in points. Second on team in power-play goals and shots. Missed two games with back spasms.

THE FINESSE GAME

Anyone who bought into the hype that Ozolinsh was playing improved defense last season ought to be ashamed of themselves. Ozolinsh is a pure "offense-man," but one who never knows when not to go. Unlike more intelligent rushing defensemen, such as Brian Leetch and Ray Bourque, Ozolinish sees only one traffic light, and it's stuck on green.

Ozolinsh likes to start things by pressing in the neutral zone, where he will gamble and try to intercept cross-ice passes. His defense partner and the forwards will always have to be alert to guard against odd-man rushes back, because Ozolinsh doesn't recognize when it's a good time to be aggressive or when to back off.

Ozolinsh will start the breakout play with his smooth skating, then spring a teammate with a crisp pass. He can pass on his forehand or backhand, which is a good thing because he is all over the ice. He will follow up the play to create an odd-man rush, trail in for a drop pass or drive to the net for a rebound.

Ozolinsh has good straightaway speed, but he can't make a lot of agile, pretty moves the way Paul Coffey can. Because he can't weave his way through a number of defenders, he has to power his way into open ice with the puck and drive the defenders back through intimidation. His speed does help him recover to get back and help out on the odd-man rushes against that he helps create.

He sometimes hangs onto the puck too long. He has a variety of shots, with his best being a one-timer from the off-side on the power play. He is not as effective when he works down low. He does not stop and start well, especially when moving backwards.

THE PHYSICAL GAME

Ozolinsh goes into areas of the ice where he gets hit a lot, and he is stronger than he looks. He is all business on the ice and pays the price to get the puck, but he needs to develop more strength to clear out his crease.

THE INTANGIBLES

Ozolinsh is a poster boy for creating a trophy for the league's best defensive defenseman. As long as he's getting Norris Trophy consideration, there's no "defense" in defenseman.

PROJECTION

Ozolinsh exceeded our prediction of 50 points, and we expect him to go-go-go to the top of the rearguard scoring list.

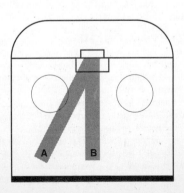

MIKE RICCI

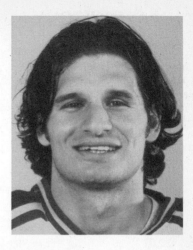

Yrs. of NHL service: 7
Born: Scarborough, Ont.; Oct. 27, 1971
Position: centre
Height: 6-0
Weight: 190
Uniform no.: 9
Shoots: left

Career statistics:

GP	G	A	TP	PIM
479	132	189	321	544

1993-94 statistics:

GP	G	A	TP	+/-	PIM	PP	SH	GW	GT	S	PCT
83	30	21	51	-9	113	13	3	6	1	138	21.3

1994-95 statistics:

GP	G	A	TP	+/-	PIM	PP	SH	GW	GT	S	PCT
48	15	21	36	+5	40	9	0	1	1	73	20.5

1995-96 statistics:

GP	G	A	TP	+/-	PIM	PP	SH	GW	GT	S	PCT
62	6	21	27	+1	52	3	0	1	0	73	8.2

1996-97 statistics:

GP	G	A	TP	+/-	PIM	PP	SH	GW	GT	S	PCT
63	13	19	32	-3	59	5	0	3	0	74	17.6

LAST SEASON

Led team in shooting percentage. Missed two games with knee surgery. Missed 11 games with shoulder injury. Missed six games with broken right thumb.

THE FINESSE GAME

Ricci is a known quantity. He has terrific hand skills, combined with hockey sense and an outstanding work ethic. He always seems to be in the right place, ready to make the right play. He sees his passing options well and is patient with the puck. Ricci can rifle it as well. He has a good backhand shot from in deep and scores most of his goals from the slot by picking the top corners. His lone drawback is his speed. He's fast enough to not look out of place and he has good balance and agility, but his lack of quickness prevents him from being more of an offensive force.

Very slick on face-offs, Ricci has good hand speed and hand-eye coordination for winning draws outright, or he can pick a bouncing puck out of the air. This serves him well in scrambles in front of the net, too, or he can deflect midair slap shots.

Ricci is a very good penalty killer, with poise and a controlled aggression for forcing the play.

THE PHYSICAL GAME

Ricci is not big, but he is so strong that it's not unusual to see him skate out from behind the net, dragging along or fending off a checker with one arm while he makes a pass or takes a shot with his other arm. He plays a tough game without being overly chippy. He is very strong in the corners and in front of the net. He plays bigger than he is.

Ricci will play hurt. He pays attention to conditioning and has a great deal of stamina.

THE INTANGIBLES

Ricci will antagonize and draw penalties. He will kill penalties and work the power play. He makes timely plays under pressure. Although he may never be as gifted offensively as Ron Francis is, he is similar to Francis in that he is a checking centre who can do so much more than just check.

Ricci's quality, character, leadership and dedication to the game and his teammates are impeccable. He is a throwback, and helps provide some grit in a finesse-laden lineup. His teammates love his upbeat off-ice attitude.

PROJECTION

Off-season shoulder surgery may end a pesky problem and allow Colorado to get a full 50-point season out of Ricci.

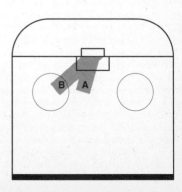

PATRICK ROY

Yrs. of NHL service: 12
Born: Quebec City, Que.; Oct. 5, 1965
Position: goaltender
Height: 6-0
Weight: 192
Uniform no.: 33
Catches: left

Career statistics:

GP	MIN	GA	SO	GAA	A	PIM
652	37921	1722	37	2.72	29	129

1993-94 statistics:

GP	MIN	GAA	W	L	T	SO	GA	S	SAPCT	PIM
68	3867	2.50	35	17	11	7	161	1956	.918	30

1994-95 statistics:

GP	MIN	GAA	W	L	T	SO	GA	S	SAPCT	PIM
43	2566	2.97	17	20	6	1	127	1357	.906	20

1995-96 statistics:

GP	MIN	GAA	W	L	T	SO	GA	S	SAPCT	PIM
61	3565	2.78	34	24	2	2	165	1797	.908	10

1996-97 statistics:

GP	MIN	GAA	W	L	T	SO	GA	S	SAPCT	PIM
62	3698	2.32	38	15	7	7	143	1861	.923	15

LAST SEASON

Led NHL goalies in wins with career high. Fourth in NHL in save percentage. Tied for second in NHL in shutouts. Seventh season with 30 or more wins. Missed three games with left shoulder injury.

THE PHYSICAL GAME

Roy is so cruel. He tempts shooters with a gaping hole between his pads, then when he has the guy suckered, snaps the pads closed at the last second to deny the goal. There is no one in the NHL better at this tantalizing technique.

Roy is tall but not broad, yet he uses his body well. He plays his angles, stays at the top of his crease and squares his body to the shooter. He is able to absorb the shot and deaden it, so there are few juicy rebounds left on his doorstep.

A butterfly goalie, he goes down much sooner than he did earlier in his career. The book on Roy is to try to beat him high. Usually there isn't much net there and it's a small spot for a shooter to hit. He gets into slumps when he allows wide-angle shots taken from the blueline to the top of the circle, but those lapses are seldom prolonged.

Roy comes back to the rest of the pack in his puck-handling, where he is merely average. As for his skating, he seldom moves out of his net. When he gets in trouble, he moves back and forth on his knees rather than trying to regain his feet. His glove hand isn't great, either. It's good, but he prefers to use his body. If he is under a strong forecheck, Roy isn't shy about freezing the puck for a draw, especially since he plays with excellent face-off men in Colorado.

THE MENTAL GAME

If you have to win one game, this is the goalie you want in the net. Roy is mentally tough, and believes he's the best. He usually is.

THE INTANGIBLES

Given the supporting cast of young studs in front of him, Roy might be able to play effectively until he's 40. Thanks to Roy, up-and-comer Marc Denis will not have to worry about getting rushed into the lineup.

PROJECTION

Another 30-win season, but Roy should stay out of goalie fights (that's how he was hurt).

JOE SAKIC

Yrs. of NHL service: 9
Born: Burnaby, B.C.; July 7, 1969
Position: centre
Height: 5-11
Weight: 185
Uniform no.: 19
Shoots: left

Career statistics:

GP	G	A	TP	PIM
655	307	513	820	261

1993-94 statistics:

GP	G	A	TP	+/-	PIM	PP	SH	GW	GT	S	PCT
84	28	64	92	-8	18	10	1	9	1	279	10.0

1994-95 statistics:

GP	G	A	TP	+/-	PIM	PP	SH	GW	GT	S	PCT
47	19	43	62	+7	30	3	2	5	0	157	12.1

1995-96 statistics:

GP	G	A	TP	+/-	PIM	PP	SH	GW	GT	S	PCT
82	51	69	120	+14	44	17	6	7	1	339	15.0

1996-97 statistics:

GP	G	A	TP	+/-	PIM	PP	SH	GW	GT	S	PCT
65	22	52	74	-10	34	10	2	5	0	261	8.4

LAST SEASON

Led team in shots. Second on team in assists, points and game-winning goals. Third on team in power-play goals. Missed 17 games with lacerated calf muscle.

THE FINESSE GAME

In Sakic's first seven seasons in the NHL, he was rightly known as one of the game's best playmakers. It's not a secret that, in the past two seasons, he has become one of the game's best shooters. Now how do you defend against him?

Sakic has one of the most explosive first steps in the league. He finds and hits the holes in a hurry, even with the puck, to create his chances. He uses a stick shaft with a little more "whip" in it, and that makes his shots more dangerous. He has one of the best wrist shots and snap shots in the NHL. He has one of the quickest releases in the game.

Sakic's most impressive gift is his great patience with the puck. He will hold it until the last minute, when he has drawn the defenders to him and opened up ice, creating — as coaches love to express it — time and space for his linemates. This makes him a gem on the power play, where last season he worked mostly down low and just off the half-boards on the right wing. Sakic can also play the point.

Sakic is a scoring threat every time he is on the ice because he can craft a dangerous scoring chance out of a situation that looks innocent. He is lethal trailing the rush. He takes a pass in full stride without slowing, then dekes and shoots before the goalie can even flinch.

Sakic is a good face-off man, and if he's tied up he uses his skates to kick the puck free.

THE PHYSICAL GAME

Sakic is not a physical player. He's stronger than he looks, and, like Wayne Gretzky, will spin off his checks when opponents take runs at him. He uses his body to protect the puck when he is carrying deep; you have to go through him to get it away. He will try to keep going through traffic or along the boards with the puck, and often squirts free with it because he is able to maintain control and his balance. He creates turnovers with his quickness and hands, but not by initiating contact. He's remarkably durable. His injury last year (the result of a skate cut) marked the first time since 1991-92 that he missed a significant number of games.

THE INTANGIBLES

Sakic is a quiet leader, a soft-spoken guy who doesn't draw much attention to himself. His game does that. He may be one of the most respected players league-wide for his talent, competive nature and class.

PROJECTION

Sakic would have hit the 100-point range we predicted for him last season if he hadn't been injured. He should easily be in the top five in scoring again. Colorado will be on a mission after failing to defend the Stanley Cup.

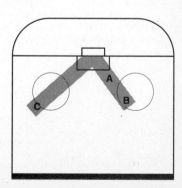

STEPHANE YELLE

Yrs. of NHL service: 2
Born: Ottawa, Ont.; May 9, 1974
Position: centre
Height: 6-1
Weight: 162
Uniform no.: 26
Shoots: left

Career statistics:

GP	G	A	TP	PIM
150	22	31	53	68

1995-96 statistics:

GP	G	A	TP	+/-	PIM	PP	SH	GW	GT	S	PCT
71	13	14	27	+15	30	0	2	1	0	93	14.0

1996-97 statistics:

GP	G	A	TP	+/-	PIM	PP	SH	GW	GT	S	PCT
79	9	17	26	+1	38	0	1	1	0	89	10.1

LAST SEASON

Missed three games with hip injuries.

THE FINESSE GAME

Yelle is a smart player who reads the play extremely well. His knowledge of the game is what has made him an NHL player. His other skills are average: he's a good skater, but he sees the ice in terms of his defensive role. He's a player you want on the ice to kill penalties or to protect a lead.

Yelle doesn't take many face-offs, usually yielding to Mike Ricci in the defensive-zone draws. He doesn't have the hands to get involved in the offense. He isn't even a real shorthanded threat because he doesn't have breakaway speed and will make the safe play instead of the glamourous one.

THE PHYSICAL GAME

Yelle is a tall and stringy-looking athlete with toothpicks for legs. He handles himself well, because even though he doesn't look very strong, he finds a way to get the puck out.

THE INTANGIBLES

Yelle will miss his checking-line partner, Mike Keane, and will assume the bulk of the club's penalty-killing duties.

PROJECTION

Yelle's absolute top end is 15 goals. His value is as a defensive forward, though he has produced in juniors.

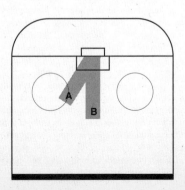

SCOTT YOUNG

Yrs. of NHL service: 8
Born: Clinton, Mass.; Oct. 1, 1967
Position: right wing
Height: 6-0
Weight: 190
Uniform no.: 48
Shoots: right

Career statistics:

GP	G	A	TP	PIM
599	173	239	412	229

1993-94 statistics:

GP	G	A	TP	+/-	PIM	PP	SH	GW	GT	S	PCT
76	26	25	51	-4	14	6	1	1	0	236	11.0

1994-95 statistics:

GP	G	A	TP	+/-	PIM	PP	SH	GW	GT	S	PCT
48	18	21	39	+9	14	3	3	0	0	167	10.8

1995-96 statistics:

GP	G	A	TP	+/-	PIM	PP	SH	GW	GT	S	PCT
81	21	39	60	+2	50	7	0	5	0	229	9.2

1996-97 statistics:

GP	G	A	TP	+/-	PIM	PP	SH	GW	GT	S	PCT
72	18	19	37	-5	14	7	0	0	0	164	11.0

LAST SEASON

Missed five games with shoulder injury.

THE FINESSE GAME

Young is a hockey machine. He has a very heavy shot that surprises a lot of goalies, and he loves to fire it off the wing. He can also one-time the puck low on the face-off, or he'll battle for pucks and tips in front of the net. He's keen to score and always goes to the net with his stick down, ready for the puck.

With all of that in mind, his defensive awareness is even more impressive, because Young is basically a checking winger. He reads plays in all zones equally well and has good anticipation. Young played defense in college, so he is well-schooled.

Young is a very fast skater, which, combined with his reads, makes him a sound forechecker. He will often outrace defensemen to touch pucks and avoid icings, and his speed allows him to recover when he gets overzealous in the attacking zone.

THE PHYSICAL GAME

Young's lone drawback is that he is not a physical player. He will do what he has to do in battles along the boards in the defensive zone, but he's more of a defensive force with his quickness and hand skills. He's not a pure grinder, but will bump and get in the way.

THE INTANGIBLES

Young underwent shoulder surgery during the off-season but he was expected to have a short recovery time. He is a complete player and a model of consistency. Players with great wheels like his tend to last a long time, so expect him to display his veteran ability for many more seasons. His only problem is playing for the talent-rich Avalanche, because he doesn't always get a huge chunk of ice time. When he does, though, Young is ready.

PROJECTION

Young's production declined by 23 points last season, and 30 to 40 points is probably a realistic range for this year.

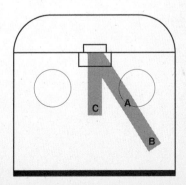

DALLAS STARS

Players' Statistics 1996-97

POS	NO	PLAYER	GP	G	A	PTS	+/-	PIM	PP	SH	GW	GT	S	PCT
C	9	MIKE MODANO	80	35	48	83	43	42	9	5	9	2	291	12.0
R	16	PAT VERBEEK	81	17	36	53	3	128	5		4		172	9.9
C	25	JOE NIEUWENDYK	66	30	21	51	-5	32	8		2	2	173	17.3
D	5	DARRYL SYDOR	82	8	40	48	37	51	2		2		142	5.6
L	33	BENOIT HOGUE	73	19	24	43	8	54	5		5		131	14.5
R	26	JERE LEHTINEN	63	16	27	43	26	2	3	1	2		134	11.9
D	56	SERGEI ZUBOV	78	13	30	43	19	24	1		3		133	9.8
L	14	DAVE REID	82	19	20	39	12	10	1	1	4		135	14.1
C	15	*JAMIE LANGENBRUNNER	76	13	26	39	-2	51	3		3		112	11.6
L	23	GREG ADAMS	50	21	15	36	27	2	5		4	1	113	18.6
C	10	TODD HARVEY	71	9	22	31	19	142	1		2		99	9.1
C	41	BRENT GILCHRIST	67	10	20	30	6	24	2		2		116	8.6
D	2	DERIAN HATCHER	63	3	19	22	8	97					96	3.1
C	21	GUY CARBONNEAU	73	5	16	21	9	36		1			99	5.1
C	7	NEAL BROTEN	42	8	12	20	-4	12	1	1	2		55	14.5
D	12	GRANT LEDYARD	67	1	15	16	31	61					99	1.0
D	3	CRAIG LUDWIG	77	2	11	13	17	62			1		59	3.4
C	28	BOB BASSEN	46	5	7	12	5	41			2		50	10.0
D	24	RICHARD MATVICHUK	57	5	7	12	1	87		2			83	6.0
L	17	BILL HUARD	40	5	6	11	5	105					34	14.7
R	29	GRANT MARSHALL	56	6	4	10	5	98					62	9.7
R	39	MIKE KENNEDY	24	1	6	7	3	13			1		26	3.8
D	18	MIKE LALOR	55	1	1	2	3	42					32	3.1
G	32	ARTURS IRBE	35		2	2	0	8						
D	22	DAN KECZMER	13		1	1	3	6					10	
G	35	ANDY MOOG	48		1	1	0	12						
L	44	*PATRICK COTE	3				0	27					1	
R	42	SERGEI MAKAROV	4				-2							
G	1	ROMAN TUREK	6				0							
L	27	MARC LABELLE	9				-4	46					2	

GP = games played; G = goals; A = assists; PTS = points; +/- = goals-for minus goals-against while player is on ice; PIM = penalties in minutes; PP = power-play goals; SH = shorthanded goals; GW = game-winning goals; GT = game-tying goals; S = no. of shots; PCT = percentage of goals to shots; * = rookie

GREG ADAMS

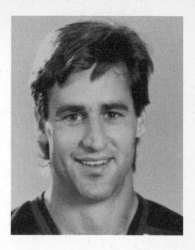

Yrs. of NHL service: 13
Born: Nelson, B.C.; Aug. 1, 1963
Position: left wing
Height: 6-3
Weight: 195
Uniform no.: 23
Shoots: left

Career statistics:

GP	G	A	TP	PIM
803	292	307	599	256

1993-94 statistics:

GP	G	A	TP	+/-	PIM	PP	SH	GW	GT	S	PCT
68	13	24	37	-1	20	5	1	2	0	139	9.4

1994-95 statistics:

GP	G	A	TP	+/-	PIM	PP	SH	GW	GT	S	PCT
43	8	13	21	-3	16	3	2	0	0	72	11.1

1995-96 statistics:

GP	G	A	TP	+/-	PIM	PP	SH	GW	GT	S	PCT
66	22	21	43	-21	33	11	1	1	0	140	15.7

1996-97 statistics:

GP	G	A	TP	+/-	PIM	PP	SH	GW	GT	S	PCT
50	21	15	36	+27	2	5	0	4	1	113	18.6

LAST SEASON

Led team in shooting percentage. Third on team in goals. Tied for third on team in power-play goals. Missed 32 games with neck injury.

THE FINESSE GAME

Adams is faster than he looks because he has a long, almost lazy stride, but he covers a lot of ground quickly and with an apparent lack of effort.

He can shoot a hard slap shot on the fly off the wing, but most of his goals come from within five feet of the net. He drives fearlessly to the goal and likes to arrive by the most expedient route possible. If that means crashing through defensemen, then so be it. Adams has good, shifty moves in deep and is an unselfish player. He played a lot of centre early in his career and is nearly as good a playmaker as finisher. One of the few knocks on him is that he doesn't shoot enough. One of his best scoring moves is a high backhand in tight. He always has his head up and is looking for the holes.

Adams has worked hard at improving his defensive awareness and has become a reliable player.

THE PHYSICAL GAME

Adams has a light frame and always plays hard, which is why he is so vulnerable to injury. He is nearly always wearing an ice pack or getting medical attention for a nick or bruise, if not a broken bone or nerve damage, yet he always comes back for more. He is physical and tough without being aggressive. He does not fight and, considering the checking attention he gets, he remains remarkably calm and determined, seldom taking bad retaliatory penalties. He just gets the job done. Adams is stronger than he looks.

THE INTANGIBLES

The problem with Adams is that he is often hurt, and usually with a serious injury. He can accomplish so much when he is in the lineup (his goals last season would prorate to 34) and meshed so well with Mike Modano and Jere Lehtinen when he was healthy that he figures prominently in the Stars' plans, but you can never count on a full season out of him. The Stars re-signed him for another year at U.S.$1.5 million after last season.

PROJECTION

In last year's *HSR* we thought 20 goals would be a stretch for Adams — because of his injury history. We'll stick to that assessment.

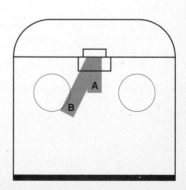

BOB BASSEN

Yrs. of NHL service: 10
Born: Calgary, Alta.; May 6, 1965
Position: centre/left wing
Height: 5-10
Weight: 185
Uniform no.: 28
Shoots: left

Career statistics:

GP	G	A	TP	PIM
615	81	137	218	857

1993-94 statistics:

GP	G	A	TP	+/-	PIM	PP	SH	GW	GT	S	PCT
59	11	17	28	+2	70	1	1	1	0	73	15.1

1994-95 statistics:

GP	G	A	TP	+/-	PIM	PP	SH	GW	GT	S	PCT
47	12	15	27	+14	33	0	1	1	0	66	18.2

1995-96 statistics:

GP	G	A	TP	+/-	PIM	PP	SH	GW	GT	S	PCT
13	0	1	1	-6	15	0	0	0	0	9	0.0

1996-97 statistics:

GP	G	A	TP	+/-	PIM	PP	SH	GW	GT	S	PCT
46	5	7	12	+5	41	0	0	2	0	50	10.0

LAST SEASON

Missed 36 games with neck surgery.

THE FINESSE GAME

Bassen doesn't have great hands or a great shot to go with his work ethic. All of his finesse skills are average at best. His few goals come from going for the puck in scrambles around the net.

Bassen has average straightaway speed, but he does have quickness and agility when healthy, which he puts to work in close quarters to avoid hits from bigger players. Don't get us wrong: if Bassen has to take a hit, he will, but he's also smart enough to avoid unnecessary punishment.

Bassen is only so-so on face-offs. He's not big enough to tie up most opposing centres, and he lacks the hand speed to win draws outright. He does try to scrunch himself low on draws to get his head under the opposing centre's, to block the sight of the puck.

THE PHYSICAL GAME

Bassen plays much bigger than his size, aware every night that if he isn't scrapping along the boards or in front of the net, someone might take his job. He is extremely fit. There isn't an ounce of body fat on him. He hates to lose.

Bassen has a low centre of gravity, which makes it tough to knock him off his feet, and he's closer to the puck than a lot of skaters. He often wins scrums just by being able to pry the puck loose from flailing feet.

THE INTANGIBLES

Bassen is a blood-and-guts competitor, a throwback to hockey's glory days with the skills of a '90s player. A reliable team man, he's one of those players who always delivers an honest effort, which is why Dallas is counting on him this season, again, despite his injury problems. He matches up night after night against most of the league's bigger, better forwards, and makes them work for what they get. He is a valuable role player, and a role model as well. Unasked, Bassen goes out of his way to help younger players.

PROJECTION

Bassen only has one gear, and that's overdrive. His point totals are negligible because he goes until he breaks, which is often. He adds grit and pushes other people to be like him.

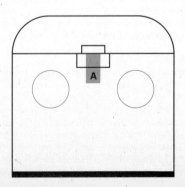

ED BELFOUR

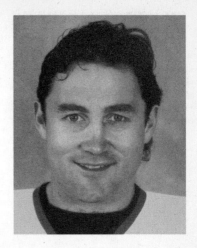

Yrs. of NHL service: 7
Born: Carman, Man.; Apr. 21, 1965
Position: goaltender
Height: 5-11
Weight: 182
Uniform no.: 20
Catches: left

Career statistics:

GP	MIN	GA	SO	GAA	A	PIM
428	24436	1090	31	2.68	15	250

1993-94 statistics:

GP	MIN	GAA	W	L	T	SO	GA	S	SAPCT	PIM
70	3998	2.67	37	24	6	7	178	1892	.906	61

1994-95 statistics:

GP	MIN	GAA	W	L	T	SO	GA	S	SAPCT	PIM
42	2450	2.28	22	15	3	5	93	990	.906	11

1995-96 statistics:

GP	MIN	GAA	W	L	T	SO	GA	S	SAPCT	PIM
50	2956	2.74	22	17	10	1	2.74	1373	.902	36

1996-97 statistics:

GP	MIN	GAA	W	L	T	SO	GA	S	SAPCT	PIM
46	2723	2.89	14	24	6	2	131	1317	.900	34

LAST SEASON

Signed by Dallas as a free agent. Acquired from Chicago for Chris Terreri, Ulf Dahlen and Michal Sykora, January 25, 1997. Missed six games with back injury. Missed 13 games with knee injury.

THE PHYSICAL GAME

Belfour's injuries and the trade to a less defense-minded team made it difficult to truly judge his season. His style relies more on athleticism than technique. He is always on his belly, his side, his back. Belfour is a runner-up only to Dominik Hasek as the best goalie with the worst style in the NHL.

Belfour has great instincts and reads the play well in front of him. He plays with an inverted V, giving the five-hole but usually taking it away from the shooter with his quick reflexes. He is very aggressive and frequently comes so far out of his crease that he gets tangled with his own defenders — as well as running interference on the opponents. He knows he is well-padded and is not afraid to use his body, though injuries have made him less aggressive than in the past.

In fact, Belfour uses his body more than his stick or glove, and that is part of his problem. He tries to make the majority of saves with his torso, making the routine saves more difficult.

Belfour tends to keep his glove low and the book on him is to shoot high, but that's the case with most NHL goalies and a lot of NHL shooters have trouble picking that spot. He sometimes gives up bad rebounds, but his defense is so good and so quick they will swoop in on the puck before the opposition gets a second or third whack. When play is developing around his net, Belfour uses the odd-looking tactic of dropping his stick low along the ice to take away low shots and lunges at the puck. It's weird, but effective.

Belfour has a lot of confidence and an impressive ability to handle the puck, though he sometimes overdoes it. He will usually go for short passes, but can go for the home-run play as well. He uses his body to screen when handling the puck for a 15-foot pass.

THE MENTAL GAME

Belfour was a lot calmer last season, but no less adept. Since the Sharks never made the playoffs, or even a serious playoff bid, there was no chance to observe Belfour under pressure.

THE INTANGIBLES

Although Belfour trained diligently as a triathlete in recent years, injuries have cut down on his physical effectiveness. San Jose made a big trade to get him, even though Belfour became an unrestricted free agent at the end of the season, and lost out big-time when he took less money to play with the Stars.

PROJECTION

Given Belfour's precarious health, the Stars must have gotten some optimistic medical reports to sign him to a lucrative three-year deal. Belfour will see fewer shots behind Dallas' impressive defense, and he'll be in the 30-win range if he gets more than 60 starts.

SHAWN CHAMBERS

Yrs. of NHL service: 9
Born: Royal Oaks, Mich.; Oct. 11, 1966
Position: left defense
Height: 6-2
Weight: 200
Uniform no.: 29
Shoots: left

Career statistics:

GP	G	A	TP	PIM
503	46	154	200	316

1993-94 statistics:

GP	G	A	TP	+/-	PIM	PP	SH	GW	GT	S	PCT
66	11	23	34	-6	23	6	1	1	0	142	7.7

1994-95 statistics:

GP	G	A	TP	+/-	PIM	PP	SH	GW	GT	S	PCT
45	4	17	21	+2	12	2	0	0	0	67	6.0

1995-96 statistics:

GP	G	A	TP	+/-	PIM	PP	SH	GW	GT	S	PCT
64	2	21	23	+1	18	2	0	1	0	112	1.8

1996-97 statistics:

GP	G	A	TP	+/-	PIM	PP	SH	GW	GT	S	PCT
73	4	17	21	+17	19	1	0	0	0	114	3.5

LAST SEASON

Signed as free agent by Dallas, July 3, 1997. Missed one game with hip injury. Missed three games with bruised right knee.

THE FINESSE GAME

As Scott Stevens's partner for 2 1/2 seasons in New Jersey, Chambers helped shoulder the load against opponents' top lines and did a creditable job. Much of Chambers's success is his ability to understand his limitations and play within them. The ill-advised gambles that plagued his early career are now a rarity.

Chambers can work on a second power-play unit. He has an awkward-looking shot, but he manages to get it away quickly, low and on net. He has the poise and the hand skills to be able to fake out a checker with a faux slapper, move to the top of the circle and drill it. Chambers has a nice touch for keeping the puck in along the blueline.

His smarts put him a cut above the rest. Although his finesse skills may be average, he has great anticipation. He understands the game well and knows where the puck is going before the play is made. He does the little things well — little wrist shots, little dump-ins, nothing that shouts out.

Chambers prefers to move the puck out of the zone with a quick pass rather than lug it. His skating isn't dazzling, but he's got some wheels and is more efficient than his style indicates.

THE PHYSICAL GAME

A big defenseman, Chambers was not much of a hitter until he joined the Devils, where the sacrifice was demanded. Confidence in his knee (he underwent arthroscopic surgery in 1993-94) showed with his willingness to play the body. Although he won't put people into the third row of the stands, he will hit often enough and hard enough so that later in a game the puck carrier will move the puck a little faster and maybe get hurried into a mistake. He has had a couple of memorable collisions with Eric Lindros during the past three seasons, and while Chambers occasionally emerged a little worse for the wear, he deserves credit for not bailing out. Many do.

He plays with a lot of enthusiasm and is a workhorse. He thrives on ice time and seems to have fun playing the game.

THE INTANGIBLES

Nearly valueless when he played for Tampa Bay, his three seasons in the Devils increased his market value and he signed a three-year, $5.9-million deal with Dallas. There is an argument that the Devils' system masked some of Chambers's flaws, but he will be equally protected in the Stars' system as long as he plays with Derian Hatcher or Richard Matvichuk and not Sergei Zubov.

PROJECTION

Chambers ended up in an ideal spot in Dallas, where he can settle in as a comfortable three or four and be part of a very strong defensive unit.

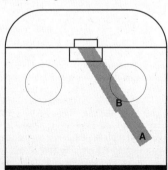

TODD HARVEY

Yrs. of NHL service: 3
Born: Hamilton, Ont.; Feb. 17, 1975
Position: centre/right wing
Height: 6-0
Weight: 195
Uniform no.: 10
Shoots: right

Career statistics:

GP	G	A	TP	PIM
180	29	51	80	345

1994-95 statistics:

GP	G	A	TP	+/-	PIM	PP	SH	GW	GT	S	PCT
40	11	9	20	-3	67	2	0	1	0	64	17.2

1995-96 statistics:

GP	G	A	TP	+/-	PIM	PP	SH	GW	GT	S	PCT
69	9	20	29	-13	136	3	0	1	0	101	8.9

1996-97 statistics:

GP	G	A	TP	+/-	PIM	PP	SH	GW	GT	S	PCT
71	9	22	31	+19	142	1	0	2	0	99	9.1

LAST SEASON

Led team in penalty minutes. Career high in points. Suspended for two games for flagrant elbow. Missed one game for personal reasons. Missed three games with knee injury.

THE FINESSE GAME

Harvey had a slow start but came on well. He was benched for a few games early in the season because he wasn't applying himself physically, but he seemed to get the message and ended the season as one of the Stars' grittier performers.

Harvey's skating is rough. In fact, it's pretty choppy, and as a result he lacks speed. To make up for that, he has good anticipation and awareness. He's clever and his hands are very good. When he gets the puck, he has patience and strength with it.

Harvey's goals are ugly ones. He works the front of the net with grit. He goes to the net and follows up shots with second and third effort. He always has his feet moving and he has good hand-eye coordination. He can't play on the top offensive lines but did an adequate job when moved to the checking line with smart veterans Dave Reid and Guy Carbonneau.

THE PHYSICAL GAME

Harvey's talent level rises when he gets more involved. He's not big enough to be a legitimate NHL heavyweight, but he doesn't back down from challenges. When he's at his best, he gets inside other people's jerseys and heads.

THE INTANGIBLES

Harvey is projected as a third-line winger, who could get the odd shift with the top two lines because the Stars lack a power winger. His progress has been gradual, but his improvement was notable last season after he took a step back in his sophomore year.

PROJECTION

To get 20 goals, Harvey will have to earn some power-play time, which could happen this season (on the second unit, at least), especially if Pat Verbeek has another rough year.

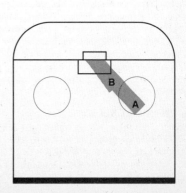

DERIAN HATCHER

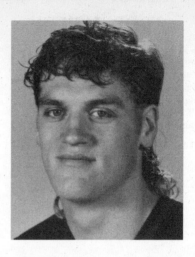

Yrs. of NHL service: 6
Born: Sterling Heights, Mich.; June 4, 1972
Position: left defense
Height: 6-5
Weight: 225
Uniform no.: 2
Shoots: left

Career statistics:

GP	G	A	TP	PIM
378	39	92	131	808

1993-94 statistics:

GP	G	A	TP	+/-	PIM	PP	SH	GW	GT	S	PCT
83	12	19	31	+19	211	2	1	2	0	132	9.1

1994-95 statistics:

GP	G	A	TP	+/-	PIM	PP	SH	GW	GT	S	PCT
43	5	11	16	+3	105	2	0	2	0	74	6.8

1995-96 statistics:

GP	G	A	TP	+/-	PIM	PP	SH	GW	GT	S	PCT
79	8	23	31	-12	129	2	0	1	0	125	6.4

1996-97 statistics:

GP	G	A	TP	+/-	PIM	PP	SH	GW	GT	S	PCT
63	3	19	22	+8	97	0	0	0	0	96	3.1

LAST SEASON

Missed 19 games with knee injury and arthroscopic knee surgery.

THE FINESSE GAME

Some players had World Cup hangovers last season, but some maintained a World Cup buzz all year long. If Hatcher hadn't had his knee problems, he would have been one of the latter. Playing a prominent role with victorious Team USA did wonders for his game, erasing the bad memories of the 1995-96 season in Dallas, and affirming that Hatcher belongs among the NHL's elite defensemen.

Hatcher plays in all key situations and has developed confidence in his decision-making process. His skating is laboured, so he lets the play come to him instead of, say, trying to chase Pavel Bure all over the ice. He is sturdy and well-balanced. The fewer strides he has to take, the better.

He has very good hands for a big man, and he has a good head for the game. Hatcher is fairly effective from the point on the power play — not because he has a big, booming slap shot, but because he has a good wrist shot and will get the puck on net quickly. He will join the rush eagerly once he gets into gear (his first few strides are sluggish), and he handles the puck nicely.

THE PHYSICAL GAME

Hatcher is a big force. He has a mean streak when provoked and is a punishing hitter, but he has a long enough fuse to stay away from bad penalties. He plays physically every night and demands respect and room. He's fearless. He's also a big horse and eats up all the ice time Dallas gives him, which can be 35 minutes a night. The more work he gets, the better.

THE INTANGIBLES

Trading Kevin Hatcher to Pittsburgh seemed to lighten an emotional load for the younger Hatcher. The excellent World Cup got him off on the right foot, but he has even more levels to attain. Hatcher will not provide big numbers, like his World Cup partner, Brian Leetch, but he and Mike Modano are the cornerstones of the franchise. Hatcher is the kind of player the team looks to for consistent effort and intensity. He is a fine role model for the younger Stars and the veterans repect him as well. He is a quiet player who wants to make a big impact.

PROJECTION

Hatcher is poised to become one of the top six defensemen in the league, though he will never have the kind of numbers that inspire Norris Trophy voters.

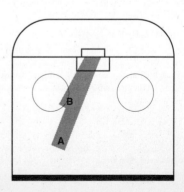

BENOIT HOGUE

Yrs. of NHL service: 9
Born: Repentigny, Que.; Oct. 28, 1966
Position: centre/right wing
Height: 5-10
Weight: 194
Uniform no.: 33
Shoots: left

Career statistics:

GP	G	A	TP	PIM
617	191	263	454	715

1993-94 statistics:

GP	G	A	TP	+/-	PIM	PP	SH	GW	GT	S	PCT
83	36	33	69	-7	73	9	5	3	0	218	16.5

1994-95 statistics:

GP	G	A	TP	+/-	PIM	PP	SH	GW	GT	S	PCT
45	9	7	16	0	34	2	0	2	1	66	13.6

1995-96 statistics:

GP	G	A	TP	+/-	PIM	PP	SH	GW	GT	S	PCT
78	19	45	64	+10	104	5	0	5	0	155	12.3

1996-97 statistics:

GP	G	A	TP	+/-	PIM	PP	SH	GW	GT	S	PCT
73	19	24	43	+8	54	5	0	5	0	131	14.5

LAST SEASON

Tied for second on team in power-play goals. Third on team in game-winning goals. Missed eight games with elbow surgery. Missed one game for disciplinary reasons.

THE FINESSE GAME

Hogue found the Stars system a bit more restrictive than he has been used to. He loves to freewheel, and there were some clashes with the coaching staff before he got the message. Once he did, he contributed as an above-average third-line winger.

Hogue's chief asset is his speed. He is explosive, leaving defenders flat-footed with his acceleration. Add to that his anticipation and ability to handle the puck at a high tempo, and he's a breakaway threat — though the Stars made sure he stopped leaving the defensive zone before the puck. Hogue is not a great puckhandler or shooter, but he capitalizes on each situation with his quickness and agility. He is a threat to score whenever he is on the ice.

Hogue plays primarily on the left side, and even when playing centre will cut to the left wing boards as he drives down the ice. He is not a great playmaker, but he creates scoring chances off his rushes.

Hogue wasn't used killing penalties as much as he has been in the past. He is an excellent, aggressive penalty killer who is a shorthanded threat, and he can also be used on the power play, though he lacks the patience to be as effective as he could be. He is very good on draws.

THE PHYSICAL GAME

Hogue is a strong one-on-one player who uses his body to lean on an opponent. He is not a big checker, but he gets involved and uses his speed as a weapon to intimidate. He is a crunch-time player, whether a team needs to protect a lead or create one. He can get into ruts where he takes bad penalties.

THE INTANGIBLES

Hogue had an adjustment to make to head coach Ken Hitchcock, and might not have always understood his boundaries. He was sent to the dressing room during one game in January, but he did not react selfishly and came back and responded well.

PROJECTION

Hogue has a tendency to change uniforms every couple of years, and Hogue, a Group 2 free agent during the off-season, is due. We figure his 45 points will be scored outside of Texas.

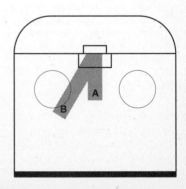

JAMIE LANGENBRUNNER

Yrs. of NHL service: 2
Born: Duluth, MN; July 24, 1975
Position: centre
Height: 5-11
Weight: 190
Uniform no.: 15
Shoots: right

Career statistics:

GP	G	A	TP	PIM
90	15	28	43	59

1994-95 statistics:

GP	G	A	TP	+/-	PIM	PP	SH	GW	GT	S	PCT
2	0	0	0	0	2	0	0	0	0	1	0.0

1995-96 statistics:

GP	G	A	TP	+/-	PIM	PP	SH	GW	GT	S	PCT
12	2	2	4	-2	6	1	0	0	0	15	13.3

1996-97 statistics:

GP	G	A	TP	+/-	PIM	PP	SH	GW	GT	S	PCT
76	13	26	39	-2	51	3	0	3	0	112	11.6

LAST SEASON

First NHL season. Longest assist streak by an NHL rookie (six games). Tied for longest point streak by an NHL rookie (eight games). Tied for third among NHL rookies in game-winning goals.

THE FINESSE GAME

Langenbrunner has terrific hand skills. He is intelligent and poised with the puck, and can play as a centre or a right wing. He has good hockey vision and can pick his spots for shots. He is also a smart passer on either his forehand or backhand.

Langenbrunner is only an average skater, so he won't be coming in with speed and driving a shot off the wing. He's not dynamic at all. He has a strong short game, with his offense generated within 15 to 20 feet of the net. He has a quick release on his shot. Any deficiencies he may have are offset by his desire to compete and succeed.

THE PHYSICAL GAME

Langenbrunner plays a very intense game, bigger than his size allows him to. He will wear down physically. He competes hard in the hard areas of the ice, to either get a puck or get himself into a space to get the puck. He is showing signs of being a tough, competitive forward. He lacks the size to be a power forward, but he may turn out to be one of the gritty types who are so annoying to play against, like Jeremy Roenick. He won't just hang on the perimeter. Langenbrunner won't back down and will even try to stir things up.

THE INTANGIBLES

Like a lot of rookies, Langenbrunner faded in the second half, with only three goals in the last 41 games.

PROJECTION

Langenbrunner is a smart, determined player who should put better numbers up than he did in his rookie year. We expect a slight improvement to the 20-goal level.

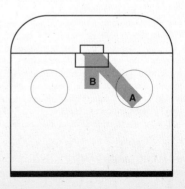

JERE LEHTINEN

Yrs. of NHL service: 2
Born: Espoo, Finland; June 24, 1973
Position: right wing
Height: 6-0
Weight: 185
Uniform no.: 26
Shoots: right

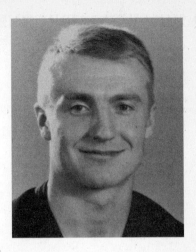

Career statistics:

GP	G	A	TP	PIM
120	22	49	71	18

1995-96 statistics:

GP	G	A	TP	+/-	PIM	PP	SH	GW	GT	S	PCT
57	6	22	28	+5	16	0	0	1	0	109	5.5

1996-97 statistics:

GP	G	A	TP	+/-	PIM	PP	SH	GW	GT	S	PCT
63	16	27	43	+26	2	3	1	2	0	134	11.9

LAST SEASON

Finalist for Selke Trophy. Second NHL season. Missed 19 games with recurring knee injury.

THE FINESSE GAME

Lehtinen is the smartest positional player on the Stars, which is why it came as no surprise that he was a candidate for the Selke in only his second NHL season. He is remarkably hockey astute. If any line was in trouble, the Stars would put Lehtinen on the unit for a couple of games to straighten them out. He is so honest and so reliable, that the other players, almost through osmosis, have to come on board.

As much as Mike Modano did on his own last season, much of his progress can be traced to his teaming with Lehtinen. Modano returned the favour, because he is enhancing the latent offensive ability of Lehtinen, who was never noted for his scoring before. Both players have become more complete because of the other.

Lehtinen's skating is well above adequate. He's not really top flight, but he has enough quickness and balance to play with highly skilled people. He controls the puck well and is an unselfish playmaker.

Lehtinen struggles only in his finishing. He appears to have a good shot with a quick release, but at times is reluctant to shoot. He is gaining more confidence, thanks to Modano.

THE PHYSICAL GAME

Lehtinen is very strong on the puck: he protects it and won't be intimidated, and he competes along the boards. He completes his checks and never stops trying. He is very durable, except for the wonky knee.

THE INTANGIBLES

Lehtinen never asks anything of the club, never complains, just asks what he can do to become better. He's a coach's dream.

PROJECTION

If he continues to play with Modano, Lehtinen will develop into a 25-goal scorer and a perennial Selke candidate.

RICHARD MATVICHUK

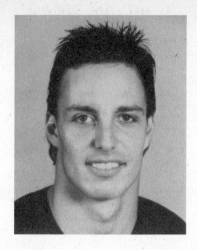

Yrs. of NHL service: 5
Born: Edmonton, Alta.; Feb. 5, 1973
Position: left defense
Height: 6-2
Weight: 195
Uniform no.: 24
Shoots: left

Career statistics:

GP	G	A	TP	PIM
222	13	31	44	220

1993-94 statistics:

GP	G	A	TP	+/-	PIM	PP	SH	GW	GT	S	PCT
25	0	3	3	+1	22	0	0	0	0	18	0.0

1994-95 statistics:

GP	G	A	TP	+/-	PIM	PP	SH	GW	GT	S	PCT
14	0	2	2	-7	14	0	0	0	0	21	0.0

1995-96 statistics:

GP	G	A	TP	+/-	PIM	PP	SH	GW	GT	S	PCT
73	6	16	22	+4	71	71	0	0	1	0	7.4

1996-97 statistics:

GP	G	A	TP	+/-	PIM	PP	SH	GW	GT	S	PCT
57	5	7	12	+1	87	0	2	0	0	83	6.0

LAST SEASON

Missed 28 games with recurring groin injury.

THE FINESSE GAME

Matvichuk is starting to find his niche as a mobile, defensive defenseman. He is a good skater with a long stride, and skates well backwards and pivots in either direction. He likes to get involved in the attack in a limited capacity. He has the hand skills and instincts to play with the offensive players to a point, but that is not a high priority with him. He uses his hockey skills defensively.

Matvichuk has a low, hard, accurate shot from the point. He makes smart, crisp passes and uses other players well. He can play either side defensively.

Matvichuk wants the ice time when the team needs a calm, defensive presence on the ice. He kills penalties and blocks shots, and appears to be physically and mentally recovered from his knee problems of two years ago. (However, the groin injuries may be a result of that surgery, since players tend to favour one leg when they are rehabbing a knee.)

THE PHYSICAL GAME

Matvichuk is aware of the importance of strength and aerobic training and wants to add even more muscle to stay competitive at the NHL level, since he is a little light by today's NHL standards. He's a hack-and-whack kind of mean guy, not a fighter. He occasionally gets into a mode where he starts fishing for the puck.

THE INTANGIBLES

Matvichuk was given the prime defending job against other teams' top lines with Derian Hatcher, and stepped up well to the challenge. He seemed to bite into the role, and always seems to be disappointed when he doesn't have a specific assignment against a top-notch line. He is part of a solid four-man corps in Dallas.

PROJECTION

Matvichuk's groin injury limited his development last season. He is still young and maturing and has a great upside, especially offensively.

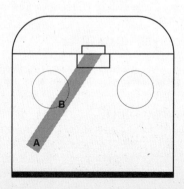

MIKE MODANO

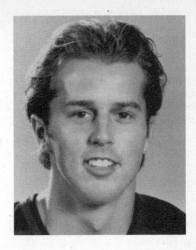

Yrs. of NHL service: 8
Born: Livonia, Mich.; June 7, 1970
Position: centre
Height: 6-3
Weight: 200
Uniform no.: 9
Shoots: left

Career statistics:

GP	G	A	TP	PIM
581	256	339	565	442

1993-94 statistics:

GP	G	A	TP	+/-	PIM	PP	SH	GW	GT	S	PCT
76	50	43	93	-8	54	18	0	4	2	281	17.8

1994-95 statistics:

GP	G	A	TP	+/-	PIM	PP	SH	GW	GT	S	PCT
30	12	17	29	+7	8	4	1	0	0	100	12.0

1995-96 statistics:

GP	G	A	TP	+/-	PIM	PP	SH	GW	GT	S	PCT
78	36	45	81	-12	63	8	4	4	1	320	11.3

1996-97 statistics:

GP	G	A	TP	+/-	PIM	PP	SH	GW	GT	S	PCT
80	35	48	83	+43	42	9	5	9	2	291	12.0

LAST SEASON

Led team in goals, assists, points and shots for second consecutive season. Led team in plus-minus, power play goals and shorthanded goals. Led team and second in NHL in plus-minus. Led team and tied for second in NHL in game-winning goals. Missed one game with flu. Missed one game with knee injury.

THE FINESSE GAME

That plus-minus in Modano's stat line is no misprint, no illusion and no mistake. Having already established himself as a steady 80- to 90-point man in the NHL, Modano brought his game to a new level by playing defense, and if you don't believe that's valuable, just look at how long Ron Francis has played at an elite level.

Modano is a different style of player than Francis, though. He has world-class skills that match up with just about any player in the NHL, and he's added a physical element. He showed in the playoffs that he will go through people, not just around them. When there is a lot of open ice, he's a thrilling player to watch. He has outstanding offensive instincts and great hands, and he is a smooth passer and a remarkable skater in all facets.

Modano makes other players around him better, which is the mark of an elite player. His speed and movement with the puck mesmerizes defenders and opens up ice for his linemates. Last season he finally found a linemate with whom he could establish some chemistry: right-winger Jere Lehtinen.

Modano has become a top penalty killer (with Lehtinen on the first unit). His anticipation and quick hands help him intercept passes. He has improved his face-offs, and became so reliable defensively that he

was thrown onto the ice in the closing minutes of a period or a game.

THE PHYSICAL GAME

In last year's *HSR* we critiqued Modano's lack of on-ice leadership, but his commitment to defense and more involved play has changed all that. Now he's the kind of leader to take his teammates into the breach. He's willing to give his all, even to the point of getting into a fight (his first since his sophomore year) with Edmonton's Kelly Buchberger. It's not something he should do every night, but don't think he didn't impress his teammates.

THE INTANGIBLES

Modano has taken some time to mature, and for a few seasons was teetering on the brink of being a player who would never live up to his potential. Now he's in full stride. He never had a teammate whose leadership he could emulate, but Joe Nieuwendyk is helping him grow in that aera. Modano also got a huge boost from playing for Team USA in the World Cup.

PROJECTION

Modano loses nothing from his offensive game by playing better defense, which might have come as a revelation to him. We love the new Modano. He could still reach 100 points, but even if he doesn't, his value to the Stars has skyrocketed.

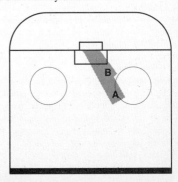

JOE NIEUWENDYK

Yrs. of NHL service: 10
Born: Oshawa, Ont.; Sept. 10, 1966
Position: centre
Height: 6-1
Weight: 195
Uniform no.: 25
Shoots: left

Career statistics:

GP	G	A	TP	PIM
695	358	341	699	389

1993-94 statistics:

GP	G	A	TP	+/-	PIM	PP	SH	GW	GT	S	PCT
64	36	39	75	+19	51	14	1	7	1	191	18.8

1994-95 statistics:

GP	G	A	TP	+/-	PIM	PP	SH	GW	GT	S	PCT
46	21	29	50	+11	33	3	0	4	0	122	17.2

1995-96 statistics:

GP	G	A	TP	+/-	PIM	PP	SH	GW	GT	S	PCT
52	14	18	32	-17	41	8	0	3	0	138	10.1

1996-97 statistics:

GP	G	A	TP	+/-	PIM	PP	SH	GW	GT	S	PCT
66	30	21	51	-5	32	8	0	2	2	173	17.3

LAST SEASON

Second on team in goals, power-play goals, shots and shooting percentage. Third on team in points. Missed 16 games due to rib injury and personal reasons.

THE FINESSE GAME

If a puck-tipping contest is ever added to the NHL All-Star-game skills competition, Nieuwendyk would be one of the favourites. He has fantastic hand-eye coordination and not only gets his blade on the puck, he acts as if he knows where he's directing it.

Nieuwendyk is aggressive, tough and aware around the net. He can finish or make a play down low. He has the good vision, poise and hand skills to make neat little passes through traffic. He's a better playmaker than finisher, but he never doubts that he will convert his chances. He has good anticipation in the neutral zone, and uses his long reach to break up passes.

Those same hand skills serve him well on draws and he's defensively sound. Once a 50-goal scorer, knee surgery a few seasons ago robbed him of the necessary quickness to produce that total again. He's become a better all-around player, though.

THE PHYSICAL GAME

He does not initiate, but he will take the punishment around the front of the net and stand his ground. He won't be intimidated, but he won't scare anyone else, either. Nieuwendyk would like to carry more weight, but recurring back and shoulder problems require him to stay on the lean side.

THE INTANGIBLES

Nieuwendyk had two lost seasons. In 1995-96, he sat out in a contract dispute. He came to last year's training camp ready to start fresh, when he was devastated by the death of his mother.

Nieuwendyk is probably the best thing to happen to Mike Modano. He is a class individual who leads by example.

PROJECTION

Nieuwendyk deserves some better luck this season. His points should be in the 70 to 80 range as a number two centre.

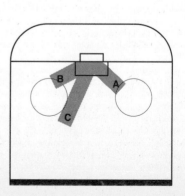

DAVE REID

Yrs. of NHL service: 13
Born: Toronto, Ont.; May 15, 1964
Position: left wing
Height: 6-1
Weight: 217
Uniform no.: 14
Shoots: left

Career statistics:

GP	G	A	TP	PIM
685	141	165	306	174

1993-94 statistics:

GP	G	A	TP	+/-	PIM	PP	SH	GW	GT	S	PCT
83	6	17	23	+10	25	0	2	1	0	145	4.1

1994-95 statistics:

GP	G	A	TP	+/-	PIM	PP	SH	GW	GT	S	PCT
38	5	5	10	+8	10	0	0	0	1	47	10.6

1995-96 statistics:

GP	G	A	TP	+/-	PIM	PP	SH	GW	GT	S	PCT
63	23	21	44	+14	4	1	6	3	1	160	14.4

1996-97 statistics:

GP	G	A	TP	+/-	PIM	PP	SH	GW	GT	S	PCT
82	19	20	39	+12	10	1	1	4	0	135	14.1

LAST SEASON

Signed as free agent, July 13, 1996. One of two Stars to appear in all 82 games.

THE FINESSE GAME

Reid fits in nicely with Dallas' team defense, and is willing to accept his role as a checking winger on the third line while adding a dollop of offense, which he has tapped into over the past two seasons. He has a lot of confidence in his game now. Where in the past he might have just dumped the puck into the corner, he is now looking to make plays without gambling.

Under normal circumstances, Reid is a defensive forward and penalty-killing specialist. He established good rapport with Guy Carbonneau on the checking line. Opposition power plays always have to be aware of taking away Reid's space if they lose the puck, because he has the ability to blow the puck by the goalie from a lot of spots on the ice. Possessing an underrated, accurate shot with a quick release, he can freeze goalies with his unexpected shot.

Reid is a good skater with surprising straight-ahead speed, especially for a big player. He has proven he can play regularly in the NHL and contribute. All of his moderate skills are enhanced by his hard work and hustle.

THE PHYSICAL GAME

Reid can create a little maelstrom on the ice. A big guy who can get his skating revved up, he causes problems once he is in motion. He isn't a big hitter, though, and doesn't threaten anybody. He is just an honest checker.

THE INTANGIBLES

Reid could have been picked up on waivers a few seasons back and he appreciates the lofty level that his U.S.$1-million contract has helped him achieve. The Stars paid Pat Verbeek three times that amount, and plugger Reid ended up with two more goals.

PROJECTION

Reid will hover around the 20-goal mark, contribute solid defense and score valuable goals.

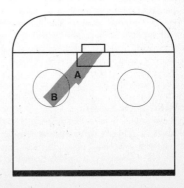

DARRYL SYDOR

Yrs. of NHL service: 5
Born: Edmonton, Alta.; May 13, 1972
Position: right defense
Height: 6-0
Weight: 195
Uniform no.: 5
Shoots: left

Career statistics:

GP	G	A	TP	PIM
396	30	131	161	338

1993-94 statistics:

GP	G	A	TP	+/-	PIM	PP	SH	GW	GT	S	PCT
84	8	27	35	-9	94	1	0	0	0	146	5.5

1994-95 statistics:

GP	G	A	TP	+/-	PIM	PP	SH	GW	GT	S	PCT
48	4	19	23	-2	36	3	0	0	1	96	4.2

1995-96 statistics:

GP	G	A	TP	+/-	PIM	PP	SH	GW	GT	S	PCT
84	3	17	20	-12	75	2	0	0	0	117	2.6

1996-97 statistics:

GP	G	A	TP	+/-	PIM	PP	SH	GW	GT	S	PCT
82	8	40	48	+37	51	2	0	2	0	142	5.6

LAST SEASON

Led team defensemen and fourth on team in scoring with career high. Second on team in plus-minus. One of two Stars to appear in all 82 games.

THE FINESSE GAME

Sydor broke into the league as an offensive defenseman in Los Angeles, lost all confidence in that aspect of his game, came to Dallas, put his defensive game in order without even thinking offense, and emerged as one of the huge surprises of the season. Dallas asked him to be more accountable defensively, and he was rewarded with more ice time. He understands his position well and is more patient.

Sydor is a very good skater with balance and agility and excellent lateral movement. He can accelerate well for a big skater and changes directions easily. He's not a dynamic defenseman, but he's better than average.

Sydor's offensive game can kick in at anytime. He has a fine shot from the point and can handle power-play time. He has good sense for jumping into the attack, and controls the puck ably when carrying it, though he doesn't always protect it well with his body. He makes nice outlet passes and has good vision of the ice. He can rush with the puck or play dump-and-chase.

THE PHYSICAL GAME

Sydor wants and needs to establish more of a physical presence. He is very intense and has to be reined in. He learned that sometimes going nowhere is better than trying to go everywhere. Sydor competes hard and could still get stronger.

THE INTANGIBLES

Sydor's hunger to improve his game paid off. He can't stop now because he can raise his game to another level. He still has to concentrate on defense. Eventually that will become second nature to him, and his game will flow.

PROJECTION

In last year's *HSR* we wrote, "He should start to regain his game this season and be a 40-point man." There's an upside: he should break through to 50 to 60 points this season.

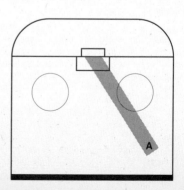

PAT VERBEEK

Yrs. of NHL service: 14
Born: Sarnia, Ont.; May 24, 1964
Position: right wing
Height: 5-9
Weight: 192
Uniform no.: 16
Shoots: right

Career statistics:

GP	G	A	TP	PIM
1065	430	444	874	2362

1993-94 statistics:

GP	G	A	TP	+/-	PIM	PP	SH	GW	GT	S	PCT
84	37	38	75	-15	177	15	1	3	1	226	16.4

1994-95 statistics:

GP	G	A	TP	+/-	PIM	PP	SH	GW	GT	S	PCT
48	17	16	33	-2	71	7	0	2	1	131	13.0

1995-96 statistics:

GP	G	A	TP	+/-	PIM	PP	SH	GW	GT	S	PCT
69	41	41	82	+29	129	17	0	6	2	252	16.3

1996-97 statistics:

GP	G	A	TP	+/-	PIM	PP	SH	GW	GT	S	PCT
81	17	36	53	+3	128	5	0	4	0	172	9.9

LAST SEASON

Second on team in assists, points and penalty minutes. Tied for third on team in power-play goals.

THE FINESSE GAME

Verbeek isn't the greatest skater in the world; it's even tougher for him to move when he's carrying the burden of huge expectations, which he was in his first season in Dallas.

Verbeek has a choppy stride, so much of his best work is done in small spaces rather than in open ice. He is very strong on his skates and likes to go into traffic zones. Larger players think they can hit him, but he's so chunky, with a low centre of gravity, that he's nearly impossible to bowl over. He's very good at carrying the puck along the boards but is no stickhandler in open ice. He has no better than fair speed.

For where Verbeek plays on the power play, low and with his righthanded shot, his power-play goal total was abysmal. He had numerous chances but nothing seemed to go in for him. He wastes few quality scoring chances, though. Most of his shots come from in tight. Nothing brings out his competitive edge more than some serious crashing around the crease, most of which he initiates. When Verbeek got off to his slow start, he became frustrated and starting cheating on his defensive responsibilities, and his game proceeded to fall apart.

Verbeek's hands are quick enough to surprise with a backhand shot. He feels the puck on his stick and looks for openings in the net instead of scrapping with his head down and taking poor shots. He is also effective coming in late and drilling the shot.

THE PHYSICAL GAME

Verbeek is among the best in the league at drawing penalties. He can cleverly hold the opponent's stick and fling himself to the ice as if he were the injured party, and it's an effective tactic. He also draws calls honestly with his hard work by driving to the net and forcing the defender to slow him down by any means possible.

Verbeek is tough, rugged and strong, with a nasty disposition that he is learning to tame without losing his ferocious edge, and he took more than his share of bad penalties.

THE INTANGIBLES

Verbeek never established a rapport with any of his Dallas teammates, and was shifted from line to line in hopes of getting his game untracked.

PROJECTION

In last year's *HSR*, we wrote: "Verbeek has a history of having an off-year in the first year of a big new contract, which is exactly the situation now in Dallas. Buyer beware."

Just as confidently, we believe Verbeek is at his best when he has something to prove, and he should be back in the 70-point range this season.

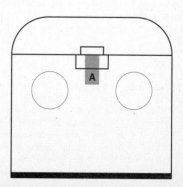

SERGEI ZUBOV

Yrs. of NHL service: 5
Born: Moscow, Russia; July 22, 1970
Position: right defense
Height: 6-1
Weight: 200
Uniform no.: 56
Shoots: right

Career statistics:

GP	G	A	TP	PIM
307	54	211	265	107

1993-94 statistics:

GP	G	A	TP	+/-	PIM	PP	SH	GW	GT	S	PCT
78	12	77	89	+20	39	9	0	1	0	222	5.4

1994-95 statistics:

GP	G	A	TP	+/-	PIM	PP	SH	GW	GT	S	PCT
38	10	26	36	-2	18	6	0	0	0	116	8.6

1995-96 statistics:

GP	G	A	TP	+/-	PIM	PP	SH	GW	GT	S	PCT
64	11	55	66	+28	22	3	2	1	0	141	7.8

1996-97 statistics:

GP	G	A	TP	+/-	PIM	PP	SH	GW	GT	S	PCT
78	13	30	43	+19	24	1	0	3	0	133	9.8

LAST SEASON

Second among team defensemen in scoring. Missed one game with back injury.

THE FINESSE GAME

How unusual is it to inquire of Zubov's first season in Dallas and be told about his defensive play. Defense? Zubov? He of the high-risk passes and the casual coverage in his own zone? Maybe Zubie just got tired of people making fun of his lapses, because he cut down on the ghastly mistakes.

Zubov remains primarily an offenseman. He has the ability to run a power play but he is not in the elite class of NHL point men, like his former teammate Brian Leetch. Zubov is still very effective, though, despite his reluctance to shoot the puck. His dropoff in points last year had less to do with his play than his teammates' failure to finish. He wasn't playing with Mario Lemieux and Jaromir Jagr, after all.

Zubov has some world-class skills. He skates with with good balance and generates power from his leg drive. He is agile in his stops and starts, even backwards. He also has a good slap shot and one-times the puck with accuracy, when he deigns to use it. He masks his intentions well, faking a shot and finding the open man with a slick pass. He's not afraid to come in deep, either. Heck, sometimes he forechecks behind the goal line on a power play. Zubov will occasionally frustrate his teammates when he slows things down with the puck on a rush or breakout while the rest of the team has already taken off like racehorses.

Zubov has very strong lateral acceleration, but he is also educated enough to keep skating stride for stride with the wing who is trying to beat him to the outside. So many other defensemen speed up a couple of strides then try to slow their men with stick-checks.

Zubov will use his reach, superior body positioning or his agility to force the play and compel the puck carrier to make a decision. However, he doesn't always search out the right man or, when he does, he doesn't always eliminate the right man. A team has to live with that, because Zubov's offensive upside is huge.

THE PHYSICAL GAME

Zubov is not physical, but he is solidly built and will take a hit to make a play. He can give a team a lot of minutes and not wear down physically.

His boyhood idol was Viacheslav Fetisov, and that role model should give you some idea of Zubov's style. He gets his body in the way with his great skating, then often strips the puck when the attacker finds no path to the net. He doesn't initiate much, but he doesn't mind getting hit to make a play.

THE INTANGIBLES

Zubov had a better second half than first. Being traded for the third time in three seasons was unsettling, but he came around to the team concept.

PROJECTION

Zubov's points won't approach his production with the flashier Penguins or Rangers, but he has the talent to improve 10 to 15 points over last year.

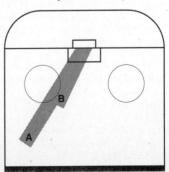

DETROIT RED WINGS

Players' Statistics 1996-97

POS.	NO.	PLAYER	GP	G	A	PTS	+/-	PIM	PP	SH	GW	GT	S	PCT
L	14	BRENDAN SHANAHAN	81	47	41	88	32	131	20	3	7	2	336	14.0
C	19	STEVE YZERMAN	81	22	63	85	22	78	8		3		232	9.5
C	91	SERGEI FEDOROV	74	30	33	63	29	30	9	2	4		273	11.0
D	5	NICKLAS LIDSTROM	79	15	42	57	11	30	8		1		214	7.0
C	8	IGOR LARIONOV	64	12	42	54	31	26	2	1	4		95	12.6
R	25	DARREN MCCARTY	68	19	30	49	14	126	5		6	1	171	11.1
L	13	VYACHESLAV KOZLOV	75	23	22	45	21	46	3		6		211	10.9
D	55	LARRY MURPHY	81	9	36	45	3	20	5		1	1	158	5.7
R	28	TOMAS SANDSTROM	74	18	24	42	6	69	1	2	2	1	139	12.9
D	16	VLAD. KONSTANTINOV	77	5	33	38	38	151					141	3.5
R	20	MARTIN LAPOINTE	78	16	17	33	-14	167	5	1	1		149	10.7
D	2	VIACHESLAV FETISOV	64	5	23	28	26	76			1		95	5.3
C	33	KRIS DRAPER	76	8	5	13	-11	73	1		1		85	9.4
R	17	DOUG BROWN	49	6	7	13	-3	8	1				69	8.7
D	3	BOB ROUSE	70	4	9	13	8	58		2			70	5.7
R	11	MATHIEU DANDENAULT	65	3	9	12	-10	28					81	3.7
D	4	*JAMIE PUSHOR	75	4	7	11	1	129					63	6.3
L	15	*TOMAS HOLMSTROM	47	6	3	9	-10	33	3				53	11.3
L	18	KIRK MALTBY	66	3	5	8	3	75					62	4.8
C	37	TIM TAYLOR	44	3	4	7	-6	52		1		2	44	6.8
D	27	*AARON WARD	49	2	5	7	-9	52					40	5.0
D	34	*ANDERS ERIKSSON	23		6	6	5	10					27	
R	26	JOEY KOCUR	34	2	1	3	-7	70			1		38	5.3
G	30	CHRIS OSGOOD	47		2	2	0	6						
R	22	*MICHAEL KNUBLE	9	1		1	-1						10	10.0
G	31	*KEVIN HODSON	6		1	1	0							
D	23	MIKE RAMSEY	2				0						3	
L	40	MARK MAJOR	2				0	5						
G	29	MIKE VERNON	33				0	35						

GP = games played; G = goals; A = assists; PTS = points; +/- = goals-for minus goals-against while player is on ice; PIM = penalties in minutes; PP = power-play goals; SH = shorthanded goals; GW = game-winning goals; GT = game-tying goals; S = no. of shots; PCT = percentage of goals to shots; * = rookie

DOUG BROWN

Yrs. of NHL service: 10
Born: Southborough, Mass.; June 12, 1964
Position: right wing
Height: 5-10
Weight: 185
Uniform no.: 17
Shoots: right

Career statistics:

GP	G	A	TP	PIM
583	113	151	264	130

1993-94 statistics:

GP	G	A	TP	+/-	PIM	PP	SH	GW	GT	S	PCT
77	18	37	55	+19	18	2	0	1	0	152	11.8

1994-95 statistics:

GP	G	A	TP	+/-	PIM	PP	SH	GW	GT	S	PCT
45	9	12	21	+14	16	1	1	2	0	69	13.0

1995-96 statistics:

GP	G	A	TP	+/-	PIM	PP	SH	GW	GT	S	PCT
62	12	15	27	+11	4	0	1	1	0	115	10.4

1996-97 statistics:

GP	G	A	TP	+/-	PIM	PP	SH	GW	GT	S	PCT
49	6	7	13	-3	8	1	0	0	0	69	8.7

LAST SEASON

Games missed were due to coaches' decision.

THE FINESSE GAME

Brown approaches the game with intelligence and enthusiasm, blocks shots fearlessly and never stops working. He always attains his level of play but seldom surpasses it, which is why coaches often give younger players ice time ahead of him at the start of the season, then tend to go back to the old reliable redhead.

A determined penalty killer and shorthanded threat, Brown never quits around the net. His goals comes from deflections or wraparounds. Because his shot isn't much of a threat at all, he seems so underconfident in his ability to create a rebound with it that he falls back to a defensive posture rather than following the play to the net.

Brown depends more on side-to-side quickness than on straight-ahead speed. Always hustling, he gets a lot of breakaways because of the quick jumps he gets on the opposition, but lacks the finishing touch to score as many goals as he should. He wipes out frequently after losing his edges. When carrying the puck, Brown does not always move it at the right time; sometimes he holds onto it too long, either because he doesn't see the proper play or cannot make it in time.

THE PHYSICAL GAME

Brown is not big or strong, but he is one of the better grinders along the wall, since he will hang in there and not give up on a puck. He keeps the puck alive with his stick or feet. He won't fight, but he won't be intimidated, either.

THE INTANGIBLES

Teams need star players and they need Doug Browns to do the support work, the glamourless, faceless stuff that trustworthy players provide. Difficult as it is to muster consistent play when dropped from the lineup for long stretches of games, Brown gets that job done. Any points he provides are a bonus, but they often come at important times. He is a very competitive player.

PROJECTION

Brown lacks world-class skills, but serves as the perfect complement to world-class players. He is just as comfortable doing the grunt work on a checking line. He hustles and grinds and does all of the little things it takes to win a hockey game. Brown has spent most of his career on the bubble. He'll be there again this fall.

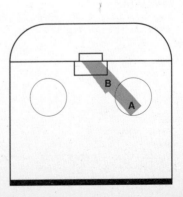

KRIS DRAPER

Yrs. of NHL service: 6
Born: Toronto, Ont.; May 24, 1971
Position: centre
Height: 5-11
Weight: 185
Uniform no.: 33
Shoots: left

Career statistics:

GP	G	A	TP	PIM
223	25	28	53	167

1993-94 statistics:

GP	G	A	TP	+/-	PIM	PP	SH	GW	GT	S	PCT
39	5	8	13	+11	31	0	1	0	0	55	9.1

1994-95 statistics:

GP	G	A	TP	+/-	PIM	PP	SH	GW	GT	S	PCT
36	2	6	8	+1	22	0	0	0	0	44	4.5

1995-96 statistics:

GP	G	A	TP	+/-	PIM	PP	SH	GW	GT	S	PCT
52	7	9	16	+2	32	0	1	0	0	51	13.7

1996-97 statistics:

GP	G	A	TP	+/-	PIM	PP	SH	GW	GT	S	PCT
76	8	5	13	-11	73	1	0	1	0	85	9.4

LAST SEASON

Career high in games played, goals.

THE FINESSE GAME

Draper seemed to set his standards higher last season; he started trying to make things happen instead of being satisfied with whatever territory defenders conceded. He ended up showing some hand quickness and cleverness with the puck in one-on-one confrontations. Rather than make the conventional play, Draper would make a fake, go to a more creative option, buy some time for teammates. And he was able to make the plays at high speed, as well.

Draper is unselfish and a good passer, especially in traffic. A good skater, he is strong on his feet and well balanced, but not fast. Clever play makes him seem much quicker than he is and heightens his usefulness as a penalty killer. He can also handle time on the power play because of his intelligent work around the net.

Still, he lacks a finisher's touch. Draper plays his position well and is proud of his checking role, but the strength of his game is his defense. His goals are hard-work goals that often come off his forecheck and his anticipation. When a linemate forces a defender into a giveaway, he's there to jump on the free puck and get a good shot away quickly.

THE PHYSICAL GAME

A no-frills defensive centre with a strong work ethic, Draper has wiry strength and uses his body well. He works the boards and corners and relishes physical play. Although short on size, he's intense, ready to play every night and completes his checks.

THE INTANGIBLES

Draper has plenty of heart. He sees limited ice time but is ready for every shift. He figures to be a role player for another season with the Red Wings thanks to his character.

PROJECTION

A hard worker, yes. A champion? Unmistakably. The scorer you need for your pool? Hardly.

ANDERS ERIKSSON

Yrs. of NHL service: 0
Born: Bolinas, Sweden; Jan. 9, 1975
Position: defense
Height: 6-3
Weight: 218
Uniform no.: 34
Shoots: left

Career statistics:

GP	G	A	TP	PIM
23	0	6	6	10

1996-97 statistics:

GP	G	A	TP	+/-	PIM	PP	SH	GW	GT	S	PCT
23	0	6	6	+5	10	0	0	0	0	27	0.0

LAST SEASON

Will be entering first NHL season. Scored 3-25 — 28 in 44 games with Adirondack (AHL).

THE FINESSE GAME

Eriksson is big for an NHL defenseman, even by today's standards, but his strength lies in his mobility and puckhandling skills. He sees the ice well; his biggest asset is his ability to get the puck out of his own end fast. He is a heads-up passer who is poised with the puck.

Eriksson is improving his defensive reads and re-actions. He doesn't jump into the play unless it's safe, and he won't pinch unless that is the correct play. He may err on the side of caution until he develops a little more confidence, but he has the skill level to provide some offense as a playmaker. He will probably limit his shots to the point.

Eriksson is a very good skater with balance and agility. He doesn't have a big turning radius and he accelerates well.

THE PHYSICAL GAME

Eriksson is not a big hitter, but he is strong and he'll tie up his man along the boards and in front of the net. His conditioning is very good, and he has adjusted to the longer North American schedule well. He should be able to handle the league's big power forwards because of his body positioning. He will force people to try to go through him.

THE INTANGIBLES

The Red Wings have brought Eriksson along slowly, but the injury to Vladimir Konstantinov and the ageing of players like Slava Fetisov will mean job openings on defense. Eriksson should be ready to step in.

PROJECTION

Eriksson will be concentrating on learning defense, but may provide 35 to 40 points while he's doing it.

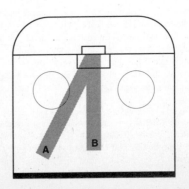

SERGEI FEDOROV

Yrs. of NHL service: 7
Born: Pskov, Russia; Dec. 13, 1969
Position: centre
Height: 6-1
Weight: 200
Uniform no.: 91
Shoots: left

Career statistics:

GP	G	A	TP	PIM
509	242	350	592	346

1993-94 statistics:

GP	G	A	TP	+/-	PIM	PP	SH	GW	GT	S	PCT
82	56	64	120	+48	34	13	4	10	0	337	16.6

1994-95 statistics:

GP	G	A	TP	+/-	PIM	PP	SH	GW	GT	S	PCT
45	20	30	50	+6	24	7	3	5	0	147	13.6

1995-96 statistics:

GP	G	A	TP	+/-	PIM	PP	SH	GW	GT	S	PCT
78	39	68	107	+49	48	11	2	11	1	306	12.7

1996-97 statistics:

GP	G	A	TP	+/-	PIM	PP	SH	GW	GT	S	PCT
74	30	33	63	+29	30	9	2	4	0	273	11.0

LAST SEASON

Third on team in points. Second on team in goals and power-play goals. Scored 30 or more goals for sixth time in seven seasons. Goals, assists and points were lowest full-season figures of his career.

THE FINESSE GAME

Versatility is a Fedorov hallmark. He has played left wing, centre and, thanks to coach Scott Bowman's eccentricity, he's also spent time on defense — which allowed his skating speed to compensate for Larry Murphy's lack of it. Fedorov is known as one of the league's outstanding defensive forwards, but Bowman took the notion to an extreme by putting him on the blueline for a regular-season experiment.

Fedorov is a tremendous package of offensive and defensive skills. He can go from checking the opponent's top centre to powering the power play from shift to shift. His skating is nothing short of phenomenal, and he can handle the puck while dazzling everyone with his blades.

He likes to gear up from his own defensive zone, using his acceleration and balance to drive wide to his right, carrying the puck on his backhand and protecting it with his body. If the defenseman lets up at all, then Fedorov is by him, pulling the puck quickly to his forehand. Nor is he by any means selfish. He has 360-degree vision of the ice and makes solid, confident passes right under opponents' sticks and smack onto the tape of his teammates'. Fedorov will swing behind the opposing net from left to right, fooling the defense into thinking he is going to continue to curl around, but he can quickly reverse with the puck on his backhand, shake his shadow and wheel around for a shot or goalmouth pass. He does it all in a flash.

Fedorov also has the strength and acceleration to drive right between two defenders, keep control of the puck and wrist a strong shot on goal. His wrist shot is an amazing, lethal weapon.

THE PHYSICAL GAME

When you are as gifted as Fedorov, opponents will do all they can to hit you and hurt you; when your medical history includes a concussion and a separated shoulder from such contact, you may become a bit gun-shy. Nonetheless, while the wiry Fedorov seems reluctant to absorb big hits or deliver any, he will leave the relative safety of open ice and head to the trenches when he has to.

Much of his power is generated from his strong skating. For the most part, his defense is dominated by his reads, anticipation and quickness in knocking down passes and breaking up plays. He is not much of a body checker, and he gets most of his penalties from stick and restraining fouls.

THE INTANGIBLES

Last year was a put-up or shut-up season for Fedorov, who had remarkably rotten regular-season numbers, but showed his mettle in the playoffs. He survived the experiment on defense, played through a demotion to the checking line, and, in the end, put up.

PROJECTION

Fedorov has the skill to dominate any game, any night. The issue is will, and, frankly, whether Bowman returns behind the Red Wings bench. Fedorov is not a great fan of Bowman's methods, and the indications were that Fedorov's point totals were a reflection of that malaise. He was "on" one night, "off" the next, and it is still difficult to know which Fedorov will appear for the contest.

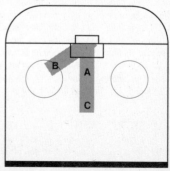

BRENT GILCHRIST

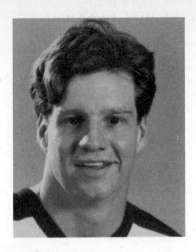

Yrs. of NHL service: 9
Born: Moose Jaw, Sask.; Apr. 3, 1967
Position: centre/left wing
Height: 5-11
Weight: 180
Uniform no.: 41
Shoots: left

Career statistics:

GP	G	A	TP	PIM
556	112	138	250	267

1993-94 statistics:

GP	G	A	TP	+/-	PIM	PP	SH	GW	GT	S	PCT
76	17	14	31	0	31	3	1	5	0	103	16.5

1994-95 statistics:

GP	G	A	TP	+/-	PIM	PP	SH	GW	GT	S	PCT
32	9	4	13	-3	16	1	3	1	0	70	12.9

1995-96 statistics:

GP	G	A	TP	+/-	PIM	PP	SH	GW	GT	S	PCT
77	20	22	42	-11	36	6	1	2	0	164	12.2

1996-97 statistics:

GP	G	A	TP	+/-	PIM	PP	SH	GW	GT	S	PCT
67	10	20	30	+6	24	2	0	2	0	116	8.6

LAST SEASON

Signed as free agent, July 7, 1997. Missed seven games with groin injury. Missed two games with hip flexor.

THE FINESSE GAME

Gilchrist is a dependable two-way forward who can play either wing or centre, and can play in any situation. In a way, his versatility has hurt him throughout his career, because he has never been able to establish himself in any one position or role. Because he can handle it he is always the player who is readily shifted. On the other hand, he will have a longer NHL career because he is so useful. At least no one's thought of putting him back on defense.

Gilchrist can play on the top line in a scoring role in a pinch, but is better on the third line as a checker. He has good knowledge of the ice. He anticipates well and is a smart and effective penalty killer.

Gilchrist was a prolific scorer in junior and in the minors, but hasn't shown the same touch at the NHL level. He has become more of a defensive specialist. He actually spent time on a fourth line last season, and there are few fourth-line players who can give you 20 goals a season, as Gilchrist can when he is healthy.

Gilchrist will work hard around the net and generates most of his scoring chances there. He has good balance and quickness in small areas, but is not a great finisher.

THE PHYSICAL GAME

Gilchrist is a strong player, though he doesn't take command of the ice. His good skating helps him move around and create a little more havoc, and he's not afraid to stand in and take a drubbing around the net. He won't back down from a challenge.

THE INTANGIBLES

Because Gilchrist is a hockey chameleon, he never seems to be given one definitive role. He can be slotted into so many situations, and he was one of the more attractive, modestly-priced restricted free agents during the off-season.

PROJECTION

Gilchrist's maximum goal production is 20, but he provides heart and effort worth more than that every night.

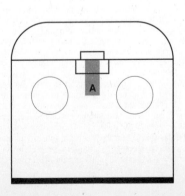

VYACHESLAV KOZLOV

Yrs. of NHL service: 4
Born: Voskresensk, Soviet Union; May 3, 1972
Position: centre/left wing
Height: 5-10
Weight: 180
Uniform no.: 13
Shoots: left

Career statistics:

GP	G	A	TP	PIM
304	110	121	231	227

1993-94 statistics:

GP	G	A	TP	+/-	PIM	PP	SH	GW	GT	S	PCT
77	34	39	73	+27	50	8	2	6	0	202	16.8

1994-95 statistics:

GP	G	A	TP	+/-	PIM	PP	SH	GW	GT	S	PCT
46	13	20	33	+12	45	5	0	3	0	97	13.4

1995-96 statistics:

GP	G	A	TP	+/-	PIM	PP	SH	GW	GT	S	PCT
82	36	37	73	+33	70	9	0	7	0	237	15.2

1996-97 statistics:

GP	G	A	TP	+/-	PIM	PP	SH	GW	GT	S	PCT
75	23	22	45	+21	46	3	0	6	0	211	10.9

LAST SEASON

Third on team in goals. Tied for second on team in game-winning goals.

THE FINESSE GAME

Kozlov can play as freewheeling offensively as the team wants. He cuts and bursts into openings and often appears at the right place at the right time. He can split the defense if it plays him too close, or drive the defense back with his speed and use the open ice to find a teammate. He has great control of the puck at high speed and plays an excellent transition game. He does not have to be coaxed into shooting, and has a quick release — generally to the top corners of the net.

That said, there also are times when Kozlov can be frustrating to watch. He will hold the puck past the point when he either should make a play with it or make a pass, then either loses control of the disk or takes himself to lesser ice. The reasonable speculation is that by holding the puck, he is buying time for teammates to break into open ice; other times, he simply appears incapable of making the necessary decision about what to do or is trying to make the perfect play instead of making a merely good play more quickly.

THE PHYSICAL GAME

Just as a defender comes to hit him, Kozlov gets rid of the puck; usually it goes to a teammate, sometimes it simply goes up for grabs. It would be easy to infer Kozlov is like a quarterback who gets rid of the ball rather than getting sacked; more likely, Kozlov is taking the hit to create space for someone else by allowing the defender to take himself — and Kozlov — out of the play.

THE INTANGIBLES

Kozlov has star-level talent, and his contribution to the Red Wings' championship in 1997 certifies his competitiveness. He regressed statistically last season as the Red Wings de-emphasized offense for defense, but was Detroit's third-leading scorer during the playoff charge to the Stanley Cup and was a major contributor on the power play.

PROJECTION

After producing a point per game in his first full season and being in that same neighbourhood the following two, Kozlov's dropoff last season was a mystery. He scored more on the road than at home, but should have scored more, regardless. He hardly seems a risky pool pick.

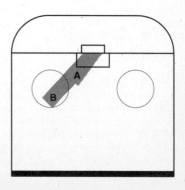

MARTIN LAPOINTE

Yrs. of NHL service: 4
Born: Ville Ste. Pierre, Que.; Sept. 12, 1973
Position: right wing
Height: 5-11
Weight: 200
Uniform no.: 20
Shoots: right

Career statistics:

GP	G	A	TP	PIM
232	34	35	69	393

1993-94 statistics:

GP	G	A	TP	+/-	PIM	PP	SH	GW	GT	S	PCT
50	8	8	16	+7	55	2	0	0	0	45	17.8

1994-95 statistics:

GP	G	A	TP	+/-	PIM	PP	SH	GW	GT	S	PCT
39	4	6	10	+1	73	0	0	1	0	46	8.7

1995-96 statistics:

GP	G	A	TP	+/-	PIM	PP	SH	GW	GT	S	PCT
58	6	3	9	0	93	1	0	0	0	76	7.9

1996-97 statistics:

GP	G	A	TP	+/-	PIM	PP	SH	GW	GT	S	PCT
78	16	17	33	-14	167	5	1	1	0	149	10.7

LAST SEASON

Missed four games due to fractured finger. Career high in points.

THE FINESSE GAME

Everything about Lapointe's game stems more from what is between his ribs than what is between his ears. It all comes from the heart: the competitiveness, the drive that sends him to the net in the straightest line possible. If a defenseman or opposing forward happens to get knocked down in the process, it's their problem.

Lapointe's goals and assists result more from his acceleration than his speed. He doesn't have breakaway speed, but his eagerness, his intensity and his willingness to compete make him seem faster than he actually is.

As important, Lapointe does not let a stick check slow him down. He'll pull a checker along like a boat tugging a water skier. He'll steam into the play to create an odd-man rush, and he creates lots of options with a nice passing touch that prevents goalies from overplaying him to shoot.

THE PHYSICAL GAME

Lapointe wants to play, wants to win and won't take an easy way out, which means a lot of opponents end up flat on the ice. He hits them all, big or small, and hits hard. He is low but wide, with a broad upper body and solid centre of gravity that powers his physical game. He can be a menace in the corners and a force in front of the net, which is why his goal total nearly tripled from the prior season's six.

THE INTANGIBLES

There is a snarl in Lapointe's game, a fire that always seems close to the fuse, and though he takes a good share of over-emotional penalties, he has better control than earlier in his career. He wakes things up, and never lets opponents take the easy way out. He never lets himself take the easy way, either. He came to the team as a big-time scorer in the Quebec League and dedicated himself to learning how to check. His approach is summarized in his statement: "I'd rather change my role and have the team win instead of being a one-man show."

PROJECTION

The Red Wings rewarded Lapointe's continued improvement, and his contribution to their championship, with a nice contract over the summer. Some fourth-year players might slip into the "I've got it made now" mode, but the feeling here is that Lapointe is still on the rise.

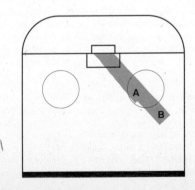

IGOR LARIONOV

Yrs. of NHL service: 7
Born: Voskresensk, Russia; Dec. 3, 1960
Position: centre
Height: 5-9
Weight: 170
Uniform no.: 8
Shoots: left

Career statistics:

GP	G	A	TP	PIM
440	107	243	350	202

1993-94 statistics:

GP	G	A	TP	+/-	PIM	PP	SH	GW	GT	S	PCT
60	18	38	56	+20	40	3	2	2	1	72	25.0

1994-95 statistics:

GP	G	A	TP	+/-	PIM	PP	SH	GW	GT	S	PCT
33	4	20	24	-3	14	0	0	0	1	69	5.8

1995-96 statistics:

GP	G	A	TP	+/-	PIM	PP	SH	GW	GT	S	PCT
73	22	51	73	+31	34	10	1	5	0	113	19.5

1996-97 statistics:

GP	G	A	TP	+/-	PIM	PP	SH	GW	GT	S	PCT
64	12	42	54	+31	26	2	1	4	0	95	12.6

LAST SEASON

Second on team in assists. Fifth on team in points. Missed seven games due to wrist injury. Missed four games due to bruised lower back. Missed one game due to flu. Missed four games due to pulled groin.

THE FINESSE GAME

Larionov is like a point guard in basketball. He moves around, holds the puck and holds the puck, encouraging his teammates to skate to an opening so he can make a creative pass. He curls back, draws defenders towards him, then sends the puck into the openings they have left for him.

When Larionov is on the ice, his team becomes a group of interchangeable parts. Everybody plays offense, everybody plays defense, and makes it look simple, as though this is the only way to play the game, and as though hockey is art, not sport.

Among the best playmakers ever to come out of the old Soviet system, Larionov is an agile, elusive skater with marvellous hand skills and a creative mind. He is extremely difficult to knock off the puck and difficult to defend because he forces an opponent to make decisions: do I go to him or hold my ground? While the opponent is thinking, Larionov is making things happen.

Larionov will not overpower many goalies with his shot but he will score with a variety of in-tight moves. He can work the point on the power play, kill penalties, and is always a threat to score a shorthanded goal.

THE PHYSICAL GAME

Larionov generally practises restraint, but a defining moment in Detroit's season came when he became entangled with Peter Forsberg — setting off the fracas in which the Red Wings settled their score with Colorado over Claude Lemieux's check on Kris Draper during the 1996 playoffs.

Larionov is wiry and fit, usually above the fray when things get nasty. He is smart enough to realize the team is better served if larger forwards win the puck and get it him, rather than the other way around.

Larionov is one of the smallest players in the league; in the dressing room, he is smaller than most of the media people interviewing him. But he has incredible wisdom and courage. He's respected, if not revered, for what he has accomplished, and the price he has paid for his success.

PROJECTION

Larionov got almost one-third of his points on the power play last season. He has played a lot of hockey over a lot of years, but remains a youthful, creative scoring threat who, with Detroit's forwards, still figures to approach a point per game as long as he can stay healthy.

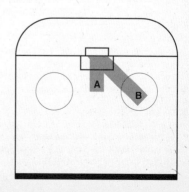

NICKLAS LIDSTROM

Yrs. of NHL service: 6
Born: Västerås, Sweden; Apr. 28, 1970
Position: left defense
Height: 6-2
Weight: 185
Uniform no.: 5
Shoots: left

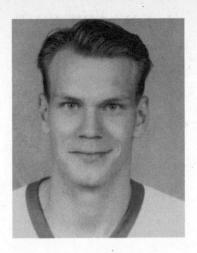

Career statistics:

GP	G	A	TP	PIM
451	70	237	307	132

1993-94 statistics:

GP	G	A	TP	+/-	PIM	PP	SH	GW	GT	S	PCT
84	10	46	56	+43	26	4	0	3	0	200	5.0

1994-95 statistics:

GP	G	A	TP	+/-	PIM	PP	SH	GW	GT	S	PCT
43	10	16	26	+15	6	7	0	0	0	90	11.1

1995-96 statistics:

GP	G	A	TP	+/-	PIM	PP	SH	GW	GT	S	PCT
81	17	50	67	+29	20	8	1	1	1	211	8.1

1996-97 statistics:

GP	G	A	TP	+/-	PIM	PP	SH	GW	GT	S	PCT
79	15	42	57	+11	30	8	0	1	0	214	7.0

LAST SEASON

Third among NHL defensemen and led team defensemen in scoring. Second on team in assists. Fourth on team in points.

THE FINESSE GAME

Lidstrom is an excellent skater and has good vision of the ice. He prefers to look for the breakout pass, rather than carry the puck, and he has a superb point shot that stays low and accurate. Lidstrom's work at the point on the power play has improved significantly. His rink management is solid, his decision-making is better and his passing — particularly to set up one-timers — is tape-to-tape. Lidstrom also is more confident about moving down low to poach for goals.

Defensively, Lidstrom uses exceptional anticipation to position himself perfectly and has improved his reads. He is tough to beat one-on-one, and sometimes even two-on-one, in open ice. He neatly breaks up passes with a quick stick. He kills penalties and willingly blocks shots. He also plays either side — an underrated asset — and is dependable in the last minute of a close period or game.

Lidstrom wants to bulk up, the way countryman Mats Sundin did, and add at least eight pounds to his wiry frame for this season. Since he has a lightning-fast metabolism, that isn't going to be easy.

THE PHYSICAL GAME

Lidstrom truly perseveres. He does not take the body much and depends on quick wits more than hard hits. But on the other side of the puck, he has little fear of contact and will accept a hit to make a play.

Although not a physical player, Lidstrom plays smart. With body positioning and stick positioning, he leaves opposing puck carriers no place to go and no alternative to giving up the puck — usually to him. He finds a way to tie up the opponent's stick. Lidstrom says he wants to play more physically this year, and dish out as much physical abuse as he absorbs.

THE INTANGIBLES

While not outwardly emotional, Lidstrom is an intense competitor. At the start of his career, he seemed poised to move into the top class of NHL offensive defensemen, but he hasn't climbed to that next step.

PROJECTION

Those exhausting wars in front of the defensive net can take a toll at the other end of the ice. Also, since he is used against the opposition's top offensive threat every night, Lidstrom's production may never rise above 60-some points. That said, he is an outstanding player. Appropriately, more people know that now after Detroit's title run last spring.

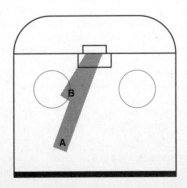

KIRK MALTBY

Yrs. of NHL service: 4
Born: Guelph, Ont.; Dec. 22, 1972
Position: right wing
Height: 6-0
Weight: 180
Uniform no.: 18
Shoots: right

Career statistics:

GP	G	A	TP	PIM
236	25	22	47	265

1993-94 statistics:

GP	G	A	TP	+/-	PIM	PP	SH	GW	GT	S	PCT
68	11	8	19	-2	74	0	1	1	0	89	12.4

1994-95 statistics:

GP	G	A	TP	+/-	PIM	PP	SH	GW	GT	S	PCT
47	8	3	11	-11	49	0	2	1	1	73	11.0

1995-96 statistics:

GP	G	A	TP	+/-	PIM	PP	SH	GW	GT	S	PCT
55	3	6	9	-16	67	0	0	1	0	55	5.5

1996-97 statistics:

GP	G	A	TP	+/-	PIM	PP	SH	GW	GT	S	PCT
66	3	5	8	+3	75	0	0	0	0	62	4.8

PROJECTION

Maltby could produce 10 to 15 goals a season and provide smart checking if he can win a full-time job in Detroit.

LAST SEASON

Penalty-minute total was a career high.

THE FINESSE GAME

Maltby's skating helps keep him in position defensively. He seldom is caught up-ice and plays well without the puck. He understands the game well and is very coachable. He kills penalties well and blocks shots.

Maltby isn't overly creative, but he works tirelessly along the boards and in the corners to keep the puck alive. He has an average wrist and snap shot, though that average shot got him five goals in the playoffs.

Astute hockey sense stamps him a two-way winger, unless, of course, he is on the bench or on the sidelines, which is where Detroit kept him from time to time during the regular season.

THE PHYSICAL GAME

There are few nights when you don't notice when Maltby is on the ice. He has good speed and just loves to flatten people with clean, hard hits, and he is fearless. He is not very big but he is solid and won't back down from a challenge.

Maltby's power emanates from his lower-body drive. He is strong and balanced and will punish with his hits. His work ethic and conditioning are strong. He wants to win the races to loose pucks.

THE INTANGIBLES

Maltby is valuable in his ability to stabilize a game. He wants to play, wants to learn, wants to do whatever he can to help the team.

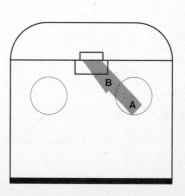

DARREN MCCARTY

Yrs. of NHL service: 4
Born: Burnaby, B.C.; April, 1972
Position: right wing
Height: 6-1
Weight: 210
Uniform no.: 25
Shoots: right

Career statistics:

GP	G	A	TP	PIM
229	48	69	117	553

1993-94 statistics:

GP	G	A	TP	+/-	PIM	PP	SH	GW	GT	S	PCT
67	9	17	26	+12	181	0	0	2	0	81	11.1

1994-95 statistics:

GP	G	A	TP	+/-	PIM	PP	SH	GW	GT	S	PCT
31	5	8	13	+5	88	1	0	2	0	27	18.5

1995-96 statistics:

GP	G	A	TP	+/-	PIM	PP	SH	GW	GT	S	PCT
63	15	14	29	+14	158	8	0	1	1	102	14.7

1996-97 statistics:

GP	G	A	TP	+/-	PIM	PP	SH	GW	GT	S	PCT
68	19	30	49	+14	126	5	0	6	1	171	11.1

LAST SEASON

Point total was a career high. Missed four games due to charley horse. Missed seven games due to hand injury.

THE FINESSE GAME

McCarty has an awkward stride and his first few steps are rather slow. But, as evidenced by his breakaways against Patrick Roy in the Western Conference finals last season, McCarty is strong on his skates. And when he reaches top speed, his acceleration is serviceable and he has decent finishing skills to go with a physical aspect.

McCarty's balance is underrated. In the Stanley Cup final, he absorbed a thunderclap hip check from Eric Lindros without even taking a backwards step; 95 per cent of the rest of the league wouldn't have landed yet.

Last season, McCarty showed the ability to execute the consummate pro's perfecta: the poise to follow a great play with a good one. He can deke a defender with an inside-outside move, then go backhand-forehand to finish the play with a huge goal that provides a huge boost to his team while utterly deflating the opposition.

McCarty has good hands and will score the majority of his goals in tight. He is not terribly creative but stays with a basic power game and is solid on the forecheck.

He led the OHL with 55 goals in 1991-92 while playing for Belleville. Although his totals at the minor-league and NHL levels have not been as impressive, he has the potential to be a solid power forward.

THE PHYSICAL GAME

Mean, big, strong, tough and fearless. All the components are there, along with the desire to throw his body at any player or puck he can reach. If a game is off to a quiet start, look for McCarty to wake everyone up. He forechecks and backchecks fiercely — tries to go through players, not just to them.

He is not a great fighter but he's willing. When there was unfinished business with Colorado's Claude Lemieux, McCarty finished it. And while *HSR* would never condone vigilante justice, McCarty's actions in that midseason game catapulted the team's chemistry to championship level.

THE INTANGIBLES

A lot has been made of McCarty's having gone to Sweden for lessons in improving his game, but that underscores his commitment to that improvement. McCarty needed to take a big step forward in his development and he made that step last season. He made himself a huge leader on his team and backed up his big heart with big plays.

PROJECTION

McCarty was a critical component of a Stanley Cup champion. The Yzermans and the Fedorovs carry so much of the load and the scrutiny, so it served as immeasurable help that McCarty took so large a step forward. He seemed to do it naturally, seemed to grow into the role, making himself an untouchable. Expect bigger things from him this season, though 60 points seems the maximum stretch to his envelope.

LARRY MURPHY

Yrs. of NHL service: 17
Born: Scarborough, Ont.; Mar. 8, 1961
Position: right defense
Height: 6-2
Weight: 210
Uniform no.: 55
Shoots: right

Career statistics:

GP	G	A	TP	PIM
1315	254	791	1051	948

1993-94 statistics:

GP	G	A	TP	+/-	PIM	PP	SH	GW	GT	S	PCT
84	17	56	73	+10	44	7	0	4	0	236	7.2

1994-95 statistics:

GP	G	A	TP	+/-	PIM	PP	SH	GW	GT	S	PCT
48	13	25	38	+12	18	4	0	3	0	124	10.5

1995-96 statistics:

GP	G	A	TP	+/-	PIM	PP	SH	GW	GT	S	PCT
82	12	49	61	-2	34	8	0	1	2	182	6.6

1996-97 statistics:

GP	G	A	TP	+/-	PIM	PP	SH	GW	GT	S	PCT
81	9	36	45	+3	20	5	0	1	1	158	5.7

LAST SEASON

Obtained from Toronto for future considerations, March 18, 1997.

THE FINESSE GAME

Murphy never has been a great skater. He actually has a rather choppy stride, but he has some agility and more quickness than speed.

He can either rush the puck out of his zone under pressure or make the nice first pass that gives his team the jump on opponents. When he snares the puck, his first impulse is to make a quick pass, then sprint up ice and join the breakout.

Murphy is smart and poised, the perfect guy to collect the puck behind his goal line and start the rush up ice on the power play. He has a fairly high panic point with the puck, and often will hold it until the last moment before passing.

Though he has been known to give away the puck, Murphy generally will not force bad passes up the middle and almost always picks the safest passing option. His pinches are well-timed, and he has the reach to prevent a lot of pucks from getting by him at the point. Murphy has the good sense, and balance, to drop to one knee and get his body in front of clearing attempts he is trying to block at the point, thus fewer pucks get past him.

Murphy's shot selection is intelligent. He loves to shoot, but he won't fire blindly. He will use a low wrist shot rather than a big slap to keep the puck on net. His positional play is where he has shown the most improvement. He reads plays well and seldom seems to be floundering on the ice.

THE PHYSICAL GAME

Murphy does not play a physical game. He will bump his man in front but doesn't make strong takeouts. He prefers to position his body and force the shooter to make a play while he himself goes for the puck or stick.

Mentally, Murphy is a tough customer. He handled a whopping workload in the finals against Philadelphia, played mostly against the toughest customers from the Legion of Doom, and was extremely effective.

THE INTANGIBLES

He added years to his career with a standout playoff that reconfirmed his credentials for steadiness and productive play. Murphy is the definition of substance over style; coaches always want veteran defensemen who can play as effectively as Murphy did for Detroit last season.

PROJECTION

Murphy seems to score the quietest points of any of the offensive-oriented NHL defensemen. He is big, but not physical. He is skilled, but not flashy. But he plays a low-maintenance game, stays healthy, gets his minutes and he's going to score goals or set them up.

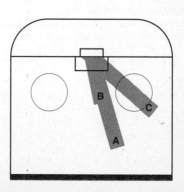

CHRIS OSGOOD

Yrs. of NHL service: 4
Born: Peace River, Alta.; Nov. 26, 1972
Position: goaltender
Height: 5-10
Weight: 175
Uniform no.: 30
Catches: left

Career statistics:

GP	MIN	GA	SO	GAA	A	PIM
157	8995	358	14	2.39	4	14

1993-94 statistics:

GP	MIN	GAA	W	L	T	SO	GA	S	SAPCT	PIM
41	2206	2.86	23	8	5	2	105	999	.895	2

1994-95 statistics:

GP	MIN	GAA	W	L	T	SO	GA	S	SAPCT	PIM
19	1087	2.26	14	5	0	1	41	496	.917	2

1995-96 statistics:

GP	MIN	GAA	W	L	T	SO	GA	S	SAPCT	PIM
50	2933	2.17	39	6	5	5	106	1190	.911	4

1996-97 statistics:

GP	MIN	GAA	W	L	T	SO	GA	S	SAPCT	PIM
47	2769	2.30	23	13	9	6	106	1175	.910	6

PROJECTION

Osgood has to pay strict attention to nutrition and conditioning because he doesn't have the big body to get him through a busy schedule and could easily wear down. He still figures to get plenty of work this season, as the Red Wings, having snapped their Cup drought, return to their long-term plan.

LAST SEASON

Sixth in NHL in goals-against average. Tied for third in NHL in shutouts. Finalist for 1996 Vezina Trophy. Led NHL in wins. Second in NHL in goals-against average. Tied for third in NHL in shutouts.

THE PHYSICAL GAME

Osgood is a small goalie, but by challenging shooters he makes himself look bigger in the net. He plays his angles well and has very quick feet. His reflexes are excellent for close shots, and he stays on his skates and doesn't flop. He has a superb glove hand and is tough to beat high.

He controls his rebounds well and doesn't have to scramble for too many second or third shots. His lateral movement is very good.

Osgood can handle the puck; in fact, he has scored a goal. He also uses his stick effectively to poke pucks off of attackers' sticks around the net.

THE MENTAL GAME

Osgood concentrates well and keeps his head in the game. He doesn't defeat himself mentally. He has been brought along slowly and allowed to grow into a position of responsibility.

THE INTANGIBLES

Osgood took a seat on the bench while Mike Vernon carried the Red Wings to the end of their Stanley Cup drought, but at 24, Osgood will get more chances to do the same thing and he, not the Conn Smythe Trophy-winning Vernon, will be the Wings' number one netminder this season.

TOMAS SANDSTROM

Yrs. of NHL service: 13
Born: Jakobstad, Finland; Sept. 4, 1964
Position: right wing
Height: 6-2
Weight: 20
Uniform no.: 28
Shoots: left

Career statistics:

GP	G	A	TP	PIM
848	370	437	807	1087

1993-94 statistics:

GP	G	A	TP	+/-	PIM	PP	SH	GW	GT	S	PCT
78	23	35	58	-7	83	4	0	3	1	193	11.9

1994-95 statistics:

GP	G	A	TP	+/-	PIM	PP	SH	GW	GT	S	PCT
47	21	23	44	+1	42	4	1	3	1	116	18.1

1995-96 statistics:

GP	G	A	TP	+/-	PIM	PP	SH	GW	GT	S	PCT
58	35	35	70	+4	69	17	1	2	0	187	18.7

1996-97 statistics:

GP	G	A	TP	+/-	PIM	PP	SH	GW	GT	S	PCT
74	18	24	42	+6	69	1	2	2	1	139	12.9

LAST SEASON

Acquired from Pittsburgh for Greg Johnson, January 27, 1997. Missed seven games with groin pull.

THE FINESSE GAME

Sandstrom is one of the few players in the league who can release a shot when the puck is in his feet. He uses a short backswing and surprises goalies with the shot's velocity and accuracy. He can beat a netminder in a number of ways, but this shot is unique. Sandstrom is also smart enough and skilled enough to work to get open and be ready for the puck.

Sandstrom combines size, speed, strength and skill. He needs to play to keep his legs going. His skating is impressive for someone of his dimensions. Quick and agile, he intimidates with his speed. He has a superb passing touch and shoots well on the fly or off the one-timer.

THE PHYSICAL GAME

Count on Sandstrom to be flat-out dirty in the corners. He'll skate on the razor's edge of the rule book, come as close as possible to hitting from behind, then collect the puck. Wildly abrasive, he gives facials with his gloves, gets his stick up and takes the body. There are times when he hits and runs, but he generally gets the last laugh as vengeance-crazed opponents take retaliatory penalties against him.

Aside from the antics, Sandstrom also pays an honest physical price, giving hits and taking them. He seems to relish the one-on-one battles on the walls and the corners; he wants to beat you there, then beat you to the front of the net.

THE INTANGIBLES

Sandstrom loves to compete, loves to battle and fully accepts the physical consequences. He gets hurt, plays hurt when he can, but through the years has retained a general disregard for safety — his own or his opponent's. Some players move around a lot because they wear out their welcomes in the dressing room; Sandstrom moves from team to team because that package is difficult to find in a veteran who can still deliver.

PROJECTION

Sandstrom's ability makes him a threat to put up points. His history of time on the sidelines all but assures he will produce those points in far less than a full complement of games.

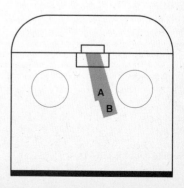

BRENDAN SHANAHAN

Yrs. of NHL service: 10
Born: Mimico, Ont.; Jan. 23, 1969
Position: left wing
Height: 6-3
Weight: 218
Uniform no.: 14
Shoots: right

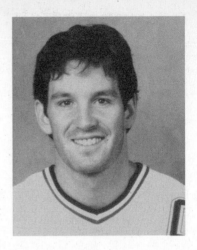

Career statistics:

GP	G	A	TP	PIM
713	335	351	686	1472

1993-94 statistics:

GP	G	A	TP	+/-	PIM	PP	SH	GW	GT	S	PCT
81	52	50	102	-9	211	15	7	8	1	397	13.1

1994-95 statistics:

GP	G	A	TP	+/-	PIM	PP	SH	GW	GT	S	PCT
45	20	21	41	+7	136	6	2	6	0	153	13.1

1995-96 statistics:

GP	G	A	TP	+/-	PIM	PP	SH	GW	GT	S	PCT
74	44	34	78	+2	125	17	2	6	0	280	15.7

1996-97 statistics:

GP	G	A	TP	+/-	PIM	PP	SH	GW	GT	S	PCT
81	47	41	88	+32	131	20	3	7	2	336	14.0

LAST SEASON

Acquired from Hartford with Brian Glynn for Keith Primeau, Paul Coffey and first-round draft pick in 1997 draft. Tenth in NHL and led team in points. Led team in power-play goals, game-winning goals and shorthanded goals. Second on team in assists and plus-minus.

THE FINESSE GAME

Skating is one of Shanahan's few flaws. He isn't very quick, isn't very agile and he often looks awkward with the puck. Most of the time, he's better off making the hit that frees the puck, passing it to a teammate and breaking to a spot, because he can score from anywhere. He is far more polished as a starter and a finisher than as the middle man who beats a couple of checkers with the puck and feeds an open man.

A wonderful package of grit, skills and smarts, Shanahan will battle in front of the net for a puck but he is also savvy enough to avoid an unnecessary thrashing. On the power play, he is one of the best in the league at staying just off the crease, waiting for a shot to come from the point, then timing his arrival at the front of the net for the moving screen, the tip or the rebound. He can get a lot on his shot even when the puck is near his feet, because of a short backswing and strong wrists.

Shanahan has wonderfully soft hands for nifty goalmouth passes, and he has a hard, accurate snap and slap shot with a quick release, which he never tires of using. He also loves the one-time shot and is a good enough athlete to bury it — even if the pass he receives isn't perfect.

He will take some face-offs, especially in the offensive zone, and succeeds by tying up the opposing centre and using his feet to control the puck. Even though he plays on the off-wing, his backhand is good enough to take passes and create some offense.

THE PHYSICAL GAME

The dilemma for rival teams: if you play Shanahan aggressively, it brings out the best in him. If you lay off and give him room, he will kill you with his skills. Shanahan spent his formative NHL years establishing his reputation by dropping his gloves with anybody who challenged him, but he has gotten smarter without losing his tough edge. He will still lose it once in awhile, which only makes rivals a little more wary.

He takes or makes a hit to create a play. He's willing to eat glass to make a pass, but would rather strike the first blow. And he does that by using his strength to overcome the hooking and holding, by fighting through checks to get himself in position to score. He sees the puck, goes and gets it, puts it towards the front of the net.

THE INTANGIBLES

Shanahan is a leader, a gamer who revels in pressure situations. Teammates thrive on his intensity. With all due respect to Steve Yzerman, Shanahan is the acting captain of the Red Wings.

Other than his willingness to hit or to scrap, no aspect of his game is super elite. But he's there when you need him to make a play that will win for you or say the right thing in the dressing room. And he's *always* there for the fans; Shanahan is one of the most popular players in the NHL.

PROJECTION

A prime-time player entering his prime production years, Shanahan will provide a definitive illustration of his maturity if he can avoid a Stanley Cup hangover and surpass last season's output.

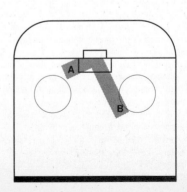

AARON WARD

Yrs. of NHL service: 1
Born: Windsor, Ont.; Jan. 17, 1973
Position: left defense
Height: 6-2
Weight: 200
Uniform no.: 27
Shoots: right

Career statistics:

GP	G	A	TP	PIM
55	3	6	9	58

1993-94 statistics:

GP	G	A	TP	+/-	PIM	PP	SH	GW	GT	S	PCT
5	1	0	1	+2	4	0	0	0	0	3	33.3

1994-95 statistics:

GP	G	A	TP	+/-	PIM	PP	SH	GW	GT	S	PCT
1	0	1	1	+1	2	0	0	0	0	0	0.0

1995-96 statistics:

P	G	A	TP	+/-	PIM	PP	SH	GW	GT	S	PC
Did not play in NHL											

1996-97 statistics:

GP	G	A	TP	+/-	PIM	PP	SH	GW	GT	S	PCT
49	2	5	7	-9	52	0	0	0	0	40	5.0

LAST SEASON

First NHL season. Missed three games due to illness.

THE FINESSE GAME

Ward's game favours finesse over physicality, but he doesn't seem to have the skills for that style. Although his quickness has improved, he could use a step in his skating. And although his puck movement has improved, he makes questionable decisions in both ends of the rink. He's still learning, but the question becomes when, exactly, does he graduate to fill out a first-rounder's promise?

Ward is adequate from a positional standpoint and plays the percentages. He makes attackers try to beat his strength and reach to the outside because he knows there aren't many forwards capable of taking the inside route.

Ward does an acceptable job in confined spaces, such as the corners, but like other big defensemen, he has trouble winning a race back to the front of the net if the puck squirts loose.

THE PHYSICAL GAME

Ward's got all kinds of size but doesn't use it particularly well. He can be physical, big-hit physical, but does not play a consistently physical game. He's not an aggressive player. Scouts question his intensity and toughness.

THE INTANGIBLES

Ward incited Colorado coach Marc Crawford to take a swing at him in a corridor at Joe Louis Arena. He also put Colorado's Rene Corbet on a stretcher with one of last season's most vicious hits. He can be a pepperpot, but doesn't seem to want to be one consistently.

Ward was a three-year collegian and now has completed four seasons in Detroit's organization. He makes impact with his hits, but has not had significant impact on the coaching staff. Since the Red Wings have been desperate to find a physical defenseman, it seems telling that Ward, with such physical promise, hasn't leaped at the chance. On the other hand, he played more games last season than any of his prior three in the Red Wings' system.

PROJECTION

It won't be too surprising if Ward ends up making a name for himself with another team that trades for him, or whichever expansion team claims him. If he stays in Detroit, the picture for this season is cloudy at best.

STEVE YZERMAN

Yrs. of NHL service: 14
Born: Cranbrook, B.C.; May 9, 1965
Position: centre
Height: 5-11
Weight: 185
Uniform no.: 19
Shoots: right

Career statistics:

GP	G	A	TP	PIM
1023	545	801	1340	694

1993-94 statistics:

GP	G	A	TP	+/-	PIM	PP	SH	GW	GT	S	PCT
58	24	58	82	+11	36	7	3	3	1	217	11.1

1994-95 statistics:

GP	G	A	TP	+/-	PIM	PP	SH	GW	GT	S	PCT
47	12	26	38	+6	40	4	0	1	0	134	9.0

1995-96 statistics:

GP	G	A	TP	+/-	PIM	PP	SH	GW	GT	S	PCT
80	36	59	95	+29	64	16	2	8	0	220	16.4

1996-97 statistics:

GP	G	A	TP	+/-	PIM	PP	SH	GW	GT	S	PCT
81	22	63	85	+22	78	8	0	3	0	232	9.5

LAST SEASON

Led team in assists. Second on team in points.

THE FINESSE GAME

Yzerman is a sensational skater. He zigs and zags all over the ice, spending very little time in the centre. He has great balance and quick feet, and is adroit at kicking the puck up onto his blade for a shot in seamless motion. He's also strong for an average-sized forward. He protects the puck well with his body and has the arm strength for wraparound shots and off-balance shots through traffic.

Yzerman prefers to stickhandle down the right side of the ice. In addition to using his body to shield the puck, he uses the boards to protect it. If a defender starts reaching in with his stick he usually ends up pulling Yzerman down for a penalty.

Yzerman's work on face-offs improved last season and his defensive play got much better, as well. He is a great penalty killer because of his speed and anticipation.

THE PHYSICAL GAME

Yzerman sacrifices his body willingly in the right circumstances and thinks nothing of diving to block a shot. He pays the price along the boards and around the net, and he's deceptively strong and durable.

Yzerman knows he isn't big enough to be an intimidating hitter, but he gets his body and stick in the way and at least makes the puck carrier change direction abruptly. He simply does not give up on a play, and he plays all 200 feet of the rink. He is just as likely to make a key play in front of his own goal as he is in front of the opponent's.

THE INTANGIBLES

A model of consistency, Yzerman's lapses during the season are few, and he seldom goes through a prolonged scoring slump. Considering how much ice time he gets and how active a skater he is, this is a great tribute to his devotion to conditioning and preparing himself for a game. He has always seemed mature than his years, even when he broke into the NHL at age 18.

Yzerman's goal production dropped significantly last season, and yet his level of determination never seemed higher. He was a man on a mission from the opening of training camp for World Cup to the moment when the Stanley Cup was placed in his hands.

PROJECTION

Although he played on a better team and had more help in the leadership aspect, it certainly seemed that it took until age 32 for Yzerman to truly come of age. He finally has admitted you can't score if you don't shoot, and he figures to shoot a lot this season.

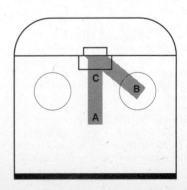

EDMONTON OILERS

Players' Statistics 1996-97

POS.	NO.	PLAYER	GP	G	A	PTS	+/-	PIM	PP	SH	GW	GT	S	PCT
C	39	DOUG WEIGHT	80	21	61	82	1	80	4		2		235	8.9
L	94	RYAN SMYTH	82	39	22	61	-7	76	20		4		265	14.7
L	51	ANDREI KOVALENKO	74	32	27	59	-5	81	14		2		163	19.6
C	7	JASON ARNOTT	67	19	38	57	-21	92	10	1	2	1	248	7.7
R	21	MARIUSZ CZERKAWSKI	76	26	21	47	0	16	4		3		182	14.3
R	16	KELLY BUCHBERGER	81	8	30	38	4	159			3		78	10.3
C	26	TODD MARCHANT	79	14	19	33	11	44		4	3		202	6.9
R	25	*MIKE GRIER	79	15	17	32	7	45	4		2		89	16.9
D	2	BORIS MIRONOV	55	6	26	32	2	85	2		1		147	4.1
L	17	*REM MURRAY	82	11	20	31	9	16	1		2		85	12.9
L	37	DEAN MCAMMOND	57	12	17	29	-15	28	4		6		106	11.3
L	14	*MATS LINDGREN	69	11	14	25	-7	12	2	3	1		71	15.5
D	23	*DANIEL MCGILLIS	73	6	16	22	2	52	2	1	2		139	4.3
D	55	*DREW BANNISTER	65	4	14	18	-23	44	1				59	6.8
D	24	BRYAN MARCHMENT	71	3	13	16	13	132	1				89	3.4
R	85	PETR KLIMA	33	2	12	14	-12	12					55	3.6
D	4	KEVIN LOWE	64	1	13	14	-1	50					46	2.2
D	22	LUKE RICHARDSON	82	1	11	12	9	91					67	1.5
L	18	*BARRIE MOORE	35	2	6	8	1	18	1				43	4.7
D	5	*GREG DE VRIES	37		4	4	-2	52					31	
L	29	LOUIE DEBRUSK	32	2		2	-6	94					10	20.0
C	9	*RALPH INTRANUOVO	8	1	1	2	-1						6	16.7
G	31	CURTIS JOSEPH	72		2	2	0	20						
C	10	*STEVE KELLY	8	1		1	-1	6				1	6	16.7
D	34	DONALD DUFRESNE	22		1	1	-1	15					10	
D	35	*CRAIG MILLAR	1				0	2					1	
D	8	*SEAN BROWN	5				-1	4					2	
C	12	JESSE BELANGER	6				-3						8	
L	15	*JOE HULBIG	6				-1						4	
G	30	BOB ESSENSA	19				0	4						

GP = games played; G = goals; A = assists; PTS = points; +/- = goals-for minus goals-against while player is on ice; PIM = penalties in minutes; PP = power-play goals; SH = shorthanded goals; GW = game-winning goals; GT = game-tying goals; S = no. of shots; PCT = percentage of goals to shots; * = rookie

JASON ARNOTT

Yrs. of NHL service: 4
Born: Collingwood, Ont.; Oct. 11, 1974
Position: centre
Height: 6-3
Weight: 220
Uniform no.: 7
Shoots: right

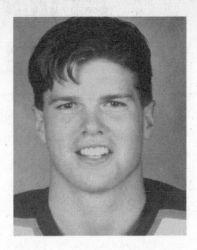

Career statistics:

GP	G	A	TP	PIM
251	95	126	221	354

1993-94 statistics:

GP	G	A	TP	+/-	PIM	PP	SH	GW	GT	S	PCT
78	33	35	68	+1	104	10	0	4	1	194	17.0

1994-95 statistics:

GP	G	A	TP	+/-	PIM	PP	SH	GW	GT	S	PCT
42	15	22	37	-14	128	7	0	1	0	156	9.6

1995-96 statistics:

GP	G	A	TP	+/-	PIM	PP	SH	GW	GT	S	PCT
64	28	31	59	-6	87	8	0	5	1	244	11.5

1996-97 statistics:

GP	G	A	TP	+/-	PIM	PP	SH	GW	GT	S	PCT
67	19	38	57	-21	92	10	1	2	1	248	7.7

LAST SEASON

Second on team in assists and shots. Worst plus-minus on team. Missed seven games with fractured ankle. Missed two games with sore ankle. Missed four games with back injury. Missed one game with flu.

THE FINESSE GAME

For the second straight season, injuries played a major role in derailing Arnott's development, and the Oilers centre remains a bit of an enigma. For a player of his size, he has tremendous skills. As a skater, he has speed, balance, a long stride and agility in turning to either side. He has also added muscle to his frame, without losing any edge in his skating.

Arnott is just as good a scorer as a passer, which makes it difficult for defenders who can't overplay him. His timing with passes is fine, as he holds onto the puck until a teammate is in the open. If the shot is his, he will use an assortment — snap, slap or wrist — and is accurate with a quick release. He can unleash a cannon shot and play the right point on the power play. He is fair on draws but will have to improve, as the Oilers rely on him more and more as a first- or second-line centre.

Arnott works down low on the power play and is on the Oilers' first unit. He can also kill penalties. His defensive play seemed adequate in his first few seasons, but he struggled with his assignments last season.

THE PHYSICAL GAME

Arnott has serious grit. He has a mean streak, and he's honest as well. He loves to hit and gets involved, especially in the attacking zone. Injuries made him less consistent in his physical play last season. Arnott came back quickly from a fractured ankle just before the All-Star break and had some lingering problems from the injury.

THE INTANGIBLES

Arnott had a sluggish finish to his season and his play-off performance was not as strong as we would have liked to see for a player of his ability and leadership potential. Arnott is entering his contract year, which could spur a return to his top form.

PROJECTION

If Arnott can stay healthy, he is capable of a 30-goal season or better. The last two seasons have been considered disappointments, but there will be plenty of teams lining up to take Arnott off the Oilers' hands if they get exasperated with him.

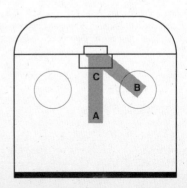

KELLY BUCHBERGER

Yrs. of NHL service: 8
Born: Langenburg, Sask.; Dec. 2, 1966
Position: left wing
Height: 6-2
Weight: 200
Uniform no.: 16
Shoots: left

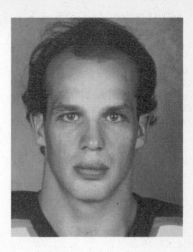

Career statistics:

GP	G	A	TP	PIM
661	72	137	199	1557

1993-94 statistics:

GP	G	A	TP	+/-	PIM	PP	SH	GW	GT	S	PCT
84	3	18	21	-20	199	0	0	0	0	93	3.2

1994-95 statistics:

GP	G	A	TP	+/-	PIM	PP	SH	GW	GT	S	PCT
48	7	17	24	0	82	2	1	5	0	73	9.6

1995-96 statistics:

GP	G	A	TP	+/-	PIM	PP	SH	GW	GT	S	PCT
82	11	14	25	-20	184	0	2	3	0	119	9.2

1996-97 statistics:

GP	G	A	TP	+/-	PIM	PP	SH	GW	GT	S	PCT
81	8	30	38	+4	159	0	0	3	0	78	10.3

LAST SEASON

Missed one game with suspension (for receiving three fight-related game misconducts), ending consecutive games-played streak at 283. Led team in penalty minutes.

THE FINESSE GAME

What's not to like? Buchberger is an ideal third-line player. Night in and night out, he faces other teams' top forwards and does a terrific shadow job, harassing without taking bad penalties.

He works hard and provides a consistent effort. He will grind, go to the net, kill penalties — all of the grunt work. He can finish off some plays now and then, but that is not his objective. The biggest change in Buchberger is that he has developed some degree of confidence in his finesse moves and is now willing to try something that looks too difficult for a "defensive" player. Sometimes it works, sometimes it doesn't, but Buchberger can suprise opponents with a saucer pass.

Buchberger has some straight-ahead speed and will go to the net and muck, but this kind of player needs some luck to get goals. He has earned a great deal of respect for his work ethic. He doesn't quit. He has five career playoff-overtime goals simply because he's a gamer.

THE PHYSICAL GAME

Buchberger is a legitimately tough customer. Honest and gritty, he won't get knocked around and is a solid hitter who likes the physical part of the game. He is a very disciplined player. He's also very determined. He keeps his legs moving constantly, and a player who lets up on this winger will be sorry, because Buchberger will keep plugging with the puck or go to the net.

THE INTANGIBLES

The heart and soul of the Oilers, Buchberger is one of the most unsung leaders in the NHL; he gets little attention playing in a small market. He is one of the best crunch-time players in the league.

PROJECTION

Point totals in this case are minimal and meaningless. Buchberger could score 10 points and be a candidate for team MVP. His point total last year was the second-highest of his career, and thanks to a better supporting cast he could net 30 points again. But Buchberger's true value lies elsewhere.

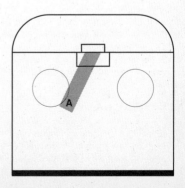

MARIUSZ CZERKAWSKI

Yrs. of NHL service: 3
Born: Radomsko, Poland; Apr. 13, 1972
Position: right wing
Height: 6-0
Weight: 195
Uniform no.: 21
Shoots: right

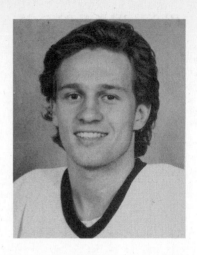

Career statistics:

GP	G	A	TP	PIM
197	57	59	116	65

1993-94 statistics:

GP	G	A	TP	+/-	PIM	PP	SH	GW	GT	S	PCT
4	2	1	3	-2	0	0	1	0	0	11	18.2

1994-95 statistics:

GP	G	A	TP	+/-	PIM	PP	SH	GW	GT	S	PCT
47	12	14	26	+4	31	1	0	2	0	126	9.5

1995-96 statistics:

GP	G	A	TP	+/-	PIM	PP	SH	GW	GT	S	PCT
70	17	23	40	-4	18	3	0	1	0	142	12.0

1996-97 statistics:

GP	G	A	TP	+/-	PIM	PP	SH	GW	GT	S	PCT
76	26	21	47	0	16	4	0	3	0	182	14.3

LAST SEASON

Career high in goals and points. Missed two games with hip pointer.

THE FINESSE GAME

While highly skilled, Czerkawski has still not shaken a common fault of gifted European puckhandlers. He will not make the simple play. Czerkawski often plays as if the objective is to dance through all five opponents on the ice before shooting or passing, leaving his teammates exasperated.

Czerkawski likes to use all of the ice, and will cut across the middle or to the right side to make the play. He is a shifty skater, not one with great straightaway speed, but he puts the slip on a defender with a lateral move and is off. This Polish import is hard to defend one-on-one because of the jitterbugging his body does, all while in full control of the puck. Unfortunately, much of his energy goes to waste when he misses out on prime scoring opportunities.

His quick wrist shot is his best weapon. With the extra room on the power play, he is at his best. He has soft hands for passes and good vision. He needs to play with someone who will get him the puck, since he will not go into the corners for it. Czerkawski was urged to shoot more last season and did, but not consistently.

THE PHYSICAL GAME

Czerkawski has to get better at protecting the puck and perform at least a willing game along the boards. He uses his body in the offensive zone, but in a perfunctory manner, and he doesn't like to get involved too much in the defensive zone. He is quick enough to peel back and help out with backchecking, since he is very smart at anticipating passes, but he will rarely knock anyone off the puck.

THE INTANGIBLES

We tend to be harder on European players if they don't produce points, but Czerkawski must score because he brings little else to the ice. His blah playoffs (two goals in 12 games) is not a promising sign.

PROJECTION

We pegged a 60-point season for Czerkawski last season, and he fell well short. Because of his skill level, much more is expected, but Czerkawski will lose power-play time to more determined players and it's starting to look like the 50-point range is more realistic.

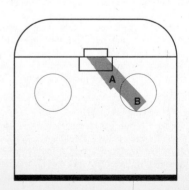

MIKE GRIER

Yrs. of NHL service: 1
Born: Detroit, Mich.; Jan. 5, 1975
Position: right wing
Height: 6-1
Weight: 232
Uniform no.: 25
Shoots: right

Career statistics:

GP	G	A	TP	PIM
79	15	17	32	45

1996-97 statistics:

GP	G	A	TP	+/-	PIM	PP	SH	GW	GT	S	PCT
79	15	17	32	+7	45	4	0	2	0	89	16.9

LAST SEASON

First NHL season. Tied for fifth among NHL rookies in goals. Led NHL rookies and second on team in shooting percentage.

THE FINESSE GAME

Grier is a hockey player in a football player's body. He is an aggressive forechecker and bores in on the unfortunate puck carrier with all of the intensity of a lineman blitzing a quarterback. But Grier doesn't waste his energy. He's intelligent about when to come in full-tilt or when to back off a bit and pick off a hasty pass. He frightens a lot of people into mistakes, and the savvier he gets at reading their reactions the better he'll be.

The knock on Grier has always been his skating, but it is getting much better. He has a slow first couple of strides, but then gets into gear and is strong and balanced with fair agility. He will score his goals like Adam Deadmarsh does, by driving to the net after loose pucks. Grier was a scorer at the collegiate level and has decent hands. He was one of the best players for the Oilers down the stretch, with 10-8 — 18 in the last 36 games.

THE PHYSICAL GAME

Grier lost about 15 pounds at the start of last season and he was a better player for it. He can't be too bulky, or he won't be agile enough for his pursuit. He isn't a fighter. It takes a lot to provoke him. He's just an honest, tough, physical winger. He played the Oilers' last two playoff games on a badly sprained ankle.

THE INTANGIBLES

Grier has dealt admirably with racism in his sport, and accepts the responsibility of being a role model for younger athletes. He made an amazing jump from college to the pros last season to become a valued member of an improving Oilers team. His attitude and work ethic are unassailable.

PROJECTION

Barring a sophomore slump, Grier should take the next step into the 20- to 25-goal range next season.

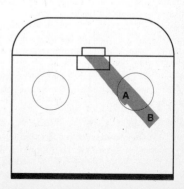

CURTIS JOSEPH

Yrs. of NHL service: 7
Born: Keswick, Ont.; Apr. 29, 1967
Position: goaltender
Height: 5-10
Weight: 182
Uniform no.: 31
Catches: left

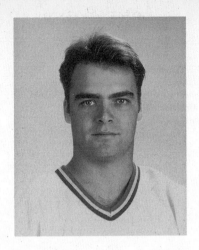

Career statistics:

GP	MIN	GA	SO	GAA	A	PIM
386	22012	1121	11	3.06	19	44

1993-94 statistics:

GP	MIN	GAA	W	L	T	SO	GA	S	SAPCT	PIM
71	4127	3.10	36	23	0	1	213	2382	.911	4

1994-95 statistics:

GP	MIN	GAA	W	L	T	SO	GA	S	SAPCT	PIM
36	1914	2.79	20	10	1	1	89	904	.902	0

1995-96 statistics:

GP	MIN	GAA	W	L	T	SO	GA	S	SAPCT	PIM
34	1936	3.44	15	16	2	0	111	971	.886	4

1996-97 statistics:

GP	MIN	GAA	W	L	T	SO	GA	S	SAPCT	PIM
72	4089	2.93	32	29	9	6	200	2144	.907	20

LAST SEASON

Career high in shutouts. Fourth in NHL in minutes played.

THE PHYSICAL GAME

Nothing Joseph does is by the book. He always looks unorthodox and off-balance, but he is one of those hybrid goalies — like Ed Belfour and Felix Potvin — whose success can't be argued with.

Joseph positions himself well, angling out to challenge the shooter, and is one of the best goalies against the breakaway in the NHL. Joseph goes to his knees quickly, but bounces back to his skates fast for the rebound. He tends to keep rebounds in front of him. His glove hand is outstanding.

A strong, if bizarre, stickhandler, Joseph has to move his hands on the stick, putting the butt-end into his catching glove and lowering his blocker. His favourite move is a weird backhand whip off the boards. He is a good skater who moves out of his cage confidently to handle the puck. He needs to improve his lateral movement. He also uses his stick to harass anyone who dares to camp on his doorstep. He's not Billy Smith, but he's getting more aggressive with his whacks.

Joseph gets into technical slumps, which seem to sprout from fatigue and usually result in his staying too deep in his net.

THE MENTAL GAME

Joseph is used to a lot of work, but last season was an exceptionally long one for him because of the World Cup. He looked like a tired goalie in the playoffs. Joseph can deal with busy nights. One of his best games of the season was a 52-save performance in Detroit in a scoreless tie.

THE INTANGIBLES

We disparaged Joseph's selection to Team Canada last year, and while he performed well in the loss, the bottom line was — he lost. That's the problem with Joseph, as it is with Ron Hextall. You're never a winner until you win the big prize. The young Oilers have improved and Joseph has been part of that, but he will be an unrestricted free agent after the 1997-98 season and unless the Oilers look like they can mount a serious Cup challenge, we expect him to go elsewhere after next season.

PROJECTION

Joseph will improve on his win total and shouldn't experience the same sort of slides he did last season. He will be a fresher goalie without the World Cup.

ANDREI KOVALENKO

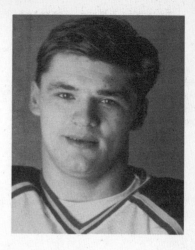

Yrs. of NHL service: 5
Born: Balakovo, Russia; June 7, 1970
Position: right wing
Height: 5-10
Weight: 215
Uniform no.: 51
Shoots: left

Career statistics:

GP	G	A	TP	PIM
335	117	123	240	264

1993-94 statistics:

GP	G	A	TP	+/-	PIM	PP	SH	GW	GT	S	PCT
58	16	17	33	-5	46	5	0	4	0	92	17.4

1994-95 statistics:

GP	G	A	TP	+/-	PIM	PP	SH	GW	GT	S	PCT
45	14	10	24	-4	31	1	0	3	0	63	22.2

1995-96 statistics:

GP	G	A	TP	+/-	PIM	PP	SH	GW	GT	S	PCT
77	28	28	56	+20	49	6	0	6	1	131	21.4

1996-97 statistics:

GP	G	A	TP	+/-	PIM	PP	SH	GW	GT	S	PCT
74	32	27	59	-5	81	14	0	2	0	163	19.6

LAST SEASON

Acquired from Montreal for Scott Thornton, September 6, 1996. Second on team in goals and power-play goals. Career high in goals. Led team and fourth in NHL in shooting percentage. Missed five games with hip pointer. Missed two games with back spasms.

THE FINESSE GAME

Kovalenko has the skills associated with many Russian forwards, but he also has a brisk, sometimes abrasive style. When he is on his best game, he plays on a number one line for the Oilers and makes things happen.

Kovalenko will bustle right into traffic. He is an intelligent player who doesn't panic with the puck and is a natural on the power play. He doesn't hang onto the puck long but likes to make short give-and-go plays in the offensive zone. He always keeps his wheels in motion. He is an accurate shooter with a quick release on his wrist shot. He should shoot more, but like many Russian players he hates to take a low-percentage shot and would rather work to get into position for a better one.

Defensive work is his downfall, but he has become more conscientious and makes fewer high-risk plays.

THE PHYSICAL GAME

Kovalenko's nickname is "the Little Tank," because of his chunky build. Checks often bounce right off him because he is so solid. He can be tough around the net and in the offensive corners. He will take some punishment in front of the net on the power play, and gets a lot of goals off the rebounds.

THE INTANGIBLES

Kovalenko has become a more reliable everyday player, but his strength is still as a power-play specialist. The Oilers have developed to the point where that is good enough to keep him in the lineup.

PROJECTION

We predicted a move for Kovalenko last season, and the switch to the Oilers made for a nice fit. We have seen his top end: another 30 goals this season is it.

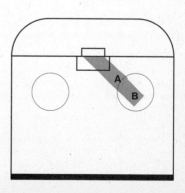

MATS LINDGREN

Yrs. of NHL service: 1
Born: Skelleftea, Sweden; Oct. 1, 1974
Position: left wing
Height: 6-2
Weight: 200
Uniform no.: 14
Shoots: left

Career statistics:

GP	G	A	TP	PIM
69	11	14	25	12

1996-97 statistics:

GP	G	A	TP	+/-	PIM	PP	SH	GW	GT	S	PCT
69	11	14	25	-7	12	2	3	1	0	71	15.5

LAST SEASON

First NHL season. Led NHL rookies and second on team in shorthanded goals. Scored 6-7 — 13 in nine games with Hamilton (AHL).

THE FINESSE GAME

Lindgren is primarily an offensive talent. He was asked to play as a defensive centre last season because of the defensive deficiencies of Doug Weight and Jason Arnott, who are ahead of Lindgren on the depth chart. With his size, hands and vision, he is a budding Mats Sundin.

Lindgren is a fine skater with balance, agility and quickness. He is especially clever in tight, moving the puck at the right moment and knowing when to shoot and when to pass. He needs to gain more confidence in his shot. He has a wrister with a lot on it.

Lindgren has terrific hockey sense, and plays equally well in all zones.

THE PHYSICAL GAME

Lindgren is solidly built and is capable of playing a power game. He'll never dominate physically, but he will battle for the puck in traffic areas.

THE INTANGIBLES

Lindgren missed almost all of the 1995-96 season with nerve damage in his leg, so his progress was slowed. He played in only 36 minor-league games before getting called up to Edmonton in November.

PROJECTION

Lindgren has great offensive upside, but where are the Oilers going to play him? If Arnott is shifted to the wing, then Lindgren can get quality ice time and notch 25 goals.

TODD MARCHANT

Yrs. of NHL service: 3
Born: Buffalo, N.Y.; Aug. 12, 1973
Position: centre
Height: 5-10
Weight: 175
Uniform no.: 26
Shoots: left

Career statistics:

GP	G	A	TP	PIM
209	46	53	99	144

1993-94 statistics:

GP	G	A	TP	+/-	PIM	PP	SH	GW	GT	S	PCT
4	0	1	1	-2	2	0	0	0	0	6	0.0

1994-95 statistics:

GP	G	A	TP	+/-	PIM	PP	SH	GW	GT	S	PCT
45	13	14	27	-3	32	3	2	2	0	95	13.7

1995-96 statistics:

GP	G	A	TP	+/-	PIM	PP	SH	GW	GT	S	PCT
81	19	19	38	-19	66	2	3	2	1	221	8.6

1996-97 statistics:

GP	G	A	TP	+/-	PIM	PP	SH	GW	GT	S	PCT
79	14	19	33	+11	44	0	4	3	0	202	6.9

LAST SEASON

Led team in shorthanded goals for second consecutive year. Missed three games with concussion.

THE FINESSE GAME

A speed merchant, Marchant is a strong one-on-one player with zippy outside speed. His quick hand skills keep pace with his feet, and he is particularly adept at tempting the defender with the puck then dragging it through the victim's legs. He then continues to the net for his scoring chances, and he is a strong finisher. Marchant is a product of the U.S. national program, which despite producing lousy results at the Olympics has been highly successful as a breeding ground for high-flying NHL stars.

Marchant is opportunistic, and with his pace reminds scouts of a young Theo Fleury. However, he has a long way to go to match Fleury's scoring touch. He will never be a 50-goal, 100-point scorer like Fleury.

Marchant is smart, sees the ice well and is a solid playmaker as well as shooter. He is no puck hog. He is an excellent penalty killer and a shorthanded threat because of his speed.

THE PHYSICAL GAME

His teammates have nicknamed him "Mighty Mouse," and Marchant is fearless in the face of bigger, supposedly tougher, opposition. Even after his concussion, Marchant hurled his body at larger foes, such as Dallas defenseman Derian Hatcher. He is really irritating to play against, because a big lug like Hatcher looks foolish trying to chase down and swat a little bitty guy like Marchant.

Marchant is average size but his grit makes him look bigger. He sacrifices his body, but, as with scrappy Jeremy Roenick, you wonder how long his body will last under the stress he puts it through. He is well-conditioned and can handle a lot of ice time. The mental toughness is there, too. He will take a hit to make a play, but has to get smarter about picking his spots in order to survive. Edmonton is a very mobile team and Marchant's lack of size might not be as much of a detriment as it could be on other teams.

THE INTANGIBLES

The problem for Marchant is finding a role on the Oilers. He spent most of last season as a fourth-line centre, but because of the Oilers' depth the position was moved to left wing, which freed him from defensive responsibilties and may be his future. He doesn't have the physical ability to match up with the league's better power centres.

PROJECTION

Marchant creates a lot of energy and excitement with his speed, but not as many points as might be expected from that quickness. He could become a consistent 20-goal scorer.

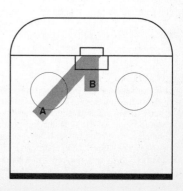

BRYAN MARCHMENT

Yrs. of NHL service: 7
Born: Toronto, Ont.; May 1, 1969
Position: left defense
Height: 6-1
Weight: 205
Uniform no.: 24
Shoots: left

Career statistics:

GP	G	A	TP	PIM
417	23	73	96	1286

1993-94 statistics:

GP	G	A	TP	+/-	PIM	PP	SH	GW	GT	S	PCT
55	4	11	15	-14	166	0	1	1	0	92	4.3

1994-95 statistics:

GP	G	A	TP	+/-	PIM	PP	SH	GW	GT	S	PCT
40	1	5	6	-11	184	0	0	0	0	57	1.8

1995-96 statistics:

GP	G	A	TP	+/-	PIM	PP	SH	GW	GT	S	PCT
78	3	15	18	-7	202	0	0	0	0	96	3.1

1996-97 statistics:

GP	G	A	TP	+/-	PIM	PP	SH	GW	GT	S	PCT
71	3	13	16	+13	132	1	0	0	0	89	3.4

LAST SEASON

Led team in plus-minus. Second on team in penalty minutes. Missed 10 games with rib injuries, including cracked ribs. Missed one game with flu.

THE FINESSE GAME

Because of Marchment's reputation as a ferocious hitter, his skills are often overlooked, but they are impressive for a big man. He loves to play, and he loves to get involved from the very first shift. He's never happier than when there's some blood on his jersey, even if it's his own.

Over the past few seasons, Marchment has started making better decisions with and without the puck. He is more aware of when it's appropriate to pinch and when to back off, but he is still overeager. He lacks the skating ability to cover up for some of his mental errors, though he is competent enough to join in on rushes. He has an underrated shot and can drill a one-timer or snap a quick shot on net. He is not much of a passer, since he doesn't sense when to feather or fire a puck to a receiver.

Marchment makes mistakes, but they are usually errors of aggression. Where he won't make mistakes is in his down-low coverage. The opposition's transition game is always a little slower when he's on the ice.

THE PHYSICAL GAME

Marchment has changed his hitting style. He used to be a dangerous, low hitter, with controversial hits that could damage knees and end careers. One scout describes Marchment as "the ultimate leg-breaker." Now Marchment stands up more. Instead of ending careers with knee injuries, he can end them with concussions. For the most part, they are clean blows, because Marchment keeps his shoulder down and his

feet on the ice.

The hits are still controversial, though, because Marchment doesn't care who is on the receiving end — a marquee name, a classy veteran or a young stud. He is a throwback to the days of the destructive open-ice hitters. This requires great strength along with good lateral mobility (or else the checker can be left spinning around at centre ice, watching the back of the puck carrier tearing up the ice on a breakaway). Marchment has become less of a headhunter and picks his spots better. The Oilers want him to be aggressive, but they also want him on the ice.

In keeping with the old-fashioned theme, Marchment is a good fighter. He also finishes every check, blocks shots and uses his upper body well. In one-on-one battles, however, he lacks drive from his legs, and he is not a balanced skater.

THE INTANGIBLES

Marchment's dedication to the game over the past few seasons has paid off in better conditioning and more intelligent play. He received one of the scariest injuries in the 1997 playoffs when he hit his head on an open door jamb and suffered a serious concussion, and that is the sole question mark to his season.

PROJECTION

If Marchment completely recovers from his injury, expect a repeat of last season, which may have been Marchment at his best.

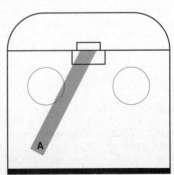

DANIEL MCGILLIS

Yrs. of NHL service: 1
Born: Hawkesbury, Ont.; July 1, 1972
Position: left defense
Height: 6-2
Weight: 220
Uniform no.: 23
Shoots: left

Career statistics:

GP	G	A	TP	PIM
73	6	16	22	52

1996-97 statistics:

GP	G	A	TP	+/-	PIM	PP	SH	GW	GT	S	PCT
73	6	16	22	+2	52	2	1	2	0	139	4.3

LAST SEASON
First NHL season.

THE FINESSE GAME
Playing alongside Kevin Lowe, as McGillis did for most of last season, is like being coached on every shift. McGillis learned by playing with the cool, smart veteran.

McGillis was an offensive defenseman in college (Northeastern University) and quickly became part of the Oilers' first power- play unit, where he switches to the left point.

He isn't a quick skater, but he is strong and agile enough for his size. He's drawn favourable comparisons to Derian Hatcher.

THE PHYSICAL GAME
McGillis steps up and challenges, and he's a big, big hitter. He's not afraid to go after the stars, either. He is powerfully built and explodes into his hits.

THE INTANGIBLES
Detroit was set to let McGillis go to L.A. for a late-round draft pick in March, 1996, when they instead made a deal with Edmonton for Kirk Maltby. Suffice it is to say that both teams were happy with the deal. Maltby became a role player on a Stanley Cup team and McGillis made the jump straight from college and, surprisingly, turned into a regular on the Oilers' defense corps.

PROJECTION
McGillis needs a little more seasoning as part of the third defensive pair, but with the loss of free agent Luke Richardson, he'll get more ice time, more responsibility and more points (30 to 40).

BORIS MIRONOV

Yrs. of NHL service: 5
Born: Moscow, Russia; March 21, 1972
Position: right defense
Height: 6-3
Weight: 220
Uniform no.: 2
Shoots: right

Career statistics:

GP	G	A	TP	PIM
241	22	81	103	336

1993-94 statistics:

GP	G	A	TP	+/-	PIM	PP	SH	GW	GT	S	PCT
79	7	24	31	-33	110	5	0	0	1	145	4.8

1994-95 statistics:

GP	G	A	TP	+/-	PIM	PP	SH	GW	GT	S	PCT
29	1	7	8	-9	40	0	0	0	0	48	2.1

1995-96 statistics:

GP	G	A	TP	+/-	PIM	PP	SH	GW	GT	S	PCT
78	8	24	32	-23	101	7	0	1	0	158	5.1

1996-97 statistics:

GP	G	A	TP	+/-	PIM	PP	SH	GW	GT	S	PCT
55	6	26	32	+2	85	2	0	1	0	147	4.1

LAST SEASON

Led team defensemen in scoring for second consecutive season. Missed 17 games with groin/abdominal strain.

THE FINESSE GAME

Mironov is basically a stay-at-home defenseman, but he has the talent to get involved offensively when he wants to. He has a huge slap shot and is a good puckhandler as well, so he can start a rush out of his own zone and finish things up at the other end. He needs a lot of time to get his shot away, and struggles against teams that pressure the points well on the penalty kill. He's not a genuine number one defenseman and certainly not a legit first-unit power-play point man, but he gets those roles by default in Edmonton.

Mironiv has improved his defensive play to the stage where he was part of the top defensive pairing (along with Luke Richardson) against other teams' top lines. He uses his size well to protect the puck, but getting it away from an attacker is another matter. Mironov tends to give up on his checks, and he doesn't always read plays coming at him well so he gets beaten wide by lesser skaters.

THE PHYSICAL GAME

Mironov is big and mobile. He isn't a thumper, but he's strong and he eliminates people. He has been compared to Viacheslav Fetisov, and though he will probably never be a checker who puts victims into the mezzanine, the Oilers' management would like to see him play more to his size.

THE INTANGIBLES

Mironov showed a big improvement in conditioning and attitude last season. In the playoffs, he was asked to handle 30 minutes (and more) of ice time and did so willingly. Last year was the first time we can recall seeing Mironov play with emotion since he came to the NHL, and it made every facet of his game better.

PROJECTION

If Mironov can sustain the momentum of last season, he could lead the Edmonton defense in scoring again with 40 to 50 points. But if the Oilers don't sign his partner, Richardson, as an unrestricted free agent, Mironov could take a step backwards.

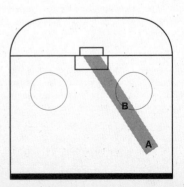

RYAN SMYTH

Yrs. of NHL service: 2
Born: Banff, Alta.; Feb. 21, 1976
Position: left wing
Height: 6-1
Weight: 195
Uniform no.: 94
Shoots: left

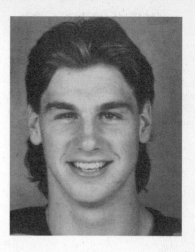

Career statistics:

GP	G	A	TP	PIM
133	41	31	72	104

1994-95 statistics:

GP	G	A	TP	+/-	PIM	PP	SH	GW	GT	S	PCT
3	0	0	0	-1	0	0	0	0	0	2	0.0

1995-96 statistics:

GP	G	A	TP	+/-	PIM	PP	SH	GW	GT	S	PCT
48	2	9	11	-10	28	1	0	0	0	65	3.1

1996-97 statistics:

GP	G	A	TP	+/-	PIM	PP	SH	GW	GT	S	PCT
82	39	22	61	-7	76	20	0	4	0	265	14.7

LAST SEASON

One of three Oilers to appear in all 82 games. Led team in goals, power-play goals and assists. Tied for NHL lead in power-play goals.

THE FINESSE GAME

One of the biggest surprises of the NHL season, Smyth in his sophomore season broke an Oilers power-play record once held by a guy named Gretzky. There is nothing remotely Gretzky-like about Smyth's game. If anything, he resembles Jeremy Roenick on his best, most reckless and headstrong nights. Smyth likes to win one-on-one battles along the boards and barrels at the net.

Smyth possesses little subtlety. Most of his goals come from the hash marks in, and probably half of them weren't the result of his shots, but tip-ins and body bounces. That's an art in itself, because Smyth has a knack for timing his moves to the net along with the shooter's release. He has a long reach for getting to rebounds and is strong on his stick for deflections.

Smyth is at a disadvantage when he is forced to shoot or make a play, because he doesn't have a quick release. When he carries the puck, he doesn't have much sense of what to do with it. Opponents may learn to "LeClair" him, forcing him to handle the puck instead of centres Jason Arnott or Doug Weight (just as Detroit made Philadelphia's John LeClair carry the puck in the Stanley Cup finals instead of Eric Lindros).

Smyth's skating is adequate. He has a fluid stride, but isn't a powerful skater. He's a glider, a hovercraft, but minus much quickness. He's an acceptable situation player, though, and coach Ron Low doesn't hesitate to use him in pressure spots.

THE PHYSICAL GAME

Smyth isn't built like a power forward, but he sure tries to play like one. He is a pesky net-crasher and can be an irritating presence. He doesn't throw bombs, but is a willing thrasher along the boards and gets good leg drive for solid hits. He's not a fighter, yet he won't back down.

THE INTANGIBLES

Smyth was able to surprise a lot of people last season (including us), but the second time around the league is always tougher. Smyth's stellar playoff performance is a good sign.

PROJECTION

Expect Smyth's power-play and goal totals to drop slightly. It's rare for a player of Smyth's inexperience to be consistent this early in his career, but his work ethic is sound and a 30-goal season is likely.

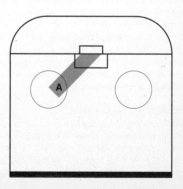

DOUG WEIGHT

Yrs. of NHL service: 6
Born: Warren, Mich.; Jan. 21, 1971
Position: centre
Height: 5-11
Weight: 191
Uniform no.: 39
Shoots: left

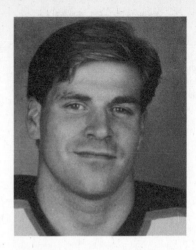

Career statistics:

GP	G	A	TP	PIM
425	102	267	378	379

1993-94 statistics:

GP	G	A	TP	+/-	PIM	PP	SH	GW	GT	S	PCT
84	24	50	74	-22	47	4	1	1	0	188	12.8

1994-95 statistics:

GP	G	A	TP	+/-	PIM	PP	SH	GW	GT	S	PCT
48	7	33	40	-17	69	1	0	1	0	104	6.7

1995-96 statistics:

GP	G	A	TP	+/-	PIM	PP	SH	GW	GT	S	PCT
82	25	70	104	-19	95	9	0	2	1	204	12.3

1996-97 statistics:

GP	G	A	TP	+/-	PIM	PP	SH	GW	GT	S	PCT
80	21	61	82	+1	80	4	0	2	0	235	8.9

LAST SEASON

Led NHL in power-play assists (35). Led team in assists and points, both for fourth consecutive season. Missed two games with ankle injury, ending consecutive games-played streak at 314.

THE FINESSE GAME

Playmaking is Weight's strong suit. He has good vision and passes well to either side. His hands are good. When he utilizes his shot he has quick and accurate wrist and snap shots. He handles the puck well in traffic, is strong on the puck and creates a lot of scoring chances. Weight is an outstanding one-on-one player, but doesn't have to challenge all the time. He will trail the play down the right wing (his preferred side) and jump into the attack late.

Weight won't win many foot races, but he keeps his legs pumping and he often surprises people on the rush who think they had him contained, only to see him push his way past. He frequently draws penalties. He has decent quickness, good balance and a fair change of direction.

Weight has improved his defensive play slightly. He is an offensive Doug Risebrough. A late bloomer, he has succeeded on a weak (but improving) team in the role of a number one centre, although a number two role would probably suit him better.

THE PHYSICAL GAME

Weight is inconsistent in his physical play. He shows flashes of grittiness but doesn't bring it to the ice every night. He is built like a fire hydrant: on the night he's on, he hits with enthusiasm, finishing every check. He initiates and annoys. Weight played the last

10 Oilers playoff games with a separated shoulder, so don't doubt his toughness.

He's also a bit of a trash talker, yapping and playing with a great deal of spirit. He can be counted on to provide a spark to the darkest of nights.

Weight has worked on his strength and conditioning and can handle a lot of ice time. He is very strong on his skates and hard to knock off the puck.

THE INTANGIBLES

Weight is going into his contract year, which can work either as a carrot (the last time he was in this situation he produced 104 points) or create stress. The young Oilers will face greater expectations this season after going two rounds in the playoffs, and Weight will be expected to produce under a brighter spotlight.

PROJECTION

Weight's dropoff in points (22) from last season is a concern, since he had just begun to establish himself as a consistent scorer. Scoring was down throughout the league last season, which might have contributed to the decline, and Weight did miss training camp. Give him the benefit of the doubt and expect a 90-point season as his supporting cast continues to improve.

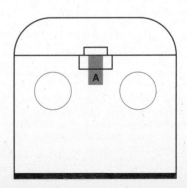

FLORIDA PANTHERS

Players' Statistics 1996-97

POS.	NO.	PLAYER	GP	G	A	PTS	+/-	PIM	PP	SH	GW	GT	S	PCT
R	26	RAY SHEPPARD	68	29	31	60	4	4	13		7		226	12.8
R	27	SCOTT MELLANBY	82	27	29	56	7	170	9	1	4		221	12.2
D	24	ROBERT SVEHLA	82	13	32	45	2	86	5		3		159	8.2
C	9	KIRK MULLER	76	21	19	40	-25	89	10	1	4		174	12.1
R	19	RADEK DVORAK	78	18	21	39	-2	30	2		1		139	12.9
C	44	ROB NIEDERMAYER	60	14	24	38	4	54	3		2		136	10.3
L	29	JOHAN GARPENLOV	53	11	25	36	10	47	1		1	2	83	13.3
L	11	BILL LINDSAY	81	11	23	34	1	120		1	3		168	6.5
L	10	DAVE LOWRY	77	15	14	29	2	51	2		2	1	96	15.6
C	28	MARTIN STRAKA	55	7	22	29	9	12	2		1		94	7.4
D	4	PER GUSTAFSSON	58	7	22	29	11	22	2		1		105	6.7
R	21	TOM FITZGERALD	71	10	14	24	7	64		2	1	1	135	7.4
D	5	GORD MURPHY	80	8	15	23	3	51	2				137	5.8
D	55	ED JOVANOVSKI	61	7	16	23	-1	172	3		1		80	8.8
C	20	BRIAN SKRUDLAND	51	5	13	18	4	48			2		57	8.8
R	12	JODY HULL	67	10	6	16	1	4	1		2	1	92	10.9
L	18	MIKE HOUGH	69	8	6	14	12	48			2		85	9.4
R	15	*DAVID NEMIROVSKY	39	7	7	14	1	32	1			1	53	13.2
D	2	TERRY CARKNER	70		14	14	-4	96					38	
D	7	RHETT WARRENER	62	4	9	13	20	88	1		1		58	6.9
D	3	PAUL LAUS	77		12	12	13	313					63	
C	22	*STEVE WASHBURN	18	3	6	9	2	4	1				21	14.3
C	23	CHRIS WELLS	47	2	6	8	5	42					29	6.9
G	34	J. VANBIESBROUCK	57		2	2	0	8						
G	30	MARK FITZPATRICK	30		1	1	0	13						
R	8	*CRAIG MARTIN	1				0	5					1	
D	25	GEOFF SMITH	3				1	2					2	
C	16	CRAIG FERGUSON	3				-1						5	
C	16	CRAIG FISHER	4				-2						2	

GP = games played; G = goals; A = assists; PTS = points; +/- = goals-for minus goals-against while player is on ice; PIM = penalties in minutes; PP = power-play goals; SH = shorthanded goals; GW = game-winning goals; GT = game-tying goals; S = no. of shots; PCT = percentage of goals to shots; * = rookie

RADEK DVORAK

Yrs. of NHL service: 2
Born: Tabor, Czech Republic; Mar. 9, 1977
Position: left wing
Height: 6-2
Weight: 187
Uniform no.: 19
Shoots: left

Career statistics:

GP	G	A	TP	PIM
153	31	35	66	50

1995-96 statistics:

GP	G	A	TP	+/-	PIM	PP	SH	GW	GT	S	PCT
77	13	14	27	+5	20	0	0	4	0	126	10.3

1996-97 statistics:

GP	G	A	TP	+/-	PIM	PP	SH	GW	GT	S	PCT
76	18	21	39	-2	30	2	0	1	0	139	12.9

LAST SEASON

Fifth on team in points. Games missed were coach's decision.

THE FINESSE GAME

Dvorak has exceptional speed. He might be one of the five fastest skaters in the Eastern Conference. He bursts down the left wing and will mix up the defenseman by sometimes driving wide and sometimes cutting through the middle. He takes the puck with him at a high tempo and creates off the rush.

Dvorak is a natural, gifted scorer who has to develop more confidence in his shot. With his speed, he should be getting over 200 shots a season, not 139. He is a heads-up passer but needs to be more of a finisher.

He needs to improve his defensive awareness and use his speed to get back. That's the only thing that is keeping him from being a complete player now.

THE PHYSICAL GAME

Dvorak could spend a little time in the weight room since he could stand to add about five pounds of muscle. He has very strong legs, which power his explosive skating, and he's not a bit intimidated by North American play. It does help that he plays on a team loaded with grinding forwards.

THE INTANGIBLES

Dvorak didn't have a goal in his first 10 games and was benched a few times in the first month of the season, but he quickly got his act together to become the team's top left wing in only his second NHL season. He is still getting acclimated to the NHL and should keep developing. He has a huge offensive upside.

PROJECTION

More consistency should result in 25 to 30 goals.

TOM FITZGERALD

Yrs. of NHL service: 9
Born: Melrose, Mass.; Aug. 28, 1968
Position: right wing/centre
Height: 6-1
Weight: 191
Uniform no.: 21
Shoots: right

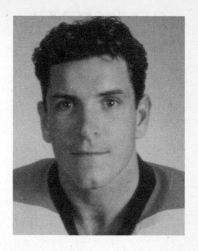

Career statistics:

GP	G	A	TP	PIM
489	69	106	165	324

1993-94 statistics:

GP	G	A	TP	+/-	PIM	PP	SH	GW	GT	S	PCT
83	18	14	32	-3	54	0	3	1	0	144	12.5

1994-95 statistics:

GP	G	A	TP	+/-	PIM	PP	SH	GW	GT	S	PCT
48	3	13	16	-3	31	0	0	0	0	78	3.8

1995-96 statistics:

GP	G	A	TP	+/-	PIM	PP	SH	GW	GT	S	PCT
82	13	21	34	-3	75	1	6	2	0	141	9.2

1996-97 statistics:

GP	G	A	TP	+/-	PIM	PP	SH	GW	GT	S	PCT
71	10	14	24	+7	64	0	2	1	1	135	7.4

LAST SEASON

Missed three games with abdominal strain. Missed five games with sprained left ankle. Missed one game with cut right eye. Missed one game with flu. Led team in shorthanded goals.

THE FINESSE GAME

Fitzgerald is a good penalty killer but has elevated his game another step above the average third-liner by becoming a reliable crunch-time player.

He is very quick and uses his outside speed to take the puck to the net. He is also less shy about using his shot, perhaps because he is working to get himself into better shooting situations, but he doesn't have the quickest release and the goalie can usually adjust in time despite Fitzgerald's speed. Fitzgerald isn't very creative. His chances come off earnest work around the net.

Fitzgerald played both centre and right wing last season, but the constant shifting doesn't faze him. There is a logjam at centre in Florida, so his versatility helps get him ice time. He is only average on draws. His hands aren't very quick and he seems to be at a disadvantage against bigger centres with the new rules regarding skate placement in the circles.

THE PHYSICAL GAME

Fitzgerald is gritty and strong. He has fairly good size and uses it along the boards and in front of the net. Although he's a pesky checker who gets people teed off, his own discipline keeps him from taking many cheap penalties. He gives his team some bang and pop and finishes his checks. He isn't huge, but he's among the best open-ice hitters in the league.

THE INTANGIBLES

Fitzgerald is one of Florida's most consistent forwards. He is developing into a top-notch checking forward who probably deserves some Selke Trophy recognition.

PROJECTION

Fitzgerald will contribute 10 to 15 goals in a checking role, but lacks the finishing touch to do much more.

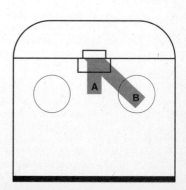

DAVE GAGNER

Yrs. of NHL service: 11
Born: Chatham, Ont.; Dec. 11, 1964
Position: centre
Height: 5-10
Weight: 180
Uniform no.: 51
Shoots: left

Career statistics:

GP	G	A	TP	PIM
799	292	351	673	898

1993-94 statistics:

GP	G	A	TP	+/-	PIM	PP	SH	GW	GT	S	PCT
76	32	29	61	+13	83	10	0	6	1	213	15.0

1994-95 statistics:

GP	G	A	TP	+/-	PIM	PP	SH	GW	GT	S	PCT
48	14	28	42	+2	42	7	0	2	1	138	10.1

1995-96 statistics:

GP	G	A	TP	+/-	PIM	PP	SH	GW	GT	S	PCT
73	21	28	49	-19	103	7	0	3	0	215	9.8

1996-97 statistics:

GP	G	A	TP	+/-	PIM	PP	SH	GW	GT	S	PCT
82	27	33	60	+2	48	9	0	4	1	228	11.8

LAST SEASON

Signed as free agent, July 4, 1997. Led Flames in plus-minus (only plus player among regulars). Second on Flames in goals, assists and points. Tied for second on Flames in power-play goals and game-winning goals. One of three Flames to appear in all 82 games.

THE FINESSE GAME

Gagner can score from just about anywhere except way out by the blueline. He can score off the rush or set up other players. He will pick up garbage goals, scoop up clean ones, finish off an outnumbered attack, or score off a drive down the wing with just his shot. He doesn't overpower goalies with his shot but he has a quick and cunning release. Defensemen will sometimes back off him on a rush because he does have some moves to slip past them. On the power play he can work down low, though he works better coming off the half-wall.

Gagner's speed isn't as noticeable as his quickness. In a 20-foot radius he's pretty quick, and he can throw in several dekes low as he drives to the net.

He is not a good defensive player. He is only average on face-offs.

THE PHYSICAL GAME

Gagner plays a tenacious, in-your-face offensive style. For a smaller player he is pretty resilient. Even after suffering two concussions in 1995-96, he still plays gung-ho. He stays in the traffic and doesn't get bounced out too easily. He can get overmatched one-on-one, but he tries to avoid battles where he can't use his quickness. His hard work is an inspiration to his teammates.

THE INTANGIBLES

Calgary gambled and lost by not trading Gagner to a contending team before the playoff stretch drive, and ended up losing him for nothing. He's not a number one centre but he's a useful support player.

PROJECTION

Gagner will find a niche in Florida as a number three centre behind Rob Niedermayer and Kirk Muller. He should improve on his 60 points.

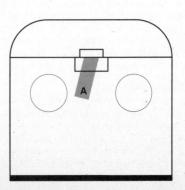

JOHAN GARPENLOV

Yrs. of NHL service: 7
Born: Stockholm, Sweden; Mar. 21, 1968
Position: left wing
Height: 5-11
Weight: 184
Uniform no.: 29
Shoots: left

Career statistics:

GP	G	A	TP	PIM
433	116	171	273	195

1993-94 statistics:

GP	G	A	TP	+/-	PIM	PP	SH	GW	GT	S	PCT
80	18	35	53	+9	28	7	0	3	0	125	14.4

1994-95 statistics:

GP	G	A	TP	+/-	PIM	PP	SH	GW	GT	S	PCT
40	4	10	14	+1	2	0	0	0	0	44	9.1

1995-96 statistics:

GP	G	A	TP	+/-	PIM	PP	SH	GW	GT	S	PCT
82	23	28	51	-10	36	8	0	7	1	130	17.7

1996-97 statistics:

GP	G	A	TP	+/-	PIM	PP	SH	GW	GT	S	PCT
53	11	25	36	+10	47	1	0	1	2	83	13.3

LAST SEASON

Missed 13 games with left knee sprain. Missed 16 games with right knee sprain.

THE FINESSE GAME

Like his linemate Rob Niedermayer, Garpenlov is a strong skater whose season was disrupted by injuries to the area where a skater is most vulnerable: his knee. In Garpenlov's case, it was both knees.

A strong skater with good balance, Garpenlov carries the puck through checks. He has a hard wrist shot from the off-wing and shoots well in stride, but he doesn't shoot often enough. His quickness gets him into high-quality scoring areas but he then looks to make a pass. He's a better playmaker than finisher. A solid forechecker, he creates turnovers and then looks to do something intelligent with the puck.

The story is different on the power play, perhaps because the open ice gives him more time and confidence. He likes to work low and use his one-timer from the left circle. If he were as eager to shoot in five-on-five situations, he could elevate his game another level. Garpenlov is one of the most creative Panthers.

THE PHYSICAL GAME

Garpenlov is not physical. His forechecking pressure comes not from physical contact but from his skating ability, which gets him in on top of a player to force a pass he can intercept.

THE INTANGIBLES

Garpenlov is not an assertive forward and doesn't have elite skills, so there are too many nights when you barely notice him in the lineup. He's the best the Panthers have on the left side, however.

PROJECTION

Garpenlov remains shot-shy, and we doubt he'll ever net more than 25 goals in a season unless he gets a little more selfish.

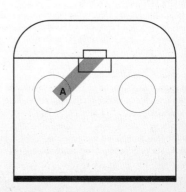

JODY HULL

Yrs. of NHL service: 9
Born: Cambridge, Ont.; Feb. 2, 1969
Position: right wing
Height: 6-2
Weight: 195
Uniform no.: 12
Shoots: right

Career statistics:

GP	G	A	TP	PIM
431	84	93	177	94

1993-94 statistics:

GP	G	A	TP	+/-	PIM	PP	SH	GW	GT	S	PCT
69	13	13	26	+6	8	0	1	5	1	100	13.0

1994-95 statistics:

GP	G	A	TP	+/-	PIM	PP	SH	GW	GT	S	PCT
46	11	8	19	-1	8	0	0	4	0	63	17.5

1995-96 statistics:

GP	G	A	TP	+/-	PIM	PP	SH	GW	GT	S	PCT
78	20	17	37	+5	25	2	0	3	1	120	16.7

1996-97 statistics:

GP	G	A	TP	+/-	PIM	PP	SH	GW	GT	S	PCT
67	10	6	16	+1	4	0	1	2	1	92	10.9

PROJECTION

Hull could probably last for another dozen NHL seasons doing what he does — scoring 10 to 15 goals — without any particular distinction, since he doesn't hurt a team.

LAST SEASON

Games missed were healthy scratches.

THE FINESSE GAME

Hull has some fine natural skills. His powerful skating stride is almost syrupy smooth. He has some range and can skate with people, slowing them down and picking off passes.

His snap shot is heavy and effective, though his release isn't the fastest. There are times when it seems you can hear him thinking. He will cut into the middle at the blueline, then outguess himself on the proper play. Even if he has skating room and could take the puck closer to the net, he does not penetrate, drive the defense and pull the goalie out to him.

Hull kills penalties well and will play positionally in a checking role. He has been given a lot more responsibility with Florida and has responded.

THE PHYSICAL GAME

Hull is a polite player. He has no mean streak to speak of. He can be goaded into an occasional slash, just to prove there's a pulse, but his lack of an aggressive game is what usually keeps him on the bubble.

THE INTANGIBLES

Hull has a lot of ability he appears not to use. He does not show much expression on the ice and tends to fade into the background. He plays a lot of quiet games, especially in the playoffs. He does more defensive than offensive things, but there are too many others of his ilk to make him anything more than a marginal player.

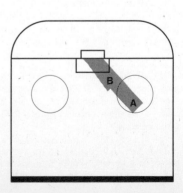

ED JOVANOVSKI

Yrs. of NHL service: 2
Born: Windsor, Ont.; June 26, 1976
Position: left defense
Height: 6-2
Weight: 205
Uniform no.: 55
Shoots: left

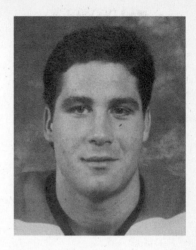

Career statistics:

GP	G	A	TP	PIM
131	17	27	44	309

1995-96 statistics:

GP	G	A	TP	+/-	PIM	PP	SH	GW	GT	S	PCT
70	10	11	21	-3	137	2	0	2	0	116	8.6

1996-97 statistics:

GP	G	A	TP	+/-	PIM	PP	SH	GW	GT	S	PCT
61	7	16	23	-1	172	3	0	1	0	80	8.8

LAST SEASON

Second NHL season. Second on team in penalty minutes. Missed 16 games with right knee sprain.

THE FINESSE GAME

Jovanovski started playing hockey later than most NHLers, and his skating, which has improved dramatically, may still be improved a notch. He already streaks through the neutral zone like a freight train. He sure isn't pretty, but he's powerful.

He is strong on his feet with a powerful, quick stride. He has more quickness than most big men, perhaps because of early soccer training, and he can use his feet to move the puck if his stick is tied up. His powerful hitting is made more wicked by the fact that he gets so much speed and leg drive. Jovanovski can make plays, too. He gets a little time because his speed forces the opposition to back off, and he has a nice passing touch.

Jovanovski can also score, but he does not possess a great decision-making process yet and still makes some bad pinches. He has an excellent point shot and good vision of the ice for passing. He may develop along Scott Stevens/Ray Bourque lines and become a defenseman who can dominate in all zones. All of his skills are quite raw and are still catching up to his body.

THE PHYSICAL GAME

If he isn't yet the best open-ice hitter in the NHL — and many scouts and GMs affirm that he is — then Jovanovski will be wearing that mantle soon. He hits to hurt. Because of his size and agility, he is able to catch people right where he wants them. They aren't dirty hits, but they are real old-time hockey throwbacks, administered by a modern-sized defenseman.

The problem is that instead of neutralizing the Brendan Shanahans and the Mark Messiers, Jovanovski is diverted from his game by the Trent Klatts and the Bill Bergs. He is so easy to distract that

it must be at the top of every team's game plan against the Panthers. He must play smarter.

THE INTANGIBLES

Too much happened too fast for Jovanovski in his rookie year (and don't blame the media; coach Doug McLean talked him up as much as anyone). Both the Panthers and the 21-year-old sophomore defenseman were due for some bumps last season after his rookie accolades and the team's four-straight disappearance from the 1996 Stanley Cup finals.

How Jovanovski will deal with it is the question.

PROJECTION

There are a lot of scouts who feel Jovanovski was one of the most overrated players in the NHL last season. We saw it as a totally expected dip in his progession chart, but he needs to reverse the trend this season. Forget about the Norris Trophy talk and the points. He can score 30 to 40 points just by playing solid two-way defense and not taking so many risks.

PAUL LAUS

Yrs. of NHL service: 4
Born: Beamsville, Ont.; Sept. 26, 1970
Position: right defense
Height: 6-1
Weight: 216
Uniform no.: 3
Shoots: right

Career statistics:

GP	G	A	TP	PIM
231	5	25	30	796

1993-94 statistics:

GP	G	A	TP	+/-	PIM	PP	SH	GW	GT	S	PCT
39	2	0	2	+9	109	0	0	1	9	15	13.3

1994-95 statistics:

GP	G	A	TP	+/-	PIM	PP	SH	GW	GT	S	PCT
37	0	7	7	+12	138	0	0	0	0	18	0.0

1995-96 statistics:

GP	G	A	TP	+/-	PIM	PP	SH	GW	GT	S	PCT
78	3	6	9	-2	236	0	0	0	0	45	6.7

1996-97 statistics:

GP	G	A	TP	+/-	PIM	PP	SH	GW	GT	S	PCT
77	0	12	12	+13	313	0	0	0	0	63	0.0

LAST SEASON

Led NHL in fighting majors (39). Led team in penalty minutes for third consecutive season. Third in NHL in penalty minutes. Missed two games with bruised left ankle. Missed one game with sprained left ankle. Missed two games with bruised left hand.

THE FINESSE GAME

People don't like to play against a club that has Laus on its side. He is a legitimate tough guy, but one who has worked at the other aspects of his game to become a more useful player.

Laus has borderline NHL skating speed. He is powerful and well-balanced for battles along the boards and in the corners. He seems to know his limitations and doesn't try to overextend himself. He needs to be paired with a mobile partner, since he doesn't cover a lot of ice. Of course, he also gets a lot of room since only the brave venture into his territory, and that buys him some time.

Laus uses his size and strength effectively at all times. He has to control both his temper and his playing style. His success in the NHL will come from him playing his position and not running around head-hunting. He doesn't have much offensive instinct, but gets some room to take shots from the point because no one wants to come near him.

THE PHYSICAL GAME

Laus hits. Anyone. At any opportunity. Since his skating isn't great, he can't catch people in open ice, but he's murder along the boards, in the corners and in front of the net. He hits to hurt. He's big, but not scary-sized like a lot of today's NHL defensemen. He

is, however, powerful and mean, and he stands up for his teammates.

THE INTANGIBLES

Laus has worked hard to become more than a mere goon, and the work has paid off. He is a perfectly serviceable fifth or sixth defenseman who has made himself a valuable member of the team. He makes his teammates braver, and if his skills keep improving as they have over the past three seasons, that will keep him on the ice. Florida rolls over its defense pairs, so Laus gets a lot of ice instead of sitting on the bench and waiting for the odd shift.

PROJECTION

If you're in a goon pool, make Laus a top choice.

BILL LINDSAY

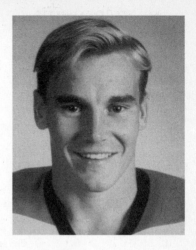

Yrs. of NHL service: 5
Born: Big Fork, Mont.; May 17, 1971
Position: left wing
Height: 5-11
Weight: 190
Uniform no.: 11
Shoots: left

Career statistics:

GP	G	A	TP	PIM
353	45	73	118	350

1993-94 statistics:

GP	G	A	TP	+/-	PIM	PP	SH	GW	GT	S	PCT
84	6	6	12	-2	97	0	0	0	0	90	6.7

1994-95 statistics:

GP	G	A	TP	+/-	PIM	PP	SH	GW	GT	S	PCT
48	10	9	19	+1	46	0	1	0	0	63	15.9

1995-96 statistics:

GP	G	A	TP	+/-	PIM	PP	SH	GW	GT	S	PCT
73	12	22	34	+13	57	0	3	2	0	118	10.2

1996-97 statistics:

GP	G	A	TP	+/-	PIM	PP	SH	GW	GT	S	PCT
81	11	23	34	+1	120	0	1	3	0	168	6.5

LAST SEASON

Only game missed was a healthy scratch.

THE FINESSE GAME

Lindsay continues to add more offensive touches to a predominantly defensive game. He has a big shot but an average release. His first instinct is to try to beat the goalie between the pads. A long reach enables him to score many of his goals from his work in front of the net. He has decent hands, but it's his second and third effort that make the difference.

Lindsay is a support player who, teamed with more offensive linemates, acts as a safety valve. He is not particularly creative, but he will follow the play to the net.

His skating speed and agility are average, but Lindsay is balanced and strong on his skates. He has good size, which he uses in a checking role. He sometimes gets a bit lazy and doesn't keep his feet moving. When he doesn't take that extra step, he takes a bad hooking or tripping penalty. There is no subtlety to his forechecking. He skates in a straight line with limited agility. Lindsay is the Panthers' best penalty-killing forward.

THE PHYSICAL GAME

Lindsay uses his body effectively but doesn't thrash people. He is sturdy and sometimes gets it into his head to stir things up, to try and give his team a bit of a spark. He plays much bigger than his size. He takes a hit to make a play, but more often initiates the contact.

THE INTANGIBLES

Lindsay's skill level makes him a borderline third-line winger, but since Florida rolls over four lines under coach Doug MacLean, he gets his fair share of ice time.

PROJECTION

Lindsay would be on the bubble if it weren't for his intensity. Scoring 20 goals would be a real stretch for him.

DAVE LOWRY

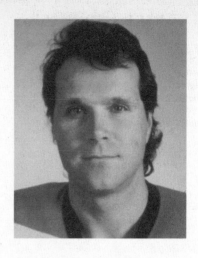

Yrs. of NHL service: 12
Born: Sudbury, Ont.; Feb. 14, 1965
Position: left wing
Height: 6-1
Weight: 200
Uniform no.: 10
Shoots: left

Career statistics:

GP	G	A	TP	PIM
741	122	132	254	965

1993-94 statistics:

GP	G	A	TP	+/-	PIM	PP	SH	GW	GT	S	PCT
80	15	22	37	-4	64	3	0	3	1	122	12.3

1994-95 statistics:

GP	G	A	TP	+/-	PIM	PP	SH	GW	GT	S	PCT
45	10	10	20	-3	25	2	0	3	0	70	14.3

1995-96 statistics:

GP	G	A	TP	+/-	PIM	PP	SH	GW	GT	S	PCT
63	10	14	24	-2	36	0	0	1	0	83	12.0

1996-97 statistics:

GP	G	A	TP	+/-	PIM	PP	SH	GW	GT	S	PCT
77	15	14	29	+2	51	2	0	2	1	96	15.6

LAST SEASON

Led team in shooting percentage. Missed three games with sprained left knee.

THE FINESSE GAME

Lowry is not a creative playmaker, and is most content in the role of an up-and-down winger. No one ever expected him to match the his phenomenal 1996 play-offs (10 goals in 22 games — the same number of goals he had scored in 63 games in the regular season), and this year Lowry was back to his customary role as a third-line checking winger.

Lowry's goals come from hard work. He pays the price in front of the net setting screens and scrapping for rebounds. He is primarily a strong forechecker and defensive forward, but doesn't limit himself and will adapt to whatever role is given him. He is opportunistic.

Skating stands out among Lowry's skills. He is fast and powerful, though he lacks subtlety. All he knows is straight ahead, whether it's to smack into an opponent or to crash the net for a scoring chance. He does little in the way of shooting from anywhere other than dead in front of the net.

THE PHYSICAL GAME

Lowry has decent size, and when he combines it with his speed he becomes an effective hitter. He will harry the puck carrier on a forechecking mission and use his stick and body to slow down a skater. He is very gritty and his effort is nonstop. He has an abrasive side.

THE INTANGIBLES

There isn't much more to Lowry's game than honest effort, but most nights that's enough.

PROJECTION

Lowry is a third-line role player who gives his team 15 to 20 goals a season.

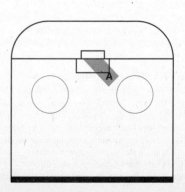

SCOTT MELLANBY

Yrs. of NHL service: 11
Born: Montreal, Que,; June 11, 1966
Position: right wing
Height: 6-1
Weight: 199
Uniform no.: 27
Shoots: right

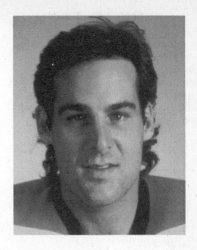

Career statistics:

GP	G	A	TP	PIM
793	223	267	490	1607

1993-94 statistics:

GP	G	A	TP	+/-	PIM	PP	SH	GW	GT	S	PCT
80	30	30	60	0	149	17	0	4	1	204	14.7

1994-95 statistics:

GP	G	A	TP	+/-	PIM	PP	SH	GW	GT	S	PCT
48	13	12	25	-16	90	4	0	5	0	130	10.0

1995-96 statistics:

GP	G	A	TP	+/-	PIM	PP	SH	GW	GT	S	PCT
79	32	38	70	+4	160	19	0	3	1	225	14.2

1996-97 statistics:

GP	G	A	TP	+/-	PIM	PP	SH	GW	GT	S	PCT
82	27	29	56	+7	170	9	1	4	0	221	12.2

LAST SEASON

One of two Panthers to appear in all 82 games. Second on team in goals, points, game-winning goals and shots. Third on team in assists and power-play goals.

THE FINESSE GAME

Not having a great deal of speed or agility, Mellanby generates most of his effectiveness in tight spaces, where he can use his size. He was the Panthers' main target on the first power-play unit, since Florida leans to the right when working the power play and looks to set Mellanby up below the hash marks. He works for screens and tips. He doesn't have many moves but he can capitalize on a loose puck. Goals don't come naturally to him, but he is determined and pays the price in front of the net.

Mellanby has developed a quicker release and more confidence in his shot, and was rewarded with a promotion to the number one line with Rob Niedermayer. Mellanby suffered when Niedermayer was out of the lineup, scoring only seven goals in the 22 games Niedermayer missed due to injury.

Mellanby is now very responsible defensively and can kill penalties, though he is not much of a short-handed threat. He lacks the speed and scoring instincts to convert turnovers into dangerous chances.

THE PHYSICAL GAME

Mellanby forechecks aggressively, using his body well to hit and force mistakes in the attacking zone. He participates in one-on-one battles in tight areas and tries to win his share. He is also willing to mix it up and takes penalties of aggression. Mellanby seldom misses an opportunity to rub his glove in an opponent's face.

He's very strong along the boards and uses his feet when battling for the puck.

THE INTANGIBLES

Mellanby's success is based on his work ethic. Any letup and the letdown will come in the scoring department. We wrongly anticipated a dropoff in his production last season. If Niedermayer hadn't been injured, Mellanby could have had a career year.

PROJECTION

A healthy Niedermayer is essential to Mellanby's game; he could score 30 goals if he maintains the effort he showed last season.

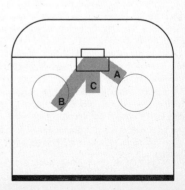

KIRK MULLER

Yrs. of NHL service: 13
Born: Kingston, Ont.; Feb. 8, 1966
Position: centre
Height: 6-0
Weight: 205
Uniform no.: 9
Shoots: left

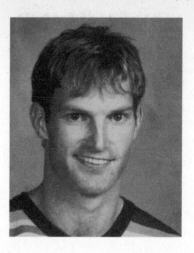

Career statistics:

GP	G	A	TP	PIM
962	326	521	847	1024

1993-94 statistics:

GP	G	A	TP	+/-	PIM	PP	SH	GW	GT	S	PCT
76	23	34	57	-1	96	9	2	3	0	168	13.7

1994-95 statistics:

GP	G	A	TP	+/-	PIM	PP	SH	GW	GT	S	PCT
45	11	16	27	-18	47	4	1	2	1	97	11.3

1995-96 statistics:

GP	G	A	TP	+/-	PIM	PP	SH	GW	GT	S	PCT
51	13	19	32	-13	57	7	0	1	0	102	12.7

1996-97 statistics:

GP	G	A	TP	+/-	PIM	PP	SH	GW	GT	S	PCT
76	21	19	40	-25	89	10	1	4	0	174	12.1

LAST SEASON

Acquired from Toronto for Jason Podollan, March 18, 1997. Worst plus-minus on team (was -23 in 66 games with Toronto; -2 in 10 games with Florida).

THE FINESSE GAME

The last two seasons haven't been kind to Muller. His reputation took a pounding from his badly handled Islanders tenure. Last year, he had to deal with a trade that took him away from home and his seriously ill father.

For most of his career, Muller has been extolled for his leadership. He is a gritty player who makes the most of his skills — which are above average, but well shy of world class — by exerting himself to the utmost.

Muller plays at his best with linemates who have keen enough hockey sense to pounce on the pucks he works free with his efforts along the wall. He does not have a clever passing touch. He is a sturdy player through traffic and has some speed, but he won't dazzle. He doesn't give up until the buzzer sounds, and he takes nothing for granted.

Muller is not an especially gifted playmaker or shooter. None of his plays will make highlight films: their ooh and ahh factor is low, but the result is in the net one way or another. It helps if he plays with at least one winger with a good burst of speed, but the Panthers haven't found him suitable partners.

Muller is defensively strong and can shut down the opposing teams' top centres. He can work both special teams.

THE PHYSICAL GAME

Muller blocks shots. He ties up players along the boards and uses his feet to kick the puck to a teammate. Ditto for his work on face-offs. Strong on his skates, he uses his skateblades almost as well as his stickblade.

THE INTANGIBLES

Can Muller be happy at last in Florida? He signed a new three-year deal after the trade, which is a good indication that he may have found a home after playing for four teams in four years.

PROJECTION

Muller's game has become slanted more and more to the defensive aspect; even though he is the number two centre in Florida behind Rob Niedermayer, anything over 40 points would be a bonus.

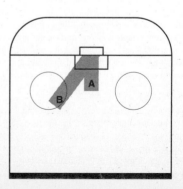

GORD MURPHY

Yrs. of NHL service: 9
Born: Willowdale, Ont.; Mar. 23, 1967
Position: right defense
Height: 6-2
Weight: 191
Uniform no.: 5
Shoots: right

Career statistics:

GP	G	A	TP	PIM
632	75	197	272	543

1993-94 statistics:

GP	G	A	TP	+/-	PIM	PP	SH	GW	GT	S	PCT
84	14	29	43	-11	71	9	0	2	3	172	8.1

1994-95 statistics:

GP	G	A	TP	+/-	PIM	PP	SH	GW	GT	S	PCT
46	6	16	22	-14	24	5	0	0	0	94	6.4

1995-96 statistics:

GP	G	A	TP	+/-	PIM	PP	SH	GW	GT	S	PCT
70	8	22	30	+5	30	4	0	0	0	125	6.4

1996-97 statistics:

GP	G	A	TP	+/-	PIM	PP	SH	GW	GT	S	PCT
80	8	15	23	+3	51	2	0	0	0	137	5.8

LAST SEASON

Two games missed were coach's decision.

THE FINESSE GAME

Robert Svehla's development took much of the offensive responsibility away from Murphy, who has concentrated on becoming a better defensive player. Murphy uses his finesse skills in a two-way role. He is a strong and agile skater, and he executes tight turns and accelerates in a stride or two. He moves the puck well and then joins the play eagerly.

Murphy also carries the puck well, though he gets into trouble when he overhandles in his own zone. He usually makes a safe pass, holding on until he is just about decked and then making a nice play. He plays the point on the power play, and uses a pull- and-drag shot, rather than a big slapper, giving him a very quick release. He is patient with the puck along the blueline, sliding laterally until he spots the open lane.

Murphy plays a smart positional game and makes intelligent defensive reads. He doesn't get suckered into pulling out of his position. He was teamed with the inexperienced Rhett Warrener most of the season and was a steady, reliable partner for the younger player.

THE PHYSICAL GAME

Murphy uses his finesse skills to defend. His long reach makes him an effective poke-checker, and he would rather wrap his arms around an attacker than move him out of the crease with a solid hit. He's more of a pusher than a hitter. He is responsible defensively and is used to killing penalties. He logs a lot of ice time and holds up well under the grind.

THE INTANGIBLES

After Ed Jovanovski took a not-unexpected step backwards in his sophomore season, Murphy was again asked to shoulder a role above his ability. Murphy is not, and will never be, a tough customer, but he has improved his positional play and can step up and provide some offensive spark. He is best with a physical, stay-at-home partner, but he can also be paired with a mobile defenseman and stay back for the defensive work himself.

PROJECTION

Murphy benefits from playing in the disciplined Florida system, and defense is his primary responsibility. He will be one of the Panthers' top four defensemen again this season.

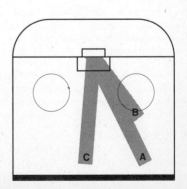

ROB NIEDERMAYER

Yrs. of NHL service: 4
Born: Cassiar, B.C.; Dec. 28, 1974
Position: centre
Height: 6-2
Weight: 201
Uniform no.: 44
Shoots: left

Career statistics:

GP	G	A	TP	PIM
410	53	82	135	248

1993-94 statistics:

GP	G	A	TP	+/-	PIM	PP	SH	GW	GT	S	PCT
65	9	17	26	-11	51	3	0	2	0	67	13.4

1994-95 statistics:

GP	G	A	TP	+/-	PIM	PP	SH	GW	GT	S	PCT
48	4	6	10	-13	36	1	0	0	0	58	6.9

1995-96 statistics:

GP	G	A	TP	+/-	PIM	PP	SH	GW	GT	S	PCT
82	26	35	61	+1	107	11	0	6	0	155	16.8

1996-97 statistics:

GP	G	A	TP	+/-	PIM	PP	SH	GW	GT	S	PCT
60	14	24	38	+4	54	3	0	2	0	136	10.3

LAST SEASON

Missed 17 games with right knee sprain. Missed two games with left groin strain. Missed three games with bruised wrist.

THE FINESSE GAME

Niedermayer's knee injury, suffered early in the season (November 22), affected most of his year. His skating is the best part of his game, and even through the second half of the season the fourth-year centre wasn't at top speed. As frequently happens, the knee injury resulted in a secondary injury, a groin strain, in March.

Niedermayer is slowly growing into the role of a number one centre in Florida, but may have another season or two to go before he really hits his stride. He's an excellent skater. He is big and strong and has the speed to stay with some of the league's best power centres. He drives to the net and is learning to play that way on a nightly basis.

Niedermayer is a strong passer and an unselfish player, probably too unselfish. He controls the puck well at tempo and can beat a defender one-on-one. He has started to finish better and play with much more authority.

Niedermayer is a mainstay on Florida's power play. One of his flaws is a slight hesitation in his shot release, but he is developing more confidence in his shot.

THE PHYSICAL GAME

Although not overly physical, Niedermayer has good size and is still growing. He has a bit of a temper, but he's an intelligent player and doesn't hurt his team by taking bad penalties. His attitude is outstanding. He is a coachable kid and a good team man. He works hard along the boards and in the corners.

THE INTANGIBLES

Niedermayer needs to develop a more well-rounded game, which should come with experience. He finished strong with four goals in his last six games, but along with his teammates had a disappointing playoffs.

PROJECTION

Niedermayer started to fulfill his promise last season, and should provide a consistent 25 goals.

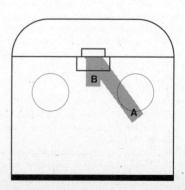

RAY SHEPPARD

Yrs. of NHL service: 10
Born: Pembroke, Ont.; May 27, 1966
Position: right wing
Height: 6-1
Weight: 195
Uniform no.: 26
Shoots: right

Career statistics:

GP	G	A	TP	PIM
625	304	238	542	169

1993-94 statistics:

GP	G	A	TP	+/-	PIM	PP	SH	GW	GT	S	PCT
82	52	41	93	+13	26	19	0	5	0	260	20.0

1994-95 statistics:

GP	G	A	TP	+/-	PIM	PP	SH	GW	GT	S	PCT
43	30	10	40	+11	17	11	0	5	1	125	24.0

1995-96 statistics:

GP	G	A	TP	+/-	PIM	PP	SH	GW	GT	S	PCT
70	37	23	60	-19	16	14	0	7	0	231	16.0

1996-97 statistics:

GP	G	A	TP	+/-	PIM	PP	SH	GW	GT	S	PCT
68	29	31	60	+4	4	13	0	7	0	226	12.8

LAST SEASON

Led team in goals and shots for second consecutive season. Led team in points, power-play goals and game-winning goals. Second on team in assists. Missed two games with sprained right shoulder. Missed 11 games with right knee sprain.

THE FINESSE GAME

There are times when Sheppard looks like a puck magnet. He is always eager to move to the puck and has good hockey sense and vision. Although he is a winger, he has a centre's view of the ice. He is also unselfish; he loves to shoot but will dish off if he spies a teammate with a better percentage shot. He has good hands with a quick release and doesn't waste time with a big backswing. He prefers efficiency and accuracy.

Sheppard has great hands, but is a liability everywhere on the ice except for a 10-foot radius around the net. He is not a great skater. He looks excruciatingly slow, but this is deceptive because he is almost always in a good scoring position. He doesn't turn quickly and doesn't have great balance, but he can curl out of the right circle on his backhand and get off a wrist or snap shot. He is also strong enough to ward off a defender with one hand and shovel a pass or push a shot towards the net with his other. He must play with a centre who will get him the puck.

Sheppard is at his best on the power play, where he moves into the open ice and converts passes. However, he is usually the last player back when play breaks back out of the offensive zone.

THE PHYSICAL GAME

Sheppard does not play a big game. He's an average-sized forward who plays below his size. He won't work along the boards but will go to the front of the net, so he has to play with one grinder to get him the puck and one quick forward to serve as the safety valve. Sheppard has improved his lower-body strength.

THE INTANGIBLES

Sheppard has a problem playing in pressure situations. He produced only two playoff goals last season after being benched in 1995 and 1996.

PROJECTION

Sheppards's days as a 40-goal scorer are long over; 30 goals will be a stretch this season. Florida doesn't play a very creative offensive game, though, so if Sheppard is traded to a team with a wide-open style his numbers will be bumped up a bit.

MARTIN STRAKA

Yrs. of NHL service: 5
Born: Plzen, Czechoslovakia; Sept. 3, 1972
Position: centre
Height: 5-10
Weight: 178
Uniform no.: 28
Shoots: left

Career statistics:

GP	G	A	TP	PIM
295	58	112	170	122

1993-94 statistics:

GP	G	A	TP	+/-	PIM	PP	SH	GW	GT	S	PCT
84	30	34	64	+24	24	2	0	6	1	130	23.1

1994-95 statistics:

GP	G	A	TP	+/-	PIM	PP	SH	GW	GT	S	PCT
37	5	13	18	-1	16	0	0	0	0	49	10.2

1995-96 statistics:

GP	G	A	TP	+/-	PIM	PP	SH	GW	GT	S	PCT
77	13	30	43	-19	41	6	0	1	0	98	13.3

1996-97 statistics:

GP	G	A	TP	+/-	PIM	PP	SH	GW	GT	S	PCT
55	7	22	29	+9	12	2	0	1	0	94	7.4

LAST SEASON

Missed 13 games with recurring groin injuries.

THE FINESSE GAME

Straka is always highly productive for a week or two, then vanishes. He shows second-line skills and fourth-line consistency. He scored seven of his 29 points in three straight games in December, then went nine games with only a single assist. You get the idea.

Straka's game is a major tease, because when he's on he can do a lot of things. He is a water bug with imagination. He makes clever passes that always land on the tape and give the recipient time to do something with the puck. He's more of a playmaker than a shooter and will have to learn to go to the net more to make his game less predictable. He draws people to him and creates open ice for his linemates.

Straka doesn't have the outside speed to burn defenders, but creates space for himself with his wheeling in tight spaces. He has good balance and is tough to knock off his feet even though he's not big.

Not a great defensive player, Straka is effective in five-on-five situations. He is an offensive threat every time he steps on the ice, but he doesn't bring much else.

THE PHYSICAL GAME

Straka has shown little inclination for the typical North American style of play. He is small and avoids corners and walls, and has to be teamed with more physical linemates to give him some room. He needs to learn to protect the puck better with his body and buy some time.

THE INTANGIBLES

Whether he plays on a bad team (Ottawa) or a good one (Florida), Straka is frustratingly inconsistent. He's worn four jerseys in the past three seasons, and it may not be long before the Panthers throw up their paws and move him, too, since he came up empty in the playoffs.

PROJECTION

Straka is a no-impact player who could score 40 of the quietest points in the NHL.

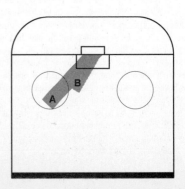

ROBERT SVEHLA

Yrs. of NHL service: 2
Born: Martin, Czech Republic; Jan. 2, 1969
Position: right defense
Height: 6-1
Weight: 190
Uniform no.: 24
Shoots: right

Career statistics:

GP	G	A	TP	PIM
168	22	82	104	180

1994-95 statistics:

GP	G	A	TP	+/-	PIM	PP	SH	GW	GT	S	PCT
5	1	1	2	+3	0	1	0	0	0	6	16.7

1995-96 statistics:

GP	G	A	TP	+/-	PIM	PP	SH	GW	GT	S	PCT
81	8	49	57	-3	94	7	0	0	0	146	5.5

1996-97 statistics:

GP	G	A	TP	+/-	PIM	PP	SH	GW	GT	S	PCT
82	13	32	45	+2	86	5	0	3	0	159	8.2

LAST SEASON

One of two Panthers to appear in all 82 games. Led team in assists for second consecutive season. Led team defensemen and third on team in points.

THE FINESSE GAME

Svehla reminds one hockey expert of Denis Potvin. We might be quick to dismiss that kind of grand statement, except that the expert in question happens to be Potvin himself. Svehla may not be destined for the Hall of Fame, but he is going to be an impact defenseman for a long time.

This Czech is among the best in the league at the lost art of the sweep-check. If he does lose control of the puck, and an attacker has a step or two on him on a breakaway, Svehla has the poise to dive and use his stick to knock the puck away without touching the man's skates.

Svehla is a terrific skater. No one, not even Jaromir Jagr, can beat Svehla wide, because he skates well backwards and laterally. He plays a quick transition. He is among the best NHL defensemen one-on-one in open ice. He pinches aggressively and intelligently. He makes high-risk plays, and is one of only two Florida players (with Johan Garpenlov) who has much of a creative clue, which makes him invaluable to the plodding Panthers.

Svehla works on the first power play, moving to the left point. He uses a long wrist shot from the point to make sure the puck will get through on net. When he kills penalties, he makes safe plays off the boards.

THE PHYSICAL GAME

Svehla does not avoid contact. He is not as strong or naturally aggressive as Potvin was, but he competes. He gets into the thick of things by battling along the wall and in the corners for the puck. He is not a huge

checker, but he pins his man and doesn't allow him back into the play. His defensive reads are impeccable.

Svehla is in peak condition and needs little recovery time between shifts, so he can handle a lot of ice time.

THE INTANGIBLES

Despite playing on a conservative team, Svehla finished among the top 13 defensemen in scoring. Last year we predicted a top 10 finish, which we (and he) missed by three points.

PROJECTION

Svehla's all-around game is improving, and his point totals may rise to 50 to 55 this season. He is one of the NHL's best-kept secrets.

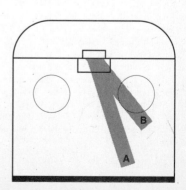

JOHN VANBIESBROUCK

Yrs. of NHL service: 13
Born: Detroit, Mich.; Sept. 4, 1963
Position: goaltender
Height: 5-8
Weight: 176
Uniform no.: 34
Catches: left

Career statistics:

GP	MIN	GA	SO	GAA	A	PIM
657	37432	1959	25	3.14	30	274

1993-94 statistics:

GP	MIN	GAA	W	L	T	SO	GA	S	SAPCT	PIM
57	3440	2.53	21	25	11	1	145	1912	.924	38

1994-95 statistics:

GP	MIN	GAA	W	L	T	SO	GA	S	SAPCT	PIM
37	2087	2.47	14	15	4	4	86	1000	.914	6

1995-96 statistics:

GP	MIN	GAA	W	L	T	SO	GA	S	SAPCT	PIM
57	3178	2.68	26	20	7	2	142	1473	.904	10

1996-97 statistics:

GP	MIN	GAA	W	L	T	SO	GA	S	SAPCT	PIM
57	3347	2.29	27	19	10	2	128	1582	.919	8

LAST SEASON

Eighth season with 20 or more wins. Fifth in NHL in goals-against average with career best. Tied for fifth in NHL in save percentage.

THE PHYSICAL GAME

There are few goalies who play a better positional game than Vanbiesbrouck. He doesn't make wild, diving saves, because he doesn't have to. He blends a strong technical game with good reflexes, anticipation and confidence. He isn't very big, so he plays his angles and squares himself to the shooter to take away as much of the net as possible. He makes himself look like a much bigger goalie. He is very aggressive, forcing the shooter to make the first move. Vanbiesbrouck doesn't beat himself often.

Vanbiesbrouck plays a butterfly-style that takes away a lot of low shots, and he has a quick glove hand, so most shooters try to go high stick-side on him, but that's a hard corner to pick. Vanbiesbrouck reads wraparound plays well and seldom gets beaten. He gets into occasional trouble when he plays too deep in his net and holds his glove hand too low.

Vanbiesbrouck is a good skater with fine lateral motion. Active with his stick, he uses it to poke-check, guide rebounds, break up passes or whack at any ankles camping out too close to his crease. He won't surrender a centimetre of his ice. Vanbiesbrouck is also confident out of his net with the puck, sometimes overly so. He'll get burned by trying to force passes up the middle.

THE MENTAL GAME

Vanbiesbrouck is unapproachable on game day because gathering his intensity and concentration is an all-day process. He is highly competitive, keeps himself in superb condition and gets better as he gets older.

THE INTANGIBLES

Playing behind the solid Panthers defensive game has probably added a year or two to Vanbiesbrouck's career, since he isn't forced to win games by himself every night — but he's still capable of doing so when needed.

PROJECTION

Vanbiesbrouck should be among the NHL's top goalies again this season.

RHETT WARRENER

Yrs. of NHL service: 2
Born: Shaunavon, Sask.; Jan. 27, 1976
Position: left defense
Height: 6-1
Weight: 209
Uniform no.: 7
Shoots: left

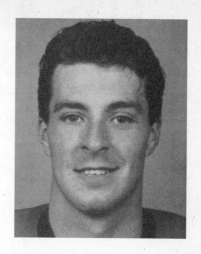

Career statistics:

GP	G	A	TP	PIM
90	4	12	16	134

1995-96 statistics:

GP	G	A	TP	+/-	PIM	PP	SH	GW	GT	S	PCT
28	0	3	3	+4	46	0	0	0	0	19	0.0

1996-97 statistics:

GP	G	A	TP	+/-	PIM	PP	SH	GW	GT	S	PCT
62	4	9	13	+20	88	1	0	1	0	58	6.9

LAST SEASON

Led team in plus-minus. Missed 14 games with groin injuries.

THE FINESSE GAME

The Panthers were patient with Warrener's development. The result is a budding two-way defenseman whose rough edges won't require that much more sanding to become polished.

Warrener started off with a foundation of good hockey sense, and completed that with size and a firm passing touch. He plays a simple game, wins a lot of the one-on-one battles and sticks within his limitations. His defensive reads are quite good for a young player. He plays his position well and moves people out from in front of the net. He blocks shots, and he can start a quick transition with a breakout pass.

Warrener might struggle a bit with his foot speed. His turns and lateral movement are okay, but he lacks quickness and acceleration.

THE PHYSICAL GAME

Warrener likes the aggressive game. Sometimes he gets a little too rambunctious and gets out of position, but that is to be expected for a young player looking to make an impact. He's a solid hitter but doesn't make the open-ice splatters like teammate Ed Jovanovski.

THE INTANGIBLES

Warrener has some offensive upside. When he is paired with a stay-at-home type like Paul Laus, he gets more involved in the attack. He can be the defensive partner, too, if he is teamed with a more offensive defensive.

PROJECTION

Warrener made a huge step forward last season and will be part of the Panthers' top four for a long time to come. His point totals won't be dazzling, but he can net 25 to 30 points.

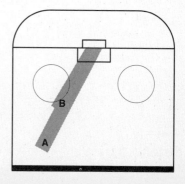

LOS ANGELES KINGS

Players' Statistics 1996-97

POS.	NO.	PLAYER	GP	G	A	PTS	+/-	PIM	PP	SH	GW	GT	S	PCT
L	8	DIMITRI KHRISTICH	75	19	37	56	8	38	3		2		135	14.1
C	20	RAY FERRARO	81	25	21	46	-22	112	11		2	1	152	16.4
L	9	VLADIMIR TSYPLAKOV	67	16	23	39	8	12	1		2		118	13.6
L	25	KEVIN STEVENS	69	14	20	34	-27	96	4		1	1	175	8.0
R	43	VITALI YACHMENEV	65	10	22	32	-9	10	2		2	1	97	10.3
D	4	ROB BLAKE	62	8	23	31	-28	82	4		1		169	4.7
R	27	GLEN MURRAY	77	16	14	30	-21	32	3		1		153	10.5
L	21	KAI NURMINEN	67	16	11	27	-3	22	4		1	1	112	14.3
C	44	YANIC PERREAULT	41	11	14	25	0	20	1	1			98	11.2
D	28	PHILIPPE BOUCHER	60	7	18	25	0	25	2		1		159	4.4
C	22	IAN LAPERRIERE	62	8	15	23	-25	102		1	2		84	9.5
D	14	MATTIAS NORSTROM	80	1	21	22	-4	84					106	.9
R	11	*BRAD SMYTH	52	9	8	17	-10	76			1	1	84	10.7
D	6	SEAN O'DONNELL	55	5	12	17	-13	144	2				68	7.4
D	27	JOHN SLANEY	32	3	11	14	-10	4	1		1		60	5.0
L	19	*JEFF SHEVALIER	26	4	9	13	-6	6	1				42	9.5
C	12	*ROMAN VOPAT	29	4	5	9	-7	60	1		2		54	7.4
D	33	*JAN VOPAT	33	4	5	9	3	22			1	1	44	9.1
L	42	*DAN BYLSMA	79	3	6	9	-15	32					86	3.5
D	5	AKI BERG	41	2	6	8	-9	24	2				65	3.1
L	23	CRAIG JOHNSON	31	4	3	7	-7	26	1				30	13.3
L	41	BRENT GRIEVE	18	4	2	6	-2	15			1		50	8.0
D	15	JAROSLAV MODRY	30	3	3	6	-13	25	1	1			32	9.4
L	40	BARRY POTOMSKI	26	3	2	5	-8	93			1		18	16.7
D	29	STEVEN FINN	54	2	3	5	-8	84			1		35	5.7
C	24	NATHAN LAFAYETTE	15	1	3	4	-8	8	1		1		26	3.8
L	17	*MATT JOHNSON	52	1	3	4	-4	194					20	5.0
C	37	PAUL DIPIETRO	6	1		1	-2	6					10	10.0
D	2	DOUG ZMOLEK	57	1		1	-22	116					28	3.6
G	32	J.C. BERGERON	1				0							
C	26	*CHRIS MARINUCCI	1				-2						1	
C	52	*JASON MORGAN	3				-3						4	
G	1	*JAMIE STORR	5				0							
D	7	*STEVE MCKENNA	9				1	37					6	
G	34	BYRON DAFOE	40				0							
G	35	STEPHANE FISET	44				0	2						

GP = games played; G = goals; A = assists; PTS = points; +/- = goals-for minus goals-against while player is on ice;
PIM = penalties in minutes; PP = power-play goals; SH = shorthanded goals; GW = game-winning goals; GT = game-tying goals; S = no. of shots; PCT = percentage of goals to shots; * = rookie

AKI-PETTERI BERG

Yrs. of NHL service: 2
Born: Turku, Finland; July 28, 1977
Position: left defense
Height: 6-3
Weight: 198
Uniform no.: 5
Shoots: left

Career statistics:

GP	G	A	TP	PIM
92	2	13	15	53

1995-96 statistics:

GP	G	A	TP	+/-	PIM	PP	SH	GW	GT	S	PCT
51	0	7	7	-13	29	0	0	0	0	56	0.0

1996-97 statistics:

GP	G	A	TP	+/-	PIM	PP	SH	GW	GT	S	PCT
41	2	6	8	-9	24	2	0	0	0	65	3.1

LAST SEASON

Missed one game with concussion. Missed one game with charley horse. Scored 1-3 — 4 in 23 games with Phoenix (IHL).

THE FINESSE GAME

It's tough enough to break into the NHL as an 18-year-old from a foreign country, let alone playing your first two seasons with a team as terrible as the Kings, but Berg is quietly managing to get better and better.

It can't hurt that Larry Robinson, one of the game's best defensemen, has been tutoring Berg, who had an especially solid second half after playing for Finland at the World Junior Championships in December.

Berg is a pleasing combination of offensive and defensive skills. His skating is top-notch. He has a powerful stride with great mobility and balance. And he gets terrific drive from perfect leg extension and deep knee bends.

He sees the ice well and has excellent passing skills. He can also rush with the puck, but he prefers to make a pass and then join the play. He quarterbacked the Kings' second power-play unit and will develop more confidence in his offensive abilities. He is a solid prospect as a two-way defenseman.

THE PHYSICAL GAME

Berg loves to hit. He's big and strong, and has the mobility to lay down some serious open-ice checks. His punishing checks have had some scouts comparing him to Scott Stevens. Berg wasn't as assertive in his rookie season, but showed better toughness last season, playing harder and finishing his checks.

THE INTANGIBLES

Some onlookers believed Berg was the top player available in the 1995 draft. He has a lot of learning to do, and, in 20-20 hindsight, he would have been better off in the minors for the last two years, learning the pro game, rather than stuck in the mire at the not-so-Great Western Forum, but the Kings were desperate for help.

PROJECTION

This season will be another struggle for Berg, whose point totals won't start going up until he has a better supporting crew. He continues to move steadily forward.

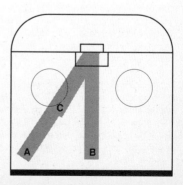

ROB BLAKE

Yrs. of NHL service: 7
Born: Simcoe, Ont.; Dec. 10, 1969
Position: right defense
Height: 6-3
Weight: 215
Uniform no.: 4
Shoots: right

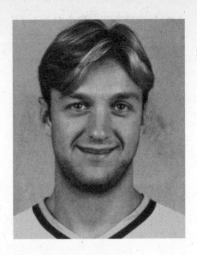

Career statistics:

GP	G	A	TP	PIM
388	68	170	238	648

1993-94 statistics:

GP	G	A	TP	+/-	PIM	PP	SH	GW	GT	S	PCT
84	20	48	68	-7	137	7	0	6	0	304	6.6

1994-95 statistics:

GP	G	A	TP	+/-	PIM	PP	SH	GW	GT	S	PCT
24	4	7	11	-16	38	4	0	1	0	76	5.3

1995-96 statistics:

GP	G	A	TP	+/-	PIM	PP	SH	GW	GT	S	PCT
6	1	2	3	0	8	0	0	0	0	13	7.7

1996-97 statistics:

GP	G	A	TP	+/-	PIM	PP	SH	GW	GT	S	PCT
62	8	23	31	-28	82	4	0	1	0	169	4.7

LAST SEASON

Led team defensemen in scoring. Worst plus-minus on team. Tied for second on team in assists and power-play goals. Missed 11 games with fractured right hand. Missed seven games with tendonitis in left knee. Missed two games due to suspension for high-sticking incident.

THE FINESSE GAME

Early in his career, Blake was projected to become a West Coast Scott Stevens, but year after year of injuries have taken their toll. November 1997 will mark the two-year anniversary of the reconstructive surgery on his left knee (the same knee that had the flare-up last season), so it will be time to see how that leg is holding up. Lower-body strength is the key to Blake's open-ice hitting, and, of course, his skating.

Blake has finesse skills that make an impact in any zone of the ice. He works the point on the power play, but lacks the vision to be as creative as he could be. He has a good, low shot and rifles it off the pass. He has quality hand skills and is not afraid to skip in deep to try to make something happen low. He is confident about attempting to force the play deep in the offensive zone, and has good enough passing skills to use a backhand pass across the goalmouth.

Before his injuries, Blake was a powerful skater, quick and agile, with good balance. He would step up and challenge at the blueline. He had great anticipation and was quite bold, forcing turnovers at the blueline with his body positioning and quick stickwork. We're unsure how much of this ability he will regain.

THE PHYSICAL GAME

When healthy, Blake is among the hardest hitters in the league. He has a nasty streak and will bring up his gloves and stick them into the face of an opponent when he thinks the referee isn't watching. He can dominate with his physical play; when he does, he opens up a lot of ice for himself and his teammates.

THE INTANGIBLES

Blake's health makes him a huge, huge question mark. The Kings need his presence but can't rely on it.

PROJECTION

If Blake stays intact and rebounds from his knee injury, he's capable of a bounce-back season, but we expect only half the total of his high-water mark of 20 goals, which he produced three seasons ago.

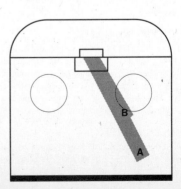

DAN BYLSMA

Yrs. of NHL service: 1
Born: Grand Rapids, MI; Sept. 19, 1970
Position: left wing
Height: 6-2
Weight: 215
Uniform no.: 42
Shoots: left

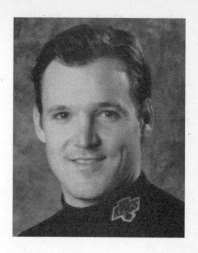

Career statistics:

GP	G	A	TP	PIM
83	3	6	9	32

1995-96 statistics:

GP	G	A	TP	+/-	PIM	PP	SH	GW	GT	S	PCT
4	0	0	0	0	0	0	0	0	0	6	0.0

1996-97 statistics:

GP	G	A	TP	+/-	PIM	PP	SH	GW	GT	S	PCT
79	3	6	9	-15	32	0	0	0	0	86	3.5

LAST SEASON

First NHL season. Missed one game with knee injury.

THE FINESSE GAME

Bylsma was an older rookie last season, and brought nothing but hard work and effort to the ice. Fortunately for him, those were qualities in short supply on the Kings.

Bylsma is best suited as a fourth-line momentum changer who can add penalty killing thanks to his speed. He plays a simple meat-and-potatoes game with very little offense. He is versatile enough to play all three forward position, and, since the Kings were slammed by injuries, simply by staying healthy Bylsma was able to rack up ice time.

Bylsma earns everything he gets. He has decent foot speed but isn't a fluid skater. In fact, he's a bit of a plodder style-wise, but he works and churns hard. His hand skills are virtually nonexistent. He has never been much of a scorer at any level.

THE PHYSICAL GAME

Bylsma is good-sized and he finishes his checks, but he doesn't have a mean streak.

THE INTANGIBLES

On any other team, Bylsma would be a career minor leaguer, but the Kings' more talented players seldom show the effort Bylsma does on a consistent basis. He is a competent role player.

PROJECTION

Bylsma's contribution doesn't show in the stats. He'll be lucky to reach double digits in points.

RAY FERRARO

Yrs. of NHL service: 13
Born: Trail, B.C.; Aug. 23, 1964
Position: centre
Height: 5-10
Weight: 185
Uniform no.: 20
Shoots: left

Career statistics:

GP	G	A	TP	PIM
915	327	364	695	934

1993-94 statistics:

GP	G	A	TP	+/-	PIM	PP	SH	GW	GT	S	PCT
82	21	32	53	+1	83	5	0	3	3	136	15.4

1994-95 statistics:

GP	G	A	TP	+/-	PIM	PP	SH	GW	GT	S	PCT
47	22	21	43	+1	30	2	0	1	2	94	23.4

1995-96 statistics:

GP	G	A	TP	+/-	PIM	PP	SH	GW	GT	S	PCT
76	29	31	60	0	92	9	0	4	0	178	16.3

1996-97 statistics:

GP	G	A	TP	+/-	PIM	PP	SH	GW	GT	S	PCT
81	25	21	46	-22	112	11	0	2	1	1	16.4

LAST SEASON

Led team in goals for second consecutive season. Led team in power-play goals. Second on team in points. Missed one game with neck injury.

THE FINESSE GAME

Ferraro excels at the short game. From the bottoms of the circles in, he uses his quickness and hand skills to work little give-and-go plays through traffic.

A streaky player, when he is in the groove he plays with great concentration and hunger around the net. He is alert to not only his first, but also his second and third options, and he makes a rapid play selection. His best shot is his wrist shot from just off to the side of the net, which is where he likes to work on the power play. He has good coordination and timing for deflections. When his confidence is down, however, Ferraro gets into serious funks.

Ferraro's skating won't win medals. He has a choppy stride and lacks rink-long speed, but he shakes loose in a few quick steps and maintains his balance well. Handling the puck does not slow him down.

Defensively, Ferraro has improved tremendously and is no longer a liability. In fact, he's a pretty decent two-way centre, though the scales still tip in favour of his offensive ability. He has particularly improved in his defensive work down low. He's good on face-offs.

THE PHYSICAL GAME

Ferraro is on the small side but is deceptively strong. Many players aren't willing to wade into the areas where they will get crunched, and he will avoid those situations when he can. But if it's the right play, he will take the abuse and whack a few ankles himself.

THE INTANGIBLES

Ferraro was terribly unhappy in L.A. and requested a trade at the deadline to a contending team. The Kings couldn't strike a deal, and Ed Olczyk — one of the few forwards happy to be in L.A. — was moved instead. The Kings would like to count on Ferraro as a leader for their young players. That will only happen if Ferraro is willing to accept his fate.

PROJECTION

Ferraro may play his heart out in the hopes of getting himself traded. Another 20-goal season is in the cards regardless.

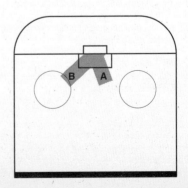

GARRY GALLEY

Yrs. of NHL service: 13
Born: Montreal, Que., Apr. 16, 1963
Position: left defense
Height: 6-0
Weight: 204
Uniform no.: 3
Shoots: left

Career statistics:

GP	G	A	TP	PIM
889	97	400	497	1014

1993-94 statistics:

GP	G	A	TP	+/-	PIM	PP	SH	GW	GT	S	PCT
81	10	60	70	-11	91	5	1	0	1	186	5.4

1994-95 statistics:

GP	G	A	TP	+/-	PIM	PP	SH	GW	GT	S	PCT
47	3	29	32	+4	30	2	0	0	0	97	3.1

1995-96 statistics:

GP	G	A	TP	+/-	PIM	PP	SH	GW	GT	S	PCT
78	10	44	54	-2	81	7	1	2	0	175	5.7

1996-97 statistics:

GP	G	A	TP	+/-	PIM	PP	SH	GW	GT	S	PCT
71	4	34	38	+10	102	1	1	1	0	84	4.8

LAST SEASON

Signed as free agent, July 6, 1997. Led Sabres defensemen in scoring for third consecutive season. Led Sabres in assists. Missed 11 games with concussion, fractured jaw, shoulder injury and abdominal muscle tear.

THE FINESSE GAME

Galley is a puck mover. He follows the play and jumps into the attack. He has decent speed to keep up with the play, though he won't be rushing the puck himself. He is mobile and has a good shot that he can get away on the fly. He will pinch aggressively, but he's also quick enough to get back if there's a counterattack.

He works well on the power play. His lateral movement allows him to slide away from the point to the middle of the blueline, and he keeps his shots low. He is a smart player and his experience shows. Galley helps any younger player he is teamed with because of his poise and communication.

Galley uses his finesse ability defensively by playing well positionally, and by using his stick for pokechecks. He has become a fairly reliable two-way defenseman.

THE PHYSICAL GAME

Galley has added a physical element to his game over the past few seasons, but he is not and will never be a big hitter. He will take his man, but not always take him out, and more physical forwards take advantage of him. He gets in the way, though, and does not back down. But there are times when he is simply overpowered. He also gets a little chippy now and then, just to keep people guessing.

THE INTANGIBLES

For the past five seasons (with Philadelphia and Buffalo) Galley led his team's defensemen in scoring, but he isn't one of the league's elite "offensemen." He simply makes the most of the opportunities given him. He would be an attractive number three or four defenseman on another team instead of a number one, but Los Angeles will be squeezing a lot of ice time out of him as the probable number two behind Rob Blake.

PROJECTION

Galley will get a lot of ice time with the Kings, but this is a very bad team and Galley may only be in the 35- to 40-point range.

DIMITRI KHRISTICH

Yrs. of NHL service: 7
Born: Kiev, Ukraine; July 23, 1969
Position: left wing
Height: 6-2
Weight: 195
Uniform no.: 8
Shoots: right

Career statistics:

GP	G	A	TP	PIM
466	167	203	370	200

1993-94 statistics:

GP	G	A	TP	+/-	PIM	PP	SH	GW	GT	S	PCT
83	29	29	58	-2	73	10	0	4	1	195	14.9

1994-95 statistics:

GP	G	A	TP	+/-	PIM	PP	SH	GW	GT	S	PCT
48	12	14	26	0	41	8	0	2	2	92	13.0

1995-96 statistics:

GP	G	A	TP	+/-	PIM	PP	SH	GW	GT	S	PCT
76	27	37	64	0	44	12	0	3	0	204	13.2

1996-97 statistics:

GP	G	A	TP	+/-	PIM	PP	SH	GW	GT	S	PCT
75	19	37	56	+8	38	3	0	2	0	135	14.1

LAST SEASON

Led team in assists and points, both for second season. Tied for team lead in plus-minus. Second on team in goals. Missed seven games with eye injury and laser surgery.

THE FINESSE GAME

Only the Buffalo Sabres had a team scoring leader with fewer points than Khristich, and the fact that their scoring leader was also matched up against other team's top lines illustrates the dearth of talent up front at the fabulous Forum.

Khristich has good hand-eye coordination for deflections and can even take draws. He is not an especially fast skater, but he has a long, strong stride and very good balance. His hockey sense is excellent, and he is responsible defensively as well.

One weakness is his tendency to put himself in a position where he gets hit, and hurt. Part of that stems from holding onto the puck to make a perfect play.

Khristich has not been as much of a factor on the power play as in recent seasons. The Kings ran a very disorganized power play last season (they ranked next-to-last in the NHL) and didn't have an effective point man, which limited the work Khristich could do down low. He likes to lurk just off to the goalie's right, with his forehand open and ready for the pass. When the puck reaches his blade, he slams the shot in one quick motion. If the penalty killers are drawn to him, then it opens ice for another forward. Either way, Khristich gets the job done.

THE PHYSICAL GAME

Khristich is a very sturdy skater but lacks physical presence. He will go into the trenches and is tough to knock off the puck. He protects the puck well.

THE INTANGIBLES

Until and unless the Kings upgrade their personnel, Khristich ranks as their best forward. He doesn't have much talent to work with, and he's not a great one-on-one player.

PROJECTION

We said last season that a 30-goal season would be amazing for Khristich under such circumstances. Nothing has changed.

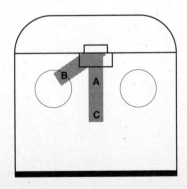

IAN LAPERRIERE

Yrs. of NHL service: 3
Born: Montreal, Que.; Jan. 19, 1974
Position: centre
Height: 6-1
Weight: 195
Uniform no.: 22
Shoots: right

Career statistics:

GP	G	A	TP	PIM
171	27	40	67	342

1993-94 statistics:

GP	G	A	TP	+/-	PIM	PP	SH	GW	GT	S	PCT
1	0	0	0	0	0	0	0	0	0	1	0.0

1994-95 statistics:

GP	G	A	TP	+/-	PIM	PP	SH	GW	GT	S	PCT
37	13	14	27	+12	85	1	0	1	0	53	24.5

1995-96 statistics:

GP	G	A	TP	+/-	PIM	PP	SH	GW	GT	S	PCT
71	6	11	17	-11	155	1	0	1	1	70	8.6

1996-97 statistics:

GP	G	A	TP	+/-	PIM	PP	SH	GW	GT	S	PCT
62	8	15	23	-25	102	0	1	2	0	84	9.5

LAST SEASON

Missed 11 games with season-ending reconstructive surgery on his right shoulder. Missed three games with shoulder strain. Missed three games with hip flexor. Missed two games with concussion.

THE FINESSE GAME

Despite some serious injuries, like a blind-side punch from Donald Brashear that resulted in a concussion for Laperriere and a four-game suspension for Brashear, Laperriere is one of the best players in the league at working hard and finishing his checks.

The knock on Laperriere earlier in his career was his skating ability, but he has improved tremendously in that department. Although he'll never be a speed demon, Laperriere doesn't look out of place at the NHL level. He will always try to take the extra stride when he is backchecking so he can make a clean check, instead of taking the easy way out and committing a lazy hooking foul. Laperriere wins his share of races for the loose puck.

Laperriere grew up watching Guy Carbonneau in Montreal, and he studied well. Laperriere knows how to win a draw between his feet. He uses his stick and his body to make sure the opposing centre doesn't get the puck. He gets his bottom hand way down on the stick and tries to win draws on his backhand. He gets very low to the ice on draws.

Laperriere is ever willing to use the backhand, either for shots or to get the puck deep. He is very reliable defensively and shows signs of becoming a two-way centre. He doesn't think the game very well, however, and his offensive reads are brutal.

THE PHYSICAL GAME

Laperriere is an obnoxious player in the Bob Bassen mold. He really battles for the puck. Although smallish, he has absolutely no fear of playing in the "circle" that extends from the lower inside of the face-off circles to behind the net. He will pay any price. He's a momentum changer. No one in the NHL hits harder on the defenseman than Laperriere when he is the first man in on the forecheck, except maybe Eric Lindros.

Laperriere played the two months before his shoulder surgery with a brace, and showed a ton of heart by maintaining his aggressive style. He will have to learn to apportion his resources better over the course of a full 82-game season, or he will be worn out before the playoffs. If the Kings are well out of the playoff race again he would make an excellent deadline-time acquisition for a Cup hopeful.

THE INTANGIBLES

Laperriere adds true grit to the lineup despite his small size, which is his major weakness. His nightly effort puts a lot of bigger guys to shame. He lost any bad habits the hard way by playing for a hard-nosed coach (Mike Keenan) early in his career. Assuming he progresses well off the shoulder surgery, he should be L.A.'s most consistent forward.

PROJECTION

Laperriere is best suited as a third- or fourth-line centre. His skills are limited, but what he does, he does well. His top range appears to be 40 points.

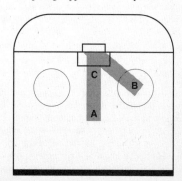

STEVE MCKENNA

Yrs. of NHL service: 0
Born: Toronto, Ont.; Aug. 21, 9173
Position: defense
Height: 6-8
Weight: 247
Uniform no.: 7
Shoots: left

Career statistics:

GP	G	A	TP	PIM
9	0	0	0	37

1996-97 statistics:

GP	G	A	TP	+/-	PIM	PP	SH	GW	GT	S	PCT
9	0	0	0	+1	37	0	0	0	0	6	0.0

LAST SEASON

Signed as free agent, May 17, 1996. Will be entering first NHL season. Scored 6-5 — 11 with 187 penalty minutes in 66 games with Phoenix (IHL).

THE FINESSE GAME

McKenna is all rough edges now, but the long-term project is for this lifetime defenseman to be converted into a mostly physical left wing. McKenna sticks his nose in and plays hard.

McKenna can play on the fourth line now. His skating is a drawback up front, but he has good lower-body strength and works hard. He's been progressing steadily and has a solid work ethic. His game isn't pretty but he thinks the game pretty well. He just needs his feet and hands to react quickly enough at the NHL level. When he has the time, he knows what to do with the puck and can make a play.

McKenna has good leadership qualities and was a captain in college (Merrimack, Hockey East). He is a heart-and-soul player.

THE PHYSICAL GAME

McKenna is believed to be the tallest player in NHL history at 6-8, and he is as tough as he is tall. In his brief NHL stint, he had dust-ups with legitimate NHL heavyweights Marty McSorley (twice) and Dave Karpa. He will take on anybody, and, most often, he'll win. He's a serious pugilist who always sticks up for his teammates.

He's a hard 247 pounds, and has a mean streak for punishing hits. Be afraid. Be very afraid.

THE INTANGIBLES

No one will come into their house and push them around — not if the Kings manage to get both McKenna and the equally mammoth (but less talented) Matt Johnson into the same lineup on a nightly basis. In a year or two, McKenna could develop enough skills to get to a third-line checking role. The Kings must be willing to live with some mistakes. He needs a lot of work, but he has a great attitude and there's a big (huge!) potential payoff.

PROJECTION

McKenna could develop into a Bob Probert-type player. He'll score 15 to 20 goals by scaring people away and getting enough room and time to bang in loose pucks.

GLEN MURRAY

Yrs. of NHL service: 5
Born: Halifax, N.S.; Nov. 1, 1972
Position: right wing
Height: 6-2
Weight: 220
Uniform no.: 27
Shoots: right

Career statistics:

GP	G	A	TP	PIM
294	59	49	108	191

1993-94 statistics:

GP	G	A	TP	+/-	PIM	PP	SH	GW	GT	S	PCT
81	18	13	31	-1	48	0	0	4	2	114	15.8

1994-95 statistics:

GP	G	A	TP	+/-	PIM	PP	SH	GW	GT	S	PCT
35	5	2	7	-11	46	0	0	2	0	64	7.8

1995-96 statistics:

GP	G	A	TP	+/-	PIM	PP	SH	GW	GT	S	PCT
69	14	15	29	+4	57	0	0	2	0	100	14.0

1996-97 statistics:

GP	G	A	TP	+/-	PIM	PP	SH	GW	GT	S	PCT
77	16	14	30	-21	32	3	0	1	0	153	10.5

LAST SEASON

Acquired from Pittsburgh for Ed Olczyk, March 18, 1997.

THE FINESSE GAME

Murray is a lumbering skater who needs a good old dump-and-chase game, on a line with a playmaker who can get him the puck and set him up in the slot. He will have to make most of his own breaks with the Kings, where he has at least been restored to the right wing. He needs to be on the right side, jamming in his forehand shots.

Murray has good size and a good short game. He has a quick release, and like a lot of great goal scorers he just plain shoots. He doesn't even have to look at the net because he feels where the shot is going. He protects the puck well with his body.

Murray is a little fragile confidence-wise, but he showed pretty good resilience after being dealt for the third time in the last three seasons. He was a welcome sight to Kings coach Larry Robinson, and Murray responded with 5-3 — 8 in 11 games with L.A.

THE PHYSICAL GAME

On nights when he's playing well, Murray is leaning on people and making his presence felt. He'll bang, but on some nights he doesn't want to pay the price and prefers to rely on his shot. When he sleepwalks, he is useless. When he's ready to rock 'n' roll, he's effective.

THE INTANGIBLES

Murray was buried on a strong Penguins team, where the European style didn't suit his North American game. The Kings play a more basic style and Murray will get a good shot at a regular job as the number one right wing.

PROJECTION

Murray scored at a nice pace after the trade. If he maintains his enthusiasm he could have a career year; 25 goals wouldn't be a bad sum.

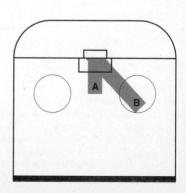

MATTIAS NORSTROM

Yrs. of NHL service: 2
Born: Mora, Sweden; Jan. 2, 1972
Position: left defense
Height: 6-1
Weight: 205
Uniform no.: 14
Shoots: left

Career statistics

GP	G	A	TP	PIM
134	3	27	30	132

1993-94 statistics:

GP	G	A	TP	+/-	PIM	PP	SH	GW	GT	S	PCT
9	0	1	1	0	6	0	0	0	0	3	0.0

1994-95 statistics:

GP	G	A	TP	+/-	PIM	PP	SH	GW	GT	S	PCT
9	0	3	3	+2	2	0	0	0	0	4	0

1995-96 statistics:

GP	G	A	TP	+/-	PIM	PP	SH	GW	GT	S	PCT
36	2	2	4	-3	40	0	0	0	0	34	5.9

1996-97 statistics:

GP	G	A	TP	+/-	PIM	PP	SH	GW	GT	S	PCT
80	1	21	22	-4	84	0	0	0	0	106	0.9

LAST SEASON

Missed one game with wrist contusion.

THE FINESSE GAME

Norstrom might not be a top four defenseman on a good team, but he has attained a fairly high level of play on a team that needs him desperately and uses him extensively. He's a good skater who is still working on his pivots and turns. He does have straight-ahead speed, to a degree, thanks to a long stride. Along the boards he delivers strong hits, but in open ice he has more misses.

His foot skills outdistance his hand skills. Norstrom can make a decent pass, but mostly he'll keep things simple with the puck — smack it around the boards if he gets into trouble, rather than try to make a play.

For so large a player, he uses a surprisingly short stick that cuts down on his reach defensively and limits some of his offensive options. However, he feels his responsibility is to break down the play, rather than create it. He will pinch down the boards occasionally, but only to drive the puck deeper, not to take the puck and make a play. And he won't jump into the play on offense until he has more confidence with his puck skills.

THE PHYSICAL GAME

Norstrom is hard-nosed, and when he hits, you feel it. He is willing to do what it takes to help his team win. He is solidly built and likes to throw big, loud hits. If he doesn't hit, he's not going to be around long because his talent is not going to carry him, and his hockey sense (especially his defensive reads) needs a lot of improvement. Norstrom sacrifices his body blocking shots.

He knows what he's good at. Norstrom has tremendously powerful legs and is strong on his skates. He has confidence in his power game and has developed a great enthusiasm for physical play.

THE INTANGIBLES

Norstrom is a hard-working athlete who loves to practise, a player acquired more for his character than for his abilities, which are average. He will be a defensive-style defenseman who will give his coach what's asked for, but won't try to do things that will put the puck, or the team, in trouble.

PROJECTION

Norstrom will continue to get a big chunk of ice time, but his offensive skills limit him to 25 to 30 points at best.

SEAN O'DONNELL

Yrs. of NHL service: 2
Born: Ottawa, Ont.; Oct. 13, 1971
Position: left defense
Height: 6-2
Weight: 225
Uniform no.: 6
Shoots: left

Career statistics:

GP	G	A	TP	PIM
141	7	19	26	320

1994-95 statistics:

GP	G	A	TP	+/-	PIM	PP	SH	GW	GT	S	PCT
15	0	2	2	-2	49	0	0	0	0	12	0.0

1995-96 statistics:

GP	G	A	TP	+/-	PIM	PP	SH	GW	GT	S	PCT
71	2	5	7	+3	127	0	0	0	0	65	3.1

1996-97 statistics:

GP	G	A	TP	+/-	PIM	PP	SH	GW	GT	S	PCT
55	5	12	17	-13	144	2	0	0	0	68	7.4

LAST SEASON

Second NHL season. Second on team in penalty minutes. Missed two games with back sprain. Missed nine games with left wrist sprain.

THE FINESSE GAME

O'Donnell has worked hard to rise above being a one-dimensional player, but his skating holds him back. He is not very good laterally and that results in his being beaten wide. He tries to line up someone and misses, because he doesn't have the quickness to get there.

It's especially tough for O'Donnell playing as a defenseman on a team that rarely scores. He has some offensive upside because he is alert and tries so hard, and that could compensate for his hand skills, which are average at best.

O'Donnell has to improve his defensive reads. He has become a fairly good shot blocker.

THE PHYSICAL GAME

O'Donnell is fearless. He is a legitimate tough guy who fights anybody. He hits anybody. He uses his stick. He's a nasty customer.

THE INTANGIBLES

O'Donnell has paid his dues in the minors, and there are a lot of rough edges to his game. He has a good distance to go yet, but under the tutelage of Larry Robinson in L.A., he could learn to supplement his game and develop along the lines of Paul Laus, who was once considered a pure goon but is now a serviceable, tough defenseman. O'Donnell is a project.

PROJECTION

O'Donnell will collect close to 200 penalty minutes if he stays healthy.

JEFF SHEVALIER

Yrs. of NHL service: 1
Born: Mississauga, Ont.; Mar. 14, 1974
Position: left wing
Height: 5-11
Weight: 185
Uniform no.: 19
Shoots: left

Career statistics:

GP	G	A	TP	PIM
27	5	9	14	6

1994-95 statistics:

GP	G	A	TP	+/-	PIM	PP	SH	GW	GT	S	PCT
1	1	0	1	+1	0	0	0	0	0	1	100

1995-96 statistics:

P	G	A	TP	+/-	PIM	PP	SH	GW	GT	S	PC
Did not play in NHL											

1996-97 statistics:

GP	G	A	TP	+/-	PIM	PP	SH	GW	GT	S	PCT
26	4	9	13	-6	6	1	0	0	0	42	9.5

LAST SEASON

First NHL season. Missed one game with concussion. Scored 15-18 — 33 in 44 games with Phoenix (IHL).

THE FINESSE GAME

Shevalier is a left-handed shot who can play both wings. He is a good skater whose major asset is getting the puck out of the corners and winning the one-on-one battles along the wall and in the trenches. Shevalier lacks quick accleration, so he has to keep his legs moving and not get caught standing still.

He has decent hands when he is in the right position. He plays a heads-up game and has good instincts around the net. He could handle some power-play time on the second unit because he makes good decisions with the puck in the offensive zone.

Defensively, Shevalier needs to work harder at getting back into his own zone and knowing what to do when he gets there.

THE PHYSICAL GAME

After an impressive rookie year in the minors, Shevalier came to training camp about 25 pounds overweight, which was his ticket right back to the minors. When the Kings told him to put on weight, they meant muscle. He is not an overly physical player. He isn't very big, strong, or feisty, but he is fairly determined in the attacking zone and will forge through checks.

THE INTANGIBLES

Shevalier's versatility (he's also played centre, but not in the NHL) will give him an edge over players that might be close to him in ability. He will be going into his contract year, which is always an incentive to show a little more.

PROJECTION

If none of the junior prospects shoulders him out of a spot, or if the Kings clear some room by moving Kevin Stevens, Shevalier has potential to play on one of the top two lines for L.A. He played well after his call-up late in the year and is a possibility for 15 to 20 goals.

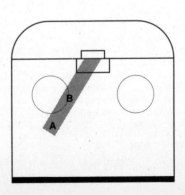

KEVIN STEVENS

Yrs. of NHL service: 9
Born: Brockton, Mass.; Apr. 15, 1965
Position: left wing
Height: 6-3
Weight: 217
Uniform no.: 25
Shoots: left

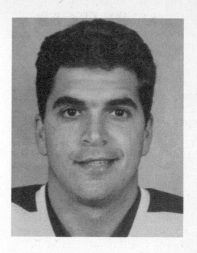

Career statistics:

GP	G	A	TP	PIM
587	278	319	597	1135

1993-94 statistics:

GP	G	A	TP	+/-	PIM	PP	SH	GW	GT	S	PCT
83	41	47	88	-24	155	21	0	4	0	284	14.4

1994-95 statistics:

GP	G	A	TP	+/-	PIM	PP	SH	GW	GT	S	PCT
27	15	12	27	0	51	6	0	4	0	80	18.8

1995-96 statistics:

GP	G	A	TP	+/-	PIM	PP	SH	GW	GT	S	PCT
61	13	23	36	-10	71	6	0	1	0	170	7.6

1996-97 statistics:

GP	G	A	TP	+/-	PIM	PP	SH	GW	GT	S	PCT
69	14	20	34	-27	96	4	0	1	1	175	8.0

LAST SEASON

Missed seven games with ankle injury. Missed two games with concussion. Missed one game with back spasms. Missed one game due to personal reasons. Led team in shots. Tied for second on team in power-play goals.

THE FINESSE GAME

Nothing has gone right for Stevens since he was traded away from the Pittsburgh Penguins and Mario Lemieux in 1995. Injuries have followed him like a plague, and he has deteriorated from an All-Star left wing to an overpaid player the Kings can't give away. Stevens is still a pretty honest sort, and he can be an effective NHL player. He just won't ever be in the elite class of left-wingers without an elite centre to play with.

Stevens has the size and strength to battle for and win position in front of the net. He has lost a lot of confidence in what used to be an astonishingly quick release on his shot. In the past, Stevens didn't think twice about where his shot was going. Now his positioning isn't as good, and he has to concentrate on where he is and where to shoot; the whole process has slowed to a crawl.

Stevens simply drops anchor in the slot on the power play. His huge frame blocks the goalie's view and he has good hand-eye coordination for tips and deflections. Those moves aren't instinctive, but came from hours of practise. He also has a devastating one-timer. He does not have to be overly clever with the puck, since he can overpower goalies with his shot. Stevens is a power-play specialist.

His play at even strength is not as strong. He is an average skater at best, and often seems overanxious to get started on the attacking rush to keep up with his fleeter linemates. His reach and range make him appear faster than he is.

THE PHYSICAL GAME

Stevens has to initiate. He doesn't react well to being knocked down. (It's surprising, given his size and strength, that he all too often is.) He isn't one of the meanest guys around, though he can throw 'em (punches and devastating hits both), but he needs to be more consistent with his physical play, and look as hungry as he did when he was breaking in.

THE INTANGIBLES

Two dreadful things have happened to Stevens in his career: Losing Lemieux as his centre, and the 1993 playoff injury in which he broke numerous facial bones. Playing in Boston, his hometown, was a nightmare because he never clicked with Adam Oates, one of the game's great centres.

Things didn't get much better in L.A., a team weak up the middle, and Stevens suffered a concussion early in the season that rattled him, followed by other minor, nagging injuries. At least coach Larry Robinson is on his side, publicly praising his leadership in an effort to get Stevens involved with some of the Kings' younger forwards.

PROJECTION

It's not likely to get any better for Stevens. He will never be a 50-goal scorer again. His top end is likely 30 goals, but only if L.A. can acquire a quality pivotman. Otherwise, Stevens will have to stay healthy and get lucky to get 20.

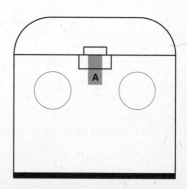

JAMIE STORR

Yrs. of NHL service: 0
Born: Brampton, Ont.; Dec. 28, 1975
Position: goaltender
Height: 6-0
Weight: 170
Uniform no.: 1
Catches: left

Career statistics:

GP	MIN	GA	SO	GAA	A	PIM
15	790	40	0	3.04	0	0

1994-95 statistics:

GP	MIN	GAA	W	L	T	SO	GA	S	SAPCT	PIM
5	263	3.88	1	3	1	0	17	152	.888	0

1995-96 statistics:

GP	MIN	GAA	W	L	T	SO	GA	S	SAPCT	PIM
5	262	2.75	3	1	0	0	12	147	.918	0

1996-97 statistics:

GP	MIN	GAA	W	L	T	SO	GA	S	SAPCT	PIM
5	265	2.49	2	1	1	0	11	147	.925	0

LAST SEASON

Will be entering first NHL season. Appeared in 44
games for Phoenix (IHL) with a 16-22-4 record and
3.62 GAA.

THE PHYSICAL GAME

Technically, Storr is pretty sound for a young player.
He plays his angles well. And he's a stand-up goalie
who challenges shooters and forces them to make the
first move, rather than scrambling and rely on his
reflexes.

Although Storr is somewhat lean, his technique
doesn't take much out of him physically, much in the
style of Kirk McLean. When he has to scramble, he
can. He had good reflexes for his size and can be in a
position for a second shot, something he will see a lot
of with the Kings.

Storr has a quick glove hand. He is adequate with
his stick but needs to improve his work out of his net.
It would help his team out immensely if he improves
in this area.

THE MENTAL GAME

Easily the weakest part of Storr's game is stored in his
head. He has trouble with his concentration, and in the
past coach Larry Robinson had to yell at him in practice to get him to wake up.

It's been Storr's misfortune to play for poor teams
at the junior and minor-league levels, but he has performed well and won two gold medals with Canada at
World Junior Championships.

THE INTANGIBLES

Storr started four of the last five games for the Kings
(he would have gotten an earlier chance to play, but
injured his heel in an off-ice accident). The last, a
35-save, 4-2 win over Colorado on the road, was the
optimistic sign the Kings have been waiting for.

PROJECTION

Storr will come into training camp as the projected
number one goalie, and would have to play himself
out of a job. Word on his minor-league play was
mixed. Expect no miracles.

VLADIMIR TSYPLAKOV

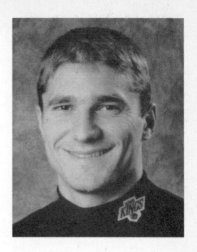

Yrs. of NHL service: 2
Born: Moscow, Russia; Apr. 18, 1969
Position: left wing
Height: 6-0
Weight: 185
Uniform no.: 19
Shoots: left

Career statistics:

GP	G	A	TP	PIM
90	21	28	49	16

1995-96 statistics:

GP	G	A	TP	+/-	PIM	PP	SH	GW	GT	S	PCT
23	5	5	10	+1	4	0	0	0	0	40	12.5

1996-97 statistics:

GP	G	A	TP	+/-	PIM	PP	SH	GW	GT	S	PCT
67	16	23	39	+8	12	1	0	2	0	118	13.6

LAST SEASON

Tied for team lead in plus-minus. Tied for second on team in assists. Third on team in points. Missed nine games with abdominal strain. Missed three games with groin strain.

THE FINESSE GAME

Tsyplakov is a highly skilled forward who likes to play an up-tempo game. He's a run-and-gun, give-and-go kind of player who'll get the puck and find the open man or jump into the holes for a pass. He has good anticipation and quick acceleration. He has very good hands and a quick release on his shot.

Tsyplakov was drafted as a 26-year-old by the Kings in 1995 to fill a specific need: scoring. He had three seasons to acclimate himself to North American hockey, but missed most of what would have been his first NHL season in 1995-96 with shoulder surgery.

He is not as effective on the power play as he should be with his shot because he shies away from the high-percentage areas where he has to pay a price to stake out his territory. He is a perimeter player, and that minimizes his NHL-calibre skills.

THE PHYSICAL GAME

Tsyplakov dislikes physical contact and is easily intimidated. The shoulder injury might have something to do with his reluctance to get involved. He underwent off-season hernia surgery, which makes him even more of a question mark.

THE INTANGIBLES

On a better team, Tsyplakov would be on the bubble or back in the IHL, pronto. The skills are there, but he appears to be unwilling to pay the price to stick on one of the top two lines.

PROJECTION

If he wins a job again, he could be a 20-goal scorer, with the potential to net 30.

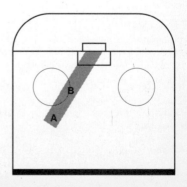

ROMAN VOPAT

Yrs. of NHL service: 1
Born: Litvinov, Czech Republic; Apr. 21, 1976
Position: centre
Height: 6-3
Weight: 216
Uniform no.: 12
Shoots: left

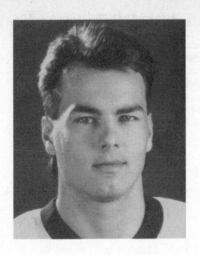

Career statistics:

GP	G	A	TP	PIM
54	6	8	14	108

1995-96 statistics:

GP	G	A	TP	+/-	PIM	PP	SH	GW	GT	S	PCT
25	2	3	5	-8	48	1	0	1	0	33	6.1

1996-97 statistics:

GP	G	A	TP	+/-	PIM	PP	SH	GW	GT	S	PCT
29	4	5	9	-7	60	1	0	2	0	54	7.4

LAST SEASON

First NHL season. Missed one game with concussion. Scored 8-8 — 16 with 139 penalty minutes in 49 games with Phoenix (IHL).

THE FINESSE GAME

Vopat is one of the players acquired from St. Louis in the 1996 Wayne Gretzky deal (along with Craig Johnson and Patrice Tardif), and he might turn out to be the most useful player of the bunch.

He is powerful skater with great lower-body strength and balance, and has surprising acceleration for a player of his size. He can handle the puck and passes well, though his creativity is limited. He's not much of a shooter, either.

Vopat understands the game well but lacks the vision and hands to get much accomplished offensively.

THE PHYSICAL GAME

Vopat has a little edge to him. He's got a big body that he needs to put to more consistent use, but he's only 21 and he's starting to get the message about what it takes to play North American-style hockey. He sticks his nose in, bumps and annoys people after the whistle, and is strong on his feet. He doesn't bowl anybody over, though, and he's capable of doing more physically.

THE INTANGIBLES

Vopat is a player you notice because of his size, and could fit in with the Kings as a hard-working third-line forward if he maintains some enthusiasm.

PROJECTION

Vopat has shown few signs of coming alive offensively in his first two years of pro hockey. He'll be a banger who can chip in 10 to 15 goals.

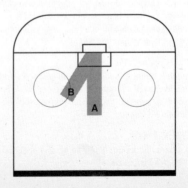

VITALI YACHMENEV

Yrs. of NHL service: 2
Born: Chelyabinsk, USSR; Jan. 8, 1975
Position: right wing
Height: 5-9
Weight: 180
Uniform no.: 43
Shoots: left

Career statistics:

GP	G	A	TP	PIM
145	29	56	85	26

1995-96 statistics:

GP	G	A	TP	+/-	PIM	PP	SH	GW	GT	S	PCT
80	19	34	53	-3	16	6	1	2	0	133	14.3

1996-97 statistics:

GP	G	A	TP	+/-	PIM	PP	SH	GW	GT	S	PCT
65	10	22	32	-9	10	2	0	2	1	97	10.3

LAST SEASON

Missed eight games with left shoulder sprain. Missed seven games with right ankle sprain. Missed one game with flu.

THE FINESSE GAME

Yachmenev's second season was a huge step back after his strong rookie year, for two major reasons: injuries, and the departure of Wayne Gretzky. The Great One actually left late in the 1995-96 season, and Yachmenev's decline can be dated from Gretzky's trade to St. Louis on February 27, 1996.

Yachmenev's shot gained him early entry to the NHL. He has a sniper's touch, and has to learn to shoot more because that is his prime skill. He has a tendency to hang onto the puck too long, a holdover from his Soviet training and his junior career when he could control the puck better, but the NHL pace is too quick for that.

He is an intelligent player with good hockey sense. He can kill penalties, where his anticipation is key.

THE PHYSICAL GAME

Yachmenev isn't very big but he is strong on his skates and solidly built. Last season he wasn't as willing to go through traffic, though he protects the puck well with his body. He showed some signs of wear and tear, and will need to work on his upper-body strength.

THE INTANGIBLES

Yachmenev needs to play with linemates who will get him the puck, but the Kings are hurting at centre. He will be on the bubble unless he brings more to the ice than he did last season.

PROJECTION

A disappointment last year, Yachmenev will have to show more to get a spot on the top two lines, the only place where he will be productive. He has produced only 15 goals in the last season and a half after notching 14 in his first half-season. What a difference a Wayne makes.

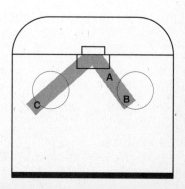

DOUG ZMOLEK

Yrs. of NHL service: 5
Born: Rochester, Minn.; Nov, 3, 1970
Position: left defense
Height: 6-2
Weight: 220
Uniform no.: 2
Shoots: left

Career statistics:

GP	G	A	TP	PIM
316	9	24	33	632

1993-94 statistics:

GP	G	A	TP	+/-	PIM	PP	SH	GW	GT	S	PCT
75	1	4	5	-8	133	0	0	0	0	32	3.1

1994-95 statistics:

GP	G	A	TP	+/-	PIM	PP	SH	GW	GT	S	PCT
42	0	5	5	-6	67	0	0	0	0	28	0.0

1995-96 statistics:

GP	G	A	TP	+/-	PIM	PP	SH	GW	GT	S	PCT
58	2	5	7	-5	87	0	0	0	0	36	5.6

1996-97 statistics:

GP	G	A	TP	+/-	PIM	PP	SH	GW	GT	S	PCT
57	1	0	1	-22	116	0	0	0	0	28	3.6

LAST SEASON

Missed six games with an irregular heartbeat. Missed one game with right hand contusion. Missed seven games with right shoulder sprain. Missed one game with right thigh contusion.

THE FINESSE GAME

Zmolek is a reliable, stay-at-home defenseman, whose value to a team is underestimated. A fine skater with a strong stride, he has good balance and agility and moves well laterally. His skating helps him angle attackers to the boards. He is a little awkward in his turning and can be victimized.

He has some nice offensive instincts. He moves the puck out of the zone well with quick, accurate passes, and he has soft hands for touch passes in tighter quarters. His understanding of the game is growing.

Zmolek is an excellent penalty killer. He is intelligent and alert.

THE PHYSICAL GAME

Zmolek developed in college (University of Minnesota) where the physical element of the game is not as important, but he realizes that to play in the NHL he has to incorporate more physical play in his game. He is defensively consistent, and he had some major battles with NHL heavyweights. He proved that he is not only a feisty player, but he can also be effective with his body work.

THE INTANGIBLES

Injuries and ailments — especially his irregular heartbeat, which is a little scary — took a toll on him last season. Zmolek is a solid, unspectacular, conservative defenseman.

PROJECTION

His point totals will be negligible, but he is seriously tough and will help stabilize a young defense in Los Angeles.

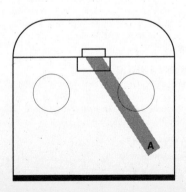

MONTREAL CANADIENS

Players' Statistics 1996-97

POS.	NO.	PLAYER	GP	G	A	PTS	+/-	PIM	PP	SH	GW	GT	S	PCT
C	25	VINCENT DAMPHOUSSE	82	27	54	81	-6	82	7	2	3	2	244	11.1
R	8	MARK RECCHI	82	34	46	80	-1	58	7	2	3		202	16.8
L	49	BRIAN SAVAGE	81	23	37	60	-14	39	5		2		219	10.5
C	11	SAKU KOIVU	50	17	39	56	7	38	5		3		135	12.6
L	26	MARTIN RUCINSKY	70	28	27	55	1	62	6	3	3	1	172	16.3
R	44	STEPHANE RICHER	63	22	24	46	0	32	2		2	1	126	17.5
R	18	VALERI BURE	64	14	21	35	4	6	4		2	1	131	10.7
D	38	VLADIMIR MALAKHOV	65	10	20	30	3	43	5		1		177	5.6
L	27	SHAYNE CORSON	58	8	16	24	-9	104	3		2		115	7.0
L	17	BENOIT BRUNET	39	10	13	23	6	14	2		2	1	63	15.9
D	5	STEPHANE QUINTAL	71	7	15	22	1	100	1				139	5.0
D	37	DAVE MANSON	75	4	18	22	-26	187	2				175	2.3
R	30	TURNER STEVENSON	65	8	13	21	-14	97	1				76	10.5
C	24	SCOTT THORNTON	73	10	10	20	-19	128	1	1	1		110	9.1
C	42	*DARCY TUCKER	73	7	13	20	-5	110	1		3	1	62	11.3
C	28	MARC BUREAU	43	6	9	15	4	16	1	1	2		56	10.7
D	3	*DAVID WILKIE	61	6	9	15	-9	63	3				65	9.2
D	43	PATRICE BRISEBOIS	49	2	13	15	-7	24			1		72	2.8
D	34	PETER POPOVIC	78	1	13	14	9	32					82	1.2
C	71	*SEBASTIEN BORDELEAU	28	2	9	11	-3	2					27	7.4
D	35	JASSEN CULLIMORE	52	2	6	8	2	44		1	1		54	3.7
D	52	*CRAIG RIVET	35		4	4	7	54					24	
C	20	*ERIC HOUDE	13		2	2	1	2					1	
G	37	*TOMAS VOKOUN	1				0							
R	51	*DAVID LING	2				0							
L	14	*TERRY RYAN	3				0							
D	48	*FRANCOIS GROLEAU	5				0	4					3	
D	32	*BRAD BROWN	8				-1	22						
L	15	PIERRE SEVIGNY	13				0	5					1	
G	60	*JOSE THEODORE	16				0							
G	41	JOCELYN THIBAULT	61				0							

GP = games played; G = goals; A = assists; PTS = points; +/- = goals-for minus goals-against while player is on ice; PIM = penalties in minutes; PP = power-play goals; SH = shorthanded goals; GW = game-winning goals; GT = game-tying goals; S = no. of shots; PCT = percentage of goals to shots; * = rookie

PATRICE BRISEBOIS

Yrs. of NHL service: 6
Born: Montreal, Que.; Jan. 27, 1971
Position: right defense
Height: 6-1
Weight: 188
Uniform no.: 43
Shoots: right

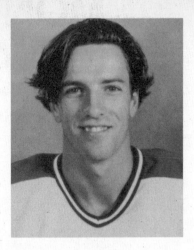

Career statistics:

GP	G	A	TP	PIM
312	29	100	129	252

1993-94 statistics:

GP	G	A	TP	+/-	PIM	PP	SH	GW	GT	S	PCT
53	2	21	23	+5	63	1	0	0	0	71	2.8

1994-95 statistics:

GP	G	A	TP	+/-	PIM	PP	SH	GW	GT	S	PCT
35	4	8	12	-2	26	0	0	2	0	67	6.0

1995-96 statistics:

GP	G	A	TP	+/-	PIM	PP	SH	GW	GT	S	PCT
69	9	27	36	+10	65	3	0	1	0	127	7.1

1996-97 statistics:

GP	G	A	TP	+/-	PIM	PP	SH	GW	GT	S	PCT
49	2	13	15	-7	24	0	0	1	0	72	2.8

LAST SEASON

Missed 27 games with separated shoulder. Missed four games with strained trapezius.

THE FINESSE GAME

Brisebois has some nice skills, but doesn't have the hockey sense to put them in a complete package to be an elite level defenseman. He has a decent first step to the puck. He has a good stride with some quickness, though he won't rush end-to-end. He carries the puck with authority, but will usually take one or two strides and look for a pass, or else make the safe dump out of the zone. He steps up in the neutral zone to slow an opponent's rush.

Brisebois plays the point well enough to be on the first power-play unit, but he doesn't have the rink vision that marks truly successful point men; basically, he gets the job in Montreal by default. Brisebois has a good point shot, with a sharp release, and he keeps it low and on target. He doesn't often venture to the circles on offense, but when he does he has the passing skills and the shot to make something happen.

Brisebois improved his positional play but often starts running around as if he is looking for someone to belt. He winds up hitting no one, while his partner is left outnumbered in the front of the net. He is a good outlet passer but will sometimes get flustered and throw the puck away.

THE PHYSICAL GAME

Brisebois did not come back from his shoulder injury at the end of the 1996-97 season and it remains to be seen if the injury will make him gun-shy. Odds are, it will. He does not take the body much and will play the puck instead of the man. He'll have to work on his conditioning since he does not appear to be a very strong player — at least, he doesn't use his body well. He's tough only when he has a stick in his hands.

THE INTANGIBLES

The Canadiens had high hopes for Brisebois, but even allowing for his physical ailments, we don't think we'll see much more out of him than has already been shown.

PROJECTION

Brisebois fits better as a number five or six defenseman than as a top four, which is what he's been asked to handle in his Canadiens career. Unless there is a better finesse defenseman on the horizon, Brisebois will continue to get his share of key power-play time, but will only be in the 40-point range.

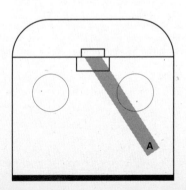

BENOIT BRUNET

Yrs. of NHL service: 5
Born: Pointe-Claire, Que.; Aug. 24, 1968
Position: left wing
Height: 5-11
Weight: 195
Uniform no.: 17
Shoots: left

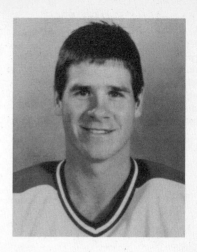

Career statistics:

GP	G	A	TP	PIM
265	49	84	133	100

1993-94 statistics:

GP	G	A	TP	+/-	PIM	PP	SH	GW	GT	S	PCT
71	10	20	30	+14	20	0	3	1	0	92	10.9

1994-95 statistics:

GP	G	A	TP	+/-	PIM	PP	SH	GW	GT	S	PCT
45	7	18	25	+7	16	1	1	2	1	80	8.8

1995-96 statistics:

GP	G	A	TP	+/-	PIM	PP	SH	GW	GT	S	PCT
26	7	8	15	-4	17	3	1	4	0	48	14.6

1996-97 statistics:

GP	G	A	TP	+/-	PIM	PP	SH	GW	GT	S	PCT
39	10	13	23	+6	14	2	0	2	1	63	15.9

LAST SEASON

Missed 21 games with fractured fibula. Missed 19 games with broken hand. Missed one game with thigh contusion. Missed one game with tonsillitis.

THE FINESSE GAME

Brunet is one of the most anonymous Montreal forwards because of his quiet, efficient role as a checking winger on the third line. Developing into a top penalty killer, he is strong on his skates and forechecks tenaciously.

When Brunet does choose to do anything offensively, he cuts to the net and uses a confident, strong touch in deep. He is always hustling back on defense, though, and seldom makes any high-risk plays deep in his own zone. He takes few chances, and seems to come up with big points. He had only 10 goals last season, but two were game-winners.

Brunet's hands aren't great, or he would be able to create more scoring off his forecheck. His goals come from hard work, not pretty finesse plays, and his game is heavily defense oriented.

THE PHYSICAL GAME

Brunet isn't very big and is overmatched when he plays against many of the league's top lines. His strength is his positional play. He takes fewer steps than other players to accomplish the same chore. He's not a big hitter, but he will tie up an opponent's stick and play smothering defense.

THE INTANGIBLES

Brunet has a strong work ethic and comes to play every night. He is like a good referee. On his best nights, you seldom notice him. His injuries over the past two seasons are a concern. He missed 56 games in 1995-96 having a benign tumor removed from his spine, and 42 games last season with a variety of ailments.

PROJECTION

Brunet is a hard worker but could slip from the third to the fourth line this season as the Canadiens' talent up front gets deeper. Even if healthy, Brunet won't produce more than 20 goals.

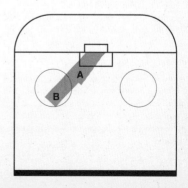

VALERI BURE

Yrs. of NHL service: 2
Born: Moscow, Russia; June 13, 1974
Position: right wing
Height: 5-10
Weight: 168
Uniform no.: 18
Shoots: right

Career statistics:

GP	G	A	TP	PIM
165	39	42	81	40

1994-95 statistics:

GP	G	A	TP	+/-	PIM	PP	SH	GW	GT	S	PCT
24	3	1	4	-1	6	0	0	1	0	39	7.7

1995-96 statistics:

GP	G	A	TP	+/-	PIM	PP	SH	GW	GT	S	PCT
77	22	20	42	+10	28	5	0	1	2	143	15.4

1996-97 statistics:

GP	G	A	TP	+/-	PIM	PP	SH	GW	GT	S	PCT
64	14	21	35	+4	6	4	0	2	1	131	10.7

LAST SEASON

Missed 11 games with bruised kidney. Missed five games with concussion. Missed two games with bruised wrist.

THE FINESSE GAME

Valeri Bure isn't as fast as his famous older brother, Pavel, but he has his own distinct qualities. He has a great sense of anticipation and wants the puck every time he's on the ice. And he can make things happen, though he sometimes tries to force the action rather than let the game flow naturally. He gets carried away in his pursuit of the puck and gets caught out of position, whereas if he just showed patience the puck would come to him.

Bure works well down low on the power play, but will also switch off and drop back to the point. He is gaining confidence in his shot and his scoring ability.

Bure has great hands to go along with his speed and seems to get a shot on goal or a scoring chance on every shift. He is smart and creative, and can make plays as well as finish.

THE PHYSICAL GAME

Bure is strong for his size, but isn't battle-tough. He can be intimidated, and if he wants to play on the top two lines he'll need to be a little grittier.

THE INTANGIBLES

Bure's development is very encouraging to the Canadiens. Unfortunately for Bure, though, most of the Canadiens' skill players are small, like him. If he had a power forward as a linemate, he would get a little more room, but he'll have to make his own space until then.

PROJECTION

This is a big year for Bure, who needs to take another step in his development to stick on one of the top two lines. Twenty goals isn't enough for a player of his skill level.

SHAYNE CORSON

Yrs. of NHL service: 11
Born: Barrie, Ont.; Aug. 13, 1966
Position: centre/left wing
Height: 6-1
Weight: 200
Uniform no.: 27
Shoots: left

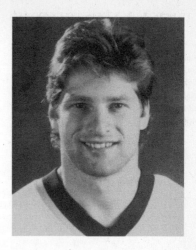

Career statistics:

GP	G	A	TP	PIM
747	200	294	494	1600

1993-94 statistics:

GP	G	A	TP	+/-	PIM	PP	SH	GW	GT	S	PCT
64	25	29	54	-8	118	11	0	3	1	171	14.6

1994-95 statistics:

GP	G	A	TP	+/-	PIM	PP	SH	GW	GT	S	PCT
48	12	24	36	-17	86	2	0	1	0	131	9.2

1995-96 statistics:

GP	G	A	TP	+/-	PIM	PP	SH	GW	GT	S	PCT
77	18	28	46	+3	192	13	0	0	2	150	12.0

1996-97 statistics:

GP	G	A	TP	+/-	PIM	PP	SH	GW	GT	S	PCT
58	8	16	24	-9	104	3	0	2	0	115	7.0

LAST SEASON

Acquired from St. Louis with Murray Baron and a fifth-round draft pick for Pierre Turgeon, Craig Conroy and Rory Fitzpatrick, October 29, 1996. Missed 10 games with sprained ankle. Missed 10 games with knee injury. Missed five games with hip flexor.

THE FINESSE GAME

Corson makes a lot of things happen by overpowering people around the net. Like Bob Probert in his prime, he has surprising scoring ability for a player who is considered a mucker. People give Corson an extra foot or two because of his muscle, which allows him extra time to pick up loose pucks out of scrums and jam his shots in tight, or lift them over a goalie's stick.

Corson gets a lot of rebound goals if he plays on a line with people who throw the puck to the net, because he will go barrelling in for it. He's free to play that style more on the left wing than at centre, but he also has some nice playmaking abilities when put in the middle. He won't do anything too fancy, but is intelligent enough to play a basic short game. Corson can win draws outright on his backhand, and Montreal used him frequently on defensive-zone draws.

Corson is a powerful skater but not very fast or agile. He has good balance for his work along the boards, and has all the attributes of a power forward. He does his dirty work in front of the net for screens and deflections, and has the hands to guide hard point shots. He is wildly inaccurate with any shots other than that at close range, so on the off nights when he is not winning his duels around the net, he is a nonfactor.

THE PHYSICAL GAME

Corson is tremendous along the wall. He has grit, and plays tough and hard every shift. He is dangerous because of his short fuse. Opponents never know when he will go off, and since he's strong and can throw punches, few people want to be around when he does. He inspires fear. He hits to hurt, and is so unpredictable he earns himself plenty of room on the ice.

THE INTANGIBLES

Corson has had two nightmarish seasons with injuries, and as if that weren't enough, the stress of the Montreal trade led to a flare-up of colitis, a condition that has affected Corson since he was 15. When Corson took medication to deal with the ailment, it produced swelling, which in turn led to painful bone spurs in both feet. The fact that he was able to play at all in the playoffs is a tribute to his perseverance.

PROJECTION

We anticipated a big bounce-back year for Corson last season, but the trade and his illness and injuries wrecked the year and make for an uncertain future. At 31, he could still have a few productive seasons left, but we doubt 40 goals is in his range. A team like the Rangers could use a player of his size up front; Corson would look pretty good alongside Wayne Gretzky.

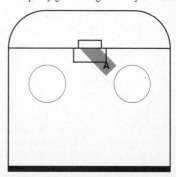

VINCENT DAMPHOUSSE

Yrs. of NHL service: 11
Born: Montreal, Que.; Dec. 17, 1967
Position: left wing
Height: 6-1
Weight: 200
Uniform no.: 25
Shoots: left

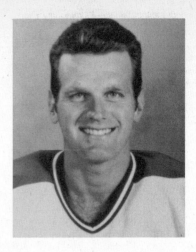

Career statistics:

GP	G	A	TP	PIM
852	310	511	821	770

1993-94 statistics:

GP	G	A	TP	+/-	PIM	PP	SH	GW	GT	S	PCT
84	40	51	91	0	75	13	0	10	1	274	14.6

1994-95 statistics:

GP	G	A	TP	+/-	PIM	PP	SH	GW	GT	S	PCT
48	10	30	40	+15	42	4	0	4	0	123	8.1

1995-96 statistics:

GP	G	A	TP	+/-	PIM	PP	SH	GW	GT	S	PCT
80	38	56	94	+5	158	11	4	3	0	254	15.0

1996-97 statistics:

GP	G	A	TP	+/-	PIM	PP	SH	GW	GT	S	PCT
82	27	54	81	-6	82	7	2	3	2	244	11.1

LAST SEASON

Led team in points, assists and shots. Tied for team lead in power-play goals and game-winning goals. One of two Canadiens to appear in all 82 games (has missed only eight games in 11 NHL seasons).

THE FINESSE GAME

Cool in tight, Damphousse has a marvellous backhand shot he can roof, and he creates opportunites low by shaking and faking checkers with his skating. He likes to set up from behind the net to make plays. Goalies need to be on the alert when he's on the attack, because he is unafraid to take shots from absurd angles just to get a shot on net and get the goalie and defense scrambling. It's an effective tactic.

Damphousse shows poise with the puck. Although he is primarily a finisher, he will also dish off to a teammate if that is a better option. He's a superb player in four-on-four situations. He has sharp offensive instincts and is good in traffic.

Damphousse won't leave any vapour trails with his skating in open ice, but he is quick around the net, especially with the puck. He has exceptional balance to hop through sticks and checks. In open ice, he uses his weight to shift and change direction, making it appear as if he's going faster than he is — and he can juke without losing the puck while looking for his passing and shooting options.

THE PHYSICAL GAME

Damphousse uses his body to protect the puck, but he is not much of a grinder and loses most of his one-on-one battles. He has to be supported with physical linemates (in short supply in Hab land) who will get him

the puck. He'll expend a great deal of energy in the attacking zone, but little in his own end of the ice, though he is more diligent about this in crunch times.

Damphousse is a well-conditioned athlete who can handle long shifts and lots of ice time. He is not shy about using his stick, as his list of stick fouls shows.

THE INTANGIBLES

Like many of his teammates, Damphousse had a dismal playoffs versus New Jersey (zero points on seven shots — he was outscored by Devils goalie Martin Brodeur). As team captain, he will have a lot to answer for this season as the Canadiens continue a slow and painful rebuilding process.

PROJECTION

We incorrectly thought a 100-point season was in the cards for Damphousse last season, but without stronger wingers, he has to do too much of the work himself. We'll call for a repeat 80-point performance. Note Damphousse's propensity for slow starts: He had only nine goals in the first 33 games last season, but 18 in the last 49.

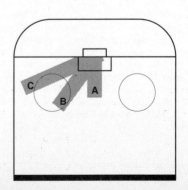

SAKU KOIVU

Yrs. of NHL service: 2
Born: Turku, Finland; Nov. 23, 1974
Position: centre
Height: 5-9
Weight: 175
Uniform no.: 11
Shoots: left

Career statistics:

GP	G	A	TP	PIM
132	37	64	101	78

1995-96 statistics:

GP	G	A	TP	+/-	PIM	PP	SH	GW	GT	S	PCT
82	20	25	45	-7	40	8	3	2	1	136	14.7

1996-97 statistics:

GP	G	A	TP	+/-	PIM	PP	SH	GW	GT	S	PCT
50	17	39	56	+7	38	5	0	3	0	135	12.6

LAST SEASON

Missed 26 games with knee injury. Missed five games with sprained shoulder. Missed one game with tonsillitis.

THE FINESSE GAME

Koivu brings brilliance and excitement to every shift. Considered one of the world's best playmakers, he makes things happen with his speed and intimidates by driving the defense back, then uses the room to create scoring chances. Koivu returned from his knee injury somewhat hobbled, but he is expected to recover well for this season with his speed intact.

Koivu has great hands and can handle the puck at a fast pace. He stickhandles through traffic and reads plays well. He is intelligent and involved.

He has a variety of shots. Like many Europeans, Koivu has an effective backhand for shooting or passing. He also has a strong wrist shot and is deadly accurate. The feisty Finn draws a lot of checking attention and fights his way through most of it, but he is small enough to get worn down.

THE PHYSICAL GAME

The lone knock on Koivu is his lack of size. He gets involved in a scrappy way, but gets shoved around. He won't be intimidated, though, and uses his stick to level the playing field a bit. He has played well in his two playoff experiences, always a positive sign for a young player.

As long as Montreal remains a smallish team, players like Koivu will get battered. Considering how valuable an asset he is, the Canadiens should acquire some big forwards as insurance.

THE INTANGIBLES

Talk about your sophomore jinx. Koivu would have sailed past his impressive rookie totals if he hadn't been decked by injuries. He possesses a strong work ethic and his skill level is world class. Gritty and de-termined, he is well-respected by his teammates and is a probable future captain of the Canadiens, if the team is daring enough to hand the "C" to a non-Francophone.

PROJECTION

If Koivu can stay physically intact, and if Montreal upgrades its size up front just a little bit, there is no reason why he can't register 30 goals.

VLADIMIR MALAKHOV

Yrs. of NHL service: 5
Born: Sverdlovsk, Russia; Aug. 30, 1968
Position: right defense
Height: 6-3
Weight: 220
Uniform no.: 38
Shoots: left

Career statistics:

GP	G	A	TP	PIM
306	43	145	188	307

1993-94 statistics:

GP	G	A	TP	+/-	PIM	PP	SH	GW	GT	S	PCT
76	10	47	57	+29	80	4	0	2	0	235	4.3

1994-95 statistics:

GP	G	A	TP	+/-	PIM	PP	SH	GW	GT	S	PCT
40	4	17	21	-3	46	1	0	0	0	91	4.4

1995-96 statistics:

GP	G	A	TP	+/-	PIM	PP	SH	GW	GT	S	PCT
61	5	23	28	+7	79	2	0	0	0	122	4.1

1996-97 statistics:

GP	G	A	TP	+/-	PIM	PP	SH	GW	GT	S	PCT
65	10	20	30	+3	43	5	0	1	0	177	5.6

LAST SEASON

Led team defensemen in scoring. Missed 16 games with fractured thumb. Missed one game with bruised ribs.

THE FINESSE GAME

Malakhov has elite pro skills and an amateur attitude. We don't mean to insult hardworking amateurs, we're just trying to make a point.

Malakhov has an absolute bullet of a shot, which he rifles off the one-timer or on the fly. He has outstanding offensive instincts for both shooting and playmaking. He moves the puck and jumps into the play, but lacks vision, lateral movement and confidence.

Malakhov is so talented he never looks like he's trying hard. Most nights he's not. He has learned on the job, and as he doesn't speak English well, he's struggled through some of the learning process. He seems discouraged at times when things aren't going smoothly. If he tries a few plays early in a game that don't work, you might as well put him on the bench the rest of the night. If he has a few good shifts early, especially offensively, odds are he'll be one of the three stars.

Malakhov can be used on both special teams. He is a mobile skater, with good agility and balance. He has huge strides, which he developed playing bandy — a Russian game similar to hockey that is played on an ice surface the size of a soccer field.

THE PHYSICAL GAME

Malakhov relies on his positioning and anticipation for his defensive plays more than his hitting. He could be a major physical force because of his size and strength, but injuries may have made him leery of getting hurt, and he really doesn't have the taste for the physical game. He gives up on the play and leaves his defense partner to his own devices.

THE INTANGIBLES

Malakhov seems to save his best hockey for when a marquee player, especially a fellow Russian, is on the opposing team. He doesn't get as pumped up the rest of the year. He is his own worst enemy, because he keeps to himself and won't allow the coaches or his teammates to help him. He has awesome talent, but we wouldn't want him on our team for an 82-game schedule. His tease is tiresome.

PROJECTION

Malakhov will get his 30 to 40 points without being much of an impact player. There isn't much depth on the Canadiens' defense, so unless he is moved he will remain one of their top three defensemen and get a big chunk of ice time.

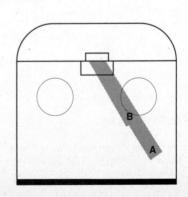

DAVE MANSON

Yrs. of NHL service: 11
Born: Prince Albert, Sask.; Jan. 27, 1967
Position: left defense
Height: 6-2
Weight: 202
Uniform no.: 37
Shoots: left

Career statistics:

GP	G	A	TP	PIM
763	87	223	310	2329

1993-94 statistics:

GP	G	A	TP	+/-	PIM	PP	SH	GW	GT	S	PCT
70	4	17	21	-14	191	1	0	0	0	180	2.2

1994-95 statistics:

GP	G	A	TP	+/-	PIM	PP	SH	GW	GT	S	PCT
44	3	15	18	-20	139	2	0	1	0	104	2.9

1995-96 statistics:

GP	G	A	TP	+/-	PIM	PP	SH	GW	GT	S	PCT
82	7	23	30	+8	205	3	0	0	0	189	3.7

1996-97 statistics:

GP	G	A	TP	+/-	PIM	PP	SH	GW	GT	S	PCT
75	4	18	22	-26	187	2	0	0	0	175	2.3

LAST SEASON

Acquired from Phoenix for Murray Baron and Chris Murray, March 18, 1997. Led team in penalty minutes. Worst plus-minus on team (-25 in 66 games with Phoenix, -1 in nine games with Montreal). Missed five games with broken toe. Missed two games with suspension. Fined $1,000 in playoffs for criticizing officiating.

THE FINESSE GAME

Manson is his own worst enemy: he makes mental errors that keep him from stepping up into the ranks of the NHL's best defensemen. He makes low-percentage plays such as skating through his own crease under a heavy forecheck. Maybe skilled Russian defensemen can get away with that. Manson can't. He can be scary in his own end when he overhandles the puck. He is conscious of helping out his goalie, communicates well and clears rebounds when he keeps the game simple.

Manson will often take himself out of position with his poor defensive reads, then has to resort to using his stick to pull attackers down. Not all of his hefty PIM total are penalties of aggression.

He is smart and effective on the power play because he will mix up his shot with a big fake and freeze. But there isn't much that's subtle about Manson. His game is power. He doesn't have much lateral mobility, so the shot isn't as effective as it would be in the hands of an Al MacInnis. He is not a bad skater for a big guy, though, and he gambles down deep and is canny enough to use an accurate wrist shot when in close.

THE PHYSICAL GAME

Manson has become more disciplined, but still has a knack for taking bad penalties at the worst times. He can throw himself off his game. He will lose control and run after people. He patrols the front of his net well, can hit to hurt and intimidates players into getting rid of the puck faster than they want to. They flinch from even the threat of a Manson body check. On a team of stick-checkers in Montreal, Manson sticks out, but he is being asked to do too much on a team that is weak defensively. His flaws can be hidden on a stronger team, but not on the Canadiens.

THE INTANGIBLES

For all of his flaws, no one can fault Manson's effort. He's a trier if not a doer. He knows his shortcomings and wants to be a better player. He plays hurt and stands up for his munchkin Montreal teammates.

PROJECTION

It's unlikely Manson will score more than 30 to 40 points, even on a team that is as offense-crazy as the Canadiens. He is part of the number one defense pairing in Montreal and has to shoulder a heavy load.

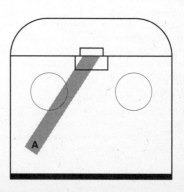

STEPHANE QUINTAL

Yrs. of NHL service: 9
Born: Boucherville, Que.; Oct. 22, 1968
Position: right defense
Height: 6-3
Weight: 225
Uniform no.: 5
Shoots: right

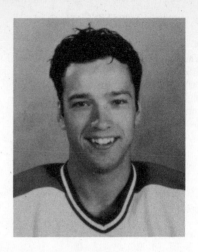

Career statistics:

GP	G	A	TP	PIM
722	32	99	131	763

1993-94 statistics:

GP	G	A	TP	+/-	PIM	PP	SH	GW	GT	S	PCT
81	8	18	26	-25	119	1	1	1	0	154	5.2

1994-95 statistics:

GP	G	A	TP	+/-	PIM	PP	SH	GW	GT	S	PCT
43	6	17	23	0	78	3	0	2	0	107	5.6

1995-96 statistics:

GP	G	A	TP	+/-	PIM	PP	SH	GW	GT	S	PCT
68	2	14	16	-4	117	0	1	1	1	104	1.9

1996-97 statistics:

GP	G	A	TP	+/-	PIM	PP	SH	GW	GT	S	PCT
71	7	15	22	+1	100	1	0	0	0	139	5.0

LAST SEASON

Missed seven games with sprained knee. Missed two games with bruised foot. Missed two games with collarbone injury.

THE FINESSE GAME

Quintal's game is limited by his lumbering skating. He has some nice touches, like a decent point shot and a good head and hands for passing, but his best moves have to be executed at a virtual standstill. He needs to be paired with a quick skater or his shifts will be spent solely in the defensive zone.

Fortunately, Quintal is aware of his flaws. He plays a smart positional game and doesn't get involved in low-percentage plays in the offensive zone. He won't step up in the neutral zone to risk an interception but will fall back into a defensive mode. He takes up a lot of ice with his body and stick, and when he doesn't overcommit, he reduces the space available to a puck carrier.

While he can exist as an NHL regular in the five-on-five mode, Quintal is a risky proposition for any specialty team play.

Quintal does not like to carry the puck, and under pressure in the right corner he will simply slam it out along the left corner boards behind the net.

THE PHYSICAL GAME

Quintal is slow but very strong on his skates. He thrives on contact and works hard along the boards and in front of the net. He hits hard without taking penalties and is a tough and willing fighter.

THE INTANGIBLES

Quintal is ideally a number five or six defenseman, but a dearth of defensive talent in Montreal requires him to play in the top four. A more limited role is in his future as the Canadiens break younger defensemen into the lineup.

PROJECTION

Quintal is a serviceable, third-pairing defenseman.

MARK RECCHI

Yrs. of NHL service: 8
Born: Kamloops, B.C.; Feb. 1, 1968
Position: right wing
Height: 5-10
Weight: 180
Uniform no.: 8
Shoots: left

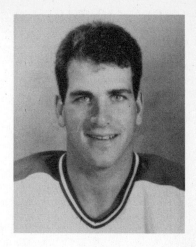

Career statistics:

GP	G	A	TP	PIM
628	285	430	715	484

1993-94 statistics:

GP	G	A	TP	+/-	PIM	PP	SH	GW	GT	S	PCT
84	40	67	107	-2	46	11	0	5	0	217	18.4

1994-95 statistics:

GP	G	A	TP	+/-	PIM	PP	SH	GW	GT	S	PCT
49	16	32	48	-9	28	9	0	3	0	121	13.2

1995-96 statistics:

GP	G	A	TP	+/-	PIM	PP	SH	GW	GT	S	PCT
82	28	50	78	+20	69	11	2	6	0	191	14.7

1996-97 statistics:

GP	G	A	TP	+/-	PIM	PP	SH	GW	GT	S	PCT
82	34	46	80	-1	58	7	2	3	0	202	16.8

LAST SEASON

The NHL's current leading iron man with 461 consecutive games played. One of two Canadiens to appear in all 82 games. Led team in goals. Tied for first on team in power-play goals and game-winning goals. Second on team in assists, points and shots.

THE FINESSE GAME

Recchi is a little package with a lot of firepower. He is one of the top small players in the game, and certainly one of the most productive. He's a feisty and relentless worker in the offensive zone. He busts into open ice, finding the holes almost before they open, and excels at the give-and-go. He's versatile enough to play wing or centre, though he is better on the wing.

Recchi has a dangerous shot from the off-wing. Although he is not as dynamic as Maurice Richard, he likes to use the Richard cut-back while rifling a wrist shot back across. It's heavy, it's on net and it requires no backswing. He follows his shot to the net for a rebound and can make a play as well. He has excellent hands, vision and anticipation for any scoring opportunity.

Recchi has worked hard to improve his defensive play. He kills penalties well because he hounds the point men aggressively and knocks the puck out of the zone. Then he heads off on a breakaway or forces the defender to pull him down.

He isn't a pretty skater but he always keeps his feet moving. While other players are coasting, Recchi's blades are in motion, and he draws penalties. He is ready to spring into any play. He resembles a puck magnet because he is always going where the puck is. He protects the puck well, keeping it close to his feet.

THE PHYSICAL GAME

Recchi gets chopped at because he doesn't hang around the perimeter. He accepts the punishment to get the job done. He is a solid player with a low centre of gravity, and is tough to knock off the puck. He is remarkably durable for the style of game he plays.

THE INTANGIBLES

Recchi is a solo artist, not a player who makes others around him better, but he can upgrade a team if he is given a decent supporting cast. Recchi might be getting a little weary of losing (he hasn't played on a strong club since the 1991 Pittsburgh Penguins) and a change of scene would boost his game. At 29, he has a number of good seasons left.

PROJECTION

No one was blameless in Montreal's poor playoff performance, but Recchi was less guilty than most. Trade rumours have plagued him for two seasons, and despite his remarkable consistency, the Canadiens might have to move him to get the goalie they so desperately need. Recchi will produce 80 points with Montreal, 90 to 100 if he is moved to a better team.

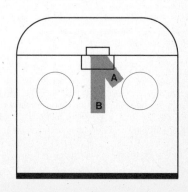

STEPHANE RICHER

Yrs. of NHL service: 12
Born: Ripon, Que.; June 7, 1966
Position: right wing
Height: 6-2
Weight: 215
Uniform no.: 44
Shoots: right

Career statistics:

GP	G	A	TP	PIM
826	366	326	692	519

1993-94 statistics:

GP	G	A	TP	+/-	PIM	PP	SH	GW	GT	S	PCT
80	36	36	72	+31	16	7	3	9	3	217	16.6

1994-95 statistics:

GP	G	A	TP	+/-	PIM	PP	SH	GW	GT	S	PCT
45	23	16	39	+8	10	1	2	5	1	133	17.3

1995-96 statistics:

GP	G	A	TP	+/-	PIM	PP	SH	GW	GT	S	PCT
73	20	12	32	-8	30	3	4	3	0	192	10.4

1996-97 statistics:

GP	G	A	TP	+/-	PIM	PP	SH	GW	GT	S	PCT
63	22	24	46	0	32	2	0	2	1	126	17.5

LAST SEASON

Acquired from New Jersey for Lyle Odelein, August 22, 1996. Missed 10 games with back spasms. Missed nine games with bruised foot.

THE FINESSE GAME

We said in last year's *HSR* that Richer's days as a 50-goal scorer were well behind him. We had no idea his days as a 20-goal scorer were in peril too.

The move back to the more wide-open style of the Canadiens put some juice back in Richer's game, and without injuries he probably would have cracked the 30-goal barrier. Unfortunately, Richer is not the dynamic force he once was, though his size, speed and shot are still in attendance. The mental toughness that once marked him as a game-breaker is absent.

Richer gets great drive from his legs. He has powerful acceleration and true rink-length speed. He can intimidate with his rush, opening up the ice for himself and his linemates. He can also be crafty, slipping in and out of the open ice. He has very good vision offensively and keen hockey sense. Richer possesses a true goal-scorer's slap shot, a wicked blur that he fires from the tops of the circles.

A player with Richer's abilities should be more successful on the power play, but he scored only twice on the power play last season. He doesn't bear down as hard as he should with the extra man. He has become a fine penalty killer, but that should enhance his value as a hockey player and not be the sum total of it.

Because Richer is so strong on his stick and has a long reach, he can strip an opponent of the puck when his body isn't even close, and the puck carrier is always surprised.

THE PHYSICAL GAME

Richer is much better in open ice than in traffic. Although he has the size, strength and balance for trench warfare, he doesn't always show the inclination, and he can be scared off. He will go to the net with the puck, though, and has a wonderful long reach that allows him to be checked and still whip off a strong shot on net. When he's determined, it is just about impossible to peel him off the puck. He is slow to rile and seldom takes bad penalties.

THE INTANGIBLES

After being singled out as one of the reasons why the Devils missed the playoffs in 1996, Richer was fingered as one of the culprits when the Canadiens were ousted in five games by the Devils and he failed to produce a point. The Habs changed coaches again during the off-season, and Alain Vigneault's arrival could give Richer a boost, though the minor-league coach is likely to prefer some of his younger players.

PROJECTION

Last season, *HSR* predicted that Richer would be moved and would score 30 goals in a less defensive-minded role. If his goal total is prorated for injuries, both of those predictions were on the mark. Richer is on the downside now. We doubt he will stay healthy enough to flirt with 30 goals.

MARTIN RUCINSKY

Yrs. of NHL service: 5
Born: Most, Czechoslovakia; March 11, 1971
Position: left wing
Height: 6-0
Weight: 198
Uniform no.: 26
Shoots: left

Career statistics:

GP	G	A	TP	PIM
311	88	133	221	255

1993-94 statistics:

GP	G	A	TP	+/-	PIM	PP	SH	GW	GT	S	PCT
60	9	23	32	+4	58	4	0	1	0	96	9.4

1994-95 statistics:

GP	G	A	TP	+/-	PIM	PP	SH	GW	GT	S	PCT
20	3	6	9	+5	14	0	0	0	0	32	9.4

1995-96 statistics:

GP	G	A	TP	+/-	PIM	PP	SH	GW	GT	S	PCT
78	29	46	75	+18	68	9	2	4	0	181	16.0

1996-97 statistics:

GP	G	A	TP	+/-	PIM	PP	SH	GW	GT	S	PCT
70	28	27	55	+1	62	6	3	3	1	172	16.3

LAST SEASON

Missed 10 games with separated shoulder. Missed one game with knee injury. Missed one game with bruised hand. Led team in shorthanded goals. Tied for team lead in game-winning goals. Second on team in goals.

THE FINESSE GAME

Rucinsky is very quick, with hand skills to match at high tempo. He is most dangerous off the rush, where he can use his speed to intimidate the defense and then use the room they give him to fire his shot.

Rucinsky's flaw is that he is not overly patient. He has nice little moves and can beat people one-on-one. He loves to shoot, though, unlike many European players.

THE PHYSICAL GAME

Rucinsky is wiry but isn't a big banger. His physical effectiveness will depend on his recovery from surgery. Confidence will allow him to continue to play in traffic and take hits to protect the puck.

THE INTANGIBLES

Rucinsky was an absolute bust in the playoffs (no points in five games), and fans were calling for his trade before the lights were turned off at Le Centre Molson. It was easier to hide his defensive flaws on a skilled team like Colorado.

PROJECTION

Rucinsky's inconsistency continues to plague him. He'll score 50 to 60 unsatisfying points.

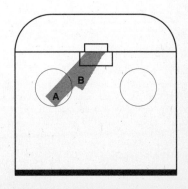

BRIAN SAVAGE

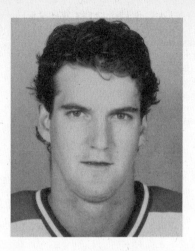

Yrs. of NHL service: 3
Born: Sudbury, Ontario; Feb. 24, 1971
Position: centre/left wing
Height: 6-1
Weight: 190
Uniform no.: 49
Shoots: left

Career statistics:

GP	G	A	TP	PIM
196	61	52	113	94

1993-94 statistics:

GP	G	A	TP	+/-	PIM	PP	SH	GW	GT	S	PCT
3	1	0	1	0	0	0	0	0	0	3	33.3

1994-95 statistics:

GP	G	A	TP	+/-	PIM	PP	SH	GW	GT	S	PCT
37	12	7	19	+5	27	0	0	0	0	64	18.8

1995-96 statistics:

GP	G	A	TP	+/-	PIM	PP	SH	GW	GT	S	PCT
75	25	8	33	-8	28	4	0	4	0	150	16.7

1996-97 statistics:

GP	G	A	TP	+/-	PIM	PP	SH	GW	GT	S	PCT
81	23	37	60	-14	39	5	0	2	0	219	10.5

LAST SEASON

Missed one game with groin injury. Career high in points. Third on team in points. Second on team in points.

THE FINESSE GAME

Savage has improved his playmaking without losing much off his finishing touch. He lacks the creativity and vision for playing centre (he suffers from a bit of tunnel vision), but his experience as a centre helps him as a left wing. He has a quick release and is accurate with his shot. He feasts from the hash marks in and seldom passes up a shot to make a play.

Savage is a streaky scorer, though, and he doesn't bring much to the game when he isn't scoring. He lets the slumps slow him down instead of working harder through the dry spells. Then it becomes a vicious circle where it's hard for him to get ice time to break out of it.

Savage has quick hands for picking up the puck and for working on face-offs. He's a good skater. Defensively, he remains a liability, which was a real drawback last year on a Montreal team that pretty much ignored positional play.

THE PHYSICAL GAME

Savage doesn't use his body well and can be intimidated when playing a team that takes the body well. Playing him with a tougher linemate, such as Turner Stevenson, gives him a bit of heart and inspiration. Savage is strong on his skates and has decent size.

THE INTANGIBLES

Savage got off to a strong start and was performing well on a line with the playmaking Pierre Turgeon, but suffered after Turgeon was dealt to St. Louis. At odds with former coach Mario Tremblay most of the season, Savage was dropped down to the fourth line. He was also moved to the right wing for a spell, which is his worst forward position. Never comfortable, Savage ended last season hoping for a trade (he became a Grade 2 free agent). A coaching change to Alain Vigneault may make Savage a happier player if he remains a Hab.

PROJECTION

We predicted 25 goals for Savage last year; that still appears to be his limit.

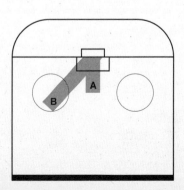

TURNER STEVENSON

Yrs. of NHL service: 3
Born: Prince George, B.C.; May 18, 1972
Position: right wing
Height: 6-3
Weight: 215
Uniform no.: 30
Shoots: right

Career statistics:

GP	G	A	TP	PIM
189	23	30	53	352

1993-94 statistics:

GP	G	A	TP	+/-	PIM	PP	SH	GW	GT	S	PCT
2	0	0	0	-2	2	0	0	0	0	0	0.0

1994-95 statistics:

GP	G	A	TP	+/-	PIM	PP	SH	GW	GT	S	PCT
41	6	1	7	0	86	0	0	1	0	35	17.1

1995-96 statistics:

GP	G	A	TP	+/-	PIM	PP	SH	GW	GT	S	PCT
80	9	16	25	-2	167	0	0	2	0	101	8.9

1996-97 statistics:

GP	G	A	TP	+/-	PIM	PP	SH	GW	GT	S	PCT
65	8	13	21	-14	97	1	0	0	0	76	10.5

PROJECTION

Stevenson can develop into a two-way winger with 20-goal potential, but "potential" is always a scary word. Stevenson has been slow to develop, like many big forwards, but Montreal believes he will be worth the wait.

LAST SEASON

Missed 16 games with knee injury.

THE FINESSE GAME

When a team as desperate for size as the Canadiens keeps a player the size of Stevenson on the third and fourth lines, that spells problems.

Effort isn't an issue, because the third-year winger was one of the few noteworthy Canadiens forwards in the playoffs, but Stevenson lacks the hand speed to combine with his decent skating speed to be more of an impact player. He doesn't shoot enough and has to take the puck to the net with more authority.

A good skater for a player of his size, he has a good long stride and is balanced and agile.

Stevenson has a variety of shots and uses all of them with power and accuracy, but his release needs improvement. He will follow the puck to the net and not give up on shots. He is also a decent passer and possesses some vision and creativity. Stevenson plays a short power game.

THE PHYSICAL GAME

Stevenson has an impressive mean streak. The problem for the coaching staff will be lighting a fire under him on a regular basis, because he doesn't bring the same intensity to the ice every night. He seems to have no idea what kind of physical presence he can add to the team.

THE INTANGIBLES

The Canadiens have a lot of small finesse players. Stevenson adds some grit and was one of the few highlights of their otherwise dismal playoff showing.

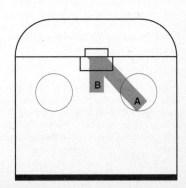

JOCELYN THIBAULT

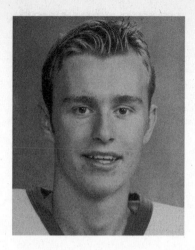

Yrs. of NHL service: 4
Born: Montreal, Que.; Jan. 12, 1975
Position: goaltender
Height: 5-11
Weight: 170
Uniform no.: 41
Catches: left

Career statistics:

GP	MIN	GA	SO	GAA	A	PIM
158	8691	420	5	2.90	0	4

1993-94 statistics:

GP	MIN	GAA	W	L	T	SO	GA	S	SAPCT	PIM
29	1504	3.31	8	13	3	0	83	768	.892	2

1994-95 statistics:

GP	MIN	GAA	W	L	T	SO	GA	S	SAPCT	PIM
18	898	2.34	12	2	2	1	35	423	.917	0

1995-96 statistics:

GP	MIN	GAA	W	L	T	SO	GA	S	SAPCT	PIM
50	2892	2.86	26	17	5	3	138	1480	.907	2

1996-97 statistics:

GP	MIN	GAA	W	L	T	SO	GA	S	SAPCT	PIM
61	3397	2.90	22	24	11	1	164	1815	.910	0

LAST SEASON

Missed nine games with fractured finger. Missed two games with flu.

THE PHYSICAL GAME

Thibault is a small goalie whose technique makes him look even smaller. He is a butterfly-style goalie, but when he goes to his knees, he doesn't keep his torso upright (as Patrick Roy does so splendidly), and that costs Thibault a big chunk of net.

He is terrible with his rebounds. He doesn't direct them, and they bounce right out into no-man's-land where he can't reach the pucks to clear them and the attackers are swooping in. Thibault's puckhandling is average on his best nights. On his worst nights, he is a giveaway machine. Put in a quarter, get a puck.

Thibault plays deep in his net and does not challenge shooters. He relies on his reflexes — which, happily for the Habs, happen to be excellent. He is a battler and doesn't give up on a puck, but he creates problems for himself by making the easy saves more difficult than they would be if his fundamentals were better. Thibault has a good glove hand, quick feet, and is a good skater with lateral mobility.

THE MENTAL GAME

Thibault wants to be a Roy clone. He embraced the trade to Montreal a season ago, despite the high stress of being a French-Canadian hockey player in that city. Thibault is very competitive and wants to perform well in pressure situations, but whether he can do it over the long haul is a huge question mark.

THE INTANGIBLES

Thibault gave way in the playoffs to Jose Theodore, another small goalie with drawbacks similar to Thibault's. He just doesn't look like a bona fide number one goalie, and won't become one without intensive goalie coaching. At one Montreal practice during the 1997 playoffs, Thibault and Theodore could both be observed standing idly in their nets without supervision while the rest of the team was congregated at centre ice. This would be unthinkable on a team like the Devils, where the goalies are always kept busy at their game.

PROJECTION

Rumours were rampant in Montreal last season that the Habs would acquire Felix Potvin to replace Thibault. If Montreal doesn't make a deal, Thibault will be number one again by default.

SCOTT THORNTON

Yrs. of NHL service: 5
Born: London, Ont.; Jan. 9, 1971
Position: left wing
Height: 6-3
Weight: 210
Uniform no.: 24
Shoots: left

Career statistics:

GP	G	A	TP	PIM
315	34	43	77	600

1993-94 statistics:

GP	G	A	TP	+/-	PIM	PP	SH	GW	GT	S	PCT
61	4	7	11	-15	104	0	0	0	0	65	6.2

1994-95 statistics:

GP	G	A	TP	+/-	PIM	PP	SH	GW	GT	S	PCT
47	10	12	22	-4	89	0	1	1	0	69	14.5

1995-96 statistics:

GP	G	A	TP	+/-	PIM	PP	SH	GW	GT	S	PCT
77	9	9	18	-25	149	0	2	3	0	95	9.5

1996-97 statistics:

GP	G	A	TP	+/-	PIM	PP	SH	GW	GT	S	PCT
73	10	10	20	-19	128	1	1	1	0	110	9.1

LAST SEASON

Acquired from Edmonton for Andrei Kovalenko, September 6, 1996. Missed five games with arthroscopic knee surgery. Missed three games with bruised hand. Missed one game with flu.

THE FINESSE GAME

Thornton's best asset is his face-off ability. He is outstanding on draws, especially in the defensive zone, and matches up against just about any centre in the league when it comes to winning puck battles. If Thornton doesn't win a draw outright, he uses his muscle to tie up the opponent and work the puck to a teammate.

He uses his toughness to get rid of a defender, then has good hands when he works in tight to get his scoring chances. Thornton is by no means a sniper, and even though he has concentrated more on the defensive aspects of the game, he is able to convert a scoring chance when the opportunity presents itself. He was a scorer at the junior level, and knows what to do with the puck around the cage, though he doesn't have an NHL release.

Thornton is a good skater, not overly fast, but no plodder. He is strong and balanced on his feet and hard to knock off the puck. He is alert positionally. If one of his defensemen goes in deep on the attack, Thornton will be the forward back covering for him.

THE PHYSICAL GAME

Thornton is a big, solid, defensive centre, a young Joel Otto but with better mobility. Tough without being chippy or taking bad penalties, he can play against just about any big number one centre in the league.

THE INTANGIBLES

Thornton will never be a major point producer, but he will fill a steady checking role for the team in many seasons to come. Thornton is the kind of reliable, defensive forward any team could use for a serious Cup run. Because he never fulfilled his offensive promise as a high draft pick (third overall in 1989 by Toronto), he may be viewed as a failure, but he delivers in other areas.

PROJECTION

Thornton's future is as a third-line checker. He'll never produce more than 10 to 15 goals a season.

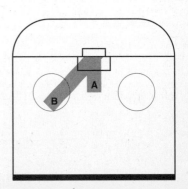

DAVID WILKIE

Yrs. of NHL service: 2
Born: Ellensburgh, WA; May 30, 1974
Position: right defense
Height: 6-2
Weight: 210
Uniform no.: 3
Shoots: right

Career statistics:

GP	G	A	TP	PIM
86	7	14	21	73

1994-95 statistics:

GP	G	A	TP	+/-	PIM	PP	SH	GW	GT	S	PCT
1	0	0	0	0	0	0	0	0	0	0	0.0

1995-96 statistics:

GP	G	A	TP	+/-	PIM	PP	SH	GW	GT	S	PCT
24	1	5	6	-10	10	1	0	0	0	39	2.6

1996-97 statistics:

GP	G	A	TP	+/-	PIM	PP	SH	GW	GT	S	PCT
61	6	9	15	-9	63	3	0	0	0	65	9.2

LAST SEASON

First NHL season. Missed four games with concussion. Missed one game with groin injury.

THE FINESSE GAME

Wilkie is a good skater on the straight but needs to improve his lateral mobility to be more effective defensively. He's an offense-oriented defenseman at this stage: intelligent, and less of a defensive liability than some of the more experienced Montreal defensemen.

Wilkie has a terrific point shot and refined offensive instincts, a result of having started his hockey career as a forward. He loves to rush with the puck and can go end-to-end. His passes are crisp and he doesn't throw the puck away under pressure.

Wilkie was hit by some injuries early in his career, which is why the Canadiens have brought him along slowly.

THE PHYSICAL GAME

Wilkie is a big skater who tends to play a little smaller than he should. He's not very aggressive, but he doesn't get knocked off the puck. He will have to use his body more because he's just too darn big to tiptoe around in his own end.

THE INTANGIBLES

Wilkie has a good offensive upside and should step in to help the Canadiens run their first-unit power play before long. Former Montreal coach Mario Tremblay didn't have much faith in Wilkie last season.

PROJECTION

Time for Wilkie to step up and step in as one of the team's top four defensemen. He could produce in the 30-point range if he does.

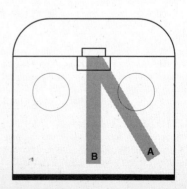

NEW JERSEY DEVILS

Players' Statistics 1996-97

POS.	NO.	PLAYER	GP	G	A	PTS	+/-	PIM	PP	SH	GW	GT	S	PCT
C	93	DOUG GILMOUR	81	22	60	82	2	68	4	1	1	1	143	15.4
C	16	BOBBY HOLIK	82	23	39	62	24	54	5		6		192	12.0
L	23	DAVE ANDREYCHUK	82	27	34	61	38	48	4	1	2	1	233	11.6
R	15	JOHN MACLEAN	80	29	25	54	11	49	5		6		254	11.4
R	12	BILL GUERIN	82	29	18	47	-2	95	7		9		177	16.4
L	14	BRIAN ROLSTON	81	18	27	45	6	20	2	2	3		237	7.6
L	25	VALERI ZELEPUKIN	71	14	24	38	-10	36	3		2		111	12.6
D	27	SCOTT NIEDERMAYER	81	5	30	35	-4	64	3		3		159	3.1
L	32	STEVE THOMAS	57	15	19	34	9	46	1		2		124	12.1
C	10	*DENIS PEDERSON	70	12	20	32	7	62	3		3		106	11.3
R	21	RANDY MCKAY	77	9	18	27	15	109			2		92	9.8
D	4	SCOTT STEVENS	79	5	19	24	26	70			1		166	3.0
D	2	DAVE ELLETT	76	6	15	21	-6	40	1		2		105	5.7
D	29	SHAWN CHAMBERS	73	4	17	21	17	19	1				114	3.5
C	19	BOB CARPENTER	62	4	15	19	6	14		1			76	5.3
C	22	PETER ZEZEL	53	4	12	16	10	16			1		62	6.5
D	24	LYLE ODELEIN	79	3	13	16	16	110	1		2		93	3.2
L	20	*JAY PANDOLFO	46	6	8	14	-1	6			1	2	61	9.8
D	3	KEN DANEYKO	77	2	7	9	24	70				1	63	3.2
D	28	KEVIN DEAN	28	2	4	6	2	6					21	9.5
R	22	*PATRIK ELIAS	17	2	3	5	-4	2					23	8.7
C	18	SERGEI BRYLIN	29	2	2	4	-13	20					34	5.9
L	33	REID SIMPSON	27		4	4	0	60					17	
G	30	MARTIN BRODEUR	67		4	4	0	8						
C	17	PETR SYKORA	19	1	2	3	-8	4					26	3.8
C	8	*PASCAL RHEAUME	2	1		1	1						5	20.0
L	26	*KRZYSZTOF OLIWA	1				-1	5						
R	9	*VADIM SHARIFIJANOV	2				0						4	
G	35	JEFF REESE	3				0							
G	1	*MIKE DUNHAM	26				0	2						

GP = games played; G = goals; A = assists; PTS = points; +/- = goals-for minus goals-against while player is on ice;
PIM = penalties in minutes; PP = power-play goals; SH = shorthanded goals; GW = game-winning goals; GT =
game-tying goals; S = no. of shots; PCT = percentage of goals to shots; * = rookie

DAVE ANDREYCHUK

Yrs. of NHL service: 15
Born: Hamilton, Ont.; Sept. 29, 1963
Position: left wing
Height: 6-3
Weight: 220
Uniform no.: 23
Shoots: right

Career statistics:

GP	G	A	TP	PIM
1099	503	557	1063	816

1993-94 statistics:

GP	G	A	TP	+/-	PIM	PP	SH	GW	GT	S	PCT
83	53	45	98	+22	98	21	5	8	0	333	15.9

1994-95 statistics:

GP	G	A	TP	+/-	PIM	PP	SH	GW	GT	S	PCT
48	22	16	38	-7	34	8	0	2	2	168	13.1

1995-96 statistics:

GP	G	A	TP	+/-	PIM	PP	SH	GW	GT	S	PCT
76	28	29	57	-9	64	14	2	3	1	241	11.6

1996-97 statistics:

GP	G	A	TP	+/-	PIM	PP	SH	GW	GT	S	PCT
82	27	34	61	+38	48	4	1	2	1	233	11.6

LAST SEASON

Scored 500th NHL goal. One of three Devils to appear in all 82 games. Led team and tied for third in NHL in plus-minus. Third on team in goals, assists and points.

THE FINESSE GAME

Andreychuk just can't get enough of the game, but defenders have certainly had their fill of him. The big winger uses a very stiff shaft on his long stick (no one was happier with the rule change allowing sticks to now be 63 inches long), enabling him to lean on it hard in front of the net. He tries to keep his blade on the ice for deflections, and by pushing his 220 pounds on the stick, he makes it almost impossible for a defender to lift it off the ice.

Andreychuk has slow feet but a cherry-picker reach, which he uses with strength and intelligence. He is a lumbering skater, but since he works in tight areas he only needs a big stride or two to plant himself where he wants. He has marvellous hand skills in traffic and can use his stick to artfully pick pucks out of midair, to slap at rebounds, or for wraparounds. He has quick and accurate wrist and snap shots. Andreychuk's hands are so quick he will frequently be used at centre for offensive-zone draws.

From the hash marks in, Andreychuk is one of the most dangerous snipers in the league. On the other four-fifths of the ice, he was once considered a liability, but he is now much more conscientious about not getting caught, as his stunning plus-minus indicates.

Increasingly, Andreychuk is becoming a power-play specialist. He needs to play with people who can get him the puck and with people who can skate, to compensate for his skating deficiencies. He gets into occasional slumps when he overhandles the puck. He is at his peak when he works the give-and-go and keeps his legs moving.

THE PHYSICAL GAME

If you're looking for someone to protect his smaller teammates, or to inspire a team with his hitting, then Andreychuk is not your man. Andreychuk is a giant shock absorber, soaking up hits without retaliating. He has a long fuse and will seldom take a bad penalty, especially when his team is on the power play.

He's tough in his own way — in front of the opponent's net, at least. He is nearly impossible to budge, and with his long arms can control pucks. He isn't dominating, but he is physically prominent within five feet of the crease. He pays the price to score goals and knows how to use his talent.

THE INTANGIBLES

The Devils acquired the perfect centre for Andreychuk — his former Toronto linemate, Doug Gilmour — but coach Jacques Lemaire stubbornly refused to put the two friends on the same line. Shouldn't the Devils have one line that puts offensive pressure on opponents? They will if Gilmour and Andreychuk are partners this season.

PROJECTION

Andreychuk was bitterly disappointed by a freak injury in the last game of the regular season, when he was dumped behind the net by Flyers rookie Janne Niinimaa and suffered a fractured ankle that forced him to miss all but the final playoff game. Since skating isn't his strong suit, Andreychuk's game won't be affected by the injury. Unless he is teamed with Gilmour, Andreychuk will score in the 60-point range. Playing with Gilmour would add 20 points.

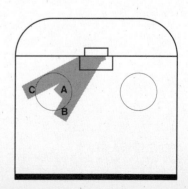

MARTIN BRODEUR

Yrs. of NHL service: 4
Born: Montreal, Que.; May 6, 1972
Position: goaltender
Height: 6-1
Weight: 205
Uniform no.: 30
Catches: left

Career statistics:

GP	MIN	GA	SO	GAA	A	PIM
149	13259	497	22	2.25	7	18

1993-94 statistics:

GP	MIN	GAA	W	L	T	SO	GA	S	SAPCT	PIM
47	2625	2.40	27	11	8	3	105	1238	.915	2

1994-95 statistics:

GP	MIN	GAA	W	L	T	SO	GA	S	SAPCT	PIM
40	2184	2.45	19	11	6	3	89	908	.902	2

1995-96 statistics:

GP	MIN	GAA	W	L	T	SO	GA	S	SAPCT	PIM
77	4434	2.34	34	30	12	6	173	1954	.911	6

1996-97 statistics:

GP	MIN	GAA	W	L	T	SO	GA	S	SAPCT	PIM
67	3838	1.88	37	14	13	10	120	1633	.927	8

LAST SEASON

Led NHL in GAA with lowest GAA in league since Tony Esposito (1.77 in 1971-72). Tied for second in NHL in wins with career high. Led NHL with 10 solo shutouts; first player since Ken Dryden (1976-77) to record 10 shutouts in a season. Tied for second in NHL in save percentage. Became second goalie in Stanley Cup history to score a playoff goal (joining Ron Hextall). Won Jennings Trophy (with Mike Dunham). Vezina Trophy finalist.

THE PHYSICAL GAME

Brodeur has developed from a strictly stand-up goalie to a hybrid, and is smart enough to adapt his style to the team or the shooter he is playing against. Brodeur makes the most of his generous size. He stands upright in the net and squares himself so well to the shooter that he looks enormous. He has become one of the game's best at using his stick around the net. He breaks up passes and will make a quick jab to knock the puck off an opponent's stick. Brodeur helps his team out immensely with this skill.

Opponents want to get Brodeur's feet moving — wraparound plays, rebounds, anything involving his skates exposes his weaknesses. Adam Graves's overtime goal, which knocked the Devils out of the playoffs, was perfect evidence of this. Because of his puck control, Brodeur prevents a lot of scrambles and minimizes his flaws. When he falls into bad streaks, it is usually because of his footwork.

Brodeur has improved his play out of the net, but has to guard against cockiness. He fulfilled a dream by scoring an empty-net goal in the playoffs against Montreal. He gets carried away in his shots through the middle of the ice, but the majority of the time he handles the puck intelligently and is effective on the penalty kill sending the puck up-ice.

THE MENTAL GAME

Bad games and bad goals don't rattle Brodeur for long. While he has a tendency to show his frustration on-ice, he also bounces back quickly with strong efforts. He concentrates and doesn't lose his intensity throughout a game. Teammates love playing in front of him because of the confidence he exudes — even through the layers of padding and the mask. When Brodeur is on, his glove saves are snappy and he bounces on his feet with flair.

No one intimidates Brodeur — with the possible exception of now-retired Mario Lemieux — and he thrives on pressure situations. His ability is often downplayed because he plays for such a strong defensive team, but the flip side is that he gets so few goals in support that he frequently needs a shutout to get a win. That's pressure.

Brodeur was knocked off-stride early in the season when the Devils manoeuvred backup Mike Dunham in and out of the lineup — in order to get Dunham the requisite number of appearances, to avoid losing him as a free agent. Brodeur lost what would have been his 11th shutout this way.

THE INTANGIBLES

Brodeur is going into the final year of a three-year, U.S.$5.2-million contract, which the Devils were so reluctant to give him. He is probably the second-best goalie in the NHL right now, bowing only to his idol, Patrick Roy, and will cost the Devils dearly after this season. He's worth every penny.

PROJECTION

Goal scoring is bound to back up at some point, so Brodeur probably will not match his absurdly low numbers. However, the Devils should score more often this season, and another 35 wins are expected.

KEN DANEYKO

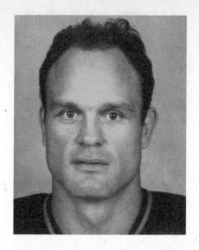

Yrs. of NHL service: 13
Born: Windsor, Ont.; Apr. 17, 1964
Position: left defense
Height: 6-0
Weight: 210
Uniform no.: 3
Shoots: left

Career statistics:

GP	G	A	TP	PIM
873	32	109	141	2118

1993-94 statistics:

GP	G	A	TP	+/-	PIM	PP	SH	GW	GT	S	PCT
78	1	9	10	+27	176	0	0	1	0	60	1.7

1994-95 statistics:

GP	G	A	TP	+/-	PIM	PP	SH	GW	GT	S	PCT
25	1	2	3	+4	54	0	0	0	0	19	3.7

1995-96 statistics:

GP	G	A	TP	+/-	PIM	PP	SH	GW	GT	S	PCT
80	2	4	6	-10	115	0	0	0	0	67	3.0

1996-97 statistics:

GP	G	A	TP	+/-	PIM	PP	SH	GW	GT	S	PCT
77	2	7	9	+24	70	0	0	0	1	63	3.2

LAST SEASON

Missed one game with hip injury. Missed one game with flu. Missed two games due to personal reasons. Second among team defensemen in plus-minus (+24).

THE FINESSE GAME

Break down Daneyko's game — average skater, average passer, below-average shooter — and he looks like someone who would have trouble getting ice time. The edge is Daneyko's competitive drive. He will do anything to win a hockey game. Add to that his strength and sound hockey sense, and the result is a powerful defensive defenseman who has been coveted by other teams for many years.

Despite his lack of footwork, Daneyko has evolved into one of the team's top penalty killers. He is a good shot blocker, though he could still use some improvement. When he goes down and fails to block a shot, he does little more than screen his goalie with his burly body.

A Daneyko rush is a rare thing. He's smart enough to recognize his limitations and he seldom joins the play or gets involved deep in the attacking zone. His offensive involvement is usually limited to a smart, safe breakout pass.

THE PHYSICAL GAME

Daneyko is powerful, with great upper and lower body strength. His legs give him drive when he's moving opposing forwards out from around the net. He is a punishing hitter; when he makes a take-out, the opponent stays out of the play. He is smart enough not to get beaten by superior skaters and will force an attacker to the perimeter. He has cut down on his bad penalties; emotions still sometimes get the better of

him, but he will usually get his two or five minutes' worth.

Daneyko is a formidable fighter, a player few are willing to tangle with, so he has to prove himself less frequently these days. His penalty-minute total was the lowest in his career, except for the lockout season. If somebody wants a scrap, though, he's willing and extremely able, and he stands up for his teammates. It helps that players such as Randy McKay and Reid Simpson are on hand, and Daneyko can spend more time on the ice than in the box.

THE INTANGIBLES

Daneyko is a classic throwback to an era when guys dragged themselves onto the ice and played on fractured ankles. His leadership on and off the ice has become even more evident. He will speak up in the dressing room to quell teammates' arguments, and a coach never has to worry about Daneyko being "up" for a game. Off nights are rare, because he knows his limitations and plays well within the boundaries. Daneyko truly takes the game of hockey to heart.

PROJECTION

Daneyko may have had one of his finest seasons last year, and in the Devils' tight defensive system can continue to function at a strong pace for at least another year. He is showing few signs of wear despite missing few games in his career.

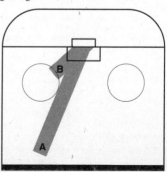

234

DOUG GILMOUR

Yrs. of NHL service: 14
Born: Kingston, Ont.; June 25, 1963
Position: centre
Height: 5-11
Weight: 172
Uniform no.: 93
Shoots: left

Career statistics:

GP	G	A	TP	PIM
1062	368	755	1123	958

1993-94 statistics:

GP	G	A	TP	+/-	PIM	PP	SH	GW	GT	S	PCT
83	27	84	111	+25	105	10	1	3	1	167	16.2

1994-95 statistics:

GP	G	A	TP	+/-	PIM	PP	SH	GW	GT	S	PCT
44	10	23	33	-5	26	3	0	1	1	73	13.7

1995-96 statistics:

GP	G	A	TP	+/-	PIM	PP	SH	GW	GT	S	PCT
81	32	40	72	-5	77	10	2	3	0	180	17.8

1996-97 statistics:

GP	G	A	TP	+/-	PIM	PP	SH	GW	GT	S	PCT
81	22	60	82	+2	68	4	1	1	1	143	15.4

LAST SEASON

Acquired from Toronto with Dave Ellett for Jason Smith, Steve Sullivan and Alyn McCauley. Led team in scoring and assists. Appeared in 1,000th NHL game. Missed three games with eye injury.

THE FINESSE GAME

A superior leader on ice (he is rather quiet in the dressing room), Gilmour is on the verge of losing that fine edge in skills and determination that put him among the league's elite. He sees a lot of ice time and battles through injuries, and looked truly worn down in the playoffs. The Devils are asking him to continue being a number one centre, and while he showed great ability in the first five games after the deal (scoring 4-5 — 9), he came up empty late in the season.

Gilmour is one of those rare individuals who feels he owes his team and teammates every dollar of his salary. For a team to have its best player possess that attitude is invaluable. The mark of a great player is that he takes his team upwards with him, and Gilmour is still capable of doing that.

A creative playmaker, he is one of those rare NHLers who has eschewed the banana blade for a nearly straight model, so he can handle the puck equally well on his forehand or backhand. He will bring people right in on top of him before he slides a little pass to a teammate, creating time and space. He is very intelligent and has great anticipation. He loves to set up from behind the net and intimidates because he plays with such supreme confidence.

Gilmour is a set-up man who needs finishers around him and doesn't shoot much. When he does, he won't use a big slapper, but instead scores from close range either as the trailer or after losing a defender with his subtle dekes and moves. He's not a smooth, gifted skater, but he is nimble and quick.

Gilmour ranks as one of the best face-off men in the NHL and routinely beats big, stronger centres on draws. In his own end, he is very sound positionally.

THE PHYSICAL GAME

Gilmour plays with passion and savvy, challenging bigger opponents regardless of where or when he plays. Although he's listed at 185 pounds, he plays at around 165 during the season and can lose up to seven pounds in a single playoff game.

The only drawback to Gilmour's competitiveness is that he can become so fierce and intense he loses his focus. He does not turn the other cheek. He goes into the trenches because that's where the puck is, and that's what he hungers for.

THE INTANGIBLES

Gilmour provides never-say-die leadership. He often responds with a big shift after his team has been scored upon and will ignite his teammates with an inspirational bump or goal. He will do everything he can to win a game, but the reservoir is only so deep. Gilmour escaped a serious eye injury late in the season when he was hit in the face with a puck, which may have been partly to blame for his late-season slump.

PROJECTION

Gilmour will be 34 when the season starts, and he will not be the 100-point performer he was in the past, especially playing for the low-scoring Devils. Like Wayne Gretzky, however, Gilmour will benefit from the easier travel schedule in the East. An 80-point season is logical.

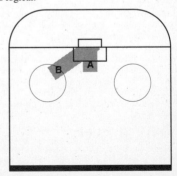

BILL GUERIN

Yrs. of NHL service: 5
Born: Wilbraham, Mass.; Nov. 9, 1970
Position: right wing
Height: 6-2
Weight: 200
Uniform no.: 12
Shoots: right

Career statistics:

GP	G	A	TP	PIM
361	103	101	204	456

1993-94 statistics:

GP	G	A	TP	+/-	PIM	PP	SH	GW	GT	S	PCT
81	25	19	44	+14	101	2	0	3	0	195	12.8

1994-95 statistics:

GP	G	A	TP	+/-	PIM	PP	SH	GW	GT	S	PCT
48	12	13	25	+6	72	4	0	3	0	96	12.5

1995-96 statistics:

GP	G	A	TP	+/-	PIM	PP	SH	GW	GT	S	PCT
80	23	30	53	+7	116	8	0	6	1	216	10.6

1996-97 statistics:

GP	G	A	TP	+/-	PIM	PP	SH	GW	GT	S	PCT
82	29	18	47	-2	95	7	0	9	0	177	16.4

LAST SEASON

Tied for team lead in goals with career high. Led team in game-winning goals and power-play goals. Led team in shooting percentage. One of three Devils to appear in all 82 games.

THE FINESSE GAME

After Guerin's contribution to Team USA in last year's World Cup, expectations for this budding power forward soared higher than ever. Now we have to wonder if what Guerin produced last season was the high end of his abilities.

Power forwards take a long time to develop, but Guerin has taken longer than most. Half the battle is confidence, which Guerin is gaining bit by bit, the other half is intelligence. Guerin has a terrifying slap shot, a wicked screamer that he unleashes off the wing in full flight. But like a young pitcher who lives off his fastball, he must master the change-up. There are times when a snap or wrist shot is the better choice, especially when he is set up for a one-timer. What he must do is keep driving to the net instead of curling around and looking to make a pass. His speed is a potent weapon, but last season, for some curious reason, he drove down his off-wing nearly half the time, and he cannot produce from the left side.

Hockey sense and creativity are lagging a tad behind his other attributes, but Guerin is a smart and conscientious player, and those qualities should develop. He is aware defensively and has worked hard at learning that part of the game, though he will still lose his checking assignments and start running around in the defensive zone.

THE PHYSICAL GAME

The more physical the game is, the more Guerin gets involved. He is big, strong and tough in every sense of the word, and, frankly, is useless when he plays the game on the perimeter. The kind of game Guerin is going to have can usually be judged in the first two or three shifts. He can play it clean or mean, with big body checks or the drop of a glove. He will move to the puck carrier and battle for control until he gets it, and he's hard to knock off his skates.

In front of the net, Guerin is at his best. He works to establish position and has the hand skills to make something happen with the puck when it gets to his stick, but he is sloppy about staying out of the crease, as was shown in the playoffs when he skated through as Doug Gilmour scored what would have been a crucial goal against the Rangers.

THE INTANGIBLES

Guerin played out his contract last season, which might have been a factor in his inconsistent play, and was a Group 2 free agent during the off-season. The Devils will re-sign him, but if the negotiations are bitter, it could affect Guerin psychologically.

PROJECTION

In last year's *HSR*, we said it would be the last year we predicted a big breakout season for Guerin, and he fell just one goal short of the 30 we pegged for him. We now believe 30 is his limit. Few players have scored bigger goals for the Devils and at the same time failed in such key situations as Guerin, which is what makes him so perplexing a player for us and coach Jacques Lemaire.

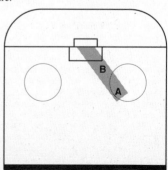

BOBBY HOLIK

Yrs. of NHL service: 7
Born: Jihlava, Czech.; Jan. 1, 1971
Position: centre
Height: 6-3
Weight: 220
Uniform no.: 16
Shoots: right

Career statistics:

GP	G	A	TP	PIM
478	121	151	272	435

1993-94 statistics:

GP	G	A	TP	+/-	PIM	PP	SH	GW	GT	S	PCT
70	13	20	33	+28	72	2	0	3	0	130	10.0

1994-95 statistics:

GP	G	A	TP	+/-	PIM	PP	SH	GW	GT	S	PCT
48	10	10	20	+9	18	0	0	2	0	84	11.9

1995-96 statistics:

GP	G	A	TP	+/-	PIM	PP	SH	GW	GT	S	PCT
63	13	17	30	+9	58	1	0	1	1	157	8.3

1996-97 statistics:

GP	G	A	TP	+/-	PIM	PP	SH	GW	GT	S	PCT
82	23	39	62	+24	54	5	0	6	0	192	12.0

LAST SEASON

One of three Devils to appear in all 82 games. Led team in assists with career high. Second on team in points with career high. Tied for second on team in game-winning goals.

THE FINESSE GAME

Holik went AWOL during training camp to make a point that he should be considered more than just the centre for the successful Crash Line, which had been one of the best fourth lines in NHL history. Holik got his wish, and for a time he performed well as a number one centre, but eventually the Devils saw the need for a true number one and made the deal for Doug Gilmour. Holik's niche as a number two centre should prove comfortable.

Holik achieved some level of chemistry with Dave Andreychuk as his winger, and his effectiveness in the playoffs diminished with Andreychuk's ankle injury. Holik is limited as a creative playmaker, because he lacks vision, but Andreychuk proved a fairly predictable partner. Holik's power game meshed with Andreychuk's willingness to get to the front of the net and battle to get his stick down.

Holik has a terrific shot, a bullet drive that he gets away quickly from a rush down the left side. He also has great hands for working in tight, in traffic and off the backhand. On the backhand (at which Europeans are so much more adept than North Americans), Holik uses his bulk to obscure the vision of his defenders, protecting the puck and masking his intentions. He has a fair wrist shot.

Playing centre (Holik played the position almost exclusively the last two season after spins on the wing the previous few years) gets Holik more consistently involved. Although he lacks the creativity to be a truly effective centre, he brings other assets to the table. He crashes the net and is a scary forechecker.

He's a powerful skater with good balance, but Holik lacks jump and agility. Once he starts churning, he can get up a good head of steam yet can be caught out of position. He is more responsible defensively, which allows Jacques Lemaire to match him against some of the league's better power centres.

THE PHYSICAL GAME

Holik is just plain big. He's a serious hitter who can hurt and who applies his bone-jarring body checks at the appropriate times. He takes few bad penalties.

THE INTANGIBLES

Few players put their faith in themselves on the line the way Holik did last season. The Devils are a club that has zero tolerance for insubordination (check the Claude Lemieux, Sean Burke and Pat Verbeek files), but it was as if the Devils had Holik penciled in for an increased role anyway, and when the time came to put up or shut up, he delivered pretty impressively. Few Devils dare to speak out as plainly and truthfully as Holik.

PROJECTION

Holik exceeded our expectations (we saw him as a steady 40-point scorer) with his production last season. Once you raise the bar, however, you have to jump it again and again.

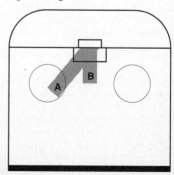

JOHN MACLEAN

Yrs. of NHL service: 13
Born: Oshawa, Ont.; Nov. 20, 1964
Position: right wing
Height: 6-0
Weight: 200
Uniform no.: 15
Shoots: right

Career statistics

GP	G	A	TP	PIM
862	327	334	661	1122

1993-94 statistics:

GP	G	A	TP	+/-	PIM	PP	SH	GW	GT	S	PCT
80	37	33	70	+30	95	8	0	4	0	277	13.4

1994-95 statistics:

GP	G	A	TP	+/-	PIM	PP	SH	GW	GT	S	PCT
46	17	12	29	+13	32	2	1	0	0	139	12.2

1995-96 statistics:

GP	G	A	TP	+/-	PIM	PP	SH	GW	GT	S	PCT
76	20	28	48	+3	91	3	3	3	0	237	8.4

1996-97 statistics:

GP	G	A	TP	+/-	PIM	PP	SH	GW	GT	S	PCT
80	29	25	54	+11	49	5	0	6	0	254	11.4

LAST SEASON

Missed one game due to personal reasons. Led team in shots. Tied for team lead in goals. Tied for second on team in game-winning goals.

THE FINESSE GAME

There is no such thing as an impossible angle for MacLean. He will shoot anytime, from anywhere on the ice, and will usually put the puck on net or out into traffic in front of the crease — where there is always a chance the puck will hit someone or something and go skittering into the net. So what if all of his scoring chances are no longer the brilliant highlight shots that characterized his presurgery (1991) career? His pure goal-scoring instincts still make MacLean a threat.

Last season saw MacLean's goal total increase — goosed by some playing time he got alongside Doug Gilmour — while he still functioned largely in a checking role. MacLean lacks the speed to be an effective shadow against the league's faster forwards, but he is an intelligent player positionally and harasses puck carriers into clumsy passes with his forechecking. He pressures the points when killing penalties. MacLean has great anticipation for picking passes out of lanes that he fools the opposition into thinking are open.

Slow in open ice but strong along the boards and in the corners, he chugs and churns and, by keeping his feet in motion, draws restraining fouls. MacLean also indulges in a bit of diving. Somehow, he gets to where he has to go, but his wheels are average on a good night.

THE PHYSICAL GAME

MacLean uses a wide-based skating stance and is tough to budge from the front of the net. He will take a lot of abuse to get the job done in traffic, and will not be intimidated. He has cut down on his retaliatory penalties, though Niklas Sundstrom might argue the point. MacLean broke Sundstrom's arm with a slash during the playoffs but escaped suspension.

Despite his problems with his knee, MacLean is remarkably durable. He is extremely competitive and fights down to the last second of a game.

THE INTANGIBLES

MacLean is heading into his option year. In an age when there is little loyalty in pro sports, MacLean — who started his Devils career in 1983 — deserves to finish in New Jersey. His is a strong presence in the dressing room.

PROJECTION

MacLean's big-number days are over as he has become more of a two-way forward, but he can still kick in 25 goals a season, as we said in last year's *HSR* and will repeat this season.

RANDY MCKAY

Yrs. of NHL service: 8
Born: Montreal, Que.; Jan. 25, 1967
Position: right wing
Height: 6-1
Weight: 205
Uniform no.: 21
Shoots: right

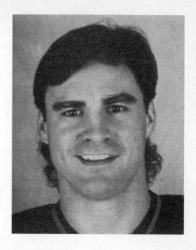

Career statistics:

GP	G	A	TP	PIM
500	69	90	159	1228

1993-94 statistics:

GP	G	A	TP	+/-	PIM	PP	SH	GW	GT	S	PCT
78	12	15	27	+24	244	0	0	1	1	77	15.6

1994-95 statistics:

GP	G	A	TP	+/-	PIM	PP	SH	GW	GT	S	PCT
33	5	7	12	+10	44	0	0	0	0	44	11.4

1995-96 statistics:

GP	G	A	TP	+/-	PIM	PP	SH	GW	GT	S	PCT
76	11	10	21	+7	145	3	0	3	1	97	11.3

1996-97 statistics:

GP	G	A	TP	+/-	PIM	PP	SH	GW	GT	S	PCT
77	9	18	27	+15	109	0	0	2	0	92	9.8

LAST SEASON

Missed four games with eye/cheekbone injury.

THE FINESSE GAME

McKay lost much of his effectiveness with the breakup of the Crash Line. Bobby Holik demanded a larger role with the team and Mike Peluso was traded to St. Louis, leaving McKay adrift.

There was never a lack of effort on McKay's part. He never cruises through a game. His reputation earns him extra ice and extra time, and he makes use of both. He has worked hard to improve his shooting and passing skills, but because he never found chemistry with other linemates, McKay became a fourth-liner with a nebulous role.

McKay is one of those rare tough guys who has enough skills to make himself a useful player in other areas, including the power play. He has the ability to beat a defender one-on-one by setting his skates wide, dangling the puck, then drawing it through the defenseman's legs and blowing past him for a shot.

McKay is also alert enough to find a linemate with a pass. He doesn't have great hockey vision, but he doesn't keep his eyes glued to the puck, either. Still, most of his points come from driving to the net.

THE PHYSICAL GAME

McKay is an absolutely ferocious fighter. He is a legitimate heavyweight who is among the first to step in to protect a teammate, yet he won't initiate with cheap nonsense. He does everything with intensity, whether it's a body check or bulling his way to the front of the net. He is astoundingly strong on his skates, tough to knock down and nearly impossible to knock out, though more of his fights last season were losses instead of wins. McKay was obviously less of a physical factor after getting hit in the face with a puck late in the season and narrowly escaping serious injury.

THE INTANGIBLES

McKay makes everyone around him braver. He will leap to the defense of a teammate, yet he seldom gets involved in histrionics. He picks his spots and doesn't hurt his team by being selfish. Throw in 10-15 goals and he is invaluable. Coaches never have to worry about McKay being up for a game.

PROJECTION

There is still a place in the game for legitimate tough guys like McKay, but he is a fourth-liner whose ice time is diminishing.

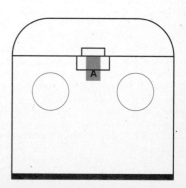

SCOTT NIEDERMAYER

Yrs. of NHL service: 5
Born: Edmonton, Alta.; Aug. 31, 1973
Position: right defense
Height: 6-0
Weight: 200
Uniform no.: 27
Shoots: left

Career statistics:

GP	G	A	TP	PIM
373	38	136	174	219

1993-94 statistics:

GP	G	A	TP	+/-	PIM	PP	SH	GW	GT	S	PCT
81	10	36	46	+34	42	5	0	2	1	135	7.4

1994-95 statistics:

GP	G	A	TP	+/-	PIM	PP	SH	GW	GT	S	PCT
48	4	15	19	+19	18	4	0	0	0	52	7.7

1995-96 statistics:

GP	G	A	TP	+/-	PIM	PP	SH	GW	GT	S	PCT
79	8	25	33	+5	46	6	0	0	0	179	4.5

1996-97 statistics:

GP	G	A	TP	+/-	PIM	PP	SH	GW	GT	S	PCT
81	5	30	35	-4	64	3	0	3	0	159	3.1

LAST SEASON

Led team defensemen in scoring. Missed one game with groin injury.

THE FINESSE GAME

Niedermayer was probably the happiest Devil when Doug Gilmour arrived in February. Thanks to Gilmour's puck control and intelligent defensive play, Niedermayer is more confident rushing the puck and pinching aggressively than at any time in his Devils career. It's no coincidence that three of Niedermayer's five goals came during the 23 games after Gilmour's arrival.

Coach Jacques Lemaire has been blamed for cementing Niedermayer to the blueline and restricting his offensive instincts, and there is some truth to that. Lemaire says he always tells Niedermayer he can go as long as he gets back. Gilmour tells him to go, and we'll score and you don't have to worry about getting back.

Niedermayer has often been compared to Paul Coffey because of his phenomenal skating, but the comparison is not apt. Niedermayer will never be the offensive force that Coffey is, but he is a better defensive player than Coffey is, or ever was.

Niedermayer carries the puck well on the rush, but is still learning to create offensive chances by using his speed in the attacking zone. The 24-year-old is an exceptional skater, one of the best-skating defensemen in the NHL. Niedermayer has it all: speed, balance, agility, mobility, lateral movement and strength. He has unbelievable edge for turns and eluding pursuers. Even when he makes a commitment mistake in the offensive zone, he can get back so quickly his de-fense partner is seldom outnumbered.

THE PHYSICAL GAME

An underrated body checker because of the focus on the glitzier parts of his game, Niedermayer has continued to improve his strength and is a willing, if not vicious, hitter. His skating ability helps him tremendously, giving more impetus to his open-ice checks. He will sacrifice his body to block shots.

THE INTANGIBLES

On a less defensive-minded team, Niedermayer would probably net 70 points, but whether he likes it or not, his tutelage under Lemaire will end up making him a better all-around defenseman than if he had just been allowed to roam at will in his first few NHL seasons. The question is how long will the Devils wait before turning him loose, on the ice or off?

Right now, Niedermayer considers himself to be making the best of a bad situation.

PROJECTION

This is not a happy camper. Niedermayer is going into the final year of a three-year contract and wants out. He will be playing to make himself more attractive to other teams (he will be a Group 2 free agent). That and a full season of playing with Gilmour should result in career-high point totals.

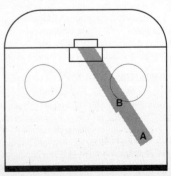

LYLE ODELEIN

Yrs. of NHL service: 7
Born: Quill Lake, Sask.; July 21, 1968
Position: right defense
Height: 5-11
Weight: 210
Uniform no.: 24
Shoots: left

Career statistics:

GP	G	A	TP	PIM
499	23	88	111	1477

1993-94 statistics:

GP	G	A	TP	+/-	PIM	PP	SH	GW	GT	S	PCT
79	11	29	40	+8	276	6	0	2	0	116	9.5

1994-95 statistics:

GP	G	A	TP	+/-	PIM	PP	SH	GW	GT	S	PCT
48	3	7	10	-13	152	0	0	0	0	74	4.1

1995-96 statistics:

GP	G	A	TP	+/-	PIM	PP	SH	GW	GT	S	PCT
79	3	14	17	+8	230	0	1	0	0	74	4.1

1996-97 statistics:

GP	G	A	TP	+/-	PIM	PP	SH	GW	GT	S	PCT
79	3	13	16	+16	110	1	0	2	0	93	3.2

LAST SEASON

Acquired from Montreal for Stephane Richer, August 22, 1996. Led team in penalty minutes. Missed three games with bruised knee.

THE FINESSE GAME

Defense is Odelein's forte. He is very calm with the puck, and able to wait until a player is on top of him and then carry the puck or find an open man. His skating is average at best, but he keeps himself out of trouble by playing a conservative game and not getting caught out of position. An attacker who comes into Odelein's piece of the ice will have to pay the price by getting through him.

Perhaps because he came from Montreal, where he was the team's number one defenseman, to a Devils defense corps where he is merely one of the gang, Odelein was less assertive, and his game suffered. His finesse skills are modest at best, but he has developed sufficient confidence to get involved in the attack if needed. He prefers to limit his contribution to shots from the point. He needs to be paired with a puck-carrying partner.

Odelein's decision-making is not always swift, and he can get his defense partner into trouble with poor defensive reads. Odelein deserves credit for having molded himself into more than an overachieving goon. He is a physical presence despite being smaller than most NHL defensemen — and smaller than many NHL forwards.

THE PHYSICAL GAME

Odelein is a banger, a limited player who knows what those limits are, stays within them and plays effec-

tively as a result. He's rugged and doesn't take chances. He takes the man at all times in front of the net and he plays tough. Heavy but not tall, he gives the impression of being a much bigger man. He will fight, but not very well.

Odelein can be taken off his game easily and gets caught up in yapping matches, which does his game no good.

THE INTANGIBLES

Odelein is credited with helping to calm the atmosphere in what had been a very tense dressing room a season ago. If he were nearly as effective on the ice as he is off it, he would be a Norris Trophy winner.

PROJECTION

There were too many nights last season when Odelein was the worst defenseman on the ice for the Devils. We know he has a better game — we've seen it in Montreal — and the Devils need a more consistent showing from him.

DENIS PEDERSON

Yrs. of NHL service: 1
Born: Prince Albert, Sask.; Sept. 10, 1975
Position: centre/left wing
Height: 6-2
Weight: 190
Uniform no.: 10
Shoots: right

Career statistics:

GP	G	A	TP	PIM
80	15	21	36	62

1995-96 statistics:

GP	G	A	TP	+/-	PIM	PP	SH	GW	GT	S	PCT
10	3	1	4	-1	0	1	0	2	0	6	50.0

1996-97 statistics:

GP	G	A	TP	+/-	PIM	PP	SH	GW	GT	S	PCT
70	12	20	32	+7	62	3	0	3	0	106	11.3

LAST SEASON

First NHL season. Missed one game with thigh injury. Missed one game with head injury. Missed two games with flu.

THE FINESSE GAME

Pederson is an intelligent hockey player who has the potential to develop into a solid two-way centre. His skills aren't elite level, but he makes the most of all of his abilities with his hockey sense.

Pederson has been groomed as a defensive forward by the Devils, but try as they might, they can't wring the offensive production out of his game. He showed some heady flashes of playmaking and is alert around the net for loose pucks. Most of his goals will come from hard work around the cage, not pretty rushing plays.

Pederson can work on the power play, where he uses his size down low and crashes the net. He works well in traffic, and has nice hands for picking the puck out of a tangle of skates and sticks. He is a puck magnet because he gives a second and third effort; the puck always seems to end up on his stick. He has a decent array of shots, including a backhand and a wrist shot, the latter being his best weapon.

He needs to improve on face-offs.

THE PHYSICAL GAME

Pederson is strong and competes hard for the puck. He has a little bit of a mean streak in him, enough to keep his opponents on their toes, and he will come unglued once in awhile. But for the most part he is a disciplined player and does not take lazy penalties. He protects the puck well with his body.

Pederson is still gaining size and strength. He should have the goods to compete against any team's power forwards on a nightly basis.

THE INTANGIBLES

Pederson is so quiet off the ice but is a season or two away from making a lot of noise on the ice. This kid was a scorer in junior, so don't pigeonhole him as strictly a defensive player, even though that is the early route the Devils are directing him along. He is a character guy and a quiet leader, with a sound work ethic.

PROJECTION

The Devils have the luxury of using Pederson as a third-line centre or converting him to left wing to add more scoring punch on a second line. What we like about Pederson is that he's not dainty. He will get down and dirty and earn his ice time honestly. He has a lot to learn yet, but a 20 to 25-goal sophomore season would not surprise us.

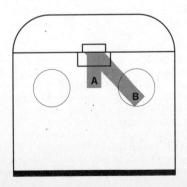

BRIAN ROLSTON

Yrs. of NHL service: 3
Born: Flint, Mich.; Feb. 21, 1973
Position: left wing
Height: 6-2
Weight: 185
Uniform no.: 14
Shoots: left

Career statistics:

GP	G	A	TP	PIM
179	38	49	87	45

1994-95 statistics:

GP	G	A	TP	+/-	PIM	PP	SH	GW	GT	S	PCT
40	7	11	18	+5	17	2	0	3	0	92	7.6

1995-96 statistics:

GP	G	A	TP	+/-	PIM	PP	SH	GW	GT	S	PCT
58	13	11	24	+9	8	3	1	4	1	139	9.4

1996-97 statistics:

GP	G	A	TP	+/-	PIM	PP	SH	GW	GT	S	PCT
81	18	27	45	+6	20	2	2	3	0	237	7.6

LAST SEASON

Career highs in goals, assists and points. Scored first career hat trick.

THE FINESSE GAME

Rolston's game is speed. He is a fast, powerful skater who drives to the net and loves to shoot. He passes well forehand and backhand, and reads breakout plays by leading his man smartly. He's better as a shooter, though. He has a cannon from the top of the circles in with a quick release. He tends to hurry his shots, even when he has time to wait, which results in wildly inaccurate shots. He wastes many odd-man rush opportunities, especially shorthanded, by not forcing the goalie to handle the puck and denying the trailing player an opportunity at a rebound. Rolston was second on the team in shots on goal but he probably led them in shots at goal — shots that went off the glass or into the crowd.

Rolston played centre during his collegiate career and in the minors, and would prefer playing that position with the Devils. However, Jacques Lemaire demands so much of his centres defensively that as long as he coaches the Devils, Rolston will remain a winger.

Rolston is an aggressive penalty killer, using his quick getaway stride to pull away for shorthanded breaks. He is starting to take some pride in this role, and works diligently. Although he doesn't like it, Rolston can also play as a defensive winger, being one of the few Devils with the speed to match strides with a Jaromir Jagr.

Rolston saw a new role this season as a point man on the power play, with mixed results. Once Dave Ellett arrived from Toronto, Rolston was taken off the point, but if the Devils don't re-sign Ellett or Shawn Chambers, or obtain a veteran point man during the off-season, Rolston could be back on the first power-play unit.

THE PHYSICAL GAME

Rolston will take a hit to make a play, and he has taken the next step to start initiating to fight for pucks. He can be intimidated. His better games are against skating clubs rather than opposite Devil clones.

THE INTANGIBLES

Adding Robbie Ftorek as an assistant coach was a boon to Rolston's shaky confidence (it was Ftorek's idea to use Rolston at the point, a position he had played on Ftorek-coached teams in the minors). Rolston has to shoulder more responsibility because, along with Bill Guerin and Scott Niedermayer, he is expected to emerge as a leader for the Devils. He still has some maturing to do.

PROJECTION

We tabbed Rolston as a potential 30-goal scorer last season but will downsize that to 25 this year. What to watch for: Rolston was a Group 2 free agent during the off-season. If his negotiations drag on or are especially bitter, Rolston may have a down year.

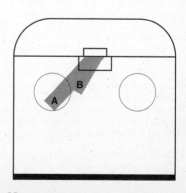

SCOTT STEVENS

Yrs. of NHL service: 15
Born: Kitchener, Ont.; Apr. 1, 1964
Position: left defense
Height: 6-2
Weight: 210
Uniform no.: 4
Shoots: left

Career statistics:

GP	G	A	TP	PIM
1120	162	584	746	2314

1993-94 statistics:

GP	G	A	TP	+/-	PIM	PP	SH	GW	GT	S	PCT
83	18	60	78	+53	112	5	1	4	0	215	8.4

1994-95 statistics:

GP	G	A	TP	+/-	PIM	PP	SH	GW	GT	S	PCT
48	2	20	22	+4	56	1	0	1	0	111	1.8

1995-96 statistics:

GP	G	A	TP	+/-	PIM	PP	SH	GW	GT	S	PCT
82	5	23	28	+7	100	2	1	1	0	174	2.9

1996-97 statistics:

GP	G	A	TP	+/-	PIM	PP	SH	GW	GT	S	PCT
79	5	19	24	+26	70	0	0	1	0	166	3.0

LAST SEASON

Led team defensemen in plus-minus. Missed one game with flu. Missed one game with stick-related suspension.

THE FINESSE GAME

Throughout most of his career, Stevens has been a hybrid defenseman who contributes offensively as well as producing in his own end. Perhaps because of the Devils' emphasis on defense first, Stevens's game has become ever more tilted towards the defensive aspect of the game, to the point where his offensive contribution last season was almost nil.

Stevens has a nice pair of hands for work in close to the net. He usually stays out at the point, and does a good job by taking something off his drive instead of spraying wild, untippable slap shots, but his release is a little slow.

A very good skater, secure and strong, he is capable both forwards and backwards and has good lateral mobility. He has a tendency to overhandle the puck in the defensive zone. Instead of quickly banging the puck off the boards to clear the zone, it seems to take Stevens an unusual amount of time to get the puck teed up and it's often kept in by the attacking team.

Stevens has a tremendous work ethic that more than makes up for some of his shortcomings (and most of those are sins of commission rather than omission). He is a bear on penalty killing because he just won't quit, and he is a fearless shot blocker. Stevens occasionally gets suckered into chasing the puck carrier behind the net at inopportune moments.

THE PHYSICAL GAME

One of the most punishing open-ice hitters in the NHL, Stevens has the skating ability to line up the puck carrier, and the size and strength to explode on impact. He simply shovels most opponents out from in front of the net and crunches them along the boards. He is one of the few NHL defensemen willing and able to tackle Eric Lindros head-on. Most of Stevens's best games occur against the Flyers because he thrives on the challenge.

Stevens fights well when provoked and other teams make a point of trying to lure him into bad penalties, which he still falls for.

THE INTANGIBLES

Stevens is heading into the option year of his contract and the Devils will have a hard decision to make. Has the 33-year-old started on the downside of his career, and will it be too big a risk to invest $10 to $12 million in a two-year deal? Or will the Devils gamble as they did in 1994, and let Stevens test the market (they will retain his rights)?

PROJECTION

Perhaps the best defenseman never to win the Norris Trophy, Stevens did not distinguish himself during the Devils' loss to the Rangers in last year's playoffs. He is an exceptionally proud athlete, and we expect an answer in his play this season, though his point total will remain in the 20-30 range.

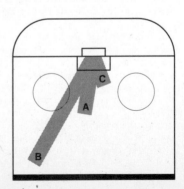

PETR SYKORA

Yrs. of NHL service: 2
Born: Plzen, Czech.; Nov. 19, 1976
Position: centre
Height: 5-11
Weight: 185
Uniform no.: 17
Shoots: left

Career statistics:

GP	G	A	TP	PIM
82	19	26	45	36

1995-96 statistics:

GP	G	A	TP	+/-	PIM	PP	SH	GW	GT	S	PCT
63	18	24	42	+7	32	8	0	3	0	128	14.1

1996-97 statistics:

GP	G	A	TP	+/-	PIM	PP	SH	GW	GT	S	PCT
19	1	2	3	-8	4	0	0	0	0	26	3.8

LAST SEASON
Missed 12 games with groin injury.

THE FINESSE GAME
There are only a few things Sykora doesn't do well technically, but what really sets him apart is his intelligence. Playing against men as a 17-year-old in the IHL in 1994-95 obviously spurred his development, and taught him how to survive as a smaller player in the mean NHL.

Sykora is a fine skater. He has a fluid stride and accelerates in a few steps. He is quick on a straightaway, with or without the puck, and is also agile in his turns. He picks his way through traffic well, and would rather try to outfox a defender and take the shortest path to the net than try to drive wide.

Sykora has excellent hands in tight, for passing or shooting. He defies the usual European stereotype of the reluctant shooter because he's a goal scorer, but he does tend to pass up a low-percentage shot to work for a better one. His wrist shot is excellent, but he also has an adequate snap and slap shot.

He sees the ice well and is a heads-up passer with a great touch. He needs to improve on his face-offs.

THE PHYSICAL GAME
Sykora won't be intimidated. He'll battle for the puck behind or in front of the net but he is simply not a big or mean player. He is strong for his size and his skating provides him with good balance. His work ethic is strong.

THE INTANGIBLES
Talk about a sophomore jinx. Sykora injured his groin on the next-to-last day of training camp, then struggled through the first part of the season trying to play with the injury before spending the bulk of the season in the American Hockey League.

Since so much of his game is derived from his skating, Sykora needs a complete recovery to hit top stride in 1997-98.

PROJECTION
The acquisition of Doug Gilmour is a dilemma for Sykora, since he has to be a number one or number two centre, and the Devils aren't likely to go with Gilmour and Sykora one-two because of their small stature. Sykora played left wing late in the season in the minors, which could be his slot. The Devils need scoring punch and he'll be given every chance to get in the lineup. If he does, he should contribute 50-60 points, but his status is iffy because of the injury.

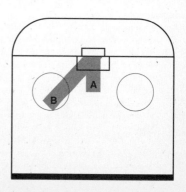

STEVE THOMAS

Yrs. of NHL service: 13
Born: Stockport, England; July 15, 1963
Position: left wing
Height: 5-11
Weight: 185
Uniform no.: 32
Shoots: left

Career statistics:

GP	G	A	TP	PIM
780	310	362	672	1032

1993-94 statistics:

GP	G	A	TP	+/-	PIM	PP	SH	GW	GT	S	PCT
78	42	33	75	-9	139	17	0	5	2	249	16.9

1994-95 statistics:

GP	G	A	TP	+/-	PIM	PP	SH	GW	GT	S	PCT
47	11	15	26	-14	60	3	0	2	0	133	8.3

1995-96 statistics:

GP	G	A	TP	+/-	PIM	PP	SH	GW	GT	S	PCT
81	26	35	61	-2	98	6	0	6	1	192	13.5

1996-97 statistics:

GP	G	A	TP	+/-	PIM	PP	SH	GW	GT	S	PCT
32	15	19	34	+9	46	1	0	2	0	124	12.1

LAST SEASON

Missed two games with flu. Missed 10 games with ankle injury. Missed 12 games with knee injury.

THE FINESSE GAME

Thomas never developed into the powerful offensive force the Devils had hoped for in return for trading away their nettlesome 1995 Conn Smythe Trophy-winner Claude Lemieux. Thomas is still aware of the disparity in their performances, since Lemieux won another Cup with Colorado in 1996 while Thomas and the Devils missed the playoffs.

This year was almost as bad. Thomas hoped to atone for his flawed season with a strong playoffs, but scored only one goal to Lemieux's 13 in the postseason. At least Colorado didn't win another Cup.

Thomas has a great shot and he loves to fire away. He looks to shoot first instead of pass, sometimes to his detriment, but subtlety is not his forte. His game is speed and power, but with his injuries he lost an edge in both departments.

He has a strong wrist shot and an excellent one-timer. He likes to win the battle for the puck in deep, feed his centre, then head for the right circle for the return pass. Playing the left side he was not as effective. Thomas has a very short backswing, which allows him to get his shots away quickly.

Thomas is a wildly intense player. His speed is straight ahead, without much deking or trying to put a move on a defender. He works along the boards and in the corners, willing to do the dirty work. He works hard and has the knack for scoring big goals, though that touch was not much in evidence last season.

THE PHYSICAL GAME

Thomas is hard-nosed and finishes his checks. He is a very good forechecker because he comes at the puck carrier like a human train. He is not big, but he is wide, and tough. He is great along the boards and among the best in the league at keeping the puck alive by using his feet. He is a feisty and fierce competitor and will throw the odd punch. On the occasions when he drops his gloves, Thomas can hold his own.

THE INTANGIBLES

Few Devils tried harder than Thomas last year, and accomplished less. Injuries were a factor, especially the midseason knee injury. Streaky in his best seasons, last year was one prolonged slump for Thomas, who is harder on himself than any coach or teammate could be.

PROJECTION

Although Thomas never fails to compete, he is not the 40-goal scorer he was four seasons ago, or even a 30-goal scorer. Frankly, he'll be lucky to surpass much more than 20 and he will be pushed by some of the younger Devil wingers.

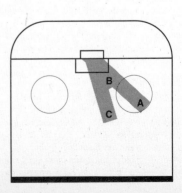

NEW YORK ISLANDERS

Players' Statistics 1996-97

POS.	NO.	PLAYER	GP	G	A	PTS	+/-	PIM	PP	SH	GW	GT	S	PCT
R	16	ZIGMUND PALFFY	80	48	42	90	21	43	6	4	6	1	292	16.4
C	39	TRAVIS GREEN	79	23	41	64	-5	38	10		3		177	13.0
C	21	ROBERT REICHEL	82	21	41	62	5	26	6	1	3		214	9.8
C	15	BRYAN SMOLINSKI	64	28	28	56	8	25	9		1	1	183	15.3
D	34	*BRYAN BERARD	82	8	40	48	1	86	3		1		172	4.7
L	32	NIKLAS ANDERSSON	74	12	31	43	4	57	1	1	1		122	9.8
D	4	BRYAN MCCABE	82	8	20	28	-2	165	2	1	2		117	6.8
R	44	TODD BERTUZZI	64	10	13	23	-3	68	3		1		79	12.7
D	3	KENNY JONSSON	81	3	18	21	10	24	1				92	3.3
C	13	CLAUDE LAPOINTE	73	13	5	18	-11	49		3	3	1	80	16.3
D	7	SCOTT LACHANCE	81	3	11	14	-7	47	1				97	3.1
C	14	*DEREK ARMSTRONG	50	6	7	13	-8	33			2		36	16.7
R	42	DAN PLANTE	67	4	9	13	-6	75	2				61	6.6
R	11	RANDY WOOD	65	6	5	11	-7	61	1	1	2		96	6.3
L	20	BRENT HUGHES	51	7	3	10	-4	57					47	14.9
D	6	DOUG HOUDA	70	2	8	10	1	99					29	6.9
L	24	PAUL KRUSE	62	6	2	8	-9	141			1		49	12.2
R	62	*STEVE WEBB	41	1	4	5	-10	144	1				21	4.8
D	2	RICHARD PILON	52	1	4	5	4	179					17	5.9
D	28	DENNIS VASKE	17		4	4	3	12					19	
C	10	DAVE MCLLWAIN	4	1	1	2	-2		1				3	33.3
L	33	*KEN BELANGER	18		2	2	-1	102					5	
D	46	*JASON HOLLAND	4	1		1	1						3	33.3
R	12	MICK VUKOTA	17	1		1	-2	71					7	14.3
G	35	TOMMY SALO	58		1	1	0	4						
G	30	TOMMY SODERSTROM	1				0							
C	25	CHRIS TAYLOR	1				0						1	
C	21	*NICK VACHON	1				-1							
L	36	*JARRETT DEULING	1				0							
L	8	MIKE DONNELLY	3				0	2					5	
C	28	JIM DOWD	3				-1							
L	42	*ANDREI VASILIEV	3				-3	2					1	
C	24	DAVID ARCHIBALD	7				-4	4					4	
D	10	COREY FOSTER	7				-2	2					1	
G	1	*ERIC FICHAUD	34				0	2						

GP = games played; G = goals; A = assists; PTS = points; +/- = goals-for minus goals-against while player is on ice; PIM = penalties in minutes; PP = power-play goals; SH = shorthanded goals; GW = game-winning goals; GT = game-tying goals; S = no. of shots; PCT = percentage of goals to shots; * = rookie

NIKLAS ANDERSSON

Yrs. of NHL service: 2
Born: Kungalv, Sweden; May 20, 1971
Position: left wing
Height: 5-9
Weight: 175
Uniform no.: 32
Shoots: left

Career statistics:

GP	G	A	TP	PIM
125	26	44	70	71

1995-96 statistics:

GP	G	A	TP	+/-	PIM	PP	SH	GW	GT	S	PCT
48	14	12	26	-3	12	3	2	1	0	89	15.7

1996-97 statistics:

GP	G	A	TP	+/-	PIM	PP	SH	GW	GT	S	PCT
74	12	31	43	+4	57	1	1	1	0	122	9.8

LAST SEASON

Second NHL season. Missed two games with right shoulder sprain. Missed two games with foot injury.

THE FINESSE GAME

If you threw Mats Sundin in the dryer for an hour on a "hot" setting, Andersson would tumble out.

Andersson is small and slick, with good offensive instincts. He's always been noted for his fine passing skills. He creates with his speed, then dishes off on the forehand or backhand with accuracy. He is less reluctant about shooting, and has a quick release on his wrist shot. His speed and anticipation make him a good penalty killer.

This Swede doesn't have the elite class skills to make opponents back off and give him some skating room. He has to play with bigger linemates as bodyguards.

THE PHYSICAL GAME

Andersson isn't thickly built, as a lot of successful small NHL players are, and he really has to keep his feet moving to steer clear of trouble. He can handle the puck in traffic.

THE INTANGIBLES

Until the Islanders can get bigger and better, Andersson is an intelligent little player who will serve as a useful stopgap. The minute a comparable player with size comes along at left wing, however, Andersson will lose his ice time.

PROJECTION

Andersson will give a plucky 10 to 15 goals if he plays a full slate, but in the Atlantic Division it's pretty tough to have a player of his size as a role player.

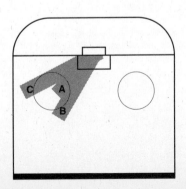

KEN BELANGER

Yrs. of NHL service: 0
Born: Sault Ste. Marie, Ont.; May 14, 1974
Position: left wing
Height: 6-4
Weight: 225
Uniform no.: 33
Shoots: left

Career statistics:

GP	G	A	TP	PIM
28	0	2	2	138

1994-95 statistics:

GP	G	A	TP	+/-	PIM	PP	SH	GW	GT	S	PCT
3	0	0	0	0	9	0	0	0	0	1	0.0

1995-96 statistics:

GP	G	A	TP	+/-	PIM	PP	SH	GW	GT	S	PCT
7	0	0	0	-2	27	0	0	0	0	0	0.0

1996-97 statistics:

GP	G	A	TP	+/-	PIM	PP	SH	GW	GT	S	PCT
18	0	2	2	-1	102	0	0	0	0	5	0.0

sure bet for 200-plus penalty minutes if he wins a regular job.

LAST SEASON

Will be entering first NHL season. Scored 10-12 — 22 with 164 penalty minutes in 38 games with Kentucky (AHL).

THE FINESSE GAME

Belanger played well during his call-up in the last three weeks of the regular season, simply by keeping things simple. He skated up and down his wing and looked like a 10-year veteran doing it.

Belanger's obvious asset is his size and his willingness to use it. But in addition to that, he's a decent skater with good enough hands to make some things happen when he stirs up the action around the net. He doesn't have very good hockey sense and isn't what we'd call an intelligent player, but he works hard and isn't a liability defensively.

THE PHYSICAL GAME

Belanger started to establish his reputation in the league by taking on the big boys like Stu Grimson. He looks for trouble, running at players, challenging them and then backing up his actions. It's what he has to do to stay in the league. He's a legitimate heavyweight.

THE INTANGIBLES

Belanger came into training camp last year 15 pounds overweight and thinking he had the world by the tail. His demotion to Kentucky was a rude awakening. But he got back into shape and played his way into a promotion. It will take that sort of attitude to make the cut this season.

PROJECTION

With his size and skating, Belanger should stick around in the league. His big body is needed by the Islanders. He'll be a fourth-line left-winger and he's a

BRYAN BERARD

Yrs. of NHL service: 1
Born: Woonsocket, R.I.; March 5, 1977
Position: left defense
Height: 6-1
Weight: 190
Uniform no.: 38
Shoots: left

Career statistics:

GP	G	A	TP	PIM
82	8	40	48	86

1996-97 statistics:

GP	G	A	TP	+/-	PIM	PP	SH	GW	GT	S	PCT
82	8	40	48	+1	86	3	0	1	0	172	4.7

LAST SEASON

Won Calder Trophy. Named to NHL All-Rookie Team. Led NHL rookie defensemen and team defensemen in scoring. Second among NHL rookies in points and assists. Third among NHL rookies in shots. One of three Islanders to appear in all 82 games.

THE FINESSE GAME

Berard entered the NHL with a lot of expectations, and he lived up to his advance billing. The youngster is a risk taker. He can win the game one night in the offensive end and maybe lose it another night in his own zone. The most important thing about Berard is that when the game is on the line, he wants the puck. He wants to make the difference.

Berard is constantly on the go and is an exciting, flashy player to watch. He has a speedy yet effortless skating style. He loves to rush with the puck, but like New Jersey's Scott Niedermayer he is so quick to recover from any counterattack that he's usually back in a defensive posture in no time. He is seldom caught out of position.

Berard carries the puck with confidence and does not panic under pressure. His shot is low and accurate. He is also a fine passer. With his combination of skills and intelligence he can control the tempo of a game. He has good vision with the puck and will make the special plays. Carrying the puck doesn't slow him down.

Berard maybe needs to tone down his dynamic game a bit to play a little more defense. He likes to go for home-run plays that can turn into big errors, but experience will make him smarter.

THE PHYSICAL GAME

While not overly physical, Berard has shown a willingness to use his body to slow people down. He is also very good using his stick to poke-check or break up passes, and opponents would be wise not to make cross-ice passes high in the attacking zone or he will easily step up and pick them off. He tends to run around and try to do too much sometimes, but coaches prefer sins of commission to sins of omission. Berard is a competitor and he battles.

THE INTANGIBLES

Berard brings people into the building and then brings them out of their seats. It's been a long time since the Islanders have had a legitimate offensive defenseman (since Denis Potvin's era). Berard has shown every indication that he will be among the league's elite offensive defensemen, but needs to add the responsible defensive play that Brian Leetch has incorporated in his game to become a well-rounded defenseman.

PROJECTION

Berard will get better as the Islanders improve over the next season or two. It won't be long before he posts a 70-point season.

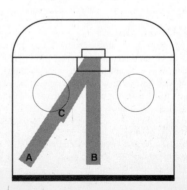

TODD BERTUZZI

Yrs. of NHL service: 2
Born: Sudbury, Ont.; Feb. 2, 1975
Position: right wing
Height: 6-3
Weight: 224
Uniform no.: 44
Shoots: left

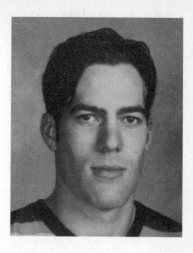

Career statistics:

GP	G	A	TP	PIM
137	28	34	62	151

1995-96 statistics:

GP	G	A	TP	+/-	PIM	PP	SH	GW	GT	S	PCT
76	18	21	39	-14	83	4	0	2	0	127	14.2

1996-97 statistics:

GP	G	A	TP	+/-	PIM	PP	SH	GW	GT	S	PCT
64	10	13	23	-3	68	3	0	1	0	79	12.7

LAST SEASON

Second NHL season. Missed one game with bone chips in elbow. Scored 5-5 — 10 in 13 games with Utah (IHL).

THE FINESSE GAME

One of the more engrossing plot lines on the Island last season was coach/GM Mike Milbury's attempt to make Bertuzzi into something he's not. Milbury wants Bertuzzi to be a physical, tough, aggresive fighter — something Bertuzzi won't become in a million years. It's not in his makeup.

What Bertuzzi could be is a poor man's John LeClair. He has physically dominating skills, but he doesn't have great vision. He has a tendency to roam all over the ice and doesn't think the game well.

Bertuzzi is instinctive, and has great power to his game. For a big man, he's quick for his size and mobile, and he's got a good, soft pair of hands to complement his skating. With the puck, he can walk over people. He is effective in the slot area, yet he's also creative with the puck and can make some plays. He can find people down low and make things happen on the power play. With the puck, he is powerful and hard to stop, though he needs to improve his game without the puck. When he's not producing, all you notice are the flaws, mentally and defensively.

THE PHYSICAL GAME

Bertuzzi wanders around and doesn't finish his checks with authority. He can beat people, but he won't beat people up. He's a solid physical specimen who shows flashes of aggression and an occasional mean streak, but he really has to be pushed and aggravated to reach a boiling point. It doesn't come naturally to him. He won't run through people or challenge them consistently, and as a result doesn't establish a physical presence.

THE INTANGIBLES

Still a relatively immature player, Bertuzzi could grow into a leader, or he could remain a frustrating enigma. He finished the season well, after coming back from his eyebrow-raising December demotion to the minors. Once the Islanders divest themselves of the notion of Bertuzzi as a challenging sort of leader, they might make the most of his size and considerable ability. He needs to be handled intelligently, with an arm around his shoulder and a kick to the butt administered at the right times. He's a big project, but there probably isn't a team in the league that wouldn't want to try. Everybody was trying to steal him from the Islanders at the last trade deadline.

PROJECTION

Bertuzzi was a bit unnerved by his treatment last season. He could come back this year and score 30 goals. Or he could score six. He's a real question mark.

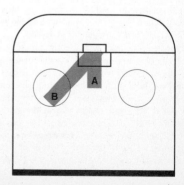

TRAVIS GREEN

Yrs. of NHL service: 5
Born: Castlegar, B.C.; Dec. 20, 1970
Position: centre
Height: 6-1
Weight: 193
Uniform no.: 39
Shoots: right

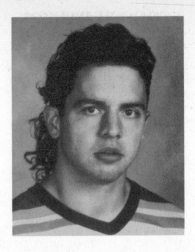

Career statistics:

GP	G	A	TP	PIM
334	77	133	210	192

1993-94 statistics:

GP	G	A	TP	+/-	PIM	PP	SH	GW	GT	S	PCT
83	18	22	40	+16	44	1	0	2	0	164	11.0

1994-95 statistics:

GP	G	A	TP	+/-	PIM	PP	SH	GW	GT	S	PCT
42	5	7	12	-10	25	0	0	0	0	59	8.5

1995-96 statistics:

GP	G	A	TP	+/-	PIM	PP	SH	GW	GT	S	PCT
69	24	45	69	-21	42	14	1	2	1	186	12.9

1996-97 statistics:

GP	G	A	TP	+/-	PIM	PP	SH	GW	GT	S	PCT
79	23	41	64	-5	38	10	0	3	0	177	13.0

LAST SEASON

Led team in power-play goals. Second on team in assists and points. Tied for second on team in game-winning goals. Third on team in goals.

THE FINESSE GAME

Green deserves a lot of credit for reinventing himself as a hockey player. Considered a pure scorer at the minor-league and junior levels, Green was taken in hand several years ago by Islanders minor-league coach Butch Goring — whose defensive play was a key factor in all four of the team's Stanley Cups — and he added a completely new dimension to Green's game. Because of the lack of depth on the Islanders, Green has frequently been asked to step in as a number one centre, but ideally he would be a superb number three centre on any NHL team.

Green is on the ice in the waning seconds of the period or the game to protect a lead. But his skating is flawed. When he stops pushing and stops moving, there's no glide to him, so his skating really falls off. He has decent balance and agility with some quickness, though he lacks straight-ahead speed.

He controls the puck well. He plays more of a finesse game than a power game. An unselfish player, Green passes equally well to either side. He sees the ice well, but he has a very heavy shot. His release needs to be quicker, which is why he'll never be the scorer at the NHL level that he was in the minors — and that makes his 10 power-play goals last season all the more admirable, because they were the result of sheer effort.

Green is the Islanders' top man on draws. He has quick hands and he uses his body to tie up an opponent, enabling his linemates to skate in for the puck.

THE PHYSICAL GAME

Green has good size and is competitive, but hockey courage doesn't come naturally to him. He talks himself into going into the corners and around the net, knowing that he has to get into the dirty areas to produce. He uses his body to get in the way. He wants to be on the ice and has learned to pay the price to be there.

THE INTANGIBLES

Green's skating keeps him from ascending to a higher quality of play, still, he has done everything the Islanders have asked of him. We would like to see him play with a little more fire, but don't anticipate that happening.

PROJECTION

As long as Green doesn't develop an inflated opinion of his game and keeps working, he can carve out a nice niche as a checking centre who can kick in 20 to 25 goals.

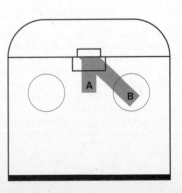

KENNY JONSSON

Yrs. of NHL service: 3
Born: Angelholm, Sweden; Oct. 6, 1974
Position: left defense
Height: 6-3
Weight: 195
Uniform no.: 3
Shoots: left

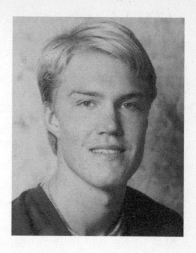

Career statistics:

GP	G	A	TP	PIM
186	9	51	60	72

1994-95 statistics:

GP	G	A	TP	+/-	PIM	PP	SH	GW	GT	S	PCT
39	2	7	9	-8	16	0	0	1	0	50	4.0

1995-96 statistics:

GP	G	A	TP	+/-	PIM	PP	SH	GW	GT	S	PCT
66	4	26	30	+7	32	3	0	1	0	130	3.1

1996-97 statistics:

GP	G	A	TP	+/-	PIM	PP	SH	GW	GT	S	PCT
81	3	18	21	+10	24	1	0	0	0	92	3.3

LAST SEASON

Second on team and led team defensemen in plus-minus. Missed one game with flu.

THE FINESSE GAME

Jonsson reads the ice and passes the puck very well. He's not overly creative. He's not a risk-taker. Players (especially defensemen) who are top point-getters are the ones who try making the moves that ordinary players can't, and don't. Jonsson is looking more like one of the pack. He moves the puck up and plays his position.

He can be used in almost every game situation. He kills penalties, works the point on the power play, plays four-on-four, and can be used in the late stages of a period or a game to protect a lead, though he needs to improve his defensive reads. He's reliable and coachable.

Jonsson is a talented skater, but part of his adjustment will be learning to protect himself by using the net in his own zone. He tends to leave himself open after passes and gets nailed.

THE PHYSICAL GAME

Jonsson needs to get stronger, because his lack of strength is an issue in his own zone. He has a tendency to follow the puck and lunge at people instead of allowing the play to come to him. He can't handle people around the net and in the corners. He is big and mobile but doesn't have a very aggressive side, so needs to be more assertive.

THE INTANGIBLES

Jonsson has levelled off after a promising start. He will still be a useful number three or four defenseman, but, after being touted as a star, that's a comedown. He's a stable defenseman but won't be a great one.

PROJECTION

There is little indication that Jonsson will push himself to do much more than he did last season.

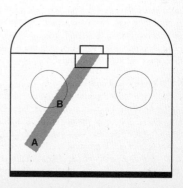

SCOTT LACHANCE

Yrs. of NHL service: 5
Born: Charlottesville, Va.; Oct. 22, 1972
Position: left defense
Height: 6-1
Weight: 196
Uniform no.: 7
Shoots: left

Career statistics:

GP	G	A	TP	PIM
328	23	60	83	240

1993-94 statistics:

GP	G	A	TP	+/-	PIM	PP	SH	GW	GT	S	PCT
74	3	11	14	-5	70	0	0	1	0	59	5.1

1994-95 statistics:

GP	G	A	TP	+/-	PIM	PP	SH	GW	GT	S	PCT
26	6	7	13	+2	26	3	0	0	0	56	10.7

1995-96 statistics:

GP	G	A	TP	+/-	PIM	PP	SH	GW	GT	S	PCT
55	3	10	13	-19	54	1	0	0	0	81	3.7

1996-97 statistics:

GP	G	A	TP	+/-	PIM	PP	SH	GW	GT	S	PCT
81	3	11	14	-7	47	1	0	0	0	97	3.1

LAST SEASON

Only game missed due to coach's decision.

THE FINESSE GAME

Lachance is the ultimate tease. He has so many good things going for him that you can't wait for him to put it all together. He came into the NHL off the 1992 Olympics with an optimistic cockiness about him, looking like future captain material. No one's been talking like that about Lachance for years.

He has good hockey sense. He moves the puck well and is poised under pressure. He's one of the few defensemen with the patience to beat a trapping team. He will never have truly impressive offensive numbers, though, because his skating isn't good enough to propel him into the elite class, but he can complement another defenseman who does have good offensive instincts. He makes a nice fit with the gifted Bryan Berard. Lachance is smart enough not to take too many chances. He doesn't have great hands.

Lachances's development has been slowed by injuries during the past two of the past three seasons. He's not an exceptional skater. He has to work on his quickness (his feet look a little heavy at times), but he is balanced and strong on his skates.

THE PHYSICAL GAME

After whistles, after his goalie is whacked, in scrums around the net, in pileups in the corner, Lachance's courage wavers. Instead of getting in people's faces or at least into a stare-down (just think of Mark Messier's defiant glare), Lachance lowers his eyes and backs away submissively. He never wants a confrontation. During play, he'll try hard and eliminate guys, but play is dead the second the whistle blows, and that prevents Lachance from staking out his territory like the NHL's more dominating defensemen do.

THE INTANGIBLES

Once thought of as a potential number two defenseman, Lachance is a solid number four on his best nights. His skill level isn't high enough to compensate for his lack of competitiveness.

PROJECTION

Even with a healthy season (and an unexpected trip to the NHL All-Star game as a sub for the injured Ziggy Palffy), Lachance mustered a meagre 14 points last season. We don't anticipate much of an improvement.

He can score 30 points a season if he can stay intact. The Islanders don't have a very strong team up front, so the defense may be relied upon to generate a lot of the scoring. Lachance should do his share.

CLAUDE LAPOINTE

Yrs. of NHL service: 6
Born: Lachine, Que.; Oct. 11, 1968
Position: centre
Height: 5-9
Weight: 181
Uniform no.: 13
Shoots: left

Career statistics:

GP	G	A	TP	PIM
361	57	83	140	368

1993-94 statistics:

GP	G	A	TP	+/-	PIM	PP	SH	GW	GT	S	PCT
59	11	17	28	+2	70	1	1	1	0	73	15.1

1994-95 statistics:

GP	G	A	TP	+/-	PIM	PP	SH	GW	GT	S	PCT
29	4	8	12	+5	41	0	0	0	0	40	10.0

1995-96 statistics:

GP	G	A	TP	+/-	PIM	PP	SH	GW	GT	S	PCT
35	4	5	9	+1	20	0	2	1	0	44	9.1

1996-97 statistics:

GP	G	A	TP	+/-	PIM	PP	SH	GW	GT	S	PCT
73	13	5	18	-11	49	0	3	3	1	80	16.3

PROJECTION

Lapointe is a useful fourth-line, role-playing centre who will be on the bubble if the Islanders are active in the free agent market during the off-season.

LAST SEASON

Second on team in shorthanded goals. Tied for second on team in game-winning goals. Third on team in shooting percentage. Matched career high in goals. Missed two games with ankle injuries. Scored 7-6 — 13 in nine games with Utah (IHL).

THE FINESSE GAME

Lapointe is one of those useful veteran forwards who will always find a spot in a lineup because of his intelligence, yet he'll always be worried about his job because he doesn't do anything special.

Lapointe is heady and aggressive. As a low draft pick (234th overall in 1988), he has always had to fight for respect. His effort is what's kept him hanging around this long.

Lapointe drives to the front of the net, knowing that that's where good things happen. He has good acceleration and quickness with the puck and decent hand skills to make things work down low. He isn't blessed with great vision, but doesn't take unnecessary chances, either, and can be used in clutch situations.

THE PHYSICAL GAME

Lapointe is small but solidly built. He uses his low centre of gravity and good balance to bump people much bigger than he is. He can surprise some of them by knocking them off the puck. He doesn't quit and is dogged in the corners and in front of the net.

Since Bowness took over as the full-time head coach of the Islanders, Lapointe has been used extensively as a penalty killer and on face-offs, and he has scored some pretty big goals.

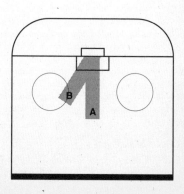

BRYAN MCCABE

Yrs. of NHL service: 2
Born: St. Catharines, Ont.; June 8, 1975
Position: left defense
Height: 6-2
Weight: 215
Uniform no.: 4
Shoots: left

Career statistics:

GP	G	A	TP	PIM
164	15	36	51	321

1995-96 statistics:

GP	G	A	TP	+/-	PIM	PP	SH	GW	GT	S	PCT
82	7	16	23	-24	156	3	0	1	0	130	5.4

1996-97 statistics:

GP	G	A	TP	+/-	PIM	PP	SH	GW	GT	S	PCT
82	8	20	28	-2	165	2	1	2	0	117	6.8

LAST SEASON

Second NHL season. One of three Islanders to appear in all 82 games. Led team in penalty minutes.

THE FINESSE GAME

McCabe's offensive game was supposed to be ahead of his defensive aspects, but he concentrated so much on his defensive game in his first two NHL seasons that the Islanders will have to urge him to produce a little more offense — he's certainly capable of it. He reads the offensive play well.

McCabe is an unorthodox skater with a bit of a hitch. He doesn't have a fluid, classic stride, but he moves his feet quickly and he can get to where he's going. When he has the puck or is jumping into the play, he has decent speed, but his lack of mobility defensively is one of his flaws. He is hesitant in his own zone when reading the rush and will get caught, but he is willing to work to improve.

McCabe needs to develop more confidence in his offensive instincts. He knows when to jump up into the attacking zone. He has a heavy, major-league slap shot. He moves the puck well and can run an NHL power play.

THE PHYSICAL GAME

MccCabe is willing to drop his gloves and can handle himself in a bout, though it's not a strong part of his game. He was asked to be one of the Islanders' top cops last season, which is really a waste of his ability. He's not tough but he is very competitive. He is a sturdy body checker, and if his skating improves he will become a more efficient hitter. He is big and strong and shows leadership. He handled a lot of tough checking assignments against other team's top physical lines.

THE INTANGIBLES

McCabe is an ideal number three defenseman. He is maturing into a reliable, all-around defender and is progressing every season. A blueline corps that includes McCabe, Bryan Berard, Kenny Jonsson, and Scott Lachance gives long-suffering Islander fans a reason to live. This is a lot to saddle a young man with, but McCabe has a wonderful attitude and is a possible future team captain.

PROJECTION

McCabe should bump up his production to 35 to 40 points without taking anything away from his defense.

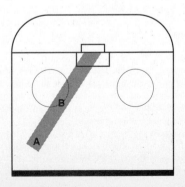

SERGEI NEMCHINOV

Yrs. of NHL service:
Born: Moscow, Russia; Jan. 14, 1964
Position: centre
Height: 6-0
Weight: 200
Uniform no.: 13
Shoots: left

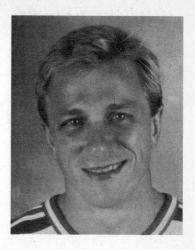

Career statistics:

GP	G	A	TP	PIM
424	107	123	230	155

1993-94 statistics:

GP	G	A	TP	+/-	PIM	PP	SH	GW	GT	S	PCT
76	22	27	49	+13	36	4	0	6	0	144	15.3

1994-95 statistics:

GP	G	A	TP	+/-	PIM	PP	SH	GW	GT	S	PCT
47	7	6	13	-6	16	0	0	3	0	67	10.4

1995-96 statistics:

GP	G	A	TP	+/-	PIM	PP	SH	GW	GT	S	PCT
78	17	15	32	+9	38	0	0	2	0	118	14.4

1996-97 statistics:

GP	G	A	TP	+/-	PIM	PP	SH	GW	GT	S	PCT
69	8	16	24	+9	16	1	0	2	0	97	8.2

LAST SEASON

Signed as a free agent July 2, 1997. Acquired from N.Y. Rangers with Brian Noonan for Esa Tikkanen and Russ Courtnall, March 8, 1997. Missed 11 games with rib injuries.

THE FINESSE GAME

If there is a five-on-three against, this is the forward who is sent out for the draw. Nemchinov backchecks well, coming back on his man, throwing him off-stride with a shoulder-check, collecting the puck and trying to do something with it.

He has the hand skills to play with almost any finesse player. Nemchinov is very fond of the backhand shot but isn't as accurate as he wants to be most of the time. Just as his strength powers his defensive game, it is critical to his offensive game as well. He will win a battle for the puck along the boards, with his stick or his skates, muscle it into the scoring zone and create a chance. He is strong enough, also, to get away a shot when his stick is being held or when he is fending off a checker. He lacks only a finishing touch.

Nemchinov carries the puck in a classic fashion, well to the side, which makes him much more difficult to forecheck. He is unpredictable in whether he will shoot or pass, because the puck is always ready for either option and he does not telegraph his moves.

He doesn't have the skating ability usually associated with players out of the old Soviet system, but he is strong and balanced and is a dedicated chopper. Nemchinov's leg strength makes him sneaky-fast.

THE PHYSICAL GAME

Powerfully built, Nemchinov forechecks with zest and drives through the boards and the corners. Linemates have to be alert, because he will churn up loose pucks. He is adept at holding an opponent's stick when the two players are tied up in a corner, and his body shields the infraction from the officials. He takes every hit and keeps coming. Nemchinov is as mentally tough as any player in the league. He is enormously strong and never stops competing.

Nemchinov gets checking assignments against behemoths such as Eric Lindros and Joel Otto, and he more than holds his own. He always seems to pin an opponent's stick to the ice at the last second when a pass is arriving in a quality scoring area.

He blocks shots, hits and takes hits to make plays and ties up his opposing centre on draws.

THE INTANGIBLES

Don't mistake his stoicism for lack of emotion or intensity. Nemchinov is a quiet leader, a player of character who is committed to winning, and the Islanders will welcome his veteran leadership and poise.

PROJECTION

Of his 15 to 20 goals per season, about half are scored in pressure situations. He is becoming more and more of a defensive specialist.

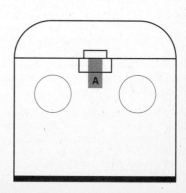

ZIGMUND PALFFY

Yrs. of NHL service: 3
Born: Skalica, Slovakia; May 5, 1972
Position: left wing
Height: 5-10
Weight: 183
Uniform no.: 16
Shoots: left

Career statistics:

GP	G	A	TP	PIM
199	101	93	194	105

1993-94 statistics:

GP	G	A	TP	+/-	PIM	PP	SH	GW	GT	S	PCT
5	0	0	0	-6	0	0	0	0	0	5	0.0

1994-95 statistics:

GP	G	A	TP	+/-	PIM	PP	SH	GW	GT	S	PCT
33	10	7	17	+3	6	1	0	1	0	75	13.3

1995-96 statistics:

GP	G	A	TP	+/-	PIM	PP	SH	GW	GT	S	PCT
81	43	44	87	-17	56	17	1	6	0	257	16.7

1996-97 statistics:

GP	G	A	TP	+/-	PIM	PP	SH	GW	GT	S	PCT
80	48	42	90	+21	43	6	4	6	1	292	16.4

LAST SEASON

Tied for eighth in NHL in scoring. Led team in goals, points, game-winning goals and shots for second consecutive season. Led team in assists and shorthanded goals. Second on team in shooting percentage. Tied for third on team in power-play goals. Missed two games with right shoulder sprain.

THE FINESSE GAME

Palffy has elite, intellectual instincts with the puck and great vision. He knows he can play in the league now and has the confidence to try the moves that only world-class players can execute.

Palffy has deceptive quickness. He is an elusive skater with a quick first step and is very shifty; he can handle the puck while dancing across the ice. He won't burn around people, but when there's an opening he can get to it in a hurry. His effort was far more consistent last season than in previous years when he flirted with making the NHL as a regular.

When you are a player of Palffy's size and surrounded on the NHL scoring list by the likes of Jaromir Jagr and Brendan Shanahan, you are doing something right. Palffy has excellent hands for passing or shooting. Earlier in his career, he would look to make a play before shooting, but he has since become a bona fide sniper.

THE PHYSICAL GAME

Palffy has a little bit of an edge to him. He wants to win — whether that will remain when he gets a $3-million contract is debatable. He's got the magic ingredient that sets the superior smaller players apart from the little guys who can't make the grade.

Palffy is decidedly on the small side. He can't afford to get into any battles in tight areas where he'll get crunched. He can jump in and out of holes and pick his spots, and he often plays with great spirit. He never puts himself in a position to get bowled over, but he has become less of a perimeter player and is more willing to take the direct route to the net, which has paid off in more quality scoring chances. He's not really a soft player, but he won't go into the corner if he's going to get crunched. Palffy's not against hacking an opponent. He wants the puck.

THE INTANGIBLES

The Islanders played hardball with Palffy in 1996 before grudgingly giving him a two-year deal, so he's playing for a new contract and a big bump from the U.S.$1.5 million he'll be earning. Palffy is establishing himself among the league's brightest, but he hasn't yet been tested in the playoff wars so we can see what he's truly made of.

PROJECTION

In last year's *HSR*, we identified Palffy as a 40-goal scorer. He is, and could even hit 50. The only thing that worries us about last season was his curious lack of production on the power play.

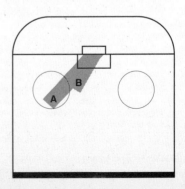

DAN PLANTE

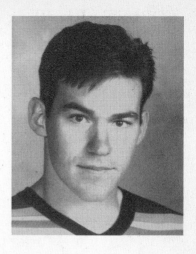

Yrs. of NHL service: 2
Born: St. Louis, Mo.; Oct. 5, 1971
Position: right wing
Height: 5-11
Weight: 202
Uniform no.: 42
Shoots: right

Career statistics:

GP	G	A	TP	PIM
152	9	13	22	129

1993-94 statistics:

GP	G	A	TP	+/-	PIM	PP	SH	GW	GT	S	PCT
12	0	1	1	-2	4	0	0	0	0	9	0.0

1994-95 statistics:

GP	G	A	TP	+/-	PIM	PP	SH	GW	GT	S	PCT
Did Not Play in NHL				4	0	0	0	0	0	9	0.0

1995-96 statistics:

GP	G	A	TP	+/-	PIM	PP	SH	GW	GT	S	PCT
73	5	3	8	-22	50	0	2	0	0	103	4.9

1996-97 statistics:

GP	G	A	TP	+/-	PIM	PP	SH	GW	GT	S	PCT
67	4	9	13	-6	75	0	2	0	0	61	6.6

LAST SEASON

Second NHL season. All games missed were coach's decision.

THE FINESSE GAME

Plante took a step backwards last season by abandoning his simple, physical style. He tried to play more of a finesse game, which he just doesn't have the skills for.

Ideally, Plante plays defense first, and does so intelligently. He is a nonstop skater whose first duty is his checking role. He was often used at centre by the Islanders last season — a mistake. He doesn't see the ice well and doesn't handle the puck well. He has to play up and down the wing, bump people, take a 25-second shift and get off to be effective.

Perhaps because Plante was a scorer at the college level, he thinks he can be the same kind of player in the NHL. He can't. He's paid a big price to get here after undergoing reconstructive knee surgery in 1994-95. He should know the value of an NHL job.

THE PHYSICAL GAME

Plante is strong but not overly tough or aggressive. When he is on his game, he skates hard and battles for the puck. He's a sparkplug and is willing to sacrifice his body. He's also very balanced and tough to knock off his feet.

THE INTANGIBLES

Plante suffered from a common sophomore syndrome. He thought he was better than he is. Every shift, he has to be out banging into people.

Plante raises the energy level of a game. He can function on a third or fourth line, kill penalties, distract some opponents and pick up a few (but not many) points.

PROJECTION

Plante's delusions to the contrary, he is a role player who will slip through the cracks unless he recaptures his energy level. Do not expect him to reach double digits in goals.

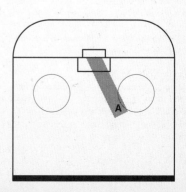

ROBERT REICHEL

Yrs. of NHL service:
Born: Litvinov, Czech Republic, June 25, 1971
Position: centre
Height: 5-9
Weight: 181
Uniform no.: 13
Shoots: left

Career statistics:

GP	G	A	TP	PIM
437	158	215	373	220

1993-94 statistics:

GP	G	A	TP	+/-	PIM	PP	SH	GW	GT	S	PCT
84	40	53	93	+20	58	14	0	6	0	249	16.1

1994-95 statistics:

GP	G	A	TP	+/-	PIM	PP	SH	GW	GT	S	PCT
48	18	17	35	-2	28	5	0	2	0	160	11.3

1995-96 statistics:

P	G	A	TP	+/-	PIM	PP	SH	GW	GT	S	PC
Did not play in NHL											

1996-97 statistics:

GP	G	A	TP	+/-	PIM	PP	SH	GW	GT	S	PCT
82	21	41	62	+5	26	6	1	3	0	214	9.8

LAST SEASON

Acquired from Calgary for Marty McInnis, Tyrone Garner and a sixth-round draft pick. One of three Islanders to appear in all 82 games. Tied for second on team in assists and game-winning goals. Second on team in shots. Third on team in points.

THE FINESSE GAME

Reichel is a good playmaker who got a boost from the trade to the Islanders, where he was paired with the speedy finisher Ziggy Palffy. Reichel scored 5-14 — 19 in 12 games with the Isles. Reichel can make a scoring opportunity materialize when there appears to be no route to the net, and Palffy read off him well. He has great control of the puck in open ice or along the boards.

Reichel likes to shoot and follows up his scoring chances. He has an explosive shot, with a lot of velocity. He pursues loose pucks in front and wheels around to the back of the net to look for an open teammate. He is good in traffic. At least that's how Reichel plays when things are going well. He is just as likely to go into a slump and doesn't add much to a team when he isn't putting up points.

THE PHYSICAL GAME

Reichel is small but sturdy. He is not a big fan of contact and there are some who question his courage. He's not a player other teams are afraid to play against. He is well-conditioned and can handle a lot of ice time.

THE INTANGIBLES

Reichel spent the 1995-96 season playing in Germany before returning to the Flames last season. He had some nice chemistry with Palffy and Bryan Smolinski after the trade, but he is a stopgap measure and not a player who will take a team to the next level in the playoffs.

PROJECTION

If he stays on a line with the peppy Palffy, Reichel should post some nice (60 to 70 points) numbers.

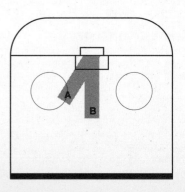

TOMMY SALO

Yrs. of NHL service: 2
Born: Surahammar, Sweden; Feb. 1, 1971
Position: goaltender
Height: 5-11
Weight: 173
Uniform no.: 35
Catches: left

Career statistics:

GP	MIN	GA	SO	GAA	A	PIM
74	4089	204	5	2.99	2	4

1994-95 statistics:

GP	MIN	GAA	W	L	T	SO	GA	S	SAPCT	PIM
6	358	3.02	1	5	0	0	18	189	.905	0

1995-96 statistics:

GP	MIN	GAA	W	L	T	SO	GA	S	SAPCT	PIM
10	523	4.02	1	7	1	0	35	250	.860	0

1996-97 statistics:

GP	MIN	GAA	W	L	T	SO	GA	S	SAPCT	PIM
58	3208	2.82	20	27	7	5	151	1576	.904	4

PROJECTION
Eric Fichaud was supposed to take over the number one role last season, and will be challenging again this year, but it's Salo's job to lose.

LAST SEASON
Tied for fifth in NHL in shutouts. Missed one game with tonsillitis.

THE PHYSICAL GAME
Salo's game is unconventional. He plays deep in his net and is excellent on low shots. He has adjusted to playing with traffic, which is one of the biggest adjustments for European goalies. Salo has quick feet but is not a great skater and needs to improve his lateral movement.

Salo has a bad habit of not holding his stick at a proper angle, and when he gets into this slump, he might as well not bother playing with a stick at all. Salo has a quick glove and tends to try to catch everything instead of using other parts of his body. Since he doesn't use his stick well, he will try to cover up on every loose pucks for face-offs. Better stickhandling work would elevate Salo's game a notch.

Because of his style, Salo makes himself appear small in the net. He is an acrobatic goalie with crowd-pleasing moves.

THE MENTAL GAME
The big knock on Salo was always his lack of concentration. He seemed to let in a bad goal or two at the worst time, but he's gotten over that hump and his effort is far more consistent.

THE INTANGIBLES
Salo has won at every level, from the Swedish Elite League to the minors to the Olympics. He has yet to prove himself in an NHL playoffs, which is the true test of an NHL goalie, but he will come into this season off an outstanding effort for Sweden in the World Championships. Salo could be a Dominik Hasek type who needs to wait until he's 27 or 28 to hit his peak.

BRYAN SMOLINSKI

Yrs. of NHL service: 4
Born: Toledo, Ohio; Dec. 27, 1971
Position: centre/right wing
Height: 6-1
Weight: 200
Uniform no.: 15
Shoots: right

Career statistics:

GP	G	A	TP	PIM
281	102	104	206	211

1993-94 statistics:

GP	G	A	TP	+/-	PIM	PP	SH	GW	GT	S	PCT
83	31	20	51	+4	82	4	3	5	0	179	17.3

1994-95 statistics:

GP	G	A	TP	+/-	PIM	PP	SH	GW	GT	S	PCT
44	18	13	31	-3	31	6	0	5	0	121	14.9

1995-96 statistics:

GP	G	A	TP	+/-	PIM	PP	SH	GW	GT	S	PCT
81	24	40	64	+6	69	8	2	1	0	229	10.5

1996-97 statistics:

GP	G	A	TP	+/-	PIM	PP	SH	GW	GT	S	PCT
64	28	28	56	+8	25	9	0	1	1	183	15.3

LAST SEASON

Acquired from Pittsburgh for Darius Kasparaitis and Andreas Johansson. Second on team in goals and power-play goals. Third on team in plus-minus. Scored 5-7 — 12 in six games with Detroit (IHL).

THE FINESSE GAME

Smolinski can play either centre or wing, but the Islanders used him predominantly on the left side after the acquisition of Robert Reichel, to give the line with Ziggy Palffy some size and grit.

Smolinski brings a centre's vision to the wing. Some scouts have compared him to a budding Jean Ratelle for his crafty play. He has a quick release and an accurate shot, and works to get himself into quality shooting areas. Confidence is a big factor; Smolinski has a history of being a streaky player. His play away from the puck has improved to where he can contribute even when the points aren't forthcoming.

His skating is adequate, but it could improve with some lower body work. He has good balance and lateral movement but is not very quick. He has a railroad-track skating base.

Smolinski has the smarts to be an asset on both specialty teams, and he has really stepped up as a penalty killer. He has good defensive awareness; his play away from the puck is sound. He is good in tight with the puck.

THE PHYSICAL GAME

Smolinski has a thick, blocky build, and he can be a solid hitter. He doesn't have much of an aggressive nature on a nightly basis. It shows up sporadically, and on those nights Smolinski is at his most effective.

THE INTANGIBLES

Smolinski has a lot going for him physically, but zero emotionally. He is not a player to be counted on at crunch time. The Islanders are his third team in three years. There's a reason for that. Teams get frustrated with him because of his lack of drive and intensity.

PROJECTION

Smolinski could bump his game up another notch. He's a nice second-line player who's a first-liner by default on the Islanders. He'll put up 60 to 70 points and have plenty left in the tank.

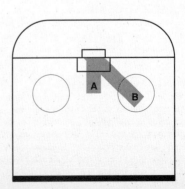

DENNIS VASKE

Yrs. of NHL service: 6
Born: Rockford, Ill.; Oct. 11, 1967
Position: left defense
Height: 6-2
Weight: 210
Uniform no.: 28
Shoots: left

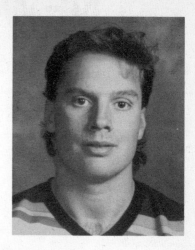

Career statistics:

GP	G	A	TP	PIM
213	5	38	43	235

1993-94 statistics:

GP	G	A	TP	+/-	PIM	PP	SH	GW	GT	S	PCT
65	2	11	13	+21	76	0	0	0	0	71	2.8

1994-95 statistics:

GP	G	A	TP	+/-	PIM	PP	SH	GW	GT	S	PCT
41	1	11	12	+3	53	0	0	0	0	48	2.1

1995-96 statistics:

GP	G	A	TP	+/-	PIM	PP	SH	GW	GT	S	PCT
19	1	6	7	-13	21	1	0	1	0	19	5.3

1996-97 statistics:

GP	G	A	TP	+/-	PIM	PP	SH	GW	GT	S	PCT
17	0	4	4	+3	12	0	0	0	0	19	0.0

PROJECTION

Vaske wasn't back in the lineup long when he went out again with a shoulder injury. He's got a big heart but a fragile body.

LAST SEASON

Missed 48 games with concussion. Missed 18 games with separated shoulder.

THE FINESSE GAME

The Islanders have already lost one young player, Brett Lindros, to premature retirement due to a severe concussion, and although Vaske returned last season after missing 111 games over the last two years with a concussion, his future is seriously in doubt.

Vaske has made progress over the past few seasons and was on his was to establishing himself as a steady, stay-at-home defenseman. He occasionally gets mesmerized and starts playing the puck instead of the body. Overall, however, he plays a sound positional game and forces attackers to try to get through him.

Although strong on his skates, Vaske doesn't have great speed or quickness, so when he stands his ground and forces the play to come to him he is the most effective.

THE PHYSICAL GAME

Vaske is a solid hitter. Because he doesn't skate well and lacks the first few steps to drive into an opponent, he doesn't bowl people over, but he is incredibly strong in the tough, close, one-on-one battles. He likes the physical play, too, but doesn't fight much.

THE INTANGIBLES

Vaske reminds us a lot of former Islander defenseman Dave "Bam Bam" Langevin. Vaske's physical play will certainly depend on his return from his injury.

NEW YORK RANGERS

Players' Statistics 1996-97

POS.	NO.	PLAYER	GP	G	A	PTS	+/-	PIM	PP	SH	GW	GT	S	PCT
C	99	WAYNE GRETZKY	82	25	72	97	12	28	6		2	1	286	8.7
C	11	MARK MESSIER	71	36	48	84	12	88	7	5	9	1	227	15.9
D	2	BRIAN LEETCH	82	20	58	78	31	40	9		2		256	7.8
L	9	ADAM GRAVES	82	33	28	61	10	66	10	4	3	5	269	12.3
L	24	NIKLAS SUNDSTROM	82	24	28	52	23	20	5	1	4		132	18.2
L	20	LUC ROBITAILLE	69	24	24	48	16	48	5		4		200	12.0
D	25	A. KARPOVTSEV	77	9	29	38	1	59	6	1			84	10.7
R	27	ALEXEI KOVALEV	45	13	22	35	11	42	1				110	11.8
R	21	RUSS COURTNALL	61	11	24	35	1	26	2	1	2		125	8.8
L	10	ESA TIKKANEN	76	13	17	30	-9	72	4	2	2	2	133	9.8
D	33	BRUCE DRIVER	79	5	25	30	8	48	2		2		154	3.2
R	8	PATRICK FLATLEY	68	10	12	22	6	26			2		96	10.4
D	5	ULF SAMUELSSON	73	6	11	17	3	138	1		1		77	7.8
L	18	BILL BERG	67	8	6	14	2	37		2	3		84	9.5
L	16	*DANIEL GONEAU	41	10	3	13	-5	10	3		2		44	22.7
D	23	JEFF BEUKEBOOM	80	3	9	12	22	167					55	5.5
C	32	MIKE EASTWOOD	60	2	10	12	-1	14					44	4.5
L	39	*VLADIMIR VOROBIEV	16	5	5	10	4	6	2				42	11.9
L	15	DARREN LANGDON	60	3	6	9	-1	195			1		24	12.5
D	6	DOUG LIDSTER	48	3	4	7	10	24					42	7.1
R	26	DAVID OLIVER	31	3	3	6	-5	8					35	8.6
R	14	*CHRIS FERRARO	12	1	1	2	1	6					23	4.3
C	19	*CHRISTIAN DUBE	27	1	1	2	-4	4	1				14	7.1
R	37	*RYAN VANDENBUSSCHE	11	1		1	-2	30					4	25.0
D	29	*ERIC CAIRNS	40		1	1	-7	147					17	
R	22	SHANE CHURLA	45		1	1	-10	106					19	
R	36	*JEFF NIELSEN	2				-1	2					1	
C	17	*PETER FERRARO	2				0						3	
D	38	*SYLVAIN BLOUIN	6				-1	18					1	
D	28	DALLAS EAKINS	7				-4	16					4	
G	30	GLENN HEALY	23				0	4						
G	35	MIKE RICHTER	61				0	4						

GP = games played; G = goals; A = assists; PTS = points; +/- = goals-for minus goals-against while player is on ice; PIM = penalties in minutes; PP = power-play goals; SH = shorthanded goals; GW = game-winning goals; GT = game-tying goals; S = no. of shots; PCT = percentage of goals to shots; * = rookie

JEFF BEUKEBOOM

Yrs. of NHL service: 11
Born: Ajax, Ont.; Mar. 28, 1965
Position: right defense
Height: 6-5
Weight: 230
Uniform no.: 23
Shoots: right

Career statistics:

GP	G	A	TP	PIM
696	30	115	145	1635

1993-94 statistics:

GP	G	A	TP	+/-	PIM	PP	SH	GW	GT	S	PCT
68	8	8	16	+18	170	1	0	0	0	58	13.8

1994-95 statistics:

GP	G	A	TP	+/-	PIM	PP	SH	GW	GT	S	PCT
44	1	3	4	+3	70	0	0	0	0	29	3.4

1995-96 statistics:

GP	G	A	TP	+/-	PIM	PP	SH	GW	GT	S	PCT
82	3	11	14	+19	220	0	0	1	1	65	4.6

1996-97 statistics:

GP	G	A	TP	+/-	PIM	PP	SH	GW	GT	S	PCT
80	3	9	12	+22	167	0	0	0	0	55	5.5

LAST SEASON

Second on team in penalty minutes. Third on team in plus-minus. Missed two games due to flu.

THE FINESSE GAME

Beukeboom is reasonably agile and covers acres of ground with a huge stride. He moves the puck fairly well, and certainly has no fear of anyone bearing down on him, but he gets burned with ill-timed or ill-advised pinches at the right point.

He takes up a lot of room on the ice, especially when he uses his long reach. A quick, active stick adds effectiveness to Beukeboom's poke-checks and sweep-checks. Often, he will lie on the ice to cut off odd-man rushes; when you add five feet of stick to more than six feet in height, Beukeboom cuts off a large portion of the defensive zone in that manner.

Content to play a simple defensive game, Beukeboom is most effective when he angles the attacker to the corners, then uses his superior size and strength to eliminate the player physically. Attackers think they can burn Beukeboom to the outside because of his lumbering style, but they find themselves running out of real estate fast.

THE PHYSICAL GAME

Beukeboom almost swaggers about his size, as though he dares you to come hit him. He makes you worry about him; he's not going to worry about you. He commands room. He takes his time getting to the puck because not many people want to throw themselves at him. He focusses on the man first, the puck second at all times.

He is most effective crunching along the boards,
and he clears the front of his net efficiently. The bigger the game, the more thunderous his hits. Beukeboom blocks shots fearlessly and often limps to the bench, only to return on his next shift.

THE INTANGIBLES

Beukeboom is a warrior in the playoffs, which makes it somewhat easier to accept the frequent giveaways and bad clears that seem to mark much of his regular-season play. This is a guy you want on your side of the trench in those playoff battles, though it remains a continuing source of frustration that he is slow to protect his meal-ticket partner, Brian Leetch, when opponents take physical liberties.

PROJECTION

Beukeboom spends virtually every minute playing with Leetch, a scoring machine, but is so committed to a strictly defensive role that it's all he can do to get 10 assists per season — not what you want if you're looking for points in your hockey pool.

ERIC CAIRNS

Yrs. of NHL service: 1
Born: Oakville, Ont.; June 27, 1974
Position: defense
Height: 6-5
Weight: 225
Uniform no.: 29
Shoots: left

Career statistics:

GP	G	A	TP	PIM
40	0	1	1	147

1996-97 statistics:

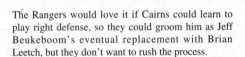

GP	G	A	TP	+/-	PIM	PP	SH	GW	GT	S	PCT
40	0	1	1	-7	147	0	0	0	0	17	0.0

LAST SEASON

First NHL season. Third on team in penalty minutes.

THE FINESSE GAME

It is natural to think a player as big as Cairns would be clumsy, but he has some smarts with the puck and enough skill to skate the puck out of the defensive zone. Occasionally, he can beat a forechecker, but Cairns knows better than to make a habit of that.

With the puck, Cairns favours backhand moves that allow him to use his body to shield the puck from defenders. He is content to get the puck deep in the zone and let the forwards do the offensive work, but his point shot is accurate when he elects to use it.

Although not a great skater, Cairns turns pretty smoothly and makes up for any shortcomings on speed by using his size and reach. He may look like someone who can be beaten easily to the outside, but Cairns generally does a nice job of angling a puck carrier to less dangerous ice.

THE PHYSICAL GAME

Cairns is a willing fighter and seems to like playing policeman if any opponent starts taking liberties with his teammates. But he had no concept of how to defend himself in his rookie tour of duty and swallowed some haymakers, which more experienced scrappers avoid by tucking their chins.

Cairns likes the big hits and mean rubouts, but does a pretty good job of avoiding the cheap hooking and holding penalties big defensemen always seem to get against smaller, quicker forwards. Larger defenders always seem more obvious in their infractions, but Cairns follows the "stride, don't glide" philosophy and keeps his feet moving.

Cairns uses his head. He knows what he can do, knows what his limitations are and plays within them. He was a total writeoff after an off-season training camp last season, but won the team's Lars-Erik Sjoberg award for the rookie who performed best at training camp, and he worked every day to improve.

The Rangers would love it if Cairns could learn to play right defense, so they could groom him as Jeff Beukeboom's eventual replacement with Brian Leetch, but they don't want to rush the process.

PROJECTION

Cairns will never be a star, and he isn't going to score much, but he has made himself a decent NHL prospect. He's going to be a project — it's going to take lots of extra work before and after practice — but size, strength and reach, sensibly packaged and deployed, are a commodity in the NHL. If he plays his cards right, Cairns can have a good career as a dependable stay-at-home and a perfect partner for the offensive guy who's going to be up ice all night.

RUSS COURTNALL

Yrs. of NHL service: 13
Born: Duncan, B.C.; June 2, 1965
Position: right wing
Height: 5-11
Weight: 185
Uniform no.: 21
Shoots: right

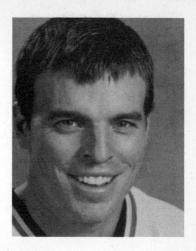

Career statistics:

GP	G	A	TP	PIM
914	279	428	707	511

1993-94 statistics:

GP	G	A	TP	+/-	PIM	PP	SH	GW	GT	S	PCT
84	23	57	80	+6	59	5	0	4	0	231	10.0

1994-95 statistics:

GP	G	A	TP	+/-	PIM	PP	SH	GW	GT	S	PCT
45	11	24	35	+2	17	2	2	2	0	132	8.3

1995-96 statistics:

GP	G	A	TP	+/-	PIM	PP	SH	GW	GT	S	PCT
81	26	39	65	+25	40	6	4	4	2	205	12.7

1996-97 statistics:

GP	G	A	TP	+/-	PIM	PP	SH	GW	GT	S	PCT
61	11	24	35	+1	26	2	1	2	0	125	8.8

LAST SEASON

Acquired from Vancouver, along with Esa Tikkanen, in exchange for Sergei Nemchinov and Brian Noonan, March 8, 1997.

THE FINESSE GAME

Courtnall gained his elite skating skills while he was growing up by doing all kinds of crossover drills without the puck. The result was intimidating speed without the puck and good speed with it. Courtnall pushes people back with sheer velocity, opening lots of room for his teammates. Once a fairly selfish player, he now uses his teammates well.

Courtnall's speed is particularly useful on the give-and-go. He can jolt into the open for a breakout pass, power up ice as a defender scrambles to survive against his speed, and make a reasonably effective pass or thread a shot through a tiny hole off the rush. He needs to play on a line with slick skaters, or else he tends to get a trifle impatient and winds up too far ahead of the play.

Defensively aware, Courtnall uses his skating assets to advantage while killing penalties, and is a shorthanded threat.

THE PHYSICAL GAME

Courtnall can play a scrappy game when he wants to, but you never know when he might want to. While he tends to stick to the open ice, where he can flash and dash — and avoid contact — he will make a hit to drive to the net. And just when you are convinced he'll never throw another check in his life, Courtnall will fling his body at someone far larger than he is.

THE INTANGIBLES

We speculated correctly that Courtnall was headed for the trade block as Vancouver looked to dump salaries. Once he got to New York, it took him an extremely long time to make the most of his abilities on a consistent basis — an affirmation that obtaining him is a high-risk proposition with only a decent chance of a high reward.

PROJECTION

In each of the past four seasons, Courtnall has alternated underproductive campaigns with acceptable output. He had only 11 goals last season after collecting 26 the year before, which suggests that this is the season you want him on your pool team. He can play enough positions, and be used in enough situations, to run up the goals and points. An unrestricted free agent, Courtnall could be on the move.

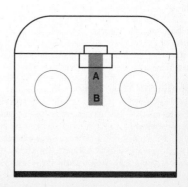

BRUCE DRIVER

Yrs. of NHL service: 13
Born: Toronto, Ont.; Apr. 29, 1962
Position: left defense
Height: 6-0
Weight: 185
Uniform no.: 33
Shoots: left

Career statistics:

GP	G	A	TP	PIM
847	34	375	466	624

1993-94 statistics:

GP	G	A	TP	+/-	PIM	PP	SH	GW	GT	S	PCT
66	8	24	32	+29	63	3	1	0	1	109	7.3

1994-95 statistics:

GP	G	A	TP	+/-	PIM	PP	SH	GW	GT	S	PCT
41	4	12	16	-1	18	1	0	1	0	62	6.5

1995-96 statistics:

GP	G	A	TP	+/-	PIM	PP	SH	GW	GT	S	PCT
66	3	34	37	+2	42	3	0	0	1	140	2.1

1996-97 statistics:

GP	G	A	TP	+/-	PIM	PP	SH	GW	GT	S	PCT
79	5	25	30	+8	48	2	0	2	0	154	3.2

LAST SEASON

Fourth on team with 12 power-play assists. Missed three games due to flu.

THE FINESSE GAME

Even on his best days now, Driver is a number four defenseman. He depends more on smarts and anticipation than on an assortment of skills, which are good on some levels but hardly great.

A fluid skater with secure strides and quick acceleration, Driver is very good moving laterally and backwards. While not particularly fast, his mobility allows him to get the jump on faster skaters.

Driver sees the ice well offensively and defensively and can kill penalties or work on the power play. He was supposed to take up some of the power-play slack left by the departure of Sergei Zubov two seasons ago, but even in his prime, Driver was never that kind of point man.

He has top-notch hand skills for passing, receiving a pass or carrying the puck, and is an above-average playmaker. He has a nice wrist shot, which he uses when he cheats into the right circle, but his point shot is hardly dangerous. He does not often venture deep into attacking territory. He plays a stable, cautious game and leaves the gambling to others.

THE PHYSICAL GAME

Driver plays defense by body position, stick position and containment, trying to occupy as much good ice space as possible by his positioning against the rush, and then using his poke-check to try to knock the puck free. He does not play a hitting game because he lacks the size, strength and temperament for it, but main-

tains an active stick that often clogs the passing lanes. And with his good finesse kills, Driver easily can start a countering rush.

He falls short in the one-on-one battles in the trenches, and frequently gets outmuscled along the boards and in front of the net. With the NHL trend towards power forwards like Eric Lindros, John LeClair and Keith Tkachuk, the weak links in Driver's game become more of a detriment. Moreover, he lacks the high-scoring numbers to offset it.

THE INTANGIBLES

Driver suffered a rib injury early in last season's playoffs and subjected himself to injections of painkillers before 10 consecutive games. While there were times during that stretch when his play seemed particularly weak from a physical standpoint, Driver never even whispered about the discomfort; he went out and played the best he could.

PROJECTION

Given the amount of power-play ice time he received, sharing the point with Brian Leetch, Driver never seemed particularly comfortable with the role. His low total of 12 man-advantage assists were not exclusively his fault, however. The Rangers don't create that much traffic in front of the net, which cuts down on the number of assists defensemen would normally get when their point shots are deflected into the net.

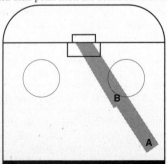

MIKE EASTWOOD

Yrs. of NHL service: 5
Born: Ottawa, Ont.; July 1, 1967
Position: centre
Height: 6-3
Weight: 205
Uniform no.: 32
Shoots: right

Career statistics:

GP	G	A	TP	PIM
264	33	53	86	123

1993-94 statistics:

GP	G	A	TP	+/-	PIM	PP	SH	GW	GT	S	PCT
54	8	10	18	+2	28	1	0	2	0	41	19.5

1994-95 statistics:

GP	G	A	TP	+/-	PIM	PP	SH	GW	GT	S	PCT
49	8	11	19	-9	36	0	0	0	0	55	14.5

1995-96 statistics:

GP	G	A	TP	+/-	PIM	PP	SH	GW	GT	S	PCT
80	14	14	28	-14	20	2	0	3	1	94	14.9

1996-97 statistics:

GP	G	A	TP	+/-	PIM	PP	SH	GW	GT	S	PCT
60	2	10	12	-1	14	0	0	0	0	44	4.5

24-goal season in the American League, Eastwood's job in the NHL is the denial of opposition offense more than the creation of offense by his team. He is a single-digit goal scorer and will remain as such until he demands more of himself, more often.

LAST SEASON
Career high in goals, assists and points.

THE FINESSE GAME
With a little more spunk, Eastwood could be a strong third-line centre. His problem is a lack of consistency. He is a big player from whom coaches always want to get more. He has some sparkling games but lacks the confidence and offensive assets, particularly when it comes to the finishing touch, to become an effective everyday player.

Eastwood is sound defensively — alert and aware. Deceptively quick as a skater, he doesn't always push himself hard and needs to be urged along by coaches. He kills penalties well and more than holds his own on face-offs.

THE PHYSICAL GAME
Eastwood will never be confused with a body builder. He doesn't have much muscular definition at all, and his temperament is equally non-descript. While he is strong and doesn't get knocked off the puck, he doesn't have much presence on the ice and could initiate more contact. He has to work on his conditioning and off-ice strengthening.

THE INTANGIBLES
During the playoffs, Eastwood showed size and spunk, and made himself play at a higher level than his easygoing nature usually requires. He can make things happen, but seems to need a lot of prodding.

PROJECTION
Although he did some scoring in college, and had one

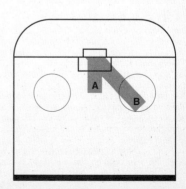

ADAM GRAVES

Yrs. of NHL service: 9
Born: Toronto, Ont.; Apr. 12, 1968
Position: left wing
Height: 6-0
Weight: 205
Uniform no.: 9
Shoots: left

Career statistics:

GP	G	A	TP	PIM
676	209	204	413	1273

1993-94 statistics:

GP	G	A	TP	+/-	PIM	PP	SH	GW	GT	S	PCT
84	52	27	79	+27	127	20	4	4	1	291	17.9

1994-95 statistics:

GP	G	A	TP	+/-	PIM	PP	SH	GW	GT	S	PCT
47	17	14	31	+9	51	9	0	3	0	185	9.2

1995-96 statistics:

GP	G	A	TP	+/-	PIM	PP	SH	GW	GT	S	PCT
82	22	36	58	+18	100	9	1	2	0	266	8.3

1996-97 statistics:

GP	G	A	TP	+/-	PIM	PP	SH	GW	GT	S	PCT
82	33	28	61	+10	66	10	4	3	5	269	12.3

LAST SEASON

Second on team in goals. Fourth on team in points. One of four Rangers to play in all 82 games. Second on team and tied for fifth in NHL in shorthanded goals. Led NHL in game-tying goals (5). Second on team in shots.

THE FINESSE GAME

Graves is a short-game player who scores a whopping percentage of his goals off deflections, rebounds and slam-dunks. A shot from the top of the circle is a long-distance effort for him. He favours the wrist shot; his rarely used slap shot barely exists. He is much better when working on instinct because, when he has time to make plays, he will out-think himself.

Although not very fast in open ice and something of an awkward skater, Graves's balance and strength are good and he can get a few quick steps on a rival. He is smart with the puck. He protects it with his body and is strong enough to fend off a checker with one arm and shovel the puck to a linemate with the other.

Graves is a former centre who can step in on draws. He is an intelligent penalty killer.

THE PHYSICAL GAME

A splendid second-effort player, Graves is all strength and sincerity. He is such a stoic, playing through unimaginable pain, that every time he has a bad game or a bad series of them, it is only natural to speculate that his back, surgically repaired three summers ago, is the source of the trouble.

Graves must be physical to be effective. He grinds and plays against other teams' top defensemen without fear. Other teams are always aware when Graves is around, because he doesn't play a quiet game. He finishes every check.

He stands up for his teammates and fights when necessary. He's so valuable that the Rangers hate to see him in the box, and he's gotten much better at con-trolling his temper and not getting goaded into bad trade-off penalties. A tenacious forechecker, he plows into the corners and plunges into his work along the boards with intelligence, but no fear. He is one of the best goalie-screeners in the league.

THE INTANGIBLES

Off the ice, the absurdly modest Graves is one of the genuine good guys. On the ice, he can be one of the meanest; he simply wants to win, and virtually nothing will deter him.

Graves is a natural leader who shows up in the grandest fashion on those nights when the rest of his teammates fail to. Those nights when the points aren't coming, Graves never hurts his club and finds other ways to contribute. A frequent winner of "Players' Player" awards, such is the respect he has earned.

PROJECTION

Graves's 52-goal season in 1993-94 looks more and more like a misprint. But his 33 goals last season were an 11-goal jump from the prior season, which was a five-goal improvement on the season before. He doesn't play an authentic scorer's game and isn't a John LeClair-style threat every time he's on the ice, yet in his five Ranger seasons he has been under 26 goals only twice — the first of which was the season following the back operation. Number one, he makes the puck go in the net. Number two, he plays virtually every game, and plays a lot. Take him, pool wizards, particularly because you're likely to get more goals than assists.

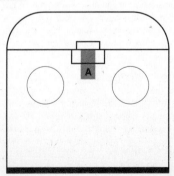

WAYNE GRETZKY

Yrs. of NHL service: 18
Born: Brantford, Ont.; Jan. 26, 1961
Position: centre
Height: 6-0
Weight: 180
Uniform no.: 99
Shoots: left

Career statistics:

GP	G	A	TP	PIM
1335	862	1843	2705	535

1993-94 statistics:

GP	G	A	TP	+/-	PIM	PP	SH	GW	GT	S	PCT
81	38	92	130	-25	20	14	4	0	1	233	16.3

1994-95 statistics:

GP	G	A	TP	+/-	PIM	PP	SH	GW	GT	S	PCT
48	11	37	48	-20	6	3	0	1	0	142	7.7

1995-96 statistics:

GP	G	A	TP	+/-	PIM	PP	SH	GW	GT	S	PCT
80	23	79	102	-13	34	6	1	3	1	195	11.8

1996-97 statistics:

GP	G	A	TP	+/-	PIM	PP	SH	GW	GT	S	PCT
82	25	72	97	+12	28	6	0	2	1	286	8.7

LAST SEASON

Signed as a free agent July 21, 1996. First on team and fourth in NHL in points. Led team, and tied for league lead, in assists. Led team in shots on goal. Led team in power-play points (31). Fifth in NHL in power-play assists. Second on club in game-winning points (13). One of four Rangers to appear in all 82 games.

THE FINESSE GAME

Almost everything is misdirection when Gretzky has the puck. If he's skating to his left, his pass will go to the right. If he's taking the puck deep in the zone, driving the defense back, bet your last dollar the late man, trailing the play, is going to get a delicious pass for a dangerous shot. Gretzky loves to create plays that go back against the grain, which is why he uses the backhand pass so extensively and so accurately.

Going against the grain also is a trademark of his shot selection, because it is easier for most goalies to step into a shot than reach back for one. If he comes down the centre of the zone and veers to his left, he almost always will shoot back to the extreme right (top corner, mostly), just in case the goalie overplays the angle and leaves a window open.

Getting the puck to the front of the net as quickly as possible is always Gretzky's priority. Be it by forehand or backhand — even if he has to kick the puck — he wants it in front before defensive positions can be established. That includes steep-angled shots from the corners or behind the net; if the goalie isn't alert and his skate isn't pinned against the goalpost, the puck might go in or bounce to someone for a putback.

Gretzky will come out from behind the net with the puck and hold it while someone else gets open. He will try the stuff shot occasionally. He also will not hesitate to use the rounded bottom of the goal frame to actually pass to himself; he will throw the puck off the net from the corner or the endboards, then try to step around the defenseman and reclaim the carom.

Particularly on the power play, Gretzky continues to operate from his "office" behind the net, which is positively the toughest play to defend for the goalie, who has to look over one shoulder at the puck, and the defense, who can't look over their shoulders to find Rangers skating to open spots. But Gretzky also operates from the right-wing circle, setting up one-timers from the point or the far circle, or working the puck deep and then cutting to the net.

THE PHYSICAL GAME

Let's face it: The guy's a weenie. But so what? Do you want him for his body or his mind? You need his genius for all 82 games, and he isn't built to withstand physical punishment.

That said, he will sneak up behind a guy, lift his stick and steal the puck. He will, at times, intentionally get in an opponent's way. And he does, once in a great while, backcheck.

THE INTANGIBLES

In spite of all the records, all the points, all the rude remarks about his whippet-thin body — and in spite of all the accolades — Gretzky never gets enough credit for his competitiveness or his desire to win.

This is an effort player, even if he doesn't scrunch up his face when he's skating. Many nights, his best period was the third, when the Rangers most needed his wizardry. And many nights, Gretzky's best moments came in the closing minutes, when he turned potential losses into ties, or turned potential ties into victories.

PROJECTION

Gretzky leads the Rangers' fast break, powers their transition game and distributes offensive chances in a manner that would stir pride in any point guard. All those big, mean centres and defensemen in the Eastern Conference didn't slow him noticeably last season, any more than they have in the past. Yes, he's slower. Yes, he's getting hit more. But he plays a lot every game and he's going to get points. He's still worth a high pick in your pool.

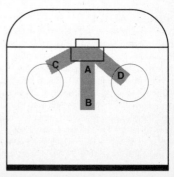

ALEXANDER KARPOVTSEV

Yrs. of NHL service: 4
Born: Moscow, Russia; Feb. 25, 1974
Position: left defense
Height: 6-1
Weight: 200
Uniform no.: 25
Shoots: left

Career statistics:

GP	G	A	TP	PIM
231	18	68	76	173

1993-94 statistics:

GP	G	A	TP	+/-	PIM	PP	SH	GW	GT	S	PCT
67	3	15	18	+12	58	1	0	1	0	78	3.8

1994-95 statistics:

GP	G	A	TP	+/-	PIM	PP	SH	GW	GT	S	PCT
47	4	8	12	-4	30	1	0	1	0	82	4.9

1995-96 statistics:

GP	G	A	TP	+/-	PIM	PP	SH	GW	GT	S	PCT
40	2	16	18	+12	26	1	0	1	0	71	2.8

1996-97 statistics:

GP	G	A	TP	+/-	PIM	PP	SH	GW	GT	S	PCT
77	9	29	28	+1	59	6	1	0	0	84	10.7

LAST SEASON
Career high in goals, assists and points.

THE FINESSE GAME
The strength of Karpovtsev's skating game is best reflected in his terrific lateral movement. He covers acres of ground with a huge stride and a long reach, has excellent balance, turns nicely in both directions and boasts a fair amount of quickness and agility. He has a quick first step to the puck.

Karpovtsev has decent puck-carrying skills and the good sense to move the puck quickly, but displays the defensive defenseman's mindset of getting to the redline and dumping the puck into the corner or making a short outlet pass. Under pressure behind his net, Karpovtsev tends to whack the puck around the boards, a play that often gets picked off.

Karpovtsev does, at times, show a good instinct for seeing a better passing option than the obvious in the attacking zone. He has an effective, hard shot from the point, and his accuracy has improved.

THE PHYSICAL GAME
Karpovtsev is extremely strong and is not shy about using his strength in front of the net or in the corners. Battling for loose pucks, he will move a player with a forearm shove, then grab the puck while his opponent is recovering from the jolt. He will also throw himself backfirst towards a player, immobilize the guy against the boards, then recover quickly and grab the puck.

Karpovtsev plays toughest against the toughest players. He does not hesitate to get involved if things turn nasty, and though hardly a polished fighter he is a willing one. He likes the big hit but doesn't mind the smaller ones.

A crease-clearer and shot-blocker, Karpovtsev is far more comfortable and poised in front of his net than when he chases to the corners or sideboards. Once he gets away from the slot, with or without the puck, he loses either confidence or focus or both, which can lead to unforced errors or turnovers that result in scoring chances.

Still, he is an effective weapon against a power forward. He can tie up the guy in front, lean on him, hit and skate with an Eric Lindros.

THE INTANGIBLES
Respect is a very important element to Karpovtsev, who has made his play more than respectable with perseverance. He can kill penalties, work the power play and is comfortable with four-on-four play, but his real value is the long, tough, bruising nights he and Ulf Samuelsson spend waging war with the Legion of Doom or any of the opposition's top offensive threats. He is a battler who has no problem with the ''heavy lifting'' assignments.

PROJECTION
Karpovtsev proved trustworthy last season, made better use of his shot and generally had a breakthrough campaign. The performance curve is upwards, which might merit late-round selection if your pool involves a lot of players.

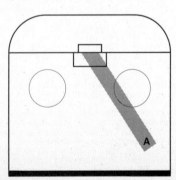

MIKE KEANE

Yrs. of NHL service: 9
Born: Winnipeg, Man.; May 28, 1967
Position: right wing
Height: 5-10
Weight: 185
Uniform no.: 25
Shoots: right

Career statistics:

GP	G	A	TP	PIM
642	100	206	316	599

1993-94 statistics:

GP	G	A	TP	+/-	PIM	PP	SH	GW	GT	S	PCT
80	16	30	46	+6	119	6	2	2	1	129	12.4

1994-95 statistics:

GP	G	A	TP	+/-	PIM	PP	SH	GW	GT	S	PCT
48	10	10	20	+5	15	1	0	0	0	75	13.3

1995-96 statistics:

GP	G	A	TP	+/-	PIM	PP	SH	GW	GT	S	PCT
73	10	17	27	-5	46	0	2	2	0	84	11.9

1996-97 statistics:

GP	G	A	TP	+/-	PIM	PP	SH	GW	GT	S	PCT
81	10	17	27	+2	63	0	1	1	0	91	11.0

LAST SEASON

Signed as free agent, July 7, 1997. Tied for Avalanche team lead in games played.

THE FINESSE GAME

Keane is one of the NHL's most underrated forwards. There are few better on the boards and in the corners, and he's the perfect linemate for a finisher. If you want the puck, he'll get it. Not only will he win the battle for it, he'll make a pass and then set a pick or screen.

He is a good skater and will use his speed to forecheck or create shorthanded threats when killing penalties. He is not much of a finisher, though he will contribute the odd goal from his work in front of the net.

Keane can play all three forward positions, but is most effective on the right side. He is a smart player who can be thrust into almost any playing situation. He can be expected to join Brian Skrudland on an effective third line with the Rangers. Keane is a valuable role player.

THE PHYSICAL GAME

Keane is a physical catalyst. He is constantly getting in someone's way. He always finishes his checks in all three zones. He is aggressive and will stand up for his teammates, though he is not a fighter. He has a ridiculously high pain threshold and has to be locked in a closet to keep him out of the lineup.

THE INTANGIBLES

Keane is a natural leader and has played on Cup winners in Montreal and Colorado. He may not have received the attention he's deserved through his career, but all that will change now that he's in New York.

PROJECTION

As a checking forward, Keane probably won't score more than 15 goals a year, but if injuries hit he can step in almost anywhere but in the net.

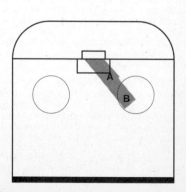

ALEXEI KOVALEV

Yrs. of NHL service: 5
Born: Togliatti, Russia; Feb. 24, 1973
Position: right wing/centre
Height: 6-0
Weight: 205
Uniform no.: 27
Shoots: left

Career statistics:

GP	G	A	TP	PIM
315	93	120	215	403

1993-94 statistics:

GP	G	A	TP	+/-	PIM	PP	SH	GW	GT	S	PCT
76	23	33	56	+18	154	7	0	3	0	184	12.5

1994-95 statistics:

GP	G	A	TP	+/-	PIM	PP	SH	GW	GT	S	PCT
48	13	15	28	-6	30	1	1	1	0	103	12.6

1995-96 statistics:

GP	G	A	TP	+/-	PIM	PP	SH	GW	GT	S	PCT
81	24	34	58	+5	98	8	1	7	0	206	11.7

1996-97 statistics:

GP	G	A	TP	+/-	PIM	PP	SH	GW	GT	S	PCT
45	13	22	35	+11	42	1	0	0	0	110	11.8

LAST SEASON

Missed 37 games of the regular season with surgery to repair torn anterior cruciate ligament in right knee.

THE FINESSE GAME

Kovalev is skilled enough to make breathtaking plays of exquisite grace, and he is stubborn enough to over-handle the puck and manoeuvre himself completely out of the play without the slightest help from an opponent.

You don't often see hands or feet as quick as Kovalev's on a player of his size. He has the dexterity, puck control, strength, balance and speed to beat the first forechecker coming out of the zone or the first line of defense once he crosses the attacking blueline. He is one of the few players in the NHL agile and balanced enough to duck under a check at the side-boards and maintain possession of the puck. Exceptional hands allow him to make remarkable moves, but his hockey thought process doesn't always finish them off well.

On many occasions, the slithery moves don't do enough offensive damage. Sometimes he overhandles, then turns the puck over. Too many times, Kovalev fails to get the puck deep. He hates to surrender the puck even when dump-and-chase is the smartest option, and as a result he causes turnovers at the blueline and has to chase any number of opposition break-aways to his team's net.

THE PHYSICAL GAME

The chippier the game, the happier Kovalev is; he'll bring his stick up and wade into the fray. He can be sneaky dirty. He'll run goalies over and try to make it look as if he was pushed into them by a defender. He's so strong and balanced on his skates that when he goes down odds are it's a dive. At the same time, he ab-sorbs all kinds of physical punishment, legal and ille-gal, and rarely receives the benefit of the doubt from the referees.

Kovalev has very good size and is a willing hitter. He likes to make highlight reel hits that splatter peo-ple. Because he is such a strong skater, he is very hard to knock down unless he's leaning. He makes exten-sive use of his edges because he combines balance and a long reach to keep the puck well away from his body, and from a defender's. But there are moments when he seems at a 45-degree angle and then he can be nudged over.

THE INTANGIBLES

Kovalev thrives on extra ice time and has to be dragged off the ice to make a line change. He was a boy of 19 when he joined the Rangers and has matured almost tangibly in the years since. A natural athlete, he remains fun-loving but has added an unmistakable professionalism and drive that was lacking when ev-erything came naturally. It is very easy to like a lot of his game. This is his sixth Ranger season and he's only 24.

PROJECTION

Season after season, Kovalev has shown glimmers of spectacular skill, has given promise that he is the Real Deal in a powerful package — only to frustrate all of Rangerdom by taking some sort of detour. Kovalev was in the middle of such a season last year when the injury struck, in the closing year of his contract. Just when he started to make you think, "This is the year he puts it all together, at last," he got hurt. Which means this will be the year GM Neil Smith's patience gets rewarded.

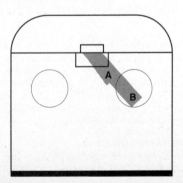

BRIAN LEETCH

Yrs. of NHL service: 9
Born: Corpus Christi, Tex.; Mar. 3, 1968
Position: left defense
Height: 5-11
Weight: 190
Uniform no.: 2
Shoots: left

Career statistics:

GP	G	A	TP	PIM
649	157	503	650	325

1993-94 statistics:

GP	G	A	TP	+/-	PIM	PP	SH	GW	GT	S	PCT
84	23	56	79	+28	67	17	1	4	0	328	7.0

1994-95 statistics:

GP	G	A	TP	+/-	PIM	PP	SH	GW	GT	S	PCT
48	9	32	41	0	18	3	0	2	0	182	4.9

1995-96 statistics:

GP	G	A	TP	+/-	PIM	PP	SH	GW	GT	S	PCT
82	15	70	85	+12	30	7	0	3	0	276	5.4

1996-97 statistics:

GP	G	A	TP	+/-	PIM	PP	SH	GW	GT	S	PCT
82	20	58	78	+31	40	9	0	2	0	256	7.8

LAST SEASON

Won 1997 Norris Trophy. Led NHL defensemen in assists and points. Led team in plus-minus. Third on team in points. Tied for team lead in power-play goals. Second on team in power-play points (30). Played every one of his team's games for fourth consecutive season.

THE FINESSE GAME

Such quick hands, feet and thoughts. Leetch is a premier passer who sees the ice clearly, identifies the optimum passing option on the move and hits his target with a forehand or backhand pass. He is terrific at picking passes out of the air and keeping attempted clearing passes from getting by him at the point.

Leetch has a fine first step that sends him towards top speed almost instantly. He can be posted at the point, then see an opportunity to jump into the play down low and bolt into action. His anticipation is superb. Leetch knows what he's going to do with the puck before he has it. He seems to be thinking about five seconds ahead of everyone else on the ice. He instantly starts a transition from defense to offense, and always seems to make the correct decision to pass or skate with the puck.

Leetch has a remarkable knack for getting his point shot through traffic and to the net. He even uses his eyes to fake. He is adept as looking and/or moving in one direction, then passing the opposite way.

Leetch smartly jumps into holes to make the most of an odd-man rush, and he is more than quick enough to hop back on defense if the puck turns the other way. He has astounding lateral movement, the best in the league among defensemen, leaving forwards completely out of room when it looked like there was open ice to get past him. He uses this as a weapon on offense to open up space for his teammates.

Leetch has a range of shots. He'll use a slap shot from the point, usually through a screen because it won't overpower any NHL goalie, but he'll also use a wrist shot from the circle. He also is gifted with the one-on-one moves that help him wriggle in front for 10-footers on the forehand or backhand, and he has worked on one-timers from close to the net.

THE PHYSICAL GAME

Leetch initiates contact and doesn't hesitate to make plays in the face of being hit. He is dependable in front of his net and responsible in his defensive zone. Although not strong enough, nor mean spirited-enough, to manhandle people, Leetch still gets physically involved. He competes for the puck and is a first-rate penalty killer.

Leetch cuts off the ice, gives the skater nowhere to go, strips the puck or steals a pass, then starts the transition game. He'll then follow the rush and may finish off the play with a goal.

THE INTANGIBLES

Leetch is a quiet leader and almost certainly will be the Rangers' first captain in the post-Messier era. His game has matured, gained a shiny lustre like fine wood. He remains the finest player at his position and boasts the hardware — two Norris trophies and a Conn Smythe — to prove it.

PROJECTION

The addition of Wayne Gretzky provided another creator to complement Leetch's ability to join the attack. From the standpoint of ice time, Leetch must be in the top five in the league — which means a shot at 80 to 90 points.

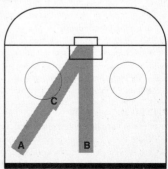

MIKE PELUSO

Yrs. of NHL service: 7
Born: Pengilly, Minn.; Nov. 8, 1965
Position: left wing
Height: 6-4
Weight: 220
Uniform no.: 20
Shoots: left

Career statistics:

GP	G	A	TP	PIM
435	39	55	94	1758

1993-94 statistics:

GP	G	A	TP	+/-	PIM	PP	SH	GW	GT	S	PCT
69	4	16	20	+19	238	0	0	0	0	44	9.1

1994-95 statistics:

GP	G	A	TP	+/-	PIM	PP	SH	GW	GT	S	PCT
46	2	9	11	+5	167	0	0	1	0	27	7.4

1995-96 statistics:

GP	G	A	TP	+/-	PIM	PP	SH	GW	GT	S	PCT
57	3	8	11	+4	146	0	0	0	0	41	7.3

1996-97 statistics:

GP	G	A	TP	+/-	PIM	PP	SH	GW	GT	S	PCT
64	2	5	7	0	226	0	0	0	0	37	5.4

LAST SEASON

Traded by St. Louis to Rangers for future considerations (compensation for the Blues' signing of GM Larry Pleau) on June 21. Traded by New Jersey to St. Louis with D Ricard Persson for D Ken Sutton and Blues' number two pick in 1998 draft on November 26, 1996. Seventh consecutive season of at least 146 penalty minutes. Surpassed 200 penalty minutes for fifth time in seven seasons.

THE FINESSE GAME

As someone who makes his living by making things happen, Peluso keeps his game simple. He works for the puck in the corners or along the wall and tries to find a way to get it to the front of the net.

Although not the world's most gifted or graceful skater, there is power in his stride for straight-ahead speed, and that's extremely useful in the pressure forecheck game Peluso likes to play. His balance is somewhat stronger now, which benefits him in those battles in front of the net. His shot, generally taken from the face-off circles or closer, is very ordinary, and his passing skills are limited.

Peluso's scoring chances are few and far between. He will create chances with his size and determination, however, far more often than not, he is the guy who worked the puck free in the corner so that someone else could knock it in.

THE PHYSICAL GAME

A bundle of energy and emotion, Peluso is most effective when given a specific task to perform. Although he is a willing, ferocious fighter, he also is trustworthy enough to be deployed for the important first shift af-

ter a goal — for or against. Peluso plays the game with a hard edge but also plays it clean. Very few of his penalty minutes result from "stupid" fouls. More often than not, he ends up getting called for hooking, holding or tripping after hauling down an opponent who has gotten a step on him.

THE INTANGIBLES

Peluso will do absolutely anything for his teammates, and his commitment to their well-being allows the finesse guys to play with more confidence — as well as a little extra breathing room. Peluso "plays big," and regularly arrives at the rink several hours early in order to properly stoke the flames of his intensity.

PROJECTION

Peluso was obtained as something of an insurance policy, because Shane Churla will be lost to the Rangers until February due to knee surgery. Still, Peluso's credentials stand on their own. He won't get many points but he will be "even" or "plus" most nights, and will serve as a much-needed bodyguard in those wars with Philadelphia, Washington and his former team, New Jersey.

MIKE RICHTER

Yrs. of NHL service: 7
Born: Abingdon, Pa.; Sept. 22, 1966
Position: goaltender
Height: 5-11
Weight: 185
Uniform no.: 35
Catches: left

Career statistics:

GP	MIN	GA	SO	GAA	A	PIM
352	20016	978	18	2.93	7	24

1993-94 statistics:

GP	MIN	GAA	W	L	T	SO	GA	S	SAPCT	PIM
68	3710	2.57	42	12	6	5	159	1758	.910	2

1994-95 statistics:

GP	MIN	GAA	W	L	T	SO	GA	S	SAPCT	PIM
35	1993	2.92	14	17	2	2	97	884	.890	2

1995-96 statistics:

GP	MIN	GAA	W	L	T	SO	GA	S	SAPCT	PIM
41	2396	2.68	24	13	3	3	107	1221	.912	4

1996-97 statistics:

GP	MIN	GAA	W	L	T	SO	GA	S	SAPCT	PIM
61	3598	2.68	33	22	6	4	161	1945	.917	4

LAST SEASON

Tied for fourth in NHL in wins. Victory total was the second-highest of his career.

THE PHYSICAL GAME

Today's goaltending "kids" are all enormously comfortable with handling the puck and with using their stick as an extension of their equipment. Richter, from a prior generation, is a stickhandling nightmare: puck exchanges with his defensemen are often laughable and, at times, life-threatening, because Richter simply cannot decide whether to leave the puck behind the net or try a cute little pass to help the cause. The results are usually calamitous. Either there is a turnover for an easy goal, or some defenseman, trying to find Richter's pass in his feet, gets creamed from behind by a forechecker.

Richter is at last starting to use his stick for poke-checks in one-on-one confrontations, but still doesn't use it enough as a pass-blocking tool. Too often, he concedes the pass across the crease and relies on his lateral movement to make a quick save he wouldn't have to make at all if he merely prevented the puck from reaching the shooter.

Nonetheless, Richter is agile, flexible and athletic and boasts exceptional post-to-post quickness. Quick reflexes allow him to reach second-chance shots off rebounds or one-timers off odd-man rushes.

Richter rarely gets beat to the low corners. Shooters beat him high on the glove side or on slam-dunks to the weak side after he has overplayed an angle. He gets a whopping percentage of the first shots, and while he catches more puck now, and holds onto them more, Richter still leaves rebounds that can be trouble.

THE MENTAL GAME

Richter may be the most patient one-on-one goalie in the NHL. Confident and fluid, he simply lets himself make whatever save is necessary. If that results in him losing his stick and at least one of his gloves, no problem. When he trusts his instincts and just flows, he is the NHL's best package of concentration, reflexes and puck-stopping skill in clutch situations.

He is exceptional at finding the puck through traffic, and able to make solid stops on close-range shots off passes from behind the net. Similarly, when the puck is moving from point to point, Richter stays focussed, stays crouched, sees the puck and stays with it.

THE INTANGIBLES

Richter has been an All-Star MVP, a World Cup MVP and a playoff hero. He wants to win, knows how to win games by himself and provides the all-important confidence a team needs. He gives his team a good-to-excellent chance to win every night and is one of the league's most entertaining at the position.

PROJECTION

His performance in the World Cup and in the playoffs against Florida and New Jersey certainly make Richter the odds-on favourite as America's Olympic starter at Nagano. The guy is a workhorse, but asking him to handle the pressures of that tournament, plus 60 games in the regular season and then the playoffs is asking too much.

LUC ROBITAILLE

Yrs. of NHL service: 11
Born: Montreal, Que.; Feb. 17, 1966
Position: left wing
Height: 6-1
Weight: 195
Uniform no.: 20
Shoots: left

Career statistics:

GP	G	A	TP	PIM
832	462	500	962	727

1993-94 statistics:

GP	G	A	TP	+/-	PIM	PP	SH	GW	GT	S	PCT
83	44	42	86	-20	86	24	0	3	0	267	16.5

1994-95 statistics:

GP	G	A	TP	+/-	PIM	PP	SH	GW	GT	S	PCT
46	23	19	42	+10	37	5	0	3	1	109	21.1

1995-96 statistics:

GP	G	A	TP	+/-	PIM	PP	SH	GW	GT	S	PCT
77	23	46	69	+13	80	11	0	4	2	223	10.3

1996-97 statistics:

GP	G	A	TP	+/-	PIM	PP	SH	GW	GT	S	PCT
69	24	24	48	+16	48	5	0	4	0	200	12.0

LAST SEASON

Tied for fourth on team in goals. Missed 13 games with stress fracture in left foot.

THE FINESSE GAME

Robitaille gets the most done when he determines one course of action and follows through on it, because he simply does not have the quickness of hand, foot or mind to do multiple tasks. Slow of foot to begin with, Robitaille's problems are magnified by questionable balance. It doesn't seem to take much to knock him off his feet.

Accordingly, carrying the puck slows Robitaille even more because it requires him to read a defense and identify a passing option. He is far better served by getting the puck, moving the puck — which was easy last year, because he spent so much of the season playing with Wayne Gretzky — and moving his feet to the holes.

Robitaille needs to be an instinctive player. When he works to an opening in the front of the net and shoots off the pass, he can be devastatingly effective because the shot is accurate and the release too quick for defensemen to block. That said, there were any number of times last season when shots that used to hit the top corners of the net started hitting every goalie in the chest.

THE PHYSICAL GAME

While considered a finesse player, the physical aspect is an under-noticed part of Robitaille's game. He's among the first — last season he was among the few on his team — to avenge any cheap shot against one of his teammates. He isn't a fighter but his sense of team is significant.

Robitaille goes to the grungy parts of the ice; he mucks for the puck. He also pays more of a physical price. He absorbs a fair amount of hits because he isn't quick enough to get out of the way, and, because he does not think or act quickly, he gets whacked while making up his mind. Still, Robitaille has such upper-body strength that a defender will think he has him wrapped up, only to see the puck in the net after Robitaille has somehow gotten his hands free.

THE INTANGIBLES

Robitaille wants to work, wants to win, tries to persevere in the face of scoring slumps that have become increasingly common, and virtually lived in the weight room while recovering from his late-season foot injury. But he and coach Colin Campbell experienced some friction last season, as both were frustrated by Robitaille's underproductive play. He's one of the world's nice guys, but he's on the spot to put up offensive numbers in better proportion to a contract that has four seasons and U.S.$13.6 million remaining.

PROJECTION

Robitaille's struggles continued despite a hefty amount of time on Wayne Gretzky's left. The limitations of his game served as reminders that this was a player claimed on the 171st pick of the 1984 draft, notwithstanding the Rookie of the Year Award that season and the several 40-goal campaigns that followed.

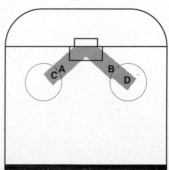

ULF SAMUELSSON

Yrs. of NHL service: 13
Born: Fagersta, Sweden; Mar. 26, 1964
Position: left defense
Height: 6-1
Weight: 195
Uniform no.: 5
Shoots: left

Career statistics:

GP	G	A	TP	PIM
887	49	256	305	2174

1993-94 statistics:

GP	G	A	TP	+/-	PIM	PP	SH	GW	GT	S	PCT
80	5	24	29	+23	199	1	0	0	1	106	4.7

1994-95 statistics:

GP	G	A	TP	+/-	PIM	PP	SH	GW	GT	S	PCT
44	1	15	16	+11	113	0	0	0	0	47	2.1

1995-96 statistics:

GP	G	A	TP	+/-	PIM	PP	SH	GW	GT	S	PCT
74	1	18	19	+9	122	0	0	0	0	66	1.5

1996-97 statistics:

GP	G	A	TP	+/-	PIM	PP	SH	GW	GT	S	PCT
73	6	11	17	+3	138	1	0	1	0	77	7.8

LAST SEASON

Missed nine games with sprained right knee.

THE FINESSE GAME

Although offense is generally an underused aspect of his game, Samuelsson started jumping to openings last season after Wayne Gretzky joined the Rangers, and scored his most goals since 1988-89. Samuelsson always picks his spots in the neutral zone, setting up cartilage-jarring hits on unsuspecting opponents. His willingness to launch himself into the play as the late man in the attacking zone caught more than a few teams by surprise, as well.

Gretzky is tailor-made for Samuelsson's game because the defenseman can't carry the puck at a high tempo and is better off making the escape pass than trying to rush it up-ice himself. Although Samuelsson likes trying to handle the puck himself, this is a mistake. He has a nice shot but lacks poise and confidence in the attacking zone. When all he needs to do is slam-dunk a Gretzky pass, though, Samuelsson is almost as good as anyone else.

Samuelsson has wonderful skills that are often overshadowed by the more irritating aspects of his nature. He is a very good skater for his size, with flat-out speed and one-step quickness, agility, mobility and balance. He skates backwards very well, generally makes good defensive reads and is always well-positioned. He is difficult to beat one-on-one and sometimes even two-on-one because of his anticipation.

THE PHYSICAL GAME

Samuelsson plays with so much extra padding that you wonder how he can even move. He looks like a kid whose overprotective parent has stuffed him into a snowsuit, with his arms sticking out at right angles. The protection does permit him to be absolutely fearless in shot-blocking, at which he is among the best in the league, and in throwing those roadblock bodyblasts.

Samuelsson is a big hitter. He will try to put someone through the wall, though sometimes a simple take-out would do. He could hit cleaner, but bringing his stick up on a hit is his most natural move, and he takes many unnecessary penalties because of this tendency.

Samuelsson absorbs a lot of punishment in addition to dishing it out. His gloves are always in an opponent's face. Some of the physical wear and tear appears to be taking a toll on him.

THE INTANGIBLES

Samuelsson has just enough goon in him to distract opponents, and enough talent to take advantage when the other team is too busy being enraged. He probably has a few seasons left as an effective defender.

PROJECTION

Samuelsson's toughness and competitiveness make him a natural matchup against the opposition's biggest and most dangerous offensive threats. But taking care of that business, plus his given offensive shortcomings, are not going to add up to much in the scoring column.

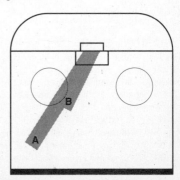

BRIAN SKRUDLAND

Yrs. of NHL service: 12
Born: Peace River, Alta.; July 31, 1963
Position: centre
Height: 6-0
Weight: 195
Uniform no.: 20
Shoots: left

Career statistics:

GP	G	A	TP	PIM
747	112	210	322	1003

1993-94 statistics:

GP	G	A	TP	+/-	PIM	PP	SH	GW	GT	S	PCT
79	15	25	40	+13	136	0	2	1	0	110	13.6

1994-95 statistics:

GP	G	A	TP	+/-	PIM	PP	SH	GW	GT	S	PCT
47	5	9	14	0	88	1	0	0	0	44	11.4

1995-96 statistics:

GP	G	A	TP	+/-	PIM	PP	SH	GW	GT	S	PCT
79	7	20	27	+6	129	0	1	1	0	90	7.8

1996-97 statistics:

GP	G	A	TP	+/-	PIM	PP	SH	GW	GT	S	PCT
51	5	13	18	+4	48	0	0	2	0	57	8.8

LAST SEASON

Signed as free agent July 7, 1997. Missed nine games with fractured rib. Missed one game with flu. Missed five games with bruised right shoulder. Missed 15 games with sprained right knee.

THE FINESSE GAME

Skrudland is among the top face-off men in the league, and that, along with his strong skating and tenacious forechecking, helps make him a reliable defensive forward.

His primary job is to keep the other team's top lines off the scoreboard, and he will get his scoring chances from forcing turnovers. He has a good short game and will look to make a creative play with the puck once he gains control. Skrudland has become less of an offensive threat in the past three seasons, settling more into a strictly defensive mode, but when he scores, he tends to tally big ones (two of his five goals were game-winners).

He is an outstanding penalty killer. He forechecks aggressively and attacks the points.

THE PHYSICAL GAME

Skrudland is tough to knock off balance. He has a wide skating stance, which also gives him a strong power base for checking. He seldom fails to get a piece of his opponent. He has a compact build and makes his presence felt.

If anything, Skrudland takes too much emotion into a game and will take a bad penalty at what always seems to be the worst time. It's a small price to pay for someone who never takes a night off unless forced to do so.

THE INTANGIBLES

Skrudland's knee injury did not allow him to play in the playoffs, and while the Panthers appeared scared off by the injury, the Rangers weren't. They've added another veteran leader to their team, one who will make an ideal third-line player. Skrudland is a quality guy, a gritty on-ice leader and a tremendous off-ice influence.

PROJECTION

Skrudland's contributions are the kind that don't show up on a scoresheet. If he's healthy, he may get 10 goals — half of which will be key in some way.

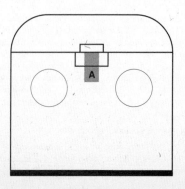

NIKLAS SUNDSTROM

Yrs. of NHL service: 2
Born: Ornskoldsvik, Sweden; June 6, 1975
Position: left wing
Height: 6-0
Weight: 185
Uniform no.: 24
Shoots: left

Career statistics:

GP	G	A	TP	PIM
164	33	40	73	34

1995-96 statistics:

GP	G	A	TP	+/-	PIM	PP	SH	GW	GT	S	PCT
82	9	12	21	+2	14	1	1	2	0	90	10.0

1996-97 statistics:

GP	G	A	TP	+/-	PIM	PP	SH	GW	GT	S	PCT
82	24	28	52	+23	20	5	1	4	0	132	18.2

LAST SEASON

Career highs in all offensive categories. Second on team in plus-minus. Third on team in goals. One of four Rangers to appear in all 82 games.

THE FINESSE GAME

Sundstrom may have a greater background as a centre but became invaluable as the right wing and defensive conscience on Wayne Gretzky's right. At least as important, Sundstrom was one of the few Rangers savvy enough to play successfully off Gretzky and convert the exceptional opportunities Gretzky creates for any teammate — each player helped provide a vital component for the other. Gretzky helped flesh out Sundstrom's reticent offensive game while Sundstrom covered Gretzky's back whenever possible.

A deceptively fast skater with good balance and a strong stride, Sundstrom plays a smart game and does a lot of subtle things well.

A puck magnet, he applies his skills to the defensive game. He reads plays very well, is aware defensively and always makes the safe decision. And when he forechecks, especially when killing penalties, he almost always comes up with the puck in a one-on-one battle.

THE PHYSICAL GAME

Sundstrom will not get much bigger and has to get stronger, but he is amoung the most persistent and consistently physical players on his team. One of Sundstrom's talents is lifting an opponent's blade to steal the puck. He absorbs way more punishment than he dishes out, since he doesn't punish anybody, but is beginning to realize that developing at least a hint of a mean streak is necessary for his survival. John MacLean broke Sundstrom's forearm with a slash in the playoffs, a painful introduction to the power of physical intimidation.

THE INTANGIBLES

Because he doesn't throw big hits or make flashy plays on the ice, and because he almost constantly is smiling off it, Sundstrom gets taken lightly a lot more than he should. He is committed to playing, and playing well. He is also committed to winning, and is enormously respected in the dressing room.

PROJECTION

Sundstrom is a passer more than a scorer. He has to learn to shoot the puck and drive to the net, to add new facets to his game and to make him less predictable.

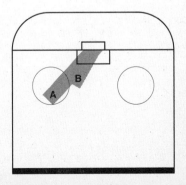

OTTAWA SENATORS

Players' Statistics 1996-97

POS.	NO.	PLAYER	GP	G	A	PTS	+/-	PIM	PP	SH	GW	GT	S	PCT
C	19	ALEXEI YASHIN	82	35	40	75	-7	44	10		5	1	291	12.0
R	11	DANIEL ALFREDSSON	76	24	47	71	5	30	11	1	1	2	247	9.7
R	91	ALEXANDRE DAIGLE	82	26	25	51	-33	33	4		5	2	203	12.8
D	28	STEVE DUCHESNE	78	19	28	47	-9	38	10	2	3		208	9.1
L	7	RANDY CUNNEYWORTH	76	12	24	36	-7	99	6		3		115	10.4
R	10	*ANDREAS DACKELL	79	12	19	31	-6	8	2		3		79	15.2
L	15	SHAWN MCEACHERN	65	11	20	31	-5	18		1	2		150	7.3
D	6	*WADE REDDEN	82	6	24	30	1	41	2		1		102	5.9
C	16	*SERGEI ZHOLTOK	57	12	16	28	2	19	5				96	12.5
L	17	TOM CHORSKE	68	18	8	26	-1	16	1	1	1		116	15.5
C	22	SHAUN VAN ALLEN	80	11	14	25	-8	35	1	1	2		123	8.9
C	25	*BRUCE GARDINER	67	11	10	21	4	49		1	2	2	94	11.7
D	33	JASON YORK	75	4	17	21	-8	67	1				121	3.3
D	27	JANNE LAUKKANEN	76	3	18	21	-14	76	2				109	2.8
L	42	DENNY LAMBERT	80	4	16	20	-4	217			1		58	6.9
C	76	RADEK BONK	53	5	13	18	-4	14	1			1	82	6.1
D	2	LANCE PITLICK	66	5	5	10	2	91			1		54	9.3
L	38	*JASON ZENT	22	3	3	6	5	9					20	15.0
D	23	CHRISTER OLSSON	30	2	4	6	-4	10	1				26	7.7
R	20	DENIS CHASSE	22	1	4	5	3	19					12	8.3
D	3	FRANK MUSIL	57		5	5	6	58					24	
C	14	DAVE HANNAN	34	2	2	4	-1	8		1	1		16	12.5
G	1	DAMIAN RHODES	50		2	2	0	2						
D	29	PHIL VONSTEFENELLI	6		1	1	-3	7					2	
L	21	DENNIS VIAL	11		1	1	0	25					4	
D	44	*RADIM BICANEK	21		1	1	-4	8					27	
R	26	PHILIP CROWE	26		1	1	0	30					8	
G	31	RON TUGNUTT	37		1	1	0							
G	35	*MIKE BALES	1				0							
D	4	SEAN HILL	5				1	4					9	
D	94	STANISLAV NECKAR	5				2	2					3	

GP = games played; G = goals; A = assists; PTS = points; +/- = goals-for minus goals-against while player is on ice; PIM = penalties in minutes; PP = power-play goals; SH = shorthanded goals; GW = game-winning goals; GT = game-tying goals; S = no. of shots; PCT = percentage of goals to shots; * = rookie

DANIEL ALFREDSSON

Yrs. of NHL service: 2
Born: Grums, Sweden; Dec. 11, 1972
Position: right wing
Height: 5-11
Weight: 187
Uniform no.: 11
Shoots: right

Career statistics:

GP	G	A	TP	PIM
158	50	82	132	58

1995-96 statistics:

GP	G	A	TP	+/-	PIM	PP	SH	GW	GT	S	PCT
82	26	35	61	-18	28	8	2	3	1	212	12.3

1996-97 statistics:

GP	G	A	TP	+/-	PIM	PP	SH	GW	GT	S	PCT
76	24	47	71	+5	30	11	1	1	2	247	9.7

LAST SEASON

Led team in assists, plus-minus and power-play goals. Second on team in points and shots. Third on team in goals. Missed six games with muscle pull in side.

THE FINESSE GAME

Alfredsson has a big-time NHL shot. His release is already hair-trigger, and it will only get better. What stamps this young Swede as more than a one-season wonder is his work ethic. He didn't make it to the NHL on cruise control. Alfredsson has to work for his space, and he does. One of the reasons why he is so good on the power play (nearly half his goals came with the extra attacker) are because of his work with the open ice. He has excellent vision and hands and is unselfish with the puck.

Alfredsson is well schooled in the defensive aspects of the game and adapted easily to the "trap" system Ottawa used for most of last season. Playing for three different coaches in his first NHL season must have been chaotic, but he remained unruffled.

THE PHYSICAL GAME

Alfredsson has a very thick and powerful lower body to fuel his skating. He is fearless and takes a lot of abuse to get into the high-scoring areas. He will skate up the wall and cut to the middle of the ice. He might get nailed by the off-side defenseman, but on the next rush he will try it again. He won't be scared off, and on the next chance he may get the shot away and in.

Alfredsson learned to handle the rigours of the NHL schedule in his second season. He pays close attention to conditioning and nutrition.

THE INTANGIBLES

Alfredsson tends to be streaky — he had two notable slumps last season — but he never stops working. His leadership was recognized with an assistant captaincy last season. He came through big-time in his first trip to the playoffs. He was involved in a very sticky con-tract situation during the off-season (he was a Group 2 free agent), which might affect training camp.

PROJECTION

Alfredsson won't be a 40-goal scorer, but he should be a reliable 30-goal man every season.

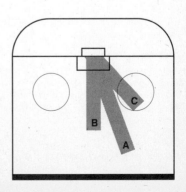

RADEK BONK

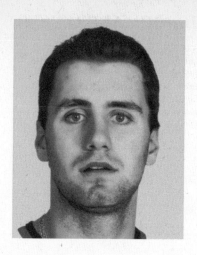

Yrs. of NHL service: 3
Born: Krnov, Czech Republic; Jan. 9, 1976
Position: centre
Height: 6-3
Weight: 215
Uniform no.: 76
Shoots: left

Career statistics:

GP	G	A	TP	PIM
171	24	40	64	78

1994-95 statistics:

GP	G	A	TP	+/-	PIM	PP	SH	GW	GT	S	PCT
42	3	8	11	-5	28	1	0	0	0	40	7.5

1995-96 statistics:

GP	G	A	TP	+/-	PIM	PP	SH	GW	GT	S	PCT
76	16	19	35	-5	36	5	0	1	0	161	9.9

1996-97 statistics:

GP	G	A	TP	+/-	PIM	PP	SH	GW	GT	S	PCT
53	5	13	18	-4	14	0	1	0	1	82	6.1

LAST SEASON

Missed 23 games with broken wrist. Missed six games with abdominal muscle strain.

THE FINESSE GAME

Bonk's skating is a detriment. He's fine when he gets a good head of speed up, but he doesn't explode in his first two strides (the way Joe Sakic does, for example). He can't utilize his skills when he can't accelerate away from stick checks.

Bonk is a puck magnet; the puck always seems to end up on his stick in the slot. He scores the majority of his goals from work in tight, getting his stick free. He has a heavy shot but doesn't have a quick release. He is a smart and creative passer and plays well in advance of his years, with a great deal of poise.

Defensively, Bonk needs to keep improving. He is decent on face-offs and can be used to kill penalties because of his anticipation.

THE PHYSICAL GAME

Although Bonk has good size, he does not show signs of becoming a power forward. He is aggressive only in his pursuit of the puck. He goes into the corners and wins many one-on-one battles because of his strength and hand skills.

THE INTANGIBLES

Bonk's injuries set him back last year. People have been quick to write him off, and it's true Bonk will never live up to the expectations that surrounded him as a first-round draft pick. He needs improvement in many areas.

PROJECTION

We once thought a healthy Bonk could produce at least 20 goals. Now, we're not so sure, though we're willing to give him one more season's grace before joining everyone else in writing him off.

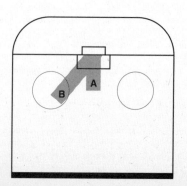

TOM CHORSKE

Yrs. of NHL service: 7
Born: Minneapolis, Minn.; Sept. 18, 1966
Position: left wing
Height: 6-1
Weight: 205
Uniform no.: 17
Shoots: right

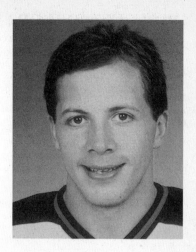

Career statistics:

GP	G	A	TP	PIM
455	102	91	193	176

1993-94 statistics:

GP	G	A	TP	+/-	PIM	PP	SH	GW	GT	S	PCT
76	21	20	41	+14	32	1	1	4	0	131	16.0

1994-95 statistics:

GP	G	A	TP	+/-	PIM	PP	SH	GW	GT	S	PCT
42	10	8	18	-4	16	0	0	2	0	59	16.9

1995-96 statistics:

GP	G	A	TP	+/-	PIM	PP	SH	GW	GT	S	PCT
72	15	14	29	-9	21	0	2	1	0	118	12.7

1996-97 statistics:

GP	G	A	TP	+/-	PIM	PP	SH	GW	GT	S	PCT
68	18	8	26	-1	16	1	1	1	0	116	15.5

LAST SEASON

Led team in shooting percentage. Missed six games with eye surgery. Missed eight games with hip injuries.

THE FINESSE GAME

Chorske has outstanding breakaway speed and considerable size — which make him a constant head-scratcher among his coaches. On any given night, he will use his body along the boards and take headman passes to key a quick attack. But those nights are rare.

Chorske has too many skills to be a mere grinder, yet when moved to a first line he never performs to those high levels. He does not play heads-up when he has the puck. He is always looking down at it, instead of at the goalie to find an opening or to a teammate for a pass. Breakaways or two-on-ones that involve him tend to get everyone excited until they realize, "Oh, it's Chorske." As one (Canadian) scout constantly mutters after Chorske's missed scoring opportunities, "American hands."

While that is an unfair slap (Pat LaFontaine and Jeremy Roenick might argue the assets of the American scoring touch), Chorske does lack the hand skills to make more of his speed. He works diligently in his checking role. With his quickness he gets many shorthanded scoring opportunities, but he doesn't bury as many as he should.

In addition to just being straight-line fast, Chorske is balanced and strong on his skates, getting great leg-drive for board and corner work. He is agile but not when carrying the puck; his moves are pretty limited.

THE PHYSICAL GAME

Chorske came out of the college ranks and doesn't play a vicious game, but he is a solid hitter and won't back down. He takes the body in all zones and hits cleanly, but his physical work is inconsistent. Some nights it's there, some nights he could skate with the proverbial eggs in his pockets and not crack a shell. He takes very few bad penalties.

THE INTANGIBLES

With his speed and size, Chorske will always go into the books as a disappointment for barely netting more than 20 goals in a season, but that appears to be his limit. He is one of those players who will always be on the bubble.

PROJECTION

Chorske will score 20 goals and be the subject of about as many trade rumours.

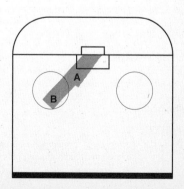

RANDY CUNNEYWORTH

Yrs. of NHL service: 14
Born: Etobicoke, Ont.; May 10, 1961
Position: left wing
Height: 6-0
Weight: 180
Uniform no.: 7
Shoots: left

Career statistics:

GP	G	A	TP	PIM
781	185	212	397	1217

1993-94 statistics:

GP	G	A	TP	+/-	PIM	PP	SH	GW	GT	S	PCT
79	13	11	24	-1	100	0	1	2	0	154	8.4

1994-95 statistics:

GP	G	A	TP	+/-	PIM	PP	SH	GW	GT	S	PCT
48	5	5	10	-19	68	2	0	0	0	71	7.0

1995-96 statistics:

GP	G	A	TP	+/-	PIM	PP	SH	GW	GT	S	PCT
81	17	19	36	-31	130	4	0	2	0	142	12.0

1996-97 statistics:

GP	G	A	TP	+/-	PIM	PP	SH	GW	GT	S	PCT
76	12	24	36	-7	99	6	0	3	0	115	10.4

LAST SEASON

Tied for third on team in game-winning goals. Missed six games with back injury and broken cheekbone.

THE FINESSE GAME

Cunneyworth has good straight-ahead speed with a decent shot. He sprints. He hustles. He competes hard every night. He played on the second line most of last season. On a stronger team, he would be a perfect third-line checking winger, but the Senators ask him to do much more.

He has above-average hand skills and scores most of his goals from in tight around the net. He is a good passer and likes to work give-and-go plays, though at this stage of his career he is not a great finisher.

Cunneyworth is also an effective penalty killer and does everything asked of him. He is consistent in his effort.

THE PHYSICAL GAME

Cunneyworth will hit and agitate. He isn't big but he will check and use his body in any zone. He is very annoying to play against.

THE INTANGIBLES

Cunneyworth wears the "C" but has already talked about turning over the leadership to the next generation. He's that classy. He gives the Senators everything he has.

PROJECTION

Cunneyworth will probably score around 30 points this season, as he is used more and more in a checking role.

ANDREAS DACKELL

Yrs. of NHL service: 1
Born: Gavle, Sweden; Dec. 29, 1972
Position: right wing
Height: 5-10
Weight: 191
Uniform no.: 10
Shoots: right

Career statistics:

GP	G	A	TP	PIM
79	12	19	31	8

1996-97 statistics:

GP	G	A	TP	+/-	PIM	PP	SH	GW	GT	S	PCT
79	12	19	31	-6	8	2	0	3	0	79	15.2

LAST SEASON

First NHL season. Second on team in shooting percentage.

THE FINESSE GAME

Dackell came into the league as a slightly older, polished rookie. Like many Europeans in their first pro year, he hit the wall after about 40 games (which is the length of the entire season in Sweden, not just the half-way mark), but he showed promise in the first half.

Dackell has good hockey sense and is very sound defensively. He does a lot of subtle things well. Tapes of his game could be used to illustrate hustling on backchecks to knock the puck away from an attacker, attacking in the neutral zone without committing yourself, playing strong along the wall and keeping your man out of the play. Dackell is a last-minute man, one of the guys put on the ice in the final minute of a period or game to protect a lead.

He has a decent, accurate shot that he could utilize more. He seems to score timely goals. He doesn't have blazing speed but he works hard to be where he's supposed to be.

THE PHYSICAL GAME

Dackell isn't overly big and he's not a banger, however, he'll make his checks and he won't be intimidated. He's not shy at all. He's good in the corner and knows how to roll off checks.

THE INTANGIBLES

Dackell has a history of not paying strict attention to his weight and conditioning during the off-season. He will need to lay off the smorgasbords while he's home in Sweden if he hopes to come into training camp and take the next step the Senators have planned.

PROJECTION

Dackell could be a 20-goal scorer in a third-line checking role.

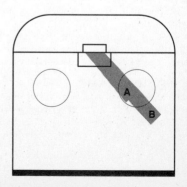

ALEXANDRE DAIGLE

Yrs. of NHL service: 4
Born: Laval, Que.; Feb. 7, 1975
Position: centre
Height: 6-0
Weight: 185
Uniform no.: 91
Shoots: left

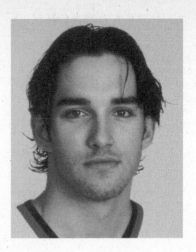

Career statistics:

GP	G	A	TP	PIM
263	67	89	156	111

1993-94 statistics:

GP	G	A	TP	+/-	PIM	PP	SH	GW	GT	S	PCT
84	20	31	51	-45	40	4	0	2	0	168	11.9

1994-95 statistics:

GP	G	A	TP	+/-	PIM	PP	SH	GW	GT	S	PCT
47	16	21	37	-22	14	4	1	2	0	105	15.2

1995-96 statistics:

GP	G	A	TP	+/-	PIM	PP	SH	GW	GT	S	PCT
50	5	12	17	-30	24	1	0	0	0	77	6.5

1996-97 statistics:

GP	G	A	TP	+/-	PIM	PP	SH	GW	GT	S	PCT
82	26	25	51	-33	33	4	0	5	2	203	12.8

LAST SEASON

Tied for team lead in game-winning goals. Second on team in goals. Third on team in assists. One of three Senators to appear in all 82 games.

THE FINESSE GAME

Daigle has NHL speed and acceleration but he doesn't have an NHL body, NHL stick skills or an NHL shot. He was such a brilliant player in certain areas at the junior level that he never had to work at many parts of his game, and he seems unaware that he can't perform the same tricks in the big leagues.

He has fine, soft hands, but he has a tough time controlling the puck in traffic. His skating, his chief asset, is compromised because he gets slower when he's carrying the puck.

Daigle demonstrates a great enthusiasm for the game, but is impatient and stubborn. He has problems with teams that play a neutral-zone trap. He has straight-on speed, but when the ice is closed off he looks bewildered, because he is not seeking the best options.

A strong forechecker, Daigle is effective as a penalty killer not because of his defensive awareness, but because he wants the puck so desperately.

THE PHYSICAL GAME

Daigle is feisty and will get involved in the offensive zone; he has learned to avoid taking dumb penalties. He could use his body better without getting creamed, but since he's not very big or strong he needs to stay out of the corners.

THE INTANGIBLES

If a game were decided on breakaways, Daigle's team would win more than its share. But there is more to hockey than that. Daigle has to improve his game on so many levels that he won't be a front-line player unless he works exceptionally hard. He wouldn't have gotten this many chances if he hadn't been a first-round draft pick.

Expectations remain high for Daigle. He will not fulfill them. He is, at best, a second-line forward whose top end is 25 to 30 goals.

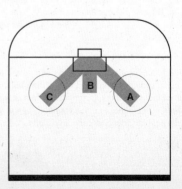

STEVE DUCHESNE

Yrs. of NHL service: 11
Born: Sept-Iles, Que.; June 30, 1965
Position: right defense
Height: 5-11
Weight: 195
Uniform no.: 28
Shoots: left

Career statistics:

GP	G	A	TP	PIM
765	188	394	582	670

1993-94 statistics:

GP	G	A	TP	+/-	PIM	PP	SH	GW	GT	S	PCT
36	12	19	31	+1	14	8	0	1	0	115	10.4

1994-95 statistics:

GP	G	A	TP	+/-	PIM	PP	SH	GW	GT	S	PCT
47	12	26	38	+29	36	1	0	1	0	116	10.3

1995-96 statistics:

GP	G	A	TP	+/-	PIM	PP	SH	GW	GT	S	PCT
62	12	24	36	-23	42	7	0	2	0	163	7.4

1996-97 statistics:

GP	G	A	TP	+/-	PIM	PP	SH	GW	GT	S	PCT
78	19	28	47	-9	38	10	2	3	0	208	9.1

LAST SEASON

Led team defensemen in scoring for second straight season. Led team in shorthanded goals. Tied for second on team in power-play goals. Tied for third in NHL for goals by a defenseman. Third on team in assists and shots. Tied for third on team in game-winning goals. Missed two games with wrist injury. Missed two games with back injury.

THE FINESSE GAME

Duchesne is a fluid, quick, smart skater who loves to join the attack. He often plays like a fourth forward. He is not afraid to gamble down deep, but he is such a good skater that he recovers quickly and is back in position in a flash. He does not waste time with the puck. He has sharp offensive sense; when the play is over he's out of there.

Duchesne has good poise and patience, and he can either drill a puck or take a little off it for his teammates to handle in front.

In the defensive zone, Duchesne uses his lateral mobility and quickness to maintain position. He is almost impossible to beat one-on-one in open ice. He helps his team out tremendously by being able to skate the puck out of danger or make a brisk headman pass. He is more interested in the puck than the man.

THE PHYSICAL GAME

Not only does Duchesne fail to knock anyone down in front of the net, most of the time he doesn't even tie them up effectively. He is not big or strong and he doesn't play tough. Positioning is the key to his defense, and he needs to play with a physical partner.

THE INTANGIBLES

The illness of his child made last year a difficult one for Duchesne, but he responded like a pro on the ice. A huge help to young players like Radim Bicanek (who will evetually take Duchesne's job) and Wade Redden, Duchesne maintained a good attitude under difficult circumstances.

PROJECTION

We pegged Duchesne for 50 points last season and will do so again, even though this is the year he will probably get moved (the Sentaors need to cut some salaries).

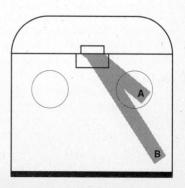

BRUCE GARDINER

Yrs. of NHL service: 1
Born: Barrie, Ont.; Feb. 11, 1971
Position: centre
Height: 6-1
Weight: 185
Uniform no.: 25
Shoots: right

Career statistics:

GP	G	A	TP	PIM
67	11	10	21	49

1996-97 statistics:

GP	G	A	TP	+/-	PIM	PP	SH	GW	GT	S	PCT
67	11	10	21	+4	49	0	1	2	2	94	11.7

LAST SEASON
First NHL season.

THE FINESSE GAME
Gardiner is versatile enough to play centre and right wing, but his future is probably as a winger, given the Senators' crowd in the middle.

Gardiner is a good skater who can do a lot of little things well. He has a good shot with a quick release. But he needs to shoot more, and he tends to be a streaky scorer. He has decent hands and vision for passing. He is adept on face-offs and has a future as a third-line checker and penalty killer. He isn't naturally gifted, but his effort makes the most of his skills.

THE PHYSICAL GAME
Gardiner is strong with good size. He's a gritty and diligent checker who takes the body well. He battles well against other teams' top centres.

THE INTANGIBLES
Gardiner's pro development was set back by a broken leg he suffered in 1995 after a strong training camp. He was supposed to miss the entire season but came back ahead of schedule to finish the season in the minors.

As an older rookie, Gardiner had a little bit of a chip on his shoulder in the dressing room, but that was mostly bravado, and he should develop legitimate confidence in his game that will eliminate the need for swagger. He works very hard in practices to improve his game.

PROJECTION
Gardiner likes the defensive part of the game and should score 15 to 20 goals in a checking role.

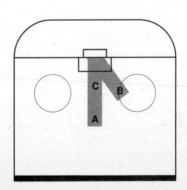

SEAN HILL

Yrs. of NHL service: 5
Born: Duluth, Minn.; Feb. 14, 1970
Position: right defense
Height: 6-0
Weight: 195
Uniform no.: 4
Shoots: right

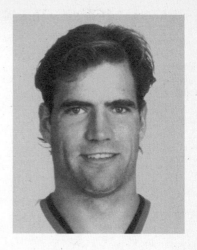

Career statistics:

GP	G	A	TP	PIM
229	17	54	71	260

1993-94 statistics:

GP	G	A	TP	+/-	PIM	PP	SH	GW	GT	S	PCT
68	7	20	27	-12	78	2	1	1	0	165	4.2

1994-95 statistics:

GP	G	A	TP	+/-	PIM	PP	SH	GW	GT	S	PCT
45	1	14	15	-11	30	0	0	0	0	107	0.9

1995-96 statistics:

GP	G	A	TP	+/-	PIM	PP	SH	GW	GT	S	PCT
80	7	14	21	-26	94	2	0	2	0	157	4.5

1996-97 statistics:

GP	G	A	TP	+/-	PIM	PP	SH	GW	GT	S	PCT
5	0	0	0	+1	4	0	0	0	0	9	0.0

posure to the Senators. He doesn't have elite skills but he can produce 25 to 30 points a season. Expect a slow first half because of his knee rehab.

LAST SEASON

Missed 77 games with knee injury and reconstructive surgery.

THE FINESSE GAME

A good skater before his injury, Hill is agile, strong and balanced, if not overly fast. He can skate the puck out of danger or make a smart first pass. He learned defense in the Montreal system but has since evolved into more of a specialty-team player.

Hill has a good point shot and good offensive sense. He likes to carry the puck and start things off a rush, or he will jump into the play. He can handle power-play time but is not exceptional. He is more suited to a second-unit role.

Hill's best quality is his competitiveness. He will hack and whack at puck carriers like an annoying terrier ripping and nipping your socks and ankles.

THE PHYSICAL GAME

For a smallish player, Hill gets his share of points, and he gets them by playing bigger than his size. He has a bit of a mean streak, and though he certainly can't overpower people, he is a solidly built player who doesn't get pushed around easily.

THE INTANGIBLES

Hill and teammate Stanislav Neckar both were injured in the same game just five games into the regular season, which makes the Senators' successful run to the playoffs even more amazing.

PROJECTION

A poor man's Al MacInnis, Hill brings a veteran com-

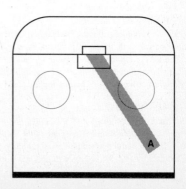

SHAWN MCEACHERN

Yrs. of NHL service: 5
Born: Waltham, Mass.; Feb. 28, 1969
Position: centre/left wing
Height: 5-11
Weight: 195
Uniform no.: 15
Shoots: left

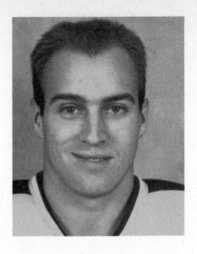

Career statistics:

GP	G	A	TP	PIM
366	96	121	217	154

1993-94 statistics:

GP	G	A	TP	+/-	PIM	PP	SH	GW	GT	S	PCT
76	20	22	42	+14	34	0	5	1	0	159	12.6

1994-95 statistics:

GP	G	A	TP	+/-	PIM	PP	SH	GW	GT	S	PCT
44	13	13	26	+4	22	1	2	1	0	97	13.4

1995-96 statistics:

GP	G	A	TP	+/-	PIM	PP	SH	GW	GT	S	PCT
82	24	29	53	-5	34	3	2	3	0	238	10.1

1996-97 statistics:

GP	G	A	TP	+/-	PIM	PP	SH	GW	GT	S	PCT
65	11	20	31	-5	18	0	1	2	0	150	7.3

PROJECTION

McEachern's speed keeps fooling people (including us here at *HSR*) into believing that he will score 60 points. We've learned. We'll downsize that to 40.

LAST SEASON

Missed 17 games with broken jaw.

THE FINESSE GAME

McEachern suffers from serious tunnel vision, which negates much of the advantage his speed brings to the lineup. He skates with his head down, looking at the ice instead of the play around him. He is strong and fast, with straightaway speed, but he tends to expend his energy almost carelessly and has to take short shifts.

McEachern's skating is what keeps him employed. He can shift speeds and direction smoothly without losing control of the puck. He can play both left wing and centre but is better on the wing. A very accurate shooter with a hard wrist shot, he has a quick release on his slap shot, which he likes to let go after using his outside speed. He is strong on face-offs and is a smart penalty killer who pressures the puck carrier.

THE PHYSICAL GAME

Generally an open-ice player, McEachern will also pursue the puck with some diligence in the attacking zone. But he is light, and although he can sometimes build up momentum with his speed for a solid bump, he loses most of the close-in battles for the puck.

THE INTANGIBLES

McEachern is a versatile player who can fill a lot of roles with his speed, but his limited playmaking skills will prevent him from being much of a producer.

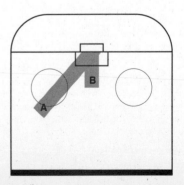

STANISLAV NECKAR

Yrs. of NHL service: 3
Born: Ceske Budejovice, Czechoslovakia; Dec. 22, 1975
Position: left defense
Height: 6-1
Weight: 196
Uniform no.: 94
Shoots: left

Career statistics:

GP	G	A	TP	PIM
135	4	12	16	93

1994-95 statistics:

GP	G	A	TP	+/-	PIM	PP	SH	GW	GT	S	PCT
48	1	3	4	-20	37	0	0	0	0	34	2.9

1995-96 statistics:

GP	G	A	TP	+/-	PIM	PP	SH	GW	GT	S	PCT
82	3	9	12	-16	54	1	0	0	0	57	5.3

1996-97 statistics:

GP	G	A	TP	+/-	PIM	PP	SH	GW	GT	S	PCT
5	0	0	0	+2	2	0	0	0	0	3	0.0

LAST SEASON

Missed 77 games with knee injury and reconstructive surgery.

THE FINESSE GAME

Neckar understands the position of defenseman, but he is fundamentally unsound when it comes time to putting all of the components together. He has to use his body more in addition to learning body position.

His offensive skills are overrated, but the Senators give Neckar a lot of time to work on them, including on the power play. He has a slow release on his point shot and doesn't do much that's creative other than put his head down and shoot. He's not a very good puckhandler or passer.

Neckar is a polished skater, especially backwards. He is not often beaten wide. His forte will be defensive play.

THE PHYSICAL GAME

Neckar is not a good open-ice hitter, but is very strong along the boards and in the corners, though he will need to develop confidence in his rebuilt knee to return to his old self. He will fight if provoked, but isn't very good at it. He needs to get much stronger. His cardiovascular conditioning is fine, and he can handle a lot of ice time (thrives on it, as a matter of fact), but he has to learn to stick and pin his man better.

THE INTANGIBLES

Neckar was showing slow but steady progress before the injury. He will need this year to regain his conditioning and timing.

PROJECTION

Don't expect much, especially in the first half, until Neckar is fully rehabbed.

CHRIS PHILLIPS

Yrs. of NHL service: 0
Born: Fort McMurray, Alta.; Mar. 9, 1978
Position: defense
Height: 6-2
Weight: 200
Uniform no.: n.a.
Shoots: left

Career junior statistics:

GP	G	A	TP	PIM
119	17	71	88	183

1995-96 junior statistics:

GP	G	A	TP	PIM
61	10	30	40	97

1996-97 junior statistics:

GP	G	A	TP	PIM
58	7	41	48	86

LAST SEASON

Named WHL Defenseman of the Year. Led team defensemen in scoring for Lethbridge with 7-41 — 48.

THE FINESSE GAME

Lots of kids in the defenseman-heavy 1996 draft were being compared to Scott Stevens. Phillips may actually be the closest to him in style and leadership. He may even turn out to be better than advertised.

Phillips is a very good skater for his size. He has all of the attributes — decent speed, lateral mobility, balance and agility. He skates well backwards and has a small turning radius. Carrying the puck doesn't slow him down much.

He will never post Ray Bourque numbers, but he can handle Bourque-like ice time. Phillips has a feel for the offensive part of the game. He joins the attack intelligently, and has a hard shot from the point as well as a good wrist shot when he goes in deep. One scout ranked his wrister as the best in the junior ranks. He is a heads-up passer and sees the ice well.

THE PHYSICAL GAME

Phillips is solidly built and there are very few question marks about his honest brand of toughness. He likes to hit, and he's mobile enough to catch a defender and drive with his legs to pack a wallop in his checks.

THE INTANGIBLES

Despite his considerable skills, Phillips ranks highest in this category. One scout said of him, "He's 18 years old, and I'm sure at his next birthday he'll be 28." Phillips cared for his ailing parents, choosing to delay his move to major junior by a year when he was just 16 to stay close to home to help. That is something that doesn't show up in the stats.

Staying in junior may have helped his leadership, since he played for a second gold-medal winner in the World Juniors. He would have been the shy kid in a room full of pros, but he was a vocal go-to guy in Lethbridge.

Now for the bad news (at least for the Senators): Shades of Bryan Berard. Phillips declared in mid-June that he could not come to a contract agreement with Ottawa and would play his last season in junior and re-enter the 1998 draft. The Sens might be forced to trade his rights.

PROJECTION

When Phillips does reach the NHL, he will be a solid two-way defenseman whose emphasis will be defense, but he could still provide 40 points a season. Being the first player picked overall carries a lot of pressure, but Phillips has already handled real pressure in his life and coped well.

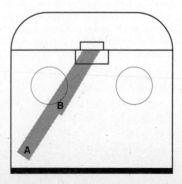

WADE REDDEN

Yrs. of NHL service: 1
Born: Lloydminster, Sask.; June 12, 1977
Position: left defense
Height: 6-2
Weight: 193
Uniform no.: 6
Shoots: left

Career statistics:

GP	G	A	TP	PIM
82	6	24	30	41

1996-97 statistics:

GP	G	A	TP	+/-	PIM	PP	SH	GW	GT	S	PCT
82	6	24	30	+1	41	2	0	1	0	102	5.9

LAST SEASON

First NHL season. Third among NHL rookie defensemen in scoring. Sixth among NHL rookies in assists. Third on team in plus-minus. One of three Senators to appear in all 82 games.

THE FINESSE GAME

Redden has tried to pattern his game after Ray Bourque, and the young defenseman has a few things in common with the Boston great. He is a good skater who can change gears swiftly and smoothly, and his superb rink vision enables him to get involved in his team's attack. He has a high skill level. His shot is hard and accurate and he is a patient and precise passer.

Redden plays older than his years and has a good grasp of the game. As he has been tested at higher and higher levels of competition he has elevated his game. His poise is exceptional.

Redden's work habits and attitude are thoroughly professional. He seems to be a player who is willing to learn in order to improve his game at the NHL level, and is a blue-chip prospect.

THE PHYSICAL GAME

Redden is not a big hitter, but he finishes his checks and stands up well. What he lacks in aggressiveness he makes up for with his competitive nature. He can handle a lot of ice time. He plays an economical game without a lot of wasted effort, is durable, and can skate all night long. He would move up a step if he dished it out instead of just taking it.

THE INTANGIBLES

Bryan Berard, for whom Redden was traded, won the Calder Trophy and was named to the All-Rookie team. Redden was ignored for any postseason honours, but he was as valuable and successful in his style as Berard was in his. Redden is a future captain and a foundation defenseman to build on.

PROJECTION

Redden will play defense first but he has good offensive upside and can produce 35 to 40 points.

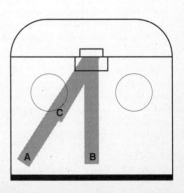

DAMIAN RHODES

Yrs. of NHL service: 3
Born: St. Paul, MN; May 28, 1969
Position: goaltender
Height: 6-0
Weight: 190
Uniform no.: 1
Catches: left

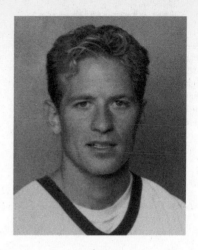

Career statistics:

GP	MIN	GA	SO	GAA	A	PIM
133	7714	348	3	2.71	4	12

1993-94 statistics:

GP	MIN	GAA	W	L	T	SO	GA	S	SAPCT	PIM
22	1213	2.62	9	7	3	0	53	541	.902	2

1994-95 statistics:

GP	MIN	GAA	W	L	T	SO	GA	S	SAPCT	PIM
13	760	2.68	6	6	1	0	34	404	.916	4

1995-96 statistics:

GP	MIN	GAA	W	L	T	SO	GA	S	SAPCT	PIM
47	2747	2.77	14	27	5	2	127	1342	.905	4

1996-97 statistics:

GP	MIN	GAA	W	L	T	SO	GA	S	SAPCT	PIM
50	2934	2.72	14	20	14	1	133	1213	.890	2

the Senators won't wait long if he shows signs of crumbling again early in the season.

LAST SEASON

Missed 19 games with calf muscle injury.

THE PHYSICAL GAME

Rhodes makes great first saves and doesn't give up bad rebounds. He either guides the pucks to the corners or deadens the puck in front of him. That is an excellent survival skill for a goalie on a team that is not strong defensively.

Rhodes is technically sound. Uncontrolled rebounds allow the shooter to drive in for the second chance, but he doesn't give away many. You have to beat him; he won't beat himself.

Rhodes is a stand-up goalie who plays his angles well and is solid in his fundamentals. He gives his team a chance to win the game.

THE MENTAL GAME

After going to the Senators in a trade in 1995-96, Rhodes looked capable of making the transition from backup goalie to number one. Now there are some question marks, however, and he will have a lot to prove in training camp. He allowed a goal on the first shot of the game seven times last season.

THE INTANGIBLES

Rhodes's calf muscle injury was curious. It seemed to get worse the better backup Ron Tugnutt played, and Rhodes lost his status as the Senators' top netminder in the playoffs. He suffered through a real crisis of confidence and went through five sets of pads.

PROJECTION

Rhodes is expected to regain the number one job, but

SHAUN VAN ALLEN

Yrs. of NHL service: 5
Born: Shaunavon, Sask.; Aug. 29, 1967
Position: centre
Height: 6-1
Weight: 200
Uniform no.: 22
Shoots: left

Career statistics:

GP	G	A	TP	PIM
277	36	81	117	178

1993-94 statistics:

GP	G	A	TP	+/-	PIM	PP	SH	GW	GT	S	PCT
80	8	25	33	0	64	2	2	1	0	104	7.7

1994-95 statistics:

GP	G	A	TP	+/-	PIM	PP	SH	GW	GT	S	PCT
45	8	21	29	-4	32	1	1	1	0	68	11.8

1995-96 statistics:

GP	G	A	TP	+/-	PIM	PP	SH	GW	GT	S	PCT
49	8	17	25	+13	41	0	0	2	0	78	10.3

1996-97 statistics:

GP	G	A	TP	+/-	PIM	PP	SH	GW	GT	S	PCT
80	11	14	25	-8	35	1	1	2	0	123	8.9

PROJECTION

Van Allen will not produce more than 30 to 35 points but will provide solid defense.

LAST SEASON

Acquired from Anaheim with Jason York for Ted Drury and Marc Moro, October 1, 1996.

THE FINESSE GAME

Van Allen always posted huge numbers in the minors, but like a lot of minor-league stars he couldn't transfer his scoring to the majors. The flaw in Van Allen's case is his skating, which is marginally NHL calibre — forcing him to change his strategy to that of a positional, defensive player.

When Van Allen does accomplish things offensively, such as on the power play, it's because of his smarts. He is a very good face-off man. If he controls the draw in the offensive zone he knows how to set up an attack. Van Allen also kills penalties. He seldom plays a poor game because he is aware of his limitations.

THE PHYSICAL GAME

Van Allen's solid, intelligent play is enhanced by his work ethic. He's not a banger but he will get in the way. He knows he would have been a career minor leaguer but for this chance, and he doesn't forget what he has to do to stay in the NHL.

THE INTANGIBLES

Van Allen will always be on the bubble. Coaches will keep trying younger, more talented guys in his spot, but he'll probably keep getting back into the lineup because he's too valuable to sit in the press box. Van Allen is a third- or fourth-line centre.

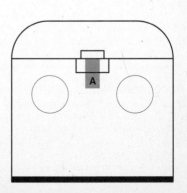

ALEXEI YASHIN

Yrs. of NHL service: 4
Born: Sverdlovsk, Russia; Nov. 5, 1973
Position: centre
Height: 6-3
Weight: 215
Uniform no.: 19
Shoots: right

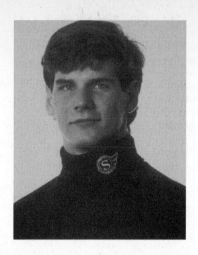

Career statistics:

GP	G	A	TP	PIM
258	101	136	237	125

1993-94 statistics:

GP	G	A	TP	+/-	PIM	PP	SH	GW	GT	S	PCT
83	30	49	79	-49	22	11	2	3	0	232	12.9

1994-95 statistics:

GP	G	A	TP	+/-	PIM	PP	SH	GW	GT	S	PCT
47	21	23	44	-20	20	11	0	1	0	154	13.6

1995-96 statistics:

GP	G	A	TP	+/-	PIM	PP	SH	GW	GT	S	PCT
46	15	24	39	-15	28	8	0	1	0	143	10.5

1996-97 statistics:

GP	G	A	TP	+/-	PIM	PP	SH	GW	GT	S	PCT
82	35	40	75	-7	44	10	0	5	1	291	12.0

LAST SEASON

Led team in goals, points and shots. Tied for team lead in game-winning goals. Second on team in assists. Tied for second on team in power-play goals. One of three Senators to appear in all 82 games.

THE FINESSE GAME

Yashin isn't a flashy skater, but he has drawn comparisons to Ron Francis in his quiet effectiveness. He is spectacular, at times, but doesn't go all-out every shift. On those occasions it looks like he's pacing himself or is fatigued. Because Yashin looks as if he isn't trying, when things go poorly for him people assume he's loafing. His protracted contract battles of the past have also made the critics quick to attack.

Yashin can be the best player on the ice one night, the next night you have to go back and check the videotape to see if he was dressed. He is a good friend of Alexei Kovalev, a player who has heard similar criticism in New York.

Yashin's skills rank with any of the new guard of players who have entered the NHL in the past three seasons. He has great hands and size. As he stickhandles in on the rush, he can put the puck through the legs of two or three defenders en route to the net. He has to learn, though, that he can go directly to the net and not wait for the defense to come to him, so that he can dazzle by using their legs as croquet wickets.

Basically, Yashin has to simply go to the net more and shoot, which he did in spells last season. He has a devastating shot. He doesn't have breakaway speed but he is powerful and balanced. He doesn't utilize his teammates well. They're not always the most talented bunch, but Mario Lemieux made a 50-goal scorer out of Warren Young, and Yashin hasn't shown signs of being able to make his teammates better.

THE PHYSICAL GAME

Yashin is big and rangy and protects the puck well. He needs to show better second effort against the other team's top checkers, because he isn't too willing to fight through the clutching and grabbing. He has little interest in defense. Other teams believe they can get in Yashin's face early and take him off his game.

THE INTANGIBLES

Yashin had an unimpressive playoffs, after playing well down the stretch to help his team get in.

PROJECTION

Yashin will continue to deal with a lot of flak because of his big contract. Given a better supporting cast, he might produce 90-plus points, but 80 is more realistic.

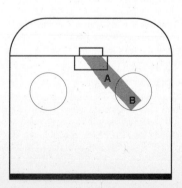

JASON YORK

Yrs. of NHL service: 4
Born: Ottawa, Ont.; May 20, 1970
Position: right defense
Height: 6-2
Weight: 195
Uniform no.: 33
Shoots: right

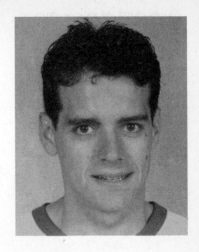

Career statistics:

GP	G	A	TP	PIM
188	9	50	59	171

1993-94 statistics:

GP	G	A	TP	+/-	PIM	PP	SH	GW	GT	S	PCT
7	1	2	3	0	2	0	0	0	0	9	11.1

1994-95 statistics:

GP	G	A	TP	+/-	PIM	PP	SH	GW	GT	S	PCT
25	1	10	11	+2	14	0	0	0	0	28	3.6

1995-96 statistics:

GP	G	A	TP	+/-	PIM	PP	SH	GW	GT	S	PCT
79	3	21	24	-7	88	0	0	0	0	106	2.8

1996-97 statistics:

GP	G	A	TP	+/-	PIM	PP	SH	GW	GT	S	PCT
75	4	17	21	-8	67	1	0	0	0	121	3.3

PROJECTION

York has some offensive upside. He belongs on a second pairing instead of a first. When he gets a little more comfortable, more points — maybe 40 — could follow.

LAST SEASON

Acquired from Anaheim with Shaun Van Allen for Ted Drury and Marc Moro, October 1, 1996. Missed six games with groin injury.

THE FINESSE GAME

York is about ready to hit his defensive prime. He is a smart, all-around defenseman who was able to put up some decent numbers at the AHL level, but is now concentrating more on his defensive play.

York's finesse skills are fine. He is a good skater with a very hard point shot, and he can handle the point on the second power- play unit — although he isn't quite good enough to step up to the first five. He's a fine penalty killer. He reads plays well (his offensive reads are far superior to his defensive reads) and has the skating ability to spring some shorthanded chances.

THE PHYSICAL GAME

York is not very physical. He is not a big checker but employs positional play to angle attackers to the boards, using his stick to sweep-check or poke pucks. Once he gains control of the puck, he moves it quickly with no panicky mistakes. He doesn't have a polished defensive game but he does work hard.

THE INTANGIBLES

York was acquired by the Senators after injuries to Sean Hill and Stanislave Neckar, and stepped up to handle checking assignments against other teams' top lines. It was asking too much but he did an admirable job.

SERGEI ZHOLTOK

Yrs. of NHL service: 2
Born: Riga, Latvia; Dec. 2, 1972
Position: centre
Height: 6-0
Weight: 190
Uniform no.: 16
Shoots: right

Career statistics:

GP	G	A	TP	PIM
82	14	18	32	21

1993-94 statistics:

GP	G	A	TP	+/-	PIM	PP	SH	GW	GT	S	PCT
24	2	1	3	-7	2	1	0	0	0	25	8.0

1994-95 statistics:

P	G	A	TP	+/-	PIM	PP	SH	GW	GT	S	PC
					Did not play in NHL						

1995-96 statistics:

P	G	A	TP	+/-	PIM	PP	SH	GW	GT	S	PC
					Did not play in NHL						

1996-97 statistics:

GP	G	A	TP	+/-	PIM	PP	SH	GW	GT	S	PCT
57	12	16	28	+2	19	5	0	0	0	96	12.5

This season will determine whether or not Zholtok can work as an NHL regular. He could have a spot on one of the top two lines and score 20 to 25 goals and 50 to 60 points — but he could be doing it in Las Vegas.

LAST SEASON

Second on team in plus-minus. Scored 13-14 — 27 in 19 games with Las Vegas (IHL).

THE FINESSE GAME

Zholtok has been a streak scorer in the minors. His first full NHL season was no different. He was sent to the minors twice and had four goals in the first half of the season. He stuck for the second half and scored eight. He had a strong playoffs and with a little better luck (he hit about a half-dozen posts) would have been more productive.

Zholtok has a funny-looking stride and kind of skates from the hips, but he generates decent speed despite his unusual style. He is an offensive player, with good hands and vision and a quick, accurate shot. He's at his best down low, from the hash marks in. He can cycle out of the corners and beat guys one-on-one.

Zholtok has to get better defensively and, in particular, make better decisions at the attacking blueline, where he often tries to force the play instead of getting the puck deep when he's under pressure.

THE PHYSICAL GAME

Zholtok needs to add strength to his upper body. He's average sized but isn't muscular.

THE INTANGIBLES

Zholtok has kicked around in the Boston system and the jury's still out on whether he's a legitimate NHL player. He has great skills and character and is a good influence on Alexei Yashin.

PROJECTION

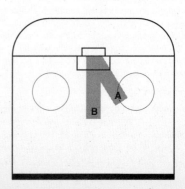

PHILADELPHIA FLYERS

Players' Statistics 1996-97

POS.	NO.	PLAYER	GP	G	A	PTS	+/-	PIM	PP	SH	GW	GT	S	PCT
L	10	JOHN LECLAIR	82	50	47	97	44	58	10		5	2	324	15.4
C	88	ERIC LINDROS	52	32	47	79	31	136	9		7	2	198	16.2
L	17	ROD BRIND'AMOUR	82	27	32	59	2	41	8	2	3	2	205	13.2
R	19	MIKAEL RENBERG	77	22	37	59	36	65	1		4	1	249	8.8
D	37	ERIC DESJARDINS	82	12	34	46	25	50	5	1	1		183	6.6
R	20	TRENT KLATT	76	24	21	45	9	20	5	5	5		131	18.3
D	44	*JANNE NIINIMAA	77	4	40	44	12	58	1		2		141	2.8
C	18	DALE HAWERCHUK	51	12	22	34	9	32	6		2		102	11.8
D	77	PAUL COFFEY	57	9	25	34	11	38	1	1	2		110	8.2
L	25	SHJON PODEIN	82	14	18	32	7	41			4		153	9.2
C	29	JOEL OTTO	78	13	19	32	12	99	1		2	1	105	12.4
D	6	CHRIS THERIEN	71	2	22	24	26	64					107	1.9
R	15	PAT FALLOON	52	11	12	23	-8	10	2		4		124	8.9
R	9	*DAINIUS ZUBRUS	68	8	13	21	3	22	1		2		71	11.3
D	24	KARL DYKHUIS	62	4	15	19	7	35	2		1		101	4.0
R	26	JOHN DRUCE	43	7	8	15	-5	12	1				73	9.6
C	45	*VACLAV PROSPAL	18	5	10	15	3	4					35	14.3
D	23	PETR SVOBODA	67	2	12	14	10	94	1				36	5.6
D	8	MICHEL PETIT	38	2	7	9	-11	71					43	4.7
C	32	DANIEL LACROIX	74	7	1	8	-1	163	1				54	13.0
L	22	SCOTT DANIELS	56	5	3	8	2	237			2		48	10.4
D	28	KJELL SAMUELSSON	34	4	3	7	17	47					36	11.1
C	11	CRAIG DARBY	9	1	4	5	2	2		1			13	7.7
L	21	DAN KORDIC	75	1	4	5	-1	210					21	4.8
L	48	*COLIN FORBES	3	1		1	0						3	33.3
D	3	*ARIS BRIMANIS	3		1	1	0						1	
D	34	JASON BOWEN	4		1	1	1	8					1	
G	30	GARTH SNOW	35		1	1	0	30						
R	38	*PAUL HEALEY	2				0							
D	2	FRANTISEK KUCERA	4				-2	2					5	
D	5	DARREN RUMBLE	10				-2						9	
G	27	RON HEXTALL	55				0	43						

GP = games played; G = goals; A = assists; PTS = points; +/- = goals-for minus goals-against while player is on ice; PIM = penalties in minutes; PP = power-play goals; SH = shorthanded goals; GW = game-winning goals; GT = game-tying goals; S = no. of shots; PCT = percentage of goals to shots; * = rookie

ROD BRIND'AMOUR

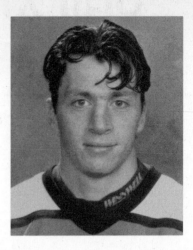

Yrs. of NHL service: 8
Born: Ottawa, Ont.; Aug. 9, 1970
Position: centre/left wing
Height: 6-1
Weight: 202
Uniform no.: 17
Shoots: left

Career statistics:

GP	G	A	TP	PIM
614	213	342	555	597

1993-94 statistics:

GP	G	A	TP	+/-	PIM	PP	SH	GW	GT	S	PCT
84	35	62	97	-9	85	14	1	4	0	230	15.2

1994-95 statistics:

GP	G	A	TP	+/-	PIM	PP	SH	GW	GT	S	PCT
48	12	27	39	-4	33	4	1	2	0	86	14.0

1995-96 statistics:

GP	G	A	TP	+/-	PIM	PP	SH	GW	GT	S	PCT
82	26	61	87	+20	110	4	4	5	4	213	12.2

1996-97 statistics:

GP	G	A	TP	+/-	PIM	PP	SH	GW	GT	S	PCT
82	27	32	59	+2	41	8	2	3	2	205	13.2

LAST SEASON

Third on team in goals, shots and power-play goals. Tied for third on team in points. Recorded 20 or more goals for sixth time in eight NHL seasons. One of four Flyers to appear in all 82 games. Raised consecutive-games streak to 320, a team record.

THE FINESSE GAME

Versatility and dependability are among Brind'Amour's trademarks. He wins face-offs. He checks. He has the strength and speed and stride to handle every defensive aspect of the game; the grit and desire to earn the loose pucks; the temperament and credibility to be on the ice in the last minute of a close game.

Brind'Amour may not beat many players one-on-one in open ice, but he outworks defenders along the boards and uses a quick burst of speed to drive to the net. He's a playmaker in the mucking sense, with scoring chances emerging from his commitment.

Brind'Amour has a long, powerful stride with a quick first step to leave a defender behind; his hand skills complement the skating assets. He drives well into a shot on the fly, has a quick-release snap shot and a strong backhand. His passes to either side are crisp.

When Brind'Amour does not have the puck, he works ferociously to get it back. An excellent penalty killer and the centre the Flyers send out if they are two men short, Brind'Amour thinks nothing of blocking shots.

THE PHYSICAL GAME

A king in the weight room, Brind'Amour uses his size well and is a strong skater. He can muck with the best in the corners and along the boards. He will carry the puck through traffic in front of the net and battle for position for screens and tip-ins. He is among the hardest workers on the team, even in practice, and is always striving to improve his game.

THE INTANGIBLES

Brind'Amour is a coach's treasure because he can be deployed in any situation and will provide trustworthy work. The fact that he provides steady play without glitter or fanfare on a high-visibility team undercuts the recognition he deserves but doesn't always receive. Brind'Amour is happiest when he's playing centre.

PROJECTION

Since he plays through the aches and pains, and plays a lot because of his work ethic and dependability, you know Brind'Amour is always going to get his 25 to 30 goals. It is difficult to understand why he fails to convert on the dozens of other glorious chances his effort creates. Although his scoring touch turned golden for a stretch of the playoffs, Brind'Amour at times remains better at not scoring than in turning those opportunities into points.

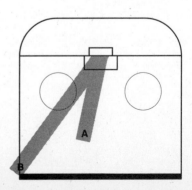

PAUL COFFEY

Yrs. of NHL service: 17
Born: Weston, Ont.; June 1, 1961
Position: right defense
Height: 6-0
Weight: 190
Uniform no.: 77
Shoots: left

Career statistics:

GP	G	A	TP	PIM
1211	381	1063	1444	1674

1993-94 statistics:

GP	G	A	TP	+/-	PIM	PP	SH	GW	GT	S	PCT
80	14	63	77	+28	106	5	0	3	0	278	5.0

1994-95 statistics:

GP	G	A	TP	+/-	PIM	PP	SH	GW	GT	S	PCT
45	14	44	58	+18	72	4	1	2	0	181	7.7

1995-96 statistics:

GP	G	A	TP	+/-	PIM	PP	SH	GW	GT	S	PCT
76	14	60	74	+19	90	3	1	3	0	234	6.0

1996-97 statistics:

GP	G	A	TP	+/-	PIM	PP	SH	GW	GT	S	PCT
57	9	25	34	+11	38	1	1	2	0	110	8.2

LAST SEASON

Acquired by Hartford, along with Keith Primeau and a number one pick in 1997, from Detroit for Brendan Shanahan and Brian Glynn, October 9, 1996. Acquired from Hartford with a third-round pick in 1997, for Kevin Haller, the Flyers' first-round pick and the Whalers' seventh-round pick, December 15, 1996. Missed three games with left shoulder separation. Missed two games with right hamstring strain. Missed five games with concussion. Missed one game with bruised left quadriceps muscle.

THE FINESSE GAME

Coffey creates a lot of open ice for his teammates because he is so intimidating as a skater: he may have the most fluid, effortless skating mechanism in the game. An agile, shifty attacker with a delicious change of pace, he has terrific balance, uses his edges well, and commands a respectable amount of space from defensemen who lack the range to step up and press the issue. With the time he buys himself, Coffey sizes up the passing options and exploits them, because he handles the puck well while whirling at top speed or changing directions.

Few players are better at the long home-run pass, and Coffey has all the finesse skills of a forward when he works down low. He has tremendous vision to make a play, feather a pass or work a give-and-go. He has a whole menu of shots, from wristers to slaps. He is a world-class point man on the power play, faking slaps and sending passes low, sliding the puck over to his point partner for a one-timer, or drilling the shot himself. He prefers to attack down the right side.

Notice all we've talked about is Coffey's offensive skills. No team has Coffey on its roster for his defense.

THE PHYSICAL GAME

Coffey uses his skating to get in an opponent's way, but he isn't going to hit as much as he is going to steer an opponent to bad ice. Like a quarterback taught to throw the ball away rather than "eat" it and accept a sack, Coffey frequently will say, "Here. Be my guest," with the puck, rather than persevering through contact.

Coffey will block shots when it counts, such as during the playoffs, but most of his defense is based on his anticipation in picking off passes and his skill with the puck.

THE INTANGIBLES

Sometimes it seems Coffey simply isn't having much fun at what he does, that the demands of the game at a top level for 17 seasons have drained him of zest. You know he's an extremely successful player, because he has played for four Stanley Cup champions and has played for Cup finalists twice in the past three seasons; but both those finalists got swept. He played a major role, and will continue to do so, as a mentor for Eric Lindros, who is still learning what it takes to lead and win in the NHL.

And while playing for six teams means those franchises valued your attributes, it seems quite significant that four teams didn't receive very much at all when they traded him. Of course Detroit, which obtained Brendan Shanahan for him, is the exception.

PROJECTION

We suspected correctly that last season would mark the start of a downslide in Coffey's production. Injuries, plus two trades — and the resultant adjustment to new cities, new teammates and new coaching philosophies — cut dramatically into his productivity.

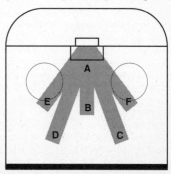

ERIC DESJARDINS

Yrs. of NHL service: 9
Born: Rouyn, Que.; June 14, 1969
Position: right defense
Height: 6-1
Weight: 200
Uniform no.: 37
Shoots: right

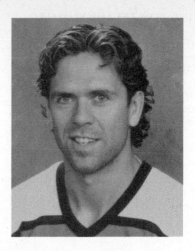

Career statistics:

GP	G	A	TP	PIM
601	67	229	296	458

1993-94 statistics:

GP	G	A	TP	+/-	PIM	PP	SH	GW	GT	S	PCT
84	12	23	35	-1	97	6	1	3	0	193	6.2

1994-95 statistics:

GP	G	A	TP	+/-	PIM	PP	SH	GW	GT	S	PCT
43	5	24	29	+12	14	1	0	1	0	93	5.4

1995-96 statistics:

GP	G	A	TP	+/-	PIM	PP	SH	GW	GT	S	PCT
80	7	40	47	+19	45	5	0	2	0	184	3.8

1996-97 statistics:

GP	G	A	TP	+/-	PIM	PP	SH	GW	GT	S	PCT
82	12	34	46	+25	50	5	1	1	0	183	6.6

LAST SEASON

Led team defensemen in scoring for third consecutive season. Goal total was a three-season high. One of four Flyers to appear in all 82 games.

THE FINESSE GAME

Desjardins has the puckhandling skills and poise to beat the first forechecker and carry the puck out of the defensive zone. He makes accurate breakout passes and also has enough savvy to keep the play simple, gain the redline and dump the puck deep in attacking ice if no other option is available. He makes the smart, safe play all the time, a reflection of his trademark consistency.

Stable and capable enough to handle power-play duty, Desjardins is wise enough to realize only the ul-tra-elite overpower NHL goalies with point shots. Although he has a strong one-timer, his slap shot is not always accurate. He is much more dangerous of-fensively when he uses his wrist shot, or simply flips deflectable pucks towards the net.

A fine skater with light, agile feet and a small turn-ing radius, Desjardins goes up ice well with the play, keeping the gap to the forwards small and remaining in good position to revert to defense if there is a turnover. A long reach helps him challenge puck car-riers to make plays more quickly, change their minds or shoot from a lower-percentage angle. Desjardins keeps his stick active while killing penalties, sweep-ing his stick on the ice to contest passing lanes and intercept pucks.

Skating skills and excellent anticipation add to Desjardins's penalty-killing ability. He seldom falls to the ice to block shots, more often dropping to one knee to challenge the shooter.

THE PHYSICAL GAME

Desjardins is a solid combination of mental and physi-cal strength. Particularly while penalty killing in front of the net, he immobilizes the opponent's stick first, then ties up the body — which separates him from the huge percentage of defensemen who are satisfied to do one or the other but not both. He plays a hard game more than a punishing one, but uses his strength in more subtle ways to gain position in front of both goals. On offense, he will venture to the corners from time to time and will beat his check to the front of the net after winning a battle for the puck.

A quiet leader on the ice and in the dressing room, Desjardins wants it more than you do, unless you prove different. He patrols the front of his net like a Doberman, but plays a clean, controlled game and rarely takes stupid penalties. He always seems to be where he is most needed, does not panic, and does not fight. He is steady and professional and easy to underappreciate.

PROJECTION

Desjardins scores consistently in the 40-point range. Although he isn't a dominating defenseman, he plays a ton because he is so dependable and versatile and makes the game easy for his partners.

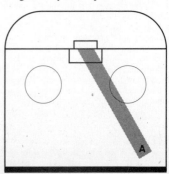

KARL DYKHUIS

Yrs. of NHL service: 4
Born: Sept-Iles, Que.,; July 8, 1972
Position: right defense
Height: 6-3
Weight: 205
Uniform no.: 24
Shoots: left

Career statistics:

GP	G	A	TP	PIM
195	12	44	56	177

1993-94 statistics:

P	G	A	TP	+/-	PIM	PP	SH	GW	GT	S	PC
Did not play in NHL											

1994-95 statistics:

GP	G	A	TP	+/-	PIM	PP	SH	GW	GT	S	PCT
33	2	6	8	+7	37	1	0	1	0	46	4.3

1995-96 statistics:

GP	G	A	TP	+/-	PIM	PP	SH	GW	GT	S	PCT
82	5	15	20	+12	101	1	0	0	0	104	4.8

1996-97 statistics:

GP	G	A	TP	+/-	PIM	PP	SH	GW	GT	S	PCT
62	4	15	19	+7	35	2	0	1	0	101	4.0

LAST SEASON

Missed 13 games with dislocated left shoulder.

THE FINESSE GAME

Another left-hand shot on the right side of the Flyers' defense, à la Janne Niinimaa, Dykhuis has learned the importance of keeping his feet moving, because it helps him stay up with the play. His game edges towards the offensive side, but he also uses his finesse skills well in his own end.

Dykhuis keeps the passes short, accurate and crisp. He banks the puck off the boards or glass if that's the only option available to get the puck out.

Dykhuis is a natural for penalty killing and four-on-four play because he has fine mobility and quickness, with a quick shift of gears that allows him to get up the ice in a hurry. Smart, with good hands for passing or drilling shots from the point, Dykhuis also leans towards conservatism; he won't venture down low unless the decision to pinch is a sound one.

THE PHYSICAL GAME

Although tall and rangy, Dykhuis isn't a heavyweight. Alhough he goes out of his way to screen off opposing forecheckers and to buy time for his partner, there regularly are times when his physical aspect is almost non-existent. Dykhuis is strong and makes solid contact on those occasions when he does hit. He is such a good skater that he can break up a play, dig out the loose puck and be off in just a stride or two to start an odd-man rush. As significant, Dykhuis uses his reach to break up plays.

THE INTANGIBLES

Dykhuis gets the puck out of the zone and keeps the game as simple as possible. He doesn't seem to be great at anything or horrible at anything. He is steady, plays a game that blends into the background. But, given the price he paid to get a full-time job in the NHL, the steps in his development seem to be smaller now.

PROJECTION

Last season was only his third full NHL campaign, and defense is one of the most difficult positions to play, so the temptation is to give him some benefit of the doubt. Nonetheless, he was a number one pick seven drafts ago; if Dykhuis was headed towards becoming an overachiever, someone would have noticed by now.

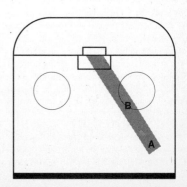

PAT FALLOON

Yrs. of NHL service: 6
Born: Foxwarren, Man.; Sept. 22, 1972
Position: centre/right wing
Height: 5-11
Weight: 190
Uniform no.: 15
Shoots: right

Career statistics:

GP	G	A	TP	PIM
345	109	124	233	91

1993-94 statistics:

GP	G	A	TP	+/-	PIM	PP	SH	GW	GT	S	PCT
83	22	31	53	-3	18	6	0	1	0	193	11.4

1994-95 statistics:

GP	G	A	TP	+/-	PIM	PP	SH	GW	GT	S	PCT
46	12	7	19	-4	25	0	0	3	0	91	13.2

1995-96 statistics:

GP	G	A	TP	+/-	PIM	PP	SH	GW	GT	S	PCT
71	25	26	51	+14	10	9	0	2	1	170	14.7

1996-97 statistics:

GP	G	A	TP	+/-	PIM	PP	SH	GW	GT	S	PCT
52	11	12	23	-8	10	2	0	4	0	124	8.9

LAST SEASON

Missed 10 games with pulled left groin muscle. Missed other games due to coaching decisions.

THE FINESSE GAME

Falloon likes to cut against the grain from the right wing to the left, and use the defenseman as a screen for a sneaky wrist shot. But that play is much more productive when his centre carries across the blueline and feeds him. When Falloon carries, he is a trifle slow, so teammates who build up some speed for a charge across the blueline either have to put on the brakes or go offside.

Falloon is better as a finisher than a creator. He employs a smart array of shots, using a wrist or slap with confidence, but does his best work jumping to an opening, keeping his forehand open and firing an accurate one-timer on net from the left-wing circle or closer. Even if he doesn't score, Falloon's release is quick enough, accurate enough, and the shot has velocity enough to force a reaction stop from a goalie who is moving to the area — that means rebounds and scrambles, and garbage goals can result.

Because he is opportunistic around the net, following up shots and pouncing on loose rebounds, Falloon needs to play with people who can get him the puck. He has soft hands and sharp instincts for the right play, but needs to work on his defensive game.

THE PHYSICAL GAME

Falloon is not physical, but he goes into traffic with the puck and will scrap in the corners for it. On a team as big and physical as the Flyers, he can take more liberties and get away with them, but does not seem inclined to be annoying.

THE INTANGIBLES

Falloon simply did not make himself special enough to get more ice time than he got from Terry Murray last season. It could be argued that Falloon might have been more special more often with more playing time. This season is his chance to be more than a quick release from the top of the circle.

Even if you factor in the groin woes, Falloon is coming off an unimpressive season. He was a first-round pick (the second player chosen after teammate Eric Lindros) when San Jose claimed him in 1991, and was obtained by the Flyers for a first-round pick in 1996, but he hasn't provided much first-round-calibre play. This, remarkably, is going to be his seventh NHL season. You can be a "late bloomer" for only so long before it becomes clear the blossom is a tad less fragrant than the gardeners had expected.

PROJECTION

Falloon fits neatly into the role of a second-line player. He has power-play skills and figures to be reasonably productive. But last year was a chance to step forward and he slid backward.

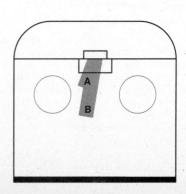

RON HEXTALL

Yrs. of NHL service: 11
Born: Brandon, Man.; May 3, 1964
Position: goaltender
Height: 6-3
Weight: 192
Uniform no.: 27
Catches: left

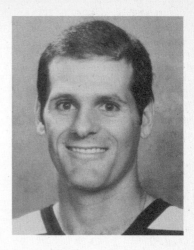

Career statistics:

GP	MIN	GA	SO	GAA	A	PIM
539	30827	1574	19	3.06	22	572

1993-94 statistics:

GP	MIN	GAA	W	L	T	SO	GA	S	SAPCT	PIM
65	3581	3.08	27	26	6	5	184	1801	.898	52

1994-95 statistics:

GP	MIN	GAA	W	L	T	SO	GA	S	SAPCT	PIM
31	1824	2.89	17	9	1	1	88	801	.890	13

1995-96 statistics:

GP	MIN	GAA	W	L	T	SO	GA	S	SAPCT	PIM
53	3102	2.17	31	13	7	4	112	1292	.913	28

1996-97 statistics:

GP	MIN	GAA	W	L	T	SO	GA	S	SAPCT	PIM
55	3094	2.56	31	16	5	5	132	1285	.897	43

LAST SEASON

Had 30 or more victories for the fifth time. Tied for fourth in NHL in shutouts.

THE PHYSICAL GAME

When he stands up, when he makes himself huge in the net, Hextall gets to the first shots and recovers position nicely for any put- backs. When he's lunging and flailing and flopping around the goalmouth, Hextall is disappointment waiting to happen.

In his stand-up, poised persona, Hextall swallows the puck and leaves no dangerous rebounds; the puck goes into his equipment and stays there. When he flops, it seems to take Hextall hours to regain his footing, and his antagonists delight in tormenting him by flipping pucks into the net off him from goofy angles, because he hasn't returned to position.

Hextall takes greater advantage of the rules protecting goaltenders than anyone at his position. Knowing full well anyone who touches him will get a penalty because goaltenders are not "fair game" when they leave the crease, Hextall roams almost arrogantly to the corners and leisurely works his will with the puck. His puckhandling ability is still among the best in the NHL, and though overconfidence leads to the occasional bad pass, Hextall never loses his faith in his ability to whip the puck off the glass or find an open teammate with a pass.

Hextall is one of the most aggressive goalies in the NHL at challenging shooters. He comes well out to the top of his crease; some teams try to tempt him to come too far out so they can get him to overcommit. He's quick down low, but has trouble on the glove side.

THE MENTAL GAME

While still extremely competitive, Hextall has matured significantly. He is far less hotheaded than he was in the past, but he will whack ankles and jump on heads if opponents are trespassing.

Teams believe, correctly, that Hextall is vulnerable mentally. There are times when he out-thinks himself, tries to make the perfect save when a merely routine one will get the job done. Too often, long, ankle-high shots tie him in knots. Rather than merely standing up and kicking those pucks into the corner, Hextall drops to his knees and in the process lifts his stick from the exact place where the puck is headed. Too often, the result is a cheap goal for which the opponent has not worked hard enough. That has a devastating impact on the bench.

THE INTANGIBLES

He is the hockey incarnation of Dr. Jekyll and Mr. Hyde, and you simply never know which personality will skate into the goal crease the night of a key game. Goalies live and die on their ability to make a difficult job as easy as possible; too often, Hextall makes his own life tougher. He wants to be perceived as solid and consistent, but isn't enough of either when the biggest chips are on the line.

PROJECTION

Hextall remains a house of cards in fat pads. He isn't a loser, by any means, but it will take a Stanley Cup championship to undo the non-winner tag he has tied around his own neck by constantly coming up short when the Flyers need him to stand tall. He wins 30 games in the regular season, but you need 16 in the playoff season to get a parade. Hextall's implosion in the finals added to already significant doubts that he'll ever come close to that magic number.

TRENT KLATT

Yrs. of NHL service: 5
Born: Robbinsdale, Minn.; Jan. 30, 1971
Position: right wing
Height: 6-1
Weight: 205
Uniform no.: 20
Shoots: right

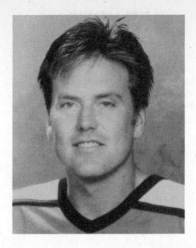

Career statistics:

GP	G	A	TP	PIM
303	61	86	147	158

1993-94 statistics:

GP	G	A	TP	+/-	PIM	PP	SH	GW	GT	S	PCT
61	14	24	38	+13	30	3	0	2	0	86	16.3

1994-95 statistics:

GP	G	A	TP	+/-	PIM	PP	SH	GW	GT	S	PCT
47	12	10	22	-2	26	5	0	3	0	91	13.2

1995-96 statistics:

GP	G	A	TP	+/-	PIM	PP	SH	GW	GT	S	PCT
71	7	12	19	+2	44	0	0	2	0	101	6.9

1996-97 statistics:

GP	G	A	TP	+/-	PIM	PP	SH	GW	GT	S	PCT
76	24	21	45	+9	20	5	5	5	0	131	18.3

LAST SEASON

Goal total was a career high. Led team in shorthanded goals. Tied for second on team in game-winning goals. Reached 20-goal plateau for the first time in five career NHL seasons. Missed two games due to concussion.

THE FINESSE GAME

Last season Klatt added a hugely important component to his game: He at last began to capitalize on some of the scoring chances created by his hard work. His hands found a finishing touch to complement the full-bore, driving style that produces such forechecking pressure and leads to so many turnovers.

Klatt is something of a choppy skater who doesn't have much use for the fancy stuff. He goes straight ahead — usually until he runs into someone from the other side.

Significantly, Klatt was a player coach Terry Murray sent onto the ice for the shift following a goal. In those situations, players are trusted to continue the momentum if the goal was scored by their team or reverse the momentum if the goal was scored by the opposition. Deployment at those times is a real compliment; Klatt earned it.

THE PHYSICAL GAME

Klatt looks harmless enough, but he is a murderous hitter. He is 210 dense-packed pounds, and his body checks can pack the wallop of a warhead. Klatt may like the regular hits but he will go for the monster hit, the one guys feel for a week, every chance he gets. Strong leg drive and a powerful upper body help Klatt make sure the hits just keep on coming.

Klatt's body slams can lift the whole bench. As important, few things please Flyer fans more than the full-speed trainwreck collisions Klatt is so good at delivering. The more Klatt hits, the more the home fans are in the game. Anything else he provides is a bonus.

Look: The guy knocked his own brother-in-law, Rangers farmhand Ken Gernander, out of the playoffs with a separated shoulder. What more do you need to know?

PROJECTION

Some checkers remain checkers because there is no pressure to score or do things on the offensive side of the puck; your job is merely to harry your opponent into a turnover or a less-dangerous play. Checkers move up a notch when they bury 24 pucks, as Klatt did last season. It is safer to pencil him in for about 15 goals, and they'll all be honest ones. He is a starter on the NHL's All-Hard-Work Team.

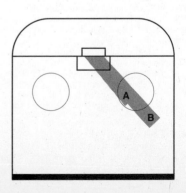

JOHN LECLAIR

Yrs. of NHL service: 6
Born: St. Albans, VT.; July 5, 1969
Position: left wing
Height: 6-3
Weight: 226
Uniform no.: 10
Shoots: left

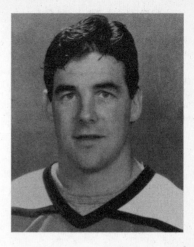

Career statistics:

GP	G	A	TP	PIM
425	175	325	361	223

1993-94 statistics:

GP	G	A	TP	+/-	PIM	PP	SH	GW	GT	S	PCT
74	19	24	43	+17	32	1	0	1	0	153	12.4

1994-95 statistics:

GP	G	A	TP	+/-	PIM	PP	SH	GW	GT	S	PCT
46	26	28	54	+20	30	6	0	7	0	131	19.8

1995-96 statistics:

GP	G	A	TP	+/-	PIM	PP	SH	GW	GT	S	PCT
82	51	46	97	+21	64	19	0	10	2	270	18.9

1996-97 statistics:

GP	G	A	TP	+/-	PIM	PP	SH	GW	GT	S	PCT
82	50	47	97	+44	58	10	0	5	2	324	15.4

LAST SEASON

Led team in points, goals, power-play goals, plus-minus and shots. Led NHL in plus-minus and in even-strength points (40-41 — 81). Tied for fourth in NHL in points. Tied for third in NHL in goals. Tied for team lead in assists. Tied for second in game-winning goals. Second in World Cup tournament in goals (6), points (10) and plus-minus (+9). Played every game for second consecutive season. One of three Flyers to appear in all 82 games.

THE FINESSE GAME

Given his finishing skills from the slot and the goal-mouth, LeClair is like the reincarnation of the immovable Tim Kerr, the skating aircraft carrier who buried pucks by the bucketfull for the Flyers of yesteryear. LeClair is big enough to post up in front and piledrive through the melees for all the rebounds, deflections and garbage goals his teammates can create. He also has enough power in his skating and confidence in his strength to cut in from the wing and drive to the net, but the left wing's attributes as a scorer far outweigh his abilities as a puckhandler; if the puck were a football, you could imagine him putting it under his arm, lowering his head and ramming it across the goal line.

LeClair's game emerged last season from whatever remained of the shell in which it resided during his Montreal days. After working on the quickness of his release, LeClair has a ferociously strong shot, and though he was, at one time, a reluctant shooter, those days clearly have passed. Now, he simply launches a rocket at the net — usually from a high-percentage area of the ice — and lets the goalie worry about the rest.

THE PHYSICAL GAME

LeClair may be the strongest man in the league, both in front of the net and behind it, and is just about impossible to push off the puck legally. He wants to win the puck, wants the puck in the net and will use every ounce of his strength to try to put it there. He always draws the attention of at least one defender, but accepts his role willingly. Because of a long reach and a big body LeClair finds a way to place himself between the puck and the defender. Those times when he has a defender under each arm behind the net, LeClair happily will kick the puck to the front.

The frequent disappointment is that he puts so much into winning the puck behind the goal line but doesn't really have the deft touch to make a smooth relay to someone who might be driving to the net. His passing skills are rather dubious and his puck-handling skills are rather erratic. Detroit succeeded in neutralizing LeClair in the Stanley Cup finals by forcing him to carry the puck, instead of driving to the net without it.

Until recently, LeClair merely was a strong hitter; now, he often is a mean hitter. With that size and strength, the combination can be devastating. More often than not, though, he remains a gentle giant. He plays hard, but clean, and really is much easier to control if you play him the same way.

THE INTANGIBLES

Displaying the durability lacked by his Legion of Doom linemate, Eric Lindros, LeClair has more than made clear that his success is not dependent on assists from his tower-tall centre. After all, LeClair was a standout at World Cup, at which his team opposed Lindros's — as it will at Nagano in February. The only thing that matches his size is the respect LeClair has gained around the league.

PROJECTION

LeClair scores goals on his knees, on his back, whatever. He isn't happy until the puck has been put in the net — either by himself or by a teammate. At 28, he is entering prime time, and should score another 50.

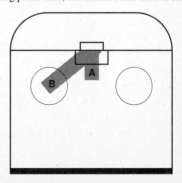

ERIC LINDROS

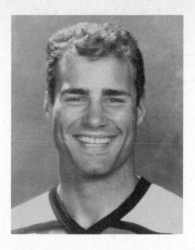

Yrs. of NHL service: 5
Born: London, Ont.; Feb. 28, 1973
Position: centre
Height: 6-4
Weight: 236
Uniform no.: 88
Shoots: right

Career statistics:

GP	G	A	TP	PIM
297	193	243	436	609

1993-94 statistics:

GP	G	A	TP	+/-	PIM	PP	SH	GW	GT	S	PCT
65	44	53	97	+16	103	13	2	9	1	197	22.3

1994-95 statistics:

GP	G	A	TP	+/-	PIM	PP	SH	GW	GT	S	PCT
46	29	41	70	+27	60	7	0	4	1	144	20.1

1995-96 statistics:

GP	G	A	TP	+/-	PIM	PP	SH	GW	GT	S	PCT
73	47	68	115	+26	163	15	0	4	0	294	16.0

1996-97 statistics:

GP	G	A	TP	+/-	PIM	PP	SH	GW	GT	S	PCT
52	32	47	79	+31	136	9	0	7	2	198	16.2

LAST SEASON

Led team in assists and game-winning goals. Second on team in goals, power-play goals and points. Third on team in plus-minus. Scored 30 or more goals for fourth time in five seasons. Missed 23 games with pulled groin. Missed one game with charley horse. Missed two games with bruised back. Missed two games with bruised right calf. Missed two games due to stick-related suspension.

THE FINESSE GAME

Those times he chooses to use it, Lindros has remarkable agility. Normally, he can bore straight ahead, freight-train you with the puck and drive to the net. There are times, though, when opponents so completely prepare themselves for his brute power that they are stunned when he puts the puck through their feet, steps around them and regains it instead of driving through them. As his game matures, Lindros will make better use of this change-up, which beautifully complements his "fastball."

Lindros has the balance and soft hands to control the puck in extremely tight quarters and make those nimble moves at the high speed he reaches quickly. That said, it remains more his nature to muscle the puck to a teammate or to the front of the net and to let his strength do most of the work because strength remains the watchword of his game.

To offset the torque his arms can generate, the stick Lindros uses has an extremely firm shaft with only a slight curve to the blade. That helps on face-offs, adds velocity to his wrist and snap shots, and makes his backhand shot a very significant weapon both for its speed and its accuracy to the upper corners from close range.

THE PHYSICAL GAME

When you go to hit Lindros, you are going to run into his stick or his elbow eight times out of 10. The remaining times, you are simply going to run into Lindros — which can be just as painful. Those times

when you do not run into Lindros, he will make a point of running into you, which makes long evenings against him even longer. And if you thought that stick was a weapon for shooting, imagine how it feels if, by some accident, you get slashed with it.

Nonetheless, a player who plays that physically pays a physical toll. Lindros already wears braces on both knees, and missed nearly half last season because of bumps, bruises and muscle pulls. Even on his most vicious nights, he still absorbs as much punishment as he administers.

THE INTANGIBLES

Lindros knows he can make things happen, wants to make things happen, but doesn't always know how to make the right things happen. He's still feeling his way as a leader, particularly in the playoffs, because the Flyers simply have not found the mentor who can show this gifted behemoth the way up the next step on his developmental ladder. As a consequence, there are nights when he gets frustrated with himself for not simply being able to will his team to victory; often those frustrations make him seem petulant and self-absorbed. Just as often, an opponent ends up with stitches, paying the price for Lindros's foul mood.

PROJECTION

This season will be a challenge for Lindros because every team in the league watched Detroit unhinge his game and knock him down to size, by "fronting" him, denying the puck, and worrying more about his stick than his hugeness. That said, not every team can execute as well as Detroit did. He'll get points by the dozens if he can stay healthier than he did last year.

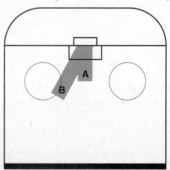

JANNE NIINIMAA

Yrs. of NHL service: 1
Born: Raahe, Finland; May 22, 1975
Position: right defense
Height: 6-1
Weight: 196
Uniform no.: 44
Shoots: left

Career statistics:

GP	G	A	TP	PIM
77	4	40	44	58

1996-97 statistics:

GP	G	A	TP	+/-	PIM	PP	SH	GW	GT	S	PCT
77	4	40	44	+12	58	1	0	2	0	141	2.8

LAST SEASON

Will be entering second NHL season. Named to NHL All-Rookie Team. First among NHL rookies in power-play assists (23). Tied for first among NHL rookies and third on the team in assists. Third among NHL rookies in points.

THE FINESSE GAME

A left-handed shot who plays the right side, Niinimaa's excellent skating and puckhandling skills allow him to handle the amount of body shifting necessary to open his body to the rink and keep the forehand available as often as possible.

A nimble, agile player, Niinimaa sets his feet wide apart for outstanding drive, power and balance, and uses a long stride and long reach to win races to the puck. He can turn the corners at near-top speed and doesn't have to slow down when carrying the puck. When the opportunity to jump into the play presents itself, Niinimaa is gone in a vapour trail.

Like Paul Kariya, Niinimaa does a great job of "framing" his stick and giving his teammate a passing target. He keeps the blade on the ice and available, his body position saying, "Put it here, so I can do something with it."

Having stepped into the league at age 21, a middle-aged rookie, Niinimaa learned that he can create just as much offensive danger by merely flipping a puck towards the net instead of taking the full-windup slap shot every time. Though his one-timers can be blistering, Niinimaa doesn't always shoot to score; sometimes, he shoots to create a rebound or possible deflection.

THE PHYSICAL GAME

For a newcomer to North American trenches, Niinimaa plays a physical game and refuses to concede territory. He bumps and jolts, and makes opponents pay a price for every inch of important ice gained. He seems to relish one-on-one battles. He wants the puck and does whatever is necessary to win it.

THE INTANGIBLES

Niinimaa's desire and youthful enthusiasm can be infectious. He wants the puck, wants to excel, wants to win and has the game to make things happen in all three zones. A dynamic, elite player, he has proved an extremely quick study.

PROJECTION

Niinimaa is going to play a lot, is going to get the power-play time and is going to get many more points. Bear in mind, he was among the rookie leaders in several categories despite a somewhat hesitant start.

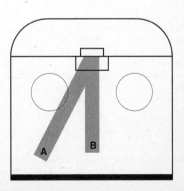

JOEL OTTO

Yrs. of NHL service: 12
Born: Elk River, Minn.; Oct. 29. 1961
Position: centre
Height: 6-4
Weight: 220
Uniform no.: 29
Shoots: right

Career statistics:

GP	G	A	TP	PIM
875	192	309	501	1860

1993-94 statistics:

GP	G	A	TP	+/-	PIM	PP	SH	GW	GT	S	PCT
81	11	12	23	-17	92	3	1	1	0	108	10.2

1994-95 statistics:

GP	G	A	TP	+/-	PIM	PP	SH	GW	GT	S	PCT
47	8	13	21	+8	130	0	2	2	1	46	17.4

1995-96 statistics:

GP	G	A	TP	+/-	PIM	PP	SH	GW	GT	S	PCT
67	12	29	41	+11	115	6	1	1	0	91	13.2

1996-97 statistics:

GP	G	A	TP	+/-	PIM	PP	SH	GW	GT	S	PCT
78	13	19	32	+12	99	0	1	2	1	105	12.4

LAST SEASON

Missed four games due to bruised ribs.

THE FINESSE GAME

Although he has the build to be a power centre, Otto's production has always been a disappointment. In addition to bulk, power forwards have to have soft hands in deep for tips and rebounds, and Otto does not have that touch. The Flyers give him occasional power-play time, using his big body as a screen, but his main value is defensive prowess.

On face-offs, he doubles over his huge frame so that his head and shoulders prevent the opposing centre from seeing the puck drop. Helmets clash on Otto's face-offs. He has lost some hand speed on the draws but is still among the best in the league.

Otto is not very fast, but he is quite agile for a player of his size, and he is so strong and balanced on his skates that he has to be dynamited out of place. Even players close to his size bounce off him when they try to check him.

THE PHYSICAL GAME

A fierce and intelligent competitor, Otto is big, strong and involved. He knows he is a brute force, and likes to make people scatter as he drives to the net. He also delivers bruising checks along the wall. He loves the hitting part of the game, and he has the work ethic to perform consistently to his own high level.

THE INTANGIBLES

Otto is a workman. He isn't a fanfare player who draws a lot of attention to himself, and he's 220 pounds of long night for any centre he's matched up against.

PROJECTION

Although strictly a defense-first player, Otto has reached double figures in goals every non-lockout season of his 12 in the NHL. He is worth between 30 and 40 points in the bank, and, although he figures to miss a few games due to bumps, bruises and age, he might be worth a late-round gamble if you're taking lots and lots of players in your pool.

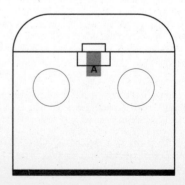

SHJON PODEIN

Yrs. of NHL service: 5
Born: Rochester, Minn.; Mar. 5, 1968
Position: left wing
Height: 6-2
Weight: 200
Uniform no.: 25
Shoots: left

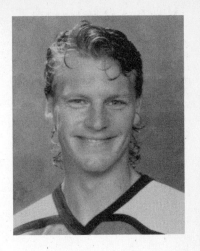

Career statistics:

GP	G	A	TP	PIM
273	32	35	67	163

1993-94 statistics:

GP	G	A	TP	+/-	PIM	PP	SH	GW	GT	S	PCT
28	3	5	8	+3	8	0	0	0	0	26	11.5

1994-95 statistics:

GP	G	A	TP	+/-	PIM	PP	SH	GW	GT	S	PCT
44	3	7	10	-2	33	0	0	1	0	48	6.3

1995-96 statistics:

GP	G	A	TP	+/-	PIM	PP	SH	GW	GT	S	PCT
79	15	10	25	+25	89	0	4	4	0	115	13.0

1996-97 statistics:

GP	G	A	TP	+/-	PIM	PP	SH	GW	GT	S	PCT
82	14	18	32	+7	41	0	0	4	0	153	9.2

LAST SEASON

One of four Flyers to play all 82 games. Assist and point totals were career highs. Tied for third on team in game-winning goals.

THE FINESSE GAME

Podein is a labourer. He works hard, loves his job and uses his size well. He started out as a centre, but he is better suited as a winger because his hands aren't great. He is happiest in a dump-and-chase game, where he can use his straightaway speed to bore in on the puck carrier.

Podein is a mucker, not a fancy scorer. He gets most of his goals from digging around the net for re-bounds and loose pucks. He doesn't have particularly good hand skills or hockey sense.

He isn't an agile skater, but he is sturdy for work along the boards and he can work up a pretty good head of steam. Just don't ask him to turn.

THE PHYSICAL GAME

Podein is antagonistic, with a bit of a mean streak, and he tends to be a bit careless with his stick. He can take bad penalties because of that tendency.

THE INTANGIBLES

Podein played well on a checking line. He is a high-energy player and penalty killer who can lift the bench with a strong shift. He has taken a long route to the NHL and will have to work to stay here.

PROJECTION

In his defensive role, Podein can pop in 15 to 20 goals a season.

VACLAV PROSPAL

Yrs. of NHL service: 0
Born: Ceske-Budejvice, Czech Republic; Feb. 17, 1975
Position: centre
Height: 6-2
Weight: 185
Uniform no.: 45
Shoots: left

Career statistics:

GP	G	A	TP	PIM
18	5	10	15	4

1996-97 statistics:

GP	G	A	TP	+/-	PIM	PP	SH	GW	GT	S	PCT
18	5	10	15	+3	4	4	0	0	0	35	14.3

LAST SEASON

Will be entering first NHL season. Second in scoring for Philadelphia (AHL) with 32-63 — 95 in 63 games.

THE FINESSE GAME

Prospal is a power-play weapon. It's not an overpowering shot that makes him effective, but his ability to thread the puck through penalty killers to an open man. Already at this stage in his career, Prospal may be as skilled at this as an NHL veteran.

The Flyers were patient with Prospal, not calling him up until the end of the season, and in the minors he handled a regular shift, power play and penalty killing. He loves to score (his wrist shot and one-timers are accurate) and loves to make plays. He had to learn to play without the puck, and he's succeeded. His defensive game took a big step forward last year. He thinks the game well.

The only rap on Prospal is his skating ability, but it's NHL calibre and his view of the ice and his hockey sense compensate for any lack of pure speed.

THE PHYSICAL GAME

Prospal is tall but lean and needs a little more muscle for one-on-one battles. Right now he gives an impression of being a little smaller than he is, but he's an eager player who will get involved.

THE INTANGIBLES

"Vinny" (apparently no one in Philadelphia can pronounce "Vaclav") has a wonderful, refreshing attitude and is well-liked by coaches and teammates. The Flyers could have used him in the playoffs (Prospal was injured in a practice after the first round).

PROJECTION

Prospal will be one of the top six Flyers forwards and a mainstay on the power play. Given what he showed in his Flyers' stint last season, he could score 25 goals and be a Calder Trophy candidate.

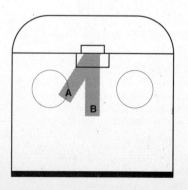

MIKAEL RENBERG

Yrs. of NHL service: 4
Born: Pitea, Sweden; May 5, 1972
Position: right wing
Height: 6-2
Weight: 218
Uniform no.: 19
Shoots: left

Career statistics:

GP	G	A	TP	PIM
258	109	132	219	166

1993-94 statistics:

GP	G	A	TP	+/-	PIM	PP	SH	GW	GT	S	PCT
83	38	44	82	+8	36	9	0	1	0	195	19.5

1994-95 statistics:

GP	G	A	TP	+/-	PIM	PP	SH	GW	GT	S	PCT
47	26	31	57	+20	20	8	0	4	0	143	18.2

1995-96 statistics:

GP	G	A	TP	+/-	PIM	PP	SH	GW	GT	S	PCT
51	23	20	43	+8	45	9	0	4	0	198	11.6

1996-97 statistics:

GP	G	A	TP	+/-	PIM	PP	SH	GW	GT	S	PCT
77	22	37	59	+36	65	1	0	4	1	249	8.8

LAST SEASON

Second on team in shots and plus-minus. Tied for third on team in points. Missed final four games of regular season due to severe facial laceration.

THE FINESSE GAME

Renberg has a long, strong stride and excellent balance, but only average speed; anticipation is the key that gives him a head start on the defense.

He drives to the net, and is strong enough to shrug off a lot of checks, or even shovel a one-handed shot or pass if one arm is tied up. He likes to come in on the off-wing, especially on the power play, and snap a strong shot off his back foot. He sees the ice well and is always looking for a teammate he can hit with a pass, but Renberg finally got it into his head that the more shots you take, the likelier it is you'll score — or that someone else might put in your rebound.

Renberg's best shots are his quick-release wrists or snaps with little backswing. He is defensively aware and is a solid two-way forward who can be on the ice in almost any situation.

THE PHYSICAL GAME

Renberg doesn't fight, but he is extremely strong, has a nasty streak and likes to hit hard. He won't be intimidated. Since he isn't a great skater, his adjustment to the smaller ice surfaces actually helped his game. Playing with John LeClair and Eric Lindros on the Legion of Doom Line has made him even braver. His quick return from a ghastly facial injury and his play through the pain of his ankle injury in the playoffs showed some grit.

THE INTANGIBLES

Players go their entire careers without suffering the way Renberg has in the past two seasons. He missed 31 games two seasons ago due to a recurring abdominal injury, then underwent off-season surgery. He missed the last few games of the 1996-97 season due to a catastrophic face cut, and was hampered throughout the playoffs by "skate bite," an ankle affliction that was corrected by off-season surgery. This year, we find out if Renberg's body can stand up to the wars.

PROJECTION

If you play with a 50-goal scorer in LeClair and someone darn close to that if Lindros plays a full season at full strength, the points are going to be there — but so are the defensive responsibilities. Renberg can handle them, and with his newfound assertiveness in shooting, he certainly should be around the 30-goal mark again.

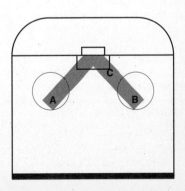

LUKE RICHARDSON

Yrs. of NHL service: 10
Born: Ottawa, Ont.; Mar. 26, 1969
Position: left defense
Height: 6-4
Weight: 210
Uniform no.: 22
Shoots: left

Career statistics:

GP	G	A	TP	PIM
714	24	101	125	1186

1993-94 statistics:

GP	G	A	TP	+/-	PIM	PP	SH	GW	GT	S	PCT
69	2	6	8	-13	131	0	0	0	0	92	2.2

1994-95 statistics:

GP	G	A	TP	+/-	PIM	PP	SH	GW	GT	S	PCT
46	3	10	13	-6	40	1	1	1	0	51	5.9

1995-96 statistics:

GP	G	A	TP	+/-	PIM	PP	SH	GW	GT	S	PCT
82	2	9	11	-27	108	0	0	0	0	61	3.3

1996-97 statistics:

GP	G	A	TP	+/-	PIM	PP	SH	GW	GT	S	PCT
82	1	11	12	+9	91	0	0	0	0	67	1.5

LAST SEASON

Signed as a free agent, July 14, 1997. One of three Oilers to appear in all 82 games.

THE FINESSE GAME

Richardson can sometimes play solid defense, but he is more often indecisive. When to step up at the blue, when to back off: you can see the thought process at work in his head, and so can the attacker.

To a degree, Richardson overcomes some of his flaws with his skating and by simply taking up as much space as he can with his size. He's a good skater with lateral mobility and balance, but not much speed. He can't carry the puck and doesn't jump up into the rush well. He seldom uses his point shot, which is merely adequate.

Defensively, Richardson doesn't know when to stay in front of his net and when to challenge in the corners. Despite his 10 years in the league, the necessary improvement hasn't always shown. Richardson played a less aggressive style last season, and wasn't always hunting for the big hit. That cut down on some of his more glaring commitment errors.

THE PHYSICAL GAME

Richardson is the kind of player you hate to play against but love to have on your side. He hits to hurt and is an imposing presence on the ice. He scares people. Richardson separates the puck carrier from the puck down low, which should help Philadelphia's transition game. When he checks, he separates the puck carrier from the puck and doesn't let the man get back into play. When he is on the ice, his teammates play a bit bigger and braver. Richardson plays hurt,

and took few bad penalties last season.

THE INTANGIBLES

Richardson has been a top defenseman for a weak team for several years, and hit the jackpot when the Flyers signed him for $12.6 million for five years. He will join a stronger defense corps in Philadelphia and will get more support than he did with the Oilers. Richardson is ideally suited as a number three, or four, defenseman. You can seldom fault his effort.

PROJECTION

Richardson's role is as a physical stay-at-home defender, and his point totals will remain low (15 to 20), even with the offensively charged Flyers.

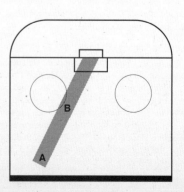

KJELL SAMUELSSON

Yrs. of NHL service: 11
Born: Tyngsryd, Sweden; Oct. 18, 1958
Position: right defense
Height: 6-6
Weight: 235
Uniform no.: 28
Shoots: right

Career statistics:

GP	G	A	TP	PIM
718	47	131	178	1159

1993-94 statistics:

GP	G	A	TP	+/-	PIM	PP	SH	GW	GT	S	PCT
59	5	8	13	+18	118	1	0	0	0	57	8.8

1994-95 statistics:

GP	G	A	TP	+/-	PIM	PP	SH	GW	GT	S	PCT
41	1	6	7	+8	54	0	0	0	0	37	2.7

1995-96 statistics:

GP	G	A	TP	+/-	PIM	PP	SH	GW	GT	S	PCT
75	3	11	14	+20	81	0	0	1	1	62	4.8

1996-97 statistics:

GP	G	A	TP	+/-	PIM	PP	SH	GW	GT	S	PCT
34	4	3	7	+17	47	0	0	0	0	36	11.1

LAST SEASON

Missed the final 39 games of the regular season due to neck surgery to repair ruptured disc. Missed one game due to virus. Missed four games with strained back. Missed three games with sore ribs.

THE FINESSE GAME

Although he made some astonishing giveaways in the playoffs (when he probably shouldn't have been playing, anyway), Samuelsson generally makes an excellent first pass out of the zone — it's one of his top skills. He doesn't always look for the home-run pass and doesn't get pinned while trying to make the perfect play; he will bank the puck off the boards if that is the safer option.

Samuelsson plays an ultraconservative style. He has a strong point shot but does not get it away quickly, and generally takes it as a last resort. He won't be found in deep, either, so don't expect to see him scrambling to get back into defensive position. He's already there.

Samuelsson's enormous stride eats up the ice. It doesn't look like he's moving fast, because he doesn't have to. He isn't very quick and doesn't get involved in the rush, but instead concentrates on his own zone. He angles the attacking player so that he runs out of room, takes him out of the play with an authoritative hit that smears the player against the boards, and uses his size to immobilize the opponent until the puck is out of danger.

THE PHYSICAL GAME

One NHL opponent said playing against Samuelsson is like playing in seaweed. He has the wingspan of a condor and is strong with his long stick, so that he can control the puck dangling miles away from his body after he has knocked it off the puck carrier's blade.

Samuelsson is a strong and nasty hitter for someone who looks so benign. In addition to using his body and powerful leg drive, he will rub his glove or elbow against an opponent's jaw or offer his stick for use as a dental device. He hits from behind. He also clutches and grabs, but does it in a smart veteran way, hanging on just long enough to provoke irritation but not long enough to merit a penalty. He will also yap to distraction.

He pays the physical price to block shots and clear his crease.

THE INTANGIBLES

There are players who make a tough job even more difficult by complicating simple tasks — Samuelsson is too smart for that. He has made an NHL career, and several million dollars, merely by using his assets, playing to his strengths and keeping things as basic as possible. He has played on many more successful teams than losing ones, and his steadiness has been a valued part of that success.

Samuelsson has great poise for pressure situations. He is slower than ever, but that wingspan of his remains a clear advantage for penalty killing; you don't need speed to clear the front of the net.

PROJECTION

You will need a microscope to find Samuelsson's point total this season, but the Flyers don't pay him for points, anyway. You never have to squint to find the "plus" in his plus/minus; it's always there.

PETR SVOBODA

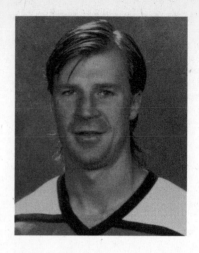

Yrs. of NHL service: 13
Born: Most, Czechoslovakia; Feb. 14, 1966
Position: left defense
Height: 6-1
Weight: 190
Uniform no.: 23
Shoots: left

Career statistics:

GP	G	A	TP	PIM
824	47	282	329	1230

1993-94 statistics:

GP	G	A	TP	+/-	PIM	PP	SH	GW	GT	S	PCT
60	2	14	16	+11	89	1	0	0	0	80	2.5

1994-95 statistics:

GP	G	A	TP	+/-	PIM	PP	SH	GW	GT	S	PCT
37	0	8	8	-5	70	0	0	0	0	39	0.0

1995-96 statistics:

GP	G	A	TP	+/-	PIM	PP	SH	GW	GT	S	PCT
73	1	28	29	+28	105	0	0	0	0	91	1.1

1996-97 statistics:

GP	G	A	TP	+/-	PIM	PP	SH	GW	GT	S	PCT
67	2	12	14	+10	94	1	0	0	0	36	5.6

PROJECTION

Svoboda has been robbed of some of his skating power by knee surgery and injuries in recent years. He seems to have less ardour than ever for offensive contribution.

LAST SEASON

Missed six games wirh separated left shoulder. Missed six games with groin injuries. Missed three games with pinched nerve in neck.

THE FINESSE GAME

Svoboda has very quick feet and is always in motion. He was never strong on his skates but he has great quickness, balance and agility — and you can't hit what you can't catch. He has a long stride. Not a very solid player, he is lean and wiry, and his skating is economical.

Svoboda has excellent instincts. He can carry the puck well and join the rush. He has a quick release on his wrist and snap shots, and also a good one-timer that he uses on the power play. He reads plays well offensively and defensively.

THE PHYSICAL GAME

Not one for physical play, Svoboda is still a feisty foe who will take the body, then use his stick to rap a player in the choppers or pull his skates out from under him. He ticks off a lot of people.

Svoboda is lean and isn't going to get much done one-on-one in a close battle. He rides an opponent out of the play well when he can use his skating to generate some power.

THE INTANGIBLES

The more teams take the body on him, the lower Svoboda's panic point with the puck seems to get as the game goes along. His body can't take the pounding, so it becomes almost a defense mechanism to get rid of the puck and take the target off his back.

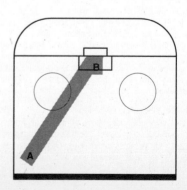

CHRIS THERIEN

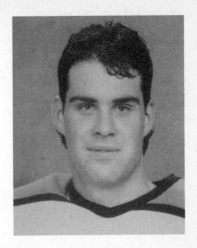

Yrs. of NHL service: 3
Born: Ottawa, Ont.; Dec. 14, 1971
Position: left defense
Height: 6-4
Weight: 230
Uniform no.: 6
Shoots: left

Career statistics:

GP	G	A	TP	PIM
201	11	49	60	191

1994-95 statistics:

GP	G	A	TP	+/-	PIM	PP	SH	GW	GT	S	PCT
48	3	10	13	+8	38	1	0	0	0	53	5.7

1995-96 statistics:

GP	G	A	TP	+/-	PIM	PP	SH	GW	GT	S	PCT
82	6	17	23	+16	89	3	0	1	0	123	4.9

1996-97 statistics:

GP	G	A	TP	+/-	PIM	PP	SH	GW	GT	S	PCT
71	2	22	24	+26	64	0	0	0	0	107	1.9

LAST SEASON

Third NHL season. Led Flyers defensemen in plus-minus. Ended consecutive game-played streak of 156 with coach's decision.

THE FINESSE GAME

Although not particularly quick, Therien is a fluid skater for his size and has improving offensive instincts. He handles the puck well and looks to move it as his first option, but can skate it out of the defensive zone and make a crisp pass while in motion. If that option is not available, he will keep it simple and bang the puck off the boards.

Good balance allows Therien to maximize his size when, rather than use the typical big-man play and slide on the ice, he takes a stride, drops to one knee and keeps his stick flat on the ice — making himself a larger and wider obstacle.

Therien doesn't have much lateral speed, but is a strong straight-ahead skater who can get up the ice in a hurry and has a good enough sense of offense that he can play the point on the power play.

THE PHYSICAL GAME

The strongest defenseman on the Flyers, Therien started using his strength to better advantage far more frequently last season. He can dominate physically and started punishing opposing forwards in front of the net in penalty-killing situations. Extremely alert away from the puck, Therien dedicates himself to gaining body position and making sure his man doesn't get it.

Therien knows big defensemen can be penalty magnets, but keeps much of his game within the rules. He keeps the elbows down, plays an effective, clean physical game. When he hits along the boards or battles in the corners, he tends to lower his body position and use his weight to smear an opponent along the boards. (Other big defensemen are too upright in those situations or try to use their arms to pin opponents, which isn't as effective.) Therien makes his heft and bulk work for him.

THE INTANGIBLES

Therien improved his defensive reads, took the hits when they were available and backed off when they weren't, and made himself a much more consistent player who figures to be a top four defensemen for years to come.

PROJECTION

Therien scored his first goal of the season on October 10, and had only one thereafter. His offensive instincts do not translate into points because usually he only takes one or two shots per game. Nonetheless, Therien improved significantly from the mistake-prone hockey he displayed in the prior season and channelled his enthusiasm into dogged, effective play that made him a key contributor.

DAINIUS ZUBRUS

Yrs. of NHL service: 1
Born: Elektrani, Lithuania; June 16, 1978
Position: right wing
Height: 6-3
Weight: 215
Uniform no.: 9
Shoots: left

Career statistics:

GP	G	A	TP	PIM
68	8	13	21	22

1996-97 statistics:

GP	G	A	TP	+/-	PIM	PP	SH	GW	GT	S	PCT
68	8	13	21	+3	22	1	0	2	0	71	11.3

LAST SEASON

First season in NHL.

THE FINESSE GAME

Zubrus plays the game in a North-South direction, goal line to goal line, rather than in the East-West fashion favoured by other imports, and is helped in that regard by a long stride that covers lots of ground. His puck control is quite impressive, as though the puck is on a very short rope that is nailed to his stick.

Splendid acceleration is a key component of Zubrus's game. He is both confident in his skating and competent enough to burst between defensemen to take the most direct path to the net. He also features enough power and balance to control a sweep behind the net, pull in front and roof a backhand shot under the crossbar from close range.

Zubrus uses his edges well and is difficult to knock off the puck. He is quite willing to zoom in off the wing, use his body to shield the puck from a defender and make something happen.

The soft touch in his hands and a quick release of his shot complements the power in Zubrus's legs. He can make a deft pass or a slick move, and can set up a goal or score one with roughly equal skill.

THE PHYSICAL GAME

Zubrus uses his size to advantage, finishes checks with authority and outmuscles as many people as he can muster. He's gritty in the corners and along the boards, and is adept at using his feet to control the puck if his upper body is tied up.

As a rookie last season, Zubrus displayed maturity and poise far beyond his 18 years. He jumped from the obscurity of Tier II hockey to the right side of the Legion of Doom when Mikael Renberg was sidelined, and made it seem he belonged there all along. Zubrus has lots of spirit and enthusiasm: he just loves playing the game, wants to "make it big" in the big leagues and certainly seems on his way.

PROJECTION

This kid hasn't even stopped growing yet, so it's natural to predict bigger things for him in 1997-98. Don't be misled by his low point total last season. He played all three forward positions and spent time on virtually every Flyer line. He figures to get steady work this season and, with a season of experience under his belt, should prove a commanding player on a commanding team if he can avoid a sophomore slump.

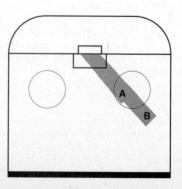

PHOENIX COYOTES

Players' Statistics 1996-97

POS.	NO.	PLAYER	GP	G	A	PTS	+/-	PIM	PP	SH	GW	GT	S	PCT
L	7	KEITH TKACHUK	81	52	34	86	-1	228	9	2	7	1	296	17.6
C	97	JEREMY ROENICK	72	29	40	69	-7	115	10	3	7		228	12.7
R	22	MIKE GARTNER	82	32	31	63	-11	38	13	1	7	1	271	11.8
D	20	OLEG TVERDOVSKY	82	10	45	55	-5	30	3	1	2		144	6.9
C	15	CRAIG JANNEY	77	15	38	53	-1	26	5		1		88	17.0
C	77	CLIFF RONNING	69	19	32	51	-9	26	8		2		171	11.1
R	11	DALLAS DRAKE	63	17	19	36	-11	52	5	1	1		113	15.0
D	27	TEPPO NUMMINEN	82	2	25	27	-3	28					135	1.5
L	34	DARRIN SHANNON	82	11	13	24	4	41	1		2		104	10.6
C	21	BOB CORKUM	80	9	11	20	-7	40		1	3		119	7.6
C	14	MIKE STAPLETON	55	4	11	15	-4	36	2		1		74	5.4
D	5	DERON QUINT	27	3	11	14	-4	4	1				63	4.8
L	17	KRIS KING	81	3	11	14	-7	185					57	5.3
D	4	GERALD DIDUCK	67	2	12	14	-7	63	1		1		80	2.5
D	44	NORM MACIVER	32	4	9	13	-11	24	1		1		40	10.0
R	19	SHANE DOAN	63	4	8	12	-3	49					100	4.0
R	23	IGOR KOROLEV	41	3	7	10	-5	28	2				41	7.3
D	8	JIM JOHNSON	55	3	7	10	5	74					51	5.9
D	26	JEFF FINLEY	65	3	7	10	-8	40	1		1		38	7.9
L	33	JIM MCKENZIE	65	5	3	8	-5	200			1		38	13.2
D	6	JAY MORE	37	1	7	8	10	62			1		28	3.6
D	36	MURRAY BARON	79	1	7	8	-20	122					64	1.6
C	18	CHAD KILGER	24	4	3	7	-5	13	1				30	13.3
D	10	BRAD MCCRIMMON	37	1	5	6	2	18					28	3.6
G	35	N. KHABIBULIN	72		3	3	0	16						
R	32	JOCELYN LEMIEUX	2	1		1	0				1		4	25.0
G	43	DARCY WAKALUK	16		1	1	0	4						
G	1	PARRIS DUFFUS	1				0							
L	38	JASON SIMON	1				-1							
D	3	BRENT THOMPSON	1				-1	7						
C	47	*TAVIS HANSEN	1				0							
D	24	KEVIN DAHL	2				0						2	
C	36	*JUHA YLONEN	2				0						2	
C	28	MIKE HUDSON	7				-4	2					9	
G	39	PAT JABLONSKI	19				0							

GP = games played; G = goals; A = assists; PTS = points; +/- = goals-for minus goals-against while player is on ice; PIM = penalties in minutes; PP = power-play goals; SH = shorthanded goals; GW = game-winning goals; GT = game-tying goals; S = no. of shots; PCT = percentage of goals to shots; * = rookie

MURRAY BARON

Yrs. of NHL service: 7
Born: Prince George, B.C., June 1, 1967
Position: left defense
Height: 6-3
Weight: 215
Uniform no.: 36
Shoots: left

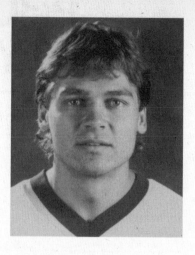

Career statistics:

GP	G	A	TP	PIM
480	23	50	73	767

1993-94 statistics:

GP	G	A	TP	+/-	PIM	PP	SH	GW	GT	S	PCT
77	5	9	14	-14	123	0	0	0	0	73	6.8

1994-95 statistics:

GP	G	A	TP	+/-	PIM	PP	SH	GW	GT	S	PCT
39	0	5	5	+9	93	0	0	0	0	28	0.0

1995-96 statistics:

GP	G	A	TP	+/-	PIM	PP	SH	GW	GT	S	PCT
82	2	9	11	+3	190	0	0	0	0	86	2.3

1996-97 statistics:

GP	G	A	TP	+/-	PIM	PP	SH	GW	GT	S	PCT
79	1	7	8	-20	122	0	0	0	0	64	1.6

LAST SEASON

Acquired from Montreal with Chris Murray for Dave Manson, March 18, 1997.

THE FINESSE GAME

Baron has developed into a steady, reliable defenseman. The Coyotes missed his presence in the playoffs, when he was hurt in the opening game against Anaheim with a fractured foot.

A strong skater with some agility, Baron jumps into the play rather than leading a rush, but he doesn't do much creatively. He concentrates on defense. He can lug the puck at a pretty good clip but does little more than stop inside the blueline and fire a shot from the point. His shot is merely average. You rarely find Baron gambling in deep. He seldom works on specialty teams.

Baron has developed more poise defensively and is now less likely to get rid of the puck in a panic. Instead, he will make a safe, if unspectacular, play. He needs to be paired with an offensive-minded partner.

THE PHYSICAL GAME

Baron has stepped up his physical play over the past three seasons. Once noted for being a rather timid player (okay, a wimp) for his size, he is doing a better job of clearing out the front of his crease. He scraps when provoked.

THE INTANGIBLES

Baron is 30, and qualifies as a late bloomer since he has played his best hockey in the past three seasons.

PROJECTION

His point totals will barely break into double digits, but Baron will be one of the Coyotes' top four defensemen this season.

BOB CORKUM

Yrs. of NHL service: 6
Born: Salisbury, Mass.; Dec. 18, 1967
Position: centre/right wing
Height: 6-2
Weight: 210
Uniform no.: 21
Shoots: right

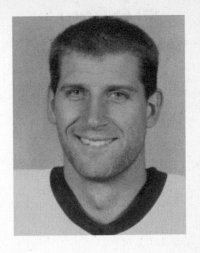

Career statistics:

GP	G	A	TP	PIM
372	61	66	127	178

1993-94 statistics:

GP	G	A	TP	+/-	PIM	PP	SH	GW	GT	S	PCT
76	23	28	51	+4	18	3	3	0	1	180	12.8

1994-95 statistics:

GP	G	A	TP	+/-	PIM	PP	SH	GW	GT	S	PCT
44	10	9	19	-7	25	0	0	1	1	100	10.0

1995-96 statistics:

GP	G	A	TP	+/-	PIM	PP	SH	GW	GT	S	PCT
76	9	10	19	+3	34	0	0	3	0	126	7.1

1996-97 statistics:

GP	G	A	TP	+/-	PIM	PP	SH	GW	GT	S	PCT
80	9	11	20	-7	40	0	1	3	0	119	7.6

LAST SEASON

Acquired on waivers from Philadelphia, September 20, 1996.

THE FINESSE GAME

Corkum has average skills but makes the most of them with his effort. He has good overall speed, balance and acceleration. He drives to the net for short-range shots and likes to use a strong wrist shot, though he doesn't get it away quickly. He also has a decent backhand. Corkum doesn't score often but tends to score meaningful goals. He's ideally suited as a third-line checking centre.

Corkum likes to use a short, sure pass. He will pass off rather than carry the puck. He anticipates well and hits the open man. He is not terribly clever with the puck, but he makes the bread-and-butter play with confidence.

THE PHYSICAL GAME

Corkum stands tough in front of the net and works hard along the boards. He is a strong forechecker who likes to take the body. He relishes the physical game and makes big hits — anyone hit by Corkum knows it. He works hard and uses his size and strength well. He takes draws and kill penalties. He'll bring energy to each shift.

THE INTANGIBLES

Corkum was a valuable waiver-draft acquisition for the Coyotes because of his hustle.

PROJECTION

Corkum can pop in 20 points in a checking role.

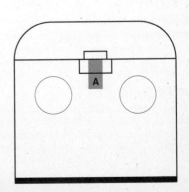

SHANE DOAN

Yrs. of NHL service: 2
Born: Halkirk, Alberta; Oct. 10, 1976
Position: right wing
Height: 6-1
Weight: 215
Uniform no.: 19
Shoots: right

Career statistics:

GP	G	A	TP	PIM
137	11	18	29	150

1995-96 statistics:

GP	G	A	TP	+/-	PIM	PP	SH	GW	GT	S	PCT
74	7	10	17	-9	101	1	0	3	0	106	6.6

1996-97 statistics:

GP	G	A	TP	+/-	PIM	PP	SH	GW	GT	S	PCT
63	4	8	12	-3	49	0	0	0	0	100	4.0

LAST SEASON

Tied for third on team in plus-minus. Missed two games with ankle injury. Missed eight games with sprained foot. Missed nine games with hand injury.

THE FINESSE GAME

Doan's game is speed. He is fast and strong, forechecking aggressively and intelligently along the wall and in the corners. He intimidates with his skating because he gets in on a defenseman fast. Once he gains control of the puck he finds the open man in front of the net. He isn't overly creative but will thrive on the dump-and-chase play, where he can just skate on his wing and race for the puck.

Doan has an acceptable wrist and slap shot but he doesn't shoot much. He will become more of a threat if he gains some confidence in his shot. He was a scorer in junior but he's now acting, thinking, and scoring like a checker. He turns away from chances or throws the puck into the corner, when he could go in and shoot or make a play.

Doan needs to see power-play time and be put into more offensive situations to revive his game. There's no question he is a fine penalty killer and can handle the checking role, but he's too talented to waste as a one-way player.

THE PHYSICAL GAME

Doan is strong and is a very good bodychecker. He seems to have a mean streak lurking under his exterior. He will lay some hard hits on people. He could play a little more abrasive.

THE INTANGIBLES

Right now Doan is a third-line player with a third-line mentality. He saw that checking would be what kept him in the NHL, so check he did. Now it's up to someone on the Coyotes' coaching staff to turn his thinking around.

PROJECTION

Doan was projected as a second-line, 30-goal scorer. If it takes sending him to the minors to get his all-around game back, the Coyotes ought to do it.

JASON DOIG

Yrs. of NHL service: 0
Born: Montreal, Que.; Jan. 29, 1977
Position: right defense
Height: 6-3
Weight: 216
Uniform no.: n.a.
Shoots: right

Career statistics:

GP	G	A	TP	PIM
15	1	1	2	28

1995-96 statistics:

GP	G	A	TP	+/-	PIM	PP	SH	GW	GT	S	PCT
15	1	1	2	-2	28	0	0	0	0	7	14.3

1996-97 statistics:

P	G	A	TP	+/-	PIM	PP	SH	GW	GT	S	PC

Did not play in NHL

LAST SEASON

Led defensemen in scoring for Granby (QMJHL) with 14-33 — 47 and 211 penalty minutes in 39 games. Scored 0-1 — 1 in 6 games with Las Vegas (IHL). Scored 0-3 — 3 in 5 games with Springfield (AHL). Missed five games with hyperextended elbow.

THE FINESSE GAME

Usually big, intimidating, tough defensemen are plodders, but that's not the case with Doig. He's a good skater who gets a little rambunctious and starts running around looking for hits. Once he learns to settle down and pick his spots he will be a much better positional defenseman. For now, just chalk it up to youthful enthusiasm.

Doig is advanced offensively. He excels on the power play and will probably develop into a second-unit power-play point man. He has a strong, heavy shot from the point, which he gets away quickly and it gets through. His lateral movement isn't great, which will keep him from ever being a top-flight offensive defenseman.

Doig loves everything about the game. He is always involved and is highly competitive.

THE PHYSICAL GAME

Doig is genuinely mean. He loves to hit and he's a punishing hitter. He uses his body well along the wall and in the corners. He is powerful and intimidating. All four of his front teeth are gone, which gives him a great hockey face when he growls at opponents. He will fight anybody, including Mike Peluso (when Doig was only 18).

Doig lifts weights and has a tendency to develop too much of a bodybuilder's physique. He needs to train like a hockey player, not Mr. Muscle Beach.

THE INTANGIBLES

Few defensemen in the NHL blend Doig's scoring ability with his penalty minutes. Chris Chelios readily comes to mind, and Doig could turn into a bigger version of Chelios. Phoenix has to guard against Doig getting too carried away with his role as a goon. He's a better player than that.

PROJECTION

Doig could probably benefit from a season in the minors, rather than making the jump directly from junior, but the Coyotes will be inclined to rush him into the lineup because of his offensive skills.

DALLAS DRAKE

Yrs. of NHL service: 5
Born: Trail, B.C.; Feb. 4, 1969
Position: centre
Height: 6-0
Weight: 180
Uniform no.: 11
Shoots: left

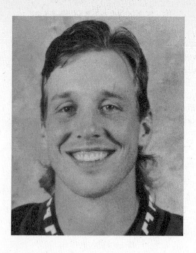

Career statistics:

GP	G	A	TP	PIM
309	75	110	185	260

1993-94 statistics:

GP	G	A	TP	+/-	PIM	PP	SH	GW	GT	S	PCT
62	13	27	40	-1	49	1	2	3	0	112	11.6

1994-95 statistics:

GP	G	A	TP	+/-	PIM	PP	SH	GW	GT	S	PCT
43	8	18	26	-6	30	0	0	1	0	66	12.1

1995-96 statistics:

GP	G	A	TP	+/-	PIM	PP	SH	GW	GT	S	PCT
69	19	20	39	-7	36	4	4	2	1	121	15.7

1996-97 statistics:

GP	G	A	TP	+/-	PIM	PP	SH	GW	GT	S	PCT
63	17	19	36	-11	52	5	1	1	0	113	15.0

PROJECTION

Drake's grit and determination set him apart from some finesse players who take too many nights off. We predicted 20 goals for Drake last season, and he would have exceeded that if he hadn't been injured.

LAST SEASON

Missed eight games with ankle injury. Missed 10 games with knee injury.

THE FINESSE GAME

Drake sees some playing time with the likes of Jeremy Roenick, playing the grinder's role by going into the corners. This is something of a reach for the overachieving Drake, who is better suited to a second-line role, but the chemistry often works because Drake does.

Drake is an aggressive forechecker, strong along the boards and in front of the net. He's on the small side, so he doesn't stand in and take a bashing, but he'll jump in and out of traffic to fight for the puck or bounce in on rebounds.

Drake is quick and powerful in his skating. He'll get outmuscled but not outhustled. His scoring chances come in deep.

THE PHYSICAL GAME

Drake gets noticed because he runs right over people. He is limited by his size but he will give a team whatever he's got. He's feisty enough to get the other team's attention, and he works to keep himself in scoring position.

Good things invariably happen when Drake takes the body. He is a strong penalty killer and forechecker.

THE INTANGIBLES

Drake is new coach Jim Schoenfeld's favourite kind of player, and he'll benefit from a game plan that is probably going to feature a heavy forecheck.

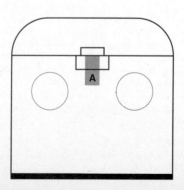

MIKE GARTNER

Yrs. of NHL service: 18
Born: Ottawa, Ont.; Oct. 29, 1959
Position: right wing
Height: 6-0
Weight: 187
Uniform no.: 22
Shoots: right

Career statistics:

GP	G	A	TP	PIM
1372	697	612	1308	1135

1993-94 statistics:

GP	G	A	TP	+/-	PIM	PP	SH	GW	GT	S	PCT
81	34	30	64	+20	62	11	5	4	0	275	12.4

1994-95 statistics:

GP	G	A	TP	+/-	PIM	PP	SH	GW	GT	S	PCT
38	12	8	20	0	6	2	1	1	1	91	13.2

1995-96 statistics:

GP	G	A	TP	+/-	PIM	PP	SH	GW	GT	S	PCT
82	35	19	54	+5	52	15	0	4	1	275	12.7

1996-97 statistics:

GP	G	A	TP	+/-	PIM	PP	SH	GW	GT	S	PCT
82	32	31	63	-11	38	13	1	7	1	271	11.8

LAST SEASON

Led team in power-play goals and tied for team lead in game-winning goals. Second on team in goals and shots. Third on team in points. One of four Coyotes to appear in all 82 games.

THE FINESSE GAME

At 38, this ageless wonder still has exceptional speed. He has flawless technical form — great stride, deep knee bend and excellent posture, which add up to power and speed. He is a human skating machine. Carrying the puck doesn't slow him down and he can still pull away from pursuers, as his 17th season with 30 or more goals will attest.

Gartner has learned to add some more crafty moves to his patented drive wide down the wing. As he slows, he can hold up and wait for a trailing teammate, because he still pushes defensemen back with his speed and opens up the ice.

Ever alert to his offensive chances, Gartner is sometimes guilty of hanging a little at the redline, looking for the break into the attacking zone. He can accept a pass in full flight. He has a clever play he uses in which he treats the boards as an extra teammate, giving himself a little pass off the wall or setting up a linemate with a smart feed.

Gartner drives his shot off the wing on the fly or uses a strong wrist shot from closer range. If his lane to the net is blocked, he will curl around behind the net — still at good speed — for a wraparound try. He isn't much of a playmaker. His assists come from teammates smart enough to follow up on his play for rebounds.

THE PHYSICAL GAME

Gartner is wiry and strong. When he doesn't beat a checker cleanly to the outside, he will manage to squeeze through along the boards and keep going forward with the puck, even if dragged to his knees.

He goes to the net and into the corners for the puck, and he has strong arms and wrists to reach into scrums and control it. He can flick a puck at the net one-handed. He seldom takes bad penalties. Even with a lot of miles on him, Gartner is very fit and durable. He hasn't missed a game in the past two seasons.

THE INTANGIBLES

Eventually Gartner will have to be spotted and may lose his role as an everyday player, but those remarkable wheels show no sign of wear yet.

PROJECTION

We predicted another 30-goal season for Gartner last season, and he did it, but we don't know if we should push our luck. Aw, why not? He's still in the wild, wild Western Conference on an improving young team.

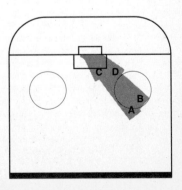

CRAIG JANNEY

Yrs. of NHL service: 9
Born: Hartford, Conn.; Sept. 26, 1967
Position: centre
Height: 6-1
Weight: 190
Uniform no.: 15
Shoots: left

Career statistics:

GP	G	A	TP	PIM
636	173	498	671	144

1993-94 statistics:

GP	G	A	TP	+/-	PIM	PP	SH	GW	GT	S	PCT
69	16	68	84	-14	24	8	0	7	0	95	16.8

1994-95 statistics:

GP	G	A	TP	+/-	PIM	PP	SH	GW	GT	S	PCT
35	7	20	27	-1	10	3	0	1	0	40	17.5

1995-96 statistics:

GP	G	A	TP	+/-	PIM	PP	SH	GW	GT	S	PCT
84	20	62	82	-33	26	7	0	2	0	91	22.0

1996-97 statistics:

GP	G	A	TP	+/-	PIM	PP	SH	GW	GT	S	PCT
77	15	38	53	-1	26	5	0	1	0	88	17.0

LAST SEASON

Tied for team lead in plus-minus. Second on team in shooting percentage. Third on team in assists.

THE FINESSE GAME

Probably one of the top five passers in the NHL, Janney finds his target, and finds him in time to allow the shooter enough room to do something with the puck. He draws the defender to him to open up ice, but by keeping the puck close to his body (he uses a very short stick) he makess it difficult for anyone fishing for the puck to knock it away. He then makes the pretty pass, usually to Keith Tkachuk, who made a nice partner with Janney much of last season.

Janney is very creative and sees the ice and all of his options well. Get into the open and he will get the puck to you. He usually disguises his intentions well enough so that the defense is caught napping. Linemates have to stay alert because he will turn what seems to be a dead play into a sudden scoring chance.

Janney's reluctance to shoot borders on the ridiculous. How can any first-line player have only 88 shots in 77 games? Martin Brodeur probably had more shots on goal. Janney has an excellent release, and could tack on an extra 10 goals a year if he took a page out of Adam Oates's book, but he would rather pass than shoot. He is patient with the puck and will wait for the goalie to commit. He has pinpoint accuracy, but he usually has to be wide open before he will take a shot.

No speed demon, Janney has slick moves that he puts on in a burst just when it appears he is about to come to a standstill. Defensively, he remains suspect.

THE PHYSICAL GAME

Janney isn't more of a scoring threat because he isn't strong enough to win the one-on-one battles in traffic. His conditioning has improved to handle all the ice time he usually gets.

The opponent's book is to hit Janney early and often. He will keep himself out of the trenches. He has fairly good size, but doesn't have the upper-body strength to knock anyone off the puck or prevent the puck being stripped from him. He is not a coward, though, and will take a hit to make a play since he controls the puck until the last moment, waiting for the perfect play.

THE INTANGIBLES

Janney isn't known as one of the most amiable people in the league, but he hasn't missed the playoffs in his 11 NHL seasons, and since he's played on some pretty awful teams (St. Louis, San Jose, Winnipeg) that's a major accomplishment. Still, Janney was benched several times last season for indifferent play.

PROJECTION

If Janney wants to keep playing with Tkachuk, he has to be more productive. Scoring 50 points is not enough.

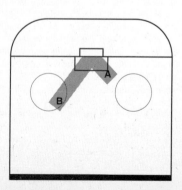

NIKOLAI KHABIBULIN

Yrs. of NHL service: 3
Born: Sverdlovsk, USSR; Jan. 13, 1973
Position: goaltender
Height: 6-1
Weight: 176
Uniform no.: 35
Catches: left

Career statistics:

GP	MIN	GA	SO	GAA	A	PIM
151	8344	421	9	3.03	4	32

1994-95 statistics:

GP	MIN	GAA	W	L	T	SO	GA	S	SAPCT	PIM
26	1339	3.41	8	9	4	0	76	723	.895	4

1995-96 statistics:

GP	MIN	GAA	W	L	T	SO	GA	S	SAPCT	PIM
53	2914	3.13	26	20	3	2	152	1656	.908	12

1996-97 statistics:

GP	MIN	GAA	W	L	T	SO	GA	S	SAPCT	PIM
72	4091	2.83	30	33	6	7	193	2094	.908	16

LAST SEASON

Third among NHL goalies in minutes played. Career high in wins. Career-best goals-against average. Tied for fourth in NHL in shutouts. Missed one game due to fatigue.

THE PHYSICAL GAME

Khabibulin is a butterfly-style goalie who positions himself like a shortstop. He gets down low and always gets his body behind the shot, and he stays on his feet and moves with the shooter. He may perform the best split-save in the league: it's stunningly graceful and athletic, and his legs look about five feet long. He leaves only the tiniest five-hole because he also gets the paddle of his stick down low across the front of the crease. Shooters have to go upstairs on him but he doesn't give away a lot of net high.

Khabibulin is solid in his fundamentals. He plays well out on the top of his crease, which is unusual for Russian goalies, who tend to stay deep in their net. He is aggressive but patient at the same time, and waits for the shooter to commit first.

Khabibulin needs to improve his work with the stick around the net and needs to control his rebounds better. He hates to move the puck. He gets himself into trouble when he does because his clearing attempts are easily picked off.

THE MENTAL GAME

Khabibulin has shown that he has the desire and the temperament to be a number one goalie. He stayed sharp despite a stretch of 42 consecutive starts.

THE INTANGIBLES

Khabibulin may be one of the most underrated goalies in the NHL and hasn't reached his prime yet.

PROJECTION

Khabibulin should get another 30-win season but will be sharper for the playoffs (he may be asked to play in the Olympics for Russia) with reduced ice time.

CHAD KILGER

Yrs. of NHL service: 2
Born: Cornwall, Ont.; Nov. 27, 1976
Position: centre
Height: 6-3
Weight: 204
Uniform no.: 18
Shoots: left

Career statistics:

GP	G	A	TP	PIM
98	11	13	24	47

1995-96 statistics:

GP	G	A	TP	+/-	PIM	PP	SH	GW	GT	S	PCT
74	7	10	17	-4	34	0	0	1	0	57	12.3

1996-97 statistics:

GP	G	A	TP	+/-	PIM	PP	SH	GW	GT	S	PCT
24	4	3	7	-5	13	1	0	0	0	30	13.3

LAST SEASON

Scored 17-28 — 45 in 52 games with Springfield (AHL). Second in Springfield in penalty minutes (234). Missed one game with thigh contusion.

THE FINESSE GAME

Kilger is getting his game back in shape after having been rushed into the NHL by Anaheim at age 18. By playing in the minors, he was able to play in all situations and regained a lot of lost confidence. He became a go-to guy and developed better hand skills.

Kilger plays an intelligent game and is poised for a youngster. He sees the ice well and is a good passer. The release on his shot is too slow for the NHL level right now but he can improve. He has a long reach, which works to his advantage in dangling the puck away from defenders.

His size and skating ability are NHL calibre. Few big players skate as well as Kilger.

THE PHYSICAL GAME

Kilger is big, but needs to fill out and get stronger. He threw his weight around well in the AHL.

THE INTANGIBLES

Kilger was sulky about his demotion to the minors, but gradually realized that it was the best thing for him. He became a leader in Springfield instead of being a lost, fringe NHLer. He should come into this year's training camp with a lot of confidence.

PROJECTION

Kilger is still raw and immature. If he's not ready to step in at the start of the season, he will be by the halfway mark. He needs to have a regular role and not be a part-timer. He might not get to be a number one centre because he won't get the points, but he will someday be a high-level number two.

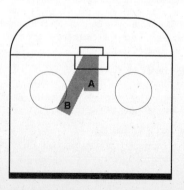

TEPPO NUMMINEN

Yrs. of NHL service: 9
Born: Tampere, Finland; July 3, 1968
Position: left defense
Height: 6-1
Weight: 190
Uniform no.: 27
Shoots: right

Career statistics:

GP	G	A	TP	PIM
629	55	237	292	243

1993-94 statistics:

GP	G	A	TP	+/-	PIM	PP	SH	GW	GT	S	PCT
57	5	18	23	-23	28	4	0	1	0	89	5.6

1994-95 statistics:

GP	G	A	TP	+/-	PIM	PP	SH	GW	GT	S	PCT
42	5	16	21	+12	16	2	0	0	0	86	5.8

1995-96 statistics:

GP	G	A	TP	+/-	PIM	PP	SH	GW	GT	S	PCT
74	11	43	54	-4	22	6	0	3	0	165	6.7

1996-97 statistics:

GP	G	A	TP	+/-	PIM	PP	SH	GW	GT	S	PCT
82	2	25	27	-3	28	0	0	0	0	135	1.5

LAST SEASON

Tied for third on team in plus-minus. One of four Coyotes to appear in all 82 games.

THE FINESSE GAME

Numminen's agility and anticipation make him look much faster than he is. A graceful skater with a smooth change of direction, he never telegraphs what he is about to do. His skating makes him valuable on the first penalty-killing unit. He will not get caught out of position and is seldom bested one-on-one.

Numminen is not afraid to give up the puck on a dump-and-chase, rather than force a neutral zone play if he is under pressure. Partnering the offensive Oleg Tverdovsky has allowed him to be the stay-at-home half of the duo, which suits his game better than trying to force offense. He would rather dish off than rush with the puck, and he is a savvy passer, moving the puck briskly and seldom overhandling it. He is not a finisher. He joins the play but doesn't lead it. Most of his offense is generated from point shots or passes in deep.

Numminen is uncannily adept at keeping the puck in at the point, frustrating opponents who try to clear it out around the boards.

THE PHYSICAL GAME

Numminen plays an acceptable physical game. He can be intimidated and doesn't scare attackers, who will attempt to drive through him to the net. Opponents get a strong forecheck on him to neutralize his smart passing game. He'll employ his body as a last resort but would rather use his stick and gain the puck. He is even-tempered and not at all nasty.

THE INTANGIBLES

Numminen is underrated but had a quality playoffs, which attracted some deserved attention.

PROJECTION

Numminen has steadily improved, season by season. He is a complete if not an elite defenseman who is capable of playing a strong all-around game and scoring 25 points.

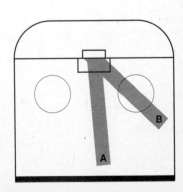

DERON QUINT

Yrs. of NHL service: 2
Born: Durham, NH; March 12, 1976
Position: left defense
Height: 6-1
Weight: 182
Uniform no.: 5
Shoots: left

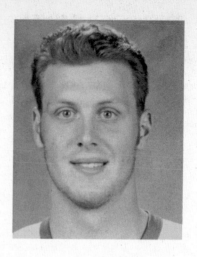

Career statistics:

GP	G	A	TP	PIM
78	8	24	32	26

1995-96 statistics:

GP	G	A	TP	+/-	PIM	PP	SH	GW	GT	S	PCT
51	5	13	18	-2	22	2	0	0	0	97	5.2

1996-97 statistics:

GP	G	A	TP	+/-	PIM	PP	SH	GW	GT	S	PCT
27	3	11	14	-4	4	1	0	0	0	63	4.8

LAST SEASON

Scored 6-18 — 24 in 43 games with Springfield (AHL).

THE FINESSE GAME

Quint has some NHL-level skills, starting with his skating. He has very good speed with a change of gears and can shift directions in a fluid motion. He also possesses a fine, accurate slap shot with a quick release. He can rush the puck end-to-end or start a rush with a smart pass and then join the attack.

The problem isn't in Quint's hands or feet, but in his head. He doesn't read the rush well and overcommits to plays. He has to learn to tune into odd-man rushes.

Quint would probably thrive if he were paired with a defense-minded partner who would feel comfortable in just telling Quint to go.

THE PHYSICAL GAME

Quint is finesse-oriented and needs to get more physically involved. He doesn't have great size for an NHL defenseman but he is big enough to bump and get in the way of people, though he's inconsistent with his body work. Quint also has a problem picking the right man to eliminate.

THE INTANGIBLES

Quint has some growing up to do, and would have been better off if the team had just let him develop in the minors for two seasons. Conditioning has been a problem with him in the past two seasons. If he can mature and take a more professional approach to his career, this season could see him move into a full-time role as a top four defenseman with the Coyotes.

PROJECTION

Quint will be a top point producer in a couple of seasons, but he's still green and 25 to 30 points is reasonable for this year.

JEREMY ROENICK

Yrs. of NHL service: 8
Born: Boston, Mass.; Jan. 17, 1970
Position: centre
Height: 6-0
Weight: 190
Uniform no.: 97
Shoots: right

Career statistics:

GP	G	A	TP	PIM
596	296	369	665	685

1993-94 statistics:

GP	G	A	TP	+/-	PIM	PP	SH	GW	GT	S	PCT
84	46	61	107	+21	125	24	5	5	1	281	16.4

1994-95 statistics:

GP	G	A	TP	+/-	PIM	PP	SH	GW	GT	S	PCT
33	10	24	34	+5	14	5	0	0	1	93	10.8

1995-96 statistics:

GP	G	A	TP	+/-	PIM	PP	SH	GW	GT	S	PCT
66	32	35	67	+9	109	12	4	2	2	171	18.7

1996-97 statistics:

GP	G	A	TP	+/-	PIM	PP	SH	GW	GT	S	PCT
72	29	40	69	-7	115	10	3	7	0	228	12.7

LAST SEASON

Tied for team lead in game-winning goals. Led team in shorthanded goals. Second on team in power-play goals. Second on team in assists and points. Missed six games with knee injury.

THE FINESSE GAME

Roenick commands a lot of attention when he is on the ice, and draws the attention of the defenders to open up ice for his teammates. He has great acceleration and can turn quickly, change directions or burn a defender with outside speed. A defenseman who plays aggressively against him will be left staring at the back of Roenick's jersey as he skips by en route to the net. Roenick has to be forced into the high traffic areas, where his lack of size and strength are the only things that derail him.

Roenick has great quickness and is tough to handle one-on-one. He won't make the same move or take the same shot twice in a row. He has a variety of shots and can score from almost anywhere on the ice. He can rifle a wrist shot from 30 feet away, or else wait until the goalie is down and lift in a backhand from in tight.

The Coyotes need to decide whether they want to use Roenick as a centre or a right wing (he was bounced around last year) and leave him alone.

THE PHYSICAL GAME

Roenick plays with such a headlong style that injuries are routine. He has trouble keeping weight on, and generally loses 15 to 20 pounds between the start of training camp and the end of the regular season.

Roenick takes aggressive penalties — smashing people into the boards, getting his elbows up — and he never backs down. He plays through pain, and is highly competitive.

THE INTANGIBLES

Things couldn't have gone much worse for Roenick, who missed the start of the season negotiating a new contract. After the big money came the big slump (Roenick is historically a slow starter), then a minor knee injury, and, in the playoffs, a serious knee injury that will require him to wear a knee brace this season. He's under a lot of heat in Phoenix (yeah, but it's a dry heat).

PROJECTION

Roenick has a lot to prove this season and needs to return to the 100-point mark to prove his worth.

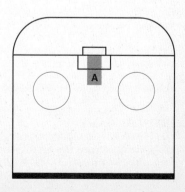

CLIFF RONNING

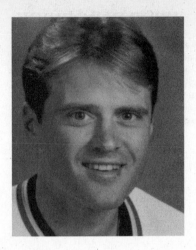

Yrs. of NHL service: 10
Born: Vancouver, B.C.; Oct. 1, 1965
Position: centre
Height: 5-8
Weight: 170
Uniform no.: 77
Shoots: left

Career statistics:

GP	G	A	TP	PIM
615	185	319	504	255

1993-94 statistics:

GP	G	A	TP	+/-	PIM	PP	SH	GW	GT	S	PCT
76	25	43	68	+7	42	10	0	4	1	197	12.7

1994-95 statistics:

GP	G	A	TP	+/-	PIM	PP	SH	GW	GT	S	PCT
41	6	19	25	-4	27	3	0	2	0	93	6.5

1995-96 statistics:

GP	G	A	TP	+/-	PIM	PP	SH	GW	GT	S	PCT
79	22	45	67	+16	42	5	0	1	1	187	11.8

1996-97 statistics:

GP	G	A	TP	+/-	PIM	PP	SH	GW	GT	S	PCT
69	19	32	51	-9	26	8	0	2	0	171	11.1

LAST SEASON

Missed 12 games with fractured hand.

THE FINESSE GAME

Ronning's forte is not scoring goals but creating chances for his wingers. He lets bigger linemates attract defenders so that he can dipsy-doodle with the puck. He's quick, shifty and smart . . . he has to be smart, otherwise he'll be flattened along the boards like an advertstisement.

Ronning likes to work from behind the net, using the cage as a shield and daring defenders to chase him. Much of his game is a dare. He is a tempting target, and even smaller-sized defensemen fantasize about smashing Ronning to the ice. But he keeps himself out of the trouble spots by dancing in and out of openings and finding free teammates.

A quick thinker and unpredictable, Ronning can curl off the wall into the slot, pass to the corners or the point and jump to the net, or beat a defender wide to the top of the circle and feed a trailing teammate coming into the play late. He's not afraid of going into traffic.

He puts a lot of little dekes into a compact area. He opens up the ice with his bursts of speed and his fakes. Unless the defense can force him along the wall·and contain him, he's all over the ice trying to make things happen.

THE PHYSICAL GAME

No one asks jockeys to tackle running backs. Ronning is built for speed and deception. He is smart enough to avoid getting crunched and talented enough to compensate for his lack of strength. He has skills and a huge heart and competes hard every night.

Ronning gets involved with his stick, hooking at a puck carrier's arm and worrying at the puck in a player's skates. He keeps the puck in his skates when he protects it, so that a checker will often have to pull Ronning down to get at the puck, which creates a power play.

THE INTANGIBLES

Tough in his own way, Ronning has excelled at a game that everyone told him he was too small to play. He would have put up much better numbers last year if he hadn't had the hand injury. He played on for several weeks with a cast that seriously hampered his flexibility.

PROJECTION

Phoenix has too many finesse centres jammed in after Jeremy Roenick, and Ronning could have trouble getting ice time this season.

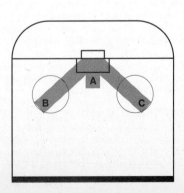

DARRIN SHANNON

Yrs. of NHL service: 7
Born: Barrie, Ont.; Dec. 8, 1969
Position: left wing
Height: 6-2
Weight: 210
Uniform no.: 34
Shoots: left

Career statistics:

GP	G	A	TP	PIM
448	85	151	236	318

1993-94 statistics:

GP	G	A	TP	+/-	PIM	PP	SH	GW	GT	S	PCT
77	21	37	58	-18	87	9	0	2	0	124	16.9

1994-95 statistics:

GP	G	A	TP	+/-	PIM	PP	SH	GW	GT	S	PCT
19	5	3	8	-6	14	3	0	1	0	26	19.2

1995-96 statistics:

GP	G	A	TP	+/-	PIM	PP	SH	GW	GT	S	PCT
63	5	18	23	-5	28	0	0	1	0	74	6.8

1996-97 statistics:

GP	G	A	TP	+/-	PIM	PP	SH	GW	GT	S	PCT
82	11	13	24	+4	41	1	0	2	0	104	10.6

LAST SEASON

One of four Coyotes to appear in all 82 games.

THE FINESSE GAME

Shannon is an up-and-down winger who doesn't do much creatively but creates off the forecheck. He doesn't have great quickness, yet he can get a solid head of steam going to plow the defenseman on the end boards. He drives to the net while letting his linemates handle the fancy stuff. His scoring chances all come from close range. He will screen the goalie for a shot or scrap for rebounds. Shannon really has to scrap, because he doesn't have very good hands.

Shannon sees limited power-play duty, picking up the last 20 seconds or so if nothing else has worked, but he doesn't create much. His defensive instincts are good enough that he can be used against some top forwards, such as Brett Hull. He does a fairly good job killing penalties.

THE PHYSICAL GAME

Shannon doesn't get into fights, just uses his big body as a battering ram. He isn't mean or even assertive. Sometimes it looks like he hits people solely because he couldn't stop.

THE INTANGIBLES

Shannon is valued for his size, even though he's not a particularly tough player and isn't very special in any sense.

PROJECTION

Shannon's range is 20 to 30 points in a checking role.

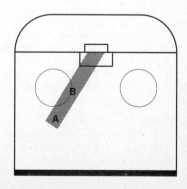

KEITH TKACHUK

Yrs. of NHL service: 5
Born: Melrose, Mass.; Mar. 28, 1972
Position: left wing
Height: 6-2
Weight: 210
Uniform no.: 7
Shoots: left

Career statistics:

GP	G	A	TP	PIM
389	196	179	375	1020

1993-94 statistics:

GP	G	A	TP	+/-	PIM	PP	SH	GW	GT	S	PCT
84	41	40	81	-12	255	22	3	3	1	218	18.8

1994-95 statistics:

GP	G	A	TP	+/-	PIM	PP	SH	GW	GT	S	PCT
48	22	29	51	-4	152	7	2	2	1	129	17.1

1995-96 statistics:

GP	G	A	TP	+/-	PIM	PP	SH	GW	GT	S	PCT
76	50	48	98	+11	156	20	2	6	0	249	20.1

1996-97 statistics:

GP	G	A	TP	+/-	PIM	PP	SH	GW	GT	S	PCT
81	52	34	86	-1	228	9	2	7	1	296	17.6

LAST SEASON

First player in NHL history to lead league in goals and have more than 200 PIM. Led team in goals, points and shots for second straight season. Led team in penalty minutes and shooting percentage. Tied for team lead in game-winning goals and plus-minus. Third on team in power-play goals.

THE FINESSE GAME

Tkachuk is among the NHL's elite power forwards, arguably the best power left wing in the game today. He's at his best when he uses his strength and scoring touch in tight. The scariest thing about him is how good he has become so young. Kevin Stevens, one of the NHL power-forward prototypes, didn't score 50 goals until he was 26 years old. Cam Neely was just shy of 25 in his first 50-goal season. Of Tkachuk's contemporaries, John LeClair and Brendan Shanahan are 28. Tkachuk is a relative baby at 25.

In front of the net, Tkachuk will bang and crash but he also has soft hands for picking pucks out of skates and flicking strong wrist shots. He can also kick at the puck with his skates without going down. He has a quick release. He looks at the net, not down at his stick, and finds the openings.

Tkachuk has improved his one-step quickness and agility. He is powerful and balanced, and often drives through bigger defensemen.

THE PHYSICAL GAME

Tkachuk is volatile and mean as a scorpion. He takes bad penalties, and since he has a reputation around the league for getting his stick up and retaliating for hits with a quick rabbit-punch to the head, referees keep a close eye on him. He will have to avoid foolish penalties. He can be tough without buying a time-share in the penalty box.

Tkachuk can dictate the physical tempo of a game with his work in the corners and along the boards.

THE INTANGIBLES

Tkachuk stepped it up when it mattered most, in the playoffs. He is a tremendous on-ice leader who is only getting better.

PROJECTION

Let's raise the bar. After all, scoring was down in the NHL last season. Tkachuk can notch 60 goals.

RICK TOCCHET

Yrs. of NHL service: 13
Born: Scarborough, Ont.; Apr. 9, 1964
Position: right wing
Height: 6-0
Weight: 205
Uniform no.: 92
Shoots: right

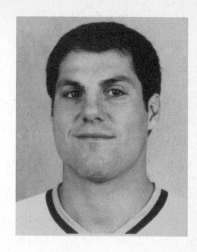

Career statistics:

GP	G	A	TP	PIM
841	359	617	776	2469

1993-94 statistics:

GP	G	A	TP	+/-	PIM	PP	SH	GW	GT	S	PCT
51	14	26	40	-15	134	5	1	2	1	150	9.3

1994-95 statistics:

GP	G	A	TP	+/-	PIM	PP	SH	GW	GT	S	PCT
36	18	17	35	-8	70	7	1	3	0	95	18.9

1995-96 statistics:

GP	G	A	TP	+/-	PIM	PP	SH	GW	GT	S	PCT
71	29	31	60	+10	181	10	0	3	1	185	15.7

1996-97 statistics:

GP	G	A	TP	+/-	PIM	PP	SH	GW	GT	S	PCT
53	21	19	40	-3	98	4	0	2	1	157	13.4

LAST SEASON

Signed as free agent, July 8, 1997. Acquired by Washington from Boston with Adam Oates and Bill Ranford for Jim Carey, Anson Carter, Jason Allison, a third-round pick in 1997 and a conditional pick in 1998, March 1, 1997. Third on Capitals in goals. Missed three games with bruised foot. Missed 17 games with knee injury. Missed two games with bruised shoulder.

THE FINESSE GAME

Tocchet managed to score 16 goals in 40 games playing on basically a three-player team in Boston. He scored 5-5 — 10 in 13 games with the Caps, and looks to do even better with a Phoenix team that is small but deep up the middle.

Tocchet has worked hard to make the most of the finesse skills he possesses and that makes everything loom larger. His skating is powerful, though he does not have great mobility. He is explosive in short bursts and is most effective in small areas. He works extremely well down low and in traffic. He drives to the front of the net and into the corners for the puck.

His shooting skills are better than his passing skills. He has limited vision of the ice for making a creative play but he is a master at the bang-bang play. He'll smack in rebounds and deflections and set screens as defenders try to knock him down.

He has a strong, accurate wrist shot and gets most of his goals from close range, though he can also fire a one-timer from the tops of the circles. He'll rarely waste a shot from the blueline. He is a good give-and-go player because his quickness allows him to jump into the holes. He will beat few people one-on-one because he lacks stickhandling prowess.

THE PHYSICAL GAME

Tocchet gets about 20 shifts a game. That's like going 20 rounds with Joe Frazier, a heavyweight who comes at you again and again with everything he's got. There is no hiding from Tocchet. He is a tough hitter and frequently gets his stick and elbows up. He has long had a history of letting his emotions get the better of him, and although he has matured somewhat, he is acutely aware of his position as one of the few tough, physical forwards on a team of finesse players. Tocchet knows he must play rugged to be effective and he can do that cleanly, but he will also get everyone's attention by bending the rules.

THE INTANGIBLES

Tocchet's work ethic is inspiring. He is always one of the last players off the ice, usually working on puck-handling drills. Before games, he's one of the first to the rink and is riding the bike; after games, he's lifting weights. He started his career as a goon but has remade himself into a solid NHL player. His health remains a huge question mark, but as long as he can stay on his feet he will be an impact player.

PROJECTION

Is Tocchet going to play 80 games? As hard as he plays, that's doubtful. But he's good for 60 points if he can play 50 with the right teammates. He's a 30-goal scorer if he can play 70 games.

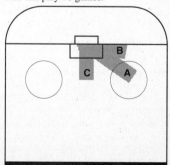

OLEG TVERDOVSKY

Yrs. of NHL service: 3
Born: Donetsk, Ukraine; May 18, 1976
Position: left defense
Height: 6-0
Weight: 185
Uniform no.: 20
Shoots: left

Career statistics:

GP	G	A	TP	PIM
200	20	77	97	85

1994-95 statistics:

GP	G	A	TP	+/-	PIM	PP	SH	GW	GT	S	PCT
36	3	9	12	-6	14	1	1	0	0	26	11.5

1995-96 statistics:

GP	G	A	TP	+/-	PIM	PP	SH	GW	GT	S	PCT
82	7	23	30	-7	41	2	0	0	0	119	5.9

1996-97 statistics:

GP	G	A	TP	+/-	PIM	PP	SH	GW	GT	S	PCT
82	10	45	55	-5	30	3	1	2	0	144	6.9

LAST SEASON

Led team defensemen and fourth among NHL defensemen in scoring. Led team in assists. One of four Coyotes to appear in all 82 games.

THE FINESSE GAME

Tverdovsky is an impressive talent. A weakness in the offensive zone is tough to find because this defenseman passes the puck well and shoots bullets. While he's clearly going to be primarily an offensive defenseman, he also settled down in his own zone. He has become a more patient player defensively, and being a partner with the underrated Teppo Numminen helped him greatly. Of course, the price to pay with an "offenseman" are defensive lapses, and Tverdovsky can make some world-class errors.

He's such a good passer that he doesn't feel the need to carry the puck all the time. And he doesn't just get the puck and go, he knows when to go. There are nights when he is simply brilliant, but he hasn't achieved consistency yet.

Tverdovsky has Brian Leetch potential. He's an explosive skater and can carry the puck at high tempo. He works the point on the power play and kills penalties. He sees his options and makes his decisions at lightning speed.

THE PHYSICAL GAME

Some of Tverdovsky's defensive weaknesses can be attributed to the fact that he sometimes plays the puck instead of the man, or tries to poke-check without backing it up with his body. Physically, when he makes the right decision, he can eliminate the man, and he looks to be improving in this area by at least tying up his man.

Tverdovsky is a devoted practice player who almost has to be wrestled off the ice. He loves to play and is enthusiastic and extremely competitive.

THE INTANGIBLES

Tverdovsky lived up to his promise in the regular season, but vanished in the playoffs after making some rather rash public statements about his former team, Anaheim.

PROJECTION

Tverdovsky took a step up last season. Is he ready to deliver more? A repeat of a 55- to 60-point season is expected and he should again rank among the top five NHL defensemen in scoring.

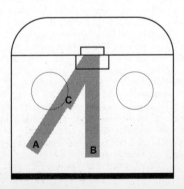

PITTSBURGH PENGUINS

Players' Statistics 1996-97

POS.	NO.	PLAYER	GP	G	A	PTS	+/-	PIM	PP	SH	GW	GT	S	PCT
C	66	MARIO LEMIEUX	76	50	72	122	27	65	15	2	7	1	327	15.3
R	68	JAROMIR JAGR	63	47	48	95	22	40	11	2	6	1	234	20.1
C	10	RON FRANCIS	81	27	63	90	7	20	10	1	2		183	14.8
C	93	PETR NEDVED	74	33	38	71	-2	66	12	3	4		189	17.5
L	27	ED OLCZYK	79	25	30	55	-14	51	5	1	6		195	12.8
D	4	KEVIN HATCHER	80	15	39	54	11	103	9		1		199	7.5
C	14	STU BARNES	81	19	30	49	-23	26	5		3	3	176	10.8
D	23	FREDRIK OLAUSSON	71	9	29	38	16	32	3		3		110	8.2
D	22	JASON WOOLLEY	60	6	30	36	4	30	2		1		86	7.0
C	9	GREG JOHNSON	75	13	19	32	-18	26	1				108	12.0
C	33	ALEX HICKS	73	7	21	28	-5	90			3		78	9.0
D	11	DARIUS KASPARAITIS	75	2	21	23	17	100					58	3.4
R	7	JOE MULLEN	54	7	15	22	0	4	1		1		63	11.1
L	8	GARRY VALK	70	10	11	21	-8	78			1		100	10.0
L	16	JOE DZIEDZIC	59	9	9	18	-4	63			1		85	10.6
R	20	ROMAN OKSIUTA	35	6	7	13	-16	26	2			1	58	10.3
C	38	*ANDREAS JOHANSSON	42	4	9	13	-12	20	1				59	6.8
L	51	DAVE ROCHE	61	5	5	10	-13	155	2				53	9.4
D	24	IAN MORAN	36	4	5	9	-11	22					50	8.0
D	2	CHRIS TAMER	45	2	4	6	-25	131		1			56	3.6
R	25	ALEK STOJANOV	35	1	4	5	3	79					11	9.1
L	15	JOSEF BERANEK	8	3	1	4	-1	4	1				15	20.0
L	72	JEFF CHRISTIAN	11	2	2	4	-3	13					18	11.1
C	29	TYLER WRIGHT	45	2	2	4	-7	70				2	30	6.7
D	28	CRAIG MUNI	64		4	4	-6	36					19	
C	9	DAN QUINN	16		3	3	-6	10					16	
D	18	FRANCOIS LEROUX	59		3	3	-3	81					5	
G	31	KEN WREGGET	46		1	1	0	6						
C	23	*DOMENIC PITTIS	1				-1							
G	30	*PHILIPPE DE ROUVILLE	2				0							
G	35	TOM BARRASSO	5				0							
D	3	*STEFAN BERGKVIST	5				-1	7						
R	44	ED PATTERSON	6				0	8					2	
D	6	NEIL WILKINSON	23				-12	36					16	
G	40	*PATRICK LALIME	39				0							

GP = games played; G = goals; A = assists; PTS = points; +/- = goals-for minus goals-against while player is on ice; PIM = penalties in minutes; PP = power-play goals; SH = shorthanded goals; GW = game-winning goals; GT = game-tying goals; S = no. of shots; PCT = percentage of goals to shots; * = rookie

STU BARNES

Yrs. of NHL service: 6
Born: Edmonton, Alta.; Dec. 25, 1970
Position: centre
Height: 5-11
Weight: 175
Uniform no.: 14
Shoots: right

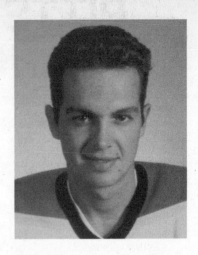

Career statistics:

GP	G	A	TP	PIM
355	91	117	208	154

1993-94 statistics:

GP	G	A	TP	+/-	PIM	PP	SH	GW	GT	S	PCT
77	23	24	47	+4	38	8	1	3	0	172	13.4

1994-95 statistics:

GP	G	A	TP	+/-	PIM	PP	SH	GW	GT	S	PCT
41	10	19	29	+7	8	1	0	2	0	93	10.8

1995-96 statistics:

GP	G	A	TP	+/-	PIM	PP	SH	GW	GT	S	PCT
72	19	25	44	-12	46	8	0	5	2	158	12.0

1996-97 statistics:

GP	G	A	TP	+/-	PIM	PP	SH	GW	GT	S	PCT
81	19	30	49	-23	26	5	0	3	3	176	10.8

PROJECTION

A checking centre who can occasionally handle playing time on the power play, Barnes can supply 20 goals in his role.

LAST SEASON

Acquired from Florida with Jason Woolley for Chris Wells, November 19, 1996.

THE FINESSE GAME

Seeing the enthusiasm with which Barnes kills penalties, it is hard to believe he had never been asked to perform in that role before playing for Florida. He pursues the puck intelligently and finishes his checks. He employs these traits at even strength, too, reading the play coming out of the zone and using his anticipation to pick off passes.

Barnes has sharply honed puck skills and offensive instincts, which he puts to especially effective use on the power play. He has good quickness and can control the puck in traffic. He uses a slap shot or a wrist shot in tight.

He has a good work ethic; his effort overcomes his deficiency in size. He's clever and plays a smart small man's game.

THE PHYSICAL GAME

Barnes is not big but he gets in the way. He brings a little bit of grit to the lineup, but what really stands out is his intensity and spirit. He can energize his team with one gutsy shift. Barnes always keeps his feet moving and draws penalties.

THE INTANGIBLES

Many people traced the beginning of the Panthers' decline to the trading away of Barnes. He is "only" a third-line centre, but he does provide a spark and helps take some of the defensive load off Ron Francis.

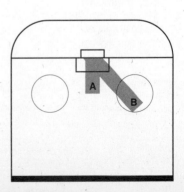

TOM BARRASSO

Yrs. of NHL service: 14
Born: Boston, Mass.; Mar. 31, 1965
Position: goaltender
Height: 6-3
Weight: 211
Uniform no.: 35
Catches: right

Career statistics:

GP	MIN	GA	SO	GAA	A	PIM
602	34624	1988	23	3.45	43	395

1993-94 statistics:

GP	MIN	GAA	W	L	T	SO	GA	S	SAPCT	PIM
44	2482	3.36	22	15	5	2	139	1304	.893	42

1994-95 statistics:

GP	MIN	GAA	W	L	T	SO	GA	S	SAPCT	PIM
2	125	3.84	0	1	1	0	8	75	.893	0

1995-96 statistics:

GP	MIN	GAA	W	L	T	SO	GA	S	SAPCT	PIM
49	2799	3.43	29	16	2	2	160	1626	.902	18

1996-97 statistics:

GP	MIN	GAA	W	L	T	SO	GA	S	SAPCT	PIM
5	270	5.78	0	5	0	0	26	186	.860	0

LAST SEASON
Missed 77 games with shoulder injury and surgery.

THE PHYSICAL GAME
The Penguins tend to give up a lot of odd-man rushes and Barrasso makes the save, handling the puck quickly to get his team going on a counterattack. It's doubtful if he would have played as well in recent years if he had been with a more conservative team. Pittsburgh's flamboyance suits him, despite his inflated goals-against average.

One of the most impressive things about Barrasso is that, although he is often on his knees, he is almost never on his side. He might be the best in the league at recovering from going down and will be back on his skates with his glove in position for the next shot. He surrenders a lot of long rebounds. He freezes the puck frequently and has one of the game's top face-off men, Ron Francis, always available for defensive-zone draws.

Barrasso loves to handle the puck; he's like a third defenseman in both his willingness to leave the crease and in his ability to pass. He's a good skater who is able to get to and control a lot of pucks that most goalies wouldn't dare try to reach. Staying on his feet more (a fundamental he has improved upon with experience) allows him to make the most of his skating skills. Most of the time he uses the boards for his passes, rather than making a risky play up the middle, but every so often he is vulnerable to the interception.

Because of Barrasso's range, teams have to adapt their attack. Hard dump-ins won't work, because he stops them behind the net and zips the puck right back out for an alert counterattack by his teammates. Since he comes out around the post to his right better than his left, teams have to aim soft dumps to his left, mak-

ing him more hesitant about making the play and giving the forecheckers time to get in on him. Barrasso's lone weakness appears to be shots low on the glove side.

THE MENTAL GAME
Barrasso is still one of the game's most intense competitors. He has battled through injuries and personal crises through the past few seasons and has lost little of his edge. He will whack guys in the ankle or get his body in the way for a subtle interference play. His concentration will slip, however, especially on long shots.

THE INTANGIBLES
Despite his physical problems, Barrasso will come into camp with as good a chance as Ken Wregget to win the number one job (rookie Patrick Lalime, despite his selection to the NHL All-Rookie Team, is not NHL-ready). This could be Barrasso's last hurrah. Wregget makes less money and is better liked by the Penguins, and most of humanity, than Barrasso is. His salary will make him difficult to unload, and his days as an elite goaltender are over, so the Pens may just be stuck with him.

PROJECTION
Barrasso resumed skating in April. It's unlikely he'll ever be as effective as he was in the Penguins' Stanley Cup days.

RON FRANCIS

Yrs. of NHL service: 16
Born: Sault Ste. Marie, Ont.; Mar. 1, 1963
Position: centre
Height: 6-2
Weight: 200
Uniform no.: 10
Shoots: left

Career statistics:

GP	G	A	TP	PIM
1166	403	944	1347	813

1993-94 statistics:

GP	G	A	TP	+/-	PIM	PP	SH	GW	GT	S	PCT
82	27	66	93	-3	62	8	0	2	1	216	12.5

1994-95 statistics:

GP	G	A	TP	+/-	PIM	PP	SH	GW	GT	S	PCT
44	11	48	59	+30	18	3	0	1	0	94	11.7

1995-96 statistics:

GP	G	A	TP	+/-	PIM	PP	SH	GW	GT	S	PCT
77	27	92	119	+25	56	12	1	4	0	158	17.1

1996-97 statistics:

GP	G	A	TP	+/-	PIM	PP	SH	GW	GT	S	PCT
81	27	63	90	+7	20	10	1	2	0	183	14.8

LAST SEASON

Tied for third in NHL and led team in assists. Third on team in points.

THE FINESSE GAME

Almost as much as Mario Lemieux, Jaromir Jagr owes much of his success to this cerebral centre, who appears ageless as long as he keeps his helmet on (it covers the grey better than Clairol). Just how much longer can the 34-year-old centre carry the number one role?

Francis can still put points on the board. Technically, he is a choppy skater who gets where he has to be with a minimum amount of style. His understanding of the game is key because he has great awareness of his positioning. He gets loads of ice time (far too much), so he has learned to pace himself to conserve his energy. There are few useless bursts of speed.

Francis is Dr. Draw. On rare nights when he is struggling with an opposing centre, he'll tinker with his changes in the neutral zone, then save what he has learned for a key draw deep in either zone. Just as a great scorer never shows a goalie the same move twice in a row, he never uses the same technique in succession. He has good hand-eye coordination and uses his body well at the dot. Pittsburgh goalies have no fear about freezing the puck because of Francis's superiority on face-offs. Few players win their draws as outright as Francis does on a consistent basis.

While he focusses on a defensive role, Francis has the hands and the vision to come out of a scramble into an attacking rush. He anticipates passes, blocks shots, then springs an odd-man breakout with a smart play. Jagr is always hanging and circling and looking for the opportunity, and Francis often finds him.

Francis doesn't have a screamingly hard shot, nor is he a flashy player. He works from the centre of the ice, between the circles and has a quick release on a one-timer. He can kill penalties or work the point on the power play with equal effectiveness. He complements any kind of player.

THE PHYSICAL GAME

Not a big, imposing hitter, Francis will use his body to get the job done. He will bump and grind and go into the trenches. Back on defense, he can function as a third defenseman; on offense, you will find him going into the corners or heading for the front of the net for tips and rebounds. He gets a lot of ice time but keeps himself in great shape. Still, he is a worn and weary player come playoff time.

THE INTANGIBLES

Francis should be a number two centre at this point in his career, but the Penguins still desperately need him as part of their top line with Jagr.

PROJECTION

Francis's 95 points last season might have been his last visit to that neighbourhood. The Penguins figure to be more defensively aware under new coach Kevin Constantine, and Francis's points should decline accordingly.

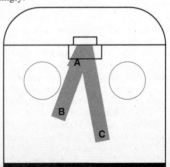

KEVIN HATCHER

Yrs. of NHL service: 12
Born: Detroit, Mich.; Sept. 9, 1966
Position: right defense
Height: 6-4
Weight: 225
Uniform no.: 4
Shoots: right

Career statistics:

GP	G	A	TP	PIM
886	189	361	550	1228

1993-94 statistics:

GP	G	A	TP	+/-	PIM	PP	SH	GW	GT	S	PCT
72	16	24	40	-13	108	6	0	3	0	217	7.4

1994-95 statistics:

GP	G	A	TP	+/-	PIM	PP	SH	GW	GT	S	PCT
47	10	19	29	-4	66	3	0	2	1	138	7.2

1995-96 statistics:

GP	G	A	TP	+/-	PIM	PP	SH	GW	GT	S	PCT
74	15	26	41	-24	58	7	0	3	2	237	6.3

1996-97 statistics:

GP	G	A	TP	+/-	PIM	PP	SH	GW	GT	S	PCT
80	15	39	54	+11	103	9	0	1	0	199	7.5

LAST SEASON

Led team defensemen in scoring.

THE FINESSE GAME

Hatcher is not among the game's elite defensemen, especially in the offensive sense. Getting as much playing time as he did with the offense-minded Penguins should have resulted in more than 54 points.

Hatcher has good anticipation in his own zone for picking off passes, which he then carries up the middle to start a counterattack. He doesn't have a quick take-off, though, and a smart checker will get to him quickly and force a turnover. He can finish in close offensively. He isn't the smartest puck carrier in the world, and is often better off making the short outlet pass or dumping the puck instead of forcing a play at the blueline. He is smart about jumping into the play, but also clever enough to make the best play the situation dictates. Hatcher moves to the left point on the power play to open up his forehand for one-timers.

Hatcher has the puck so much during a game that there are times when he'll turn the puck over or carry it dangerously in front of his own net. He makes decisions quickly in all zones. If the heat is on him in his own zone, he is aware of his teammates' positions on the ice and makes the smart outlet pass or bangs the puck off the glass. He is constantly looking to see which attackers might be bearing in on him.

THE PHYSICAL GAME

Who wants a finesse defenseman this big? He's not very brave, and doesn't use his body as well as he should.

THE INTANGIBLES

Hatcher has yet to prove he can be a dominating defenseman. Maybe new coach Kevin Constantine will be able to draw a better game out of Hatcher than we've seen so far. We're not holding our breath. Hatcher was a second-half disappointment and had an average playoffs.

PROJECTION

In last year's *HSR* we told you "He is only a legitimate 50-point man at best." Even with the inflated stats defensemen can pick up with the Penguins, that's his limit.

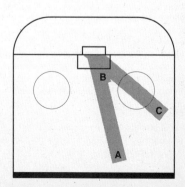

ALEX HICKS

Yrs. of NHL service: 2
Born: Calgary, Alberta; Sept. 4, 1969
Position: left wing
Height: 6-1
Weight: 195
Uniform no.: 33
Shoots: left

Career statistics:

GP	G	A	TP	PIM
137	17	32	49	127

1995-96 statistics:

GP	G	A	TP	+/-	PIM	PP	SH	GW	GT	S	PCT
64	10	11	21	+11	37	0	0	2	1	83	12.0

1996-97 statistics:

GP	G	A	TP	+/-	PIM	PP	SH	GW	GT	S	PCT
73	7	21	28	-5	90	0	0	3	0	78	9.0

LAST SEASON

Acquired from Anaheim with Fredrik Olausson for Shawn Antoski and Dmitri Mironov, November 19, 1996. Missed four games with hip pointer. Missed two games with groin injury. Missed one game with bruised leg.

THE FINESSE GAME

Meet Pat Conacher, 10 years ago. After years of slogging through the minors in Toledo and Las Vegas, Hicks has gotten an NHL job and earned it with his intelligence and work ethic.

Hicks drives to the net and gets his goals from his second effort. He has a decent shot but scores mostly from within 10 feet of the net. He excels at goalmouth scrambles. Hicks was a good scorer in the minors, but doesn't have the big-time speed and shot to make a serious splash in the NHL.

He can be used to kill penalties, though he doesn't have great speed. He looks faster because he's always hustling.

THE PHYSICAL GAME

Hicks is strong and sturdy, and never quits trying for the puck along the wall or behind the net. If he had better hands, he could make things happen, but he can stir things up and is a very busy player who can rattle the defense into a bad pass.

THE INTANGIBLES

Hicks will always be on the bubble, but he's a momentum changer who can handle limited shifts on the fourth line and fill in as a penalty killer. He doesn't score many goals, but they tend to be big ones.

PROJECTION

Hicks will probably end up on about 10 NHL teams before his career is over, but he'll always have value as a character role player.

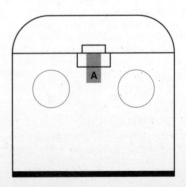

JAROMIR JAGR

Yrs. of NHL service: 7
Born: Kladno, Czechoslovakia; Feb. 15, 1972
Position: right wing
Height: 6-2
Weight: 216
Uniform no.: 68
Shoots: left

Career statistics:

GP	G	A	TP	PIM
504	266	367	633	371

1993-94 statistics:

GP	G	A	TP	+/-	PIM	PP	SH	GW	GT	S	PCT
80	32	67	99	+15	61	9	0	6	2	298	10.7

1994-95 statistics:

GP	G	A	TP	+/-	PIM	PP	SH	GW	GT	S	PCT
48	32	38	70	+23	37	8	3	7	0	192	16.7

1995-96 statistics:

GP	G	A	TP	+/-	PIM	PP	SH	GW	GT	S	PCT
82	62	87	149	+31	96	20	1	12	1	403	15.4

1996-97 statistics:

GP	G	A	TP	+/-	PIM	PP	SH	GW	GT	S	PCT
63	47	48	95	+22	40	11	2	6	1	234	20.1

LAST SEASON

Led team in shooting percentage. Second in team in goals, points and plus-minus. Tied for second on team in game-winning goals and shorthanded goals. Third on team in assists and power-play goals. Missed 19 games with groin injury.

THE FINESSE GAME

Jagr creates a terrible quandary for opposing coaches, because there is simply no defense for him. He can't be shadowed — there is not a player on earth who can stay with him — and when he beats his shadow he creates an odd-man situation. Teams have to concentrate on playing positionally, to try to cut down his passing lanes.

Jagr is as close to a perfect skater as there is in the NHL. He keeps his body centred over his skates, giving him a low centre of gravity and making it very tough for anyone to knock him off the puck. He has a deep knee bend, for quickness and power. His strokes are long and sure, he has control over his body and exceptional lateral mobility. He dazzles with his footwork and handles the puck at high tempo.

He brings sheer joy and a dynamic energy to the game every night. Jagr lives and loves to play hockey. His long hair flowing out from beneath his helmet, he's poetry is motion with his beautifully effortless skating style. Playing with the more defensive-minded Ron Francis as his safety valve last season again gave him even more freedom to freewheel, but the loss of Mario Lemieux will be keenly felt.

With his Lemieux-like reach, Jagr can dangle the puck while he's gliding and swooping. He will fake the backhand and go to his forehand in a flash. He is also powerful enough to drag a defender with him to the net and push off a strong one-handed shot. He has a big slap shot and can drive it on the fly or fire it with a one-timer off a pass.

One of the reasons for Jagr's wicked shots is that he plays with barely legal sticks. He gets them illegally curved on order from the factory, and sharp-eyed opposing coaches should keep a lookout for those he hasn't doctored to NHL specifications.

THE PHYSICAL GAME

Considering how often he gets pounded and how much ice time he logs, Jagr's durability over the past four seasons is remarkable. His physical problems last year were attributed to an ill-fitting skate on his right foot. Earlier in his career, he could be intimidated physically, and he still doesn't like to get hit, but he's not as wimpy as he used to be. He's confident, almost cocky, and he's tough to catch — impossible to hit in open ice.

THE INTANGIBLES

Jagr will have to cope with two major changes in 1997-98. He's been able to carry the team through Lemieux's temporary absences, but now that it's permanent (or seems to be), how will Jagr react emotionally and professionally? And what impact will strict new coach Kevin Constantine have on the country-club Penguins, who have essentially been coaching themselves for years?

PROJECTION

Assuming Jagr can find skates that will cure his nagging groin problems, he's sure to net 90 to 100 points, but the Penguins better get him some help. Fast.

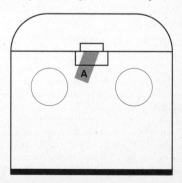

DARIUS KASPARAITIS

Yrs. of NHL service: 5
Born: Elektrenai, Lithuania; Oct. 16, 1972
Position: right defense
Height: 5-10
Weight: 205
Uniform no.: 11
Shoots: left

Career statistics:

GP	G	A	TP	PIM
289	8	56	64	523

1993-94 statistics:

GP	G	A	TP	+/-	PIM	PP	SH	GW	GT	S	PCT
76	1	10	11	-6	142	0	0	0	0	81	1.2

1994-95 statistics:

GP	G	A	TP	+/-	PIM	PP	SH	GW	GT	S	PCT
13	0	1	1	-11	22	0	0	0	0	8	0.0

1995-96 statistics:

GP	G	A	TP	+/-	PIM	PP	SH	GW	GT	S	PCT
46	1	7	8	-12	93	0	0	0	0	34	2.9

1996-97 statistics:

GP	G	A	TP	+/-	PIM	PP	SH	GW	GT	S	PCT
75	2	21	23	+17	100	0	0	0	0	58	3.4

LAST SEASON

Acquired from N.Y. Islanders with Andreas Johansson for Bryan Smolinski, November 17, 1996. Third on team in plus-minus. Missed five games with two concussions.

THE FINESSE GAME

Kasparaitis is a strong, powerful skater and he can accelerate in all directions. You can run but you can't hide from this defenseman, who accepts all challenges. He is aggressive in the neutral zone, sometimes overly so, stepping up to break up a team's attack.

He concentrates mainly on his defensive role, but Kasparaitis has the skills to get more involved in the offense. He will make a sharp outlet pass and then follow up into the play. He also has good offensive instincts, moves the puck well and, if he plays on his off-side, will open up his forehand for the one-timer.

Kasparaitis has infectious enthusiasm, which is an inspiration to the rest of his team. There is a purpose to whatever he does. He's highly competitive.

THE PHYSICAL GAME

Kasparaitis is well on his way to succeeding Ulf Samuelsson as the player most NHLers would like to see run over by a bus. It's always borderline interference with Kasparaitis, who uses his stick liberally, waiting three or four seconds after a victim has gotten rid of the puck to apply the lumber. Cross-check, butt-end, high stick — through the course of a season Kasparaitis will illustrate all of the stick infractions.

His timing isn't always the best, and he has to think about the good of the team rather than indulging his own vendettas.

Kasparaitis is legitimately tough. It doesn't matter whose name is on back of the jersey — Lemieux, Tocchet, McKay, Messier — he will goad the stars and the heavyweights equally. He yaps, too, and is as irritating as a car alarm at 3 a.m.

THE INTANGIBLES

Kasparaitis's grit is badly needed in Pittsburgh, and he should hit it off with new coach Kevin Constantine because of his abrasive style.

PROJECTION

Those two concussions are troubling. Kasparaitis plays the game tough and won't change his style. He's good for 30 points and 100 penalty minutes if he's healthy.

PETR NEDVED

Yrs. of NHL service: 7
Born: Liberec, Czech Republic; Dec. 9, 1971
Position: centre
Height: 6-3
Weight: 195
Uniform no.: 93
Shoots: left

Career statistics:

GP	G	A	TP	PIM
441	158	179	337	320

1993-94 statistics:

GP	G	A	TP	+/-	PIM	PP	SH	GW	GT	S	PCT
19	6	14	20	+2	8	2	0	0	1	63	9.5

1994-95 statistics:

GP	G	A	TP	+/-	PIM	PP	SH	GW	GT	S	PCT
46	11	12	23	-1	26	1	0	3	0	123	8.9

1995-96 statistics:

GP	G	A	TP	+/-	PIM	PP	SH	GW	GT	S	PCT
80	45	54	99	+37	68	8	1	5	1	204	22.1

1996-97 statistics:

GP	G	A	TP	+/-	PIM	PP	SH	GW	GT	S	PCT
74	33	38	71	-2	66	12	3	4	0	189	17.5

LAST SEASON

Led team in shorthanded goals. Second on team in power-play goals and shooting percentage. Fourth on team in points. Missed eight games with wrist injury and charley horse.

THE FINESSE GAME

Tall but slightly built, Nedved can handle the puck well in traffic or in open ice at tempo. He uses his forehand and backhand equally well for a pass or a shot. He sees the ice very well and has a creative mind. He plays his best hockey at left wing with Ron Francis and Jaromir Jagr, though Mario Lemieux took that spot most of last year. It's a dream job for Nedved because Francis is a conscientious two-way player and Jagr opens up a lot of ice.

Nedved makes use of the time and space. He may have the best wrist shot in the NHL, with a hair-trigger release and radar-like accuracy. He likes to go high on the glove side, picking the corner. Although he lacks a big slap shot, he has the vision to handle the power play from the point.

Nedved's drawback is his lack of consistency. He will pay the price occasionally along the boards if he's not the inside man, the guy who will get hit. If there's a chance of contact he generally won't be the first to the puck.

THE PHYSICAL GAME

Good on attacking-zone draws, he knows his way around a face-off. He has good hand quickness and cheats well. On offensive-zone draws, he turns his body so that he's almost facing the boards; he has improved enough to take some defensive-zone draws (probably learning from Francis). That is about it for his defensive contribution, though he can kill penalties because of his quickness and anticipation.

THE INTANGIBLES

Nedved played well in Pittsburgh because he was afraid Mario Lemieux would kill him if he didn't. That's a bit of an exaggeration, but not much. Nedved's point total fell off last season, as expected, and we're skeptical of how long Nedved will last under Kevin Constantine.

PROJECTION

The Penguins need someone to step up big time after Lemieux's retirement, but Nedved is a good-time, not a big-time player. If Pittsburgh can find someone to take him, he's gone.

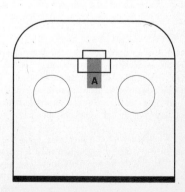

ROMAN OKSIUTA

Yrs. of NHL service: 3
Born: Murmansk, Soviet Union; Aug. 21, 1970
Position: right wing
Height: 6-3
Weight: 229
Uniform no.: 20
Shoots: left

Career statistics:

GP	G	A	TP	PIM
153	46	41	87	100

1993-94 statistics:

GP	G	A	TP	+/-	PIM	PP	SH	GW	GT	S	PCT
10	1	2	3	-1	4	0	0	0	0	18	5.6

1994-95 statistics:

GP	G	A	TP	+/-	PIM	PP	SH	GW	GT	S	PCT
38	16	4	20	-12	10	6	0	1	0	67	23.9

1995-96 statistics:

GP	G	A	TP	+/-	PIM	PP	SH	GW	GT	S	PCT
70	23	28	51	+4	60	11	0	1	0	119	19.3

1996-97 statistics:

GP	G	A	TP	+/-	PIM	PP	SH	GW	GT	S	PCT
35	6	7	13	-16	26	2	0	0	1	58	10.3

LAST SEASON

Acquired from Anaheim for Richard Park, March 18, 1997. Missed two games for personal reasons. Healthy scratch 28 games.

THE FINESSE GAME

Oksiuta has a long reach, and he needs it, because he is slow afoot. He's very powerful on his skates and once he is established in front of the net is extremely tough to budge. He has soft hands and good scoring instincts. He sees the ice well and moves the puck with assurance. The lumbering Russian could truly become a force on the power play because of his size and touch, but he doesn't indicate a consistent level of intensity.

Oksiuta's clunky skating makes him a liability defensively and keeps him from getting any four-on-four time, though he thrives with the open ice on the power play.

While he is outstanding with the puck, he has to work on his game without the puck to be a factor.

THE PHYSICAL GAME

Oksiuta has never been known as a fitness nut, which is why his progress has been minimal. Ron Wilson had a fit with him in Anaheim because Oksiuta failed to pursue proper treatment for a groin injury. He will take a beating but doesn't retaliate or initiate. He needs to keep weight off, to help his mobility.

THE INTANGIBLES

Oksiuta has been on four teams in three seasons; each organization that trades for him thinks their coaches will be the ones to find the key to unlock the "real" Oksiuta. He is a high-maintenance athlete. What he really needs is a coach who will ride herd on him, to make him more professional in his approach to the sport. Some of that has to come from Oksiuta. This may be his last chance to prove that he really wants an NHL job.

PROJECTION

Too tough to call. Oksiuta can score in spurts and look like a 30-goal man, or just as easily look like a minor leaguer.

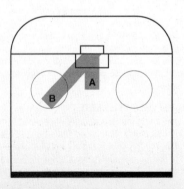

FREDRIK OLAUSSON

Yrs. of NHL service: 11
Born: Dadsejo, Sweden; Oct. 5, 1966
Position: right defense
Height: 6-2
Weight: 195
Uniform no.: 23
Shoots: right

Career statistics:

GP	G	A	TP	PIM
711	106	329	435	296

1993-94 statistics:

GP	G	A	TP	+/-	PIM	PP	SH	GW	GT	S	PCT
73	11	24	35	-7	30	7	0	1	0	126	8.7

1994-95 statistics:

GP	G	A	TP	+/-	PIM	PP	SH	GW	GT	S	PCT
33	0	10	10	-4	20	0	0	0	0	52	0.0

1995-96 statistics:

GP	G	A	TP	+/-	PIM	PP	SH	GW	GT	S	PCT
56	2	22	24	-7	38	1	0	0	0	83	2.4

1996-97 statistics:

GP	G	A	TP	+/-	PIM	PP	SH	GW	GT	S	PCT
71	9	29	38	+16	32	3	0	3	0	110	8.2

PROJECTION

Olausson will be a 30- to 35-point producer.

LAST SEASON

Acquired from Anaheim with Alex Hicks for Shawn Antoski and Dmitri Mironov, November 19, 1996. Second among team defensemen in scoring. Missed nine games with fractured cheekbone.

THE FINESSE GAME

Olausson is a power-play specialist. With the hand skills to cradle the puck when he is heading up-ice, he has decent hockey vision. He plays the right (off) side at full strength and on the power play.

Olausson gambles low on rare occasions, and usually stays at the point to prevent breakouts. He is adept at keeping the puck in at the point.

He has some glaring defensive lapses, though his skating does help him to recover from some of his mistakes. He has pretty good jets, but is more determined on the attack than when backchecking, when he tends to let an opponent go, leaving his defense partner outnumbered.

THE PHYSICAL GAME

Olausson's work ethic is more evident in the attacking zone than in the defensive zone. His physical involvement is minimal.

THE INTANGIBLES

Olausson's stock has dropped rapidly over the past two seasons. He ended the year as a number five or six defenseman for Pittsburgh, and, if the Penguins have any young two-way defensemen who show something in training camp, Olausson could be in jeopardy.

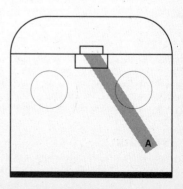

ED OLCZYK

Yrs. of NHL service: 13
Born: Chicago, Ill.; Aug. 16, 1966
Position: centre
Height: 6-1
Weight: 205
Uniform no.: 27
Shoots: left

Career statistics:

GP	G	A	TP	PIM
881	319	424	743	798

1993-94 statistics:

GP	G	A	TP	+/-	PIM	PP	SH	GW	GT	S	PCT
37	3	8	11	-1	28	0	0	1	0	40	7.5

1994-95 statistics:

GP	G	A	TP	+/-	PIM	PP	SH	GW	GT	S	PCT
33	4	9	13	-1	12	2	0	0	0	56	7.1

1995-96 statistics:

GP	G	A	TP	+/-	PIM	PP	SH	GW	GT	S	PCT
51	27	22	49	0	65	16	0	1	0	147	18.4

1996-97 statistics:

GP	G	A	TP	+/-	PIM	PP	SH	GW	GT	S	PCT
79	25	30	55	-14	51	5	1	6	0	195	12.8

PROJECTION

We said in last year's *HSR* that if Olczyk ended up in the right spot, he could be a 60-point scorer again. He did and he will.

LAST SEASON

Acquired from Los Angeles for Glen Murray, March 18, 1997.

THE FINESSE GAME

It's been hard for Olczyk to get playing time in recent seasons, until he signed as a free agent with Los Angeles. He was then traded to Pittsburgh, where he became a number two centre with quality power ice time. Olczyk responded by scoring nearly a point per game (4-7 — 11 in 12 games) after the trade.

Olcyzk doesn't have great speed but he is deceptive, and works hard to get open. He loves to shoot, without being selfish. He can play all three forward positions and brings a centre's playmaking sense to the wing. He is most effective from the left side, from the top of the circle in. Olczyk has a long reach with a fair backhand shot.

Olczyk is at his best on the power play. He likes the extra open ice and is creative. He'll probably inherit some of the ice time left by Mario Lemieux's retirement.

THE PHYSICAL GAME

The reason Olczyk falls out of favour with so many coaches is that he is a big guy who doesn't play big. He fights for the puck, but isn't as determined in his play away from the puck. He will take a hit to make a play, yet he doesn't initiate and isn't strong along the wall.

THE INTANGIBLES

Olczyk is a likable and upbeat guy who will be used on the top two lines in Pittsburgh.

CHRIS TAMER

Yrs. of NHL service: 3
Born: Dearborn, Mich.; Nov. 17, 1970
Position: left defense
Height: 6-2
Weight: 212
Uniform no.: 2
Shoots: left

Career statistics:

GP	G	A	TP	PIM
163	8	14	22	375

1993-94 statistics:

GP	G	A	TP	+/-	PIM	PP	SH	GW	GT	S	PCT
12	0	0	0	+3	9	0	0	0	0	10	0.0

1994-95 statistics:

GP	G	A	TP	+/-	PIM	PP	SH	GW	GT	S	PCT
36	2	0	2	0	82	0	0	0	0	26	7.7

1995-96 statistics:

GP	G	A	TP	+/-	PIM	PP	SH	GW	GT	S	PCT
70	4	10	14	+20	153	0	0	1	0	75	5.3

1996-97 statistics:

GP	G	A	TP	+/-	PIM	PP	SH	GW	GT	S	PCT
45	2	4	6	-25	131	0	1	0	0	56	3.6

LAST SEASON

Second on team in penalty minutes. Missed 33 games with pulled abdominal muscle and hip flexor.

THE FINESSE GAME

Tamer is a conservative, stay-at-home defenseman. He has limited skating and stick skills but is smart enough to stay within his limitations and play a positional game.

Tamer plays a poised game and learned from his mistakes. He does the little things well, chipping a puck off the boards or angling an attacker to the wall. Injuries prevented him from maintaining the progress he showed from his first to second NHL seasons.

Tamer is smart enough when he is shooting from the point to make sure his shot doesn't get blocked. He will take something off his shot, or put it wide so the forwards could attack the puck off the end boards.

THE PHYSICAL GAME

Tamer doesn't nail people, but he has some strength and will use it to push people out of the crease and battle in the corners. He doesn't have a good skating base to be a punishing open-ice hitter. He defends himself or sticks up for a teammate. He doesn't have a serious nasty side, though he is often guilty of late hits.

Tamer is a well-conditioned athlete and can handle a lot of ice time. He kills penalties well and blocks shots.

THE INTANGIBLES

Tamer is a fixture among the team's top four defensemen. He will never be a star, but he gives solid support and can complement a more offensive player. His point production will be low, but he is an intelligent defenseman who will only get better.

PROJECTION

Tamer underwent off-season surgery to correct his abdominal muscle injury. His progress hinges on his recovery.

GARRY VALK

Yrs. of NHL service: 7
Born: Edmonton, Alberta; Nov. 27, 1967
Position: left wing
Height: 6-1
Weight: 205
Uniform no.: 8
Shoots: left

Career statistics:

GP	G	A	TP	PIM
435	67	91	158	537

1993-94 statistics:

GP	G	A	TP	+/-	PIM	PP	SH	GW	GT	S	PCT
78	18	27	45	+8	100	4	1	5	0	165	10.9

1994-95 statistics:

GP	G	A	TP	+/-	PIM	PP	SH	GW	GT	S	PCT
36	3	6	9	-4	34	0	0	0	0	53	5.7

1995-96 statistics:

GP	G	A	TP	+/-	PIM	PP	SH	GW	GT	S	PCT
79	12	12	24	+8	125	1	1	2	0	108	11.1

1996-97 statistics:

GP	G	A	TP	+/-	PIM	PP	SH	GW	GT	S	PCT
70	10	11	21	-8	78	0	0	1	0	100	10.0

PROJECTION

Valk can do an adequate job defensively, but he'll always be pushed for a job.

LAST SEASON

Acquired from Anaheim for J.J. Daigneault, February 21, 1997. Missed four games with rib injury.

THE FINESSE GAME

Not much about Valk's game is pretty, but it is gritty. He is a defensive specialist with a knock-kneed stance (the opposite of the many bowlegged skaters in the league). Through determination, Valk gets to where he has to go. He has a great deal of drive in his skating. He is strong on his skates but not fast.

Very streaky, Valk will go forever without getting a goal, then will pop home several in a week. He goes to the net hard but he doesn't have great hands. Most of his goals come from second and third efforts around the net.

Valk is a defensive forward. He kills penalties well and has good jump forechecking. He keeps himself in excellent physical condition and mentally accepts his role as a checker.

THE PHYSICAL GAME

Valk has a strong work ethic and likes to get out on the ice and provide a spark for his team. He throws his body around with enthusiasm and will get into altercations. He can be very annoying to play against. Nothing Valk does is flashy, but he gets the job done in a blue-collar fashion.

THE INTANGIBLES

Valk has found a niche as a third-line checking forward, with sufficient offensive awareness to score once in a blue moon.

NEIL WILKINSON

Yrs. of NHL service: 8
Born: Selkirk, Man.; Aug. 15, 1967
Position: left defense
Height: 6-3
Weight: 190
Uniform no.: 6
Shoots: right

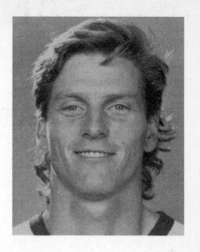

Career statistics:

GP	G	A	TP	PIM
399	14	63	77	755

1993-94 statistics:

GP	G	A	TP	+/-	PIM	PP	SH	GW	GT	S	PCT
72	3	9	12	+2	114	1	0	0	0	72	4.2

1994-95 statistics:

GP	G	A	TP	+/-	PIM	PP	SH	GW	GT	S	PCT
40	1	4	5	-26	75	0	0	0	0	25	4.0

1995-96 statistics:

GP	G	A	TP	+/-	PIM	PP	SH	GW	GT	S	PCT
62	3	14	17	+12	120	0	1	1	0	59	5.1

1996-97 statistics:

GP	G	A	TP	+/-	PIM	PP	SH	GW	GT	S	PCT
23	0	0	0	-12	36	0	0	0	0	16	0.0

LAST SEASON

Missed 42 games with abdominal injury and surgery. Missed nine games with fractured cheekbone.

THE FINESSE GAME

Wilkinson is solid in most areas of the game, though nothing really stands out. He carries the puck but wouldn't be categorized as a rushing defenseman. He will play back, but his defensive reads are in serious need of improvement. He does not complete easy passes and doesn't have much of a shot.

Wilkinson is an average skater and has some difficulty with his foot speed when backskating. He is vulnerable to outside speed. He has to learn to angle his man to the boards.

He has a good attitude and will try anything the coaching staff ask, but he is a high-risk defenseman.

THE PHYSICAL GAME

Wilkinson is tall and gives the impression that he will be more of a bruiser, but he isn't that solid and his checks aren't that jarring. He will play tough and help his teammates. He is not a great fighter but he will give it a go if provoked. Because he isn't a good skater he can't hit a moving target.

THE INTANGIBLES

The Penguins acquired Wilkinson to add some toughness to their lineup, and he figures in among their top four defensemen this season. Last season was kind of a lost one due to injuries.

PROJECTION

Wilkinson will barely scratch double digits in points.

SAN JOSE SHARKS

Players' Statistics 1996-97

POS.	NO.	PLAYER	GP	G	A	PTS	+/-	PIM	PP	SH	GW	GT	S	PCT
R	11	OWEN NOLAN	72	31	32	63	-19	155	10		3	1	225	13.8
C	39	JEFF FRIESEN	82	28	34	62	-8	75	6	2	5	2	200	14.0
C	9	BERNIE NICHOLLS	65	12	33	45	-21	63	2	1		1	137	8.8
L	25	VIKTOR KOZLOV	78	16	25	41	-16	40	4		4		184	8.7
L	21	TONY GRANATO	76	25	15	40	-7	159	5	1	4		231	10.8
C	8	DARREN TURCOTTE	65	16	21	37	-8	16	3	1	4		126	12.7
R	62	ANDREI NAZAROV	60	12	15	27	-4	222	1		1		116	10.3
L	17	*STEPHEN GUOLLA	43	13	8	21	-10	14	2		1	1	81	16.0
D	23	TODD GILL	79		21	21	-20	101					101	
D	4	GREG HAWGOOD	63	6	12	18	-22	69	3			1	83	7.2
D	10	MARCUS RAGNARSSON	69	3	14	17	-18	63	2				57	5.3
D	33	MARTY MCSORLEY	57	4	12	16	-6	186		1	1	1	74	5.4
D	3	DOUG BODGER	81	1	15	16	-14	64			1		96	1.0
R	42	SHEAN DONOVAN	73	9	6	15	-18	42		1			115	7.8
D	43	AL IAFRATE	38	6	9	15	-10	91	3				91	6.6
C	12	RON SUTTER	78	5	7	12	-8	65	1	2	1		78	6.4
L	22	BOB ERREY	66	4	8	12	-5	47					72	5.6
D	44	VLASTIMIL KROUPA	35	2	6	8	-17	12	2		1		24	8.3
D	40	MIKE RATHJE	31		8	8	-1	21					22	
C	16	DODY WOOD	44	3	2	5	-3	193					43	7.0
L	7	VILLE PELTONEN	28	2	3	5	-8		1				35	5.7
L	18	CHRIS TANCILL	25	4		4	-5	8	1				20	20.0
R	19	TIM HUNTER	46		4	4	0	135					13	
L	14	RAY WHITNEY	12		2	2	-6	4					24	
R	36	TODD EWEN	51		2	2	-5	162					22	
D	5	*JASON WIDMER	2		1	1	1							
R	15	*ALEXEI YEGOROV	2		1	1	1							
C	28	IAIN FRASER	2				-1	2						
R	91	*JAN CALOUN	2				-2						3	
G	31	WADE FLAHERTY	7				0							
D	26	CHRIS LIPUMA	8				-2	22					4	
G	20	ED BELFOUR	46				0	34						
G	32	KELLY HRUDEY	48				0							

GP = games played; G = goals; A = assists; PTS = points; +/- = goals-for minus goals-against while player is on ice; PIM = penalties in minutes; PP = power-play goals; SH = shorthanded goals; GW = game-winning goals; GT = game-tying goals; S = no. of shots; PCT = percentage of goals to shots; * = rookie

DOUG BODGER

Yrs. of NHL service: 13
Born: Chemainus, B.C.; June 18, 1966
Position: left defense
Height: 6-2
Weight: 210
Uniform no.: 3
Shoots: left

Career statistics:

GP	G	A	TP	PIM
916	94	399	493	912

1993-94 statistics:

GP	G	A	TP	+/-	PIM	PP	SH	GW	GT	S	PCT
75	7	32	39	+8	76	5	1	1	0	144	4.9

1994-95 statistics:

GP	G	A	TP	+/-	PIM	PP	SH	GW	GT	S	PCT
44	3	17	20	-3	47	2	0	0	0	87	3.4

1995-96 statistics:

GP	G	A	TP	+/-	PIM	PP	SH	GW	GT	S	PCT
73	4	24	28	-24	68	3	0	0	0	121	3.3

1996-97 statistics:

GP	G	A	TP	+/-	PIM	PP	SH	GW	GT	S	PCT
81	1	15	16	-14	64	0	0	1	0	96	1.0

LAST SEASON

Missed one game with flu.

THE FINESSE GAME

Bodger is a smooth skater with good quickness, and he can make tight pivots while carrying the puck. Although age is taking its toll, he remains among the better-skating defensemen in the league. It is Bodger who will collect the puck from the goalie behind the net, let his teammates wheel back and get ready to attack, then move out with the puck. He can either carry up, or feed one of the forwards with a smooth pass and then jump into the play. Bodger sees his passing options well and is very clever with the puck.

Bodger has a big slapper that he keeps down for tips and scrambles in front. He generally takes something off his shot for the forwards in front to work with. His best shot is a one-timer off a feed. Bodger saw second-unit power-play time last season. He has great poise with the puck, and gives his team a sense of control when he is quarterbacking.

THE PHYSICAL GAME

Bodger takes the body when he absolutely must, but he is not by nature a hitter. He has never used his size as well as he should. Because his hand skills are so good, he prefers to position himself and try to poke- or sweep-check. He's a strong one-on-one defender because of his skating, but he will not clear people out from in front of his net as well as he should. He is aggressive stepping up into the neutral zone and challenges on penalty killing as well.

THE INTANGIBLES

Bodger has begun to play less of an offensive role but will help the Sharks develop some of their younger defensemen, even though his role is much reduced.

PROJECTION

Bodger's point totals have fallen off to the 15- to 20-point range and can be expected to stay there.

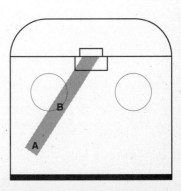

SHAWN BURR

Yrs. of NHL service: 12
Born: Sarnia, Ont.,; July 1, 1966
Position: left wing
Height: 6-1
Weight: 202
Uniform no.: 11
Shoots: left

Career statistics:

GP	G	A	TP	PIM
814	175	250	425	990

1993-94 statistics:

GP	G	A	TP	+/-	PIM	PP	SH	GW	GT	S	PCT
51	10	12	22	+12	31	0	1	1	0	64	15.6

1994-95 statistics:

GP	G	A	TP	+/-	PIM	PP	SH	GW	GT	S	PCT
42	6	8	14	+13	60	0	0	3	0	65	9.2

1995-96 statistics:

GP	G	A	TP	+/-	PIM	PP	SH	GW	GT	S	PCT
81	13	15	28	+4	119	1	0	2	0	122	10.7

1996-97 statistics:

GP	G	A	TP	+/-	PIM	PP	SH	GW	GT	S	PCT
74	14	21	35	+5	106	1	0	3	0	128	10.9

LAST SEASON

Acquired from Tampa Bay for a 1997 fifth-round draft pick. Second on Lightning in plus-minus. Missed eight games with finger injury.

THE FINESSE GAME

Burr is an aggressive forechecker. His skating isn't the best, but he is a diligent enough plugger to stick with all but the fastest NHL forwards. He goes hard to the nets and along the boards, trying to make up with energy what he lacks in acceleration.

Burr is a smart hockey player, which makes him a natural in the defensive role, either as a checker or as the safety valve on a scoring line. He creates turnovers with his aggressive checking, though he lacks the finishing touch to bury his chances. He was a scorer at the junior and minor-league level; that touch has not manifested itself in the majors. Most of Burr's scoring chances come from scrums around the net. His shot scares no one.

Burr is a solid penalty killer who can take defensive-zone draws.

THE PHYSICAL GAME

Burr has to be involved every night, using his muscle along the boards and in front of the net. He makes puck carriers rush their passes because he sticks to them tenaciously. Because he is not a very good skater and has limited range, he does not hit in open ice. He is scrappy, yappy, and can be very annoying to play against.

THE INTANGIBLES

Burr is respected for his honest defensive work despite his lack of production, but he has to bring a lot to the ice when he only scores 10 goals a year.

PROJECTION

Burr will get a lot of ice time with a weak Sharks team but even so, 15 to 20 goals is his max.

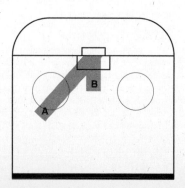

SHEAN DONOVAN

Yrs. of NHL service: 2
Born: Timmins, Ont.; Jan. 22, 1975
Position: right wing
Height: 6-2
Weight: 190
Uniform no.: 42
Shoots: right

Career statistics:

GP	G	A	TP	PIM
161	22	14	36	87

1994-95 statistics:

GP	G	A	TP	+/-	PIM	PP	SH	GW	GT	S	PCT
14	0	0	0	-6	6	0	0	0	0	13	0.0

1995-96 statistics:

GP	G	A	TP	+/-	PIM	PP	SH	GW	GT	S	PCT
74	13	8	21	-17	39	0	1	2	0	73	17.8

1996-97 statistics:

GP	G	A	TP	+/-	PIM	PP	SH	GW	GT	S	PCT
73	9	6	15	-18	42	0	1	0	0	115	7.8

LAST SEASON

Second NHL season. Missed two games with concussion. Missed two games with knee injury.

THE FINESSE GAME

Donovan has big-league speed, but lacks the hand skills to make the best use of it. His quickness and powerful stride allow him to shift directions with agility. And he doesn't waste energy. He knows where he is supposed to be positioned and reads plays well. He has good anticipation, which stamps him as a strong penalty killer, though he is not a real short-handed scoring threat yet because of his lack of moves on a breakaway.

Donovan may never be a great point-getter because of his lack of scoring or playmaking touch. Donovan showed a few lapses in effort last season, which led to a couple of benchings and a short (two-game) stint in the minors. He has a future as a third-line checking winger, but has to become more consistent. He isn't fazed by facing some of the league's better wingers, and has the skating ability to shadow almost anyone.

THE PHYSICAL GAME

Donovan is always busy making hits, and brings a lot of energy to a game when he is in the mood. He doesn't have much of a mean streak, but he showed an occasional willingness to agitate last season; he needs to get under opponents' skin a little more. He takes the body, but doesn't punish people. He is well-conditioned and has good stamina. He doesn't get pushed off the puck easily.

THE INTANGIBLES

Donovan could be another Shawn McEachern unless he is able to capitalize on more of his chances. Of all the players the Sharks have tested for skating speed over the years, Donovan ranks right at the top with noted NHL speedster Mike Gartner. A player with Donovan's kind of speed can have a comfortable, 10-year NHL career, but he'll only be successful if he can add more scoring.

PROJECTION

It's too soon to give up on Donovan. If he can bump his goals up to 15 to 20, he'll be a valuable piece in the San Jose puzzle.

JEFF FRIESEN

Yrs. of NHL service: 3
Born: Meadow Lake, Sask.; Aug. 5, 1976
Position: left wing/centre
Height: 6-0
Weight: 185
Uniform no.: 39
Shoots: left

Career statistics:

GP	G	A	TP	PIM
209	58	75	133	131

1994-95 statistics:

GP	G	A	TP	+/-	PIM	PP	SH	GW	GT	S	PCT
48	15	10	25	-8	14	5	1	2	0	86	17.4

1995-96 statistics:

GP	G	A	TP	+/-	PIM	PP	SH	GW	GT	S	PCT
79	15	31	46	-19	42	2	0	0	0	123	12.2

1996-97 statistics:

GP	G	A	TP	+/-	PIM	PP	SH	GW	GT	S	PCT
82	28	34	62	-8	75	6	2	5	2	200	14.0

LAST SEASON

The only Shark to play in all 82 games. Led team in assists with career high. Led team in game-winning goals and shooting percentage. Tied for team lead in shorthanded goals. Second on team with career highs in goals and points. Second on team in power-play goals.

THE FINESSE GAME

Friesen developed from a pure scorer in junior, to a third-line checking winger as a freshman and sophomore NHLer, to where he is today: one of the youngest first-line centres in the league. Few players in his age group were given as much responsibility as Friesen was last year at age 20 — and responded as handsomely as Friesen did.

Friesen is a fast, strong skater, handles the puck well and has the size to go with those qualities. He is a better finisher than playmaker. Viktor Kozlov, the left-winger who has a future with Friesen and Owen Nolan, is actually the playmaker of the three. Friesen has a quick, strong release on his snap or wrist shot and is shifty with a smooth change of speed. Carrying the puck doesn't slow him down.

Friesen never seems to get rattled or forced into making bad plays. In fact, he's the one who forces opponents into panic moves with his pressure. He draws penalties by keeping his feet moving as he drives to the net or digs for the puck along the boards. He is strong on face-offs.

THE PHYSICAL GAME

Friesen added good weight in the past season, and needs the muscle to handle the checking attention other teams will be assigning him from now on (or until the Sharks concoct a dangerous second line). He doesn't have much of a mean streak, but plays tough

and honest.

THE INTANGIBLES

Friesen is a potential future captain of the Sharks. Tabbed with a lazy label in his junior days, he has matured into a hard-working player who cares. Losing may wear on him if the Sharks don't get better in the next season or two, but we see a great upside to Friesen.

PROJECTION

In last year's *HSR*, we predicted a bounce-back 55- to 60-point season for Friesen, and he delivered. Now it's time to up the ante a bit. Friesen will never be a 100-point scorer, but 70 is surely within his scope.

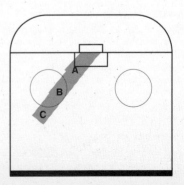

TODD GILL

Yrs. of NHL service: 12
Born: Cardinal, Ont.; Nov. 9, 1965
Position: right defense
Height: 6-0
Weight: 180
Uniform no.: 23
Shoots: left

Career statistics:

GP	G	A	TP	PIM
718	59	229	288	1023

1993-94 statistics:

GP	G	A	TP	+/-	PIM	PP	SH	GW	GT	S	PCT
45	4	23	27	+8	44	2	0	1	0	74	5.4

1994-95 statistics:

GP	G	A	TP	+/-	PIM	PP	SH	GW	GT	S	PCT
47	7	25	32	-8	64	3	1	2	0	82	8.5

1995-96 statistics:

GP	G	A	TP	+/-	PIM	PP	SH	GW	GT	S	PCT
74	7	18	25	-15	116	1	0	2	0	109	6.4

1996-97 statistics:

GP	G	A	TP	+/-	PIM	PP	SH	GW	GT	S	PCT
79	0	21	21	-20	101	0	0	0	0	101	0.0

LAST SEASON

Led team defensemen in scoring. Missed three games with knee injury.

THE FINESSE GAME

Gill is a good number three defenseman being asked to serve as a number one. He's not quite equal to the task, but he gives an honest account of himself every night. He's a gamer, and a player who knows his limitations and seldom tries to do what he can't.

Gill has sufficient offensive skills to get involved in the attack. He has good hockey sense and can do some things with the puck, like making a short, smart pass or taking a well-timed point shot. He doesn't like the puck to linger in his own zone. He'll carry it out and make smart plays. He has faith in his partners and lets them and the puck do the work.

Gill is not afraid to venture deep and use a wrist or snap shot from the left circle. Once in awhile he'll brave the front of the net (though he has to be darned sure when he tries it). He's smart and talented enough to work the point on the power play on the second unit and works on the second penalty-killing unit.

THE PHYSICAL GAME

Gill is a tough defenseman with a ton of heart and spunk. He's on the slight side for an NHL defense-man, and has to be mindful of conditioning and nutrition to keep up with the grind. And grind is what he has to do to be effective. He will drop the gloves and go if he has to, and he stands up for his teammates, taking on the biggest guy on the ice.

THE INTANGIBLES

Being named captain of the Sharks last season was an honour Gill did not take lightly. He's a respected competitor who added stability to the Sharks' blueline and some character to the room. He plays with enthusiasm and intensity on a game-by-game basis.

PROJECTION

Gill's top priority is defense. His top end points-wise is probably 30 points, but that's only if the Sharks improve their overall play this season.

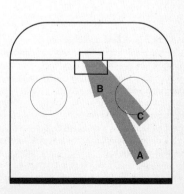

BILL HOULDER

Yrs. of NHL service: 10
Born: Thunder Bay, Ont.; Mar. 11, 1967
Position: left defense
Height: 6-3
Weight: 211
Uniform no.: 2
Shoots: left

Career statistics:

GP	G	A	TP	PIM
372	34	105	139	170

1993-94 statistics:

GP	G	A	TP	+/-	PIM	PP	SH	GW	GT	S	PCT
80	14	25	39	-18	40	3	0	3	0	187	7.5

1994-95 statistics:

GP	G	A	TP	+/-	PIM	PP	SH	GW	GT	S	PCT
41	5	13	18	+16	20	1	0	0	0	59	8.5

1995-96 statistics:

GP	G	A	TP	+/-	PIM	PP	SH	GW	GT	S	PCT
61	5	23	28	+1	22	3	0	0	1	90	5.6

1996-97 statistics:

GP	G	A	TP	+/-	PIM	PP	SH	GW	GT	S	PCT
79	4	21	25	+16	30	0	0	2	0	116	3.4

LAST SEASON

Signed as free agent, July 9, 1997. Led Lightning in plus-minus. Missed three games with wrist injury.

THE FINESSE GAME

Houlder has a big shot, but otherwise his overall skills are average. Although he struggles as a skater, especially in his turns, he has a decent first step to the puck and is strong on his skates.

He makes smart options with his passes. He does not like to carry the puck but is a stay-at-home type who is aware he is limited by his range; he will make a pass to a teammate or chip the puck out along the wall rather than try to carry it past a checker.

Houlder's offensive input is minimal (he can get five to 10 goals a year) and is mostly limited to point shots, though he will get brave once in awhile and gamble to the top of the circle. Most of his goals come from 60 feet out with some traffic in front. He can play on the second units on power play and penalty killing, but is best in five-on-five situations.

THE PHYSICAL GAME

Houlder is a gentle giant. There is always the expectation with bigger players that they will make monster hits, but we have the feeling that a lot of them were big as youngsters and were told by their parents not to go around picking on smaller kids. Houlder is definitely among the big guys who don't hit to hurt. If he did get involved he would be a dominating defenseman, but that's not about to happen at this stage of his career.

He will take out his man with quiet efficiency. He has to angle the attacker to the boards because of his lack of agility. He is vulnerable to outside speed when he doesn't close off the lane.

THE INTANGIBLES

Houlder rates as a reliable fifth or sixth defenseman, but he is a top four in San Jose because of the team's lack of depth. He doesn't have much upside at this stage of his career.

PROJECTION

Houlder will provide solid defense and 20 to 25 points.

KELLY HRUDEY

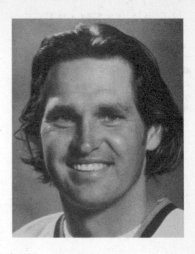

Yrs. of NHL service: 14
Born: Edmonton, Alta,; Jan. 13, 1961
Position: goaltender
Height: 5-10
Weight: 189
Uniform no.: 20
Catches: left

Career statistics:

GP	MIN	GA	SO	GAA	A	PIM
649	36724	2112	16	3.45	17	171

1993-94 statistics:

GP	MIN	GAA	W	L	T	SO	GA	S	SAPCT	PIM
64	3712	3.68	22	31	7	1	228	2219	.897	6

1994-95 statistics:

GP	MIN	GAA	W	L	T	SO	GA	S	SAPCT	PIM
35	1894	3.14	14	13	5	0	99	1099	.910	0

1995-96 statistics:

GP	MIN	GAA	W	L	T	SO	GA	S	SAPCT	PIM
36	2077	3.26	7	15	10	0	113	1214	.907	4

1996-97 statistics:

GP	MIN	GAA	W	L	T	SO	GA	S	SAPCT	PIM
48	2631	3.19	16	24	5	0	140	1263	.889	0

PROJECTION

At press time, Hrudey was the only goalie the Sharks had under contract, after losing Ed Belfour to free agency. He is no longer a number one goalie and San Jose should go all-out to acquire another netminder.

LAST SEASON

Most wins in three seasons.

THE PHYSICAL GAME

It's never helped Hrudey's game that his last two teams, Los Angeles and San Jose, have been among the worst defensive teams in the NHL every year. Even at his best, Hrudey is prone to lapses in discipline, and when 40 to 45 shots a night is routine a goalie can get sloppy.

Hrudey lives by his reflexes. On his worst nights, when he feels he has to stop shots and play defense, he's a sprawling, lunging mess. On wide drives, he will lie down, leaving the short side open for a shot.

Hrudey is aggressive, sometimes overly so, and loves to challenge the shooter. He likes to handle the puck and is fairly adept at it. He's a good athlete and a good skater. He moves confidently out of his net.

Like many of today's goalies, Hrudey puts the paddle of his stick low across the front of his net on wraprounds.

THE MENTAL GAME

Hrudey plays on emotion, and it can be draining when you feel you're doing your utmost but you're still losing on a consistent basis. However, Hrudey stays fairly upbeat. He gets mad and takes it out on an opponent with his stick.

THE INTANGIBLES

Hrudey is 36 and asking for 60 games out of him may be a bit much.

AL IAFRATE

Yrs. of NHL service: 11
Born: Dearborn, Mich.; Mar. 21, 1966
Position: right defense
Height: 6-3
Weight: 235
Uniform no.: 43
Shoots: left

Career statistics:

GP	G	A	TP	PIM
778	150	304	454	1273

1993-94 statistics:

GP	G	A	TP	+/-	PIM	PP	SH	GW	GT	S	PCT
79	15	43	58	+16	163	6	0	4	0	299	5.0

1994-95 statistics:

Did not play in NHL

1995-96 statistics:

Did not play in NHL

1996-97 statistics:

GP	G	A	TP	+/-	PIM	PP	SH	GW	GT	S	PCT
38	6	9	15	-10	91	3	0	0	0	91	6.6

LAST SEASON

Misses 12 games with toe injury and broken toe. Missed 30 games with back surgery.

THE FINESSE GAME

If you really want to know what's going on with Iafrate, don't read the rest of this page. You would do just as well calling a psychic hotline.

Iafrate returned to the NHL after missing two full seasons with injuries. He wasn't quite his old self, but his two best assets, his skating and his scary shot, were suprisingly intact when he was healthy, and the Sharks were 17-17-4 with him in the lineup. His knee injuries have led to his back problems, which forced surgery last season, so again we'll head into this season with question marks about the deterioration of his skills.

Will he still have his big-time slap shot? Can he still leave a defender flat-footed with his skating?

Iafrate can play an all-out offensive game, which is his strength, or settle back and provide some solid defense. He is capable of rushing end to end but is better at jumping up into the play. He moves the puck quickly out of his own zone, often taking it himself. He can stickhandle and uses all of the ice.

Iafrate can play either point on the power play. He has a deadly one-timer. His point shot is intimidating, and he will fake the shot, freeze the defense, then move around for a snap shot (even that hurts when a defender tries to block it) or slide the puck in deep. There isn't much he can't do as far as finesse skills are concerned.

THE PHYSICAL GAME

For a big guy, Iafrate does not hit with much intensity,

and after his back woes will be even less inclined to do so. He does not enjoy the one-on-one battles. He can be a booming open-ice hitter when the spirit moves him, but just as often he will be wiped out along the boards. Of course, his conditioning will be a huge question mark.

THE INTANGIBLES

Iafrate is enthusiastic playing in San Jose, but he is the riskiest of propositions.

PROJECTION

Because of the dearth of defensive talent on the team, San Jose gave Iafrate a one-year contract at U.S.$2 million, hardly a safe investment.

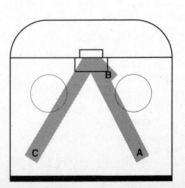

VIKTOR KOZLOV

Yrs. of NHL service: 2
Born: Togliatti, Russia; Feb. 14, 1975
Position: right wing
Height: 6-5
Weight: 225
Uniform no.: 25
Shoots: right

Career statistics:

GP	G	A	TP	PIM
156	24	38	62	48

1994-95 statistics:

GP	G	A	TP	+/-	PIM	PP	SH	GW	GT	S	PCT
16	2	0	2	-5	2	0	0	0	0	23	8.7

1995-96 statistics:

GP	G	A	TP	+/-	PIM	PP	SH	GW	GT	S	PCT
62	6	13	19	-15	6	1	0	0	0	107	5.6

1996-97 statistics:

GP	G	A	TP	+/-	PIM	PP	SH	GW	GT	S	PCT
78	16	25	41	-16	40	4	0	4	0	184	8.7

LAST SEASON

Missed four games with ankle injury. Career highs in goals, assists and points. Tied for second on team in game-winning goals.

THE FINESSE GAME

Kozlov played centre when he started out with the Sharks, and he brings a centre's vision and creativity to the left-wing position he played last season. He's a beautiful skater for his size. He has the moves of a 150-pounder, with quickness and agility. He has learned to come off the boards much quicker. As a huge right-handed shooter attacking the left side, he has a move that — dare we say it? — makes him look like Mario Lemieux. He can undress a defender with his stickhandling and create a scoring chance down low. He has a keen sense of timing and pace.

Unlike Lemieux, however, Kozlov is a reluctant shooter. Playing with Jeff Friesen and Owen Nolan gave him two good finishers as partners, but Kozlov must become more unpredictable, because he possesses an accurate wrist shot.

Kozlov won't float and he has defensive principles. He won't hang at the redline, but is an attentive backchecker. With deceptively quick acceleration for a player of his size, he excels at the transition game.

Kozlov needs to learn to protect the puck better by keeping it closer to his feet. He often makes it too easy for a defender to strip the puck.

THE PHYSICAL GAME

Kozlov's physique makes him sturdy in contact, and when he goes down on a hook or a hold, nine times out of 10 it's a dive.

He has a long reach but doesn't care to play the body defensively, though offensively he will work with the puck to get in front of the net and into scoring position. He handles the puck well in traffic.

THE INTANGIBLES

There wasn't much to get excited about in the Shark tank last season, but Kozlov's progress was one of the few positive developments. The next step will be to see how he handles the checking attention his line will receive this season.

PROJECTION

No reason for Kozlov not to make the jump to 60 points this season if he stays on the top line with Friesen and Nolan. There is good chemistry brewing there.

MARTY MCSORLEY

Yrs. of NHL service: 14
Born: Hamilton, Ont.; May 18, 1963
Position: right defense
Height: 6-1
Weight: 225
Uniform no.: 33
Shoots: right

Career statistics:

GP	G	A	TP	PIM
832	102	235	337	3080

1993-94 statistics:

GP	G	A	TP	+/-	PIM	PP	SH	GW	GT	S	PCT
65	7	24	31	-12	194	1	0	1	1	160	4.4

1994-95 statistics:

GP	G	A	TP	+/-	PIM	PP	SH	GW	GT	S	PCT
41	3	18	21	-14	83	1	0	0	1	75	4.0

1995-96 statistics:

GP	G	A	TP	+/-	PIM	PP	SH	GW	GT	S	PCT
68	10	23	33	-20	169	1	1	1	0	130	7.7

1996-97 statistics:

GP	G	A	TP	+/-	PIM	PP	SH	GW	GT	S	PCT
57	4	12	16	-6	186	0	1	1	1	74	5.4

LAST SEASON

Missed 17 games following hip surgery. Missed eight games with groin injuries.

THE FINESSE GAME

One of the first things you notice about McSorley is his feet. His skates are big and heavy (he has custom-made skates that are more cumbersome than the average player's). Add to that his sluggish skating and you get a player whose rushes can be timed with a calendar.

Despite those drawbacks, McSorley — when healthy — saw prime ice time last season with a woeful Sharks squad. He saw power-play and penalty-killing time and often drew top checking assignments. He works hard and plays a pretty smart game, and has been used almost exclusively on the backline over the past four seasons, though he can go up front on the power play at times.

McSorley's finesse skills are average at best. He does not have good vision of the ice for creative play-making. Unfortunately, every so often he tries to make the fancy play instead of the safe shot; he gets burned because he can't recover quickly defensively. He has to be paired with a mobile defense partner.

THE PHYSICAL GAME

McSorley works hard at his conditioning but couldn't overcome his injuries last season. He has a lot of hockey miles on him.

He also ranks among the best fighters in the league. He does annoying things after the whistle — well after the whistle — such as shooting the puck at the goalie on an offside call or giving an attacker a shove after a save.

THE INTANGIBLES

McSorley's a gritty sort who should have a number five, or six role, but with the Sharks he has to handle more responsibility than he should be given. We can't blame McSorley when he falls short.

PROJECTION

McSorley is a 20-point role player whose health is a continuing question mark.

ANDREI NAZAROV

Yrs. of NHL service: 3
Born: Chelyabinsk, Soviet Union; May 22, 1974
Position: right wing
Height: 6-5
Weight: 230
Uniform no.: 62
Shoots: right

Career statistics:

GP	G	A	TP	PIM
129	22	27	49	378

1993-94 statistics:

GP	G	A	TP	+/-	PIM	PP	SH	GW	GT	S	PCT
1	0	0	0	0	0	0	0	0	0	0	0.0

1994-95 statistics:

GP	G	A	TP	+/-	PIM	PP	SH	GW	GT	S	PCT
26	3	5	8	-1	94	0	0	0	0	19	15.8

1995-96 statistics:

GP	G	A	TP	+/-	PIM	PP	SH	GW	GT	S	PCT
42	7	7	14	-15	62	2	0	1	0	55	12.7

1996-97 statistics:

GP	G	A	TP	+/-	PIM	PP	SH	GW	GT	S	PCT
60	12	15	27	-4	222	1	0	1	0	116	10.3

LAST SEASON

Led team in penalty minutes and plus-minus. Missed 14 games with facial injury. Missed six games with suspension for shoving a linesman.

THE FINESSE GAME

Nazarov isn't overly creative with the puck, but with his size, does he have to be? This giant has decent hand skills around the net, though he does have some trouble fishing out loose pucks from his feet in goal-mouth scrambles, presumably because his head is so far from the ice it's tough to see.

The biggest improvement in Nazarov's game last year was in his skating. He can handle second-line and second-unit power-play time with assurance. Nazarov is not at his best handling the puck for long. He is insecure if forced to rush with it and defenders have a relatively easy time stripping it from him because the puck is so far from his feet. He plops himself in front of the net on power plays and creates a wall that is nearly impossible for the goalie to see around.

Nazarov is smart and understands the game well. He is aware of his limitations and won't try to do too much. He has an obvious love for the game.

THE PHYSICAL GAME

How scary is the spectre of Nazarov? One scout says of him, "He's sick." Nazarov is rattlesnake-mean and he has a short fuse. He will fight anyone, and his long reach makes him tough for even some of the league's best fighters to cope with. He will protect his team-mates. Anyone checked by Nazarov does not get back into the play quickly. He could star in a lot of very ugly highlight tapes.

Nazarov's toughness showed when he suffered a facial injury (including broken bones) and still wanted back in the lineup for the next game. None of his orneriness was lost when he came back from the injury.

THE INTANGIBLES

Nazarov was sent to the minors for a two-game stint in December and came back with the desire to improve to stay in the NHL. His game is still rough, but he took a big step forward last season. He was a Group 2 free agent in the off-season, but the Sharks won't let this big fish get away.

PROJECTION

Continued work on the second line will translate into fatter point totals (40 is a possibility); continued ill temper will mean another 200 PIM season.

OWEN NOLAN

Yrs. of NHL service: 7
Born: Belfast, N. Ireland; Sept. 22, 1971
Position: right wing
Height: 6-1
Weight: 201
Uniform no.: 11
Shoots: right

Career statistics:

GP	G	A	TP	PIM
406	175	169	354	827

1993-94 statistics:

GP	G	A	TP	+/-	PIM	PP	SH	GW	GT	S	PCT
6	2	2	4	+2	8	0	0	0	0	15	13.3

1994-95 statistics:

GP	G	A	TP	+/-	PIM	PP	SH	GW	GT	S	PCT
46	30	19	49	+21	46	13	2	8	0	137	21.9

1995-96 statistics:

GP	G	A	TP	+/-	PIM	PP	SH	GW	GT	S	PCT
81	33	36	69	-33	146	16	1	2	0	207	15.9

1996-97 statistics:

GP	G	A	TP	+/-	PIM	PP	SH	GW	GT	S	PCT
72	31	32	63	-19	155	10	0	3	1	225	13.8

LAST SEASON

Led team in goals, points and power-play goals for second consecutive season. Missed three games with groin injury. Missed four games with ankle injury. Missed two games with shoulder injury. Missed one game with flu.

THE FINESSE GAME

What better indicator of Nolan's confidence in his shot is there than his "called" goal in last year's All-Star game? Nolan rips one-timers from the circle with deadly speed and accuracy — a pure shooter with good hands. His game suffers when he tries to get too fancy and ventures away from a meat-and-potatoes game. When that happens, he holds onto the puck too long and tries to make plays instead of shooting. Nobody knows where Nolan's shot is headed, except Nolan.

He has an amazing knack for letting the puck go at just the right moment. He has a little move in tight to the goal with a forehand to backhand, and around the net he is about as good as anyone in the game.

Nolan is a strong skater with good balance and fair agility. He is quick straight ahead but won't split the defense when carrying the puck. He's better without the puck, driving into open ice for the pass and quick shot. Defensively, he has improved tremendously. Don't let the poor plus-minus deceive you. The Sharks were a terrible defensive team last season.

Nolan played on a huge and hugely impressive line with Jeff Friesen and Viktor Kozlov for part of last season. San Jose is pretty much a one-line team, but if this trio stays intact, they will be one tough line

to stop, especially on the power play.

THE PHYSICAL GAME

Nolan needs to use his body to be effective, but has a nagging shoulder injury that sometimes makes him a little shy about getting involved.

THE INTANGIBLES

Nolan could have gone up or down after the trade from Colorado, but he appears to be moving in a positive direction. He is maturing into a leader; the Sharks giving him an assistant captain's role at midseason was another big step. How Nolan will adjust to a new coach in Darryl Sutter is the only question mark.

PROJECTION

Nolan has the skills and, we believe, the drive to become a 50-goal player. He suffers from San Jose's lack of a talented puck-carrying defenseman (he was traded for the only one they had, Sandis Ozolinsh). He's just 26, and about to come into his own.

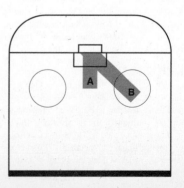

MARCUS RAGNARSSON

Yrs. of NHL service: 2
Born: Ostervala, Sweden; Aug. 13, 1971
Position: left defense
Height: 6-1
Weight: 200
Uniform no.: 10
Shoots: left

Career statistics:

GP	G	A	TP	PIM
140	11	45	56	105

1995-96 statistics:

GP	G	A	TP	+/-	PIM	PP	SH	GW	GT	S	PCT
71	8	31	39	-24	42	4	0	0	0	94	8.5

1996-97 statistics:

GP	G	A	TP	+/-	PIM	PP	SH	GW	GT	S	PCT
69	3	14	17	-18	63	2	0	0	0	57	5.3

LAST SEASON

Second NHL season. Missed two games with leg injury. Missed two games with toe injury.

THE FINESSE GAME

Ragnarsson has a lot of poise, hand skills and skating ability. He has very quick feet and moves the puck well. He makes a good first pass and also makes some good decisions at the blueline to get the puck through.

He controls a lot of the breakout for San Jose and made smart choices in the neutral zone. He was given a lot of responsibility on the power play, and while he is not in the elite class of quarterbacks, he has a decent, if not outstanding, point shot and isn't afraid to shoot. Ragnarsson gets time on the first power-play unit but could benefit from learning from a more skilled point man. The Sharks simply don't have one.

Defensively, Ragnarsson still has some work to do. He uses his body positionally to take up space, but isn't much of a hitter. He will get the puck out in a hurry when he has time but is vulnerable to a strong forecheck.

THE PHYSICAL GAME

Ragnarsson is built solidly and will play a physical game, though finesse is his forte. Oddly, playing alongsize Marty McSorley seemed to make him more tentative instead of braver.

THE INTANGIBLES

The sophomore jinx struck Ragnarsson, who was benched for eight of the first 13 games after a subpar start to his season. How much desire does Ragnarsson have to improve his game? We'll find out this season.

PROJECTION

Ragnarsson showed so much promise in his rookie year that we'll chalk up last season to part of his learning process and predict a 40-point season.

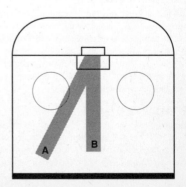

MIKE RATHJE

Yrs. of NHL service: 4
Born: Mannville, Alta.; May 11, 1974
Position: left defense
Height: 6-6
Weight: 220
Uniform no.: 40
Shoots: left

Career statistics:

GP	G	A	TP	PIM
147	3	31	34	123

1993-94 statistics:

GP	G	A	TP	+/-	PIM	PP	SH	GW	GT	S	PCT
47	1	9	10	-9	59	1	0	0	0	30	3.3

1994-95 statistics:

GP	G	A	TP	+/-	PIM	PP	SH	GW	GT	S	PCT
42	2	7	9	-1	29	0	0	0	0	38	5.3

1995-96 statistics:

GP	G	A	TP	+/-	PIM	PP	SH	GW	GT	S	PCT
27	0	7	7	-16	14	0	0	0	0	26	0.0

1996-97 statistics:

GP	G	A	TP	+/-	PIM	PP	SH	GW	GT	S	PCT
31	0	8	8	-1	21	0	0	0	0	22	0.0

LAST SEASON

Missed 51 games with groin surgery and related injuries.

THE FINESSE GAME

Gauging Rathje's performance was difficult because of the limited playing time due to his injuries and surgery, but Rathje finished up strong when he returned to the lineup for the last 15 games of the season.

A stay-at-home defenseman, Rathje is a cornerstone for a new and improved defense. He will become even more effective once he learns to use his reach and eliminate more of the ice.

Rathje has the ability to get involved in the attack but is prized primarily for his defense. He helps get the puck out of the zone quickly. He can either carry the puck out and make a smart headman pass, then follow the play, or make the safe move and chip the puck out along the wall.

Rathje has great poise for a young player. He will probably have to be paired with a more offensive defenseman, though he does a nice job on the right point on the power play. He combines his lateral mobility with a good low shot to get the puck on the net without being blocked. He has to improve his defensive reads, but that should come with experience.

THE PHYSICAL GAME

Rathje has good size and he's adding more muscle. He's only 23, but has built himself up to about 6-5, 220. What Rathje has to learn is controlled aggression. He has a tendency to try to do too much, which is a happier problem than the reverse. He has a little bit of mean in him, and he likes to hit, but he doesn't eliminate as well as he should; he has to concentrate on the takeout instead of the knockout. He has unbelievable strength and good mobility for his size. As he gains confidence in his body after last season's surgery, he should be back to his old physical self.

THE INTANGIBLES

Potential exists for Rathje to step up and prove himself as a blue-chip prospect. Last year was a setback, but there is good buzz about him coming from San Jose and he's due for a big bounce-back season.

PROJECTION

Defensemen take longer to develop than other position players, and Rathje may be a year away yet from becoming one of the Sharks' top two defensemen, but he will be given every opportunity to do so. If he can stay healthy and net 20 to 25 points this season, that will be serious progress.

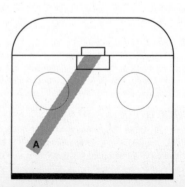

ANDREI ZYUZIN

Yrs. of NHL service: 0
Born: Ufa, Russia; Jan. 21, 1978
Position: left defense
Height: 6-1
Weight: 187
Uniform no.: n.a.
Shoots: left

	Career statistics (Russia):			
GP	G	A	TP	PIM
103	16	13	29	68

	1995-96 statistics (Russia):			
GP	G	A	TP	PIM
41	6	3	9	24

	1996-97 statistics (Russia):			
GP	G	A	TP	PIM
32	7	10	17	28

LAST SEASON

Will be entering first NHL season.

THE FINESSE GAME

Zyuzin is an offensive-minded defenseman with the kind of speed and anticipation that will prevent him from being too much of a liability on defense — because of his ability to recover and position himself.

Zyuzin could well prove to be the kind of player who can dictate the tempo of a game, or break it wide open with one end-to-end rush, a la Brian Leetch. At the moment, he doesn't seem to possess the exceptional lateral movement along the blueline that sets Leetch apart from most of his NHL brethren, but Zyuzin has a big upside.

The young Russian is a fast skater with quick acceleration and balance. He handles the puck well at a high pace and will pass or shoot: a smart playmaker, but one who will not pass up a golden scoring opportunity. He has a hard point shot and will become a good power-play quarterback. Zyuzin is just what San Jose has been missing since the trade of Sandis Ozolinsh.

THE PHYSICAL GAME

Zyuzin is not a physical player. He has adequate size but will need a streak of Chris Chelios-like aggressiveness to make the best use of his ability. Zyuzin does have a desire to excel, and if it means stepping up his game physically he will probably be able to make that transition.

THE INTANGIBLES

Zyuzin has been compared to Ray Bourque, a do-it-all defenseman, but he will need more bulk before he can fulfill those lofty expectations. He will need at least one year's grace in North America (he speaks almost no English) before becoming an impact player. Scouts are high on his character and his drive to be a successful NHLer. Having two other Russians on the team will help his transition.

PROJECTION

Everything is in place for Zyuzin to step in this year except his contract. If that is ironed out, he will be given prime power-play ice time and every chance to produce. Indications are he could be a Calder Trophy contender.

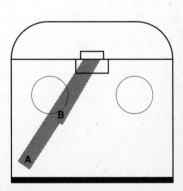

ST. LOUIS BLUES

Players' Statistics 1996-97

POS.	NO.	PLAYER	GP	G	A	PTS	+/-	PIM	PP	SH	GW	GT	S	PCT
C	77	PIERRE TURGEON	78	26	59	85	8	14	5		7	1	216	12.0
R	16	BRETT HULL	77	42	40	82	-9	10	12	2	6	2	302	13.9
L	14	GEOFF COURTNALL	82	17	40	57	3	86	4		2		203	8.4
R	17	JOE MURPHY	75	20	25	45	-1	69	4	1	2	1	151	13.2
R	10	*JIM CAMPBELL	68	23	20	43	3	68	5		6	1	169	13.6
D	2	AL MACINNIS	72	13	30	43	2	65	6	1	1		296	4.4
L	32	STEPHANE MATTEAU	74	16	20	36	11	50	1	2	2		98	16.3
D	44	CHRIS PRONGER	79	11	24	35	15	143	4				147	7.5
C	37	*HARRY YORK	74	14	18	32	1	24	3	1	3		86	16.3
D	5	IGOR KRAVCHUK	82	4	24	28	7	35	1				142	2.8
C	36	ROBERT PETROVICKY	44	7	12	19	2	10			1		54	13.0
R	39	SCOTT PELLERIN	54	8	10	18	12	35		2	2		76	10.5
C	22	CRAIG CONROY	61	6	11	17	0	43			1		74	8.1
D	28	RICARD PERSSON	54	4	8	12	-2	45	1				70	5.7
D	6	*JAMIE RIVERS	15	2	5	7	-4	6	1				9	22.2
C	23	CRAIG MACTAVISH	50	2	5	7	-12	33					26	7.7
L	20	MIKE PELUSO	64	2	5	7	0	226					37	5.4
D	43	*LIBOR ZABRANSKY	34	1	5	6	-1	44			1		26	3.8
L	26	SERGIO MOMESSO	40	1	3	4	-6	48					43	2.3
D	4	MARC BERGEVIN	82		4	4	-9	53					30	
R	38	PAVOL DEMITRA	8	3		3	0	2	2		1		15	20.0
R	26	KONSTANTIN SHAFRANOV	5	2	1	3	1						8	25.0
R	27	STEPHEN LEACH	17	2	1	3	-2	24					33	6.1
R	12	ROB PEARSON	18	1	2	3	-5	37					14	7.1
L	18	TONY TWIST	64	1	2	3	-8	121					21	4.8
D	33	TRENT YAWNEY	39		2	2	2	17					8	
G	31	GRANT FUHR	73		2	2	0	6						
L	13	YURI KHMYLEV	2	1		1	-1	2					3	33.3
R	38	GARY LEEMAN	2		1	1	0						3	
C	21	*JAMAL MAYERS	6		1	1	-3	2					7	
D	42	RORY FITZPATRICK	8		1	1	-4	8					6	
R	15	*ALEXANDER VASILEVSKI	3				-1	2					3	
G	30	JON CASEY	15				0							
D	19	*CHRIS MCALPINE	15				-2	24					3	

GP = games played; G = goals; A = assists; PTS = points; +/- = goals-for minus goals-against while player is on ice; PIM = penalties in minutes; PP = power-play goals; SH = shorthanded goals; GW = game-winning goals; GT = game-tying goals; S = no. of shots; PCT = percentage of goals to shots; * = rookie

JIM CAMPBELL

Yrs. of NHL service: 1
Born: Worcester, Mass.; Apr. 3, 1973
Position: right wing
Height: 6-2
Weight: 185
Uniform no.: 10
Shoots: right

Career statistics:

GP	G	A	TP	PIM
84	25	23	48	104

1995-96 statistics:

GP	G	A	TP	+/-	PIM	PP	SH	GW	GT	S	PCT
16	2	3	5	0	36	1	0	0	0	25	8.0

1996-97 statistics:

GP	G	A	TP	+/-	PIM	PP	SH	GW	GT	S	PCT
68	23	20	43	+3	68	5	0	6	1	169	13.6

LAST SEASON

Calder Trophy finalist. Second among NHL rookies and third on team in goals. Tied for NHL lead among rookies and tied for second on team in game-winning goals. Fourth among NHL rookies in scoring and shooting percentage. Missed 14 games with thumb surgery and related injuries.

THE FINESSE GAME

Campbell has great speed and quickness, with a two-step acceleration that allows him to pull away from checks. He came through the U.S. national program (he was a 1994 Olympian), which has traditionally been a breeding ground for fine skaters. Campbell is no exception.

He has an underrated shot, with very good hand skills. Rather than create anything fancy, he intimidates with his speed and takes advantage of turnovers and loose pucks. He is an opportunistic scorer.

Campbell does not distribute the puck well. He is more of a scorer than a playmaker. Last year, he played on the second power-play unit, behind Brett Hull.

THE PHYSICAL GAME

Campbell doesn't play a very physical game, and this coming year will be a huge indicator as to how big a price he will pay to stay in the NHL. He has good size and has to make a commitment to play bigger. Opponents will start to pay more attention to him now, and he will have to work through it.

THE INTANGIBLES

Like many rookies (and not a few veterans), Campbell struggled with his consistency last year and went nearly a month without a goal in the first half of the season. He could have a career as an average player or take the next step up. He also slowed down at the end of the season, even before the injury took effect.

PROJECTION

Campbell will continue to get ice time on the second line. After filtering through two organizations (Montreal and Anaheim), he realizes this is his chance to establish himself, and a follow-up 20-25 goal season is expected.

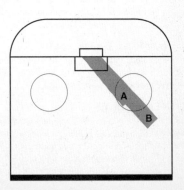

CRAIG CONROY

Yrs. of NHL service: 2
Born: Potsdam, NY; Sept. 4, 1971
Position: centre
Height: 6-2
Weight: 198
Uniform no.: 22
Shoots: right

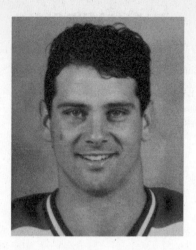

Career statistics:

GP	G	A	TP	PIM
74	7	11	18	45

1994-95 statistics:

GP	G	A	TP	+/-	PIM	PP	SH	GW	GT	S	PCT
6	1	0	1	-1	0	0	0	0	0	4	25.0

1995-96 statistics:

GP	G	A	TP	+/-	PIM	PP	SH	GW	GT	S	PCT
7	0	0	0	-4	2	0	0	0	0	1	0.0

1996-97 statistics:

GP	G	A	TP	+/-	PIM	PP	SH	GW	GT	S	PCT
61	6	11	17	0	43	0	0	1	0	74	8.1

LAST SEASON

Acquired from Montreal with Pierre Turgeon and Rory Fitzpatrick for Shayne Corson, Murray Baron and a fifth-round draft pick, October 29, 1996. Scored 15-12 — 27 in 14 games with Worcester (AHL).

THE FINESSE GAME

Conroy is a determined player who needs a little more confidence in his game to bring out some assets he has yet to display at the NHL level. A numbers man early in his career, he has worked hard at the defensive aspect of the game to become a more well-rounded player.

Conroy kills penalties well, using his speed, size and anticipation. He is a smart player who can make the little hook or hold to slow down an opponent without getting caught. Conroy has quick hands and is good on draws, taking most of the Blues' key defensive-zone face-offs.

Conroy has been a scorer at the college and minor-league levels (he was leading the AHL in scoring when St. Louis obtained him) and is just starting to come into his own. He's reliable in all key situations, defending a lead, in the closing minutes of a period, and killing penalties at crucial times.

THE PHYSICAL GAME

Conroy isn't mean, but he is tough in a quiet way. He uses his size well and accepts checking roles against elite players without being intimidated.

THE INTANGIBLES

Essentially a throw-in in the Turgeon deal, Conroy emerged as a valuable role player in the second half of the season for the Blues. Conroy gave St. Louis a trusted third-line checking centre who could handle the duties of playing against other teams' top lines. He played well in the playoffs against Detroit's skilled Russian unit. He loves the game and will do anything to play. He is malleable and easy to coach.

PROJECTION

Conroy has considerable upside, and after watching less determined Canadiens flounder in the playoffs, it's a wonder Montreal kept him buried in their farm system before letting him go. He has the potential to score 15 to 20 goals in a checking role. Few NHL teams would pass that up.

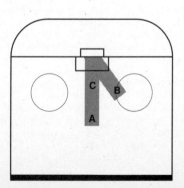

GEOFF COURTNALL

Yrs. of NHL service: 13
Born: Victoria, B.C.; Aug. 18, 1962
Position: left wing
Height: 6-1
Weight: 195
Uniform no.: 14
Shoots: left

Career statistics:

GP	G	A	TP	PIM
939	329	392	721	1339

1993-94 statistics:

GP	G	A	TP	+/-	PIM	PP	SH	GW	GT	S	PCT
82	26	44	70	+15	123	12	1	2	0	264	9.8

1994-95 statistics:

GP	G	A	TP	+/-	PIM	PP	SH	GW	GT	S	PCT
45	16	18	34	+2	81	7	0	1	0	144	11.1

1995-96 statistics:

GP	G	A	TP	+/-	PIM	PP	SH	GW	GT	S	PCT
69	24	16	40	-9	101	7	1	1	2	228	10.5

1996-97 statistics:

GP	G	A	TP	+/-	PIM	PP	SH	GW	GT	S	PCT
82	17	40	57	+3	86	4	0	2	0	203	8.4

LAST SEASON

One of three Blues to appear in all 82 games. Tied for second on team in assists. Third on team in points.

THE FINESSE GAME

Throughout his NHL career, Courtnall has been a streaky scorer. When he's hot he uses a variety of shots to pepper the net. He can score off the backhand, muscle a close-range shot to the top shelf, use a snap shot off the wing on the fly, or wrist in a rebound. He had some of his best games last season on a line with Pierre Turgeon and Brett Hull, but there is no guarantee that the threesome will be together this year.

Courtnall finds the holes and is a textbook give-and-go player. He makes the first pass, burns for the opening, then rips a one-timer from the circle to complete the play. But when he's cold, he's frigid. Courtnall doesn't finish as well as he should for a player with his speed and skill level.

Courtnall has good hands for passing, making especially nice touch passes to breaking teammates on a give-and-go. He has sharp hand-eye coordination to play up front on the power play. He doesn't stand in front of the net to take punishment, but instead times his moves in for deflections with his stick.

THE PHYSICAL GAME

Courtnall is a good-sized forward who has never had much of a physical element to his game. He goes to his stick first when he he's trying to intimidate an opponent or battle along the boards for the puck. He sometimes uses his body, but not consistently. If opponents come at him hard enough early in the game, he mails in the rest of the game. When Courtnall is involved, his forechecking speed is intimidating and he forces turnovers.

THE INTANGIBLES

Consistency continues to elude Courtnall, and the fact that he has the skills to be a 30-goal scorer is very frustrating for coaches. At least he acquitted himself well in the playoffs.

PROJECTION

Courtnall continues to fool us, so we'll drop his estimated goal production to 20 to 25 this season, the lower end if he doesn't get much ice time with Turgeon and Hull.

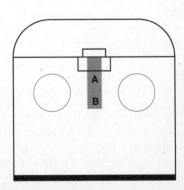

PAVOL DEMITRA

Yrs. of NHL service: 3
Born: Dubnica, Czech; Nov. 29, 1974
Position: left wing
Height: 6-0
Weight: 189
Uniform no.: 38
Shoots: left

Career statistics:

GP	G	A	TP	PIM
67	15	14	29	12

1993-94 statistics:

GP	G	A	TP	+/-	PIM	PP	SH	GW	GT	S	PCT
12	1	1	2	-7	4	1	0	0	0	10	10.0

1994-95 statistics:

GP	G	A	TP	+/-	PIM	PP	SH	GW	GT	S	PCT
16	4	3	7	-4	0	1	0	0	0	21	19.0

1995-96 statistics:

GP	G	A	TP	+/-	PIM	PP	SH	GW	GT	S	PCT
31	7	10	17	-3	6	2	0	1	0	66	10.6

1996-97 statistics:

GP	G	A	TP	+/-	PIM	PP	SH	GW	GT	S	PCT
8	3	0	3	0	2	2	0	1	0	15	20.0

LAST SEASON

Rights acquired for Christer Olsson, November 27, 1996. Signed as a free agent, March 14, 1997.

THE FINESSE GAME

Demitra is a one-dimensional offensive player who spent most of last season in the minors before finding the perfect home with the needy Blues. He has good stick skills and loves to shoot. He can really find the top of the net, especially with his one-timer. He is well-versed at picking the top corners and he can do it at speed.

Demitra is an exceptional puckhandler, and has a quick, deceptive shot. He's not shy about letting the puck go, either — he had seven shots on goal in one game and needs more nights like that. He likes to drag the puck into his skates and then shoot it through a defenseman's legs. The move gets the rearguard to move up a little bit, and Demitra gets it by him on net.

He is actually better on his off (right) wing, and will move to the middle on his forehand and throw the puck back against the grain. Because the Blues are deep on the right side with Brett Hull, Joe Murphy, and Jim Campbell, Demitra will more likely be used on the left side. He needs to improve his explosive speed to build momentum through the neutral zone, and he needs to work on his puck protection skills. Sometimes he exposes the puck too much and what should be a scoring chance for him gets knocked away.

THE PHYSICAL GAME

Demitra is not very big, but he has built up his body, adding 10 to 12 pounds of legitimate muscle weight.

He is much stronger than he was in his first tour of NHL duty with the Ottawa Senators, and is more mature and smarter, too. He needs to use his speed to stay out of situations where he will get crunched. Demitra has a high pain threshold and played in the playoffs with a broken right hand.

THE INTANGIBLES

If he plays on the first two lines, Demitra will get his fair share of goals. If he is used in a checking role, he is not going to fare as well. St. Louis was forced to use him as a centre because of injuries, but Demitra is a gunner and needs to play on the wing. He wants to succeed and appears to be willing to pay the price to stay in the NHL. The Blues are so thin on the left wing that Demitra has a chance at being number one or number two with Geoff Courtnall as his main competition.

PROJECTION

Demitra could be a sleeper, but we don't see many more than 20 goals a season in his future.

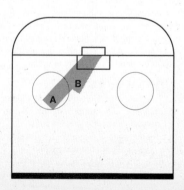

RORY FITZPATRICK

Yrs. of NHL service: 2
Born: Rochester, NY; Jan. 11, 1975
Position: right defense
Height: 6-1
Weight: 205
Uniform no.: 42
Shoots: right

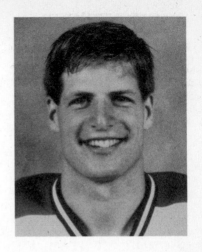

Career statistics:

GP	G	A	TP	PIM
50	0	3	3	26

1995-96 statistics:

GP	G	A	TP	+/-	PIM	PP	SH	GW	GT	S	PCT
42	0	2	2	-7	18	0	0	0	0	31	0.0

1996-97 statistics:

GP	G	A	TP	+/-	PIM	PP	SH	GW	GT	S	PCT
8	0	1	1	-4	8	0	0	0	0	6	0.0

LAST SEASON

Acquired from Montreal with Pierre Turgeon and Craig Conroy for Shayne Corson, Murray Baron and a fifth-round draft pick, October 29, 1996. Scored 4-13 — 17 with 78 penalty minutes in 49 games with Worcester (AHL).

THE FINESSE GAME

Fitzpatrick has the ability to play right or left defense, which is a considerable skill for a young defenseman and underscores his knowledge of the game.

Fitzpatrick's other assets lie in his skill and his willingness to use his talent defensively. He is strong in the corners and along the boards. He moves the puck well, but is more interested in clearing his zone than in getting involved at the other end of the ice.

Fitzpatrick was a captain in junior and will develop a commanding presence on the ice in the NHL in time. He communicates well with his partner and goalie. His defensive reads are well advanced for a player of his experience.

THE PHYSICAL GAME

Fitzpatrick is strong for his age and getting stronger. Think of him as a potential Rod Langway. Fitzpatrick isn't a pugilist, but he is rock-solid and won't be intimidated. He gets in people's faces without getting into scraps. He plays a tough and honest game.

THE INTANGIBLES

Fitzpatrick plays a sturdy, stay-at-home style and will get a long look in training camp as the Blues try to upgrade their defense. Fitzpatrick was slowed by two shoulder injuries last season. If healthy, he could make the jump this year.

PROJECTION

The comparison to Langway is apt. Fitzpatrick's plus-minus will easily outpace his scoring. His contributions will be subtle as he learns to adjust to the NHL.

GRANT FUHR

Yrs. of NHL service: 16
Born: Spruce Grove, Alta.; Sept. 28, 1962
Position: goaltender
Height: 5-9
Weight: 190
Uniform no.: 31
Catches: right

Career statistics:

GP	MIN	GA	SO	GAA	A	PIM
748	42273	2452	20	3.48	44	120

1993-94 statistics:

GP	MIN	GAA	W	L	T	SO	GA	S	SAPCT	PIM
32	1726	3.68	13	12	3	2	106	907	.883	16

1994-95 statistics:

GP	MIN	GAA	W	L	T	SO	GA	S	SAPCT	PIM
17	878	4.03	2	9	3	0	59	464	.873	2

1995-96 statistics:

GP	MIN	GAA	W	L	T	SO	GA	S	SAPCT	PIM
79	4365	2.87	30	28	16	3	209	2157	.903	8

1996-97 statistics:

GP	MIN	GAA	W	L	T	SO	GA	S	SAPCT	PIM
73	4261	2.72	33	27	11	3	193	1940	.901	6

LAST SEASON

Second among NHL goalies in minutes played. Fourth season with 30 or more wins. Tied for fourth in NHL in wins. Missed two games with neck injury.

THE PHYSICAL GAME

Fuhr probably never got enough credit when the Oilers were winning all those Stanley Cups, but now that he has been toiling for a less talented and less successful team in St. Louis, he is finally getting his due. Fuhr was always spectacularly quick, and after dedicating himself to a fitness regimen two seasons ago, his reflexes are that of a goalie 10 years younger. Injuries and age have conspired to slow him down a bit, but Fuhr remains a master at letting a shooter think he has him beaten, and then making the save at the last split-second.

Fuhr is a great skater with outstanding balance. He catches with his right hand, which is disconcerting to some shooters, and his strength is his glove side.

Fuhr recovers well for second shots and is so efficient about it that he never seems to be scrambling or panicky. He controls his rebounds well. He isn't overly active with his stick.

THE MENTAL GAME

Fuhr has always possessed a very laid-back demeanour, and that calmness gives his defense confidence even when he's under siege. But the cool exterior masks a very determined personality. Fuhr maintains his concentration well through screens and scrambles. He doesn't allow many soft goals because his attention doesn't waver.

Fuhr is very smart. He reads plays coming at him

as well as any top defenseman, and is a master of the read and react.

THE INTANGIBLES

Fuhr is still an effective goalie, if not an elite one. The Blues would dearly love to find a trustworthy backup goalie to reduce his workload, because he will be 35 at the start of this season and has to be given a more realistic schedule of 60 games.

PROJECTION

Fuhr could still net 30 wins, but given his expected reduced playing time, 25 is a more likely target.

BRETT HULL

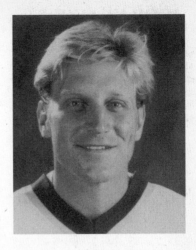

Yrs. of NHL service: 10
Born: Belleville, Ont.; Aug. 9, 1964
Position: right wing
Height: 5-10
Weight: 201
Uniform no.: 16
Shoots: right

Career statistics:

GP	G	A	TP	PIM
735	527	388	915	272

1993-94 statistics:

GP	G	A	TP	+/-	PIM	PP	SH	GW	GT	S	PCT
81	57	40	97	-3	38	25	3	6	1	392	14.5

1994-95 statistics:

GP	G	A	TP	+/-	PIM	PP	SH	GW	GT	S	PCT
48	29	21	50	+13	10	9	3	6	0	200	14.5

1995-96 statistics:

GP	G	A	TP	+/-	PIM	PP	SH	GW	GT	S	PCT
70	43	40	83	+4	30	16	5	6	0	327	13.1

1996-97 statistics:

GP	G	A	TP	+/-	PIM	PP	SH	GW	GT	S	PCT
77	42	40	82	-9	10	12	2	6	2	302	13.9

LAST SEASON

Scored 500th NHL goal. Led team in goals and power-play goals for fourth consecutive season. Led team in shots. Second on team in assists and points. Tied for second on team in game-winning goals. Missed four games with groin injury.

THE FINESSE GAME

Few players win a showdown with a coach, especially one as powerful and well-paid as Mike Keenan. The pressure on a player to produce after winning such a war is tremendous, but Hull got even better after Keenan left town and it's no small coincidence that Hull's 500th goal was scored three days after Keenan's ouster.

Hull was supposed to wear down late in the season because of World Cup fatigue, but instead he got stronger. Except for a recurrence of his groin problem, he was strong through the finish of the season and the playoffs.

Hull's overall game continues to improve, and he was obviously happy with the arrival of the playmaking Pierre Turgeon. Hull plays well in all three zones, but he'll never be mistaken for Doug Gilmour, because he is a shooter first. His shot is seldom blocked because he gets it away so quickly that the defense doesn't have time to react. Hull's shots have tremendous velocity, especially his one-timers from the tops of the circles in.

Hull is always working to get himself in position for a pass, but he doesn't look like he's working. He sort of drifts into open ice and before a defender can react, he is firing off any kind of shot accurately. He usually moves to his off-wing on the power play. Hull was used briefly on the point on the power play last season but is a better asset down low.

Hull is an underrated playmaker who can thread a pass through traffic right onto the tape of a teammate. He will find the open man because he has soft hands and good vision. When the opponent overplays him, he makes smart decisions about whether to shoot or pass. He has become a serviceable penalty killer as well and is a shorthanded threat.

THE PHYSICAL GAME

Hull is compact and when he wants to hit, it's a solid check. He is not as physically involved as he was when he was scoring goals at an absurd rate, but he will bump people. His conditioning has improved, and he routinely plays up to 30 minutes a game.

THE INTANGIBLES

Hull might not be the prototypical team leader, but once he's on the ice, he's as competitive as any of the elite players. His performance in the World Cup was dazzling. Too bad he won't have as talented a group around him with the Blues.

PROJECTION

In last year's *HSR*, we said Hull wouldn't score 86 points again. He didn't, but that's only because he missed five games and the first quarter of the season was wasted sulking under the Keenan regime. With a healthy Turgeon, Hull could get back into the 100-point neighbourhood.

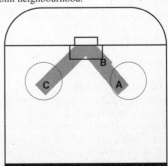

IGOR KRAVCHUK

Yrs. of NHL service: 5
Born: Ufa, Russia; Sept. 13, 1966
Position: right defense
Height: 6-1
Weight: 200
Uniform no.: 5
Shoots: left

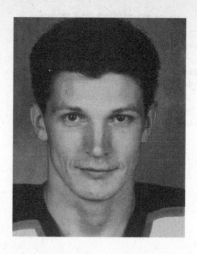

Career statistics:

GP	G	A	TP	PIM
338	41	114	155	150

1993-94 statistics:

GP	G	A	TP	+/-	PIM	PP	SH	GW	GT	S	PCT
81	12	38	50	-12	16	5	0	2	0	197	6.1

1994-95 statistics:

GP	G	A	TP	+/-	PIM	PP	SH	GW	GT	S	PCT
36	7	11	18	-15	29	3	1	0	0	93	7.5

1995-96 statistics:

GP	G	A	TP	+/-	PIM	PP	SH	GW	GT	S	PCT
66	7	16	23	-19	34	3	0	1	0	173	4.0

1996-97 statistics:

GP	G	A	TP	+/-	PIM	PP	SH	GW	GT	S	PCT
82	4	24	28	+7	35	1	0	0	0	142	2.8

LAST SEASON

One of three Blues to appear in all 82 games.

THE FINESSE GAME

Kravchuk is a big defenseman who does a lot of little things well. There is no one facet of his game that stands out from the rest, but there are no serious flaws, either. Kravchuk's skills are subtle. He has good offensive instincts, but his sound defensive game is the basis for his world-class skills.

An exceptionally mobile skater, Kravchuk can pivot like a figure skater with the puck and accelerate quickly. He likes to jump into the play and keep the puck moving. He sees the ice well. He is able to carry the puck out of the defensive zone to alleviate pressure on his goalie. St. Louis goalie Grant Fuhr does not handle the puck much, and Kravchuk is quick to help out around the net. But he will sometimes make a mistake in joining the rush too soon, and he often gets caught when there's a turnover. He has become less aggressive offensively.

Kravchuk will freeze a defenseman with a fake slap shot before sliding a pass down low. He can also fire, and he has the moves to beat a defender in open ice. He's an intelligent penalty killer and utilizes his skating well. He is strong in four-on-four team play.

THE PHYSICAL GAME

Kravchuk has some strength but he is a pusher, not a hitter. He will tie up his man in front of the net, or lean with his stick on top of an opponent's to keep that player from doing something with the puck, but Kravchuk won't wipe anyone out. It won't hurt to keep him paired with a more physical partner.

THE INTANGIBLES

Kravchuk suffered torn rib cartilage in the playoffs, but the injury is not expected to affect him this season.

PROJECTION

Kravchuk would be a strong number five defenseman on a better team. He's a three or four with St. Louis, and sometimes has to overdo. He has the skills to get involved more offensively, but his game has become strongly weighted on defense.

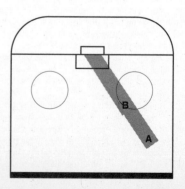

AL MACINNIS

Yrs. of NHL service: 15
Born: Inverness, N.S.; July 11, 1963
Position: right defense
Height: 6-2
Weight: 196
Uniform no.: 2
Shoots: right

Career statistics:

GP	G	A	TP	PIM
989	251	703	954	1149

1993-94 statistics:

GP	G	A	TP	+/-	PIM	PP	SH	GW	GT	S	PCT
75	28	54	82	+35	95	12	1	5	0	324	8.6

1994-95 statistics:

GP	G	A	TP	+/-	PIM	PP	SH	GW	GT	S	PCT
32	8	20	28	+19	43	2	0	0	0	110	7.3

1995-96 statistics:

GP	G	A	TP	+/-	PIM	PP	SH	GW	GT	S	PCT
82	17	44	61	+5	88	9	1	1	1	317	5.4

1996-97 statistics:

GP	G	A	TP	+/-	PIM	PP	SH	GW	GT	S	PCT
72	13	30	43	+2	65	6	1	1	0	296	4.4

LAST SEASON

Led team defensemen in scoring. Tied for seventh among NHL defensemen in goals. Second on team in shots and power-play goals. Missed nine games with shoulder injury.

THE FINESSE GAME

What makes his shot so good is that MacInnis knows the value of a change-up, and he won't always fire with the same velocity. If there is traffic in front, he will take a little off his shot to make it more tippable (and so he doesn't break too many teammates' ankles). One-on-one, of course, MacInnis will fire the laser and can just about knock a goalie into the net.

MacInnis knows when to jump into the play and when to back off. He can start a rush with a rink-wide pass, then be quick enough to burst up-ice and be in position for a return pass. Because his shot is such a formidable weapon, he can freeze the opposition by faking a big windup, then quickly dish a pass in low to an open teammate. Even when he merely rings the puck off the boards, he's a threat, since there is so much on the shot the goaltender has to be careful to stop it.

MacInnis skates well with the puck. He is not very mobile, but he gets up to speed in a few strides and can hit his outside speed to beat a defender one-on-one. He will gamble and is best paired with a defensively alert partner, though he has improved his defensive play and is very smart against a two-on-one.

THE PHYSICAL GAME

MacInnis will use his finesse skills in a defensive posture, always looking for the counterattack. He reads defenses alertly, and positions himself to tie up attackers rather than try to knock them down. He gets caught fishing for the puck instead of taking the body, an especially dangerous habit at his own blueline. In his own way, he is a tough competitor who will pay the price to win. After one healthy season, MacInnis reinjured his surgically repaired shoulder, an injury that bears watching.

THE INTANGIBLES

MacInnis is one of the elder statesmen who should stick around while the Blues continue to rebuild with younger talent. He is still one of the best offensive defensemen in the game and is helping with Chris Pronger's growth. Along with Brett Hull, MacInnis was one of the happier Blues when Mike Keenan departed.

PROJECTION

At 34, MacInnis won't be among the league leaders in defense scoring, and it's unlikely he'll improve much over his point totals from last season.

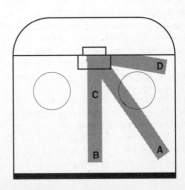

STEPHANE MATTEAU

Yrs. of NHL service: 6
Born: Rouyn-Noranda, Que.; Sept. 2, 1969
Position: left wing
Height: 6-3
Weight: 215
Uniform no.: 32
Shoots: left

Career statistics:

GP	G	A	TP	PIM
451	85	104	189	474

1993-94 statistics:

GP	G	A	TP	+/-	PIM	PP	SH	GW	GT	S	PCT
77	19	19	38	+15	57	3	0	2	1	135	14.1

1994-95 statistics:

GP	G	A	TP	+/-	PIM	PP	SH	GW	GT	S	PCT
41	3	5	8	-8	25	0	0	0	0	37	8.1

1995-96 statistics:

GP	G	A	TP	+/-	PIM	PP	SH	GW	GT	S	PCT
78	11	15	26	-8	87	4	0	2	1	109	10.1

1996-97 statistics:

GP	G	A	TP	+/-	PIM	PP	SH	GW	GT	S	PCT
74	16	20	36	+11	50	1	2	2	0	98	16.3

LAST SEASON

Led team in shooting percentage.

THE FINESSE GAME

Matteau has never clearly defined himself as a physical player or an offensive player, which means he's inconsistent even in his inconsistency. It's the kind of dilemma that drives coaches batty, and it should be Matteau's ticket out of St. Louis as soon as his pal Mike Keenan lands another NHL coaching job. Keenan develops inexplicable loyalties to some players, and Matteau is one of his guys.

Matteau's most valuable asset is his ability to get to the boards, hurry a defenseman into a turnover, then get to the front of the net for a deflection or to set a screen. The problem is, you might see that play out of him once in a game, then maybe not again for a week or more. He is mentally fragile. He gets down on himself, which leads to catastrophic slumps. Some players need a pat on the back, some need a kick in the pants. Matteau needs both at different times.

Matteau is not going to overpower goalies with many shots. His goals come from short range — rebounds, deflections, backhands, wraparounds — which explains his high shooting percentage. More often, though, he's the player causing a distraction and getting cross-checked while a teammate converts the garbage. He shows good hustle and works hard to get into scoring position in front of the net, but he doesn't have the touch to finish off the play. When he wants to, he will skate through a check. Too often, it takes too little to stop his legs. He's got a big reach and is reasonably quick with the puck.

THE PHYSICAL GAME

Matteau is big enough to make himself useful, strong enough to make himself a force, fast enough to be intimidating, but he's also inconsistent enough to make you understand why so many teams have given up on him.

He finishes his checks, hard at times, but tends to use his size in more subtle ways. He makes the defenseman tie him up in front of the net, which leaves openings down low for teammates. He does a decent job along the boards, shielding the puck and kicking it to his stick.

THE INTANGIBLES

Matteau is supposed to be Mr. Spring, but he's had three straight nonproductive playoffs. He should be with another team soon.

PROJECTION

A limited role, and no more than 10 to 15 goals.

JOE MURPHY

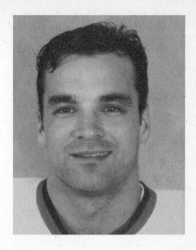

Yrs. of NHL service: 10
Born: London, Ont.; Oct. 16, 1967
Position: right wing
Height: 6-1
Weight: 190
Uniform no.: 17
Shoots: left

Career statistics:

GP	G	A	TP	PIM
597	186	203	389	587

1993-94 statistics:

GP	G	A	TP	+/-	PIM	PP	SH	GW	GT	S	PCT
81	31	39	70	+1	111	7	4	4	0	222	14.0

1994-95 statistics:

GP	G	A	TP	+/-	PIM	PP	SH	GW	GT	S	PCT
40	23	18	41	+7	89	7	0	3	0	120	19.2

1995-96 statistics:

GP	G	A	TP	+/-	PIM	PP	SH	GW	GT	S	PCT
70	22	29	51	-3	86	8	0	3	0	212	10.4

1996-97 statistics:

GP	G	A	TP	+/-	PIM	PP	SH	GW	GT	S	PCT
75	20	25	45	-1	69	4	1	2	1	151	13.2

LAST SEASON

Fourth on team in scoring. Missed five games with virus. Missed one game with groin strain.

THE FINESSE GAME

Murphy will have teasing spurts when coaches begin to daydream about what he could deliver on a team night after night, but inconsistency has been the hallmark of Murphy's career and nothing changed after he signed a lucrative free-agent contract with the Blues last year.

Murphy can be dangerous. He is a goal scorer, and when he's on his game there aren't many better. He has an explosive burst of speed and can take the puck to the net. He has great hands. He is creative off the forecheck and has confidence with the puck. He is sometimes too selfish and single-minded when he has made the decision to shoot, even when a better option to pass suddenly presents itself. He needs a pivot who can get him the puck at the right times, but the Blues don't have anyone behind Pierre Turgeon — Brett Hull's centreman — to fill that role.

Murphy has a lot of zip on his slap and wrist shots. He gets both away quickly and through a crowd, and he's been a high-percentage shooter through much of his career.

THE PHYSICAL GAME

Murphy makes preemptive hits when going for the puck in the corners — which is a nice way of saying he picks and interferes. He will use his size and strength in front of the net to establish position, and he'll fight along the wall and in the corners. He's not a big banger or crasher, but he does have a nasty streak.

THE INTANGIBLES

The Blues would love to unload Murphy, who has two years remaining for more than $7 million, but they got themselves into this mess by overpaying for him in the first place and they're stuck. He's not a total stiff. Murphy will have his moments of brilliance but consistency has never been his strong suit. He has the ability to notch 30 to 35 goals, but he has never done it in 10 NHL seasons. He has a knack for scoring the occasional big goal (he has four overtime winners in the playoffs). He's always a potential game-breaker, but the key to Murphy is "potential," and he's never fulfilled his.

PROJECTION

A 20-goal season, with the skill level for twice that number.

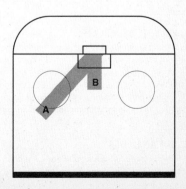

SCOTT PELLERIN

Yrs. of NHL service: 4
Born: Shediac, N.B.; Jan. 9, 1970
Position: right wing
Height: 5-11
Weight: 195
Uniform no.: 39
Shoots: left

Career statistics:

GP	G	A	TP	PIM
106	20	22	42	78

1993-94 statistics:

GP	G	A	TP	+/-	PIM	PP	SH	GW	GT	S	PCT
1	0	0	0	0	2	0	0	0	0	0	0.0

1994-95 statistics:

P	G	A	TP	+/-	PIM	PP	SH	GW	GT	S	PC
				Did not play in NHL							

1995-96 statistics:

GP	G	A	TP	+/-	PIM	PP	SH	GW	GT	S	PCT
6	2	1	3	+1	0	0	0	0	0	9	2.2

1996-97 statistics:

GP	G	A	TP	+/-	PIM	PP	SH	GW	GT	S	PCT
54	8	10	18	+12	35	0	2	2	0	76	10.5

LAST SEASON

Signed as a free agent, July 10, 1996. Second on team in plus-minus. Scored 10-16 — 26 in 24 games with Worcester (AHL).

THE FINESSE GAME

Pellerin was a Hobey Baker Award winner as the top U.S. collegiate player with the University of Maine in 1992, and shares the traits most often associated with those so honoured — quickness, intelligence and decent hand skills.

Pellerin worked well with Craig Conroy, a player of similar style and temperament, on the Blues' third line, handling most of the first-unit power-play responsibilities.

Pellerin is a heart-and-soul guy who gives you everything he has. Offensively, his biggest asset is his playmaking ability. He was a scorer at the college and minor-league levels, and has a fairly good touch with the pucks, though his shot isn't quick enough by NHL standards.

THE PHYSICAL GAME

Pellerin is small but stocky, and size is never an issue with him. He plays the same way all the time against opponents both large and small. He's feisty and won't be intimidated. He is a sturdy skater who is hard to knock off his feet. He can handle a lot of ice time. Pellerin usually ends up with the most hits in a game for the Blues.

THE INTANGIBLES

Pellerin was lost in the deep New Jersey system, but always showed up with a big effort when he did get a chance to play at the major-league level. Getting new life with the St. Louis organization at age 26 was not lost on Pellerin, who gives an honest effort every night and was one of the Blues' most consistent forwards last season.

PROJECTION

Pellerin is a favorite of new coach Joel Quenneville and will get prime checking time against other teams' top lines. He won't score much at this level — 15 to 20 goals would be huge — but he has a knack for scoring at the right time.

CHRIS PRONGER

Yrs. of NHL service: 4
Born: Dryden, Ont.; Oct. 10, 1974
Position: left defense
Height: 6-5
Weight: 220
Uniform no.: 44
Shoots: left

Career statistics:

GP	G	A	TP	PIM
281	28	77	104	335

1993-94 statistics:

GP	G	A	TP	+/-	PIM	PP	SH	GW	GT	S	PCT
81	5	25	30	-3	113	2	0	0	0	174	2.9

1994-95 statistics:

GP	G	A	TP	+/-	PIM	PP	SH	GW	GT	S	PCT
43	5	9	14	-12	54	3	0	1	0	94	5.3

1995-96 statistics:

GP	G	A	TP	+/-	PIM	PP	SH	GW	GT	S	PCT
78	7	18	25	-18	110	3	1	1	0	138	5.1

1996-97 statistics:

GP	G	A	TP	+/-	PIM	PP	SH	GW	GT	S	PCT
79	11	25	35	+15	143	4	0	0	0	147	7.5

LAST SEASON

Second among team defensemen in scoring. Led team in plus-minus. Missed three games with thumb injury.

THE FINESSE GAME

Pronger has been touted as a young Larry Robinson, and although he has a long way and a handful of Stanley Cup rings to go before he can live up to that comparison, there are similarities in their physique and style. Pronger is lanky, almost weedy, with a powerful skating stride for angling his man to the boards for a take-out. He blends his physical play with good offensive instincts and skills.

Pronger also handles the puck well when skating and is always alert for passing opportunities. His vision shows in his work on the power play. He patrols the point smartly, using a low, tippable shot. Like many tall defensemen, Pronger doesn't get his slap shot away quickly, but he compensates with a snap shot that he uses liberally. He has good enough hands for a big guy that the Blues occasionally use him in front of the net on the power play.

Pronger not only jumps into the rush, he knows when to, which is an art. He'll back off if the opportunity is not there. The club has been encouraging him to participate on offense more and, playing with Al MacInnis, one of the game's great offensive defensemen, has helped Pronger in this area. He makes unique plays that make him stand out, great breakout passes and clever feeds through the neutral zone. He is also wise enough to dump-and-chase rather than hold onto the puck and force a low-percentage pass. Pronger focuses more on his defensive role, but there is a considerable upside to his offense.

Disciplined away from the puck and alert defen-sively, Pronger shows good anticipation, going where the puck is headed before it's shot there. He is very confident with the puck in his own end. His defensive reads are excellent for such a young player.

THE PHYSICAL GAME

Pronger will finish every check with enthusiasm, and shows something of a nasty streak with his stick. He makes his stand between the blueline and the top of the circle, forcing the forward to react. His long reach helps to make that style effective. He also uses his stick and reach when killing penalties. Pronger averages 25 to 32 minutes a game and doesn't mind it at all.

THE INTANGIBLES

Pronger has continued to get better every season, and in last year's playoffs was as good a defenseman as there was in the NHL. At this rate of improvement, Pronger will start getting notices as a Norris Trophy candidate in a season or two. He is maturing and realizing his leadership abilities.

PROJECTION

Pronger is a step away from becoming an elite defenseman. Although he benefited from Mike Keenan's coaching, he made a successful adjustment to the coaching change. Joel Quenneville, an ex-defenseman, can help Pronger continue to progress. Look for a 40- to 45-point season.

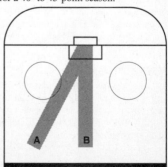

JAMIE RIVERS

Yrs. of NHL service: 1
Born: Ottawa, Ont.; March 16, 1975
Position: defense
Height: 6-0
Weight: 190
Uniform no.: 6
Shoots: left

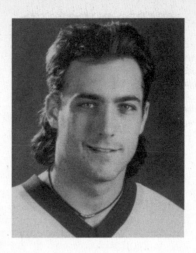

Career statistics:

GP	G	A	TP	PIM
18	2	5	7	8

1995-96 statistics:

GP	G	A	TP	+/-	PIM	PP	SH	GW	GT	S	PCT
3	0	0	0	-1	2	0	0	0	0	5	0.0

1996-97 statistics:

GP	G	A	TP	+/-	PIM	PP	SH	GW	GT	S	PCT
15	2	5	7	-4	6	1	0	0	0	9	22.2

LAST SEASON

Will be entering first NHL season. Scored 8-35 — 43 in 63 games with Worcester (AHL), leading team defensemen in scoring.

THE FINESSE GAME

Rivers has had two seasons of seasoning in the minors, and has thus far shown an in-between style and physique that makes him difficult to read. He's not real fast, but not too slow. Not real big, but not too small. Not super tough, but not a wimp.

There is no doubt Rivers has a big-league shot. It is low, hard and accurate from the left point, and he shoots off the pass with a fine one-timer. He skates well with the puck. He starts his team on the attack and is an accurate passer. He reads plays well offensively but has to be more intelligent about when to jump into the attack and when to back off. When he was a young teenager, there were whispers that Rivers would be the next Bobby Orr, but as other players around him matured and got quicker, his talent levelled off. Rivers's lack of foot speed hurts him, because he's not big enough to get away from stick checks and not fast enough to elude the first forechecker.

Rivers played some forward in junior, evidence of his hockey sense and hand skills. He has some defensive weaknesses, not unusual for a young player who has relied on his scoring. He is inconsistent in his defensive play, trying to make the high-risk plays up the middle in his own end.

THE PHYSICAL GAME

Rivers was a skinny, small-boned kid, and he's had to work hard to make his body big enough to play. Improvement in this department will be necessary before he wins an NHL job. Rivers won't be intimidated and has a quiet toughness to him.

THE INTANGIBLES

Rivers is an offensive defenseman who will be on the bubble unless his skating improves.

PROJECTION

If he does make the team and become a full-timer, Rivers will get second-unit power-play time. He could be expected to contribute 30 to 35 points.

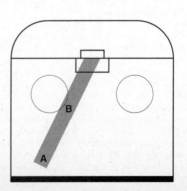

DARREN TURCOTTE

Yrs. of NHL service: 8
Born: Boston, Mass.; Mar. 2, 1968
Position: centre
Height: 6-0
Weight: 178
Uniform no.: 8
Shoots: left

Career statistics:

GP	G	A	TP	PIM
524	179	204	383	255

1993-94 statistics:

GP	G	A	TP	+/-	PIM	PP	SH	GW	GT	S	PCT
32	4	15	19	-13	17	0	0	0	0	60	6.7

1994-95 statistics:

GP	G	A	TP	+/-	PIM	PP	SH	GW	GT	S	PCT
47	17	18	35	+1	22	3	1	3	0	121	14.0

1995-96 statistics:

GP	G	A	TP	+/-	PIM	PP	SH	GW	GT	S	PCT
68	22	21	43	+5	30	2	1	4	0	167	13.2

1996-97 statistics:

GP	G	A	TP	+/-	PIM	PP	SH	GW	GT	S	PCT
65	16	21	37	-8	16	3	1	4	0	126	12.7

LAST SEASON

Acquired from San Jose for Stephane Matteau, July 25, 1997. Missed 13 games with punctured eardrum. Missed three games with knee injury. Missed one game with flu. Tied for second on team in game-winning goals.

THE FINESSE GAME

Back in elementary school, one memorable health class film contained the warning, "Never put anything bigger than your elbow in your ear." Apparently, Turcotte was absent that day, because he missed 13 games this season with one of the weirdest injuries of the year: he punctured his eardrum with a cotton swab. The injury affected his balance, and balance is the key to Turcotte's contribution to a team. He does a little bit of everything.

Turcotte is much better on special teams than at even strength, though he is a capable five-on-five player. With the extra open ice — even when his team is shorthanded — he makes things happen. He's a fine skater who appears to hover over the ice. He takes long, fluid strides that cover a lot of territory, and creates space with his speed, driving the defenders back and daring them to come up to challenge him.

Turcotte kills penalties aggressively. He forces the play and when he gets a turnover he springs down-ice on a break. He makes point men nervous, and teams who use forwards at the point are especially vulnerable to his pressure.

On the power play, Turcotte works down low but can drop back to handle the point if the defenseman comes in deep. He has a fine snap shot, as well as a good wrister and one-timer. He has sharp hand-eye coordination and is skilled on draws. He's a centre who prefers to shoot rather than pass.

THE PHYSICAL GAME

Turcotte will take a hit to make a play but he's not a physical player. He goes into traffic with the puck and has the hand skills to control the puck in a crowd.

THE INTANGIBLES

Turcotte didn't show much last season and the Blues became his fifth team in the last four seasons, giving him yet another fresh start. There is little chance he'll get playing time with Brett Hull as long Pierre Turgeon is healthy.

PROJECTION

Tough call. Turcotte has the skills to produce at least 50 points, but hasn't reached that mark in four seasons.

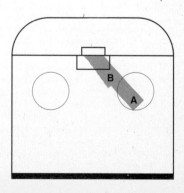

PIERRE TURGEON

Yrs. of NHL service: 10
Born: Rouyn, Que.; Aug. 28, 1969
Position: centre
Height: 6-1
Weight: 195
Uniform no.: 77
Shoots: left

Career statistics:

GP	G	A	TP	PIM
750	344	520	864	251

1993-94 statistics:

GP	G	A	TP	+/-	PIM	PP	SH	GW	GT	S	PCT
69	38	56	94	+14	18	10	4	6	0	254	15.0

1994-95 statistics:

GP	G	A	TP	+/-	PIM	PP	SH	GW	GT	S	PCT
49	24	23	47	0	14	5	2	4	0	160	15.0

1995-96 statistics:

GP	G	A	TP	+/-	PIM	PP	SH	GW	GT	S	PCT
80	38	58	96	+19	44	17	1	6	0	297	12.8

1996-97 statistics:

GP	G	A	TP	+/-	PIM	PP	SH	GW	GT	S	PCT
78	26	59	85	+8	14	5	0	7	1	216	12.0

LAST SEASON

Acquired from Montreal with Craig Conroy and Rory Fitzpatrick for Shayne Corson, Murray Baron and a fifth-round draft pick, October 29, 1996. Led team in assists, points and power-play goals. Second on team in goals.

THE FINESSE GAME

The move out of Montreal was a positive one for the sensitive Turgeon, who ended up in a good spot in St. Louis — once coach Mike Keenan was excised — as the centre for Brett Hull.

Turgeon's skills are amazing. He never seems to be looking at the puck yet he is always in perfect control of it. He has a style unlike just about anyone else in the NHL. He's not a fast skater, but he can deke a defender or make a sneaky-Pete surprise pass. He is tough to defend against, because if you aren't aware of where he is on the ice and don't deny him the pass, he can kill a team with several moves.

Turgeon can slow or speed up the tempo of a game. He lacks the breakout speed of a Pat LaFontaine, but because he is slippery and can change speeds so smoothly, he's deceptive. His control with the puck down low is remarkable. He protects the puck well with the body and has good anticipation, reads plays well and is patient with the puck.

While best known for his playmaking, Turgeon has an excellent shot. He will curl out from behind the net with a wrist shot, shoot off the fly from the right wing (his preferred side of the ice) or stand off to the side of the net on a power play and reach for a tip or redirection of a point shot. He doesn't have a bazooka shot, but he uses quick, accurate wrist and snap shots.

He has to create odd-man rushes. This is when he is at his finest.

THE PHYSICAL GAME

Turgeon has to decide if he wants to be a good statistical player or a winner, and to be the latter he will have to add a more physical element to his game. He is strong, but clearly does not like the contact part of the game; he can be taken out of a game by a team that hounds him. Turgeon must play through it. He had another disappointing playoffs (and was sidelined for one game by recurring headaches).

THE INTANGIBLES

Turgeon isn't Wayne Gretzky or Doug Gilmour. He isn't a leader. That makes St. Louis a nice fit for him because veterans Hull and Al MacInnis and the young Chris Pronger bear the brunt of the leadership role and Turgeon can do his finesse thing. He will create a considerable amount of brilliance, but never take his game to the next level. A Group 2 free agent during the off-season, he is due for a hefty raise.

PROJECTION

Playing with Hull for a full season could push Turgeon near the 100-point mark he's attained twice before in his career, but the Blues need a number two centre to take some of the checking heat off their top line.

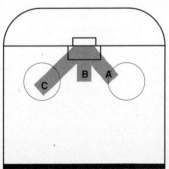

HARRY YORK

Yrs. of NHL service: 1
Born: Ponoka, Alta.; May 20, 1970
Position: centre
Height: 6-2
Weight: 215
Uniform no.: 37
Shoots: left

Career statistics:

GP	G	A	TP	PIM
74	14	18	32	24

1996-97 statistics:

GP	G	A	TP	+/-	PIM	PP	SH	GW	GT	S	PCT
74	14	18	32	+1	24	3	1	3	0	86	16.3

LAST SEASON

First NHL season. Missed one game with flu. Second among NHL rookies in shooting percentage. Tied for longest point-scoring streak by a rookie (eight games).

THE FINESSE GAME

York's strength is his strength. His skills are minimal by NHL standards, but he has the size to make some good things happen. York can create a forecheck because he can wipe out the defensemen and stir up loose pucks.

York played as a second-line centre by default. He's more of a setup man than a scorer. Although not a great playmaker and not a great shooter, he has deceiving hands. There are games when York gets his physical game rolling and his confidence grows, and when that happens he is going to get points. He has the ability to make a pretty passing play now and then.

York has to pick up his skating. He is a poor man's Adam Oates, but lacks Oates's ability to break away with his skating.

THE PHYSICAL GAME

York has to establish his physical game in the NHL in order to feel comfortable, and he didn't quite achieve that level last season. He is basically a banger, and on a more talented team would play as a third- or fourth-line forward, as a momentum changer. York has tremendous size and natural strength.

THE INTANGIBLES

York slowed down at the end of the season, which was to be expected from a player making the huge jump he did from the ECHL to the NHL. York was a free agent signing, and a player who took advantage of the opportunity given him in St. Louis. Now he has to prove he can be an everyday player in the NHL and not just a pleasant surprise. Early in his career, he wasn't the hardest worker around, and there are probably players who played with him in the ECHL who are shocked at his development.

PROJECTION

Despite the strong impression he made in his rookie season, York can't think he can walk into camp this year and claim a roster spot. With some improvement in his skating and continued effort, however, he could become a 25-goal second-line centre for the Blues, who are thin up the middle.

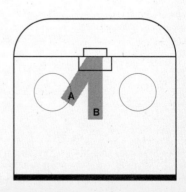

TAMPA BAY LIGHTNING

Players' Statistics 1996-97

POS.	NO.	PLAYER	GP	G	A	PTS	+/-	PIM	PP	SH	GW	GT	S	PCT
C	77	CHRIS GRATTON	82	30	32	62	-28	201	9		4		230	13.0
R	22	DINO CICCARELLI	77	35	25	60	-11	116	12		6		229	15.3
C	12	JOHN CULLEN	70	18	37	55	-14	95	5		2	1	116	15.5
L	7	ROB ZAMUNER	82	17	33	50	3	56		4	3		216	7.9
D	44	ROMAN HAMRLIK	79	12	28	40	-29	57	6			1	238	5.0
L	11	SHAWN BURR	74	14	21	35	5	106	1		3		128	10.9
R	29	ALEXANDER SELIVANOV	69	15	18	33	-3	61	3		4		187	8.0
C	18	*DAYMOND LANGKOW	79	15	13	28	1	35	3	1	1	1	170	8.8
L	28	PATRICK POULIN	73	12	14	26	-16	56	2	3	1		124	9.7
D	2	BILL HOULDER	79	4	21	25	16	30			2		116	3.4
C	19	BRIAN BRADLEY	35	7	17	24	2	16	1	2	1		93	7.5
L	34	MIKAEL ANDERSSON	70	5	14	19	1	8		3	1		102	4.9
D	6	JEFF NORTON	75	2	16	18	-7	58					81	2.5
L	15	PAUL YSEBAERT	39	5	12	17	1	4	2				91	5.5
L	24	JASON WIEMER	63	9	5	14	-13	134	2				103	8.7
D	27	DAVID SHAW	57	1	10	11	1	72					59	1.7
L	9	*JEFF TOMS	34	2	8	10	2	10			1		53	3.8
D	4	CORY CROSS	72	4	5	9	6	95			2		75	5.3
D	5	IGOR ULANOV	59	1	7	8	2	108			1		56	1.8
R	20	RUDY POESCHEK	60		6	6	-3	120					30	
D	8	JAMIE HUSCROFT	52		5	5	-2	151					40	
R	74	*BRANTT MYHRES	47	3	1	4	1	136			1		13	23.1
L	17	*BRENT PETERSON	17	2		2	-4	4					11	18.2
G	32	*COREY SCHWAB	31		1	1	0	10						
G	31	RICK TABARACCI	62		1	1	0	12						
C	25	*ALAN EGELAND	4				-3	5					1	
G	35	*DEREK WILKINSON	5				0							
G	93	DAREN PUPPA	6				0	2						
R	10	*PAUL BROUSSEAU	6				-4						3	
D	26	JAY WELLS	21				-3	13					16	

GP = games played; G = goals; A = assists; PTS = points; +/- = goals-for minus goals-against while player is on ice; PIM = penalties in minutes; PP = power-play goals; SH = shorthanded goals; GW = game-winning goals; GT = game-tying goals; S = no. of shots; PCT = percentage of goals to shots; * = rookie

DINO CICCARELLI

Yrs. of NHL service: 17
Born: Sarnia, Ont.; Feb. 18, 1960
Position: right wing
Height: 5-10
Weight: 185
Uniform no.: 22
Shoots: right

Career statistics:

GP	G	A	TP	PIM
1156	586	574	1160	1328

1993-94 statistics:

GP	G	A	TP	+/-	PIM	PP	SH	GW	GT	S	PCT
66	28	29	57	+10	73	12	0	1	2	153	18.3

1994-95 statistics:

GP	G	A	TP	+/-	PIM	PP	SH	GW	GT	S	PCT
42	16	27	43	+12	39	6	0	3	0	106	15.1

1995-96 statistics:

GP	G	A	TP	+/-	PIM	PP	SH	GW	GT	S	PCT
64	22	21	43	+14	99	13	0	5	0	107	20.6

1996-97 statistics:

GP	G	A	TP	+/-	PIM	PP	SH	GW	GT	S	PCT
77	35	25	60	-11	116	12	0	6	0	229	15.3

LAST SEASON

Acquired from Detroit for a 1998 draft pick, August 28, 1996. Led team in goals, power-play goals and game-winning goals. Second on team in points and shooting percentage. Third on team in shots. Missed three games with concussion. Missed on game with back injury.

THE FINESSE GAME

For a smallish player, Ciccarelli casts a big shadow. Yapping and jabbing, he plays few invisible games. His attitude and aggressive style enhance his skills, which are highlighted by his quickness and his scoring knack. Last season, he scored his most goals since 1992-93.

Ciccarelli has great hands for finishing plays. Although he has a big slap shot he is more effective down low. He creates havoc for goalies: digging for loose pucks, deflecting shots and screening the netminder. His offensive game is straightforward. He's not a very creative playmaker, so he shoots first and asks questions later. Somehow, he always seems to get a piece of the puck.

A strong forechecker, Ciccarelli takes the body well despite his small size, and he can do something with the puck when it does squirt free. He doesn't have breakaway speed and dazzling moves, but he is a strong and well-balanced skater who is very quick in small spaces.

THE PHYSICAL GAME

"Dino the Disturber." Ciccarelli is starved for attention and isn't happy unless he's got a goaltender in a tizzy or a goal judge pushing that red-light button. He isn't a very good skater so he can't afford to be a perimeter player. He has to be parked right on the paint in front of the net, his heels on the crease, taking the punishment and dishing it out. Intimidation is a huge part of his game. He will check goalies out of their crease and try to get a piece of them while they're still in it.

Ciccarelli plays as if he has to prove his courage every night; pound for pound he's as strong as most bigger players. He has a low centre of gravity and is difficult to move. Defensemen may think, "No problem, I can move this guy," only to find Ciccarelli impossible to budge. Punish him as much as you want. He'll keep coming back.

THE INTANGIBLES

Ciccarelli filled an important niche on a Tampa Bay team that needed some grit and energy up front, and he considerably upgraded the team's power play. He remains the quintessential hockey brat. He's slowed a bit, but then he was never known for his speed anyway. With sufficient power-play time, Ciccarelli should be productive again. His desire and competitive nature are big plusses.

PROJECTION

Ciccarelli still has the hands and the guts for another 30-goal season.

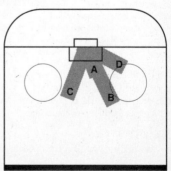

CORY CROSS

Yrs. of NHL service: 3
Born: Lloydminster, Alta.; Jan. 3, 1971
Position: left defense
Height: 6-5
Weight: 212
Uniform no.: 4
Shoots: left

Career statistics:

GP	G	A	TP	PIM
195	7	24	31	208

1993-94 statistics:

GP	G	A	TP	+/-	PIM	PP	SH	GW	GT	S	PCT
5	0	0	0	-3	6	0	0	0	0	5	0.0

1994-95 statistics:

GP	G	A	TP	+/-	PIM	PP	SH	GW	GT	S	PCT
43	1	5	6	-6	41	0	0	1	0	35	2.9

1995-96 statistics:

GP	G	A	TP	+/-	PIM	PP	SH	GW	GT	S	PCT
75	2	14	16	+4	66	0	0	0	0	57	3.5

1996-97 statistics:

GP	G	A	TP	+/-	PIM	PP	SH	GW	GT	S	PCT
72	4	5	9	+6	95	0	0	2	0	75	5.3

LAST SEASON

Missed three games with wrist injury.

THE FINESSE GAME

Cross's most impressive asset is his intelligence. He is smart enough to recognize the mistakes he makes and learn from them. He is highly skilled: a fine skater who can either lug the puck out of his zone or start things with a pass and then jump up into the play. He has a good shot and will make wise pinches to keep the puck in the zone.

Cross was the first player taken in the 1992 supplemental draft and he shot his way up the Lightning depth chart. He may be good enough with the puck to merit more power-play time on the point on the second unit, but he is not a real offensive defenseman.

THE PHYSICAL GAME

Cross did not play in a physical environment at the collegiate level, and he's learned that it's okay to hit people hard. He has taken a real shine to NHL play, showing a latent aggressive streak. He is a solid skater with good size and is still discovering how truly big and powerful he is. He can get his stick up at times. He can develop even more upper-body strength.

THE INTANGIBLES

Cross continues to quietly develop into a very effective NHL defenseman. He is probably the number three or four man on the depth chart now.

PROJECTION

Cross has the ability to score more than single digits in points.

CHRIS GRATTON

Yrs. of NHL service: 4
Born: Brantford, Ont.; July 5, 1975
Position: centre
Height: 6-4
Weight: 218
Uniform no.: 77
Shoots: left

Career statistics:

GP	G	A	TP	PIM
294	67	102	169	518

1993-94 statistics:

GP	G	A	TP	+/-	PIM	PP	SH	GW	GT	S	PCT
84	13	29	42	-25	123	5	1	2	1	161	8.1

1994-95 statistics:

GP	G	A	TP	+/-	PIM	PP	SH	GW	GT	S	PCT
46	7	20	27	-2	89	2	0	0	0	91	7.7

1995-96 statistics:

GP	G	A	TP	+/-	PIM	PP	SH	GW	GT	S	PCT
82	17	21	38	-13	105	7	0	3	0	183	9.3

1996-97 statistics:

GP	G	A	TP	+/-	PIM	PP	SH	GW	GT	S	PCT
82	30	32	62	-28	201	9	0	4	0	230	13.0

LAST SEASON

Led team in points and penalty minutes with career highs. Second on team in goals with career high. Second on team in power-play goals and shots. Tied for second on team in game-winning goals. Third on team in assists and shooting percentage. One of two Lightning players to appear in all 82 games for second consecutive season.

THE FINESSE GAME

Gratton was supposed to be a power centre, and is happier playing there than when he is shuffled to the wing, but he is clearly overmatched in the middle. One of the major reasons is his lack of foot speed, which really hurts him despite a lot of coaching in this area.

Gratton's game is meat and potatoes. He's a grinder and needs to work hard every shift, every night, to make an impact. He has a hard shot, which he needs to use more. He gets his goals from digging around the net, and there's some Cam Neely in him, but he lacks the long, strong stride that Neely uses in traffic. He has good hand-eye coordination and can pick passes out of midair for a shot.

Gratton is an unselfish playmaker. He's not the prettiest of passers, but he has some poise with the puck and knows when to pass and when to shoot. He has shown an ability to win face-offs, and works diligently in his own end.

THE PHYSICAL GAME

Gratton is a hard-working sort who doesn't shy from contact, but he has to initiate more. If his skating improves, he will be able to establish a more physical presence. He doesn't generate enough speed from leg drive to be much of a checker. He won't be an impact player in the NHL until he does.

Gratton was challenged frequently last season and responded by dropping his gloves.

THE INTANGIBLES

Gratton took a big step up last season, but because so much is expected of him his season was considered a disappointment in some quarters. A restricted free agent, he was the subject of some trade rumours. However, it would take a pretty good deal in our book to pry away a 30-goal scorer with his size.

Gratton is a quiet kid and the coaching staff has to work hard at keeping his confidence level up.

PROJECTION

Gratton isn't an elite number one centre, but he's a pretty good one. If he can become a consistent 30- to 35-goal scorer most teams would be happy to have him.

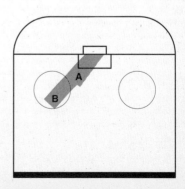

ROMAN HAMRLIK

Yrs. of NHL service: 5
Born: Gottwaldov, Czech.; Apr. 12, 1974
Position: left defense
Height: 6-2
Weight: 202
Uniform no.: 44
Shoots: left

Career statistics:

GP	G	A	TP	PIM
340	49	121	170	452

1993-94 statistics:

GP	G	A	TP	+/-	PIM	PP	SH	GW	GT	S	PCT
64	3	18	21	-14	135	0	0	0	0	158	1.9

1994-95 statistics:

GP	G	A	TP	+/-	PIM	PP	SH	GW	GT	S	PCT
48	12	11	23	-18	86	7	1	2	0	134	9.0

1995-96 statistics:

GP	G	A	TP	+/-	PIM	PP	SH	GW	GT	S	PCT
82	16	49	65	-24	103	12	0	2	3	281	5.7

1996-97 statistics:

GP	G	A	TP	+/-	PIM	PP	SH	GW	GT	S	PCT
79	12	28	40	-29	57	6	0	0	1	238	5.0

LAST SEASON

Led team defensemen in scoring for third consecutive season. Led team in shots for third consecutive season. Third on team in power-play goals. Worst plus-minus on team. Missed two games with back injury.

THE FINESSE GAME

Hamrlik is drawing comparisons to Ray Bourque and Chris Chelios for his marathon ice time and his desire to control a game. Despite his step backwards last season, he is very close to becoming the NHL's next star defenseman. He probably has to get out of Tampa Bay to do it. He has all the tools. He is a fast, strong skater forwards and backwards. Although he still needs to improve his reads, he's getting better.

He is a mobile defenseman with a solid shot and good passing skills, though he is not very creative. Right now, the young Czech thinks he can just overpower people, and he frequently can, but he could also learn to outsmart them and not make the game so difficult. He loves to get involved offensively. He plays nearly the full two minutes of a power play on the point, but he won't hesitate to jump into the play low. He has an excellent shot with a quick release.

He has adjusted to the NHL pace because of his strong skating. He makes high-risk plays, however. Defensively, Hamrlik runs into problems when he is trying to move the puck out of his zone and when forced to handle the puck on his backhand, but that is about the only way the opposition can cope with him.

THE PHYSICAL GAME

Hamrlik is aggressive and likes physical play, though he is not a huge, splashy hitter. He is in great shape and routinely plays 27 to 30 minutes a night, or wants to, but that's a major source of contention with coach Terry Crisp.

THE INTANGIBLES

Hamrlik is a high-maintenance defenseman, and it's pretty clear his marriage with Crisp won't survive. Hamrlik lost his man, assistant Wayne Cashman, prior to last season, and lost pal Petr Klima as well.

PROJECTION

Hamrlik underachieved last season. He should be a 20-goal, 50-point scorer and be among the top 10 defensemen in scoring, but his game and his head have to be straightened out first.

DAYMOND LANGKOW

Yrs. of NHL service: 1
Born: Edmonton, Alberta; Sept. 27, 1976
Position: centre
Height: 5-11
Weight: 175
Uniform no.: 18
Shoots: left

Career statistics:

GP	G	A	TP	PIM
83	15	14	29	35

1995-96 statistics:

GP	G	A	TP	+/-	PIM	PP	SH	GW	GT	S	PCT
4	0	1	1	-1	0	0	0	0	0	4	0.0

1996-97 statistics:

GP	G	A	TP	+/-	PIM	PP	SH	GW	GT	S	PCT
79	15	13	28	-1	35	3	1	1	1	170	8.8

LAST SEASON

First NHL season. Tied for fifth among NHL rookies in goals. Fourth among NHL rookies in shots. Scored 1-1 — 2 in 2 games with Springfield (AHL).

THE FINESSE GAME

Langkow is the complete package. The only problem is, it's such a darned small package.

Small men can succeed in the NHL, however, and it appears that Langkow could be one of them. He has terrific hockey sense, which is probably his chief asset, to go along with his stickhandling ability and shot. He is a fine passer with good vision and is patient with the puck. He is not shy about shooting and possesses a good wrist shot and slap shot.

Langkow has good speed, spies his options quickly and works hard. He knows what's going to happen before it does, which is the mark of an elite playmaker. He will harass opponents on the forecheck and create turnovers. He could become a very good two-way forward. His defensive awareness is above average for a young player.

THE PHYSICAL GAME

Langkow is a spunky, fast, in-your-face kind of forward. He has a little sandpaper in his game, which gives him an edge over small forwards who rely only on their finesse skills. He doesn't mind aggravating people, and he'll throw punches at far bigger men. He won't be intimidated, either, and does his scoring in the trenches despite getting hit. He has a high pain threshhold.

THE INTANGIBLES

Because of the unfortunate John Cullen situation (Cullen is battling cancer), Langkow will get a chance to see quality ice time this season. He will need to play with some wingers of size. Langkow was a captain in junior and is determined to be an NHL player.

PROJECTION

Langkow will eventually become a 30- to 40-goal scorer. This season will still be a learning experience, but he projects as a second-line forward.

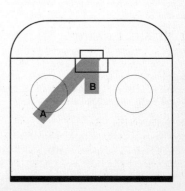

JEFF NORTON

Yrs. of NHL service: 9
Born: Acton, Mass.; Nov. 25, 1965
Position: right defense
Height: 6-2
Weight: 200
Uniform no.: 6
Shoots: left

Career statistics:

GP	G	A	TP	PIM
535	42	265	307	440

1993-94 statistics:

GP	G	A	TP	+/-	PIM	PP	SH	GW	GT	S	PCT
64	7	33	40	+16	36	1	0	0	0	92	7.6

1994-95 statistics:

GP	G	A	TP	+/-	PIM	PP	SH	GW	GT	S	PCT
48	3	27	30	+22	72	0	0	1	0	48	6.3

1995-96 statistics:

GP	G	A	TP	+/-	PIM	PP	SH	GW	GT	S	PCT
66	8	23	31	+9	42	1	0	2	0	85	9.4

1996-97 statistics:

GP	G	A	TP	+/-	PIM	PP	SH	GW	GT	S	PCT
75	2	16	18	-7	58	0	0	0	0	81	2.5

PROJECTION

A fresh start could make a difference, with Norton capable of reaching the 40- to 50-point range.

LAST SEASON

Acquired from Edmonton for Drew Bannister and a conditional draft pick, March 18, 1997.

THE FINESSE GAME

An offensive defenseman, Norton has deep edges and seems to make his turns and cuts with his body set at a 45-degree angle to the ice. His skating ability allows him to cover up for some of his more erratic defensive play. He gets too excited about joining the attack and forgets gap control or makes ill-timed pinches. Many times, he is able to gallop back into position but he still makes a risky defensive proposition. His knee injury may affect his skating, which is his chief asset.

His hockey sense is good, especially offensively, but Norton has never been able to combine his skating with the kind of scoring impact he should. He doesn't have a great shot. He will generate a play with his skating and puckhandling and get the puck into the attacking zone, but he never seems to have the finishing touch.

THE PHYSICAL GAME

Norton is not strong in his own end of the ice. On many nights, he will drift up as if he is ready to leave the zone prematurely and leave his teammates scrambling behind. His mental toughness is a question mark, and his focus and concentration waver.

THE INTANGIBLES

Norton never recovered from a terrible start in Edmonton. Even though he was happy with the trade, he only scored five assists in 13 games with the Lightning.

PATRICK POULIN

Yrs. of NHL service: 5
Born: Vanier, Que.; Apr. 23, 1973
Position: left wing
Height: 6-1
Weight: 210
Uniform no.: 28
Shoots: left

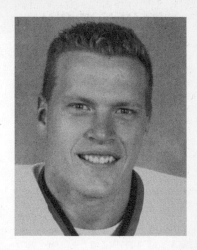

Career statistics:

GP	G	A	TP	PIM
313	68	83	151	215

1993-94 statistics:

GP	G	A	TP	+/-	PIM	PP	SH	GW	GT	S	PCT
67	14	14	28	-8	51	2	0	3	0	96	14.6

1994-95 statistics:

GP	G	A	TP	+/-	PIM	PP	SH	GW	GT	S	PCT
45	15	15	30	+13	53	4	0	2	0	77	19.5

1995-96 statistics:

GP	G	A	TP	+/-	PIM	PP	SH	GW	GT	S	PCT
46	7	9	16	+7	16	1	0	0	1	51	13.7

1996-97 statistics:

GP	G	A	TP	+/-	PIM	PP	SH	GW	GT	S	PCT
73	12	14	26	-16	56	2	3	1	0	124	9.7

LAST SEASON

Missed seven games with knee injuries.

THE FINESSE GAME

Poulin has all the tools — size, strength, speed, shot, hands — to be an elite player, but he never uses all of those qualities on a nightly basis.

He is intelligent and attentive, but Pouilin is also high maintenance, since he gets down on himself and needs to be shored up mentally. As he matures, he has to take more of the burden upon himself to motivate his game. It's not an uncommon tendency for a player who starred at the junior level with little effort, as Poulin did, to try to cruise on talent alone his first season or two in the NHL, but Poulin is not in that elite group of athletes and he has shown little improvement over the past few seasons.

Possessing explosive speed, Poulin can peel off the wing and barrel in with a rifle shot from the circle. He has an excellent shot with a quick release, and his wrist shot is very strong. However, he does not skate well with the puck. He has a fluid stride and a good eye for the openings.

Poulin needs a great deal of work on his defensive game, but he has good hockey instincts and a grasp of positional play.

THE PHYSICAL GAME

Poulin is large in stature but not in on-ice presence. He does not use his body well, doesn't finish his checks and doesn't create the openings a player of his ability should. Floating should be something he does in the pool, not on the ice. Coaches keep hoping Poulin will become a Kevin Stevens type, but he lacks that ag-gressive streak. He doesn't drive to the net or fight through checks.

THE INTANGIBLES

Poulin will never develop the mental toughness to enhance his skills.

PROJECTION

Poulin is a 15-goal scorer in the body of a 40-goal scorer.

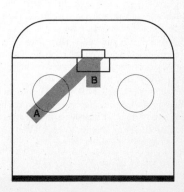

DAREN PUPPA

Yrs. of NHL service: 11
Born: Kirkland Lake, Ont.; Mar. 23, 1965
Position: goaltender
Height: 6-3
Weight: 205
Uniform no.: 93
Catches: right

Career statistics:

GP	MIN	GA	SO	GAA	A	PIM
385	21423	1086	17	3.04	17	36

1993-94 statistics:

GP	MIN	GAA	W	L	T	SO	GA	S	SAPCT	PIM
63	3653	2.71	22	33	6	4	165	1637	.899	2

1994-95 statistics:

GP	MIN	GAA	W	L	T	SO	GA	S	SAPCT	PIM
36	2013	2.68	14	19	2	1	90	946	.905	2

1995-96 statistics:

GP	MIN	GAA	W	L	T	SO	GA	S	SAPCT	PIM
57	3189	2.46	29	16	9	5	131	1605	.918	4

1996-97 statistics:

GP	MIN	GAA	W	L	T	SO	GA	S	SAPCT	PIM
6	325	2.58	1	1	2	0	14	150	.907	2

LAST SEASON

Missed 50 games with back injury and surgery.

THE PHYSICAL GAME

A big player, with big pads, Puppa stands up well to make himself look even bigger in the nets. He tries to stay on his feet and play his angles, and he challenges shooters. He plays a butterfly style, and even when he drops to his knees there is still a lot of torso blocking the net.

Puppa has a good glove. He catches right-handed, which is an advantage (much like left-handed tennis players and pitchers have) because shooters are used to looking at left-gloved goalies. His weakness is high stick-side (as with most goalies), but shooters who think they are going stick-side on him are actually shooting to his glove side.

He is very good on low shots, though he gets in trouble when he drops down too early, and flounders. He occasionally gets into a bad habit of staying too deep in his net and playing a passive game. He has to be aggressive to be successful.

Puppa moves in and out of his net well. He sets picks and will interfere with the opposition trying to get in. He also helps his defensemen by holding up forwards (illegal, but he gets away with it). He does not handle the puck well, however, and since he isn't playing behind a mobile defense corps it would really help his cause if he could improve in this area. He uses his stick well around the net to knock away loose pucks and cut off passes near the crease.

THE MENTAL GAME

Finally getting recognition around the league as a quality netminder has meant a great deal to Puppa, who toiled for years in Buffalo and Toronto as a backup. Confidence is a major part of any goalie's game, and Puppa has become less fragile mentally and much more resilient.

THE INTANGIBLES

Puppa has been so injury-prone that it's tough to get a good read on him. Tampa gambled heavily by signing him to a new three-year deal, and they are sunk unless he plays well. He is the key to the hockey club. The Lightning doesn't win unless Puppa is one of the best players on the ice every night.

PROJECTION

Puppa is so fragile that whoever wins the backup role should be prepared to play 40 games.

ALEXANDER SELIVANOV

Yrs. of NHL service: 3
Born: Moscow, Russia; March 23, 1971
Position: right wing
Height: 6-1
Weight: 206
Uniform no.: 29
Shoots: left

Career statistics:

GP	G	A	TP	PIM
191	56	45	101	168

1994-95 statistics:

GP	G	A	TP	+/-	PIM	PP	SH	GW	GT	S	PCT
43	10	6	16	-2	14	4	0	3	0	94	10.6

1995-96 statistics:

GP	G	A	TP	+/-	PIM	PP	SH	GW	GT	S	PCT
79	31	21	52	+3	93	13	0	5	2	215	14.4

1996-97 statistics:

GP	G	A	TP	+/-	PIM	PP	SH	GW	GT	S	PCT
69	15	18	33	-3	61	3	0	4	0	187	8.0

LAST SEASON

Tied for second on team in game-winning goals. Missed 10 games with knee injury.

THE FINESSE GAME

Selivanov is very clever with the puck. He can beat people one-on-one with his speed and puckhandling, but needs to learn to use his teammates better. Once he does, he will be much more productive. He loves to score, and he works to get himself in position for a quality shot. He needs to play with a creative centre who will get the puck to him, because he can finish.

Selivanov tends to take very long shifts (which drives his coaches crazy), but that's a common tendency with Russian players. He is strong on the puck. He has some defensive lapses, but it's not as much of a liability with him as it is with many young players.

Selivanov has an excellent release on his shot, and is one of the many NHL players who get away with playing with a stick that has an illegal curve. He's a left-hand shot who plays right wing. Playing with a straighter stick would help him receive passes and handle the puck on his backhand.

THE PHYSICAL GAME

Selivanov is wiry but he is not terribly strong or aggressive. He is not intimidated, however, he will probably need at least one bodyguard on his line. He is quick and smart enough to stay out of trouble.

THE INTANGIBLES

Even before his injury, Selivanov was off to a poor start and was demoted to the fourth line. Guess it's not so easy being the boss's son-in-law (he's married to the daughter of GM Phil Esposito).

PROJECTION

Selivanov has some rebounding to do. There is still more upside to his game because of his tremendous creativity, and he should score 25 to 30 goals.

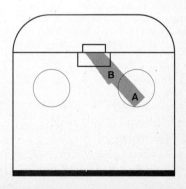

IGOR ULANOV

Yrs. of NHL service: 6
Born: Krasnokamsk, USSR; Oct. 1, 1969
Position: left defense
Height: 6-1
Weight: 205
Uniform no.: 5
Shoots: left

Career statistics:

GP	G	A	TP	PIM
302	9	60	69	609

1993-94 statistics:

GP	G	A	TP	+/-	PIM	PP	SH	GW	GT	S	PCT
74	0	17	17	-11	165	0	0	0	0	46	0.0

1994-95 statistics:

GP	G	A	TP	+/-	PIM	PP	SH	GW	GT	S	PCT
22	1	4	5	+1	29	0	0	0	0	13	7.7

1995-96 statistics:

GP	G	A	TP	+/-	PIM	PP	SH	GW	GT	S	PCT
64	3	9	12	+11	116	0	0	1	0	37	8.1

1996-97 statistics:

GP	G	A	TP	+/-	PIM	PP	SH	GW	GT	S	PCT
59	1	7	8	+2	108	0	0	1	0	56	1.8

LAST SEASON

Missed four games with rib injuries. Missed six games with groin injury.

THE FINESSE GAME

Ulanov's skills are magnified by the kind of tough physical game he is capable of playing. A player who can skate and handle the puck as well as he can, or level you with a hit, is going to command a lot of space. Ulanov knows what to do with that space once he gets it. He loves to join the attack. He has good first-step quickness, with agility and balance.

He anticipates well. He will break up a rush at his own blueline and start a quick counterattack. He has very good puck skills, but he's not a real offensive defenseman because he does not finish and has only a modest point shot. He starts breakouts with a smart, short pass. He can carry the puck, though he would rather have a teammate lug it.

THE PHYSICAL GAME

Ulanov is inconsistent in his physical play; last season he was seldom much of a factor. He is a punishing open-ice hitter and has a real nasty streak. Some nights he won't hesitate to make a vicious hit right in front of the opponent's bench. But in the same game he'll lose an attacker by failing to make a simple take-out check, leaving his defense partner outnumbered. He raises the temperature of the opposition by raising his stick, too.

THE INTANGIBLES

Ulanov is too unreliable to be much more than a fifth defenseman. He is scary when he plays like a head-hunter, but gets too involved in running around instead of playing his game.

PROJECTION

Ulanov is on the bubble in Tampa Bay.

JASON WIEMER

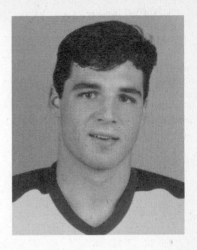

Yrs. of NHL service: 3
Born: Kimberley, B.C.; Apr. 14, 1976
Position: left wing
Height: 6-1
Weight: 215
Uniform no.: 24
Shoots: left

Career statistics:

GP	G	A	TP	PIM
165	19	18	47	259

1994-95 statistics:

GP	G	A	TP	+/-	PIM	PP	SH	GW	GT	S	PCT
36	1	4	5	-2	44	0	0	0	0	10	10.0

1995-96 statistics:

GP	G	A	TP	+/-	PIM	PP	SH	GW	GT	S	PCT
66	9	9	18	-9	81	4	0	1	0	89	10.1

1996-97 statistics:

GP	G	A	TP	+/-	PIM	PP	SH	GW	GT	S	PCT
63	9	5	14	-13	134	2	0	0	0	103	8.7

LAST SEASON

Appeared in four games with Adirondack (AHL), scoring 1-0 — 1.

THE FINESSE GAME

The Lightning look at Wiemer as a budding power forward, and while he might someday be that player, right now his contributions are far more subtle. His game is getting the puck out of the corners and onto the stick of Chris Gratton or a more skilled player.

He has the build and the touch for standing in the traffic areas and picking pucks out of scrambles. He also has a touch of mean that merits him some room and time to execute. His release has improved, but he may not have an NHL shot.

Wiemer's major shortcoming is his skating (although his foot speed is improving), but this shouldn't hold him back from being an impact player. He is very strong and well balanced for work around the net. He doesn't play a creative game but relies on his strength and his reach.

THE PHYSICAL GAME

Wiemer is starting to get the idea that what he does off-ice and in the off-season will pay dividends (remember, this is a young guy).

Wiemer relishes body contact and will usually initiate checks to intimidate. He is very strong and can hit to hurt. He drives to the net and pushes defenders back, and isn't shy about dropping his gloves or raising his elbows. He functions as the grinder on a line, since he will scrap along the boards and in the corners for the puck. He can complement almost any linemate.

THE INTANGIBLES

It will probably take another season or two for Wiemer to start hitting his stride. He needs to get qual-ity ice time this season (not just token fourth-line shifts) to improve.

PROJECTION

Power forwards take a long time to advance to the 20- to 25-goal range. Wiemer isn't quite there yet.

PAUL YSEBAERT

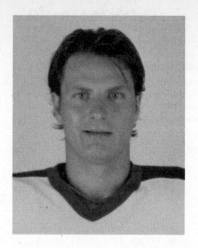

Yrs. of NHL service: 7
Born: Sarnia, Ont.; May 15, 1966
Position: left wing
Height: 6-1
Weight: 190
Uniform no.: 15
Shoots: left

Career statistics:

GP	G	A	TP	PIM
440	136	159	295	183

1993-94 statistics:

GP	G	A	TP	+/-	PIM	PP	SH	GW	GT	S	PCT
71	14	21	35	-7	26	3	0	1	0	151	9.3

1994-95 statistics:

GP	G	A	TP	+/-	PIM	PP	SH	GW	GT	S	PCT
44	12	16	28	+3	18	0	0	1	0	93	12.9

1995-96 statistics:

GP	G	A	TP	+/-	PIM	PP	SH	GW	GT	S	PCT
55	16	15	31	-19	16	4	1	1	0	135	11.9

1996-97 statistics:

GP	G	A	TP	+/-	PIM	PP	SH	GW	GT	S	PCT
39	5	12	17	+1	4	2	0	0	0	91	5.5

LAST SEASON

Missed 43 games with groin injury.

THE FINESSE GAME

Ysebaert thrives on his skating, which made the last two seasons a nightmare because of recurring groin problems. When healthy, he accelerates in a heartbeat and has the speed and balance to beat defenders wide. He has a wide skating stance, which makes him tough to knock off the puck. He also has a good array of shots and will work diligently for his scoring opportunities around the net. He goes to the net hard with the puck, but last season he showed more of a tendency to hurry his shots and to not work to get into the high-percentage scoring areas. He has a quick release and his shot is heavy.

Ysebaert needs someone to open up a bit of ice so he can use his skating to jump into the holes. He can kill penalties and contribute shorthanded.

THE PHYSICAL GAME

Ysebaert's injury has deprived him of any strength and power.

THE INTANGIBLES

Tampa Bay is in a quandary with Ysebaert. The team wants him in the lineup because of his leadership and his solid all-around play. His attitude and consistent effort is a bonus. He can show the way, but the team just doesn't know if it will have him in the lineup and how effective he will be.

PROJECTION

A risky proposition, for your pool or for Tampa Bay.

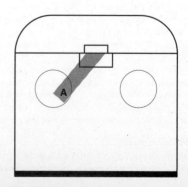

ROB ZAMUNER

Yrs. of NHL service: 5
Born: Oakville, Ont.; Sept. 17, 1969
Position: left wing
Height: 6-2
Weight: 202
Uniform no.: 7
Shoots: left

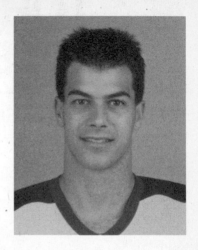

Career statistics:

GP	G	A	TP	PIM
349	63	95	158	260

1993-94 statistics:

GP	G	A	TP	+/-	PIM	PP	SH	GW	GT	S	PCT
59	6	6	12	-9	42	0	0	1	0	109	5.5

1994-95 statistics:

GP	G	A	TP	+/-	PIM	PP	SH	GW	GT	S	PCT
43	9	6	15	-3	24	0	3	1	0	74	12.2

1995-96 statistics:

GP	G	A	TP	+/-	PIM	PP	SH	GW	GT	S	PCT
72	15	20	35	+11	62	0	3	4	0	152	9.9

1996-97 statistics:

GP	G	A	TP	+/-	PIM	PP	SH	GW	GT	S	PCT
82	17	33	50	+3	56	0	4	3	0	216	7.9

LAST SEASON

Led team in shorthanded goals. Second on team in assists. Career high in goals. One of two Lightning players to appear in all 82 games.

THE FINESSE GAME

Zamuner doesn't have great speed, but he compensates for it in other ways, including all-out effort. He is a complementary player, a grinder who can also handle the puck and has some good hand skills. He isn't quite good enough to play as a third-line checking winger, because of his lack of speed, and has to be spotted cautiously by his coaches. Lacking speed, he plays well positionally and takes away the attacker's angles to the net.

Zamuner was a sniper at the minor-league level but has not been able to make the same impact in the NHL. He has a decent touch for scoring or passing, however, it's average at best. He is a shorthanded threat because of his anticipation and work ethic. He has a knack for scoring key goals, and was big for the Lightning in the playoff stretch run.

THE PHYSICAL GAME

Zamuner had problems in the past with fitness, until he realized what a big edge he could have with better conditioning. He has good size and uses it effectively. He is pesky and annoying to play against. On many nights he will be the most physically active forward on the Lightning, adding a real spark with his effort.

THE INTANGIBLES

Zamuner is a tough guy to keep in the lineup because of his marginal skating. He's a tough guy to keep out of the lineup, though, because few players try as hard as he does. He's a gamer.

PROJECTION

Zamuner has become a checking winger who can provide a steady 15 to 20 goals a season.

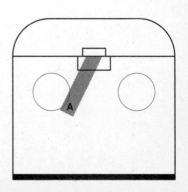

TORONTO MAPLE LEAFS

Players' Statistics 1996-97

POS	NO.	PLAYER	GP	G	A	PTS	+/-	PIM	PP	SH	GW	GT	S	PCT
C	13	MATS SUNDIN	82	41	53	94	6	59	7	4	8	1	281	14.6
L	17	WENDEL CLARK	65	30	19	49	-2	75	6		6		212	14.2
R	94	*SERGEI BEREZIN	73	25	16	41	-3	2	7		2		177	14.1
C	11	*STEVE SULLIVAN	54	13	25	38	14	37	3		3	1	108	12.0
L	8	TODD WARRINER	75	12	21	33	-3	41	2	2		1	146	8.2
R	28	TIE DOMI	80	11	17	28	-17	275	2		1		98	11.2
R	9	MIKE CRAIG	65	7	13	20	-20	62	1				128	5.5
C	14	DARBY HENDRICKSON	64	11	6	17	-20	47		1		2	105	10.5
C	16	JAMIE BAKER	58	8	8	16	2	28	1		3		69	11.6
D	36	DIMITRI YUSHKEVICH	74	4	10	14	-24	56	1	1	1		99	4.0
D	2	ROB ZETTLER	48	2	12	14	8	51					31	6.5
L	19	*FREDRIK MODIN	76	6	7	13	-14	24					85	7.1
D	72	MATHIEU SCHNEIDER	26	5	7	12	3	20	1		1		63	7.9
D	34	JAMIE MACOUN	73	1	10	11	-14	93			1		64	1.6
C	12	*BRANDON CONVERY	39	2	8	10	-9	20					41	4.9
R	10	*ZDENEK NEDVED	23	3	5	8	4	6	1				22	13.6
D	25	JASON SMITH	78	1	7	8	-12	54					74	1.4
D	42	*DAVID COOPER	19	3	3	6	-3	16	2				23	13.0
L	32	NICK KYPREOS	35	3	2	5	1	62					18	16.7
R	26	*JAMIE HEWARD	20	1	4	5	-6	6					23	4.3
C	7	*JASON PODOLLAN	29	1	4	5	-5	10	1				30	3.3
R	20	*MIKE JOHNSON	13	2	2	4	-2	4		1	1		27	7.4
D	3	MATT MARTIN	36		4	4	-12	38					30	
D	26	CRAIG WOLANIN	38		4	4	-6	21					43	
D	24	TOM PEDERSON	15	1	2	3	0	9	1				23	4.3
R	39	KELLY CHASE	30	1	2	3	2	149					6	16.7
G	29	FELIX POTVIN	74		3	3	0	19						
L	43	*NATHAN DEMPSEY	14	1	1	2	-2	2					11	9.1
C	7	*KELLY FAIRCHILD	22		2	2	-5	2					14	
D	4	*D.J. SMITH	8		1	1	-5	7					4	
G	31	*MARCEL COUSINEAU	13		1	1	0							
L	22	SCOTT PEARSON	1				0	2						
D	25	GREG SMYTH	2				0						1	
G	33	DON BEAUPRE	3				0							
C	15	*BRIAN WISEMAN	3				0						1	
R	41	*SHAYNE TOPOROWSKI	3				0	7					3	
D	38	*YANNICK TREMBLAY	5				-4						2	
R	44	*JOHN CRAIGHEAD	5				0	10						
R	37	*MARK KOLESAR	7				-3						3	
D	23	*JEFF WARE	13				2	6					4	

GP = games played; G = goals; A = assists; PTS = points; +/- = goals-for minus goals-against while player is on ice; PIM = penalties in minutes; PP = power-play goals; SH = shorthanded goals; GW = game-winning goals; GT = game-tying goals; S = no. of shots; PCT = percentage of goals to shots; * = rookie

JAMIE BAKER

Yrs. of NHL service: 6
Born: Ottawa, Ont.; Aug. 31, 1966
Position: centre
Height: 6-0
Weight: 195
Uniform no.: 16
Shoots: left

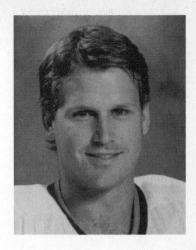

Career statistics:

GP	G	A	TP	PIM
390	71	73	144	261

1993-94 statistics:

GP	G	A	TP	+/-	PIM	PP	SH	GW	GT	S	PCT
65	12	5	17	+2	38	0	0	2	0	68	17.6

1994-95 statistics:

GP	G	A	TP	+/-	PIM	PP	SH	GW	GT	S	PCT
43	7	4	11	-7	22	0	1	0	0	60	11.7

1995-96 statistics:

GP	G	A	TP	+/-	PIM	PP	SH	GW	GT	S	PCT
77	16	17	33	-19	79	2	6	0	0	117	13.7

1996-97 statistics:

GP	G	A	TP	+/-	PIM	PP	SH	GW	GT	S	PCT
58	8	8	16	+2	28	1	0	3	0	69	11.6

LAST SEASON

Missed five games with separated shoulder. Missed 14 games with severe facial injury (broken orbital bone and concussion).

THE FINESSE GAME

Baker had a tough year. He was inconsistent and second-guessed himself. Instead of initiating, he was sitting back and reacting to the situation, and wasn't involved in the play. Just when it looked like Baker was picking up his game and might be able to redeem himself with a solid second half, he went down to block a Greg Hawgood shot and took a puck in the face.

Baker plays a largely defensive role, but he also has the skills to pop in some points even when he is working as a checker. That's what makes Baker a "tweener" — between defense and offense — because he always looks like he has the ability to deliver more than he shows on the stat sheet.

Baker does his best work in the corners. He hustles and is always quickly onto the puck carrier on the forecheck. He reads offensive plays nicely, so if he is able to force a turnover, he knows where to make the pass and whether or not to head to the net. He protects the puck well along the boards and while skating. This is his biggest asset.

Baker will keep the puck alive with his stick even when he's been knocked flat to the ice. He won't just cough it up. He's a better playmaker than scorer, but he can finish around the net when given the chance. He passes off his forehand or backhand, and is effective down low. He has a choppy stride but can move quickly for the first step or two.

Baker is average on draws. He is a determined and aggressive penalty killer and a shorthanded threat. He is a reliable man to have on the ice at crunch time.

THE PHYSICAL GAME

Baker has good size and has added some strength to make himself a more effective hitter, but continued work in the muscle department would help his career. He goes full out, regardless of the score.

THE INTANGIBLES

Baker can score more than he thinks he can. He's been groomed to be a defensive player so that he is looking to prevent instead of score, but he has good hands in close and a good shot — which he seldom uses. He has a point to prove this season.

PROJECTION

Baker is a character guy, an intelligent player who won't hurt a team, and he can score 30 points or so as a checking forward.

SERGEI BEREZIN

Yrs. of NHL service: 1
Born: Voskresensk, USSR; Nov. 5, 1971
Position: right wing
Height: 5-10
Weight: 197
Uniform no.: 94
Shoots: right

Career statistics:

GP	G	A	TP	PIM
73	26	16	41	2

1996-97 statistics:

GP	G	A	TP	+/-	PIM	PP	SH	GW	GT	S	PCT
73	26	16	41	-3	2	7	0	2	0	177	14.1

LAST SEASON

Named to NHL All-Rookie Team. Led NHL rookies and third on team in goals. Second among NHL rookies in power-play goals and shots. Tied for team lead in power-play goals. Third among NHL rookies and third on team in shooting percentage. Fourth among NHL rookies in power-play points. Fifth among NHL rookies and third on team in points. Missed seven games with hand surgery. Missed two games with knee strain.

THE FINESSE GAME

Berezin is strictly an offensive player, and is a pure goal scorer. He knows where the net is, and while he is less reluctant to shoot than a lot of Russian players, sometimes he has to see the whites of the goalie's eyes before he will let it go. He shoots one-timers and is pretty greedy with the puck. He knows he's a sniper. Sometimes he overhandles the puck.

Berezin is one of those scorers who seems to suddenly materialize in the right spot, like Mike Bossy used to do. Berezin can seem to disappear during a game, then he gets a scoring chance and it's in the net.

Berezin is a deceptive, quick skater with good balance. He is aware of his defensive shortcomings, and showed improvement in that facet of his game near the end of the season. He realizes what it means to his team to pick up his wing and watch his point man.

THE PHYSICAL GAME

Berezin is small but stocky. He tends to use his body only in the offensive zone. He isn't intimidated by physical play and doesn't change his game, but he also doesn't initiate. Berezin started to wear down at mid-season (adapting to the rigours of an NHL schedule instead of a 40-game European slate is a major adjustment).

THE INTANGIBLES

Sometimes there is gold in those late-round draft picks. Berezin was selected 256th overall by the Leafs in 1994. After playing for Russia in the World Cup (the only player on the team without any previous NHL experience), Berezin was the surprise of training camp. He's not a surprise anymore, which always makes the second-year trip through the league tougher. Despite his numbers, Berezin was disappointed with his year and wants to play better. That shows he cares and wants to find ways to get better.

PROJECTION

Berezin is slotted in as the number one right wing. Barring a sophomore slump he should score in the 25- to 30-goal range.

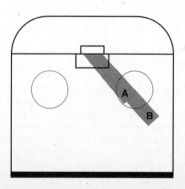

WENDEL CLARK

Yrs. of NHL service: 12
Born: Kelvington, Sask.; Oct. 25, 1966
Position: left wing
Height: 5-11
Weight: 194
Uniform no.: 17
Shoots: left

Career statistics:

GP	G	A	TP	PIM
636	312	209	645	1539

1993-94 statistics:

GP	G	A	TP	+/-	PIM	PP	SH	GW	GT	S	PCT
64	46	30	76	+10	115	21	0	8	0	275	16.7

1994-95 statistics:

GP	G	A	TP	+/-	PIM	PP	SH	GW	GT	S	PCT
37	12	18	30	-1	45	5	0	0	0	95	12.6

1995-96 statistics:

GP	G	A	TP	+/-	PIM	PP	SH	GW	GT	S	PCT
71	32	26	58	-5	76	8	0	3	1	237	13.5

1996-97 statistics:

GP	G	A	TP	+/-	PIM	PP	SH	GW	GT	S	PCT
65	30	19	49	-2	75	6	0	6	0	212	14.2

LAST SEASON

Second on team in goals, points, game-winning goals, shots and shooting percentage. Third on team in power-play goals. Missed 16 games with fractured thumb. Missed one game with tailbone injury.

THE FINESSE GAME

Clark gives you everything his body will allow. Returning early from a thumb injury and playing for several weeks with a plastic splint on the thumb, he still managed to accomplish more in 65 games than many players do over a complete season. Playing in the Western Conference, with its difficult travel schedule, allows Clark little time for recovery, yet he still soldiers on.

Clark is an accurate shooter. He uses a slightly shorter stick than he did early in his career and keeps his hands higher on the stick than most, like Brett Hull. He is shooting from close to his feet, and his snap shots are quick and accurate. He can still overpower a goalie from the blueline, even with his wrist shot, which has tremendous power.

Not a clever player, Clark rarely passes the puck. His effectiveness depends on him charging down the ice, wreaking havoc and letting his teammates trail in his wake, picking through the debris to make a play. When Clark gets the puck, he has to shoot it in. He gets into trouble when he makes plays.

Clark is not a smart player positionally, either. Although a strong skater, he's not agile, fast or mobile. When he's playing well, he uses his leg drive like a linebacker in football to hit hard.

THE PHYSICAL GAME

Clark is just plain mean. He hits when it's least expected, often well away from the play. And he's a big, big hitter who hurts. He's a strong forechecker, but he gets frustrated when his scoring touch deserts him and he'll run around and take bad penalties.

THE INTANGIBLES

Clark never shortchanges his coaches or his teammates, but his body gets tapped out because of his heart-and-soul style, which never allows him to play at half-speed. Clark isn't very vocal, but he provides veteran leadership on what has quickly become a young team. When Clark speaks up on the bench or in the room, his teammates listen.

PROJECTION

If he can stay healthy — a big if — Clark will retain his role on the top line and is capable of another 30-goal season.

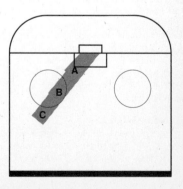

MIKE CRAIG

Yrs. of NHL service: 7
Born: London, Ont.; June 6, 1971
Position: right wing
Height: 6-1
Weight: 180
Uniform no.: 9
Shoots: right

Career statistics:

GP	G	A	TP	PIM
420	71	97	168	548

1993-94 statistics:

GP	G	A	TP	+/-	PIM	PP	SH	GW	GT	S	PCT
72	13	24	37	-14	139	3	0	2	0	150	8.7

1994-95 statistics:

GP	G	A	TP	+/-	PIM	PP	SH	GW	GT	S	PCT
37	5	5	10	-21	12	1	0	1	0	61	8.2

1995-96 statistics:

GP	G	A	TP	+/-	PIM	PP	SH	GW	GT	S	PCT
70	8	12	20	-8	42	1	0	1	0	108	7.4

1996-97 statistics:

GP	G	A	TP	+/-	PIM	PP	SH	GW	GT	S	PCT
65	7	13	20	-20	62	1	0	0	0	128	5.5

LAST SEASON

Missed two games with stick-related suspension. Missed three games with groin injury.

THE FINESSE GAME

The problem with Craig is finding a role for him. He is a tweener, who can't kill penalties and can't work the power play. He is a great practice player, and has a terrific shot in the mornings, but in games he can't seem to find a position to shoot the puck. He didn't have a goal after January 4.

Craig is a choppy skater, but he chops with enthusiasm. He has good hands and tenacity and can play well with top offensive people because he will do the grunt work for them in the corners and along the boards. His wrist shot is especially effective, accurate and quickly unleashed.

The problem with Craig continues to be his inconsistency, which is why he had trouble getting into the lineup and why he played on the fourth line when he did.

THE PHYSICAL GAME

Craig needs to play bigger than he is. He has to continue gaining more strength so he can hold that game through a full schedule — either that or he has to learn to pace himself better, because he tends to wear down in the second half.

THE INTANGIBLES

Craig has continued a downward spiral. He has too much talent to let his game slip away, but he has to find the tenacity to earn a spot. The Leafs would like to move him where he can tempt another coaching staff with his potential and frustrate them with his output.

PROJECTION

Craig will be on the bubble wherever he ends up.

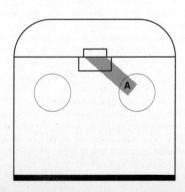

TIE DOMI

Yrs. of NHL service: 7
Born: Windsor, Ont.; Nov. 1, 1969
Position: right wing
Height: 5-10
Weight: 200
Uniform no.: 28
Shoots: right

Career statistics:

GP	G	A	TP	PIM
406	38	53	91	1895

1993-94 statistics:

GP	G	A	TP	+/-	PIM	PP	SH	GW	GT	S	PCT
81	8	11	19	-8	347	0	0	1	0	98	8.2

1994-95 statistics:

GP	G	A	TP	+/-	PIM	PP	SH	GW	GT	S	PCT
40	4	5	9	-5	159	0	0	0	0	46	8.7

1995-96 statistics:

GP	G	A	TP	+/-	PIM	PP	SH	GW	GT	S	PCT
72	7	6	13	-3	297	0	0	1	0	61	11.5

1996-97 statistics:

GP	G	A	TP	+/-	PIM	PP	SH	GW	GT	S	PCT
80	11	17	28	-17	275	2	0	1	0	98	11.2

LAST SEASON

Career highs in goals, assists and points. Fifth in NHL and led team in penalty minutes. Second in NHL in fighting majors (26). Missed two games with ankle injury, ending consecutive games-played streak at 135.

THE FINESSE GAME

Finesse? Should that be discussed in context with this rock-hard (some might say rock-headed) right-winger? Yep, because Domi played his best hockey last season.

Domi has some skills that elevate him above the level of a mere goon. He is a pretty nifty skater, and in a role as a third-line checker will often be in quickly on the opposing goalie behind the net, trying to force a bad pass or a turnover by the netminder. He barrels in on defensemen, too (the obstruction crackdown is ideal for forecheckers like Domi).

When he gets the puck, he has the presence of mind to try to do something useful. Bang-bang reaction plays, whether shots or passes, are his strong suit. He shouldn't think too much. Domi has a short-range shot. He'll wallow into the activity around the crease. He is surprisingly good with his feet, and if his stick is tied up or dropped he will attempt to kick the puck to a teammate.

THE PHYSICAL GAME

Short but burly, Domi is one of the most eager fighters in the NHL. He talks trash and builds up some of his upcoming "bouts" as if he were Don King, which doesn't exactly endear him to the NHL hierarchy. Domi was actually a little restrained in his conduct last season, and managed to get through the year without a suspension.

THE INTANGIBLES

Domi can play with controlled aggression, but the knowledge that he could snap at any moment makes opponents leery of him, and he earns some time and space. His key role, though, is to make some of his skilled teammates braver.

PROJECTION

Penalties and points, too. What a combo. Domi should again reach the 25- to 30-point mark in 1997-98.

DARBY HENDRICKSON

Yrs. of NHL service: 2
Born: Richfield, Minn.; Aug. 28, 1972
Position: centre/left wing
Height: 6-0
Weight: 185
Uniform no.: 14
Shoots: right

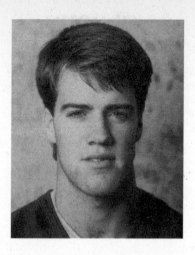

Career statistics:

GP	G	A	TP	PIM
134	18	17	35	131

1994-95 statistics:

GP	G	A	TP	+/-	PIM	PP	SH	GW	GT	S	PCT
8	0	1	1	0	4	0	0	0	0	4	0.0

1995-96 statistics:

GP	G	A	TP	+/-	PIM	PP	SH	GW	GT	S	PCT
62	7	10	17	-8	80	0	0	1	0	73	9.6

1996-97 statistics:

GP	G	A	TP	+/-	PIM	PP	SH	GW	GT	S	PCT
64	11	6	17	-20	47	0	1	0	2	105	10.5

LAST SEASON

Acquired from the Islanders for a conditional 1998 draft pick, October 11, 1996. Career high in goals. Missed five games with back spasms. Scored 5-4 — 9 in 12 games with St. John's (AHL).

THE FINESSE GAME

Hendrickson works hard and gives an honest effort that maximizes his modest skills. He is an in-between forward, since he isn't big enough to play an effective power game, but his skills aren't elite enough for him to be considered a pure finesse playmaker.

Hendrickson is a two-way forward with better-than-average skills for a checking role. He is a good, quick skater in small areas. He is clever with the puck and will look to make a pass rather than shoot.

Hendrickson is defensively alert, and with increased ice time could develop into a more confident all-around player. He's young and still learning the game. He can play any forward position, which is a plus.

THE PHYSICAL GAME

Hendrickson has a feisty side, and isn't afraid to get involved with some of the league's tougher players (like Keith Tkachuk) if not the heavyweights. He is learning to play in-your-face hockey, which will get him more ice time.

THE INTANGIBLES

Hendrickson was shipped to the Islanders in the Wendel Clark deal, then reacquired after the start of last season. The temporary change of scene seems to have done him some good in the maturity department.

Hendrickson is best suited as a third-line centre or winger, or as a safety-valve winger on a second line. He was a star scorer as a Minnesota schoolboy, but hasn't been able to display the same touch at the pro level.

PROJECTION

Hendrickson should produce 20 to 25 points in a largely defensive role.

MIKE JOHNSON

Yrs. of NHL service: 0
Born: Scarborough, Ont.; Oct. 3, 1974
Position: right wing
Height: 6-2
Weight: 180
Uniform no.: 20
Shoots: right

Career statistics:

GP	G	A	TP	PIM
13	2	2	4	4

1996-97 statistics:

GP	G	A	TP	+/-	PIM	PP	SH	GW	GT	S	PCT
13	2	2	4	-2	4	0	1	1	0	27	7.4

LAST SEASON

Signed as free agent, March 16, 1997. Led team and fourth in CCHA in scoring with 30-32 — 62 in 38 games played for Bowling Green.

THE FINESSE GAME

Johnson has an amazing, advanced knowledge of how to use the ice offensively and defensively. He protects the puck on the boards. When he's down low in his own end on defensive-zone coverage, he's strong and supports the puck well.

Offensively, he'll take the puck to the net. He knows when to move and doesn't just stand around and stay checked. He moves into scoring positions. His puck movement on the power play is exceptional. Johnson has to get a stronger shot, which should come with physical maturity.

Johnson is a terrific skater with the kind of ability that instantly stamps him as a 10-year pro. He can harry puck carriers when killing penalties and has the one-step breakaway quickness to be a shorthanded threat.

THE PHYSICAL GAME

Johnson has to get bigger and stronger. He is tall and reedy, and if he stands too still near the stick rack he'll get packed away for the next road trip.

THE INTANGIBLES

Johnson could be one of the best players to come out of the college ranks. He was thrown to the wolves in his brief stint with the Leafs and did a terrific job killing penalties, keeping the puck to the outside and protecting the slot. He should get more time on the second-unit power play.

PROJECTION

He could be a sleeper pool pick with 25-goal potential.

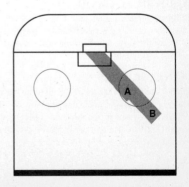

DEREK KING

Yrs. of NHL service: 10
Born: Hamilton, Ont.; Feb. 11, 1967
Position: left wing
Height: 6-0
Weight: 212
Uniform no.: 27
Shoots: left

Career statistics:

GP	G	A	TP	PIM
650	214	291	505	346

1993-94 statistics:

GP	G	A	TP	+/-	PIM	PP	SH	GW	GT	S	PCT
78	30	40	70	+18	59	10	0	7	1	171	17.5

1994-95 statistics:

GP	G	A	TP	+/-	PIM	PP	SH	GW	GT	S	PCT
43	10	16	26	-5	41	7	0	0	0	118	8.5

1995-96 statistics:

GP	G	A	TP	+/-	PIM	PP	SH	GW	GT	S	PCT
61	12	20	32	-10	23	5	1	0	1	154	7.8

1996-97 statistics:

GP	G	A	TP	+/-	PIM	PP	SH	GW	GT	S	PCT
82	26	33	59	-6	22	6	0	3	0	181	14.4

PROJECTION

King is a 20-goal skater with 40-goal hands. His output should fall somewhere in between.

LAST SEASON

Signed as free agent, July 3, 1997. Acquired by Hartford from N.Y. Islanders for a 1997 fifth-round draft pick, March 18, 1997. Second on Whalers in goals and assists. Third on Whalers in points. Appeared in all 82 games.

THE FINESSE GAME

There is only one thing King does well, and that is score goals. He is at his best from the face-off dot of the left circle to the front of the net. He has great concentration through traffic and soft, soft hands for cradling passes and then snapping off the shot the instant the puck hits his blade. He has to play with someone who will get him the puck.

Among the best in the league on the power play, King has good anticipation and reads the offensive plays well. He is not a great skater but has improved his defensive awareness.

THE PHYSICAL GAME

A solid and durable player who takes a pounding in front of the net, King doesn't use his body well in other areas of the ice, which is one of the reasons for his defensive problems.

THE INTANGIBLES

If King is to have a comeback, Toronto is the place for it. He was excited by the chance to play for the Maple Leafs, who have two gifted centres — Mats Sundin and Steve Sullivan — either of whom could click with King.

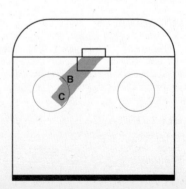

KRIS KING

Yrs. of NHL service: 8
Born: Bracebridge, Ont.; Feb. 18, 1966
Position: left wing
Height: 5-11
Weight: 208
Uniform no.: 17
Shoots: left

Career statistics:

GP	G	A	TP	PIM
648	58	76	134	1665

1993-94 statistics:

GP	G	A	TP	+/-	PIM	PP	SH	GW	GT	S	PCT
83	4	8	12	-22	205	0	0	1	0	86	4.7

1994-95 statistics:

GP	G	A	TP	+/-	PIM	PP	SH	GW	GT	S	PCT
48	4	2	6	0	85	0	0	0	0	58	6.9

1995-96 statistics:

GP	G	A	TP	+/-	PIM	PP	SH	GW	GT	S	PCT
81	9	11	20	-7	151	0	1	2	0	89	10.1

1996-97 statistics:

GP	G	A	TP	+/-	PIM	PP	SH	GW	GT	S	PCT
81	3	11	14	-7	185	0	0	0	0	57	5.3

PROJECTION

Points will be negligible, but King's contribution will be considerable.

LAST SEASON

Signed as free agent, July 8, 1997. Third on Coyotes in penalty minutes.

THE FINESSE GAME

King is a checking winger, a role that can wear on a player night after night, but he brings enthusiasm and hustle to every shift. He has to play that way to stay in the NHL, and he knows it. He doesn't possess many skills. He will generate some scoring chances with his speed but can't do much with the puck at tempo. He's more intent on chasing the puck carrier. He will create turnovers but doesn't do much with the puck when he gets it. Most of his scoring chances will be garbage goals off the scrums in front of the net.

A superb crunch-time player, whether protecting a lead or needing a big play in overtime, he'll do his utmost to deliver. He is a gamer.

THE PHYSICAL GAME

King knows somebody's got to do the grunt work, and he's willing and able. He's relentless along the boards and in the corners, and anyone who has his back to King or his head down will pay the physical price. King takes no prisoners and will stand up for his teammates. He will fight if needed, but his reputation as a clean, hard checker is no secret.

THE INTANGIBLES

King brings sandpaper and leadership to a team in desperate need of both. Although he is "only" a third-line winger, the Maple Leafs can use his character on and off the ice.

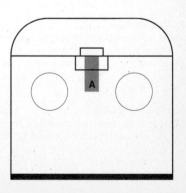

ALYN MCCAULEY

Yrs. of NHL service: 0
Born: Brockville, Ont.; May 29, 1977
Position: centre
Height: 5-11
Weight: 185
Uniform no.: n.a.
Shoots: left

		Career junior statistics:		
GP	G	A	TP	PIM
208	119	165	254	70

		1993-94 junior statistics:		
GP	G	A	TP	PIM
38	13	23	36	10

		1994-95 junior statistics:		
GP	G	A	TP	PIM
65	16	38	54	20

		1995-96 junior statistics:		
GP	G	A	TP	PIM
55	34	48	52	24

		1996-97 junior statistics:		
GP	G	A	TP	PIM
50	56	56	112	16

LAST SEASON

Rights acquired from New Jersey with Jason Smith and Steve Sullivan for Doug Gilmour and Dave Ellett, February 27, 1997. Named Canadian Hockey League Player of the Year. Second on team and third in OHL in scoring with 56-56 — 112 for Oshawa. Scored 0-1 — 1 in three playoff games for St. John's (AHL).

THE FINESSE GAME

McCauley is all finesse. His skating, scoring touch and vision stamped him as one of the most exciting players in major junior hockey last season.

He's a one-way player, equally adept at shooting and playmaking. He's at his best in an up-tempo game because he skates well and can handle the puck at speed. He makes and accepts passes at a quick pace. He has hockey smarts and sees the ice well, weighing his options in a flash.

McCauley needs to improve his defensive play. He uses his stick, not his body, to check.

THE PHYSICAL GAME

McCauley is a small, blocky player without much ferocity. If he were playing on a tougher team that might not be such a drawback, but he will have to fight a lot of his own battles on a finesse-laden Leafs squad (Tie Domi excepted, of course).

THE INTANGIBLES

McCauley has a great deal of confidence in his ability and is an intelligent player who knows the deck is stacked against him because of his size. He has a history of stepping up in big games (World Juniors, OHL playoffs). He has already suffered several concussions in his young career, which is a bit troublesome.

It's also interesting to note that the Devils, desperate for young scoring, were not planning on signing McCauley and packaged him in the Doug Gilmour trade.

PROJECTION

McCauley could use at least a half-season in the minors to adjust to the pro game, but the Leafs may not have that luxury.

FREDRIK MODIN

Yrs. of NHL service: 1
Born: Sundsvall, Sweden; Oct. 8, 1974
Position: left wing
Height: 6-3
Weight: 202
Uniform no.: 19
Shoots: left

Career statistics:

GP	G	A	TP	PIM
76	6	7	13	24

1996-97 statistics:

GP	G	A	TP	+/-	PIM	PP	SH	GW	GT	S	PCT
76	6	7	13	-14	24	0	0	0	0	85	7.1

LAST SEASON

First NHL season. Missed three games with concussion. Missed one game with flu. Missed one game with knee injury.

THE FINESSE GAME

Modin would have been better off getting acclimated to North American hockey in the minors last season, but the desperately depleted Maple Leafs pushed the Swedish rookie winger into part-time duty.

Modin came here with the reputation of being a playmaker, but he has a heavy, cannon shot. He doesn't use it enough and sometimes takes too long to get it away, so it gets deflected frequently. He has a bit of a knock-kneed skating style and isn't very pretty to watch, but his speed is NHL calibre and he's very strong.

THE PHYSICAL GAME

Modin has good size and will hit. He plays his best hockey when he gets physically involved and goes to the net.

THE INTANGIBLES

The young Swede played a fourth-line role but has some offensive skill that occasionally earned him a promotion to the second line. One scout called him a "Jethro," big, but very raw and green. He has a lot to learn about the game. His adjustment was made easier by his personality and good command of English.

PROJECTION

Modin has an upside and can play regularly on a third line for the Leafs. He has terrific hands, so he should be able to push his goals into double digits.

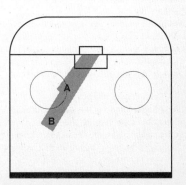

FELIX POTVIN

Yrs. of NHL service: 5
Born: Anjou, Que.; June 23, 1971
Position: goaltender
Height: 6-0
Weight: 190
Uniform no.: 29
Catches: left

Career statistics:

GP	MIN	GA	SO	GAA	A	PIM
297	17298	831	7	2.88	8	35

1993-94 statistics:

GP	MIN	GAA	W	L	T	SO	GA	S	SAPCT	PIM
66	3883	2.89	34	22	9	3	187	2010	.907	4

1994-95 statistics:

GP	MIN	GAA	W	L	T	SO	GA	S	SAPCT	PIM
36	2144	2.91	15	13	7	0	104	1120	.907	4

1995-96 statistics:

GP	MIN	GAA	W	L	T	SO	GA	S	SAPCT	PIM
69	4009	2.87	30	26	11	2	192	2135	.910	4

1996-97 statistics:

GP	MIN	GAA	W	L	T	SO	GA	S	SAPCT	PIM
74	4271	3.15	27	36	7	0	224	2438	.908	19

LAST SEASON

Led NHL goalies in minutes played. Faced most shots by any NHL goalie. Goals-against average above 3.00 for first time in five-year career.

THE PHYSICAL GAME

The Leafs worked hard in breaking Potvin of his habit of playing deep in his net, to the point where Rick Wamsley was pulled in from his pro scouting duties and travelled with the team the last few months of the season to school Potvin. He prefers to keep his skates in the paint at all times, but seems to be honestly trying to play at the top of his crease instead of back on his goal line, but it's been a battle getting Potvin out of his comfort zone.

Potvin is excellent on low shots. His style is similar to that of his idol, Patrick Roy, in that Potvin likes to butterfly and flirt with leaving a five-hole for shooters. The best place to beat Potvin is high, but shooters see that tempting gap between the pads and go for it, and he snaps the pads shut.

Potvin allows very few bad rebounds. He either controls them into the corners or deadens them in front of him. He's still weak with his stick. He doesn't use it well around the net to break up passes and hates to come out of his net to try to move the puck.

THE MENTAL GAME

Potvin is understanding the game better, and has maintained his calm despite the prevalent trade rumours. He needs to be more consistent. Players love to play for him because of his unruffled temperament.

THE INTANGIBLES

Potvin's last two years have been very average, but those trade rumours are just plain silly. Just who would replace Potvin? The new Leafs president Ken Dryden?

Potvin is still young and capable of shoring up the weaker parts of his game. He is a player who cares not only about his own game but about the team.

PROJECTION

Potvin had a strong final quarter of the season and is due for a major improvement in his goals-against this year.

MATHIEU SCHNEIDER

Yrs. of NHL service: 8
Born: New York, N.Y.; June 12, 1969
Position: left defense
Height: 5-11
Weight: 192
Uniform no.: 72
Shoots: left

Career statistics:

GP	G	A	TP	PIM
480	84	190	274	467

1993-94 statistics:

GP	G	A	TP	+/-	PIM	PP	SH	GW	GT	S	PCT
75	20	32	52	+15	62	11	0	4	0	193	10.4

1994-95 statistics:

GP	G	A	TP	+/-	PIM	PP	SH	GW	GT	S	PCT
43	8	21	29	-8	79	3	0	2	0	118	6.8

1995-96 statistics:

GP	G	A	TP	+/-	PIM	PP	SH	GW	GT	S	PCT
78	13	41	54	-20	103	7	0	1	0	191	6.8

1996-97 statistics:

GP	G	A	TP	+/-	PIM	PP	SH	GW	GT	S	PCT
26	5	7	12	+3	20	1	0	1	0	63	7.9

LAST SEASON

Missed 52 games with groin injuries and surgery. Suspended three games for flagrant elbow foul.

THE FINESSE GAME

Schneider's lost season left the Leafs bereft of much help on the blueline. He has developed into a good two-way defenseman with the offensive skills to get involved in the attack and to work the point on the power play; his major concern is his solid positional play. He makes fewer high-risk plays as he has gained more experience.

A talented skater, strong, balanced and agile, Schneider lacks breakaway speed but is quick with his first step and changes directions smoothly. He can carry the puck but does not lead many rushes. He gets the puck out of the corner quickly. He makes good defensive decisions.

Schneider has improved his point play, doing more with the puck than just drilling shots. He handles the puck well and looks for the passes down low. Given the green light, he is likely to get involved down low more often. He has the skating ability to recover quickly when he takes a chance.

THE PHYSICAL GAME

Schneider plays with determination, but he lacks the size and strength to be an impact defenseman physically. His goal is to play a containment game and move the puck quickly and intelligently out of the zone, which he does well. He is often matched against other teams' top scoring lines and always tries to do the job. He is best when paired with a physical defenseman. Schneider has a tendency to hit high and

gets penalties because of it.

THE INTANGIBLES

Schneider was scheduled to begin skating in midsummer. Expect a period of adjustment for him in the first half of the season as he rehabs and builds confidence in the injured area.

PROJECTION

Schneider is the Leafs' top defenseman and will get a lot of ice time. His production should be in the 45- to 50-point range.

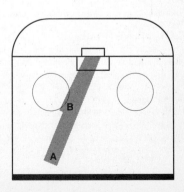

JASON SMITH

Yrs. of NHL service: 4
Born: Calgary, Alta.; Nov. 2, 1973
Position: right defense
Height: 6-3
Weight: 205
Uniform no.: 25
Shoots: right

Career statistics:

GP	G	A	TP	PIM
185	3	8	11	183

1993-94 statistics:

GP	G	A	TP	+/-	PIM	PP	SH	GW	GT	S	PCT
41	0	5	5	+7	43	0	0	0	0	47	0.0

1994-95 statistics:

GP	G	A	TP	+/-	PIM	PP	SH	GW	GT	S	PCT
2	0	0	0	-3	0	0	0	0	0	5	0.0

1995-96 statistics:

GP	G	A	TP	+/-	PIM	PP	SH	GW	GT	S	PCT
64	2	1	3	+5	86	0	0	0	0	52	3.8

1996-97 statistics:

GP	G	A	TP	+/-	PIM	PP	SH	GW	GT	S	PCT
78	1	7	8	-12	54	0	0	0	0	74	1.4

LAST SEASON

Acquired from New Jersey with Steve Sullivan and rights to Alyn McCauley for Doug Gilmour and Dave Ellett, February 25, 1997.

THE FINESSE GAME

Smith could be a poster boy for a campaign to start a trophy for best defensive defenseman. Like Sylvain Lefebvre, Smith will make his reputation along his own blueline with little fanfare and a lot of success.

Smith has a low-key personality and will never be the kind of defenseman who can control a game. Knee surgery has affected his skating somewhat, but he has better than average speed and fair mobility. He can be erratic in his defensive reads, but is showing constant improvement and making better decisions.

Smith won't make anyone forget Brian Leetch. He has a fairly heavy shot, but it has little movement on it. He's not very creative offensively and doesn't gamble. However, he can kill penalties, though he'll get into trouble against a team that cycles well down low.

THE PHYSICAL GAME

Smith is a solid hitter with a latent mean streak; his takeouts are effective along the boards and in front of the net. He's not as good in open ice because his mobility is not exceptional. He has a fairly long fuse but is a capable fighter.

Smith worked hard to make a speedy recovery from reconstructive knee surgery two seasons ago. He is very fit and can handle 26 to 28 minutes a game.

THE INTANGIBLES

Although he was somewhat buried on a team of veteran defensemen in New Jersey, Smith can be a top four defenseman on any NHL team. He wants to learn and will work hard to improve. He is very coachable, quietly confident and has good leadership ability. He will work best paired with an offensive defenseman.

PROJECTION

Smith is evolving into a reliable crunch-time player but his numbers will never be gaudy.

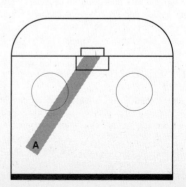

STEVE SULLIVAN

Yrs. of NHL service: 1
Born: Timmins, Ont.; July 6, 1974
Position: centre
Height: 5-9
Weight: 155
Uniform no.: 11
Shoots: right

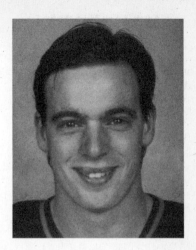

Career statistics:

GP	G	A	TP	PIM
70	18	29	47	45

1995-96 statistics:

GP	G	A	TP	+/-	PIM	PP	SH	GW	GT	S	PCT
16	5	4	9	+3	8	2	0	1	0	23	21.7

1996-97 statistics:

GP	G	A	TP	+/-	PIM	PP	SH	GW	GT	S	PCT
54	13	25	38	+14	37	3	0	3	1	108	12.0

LAST SEASON

Acquired from New Jersey with Jason Smith and rights to Alyn McCauley for Doug Gilmour and Dave Ellett, February 25, 1997. Fourth on team and seventh among NHL rookies in points. Second on team and fifth among NHL rookies in assists. Second among NHL rookies in plus-minus. Scored 8-7 — 15 in 15 games with Albany (AHL).

THE FINESSE GAME

One advantage to being as small as Sullivan, is that you are closer to the puck than a lot of your rivals. Sullivan complicates matters by using a short stick — short even by his standards — to keep the puck in his feet. He draws penalties by protecting the puck so well; foes usually have to foul him to get the puck.

By nature a centre, Sullivan has terrific hands, vision and anticipation. However, he will probably have to make his way in the NHL as a left wing, even though that means sending him into the wars along the boards. Playing wing, he doesn't have to be down low on defensive-zone coverage.

Sullivan is quick and smart enough to get himself out of pending jams, but he is so determined to get the puck and so patient once he has it that he will make a physical sacrifice to make the play.

THE PHYSICAL GAME

Sullivan will get bounced around but he will always get back up and dig for the puck along the wall or around the net. He is fiery and will get his stick up if he feels opponents are taking liberties. He will lose battles because of his size, but there won't be a Leaf ticket-holder who goes home thinking he or she was cheated by Sullivan's nonstop effort.

THE INTANGIBLES

Sullivan has great confidence in his ability, which will give him a needed edge against the larger players in the NHL. His talent level is a cut below the elite, or he would be a sure bet to succeed despite his stature. He has determination and grit.

PROJECTION

Sullivan's season was slowed by his injury in training camp. A full, healthy year on Toronto's second line could translate into a 60-point season for this dynamic player.

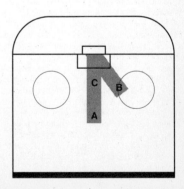

MATS SUNDIN

Yrs. of NHL service: 7
Born: Bromma, Sweden; Feb. 13, 1971
Position: right wing/centre
Height: 6-4
Weight: 215
Uniform no.: 13
Shoots: right

Career statistics:

GP	G	A	TP	PIM
529	232	326	558	438

1993-94 statistics:

GP	G	A	TP	+/-	PIM	PP	SH	GW	GT	S	PCT
84	32	53	85	+1	60	6	2	4	0	226	14.2

1994-95 statistics:

GP	G	A	TP	+/-	PIM	PP	SH	GW	GT	S	PCT
47	23	24	47	-5	14	9	0	4	1	173	13.3

1995-96 statistics:

GP	G	A	TP	+/-	PIM	PP	SH	GW	GT	S	PCT
76	33	50	83	+8	46	7	6	7	1	301	11.0

1996-97 statistics:

GP	G	A	TP	+/-	PIM	PP	SH	GW	GT	S	PCT
82	41	53	94	+6	59	7	4	8	1	281	14.6

LAST SEASON

Led team in points and game-winning goals for third consecutive season. Lead team in assists and shots for second consecutive season. Led team in goals and shorthanded goals. Tied for team lead in power-play goals. Second on team in plus-minus. Only Leaf to appear in all 82 games.

THE FINESSE GAME

Sundin played as a winger until the Doug Gilmour trade in February, when he was moved to centre. His best position is probably the off (left) wing, where he can come off the boards with speed and he's hard to check. As a centre, he gets the puck low in his own end; people can move to him right away, and he has to move the puck. If a checker stays with him Sundin can't get the puck back. But he is an elite player who has handled the changes with little complaint and with no damage to his effectiveness.

Sundin is a big skater who looks huge, as he uses an ultralong stick that gives him a broad wingspan. For a big man, he is an agile skater, and his balance has improved. He has good lower-body strength, supplying drive for battles along the boards. He doesn't stay checked. He's evasive, and once he is on the fly he is hard to stop. Sundin is less effective when carrying the puck. His best play is to get up a head of steam, jump into the holes and take a quick shot.

Sundin can take bad passes in stride, either kicking an errant puck up onto his stick or reaching behind to corral it. He isn't a clever stickhandler. His game is power and speed. Sundin doesn't look fast, but he has ground-eating strides that allow him to cover in two strides what other skaters do in three or four. He is quick, too, and can get untracked in a heartbeat.

His shot is excellent. He can use a slap shot, one-timer, wrister, or backhand. The only liability to his reach is that he will dangle the puck well away from his body and he doesn't always control it, which makes him vulnerable to a poke-check.

THE PHYSICAL GAME

Sundin is big and strong. He has shown better attention to off-ice work to improve his strength. His conditioning is excellent — he can skate all night. He has even shown a touch of mean, but mostly with his stick.

THE INTANGIBLES

Rumours about trading Sundin always seem to pop up, but who would you trade for him? It would take another elite player, like a Paul Kariya, to be worth a Sundin, and because of his size, Sundin is an untouchable. He may be the most underrated player in the NHL (and underpublicized, despite playing in a media centre that makes superstars out of far lesser players). Sundin is a quality player who is liked and respected by his coaches and teammates. He will become the captain of the Leafs, and this is his team now.

PROJECTION

Last season we doubted Sundin would reach the 100-point mark again, but he nearly made it. Playing without Gilmour this season will hurt his goal total, because the Swedish star will have to play a more unselfish role at centre. He scored only eight goals in 21 games after the trade after compiling 33 in 61. Unless some young Leaf winger turns into a bona fide sniper, or if Toronto can get more than 60 games out of Wendel Clark, Sundin's point totals will fall off this season to the 80-point range.

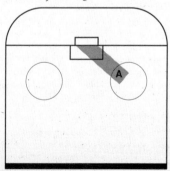

TODD WARRINER

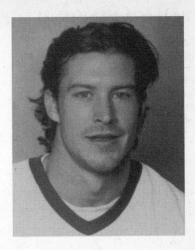

Yrs. of NHL service: 2
Born: Blenheim, Ont.; Jan. 3, 1974
Position: left wing
Height: 6-1
Weight: 188
Uniform no.: 8
Shoots: left

Career statistics:

GP	G	A	TP	PIM
137	19	29	48	41

1994-95 statistics:

GP	G	A	TP	+/-	PIM	PP	SH	GW	GT	S	PCT
5	0	0	0	-3	0	0	0	0	0	1	0.0

1995-96 statistics:

GP	G	A	TP	+/-	PIM	PP	SH	GW	GT	S	PCT
57	7	8	15	-11	26	1	0	0	0	79	8.9

1996-97 statistics:

GP	G	A	TP	+/-	PIM	PP	SH	GW	GT	S	PCT
75	12	21	33	-3	41	2	2	0	1	146	8.2

LAST SEASON

Second NHL season. Second on team in shorthanded goals. Third on team in assists. Missed five games with hip injuries.

THE FINESSE GAME

Warriner went through some horrendous slumps last season (including a 14-game goalless streak) when he failed to make use of his best asset, his shot. He has to shoot off the wing, driving wide on the defenseman, but he gets into the bad habit of cutting to the middle, where he is less effective.

Warriner releases his shot quickly from the circles, and although he doesn't have blinding speed he is slick enough to jump into holes, accept a pass and throw it quickly on net. He knows that the element of surprise is more important than winding up for a blast. On the flip side, however, he needs to read his options better, and learn to take his time with his shot when he does have the room. He has a tendency to panic and get rid of the puck when there might be a better play. The Leafs would like to see him develop the Dave Andreychuk style of shooting intentionally at the goalie's pads from tough angles and following the puck to the net for rebounds.

Warriner has relied on his natural ability through most levels of the sport, but will need to push himself to succeed at the NHL level. He had a splendid two months with the Leafs last season where he was able to handle any responsibility, then curiously went off his game.

Warriner's defensive game needs to improve, but he is a clever player who should be able to grasp the intricacies of a well-rounded game.

THE PHYSICAL GAME

Warriner is wiry, a little on the light side, and he'll need to add some muscle, since he lacks the top-shelf finesse skills to play a perimeter game. He maintains himself well.

THE INTANGIBLES

Warriner needs to mature. His problems last season seemed more mental than physical. He seemed to be a little too comfortable in a second-line role instead of pushing himself to challenge for a job on the number two line.

PROJECTION

Still an intriguing prospect, Warriner could jump past 50 points if he pushes himself, or settle into a 20- to 30-point third-line role.

DIMITRI YUSHKEVICH

Yrs. of NHL service:
Born: Barrie, Ont.; Dec. 8, 1969
Position: left wing
Height: 6-2
Weight: 210
Uniform no.: 34
Shoots: left

Career statistics:

GP	G	A	TP	PIM
340	20	81	101	370

1993-94 statistics:

GP	G	A	TP	+/-	PIM	PP	SH	GW	GT	S	PCT
75	5	25	30	-8	86	1	0	2	0	136	3.7

1994-95 statistics:

GP	G	A	TP	+/-	PIM	PP	SH	GW	GT	S	PCT
40	5	9	14	-4	47	3	1	1	0	80	6.3

1995-96 statistics:

GP	G	A	TP	+/-	PIM	PP	SH	GW	GT	S	PCT
69	1	10	11	-14	54	1	0	0	0	96	1.0

1996-97 statistics:

GP	G	A	TP	+/-	PIM	PP	SH	GW	GT	S	PCT
74	4	10	14	-24	56	1	1	1	0	99	4.0

LAST SEASON

Tied for team lead in scoring among defensemen. Worst plus-minus on team. Missed four games with hamstring injury. Missed two games with knee injury. Benched two games for disciplinary reasons.

THE FINESSE GAME

When Yushkevich pulls eveything together mentally and physically, he steps up into a level that isn't elite but is a solid "B" game. It's just frustrating that he does so infrequently.

Yushkevich is a good skater with a decent shot. It's a real good shot in practice, but in games, he takes too long to get it away. He is strong and well-balanced on his feet. He can move laterally, pivot and put on a short burst of speed, or sustain a rush the length of the rink. Occasionally he can be beaten with outside speed, but it takes a pretty good skater to do it.

Yushkevich doesn't react quickly enough in game situations. He is still fairly young for a defenseman but has enough experience to play better than he does. The problem is part reads and part stubbornness. He also tends to make some maddening nonchalant plays.

He can work the point on a second power-play unit and will kill penalties.

THE PHYSICAL GAME

Yushkevich is very fit and, if asked, can play 30 minutes a game. He'll grind. When the mood strikes him, he can play with an edge and use his body to win puck battles. He can hit to hurt and can be annoying to play against. Last season, he was mostly annoying to play with.

THE INTANGIBLES

Yushkevich has a lot of inconsistencies in his game and hasn't made friends with his coaches or teammates in Toronto. He was benched for swearing at an assistant coach and missed a team flight. Not exactly a team guy.

PROJECTION

Yushkevich has been in and out in five NHL seasons and could be out — of Toronto. He had two seasons with 30-plus points with the Flyers but hasn't found that groove since.

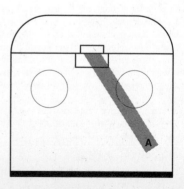

VANCOUVER CANUCKS

Players' Statistics 1996-97

POS.	NO.	PLAYER	GP	G	A	PTS	+/-	PIM	PP	SH	GW	GT	S	PCT
R	89	ALEXANDER MOGILNY	76	31	42	73	9	18	7	1	4	1	174	17.8
L	23	MARTIN GELINAS	74	35	33	68	6	42	6	1	3	1	177	19.8
R	96	PAVEL BURE	63	23	32	55	-14	40	4	1	2		265	8.7
C	17	MIKE RIDLEY	75	20	32	52	0	42	3		5		79	25.3
L	19	MARKUS NASLUND	78	21	20	41	-15	30	4		4		120	17.5
R	16	TREVOR LINDEN	49	9	31	40	5	27	2	2	2		84	10.7
R	26	MIKE SILLINGER	78	17	20	37	-3	25	3	3	2		112	15.2
D	21	JYRKI LUMME	66	11	24	35	8	32	5		2		107	10.3
R	28	BRIAN NOONAN	73	12	22	34	-3	34	3	1	1	1	100	12.0
L	7	DAVID ROBERTS	58	10	17	27	11	51	1	1	1		74	13.5
D	44	DAVE BABYCH	78	5	22	27	-2	38	2		1		105	4.8
C	13	SERGEI NEMCHINOV	69	8	16	24	9	16	1		2		97	8.2
R	14	*LONNY BOHONOS	36	11	11	22	-3	10	2		1		67	16.4
D	6	ADRIAN AUCOIN	70	5	16	21	0	63	1				116	4.3
D	3	BRET HEDICAN	67	4	15	19	-3	51	2		1		93	4.3
C	24	SCOTT WALKER	64	3	15	18	2	132					55	5.5
D	25	*STEVE STAIOS	63	3	14	17	-24	91			1		66	4.5
D	32	CHRIS JOSEPH	63	3	13	16	-21	62	2		1		99	3.0
L	8	DONALD BRASHEAR	69	8	5	13	-8	245			2		61	13.1
L	29	GINO ODJICK	70	5	8	13	-5	371	1				85	5.9
D	27	LEIF ROHLIN	40	2	8	10	4	8					37	5.4
D	4	*MARK WOTTON	36	3	6	9	8	19		1			41	7.3
D	5	DANA MURZYN	61	1	7	8	7	118					70	1.4
C	20	ALEXANDER SEMAK	18	2	1	3	-2	2	1				12	16.7
R	18	TROY CROWDER	30	1	2	3	-6	52					11	9.1
L	22	*LARRY COURVILLE	19		2	2	-4	11					11	
G	1	KIRK MCLEAN	44		2	2	0	2						
G	31	COREY HIRSCH	39		1	1	0	6						
D	2	YEVGENY NAMESTNIKOV	2				-1	4					1	
G	30	*MICHAEL FOUNTAIN	6					0						

GP = games played; G = goals; A = assists; PTS = points; +/- = goals-for minus goals-against while player is on ice; PIM = penalties in minutes; PP = power-play goals; SH = shorthanded goals; GW = game-winning goals; GT = game-tying goals; S = no. of shots; PCT = percentage of goals to shots; * = rookie

ADRIAN AUCOIN

Yrs. of NHL service: 2
Born: Ottawa, Ont.; July 3, 1973
Position: right defenseman
Height: 6-1
Weight: 194
Uniform no.: 6
Shoots: right

Career statistics:

GP	G	A	TP	PIM
120	10	30	40	97

1994-95 statistics:

GP	G	A	TP	+/-	PIM	PP	SH	GW	GT	S	PCT
1	1	0	1	+1	0	0	0	0	0	2	50.0

1995-96 statistics:

GP	G	A	TP	+/-	PIM	PP	SH	GW	GT	S	PCT
49	4	14	18	+8	34	2	0	0	0	85	4.7

1996-97 statistics:

GP	G	A	TP	+/-	PIM	PP	SH	GW	GT	S	PCT
70	5	16	21	0	63	1	0	0	0	116	4.3

LAST SEASON

Missed six games with shoulder injury.

THE FINESSE GAME

Aucoin was a low draft pick (117th overall in 1992), but by playing with the Canadian national team and in the 1994 Olympics, he has upgraded his offensive skills and developed into a promising offensive defenseman. His major flaw is that he has added little else to his game in his two NHL seasons.

Aucoin is a mobile, agile skater who moves well with the puck. He doesn't have breakaway speed, but he jumps alertly into the play. On the power play, he smartly switches off with a forward to cut in deep, and he has good hands for shots in tight. He also has a good point shot, though it is not elite.

THE PHYSICAL GAME

Aucoin is a strong, good-sized defenseman who often plays smaller. He needs to be more assertive around the net to earn himself more ice time. He has no mean streak to speak of; opponents know he can be pushed around and they take advantage of that. Aucoin just wants to play and have nobody notice him, which is usually what happens.

THE INTANGIBLES

Aucoin would be a depth guy on a stronger NHL team, but instead of being a sixth or seventh defenseman he lingers in the Canucks' top four by default.

PROJECTION

Aucoin is a bubble guy who will get 20 of the quietest NHL points you'll see next season.

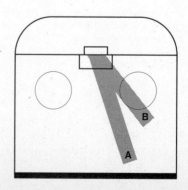

LONNY BOHONOS

Yrs. of NHL service: 1
Born: Winnipeg, Man.; May 20, 1973
Position: right wing
Height: 5-11
Weight: 190
Uniform no.: 14
Shoots: right

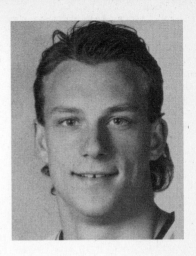

Career statistics:

GP	G	A	TP	PIM
39	11	12	23	10

1995-96 statistics:

GP	G	A	TP	+/-	PIM	PP	SH	GW	GT	S	PCT
3	0	1	1	+1	0	0	0	0	0	3	0.0

1996-97 statistics:

GP	G	A	TP	+/-	PIM	PP	SH	GW	GT	S	PCT
36	11	11	22	-3	10	2	0	1	0	67	16.4

LAST SEASON

First NHL season. Led Syracuse (AHL) in goals and second in scoring with 22-30 — 52 in 41 games played.

THE FINESSE GAME

Bohonos's idol is Brett Hull, and, like Hull, he has a big-time shot and major-league scoring ability. Just look at the numbers Bohonos posted in under half a season with the Canucks and you get an idea of his tantalizing talent. He lacks consistency, however. Like Hull in his early days, Bohonos plays when he wants to. You can float when you're Hull, but not when you're trying to establish yourself as an NHL player.

Bohonos has a heavy, quick shot, the hands, and the skating ability to stick at the NHL level. His defensive work isn't great, but the Canucks would live with it if they believed they could get a consistent effort. His mental approach is the only thing holding him back.

THE PHYSICAL GAME

Bohonos does his damage with the puck, not his body. On nights when he's on, he pushes his way through checks, but he could use some work in the strength department.

THE INTANGIBLES

Bohonos is a smallish skill guy, which unfortunately for him is a category the Canucks are overstocked in. He will have to show something really special in training camp to earn a full-time job, or hope Alexander Mogilny is traded, or be ready in case of injury to Pavel Bure, which is how Bohonos got his break last season.

PROJECTION

A scorer at the junior- and minor-league levels, Bohonos has been loitering on the fringe of the Canucks' depth chart. If he is able to get into the lineup, he could score 25 to 30 goals.

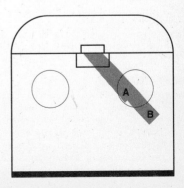

DONALD BRASHEAR

Yrs. of NHL service: 3
Born: Bedford, Ind.; Jan. 7, 1972
Position: left wing
Height: 6-2
Weight: 220
Uniform no.: 8
Shoots: left

Career statistics:

GP	G	A	TP	PIM
170	11	12	23	565

1993-94 statistics:

GP	G	A	TP	+/-	PIM	PP	SH	GW	GT	S	PCT
14	2	2	4	0	34	0	0	0	0	15	13.3

1994-95 statistics:

GP	G	A	TP	+/-	PIM	PP	SH	GW	GT	S	PCT
20	1	1	2	-5	63	0	0	1	0	10	10.0

1995-96 statistics:

GP	G	A	TP	+/-	PIM	PP	SH	GW	GT	S	PCT
67	0	4	4	-10	223	0	0	0	0	25	0.0

1996-97 statistics:

GP	G	A	TP	+/-	PIM	PP	SH	GW	GT	S	PCT
69	8	5	13	-8	245	0	0	2	0	61	13.1

LAST SEASON

Acquired from Montreal for Jassen Cullimore, November 13, 1996. Second on team in penalty minutes. Served four-game suspension. Missed games with back injury.

THE FINESSE GAME

Brashear scored 38 goals in the AHL in 1993-94, proving he can do more with his hands than just wallop the daylights out of some victim. The trade that brought him to Vancouver looked like little more than a swap-meet transaction, but Brashear brought an energy to his game after the move and was surprisingly effective in a third-line role.

Brashear had no points in 10 games with Montreal, then scored 8-15-23 in just 59 with the Canucks. He can play on the third and fourth lines, and has to work hard for his scoring chances, most of which come from his churning around the net. He has a hard but predictable shot from the left circle.

THE PHYSICAL GAME

Brashear has improved his fighting. He's big, tough and mean. He hits to hurt and creates a lot of room for himself.

THE INTANGIBLES

Brashear was ticketed out of Montreal for an ugly row with then-coach Mario Tremblay. The Habs would probably be happy to take him back, given the way they are pushed around on a nightly basis. The Canucks lineup is loaded with small, weenie forwards (and defensemen), and Brashear and Gino Odjick are valuable insurance. He'll come into this year's training camp after playing for Team USA in the World Championships, and his confidence has never been higher.

PROJECTION

Brashear will get the most quality ice time of his career if he re-signs with the Canucks (he was a restricted free agent during the off-season). If your pool includes penalty minutes, take him.

PAVEL BURE

Yrs. of NHL service: 6
Born: Moscow, Russia; Mar. 31, 1971
Position: right wing
Height: 5-10
Weight: 189
Uniform no.: 96
Shoots: left

Career statistics:

GP	G	A	TP	PIM
346	203	185	388	280

1993-94 statistics:

GP	G	A	TP	+/-	PIM	PP	SH	GW	GT	S	PCT
76	60	47	107	+1	86	25	4	9	0	374	16.0

1994-95 statistics:

GP	G	A	TP	+/-	PIM	PP	SH	GW	GT	S	PCT
44	20	23	43	-8	47	6	2	2	0	198	10.1

1995-96 statistics:

GP	G	A	TP	+/-	PIM	PP	SH	GW	GT	S	PCT
15	6	7	13	-2	8	1	1	0	0	78	7.7

1996-97 statistics:

GP	G	A	TP	+/-	PIM	PP	SH	GW	GT	S	PCT
63	23	32	55	-14	40	4	1	2	0	265	8.7

LAST SEASON

Led team in shots. Third on team in goals, assists and points. Missed one game due to suspension. Missed one game with flu. Missed seven games with neck injury.

THE FINESSE GAME

Every time Bure touches the puck, fans in his home rink move to the edge of their seats. The Russian Rocket's quickness — and his control of the puck at supersonic speed — means anything is possible. He intimidates with his skating, driving back defenders who must play off him or risk being deked out of their skates at the blueline. He opens up tremendous ice for his teammates and will leave a drop pass or, more often, try to do it himself.

Bure's major weakness is his failure to use his teammates better. He will attempt to go through a team one-on-five rather than use his support. Of course, once in awhile he can actually do it. That's the scary part. He has great balance and agility and he seems to move equally well with the puck or without it. The puck doesn't slow him down a fraction.

Bure doesn't do much defensively. He prefers to hang out at centre ice, and when he is going through a slump he doesn't do the other little things that can make a player useful until the scoring starts to click again. He is a shorthanded threat because of his break-away speed and anticipation.

His explosive skating comes from his thick, powerful thighs, which look like a speed skater's.

THE PHYSICAL GAME

Bure's neck injury caused him a great deal of pain all season, and prevented him from making any contact. Bure has a little nasty edge to him (the suspension came for a flagrant elbow), and will make solid hits for the puck, though he doesn't apply himself as enthusiastically in a defensive role even when he is healthy. He has to play a reckless game to drive to the net and score goals. He takes a lot of punishment getting there and that's what makes him vulnerable to injuries.

THE INTANGIBLES

Injuries have robbed Bure of two seasons, and it's questionable how effective he'll be this year. He was still suffering from headaches and neck pain after a whiplash-type injury at the start of the season. Bure missed almost the entire 1995-96 season with a knee injury and surgery.

Like Alexander Mogilny, Bure has had his run-ins with new coach Tom Renney, and hasn't had a happy couple of years in Vancouver.

PROJECTION

Bure still has 60 goals in him, but not this season. A more reliable bet is 30.

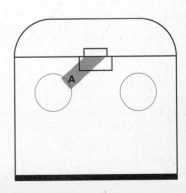

MARTIN GELINAS

Yrs. of NHL service: 8
Born: Shawinigan, Que.; June 5, 1970
Position: left wing
Height: 5-11
Weight: 195
Uniform no.: 23
Shoots: left

Career statistics:

GP	G	A	TP	PIM
523	152	143	295	327

1993-94 statistics:

GP	G	A	TP	+/-	PIM	PP	SH	GW	GT	S	PCT
64	14	14	28	-8	34	3	0	1	2	107	13.1

1994-95 statistics:

GP	G	A	TP	+/-	PIM	PP	SH	GW	GT	S	PCT
46	13	10	23	+8	36	1	0	4	0	75	17.3

1995-96 statistics:

GP	G	A	TP	+/-	PIM	PP	SH	GW	GT	S	PCT
81	30	26	56	+8	59	3	4	5	1	181	16.6

1996-97 statistics:

GP	G	A	TP	+/-	PIM	PP	SH	GW	GT	S	PCT
74	35	33	68	+6	42	6	1	3	1	177	19.8

Canuck who had a season to be proud of last year.

PROJECTION

Gelinas needs to play with someone who'll put the puck on the net and keep the game simple. His work ethic should keep him in the low 30-goal range.

LAST SEASON

Led team in goals with career high. Second on team in assists and points, both career highs. Second on team in power-play goals and shooting percentage. Missed six games with fractured ribs.

THE FINESSE GAME

Gelinas has come into his own as a confident scorer and a competent two-way forward. He has improved over each of the last two seasons and has found a home in Vancouver after being bounced around several organizations. The Canucks picked him up on waivers in 1994.

Gelinas plays a grinding game on the dump-and-chase. Much of his scoring is generated by his forechecking, with the majority of his goals tap-ins from about five feet out. He is strong along the boards and in front of the net. He is not a natural scorer, but he has good instincts and works hard for his chances. He is a good penalty killer.

Gelinas is ideally a third-line winger, but he has played on the top lines with the Canucks because they needed help. His hockey sense and puckhandling prevent him from blossoming in a bigger role.

THE PHYSICAL GAME

Gelinas is a small player and seems to get himself into situations where he just gets flattened. He isn't intimidated, but he does get wiped out of the play and he needs to be smarter about jumping in and out of holes, paying the price only when necessary.

THE INTANGIBLES

Gelinas is coming into his prime and is about the only

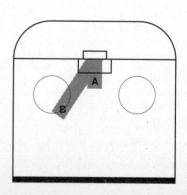

BRET HEDICAN

Yrs. of NHL service: 5
Born: St. Paul, Minn.; Aug. 10, 1970
Position: left defense
Height: 6-2
Weight: 195
Uniform no.: 3
Shoots: left

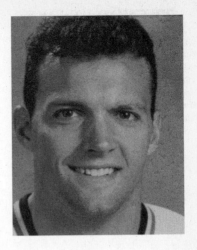

Career statistics:

GP	G	A	TP	PIM
304	13	69	82	241

1993-94 statistics:

GP	G	A	TP	+/-	PIM	PP	SH	GW	GT	S	PCT
69	0	12	12	-7	64	0	0	0	0	88	0.0

1994-95 statistics:

GP	G	A	TP	+/-	PIM	PP	SH	GW	GT	S	PCT
45	2	11	13	-3	34	0	0	0	0	56	3.6

1995-96 statistics:

GP	G	A	TP	+/-	PIM	PP	SH	GW	GT	S	PCT
77	6	23	29	+8	83	1	0	0	0	113	5.3

1996-97 statistics:

GP	G	A	TP	+/-	PIM	PP	SH	GW	GT	S	PCT
67	4	15	19	-3	51	2	0	1	0	93	4.3

LAST SEASON

Missed four games with groin injury. Missed 11 games with back injury.

THE FINESSE GAME

A well-kept secret in Vancouver, Hedican is among the best-skating defensemen in the league. He has a nice, deep knee bend and his fluid stride provides good acceleration; each stride eats up lots of ice. His steady balance allows him to go down to one knee and use his stick to challenge passes from the corners. He uses quickness, range and reach to make a confident stand at the defensive blueline.

Hedican happily uses his speed with the puck to drive down the wing and create trouble in the offensive zone. He also varies the attack. He seems to prefer the left wing boards but will also take the right-wing route to try to make plays off the backhand.

Hedican is a good enough stickhandler to try one-on-one moves. He is eager to jump into the play. He will never be a great point- getter or playmaker because he doesn't think the game well enough, but he tries to help his team on the attack. He simply doesn't have elite ability. He is a better player in the playoffs because he doesn't think as much and lets his natural instincts rule.

Hedican knows that if an attacker beats him, he will be able to keep up with him and steer him to bad ice. He is the perfect guy to pick up the puck behind the net and get it to the redline and start the half-court game. He doesn't always just put his head down and go. He will move up the middle and look for a pass to a breaking wing.

THE PHYSICAL GAME

Hedican is one of the most fit athletes on the team. He has decent size but not a great deal of strength or toughness. He won't bulldoze people in front of the net, preferring to tie people up and go for the puck. He is more of a stick checker than a body checker, but will sometimes knock a player off the puck at the blueline, control it and make a smart first pass. His preference is to use body positioning to nullify an opponent rather than initiate hard body contact.

THE INTANGIBLES

Hedican played his best hockey when he was partner to the departed Jeff Brown. His game would shine if the Canucks could find another sleek offensive defenseman to pair with him, because then the partner could move the puck and Hedican could hit the holes, be the release guy and get the puck out of the zone. He's one of the first players other teams ask about when trying to make a trade.

PROJECTION

Hedican's numbers are improving gradually from season to season, but we doubt he'll surpass the 40-point mark. He is developing into a solid two-way defenseman and can be expected to improve sharply over the next few seasons as he gains confidence and experience. He won't lead the team in scoring, but don't be surprised if he ranks first or second among Canucks defensemen.

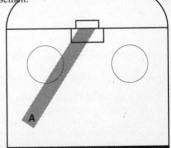

TREVOR LINDEN

Yrs. of NHL service: 9
Born: Medicine Hat, Alta.; Apr. 11, 1970
Position: centre/right wing
Height: 6-4
Weight: 210
Uniform no.: 16
Shoots: right

Career statistics:

GP	G	A	TP	PIM
660	240	307	547	520

1993-94 statistics:

GP	G	A	TP	+/-	PIM	PP	SH	GW	GT	S	PCT
84	32	29	61	+6	73	10	2	3	0	234	13.7

1994-95 statistics:

GP	G	A	TP	+/-	PIM	PP	SH	GW	GT	S	PCT
48	18	22	40	-5	40	9	0	1	3	129	14.0

1995-96 statistics:

GP	G	A	TP	+/-	PIM	PP	SH	GW	GT	S	PCT
82	33	47	80	+6	42	12	1	2	0	202	16.3

1996-97 statistics:

GP	G	A	TP	+/-	PIM	PP	SH	GW	GT	S	PCT
49	9	31	40	+5	27	2	2	2	0	84	10.7

LAST SEASON

Missed 24 games with left knee injury, ending "iron man" streak at 482 consecutive games (longest active in NHL at time of injury). Missed 16 games with rib injury.

THE FINESSE GAME

Linden is a good player during the regular season, who lifts his game a notch in the playoffs or in other big games. He would be much more effective as a winger than a centre, but the Canucks are very weak up the middle and need a pivot with good size to match up against many of the NHL's power centres, so he is pretty much stuck. Not a graceful skater, at times Linden looks very awkward, and he's not as strong on his skates as a player of his size should be. Despite his heavy feet his agility is satisfactory, but he lacks first-step quickness and doesn't have the all-out speed to pull away from a checker. He has a big turning radius.

Linden has improved his release, but it is not quick. He has a long reach, but unlike, say, Dave Andreychuk (who is built along similar lines), his short game is not as effective as it should be.

Linden is unselfish and makes quick, safe passing decisions that help his team break smartly up the ice, often creating odd-man rushes. He has improved tremendously in his defensive coverage.

THE PHYSICAL GAME

Last season's two prolonged absences might be a blessing in disguise, because Linden played through injuries to keep his streak alive. He can afford to back off and take a night if he has to.

Linden is big but doesn't always play tough, and so doesn't make good use of his size. He will attack the blueline and draw the attention of both defensemen, but will pull up rather than try to muscle through and earn a holding penalty. There are people he should

nullify who still seem able to get away from him. He does not skate through the physical challenges along the boards.

If only he would keep his feet moving, Linden would be so much more commanding. Instead, he can be angled off the play fairly easily because he will not battle for better ice. He uses his body more to defend than to help create offense. He will use his range to cut down the ice on a player, then merely stick out his stick to slow him down, rather than throw a shoulder into him.

When Linden is throwing his weight around, he drives to the net and drags a defender or two with him, opening up a lot of ice for his teammates. He creates havoc in front of the net on the power play, planting himself for screens and deflections. When the puck is at the side boards, he's smart enough to move up higher, between the circles, and force the penalty killers to make a decision. If the defenseman on that side steps up to cover him, space will open behind the defenseman; if a forward collapses to cover him, a point shot will open up.

THE INTANGIBLES

Linden is very likable and is a team leader. He faces other team's top checking attention night after night. His injuries never allowed him to play at his best last season.

PROJECTION

Linden won't be a 100-point scorer. He'll get his 25 to 30 goals and 65 to 70 points on a regular basis.

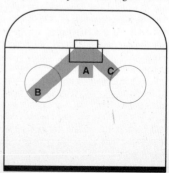

JYRKI LUMME

Yrs. of NHL service: 9
Born: Tampere, Finland; July 16, 1966
Position: right defense
Height: 6-1
Weight: 205
Uniform no.: 21
Shoots: left

Career statistics:

GP	G	A	TP	PIM
580	76	239	315	396

1993-94 statistics:

GP	G	A	TP	+/-	PIM	PP	SH	GW	GT	S	PCT
83	13	42	55	+3	50	1	3	3	0	161	8.1

1994-95 statistics:

GP	G	A	TP	+/-	PIM	PP	SH	GW	GT	S	PCT
36	5	12	17	+4	26	3	0	1	0	78	6.4

1995-96 statistics:

GP	G	A	TP	+/-	PIM	PP	SH	GW	GT	S	PCT
80	17	37	54	-9	50	8	0	2	2	192	8.9

1996-97 statistics:

GP	G	A	TP	+/-	PIM	PP	SH	GW	GT	S	PCT
66	11	24	35	+8	32	5	0	2	0	107	10.3

LAST SEASON

Led team defensemen in scoring for second straight season. Missed 16 games with muscle tear in shoulder.

THE FINESSE GAME

Lumme is one of the Canucks' more mobile defenseman, an accomplished puck carrier who can rush the puck out of danger and make a smart first pass to start the attack. He likes to gamble a bit offensively, but he has the good skating ability to be able to wheel back into a defensive mode.

He plays the right point on the power play. His shot isn't overpowering, but he keeps it low and on net and times it well. He has very good hands and is adept at keeping the puck in. He also uses his lateral mobility to slide along the blueline into the centre to quarterback the power play. Lumme will also glide to the top of the circle for a shot. He can control a game and make everyone play at his pace.

Defensively, he uses his hand skills for sweep- and poke-checks. He will challenge at the blueline to try to knock the puck free. He is tough to beat one-on-one, and always comes out of the corner with the puck. Lumme is a strong penalty killer because of his range and anticipation.

THE PHYSICAL GAME

Lumme is all finesse. He will take a hit to protect the puck or make a play, but he won't throw himself at anybody. Other teams like to key on Lumme, because if he gets hit often and hard enough, he can be taken out of a game early, depriving the Canucks of a valuable component of their offense.

THE INTANGIBLES

This is a contract year for Lumme, and if he doesn't get the deal done before the season starts, he will struggle because he is not the kind of guy who wants to play without that security.

He's not a number one defenseman because his all-around skills aren't good enough, but he's just a cut below the NHL's best rearguards. He has improved defensively, but his key value remains his open-ice play and his involvement in the attack.

PROJECTION

If the Canucks make Lumme happy with a new contract, he should produce close to 60 points if healthy.

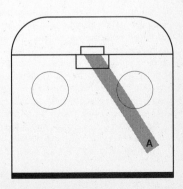

KIRK MCLEAN

Yrs. of NHL service: 10
Born: Willowdale, Ont.; June 26, 1966
Position: goaltender
Height: 6-0
Weight: 195
Uniform no.: 1
Catches: left

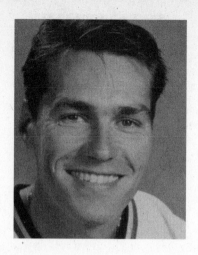

Career statistics:

GP	MIN	GA	SO	GAA	A	PIM
493	28677	1561	19	3.27	20	54

1993-94 statistics:

GP	MIN	GAA	W	L	T	SO	GA	S	SAPCT	PIM
52	3128	2.99	23	26	3	3	156	1430	.891	2

1994-95 statistics:

GP	MIN	GAA	W	L	T	SO	GA	S	SAPCT	PIM
40	2374	2.75	18	12	10	1	109	1140	.904	4

1995-96 statistics:

GP	MIN	GAA	W	L	T	SO	GA	S	SAPCT	PIM
45	2645	3.54	15	21	9	2	156	1292	.879	6

1996-97 statistics:

GP	MIN	GAA	W	L	T	SO	GA	S	SAPCT	PIM
44	2581	3.21	21	18	3	0	138	1247	.889	2

LAST SEASON

Missed 30 games with knee injury.

THE PHYSICAL GAME

McLean stays on his feet more than any goalie in the NHL. He has great lateral movement. Maybe because of his soccer training, his movement and balance are advanced. He is smooth, almost casual, in his post-to-post moves.

McLean makes himself look big in the net because of his positioning and stand-up play. He is very solid technically and has good reflexes. His solid foundation means few bad stretches of play. He will blow the occasional angle, especially on the stick side, but he has a great deal of confidence in his game and does not rattle easily. His bad streaks are usually caused by playing too deep in the net and being passive.

He's good up high, with a quick glove hand. He is strong on his stick and uses it well around the net for jabbing at puckhandlers or breaking up passes. He makes shooters try to be too perfect. McLean doesn't waste any motion, which makes him seem downright lethargic at times, but the lack of dramatics should not detract from appreciation of his overall technical skill. There's nothing objectionable about making the job easier; the job is tough enough without adding unnecessary flourishes. He does not showboat.

McLean handles the puck well, again, without much excitement, but enough to help out his team defensively. He is smart with the puck on his forehand and backhand, and recognizes when to move it and when to leave it for his defense.

THE MENTAL GAME

The key to McLean is to fluster him early. He is a big goalie, who usually needs to handle some shots to get into the flow of the game, and he tends to get better as the game moves along.

THE INTANGIBLES

McLean has had surgery on both of his knees in the past two seasons.

PROJECTION

Challenges from Corey Hirsch and Mike Fountain have fallen flat. The Canucks missed the playoffs because they didn't have a healthy McLean. He is not among the NHL's elite goalies, but he's a serviceable number one.

MARK MESSIER

Yrs. of NHL service: 18
Born: Edmonton, Alta.; Jan. 18, 1961
Position: centre
Height: 6-1
Weight: 205
Uniform no.: 11
Shoots: left

Career statistics:

GP	G	A	TP	PIM
1272	575	977	1552	1596

1993-94 statistics:

GP	G	A	TP	+/-	PIM	PP	SH	GW	GT	S	PCT
76	26	58	84	+25	76	6	2	5	0	216	12.0

1994-95 statistics:

GP	G	A	TP	+/-	PIM	PP	SH	GW	GT	S	PCT
46	14	39	53	+8	40	3	3	2	0	126	11.1

1995-96 statistics:

GP	G	A	TP	+/-	PIM	PP	SH	GW	GT	S	PCT
74	47	52	99	+29	122	14	1	5	1	241	19.5

1996-97 statistics:

GP	G	A	TP	+/-	PIM	PP	SH	GW	GT	S	PCT
71	36	48	84	+12	88	7	5	9	1	227	15.9

LAST SEASON

Signed as free agent, July 28, 1997. Led Rangers in goals. Second on Rangers in points. Fifth in NHL in shorthanded goals. Led NHL in shorthanded points (11). Missed four games due to sprained elbow. Missed two games due to back spasms. Missed two games due to charley horse. Served two-game suspension for hitting from behind.

THE FINESSE GAME

Messier will use his speed to drive defenders back, then stop and quickly check his options, making the most of the time and space he has earned. He is unlikely to try many one-on-one moves; he prefers to makes the utmost use of his teammates.

Messier is strong on his skates: he changes directions, pivots, bursts into open ice and, when his game is at its strongest, does it all with or without the puck. Messier still has tremendous acceleration and a powerful burst of straightaway speed, which is tailor-made for killing penalties and scoring shorthanded goals — even if he cheats into the neutral zone, looking for a breakaway pass, too often.

Messier's shot of choice is a wrister off the back foot from the right-wing circle, which is where he always seems to gravitate. He also makes as much use of the backhand, for passing and shooting, as any other North American player in the league. Messier will weave to the right-wing circle, fake a pass to the centre, get the goalie to cheat away from the post, then flip a backhand under the crossbar. He shoots from almost anywhere and is unpredictable in his shot selection when the back-foot wrist is not available.

THE PHYSICAL GAME

The Messier mean streak is legendary, even if less frequently evident. He is a master of the preemptive strike, the elbows or stick held teeth-high when a checker is coming towards him. Anyone who goes into the corner with him pays the price. But last season, he was far too easily ridden off the play far too many times.

THE INTANGIBLES

There are few better big-game players in NHL history than Messier, but the past is the past, and at 36 he is simply overtaxed by the amount of playing time he sees night after night. Messier wants to be on the ice, which makes it tough for a coach to tell him "No."

PROJECTION

Messier spent enough of his time on the perimeter to make you wonder if that next level is gone forever. Clearly the Canucks don't think so, as evidenced by their $20-million, three-year contract offer. Messier will get his points — he always does, and his output of 47 and 36 goals over the past two years is proof of that. But, particularly as this is an Olympic year, he figures once again to be either exhausted or injured when the playoffs begin.

ALEXANDER MOGILNY

Yrs. of NHL service: 8
Born: Khabarovsk, Russia; Feb. 18, 1969
Position: right wing
Height: 5-11
Weight: 187
Uniform no.: 89
Shoots: left

Career statistics:

GP	G	A	TP	PIM
536	297	327	624	237

1993-94 statistics:

GP	G	A	TP	+/-	PIM	PP	SH	GW	GT	S	PCT
66	32	47	79	+8	22	17	0	7	1	258	12.4

1994-95 statistics:

GP	G	A	TP	+/-	PIM	PP	SH	GW	GT	S	PCT
44	19	28	47	0	36	12	0	2	1	148	12.8

1995-96 statistics:

GP	G	A	TP	+/-	PIM	PP	SH	GW	GT	S	PCT
79	55	52	107	+14	16	10	5	6	3	292	18.8

1996-97 statistics:

GP	G	A	TP	+/-	PIM	PP	SH	GW	GT	S	PCT
76	31	42	73	+9	18	7	1	4	1	174	17.8

LAST SEASON

Led team in points for fifth consecutive season. Led team in assists and power-play goals. Second on team in goals. Tied for second on team in plus-minus and game-winning goals.

THE FINESSE GAME

Mogilny's biggest problems are his inconsistency and motivation. He has so many wondrous skills, but most of the time just doesn't seem interested. What a waste.

Skating is the basis of Mogilny's game. He has a burst of speed from a standstill and hits his top speed in just a few strides. When he streaks down the ice, there is a good chance you'll see something new, something you didn't expect. He is unbelievably quick. Mogilny may hate to fly in a plane but he loves to fly over the ice.

Mogilny's anticipation sets him apart from other players who are merely fast. He won't skate deeply into his own defensive zone, instead awaiting a turnover and a chance to get a jump on the defenseman, with a preferred move to the outside. But he is not afraid to go inside either, so a defenseman intent on angling him to the boards could just as easily get burned inside.

Mogilny can beat you in so many ways. He has a powerful and accurate wrist shot from the tops of the circles in. He shoots without breaking stride. He can work a give-and-go that is a thing of beauty. He one-times with the best of them. And everything is done at racehorse speed. The game comes easy to him.

THE PHYSICAL GAME

Mogilny doesn't work as hard as he should, and there always seems to be something left in the tank. He doesn't push himself to the limit, and no one knows on a nightly basis if Mogilny is going to show up. There are nights when he is invisible on the ice, and that is unpardonable for a player of his ability and importance.

Mogilny intimidates with his speed but will also add a physical element. He has great upper body strength and will drive through a defender to the net.

THE INTANGIBLES

Mogilny's expected teaming with Pavel Bure (both prefer the right wing) has never materialized in Vancouver, and neither has a centre whose game complements Mogilny's. He wants a playmaker, or he wants out, so he says.

PROJECTION

Mogilny's on the move on the ice, and for the right price, will be on the move off the ice. He has about worn out his welcome in Vancouver, though the Canucks are leery of letting him go only to watch him score 50 goals elsewhere.

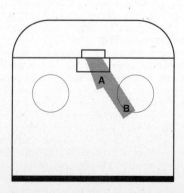

MARKUS NASLUND

Yrs. of NHL service: 4
Born: Bonassund, Sweden; July 30, 1973
Position: left/right wing
Height: 6-0
Weight: 186
Uniform no.: 19
Shoots: left

Career statistics:

GP	G	A	TP	PIM
239	49	62	111	101

1993-94 statistics:

GP	G	A	TP	+/-	PIM	PP	SH	GW	GT	S	PCT
71	4	7	11	-3	27	1	0	0	0	80	5.0

1994-95 statistics:

GP	G	A	TP	+/-	PIM	PP	SH	GW	GT	S	PCT
14	2	2	4	0	2	0	0	0	0	13	15.4

1995-96 statistics:

GP	G	A	TP	+/-	PIM	PP	SH	GW	GT	S	PCT
76	22	33	55	+20	42	4	0	5	0	144	15.3

1996-97 statistics:

GP	G	A	TP	+/-	PIM	PP	SH	GW	GT	S	PCT
78	21	20	41	-15	30	4	0	4	0	120	17.5

PROJECTION

Naslund can either be an underachieving 20-goal scorer, or he can take the next step, like Martin Gelinas, and become a reliable 30-goal scorer. It's up to him.

LAST SEASON

Tied for team lead in game-winning goals. Fourth on team in points.

THE FINESSE GAME

Naslund is a pure sniper. He has excellent snap and wrist shots, and can score in just about every way imaginable, including the backhand in tight. He has quick hands and an accurate touch.

Naslund needs to play with people who will get him the puck. He will not play aggressively and dig in the corners for the puck, and is a little shy in traffic. He is a jitterbug on the ice, and he can keep up with the fastest linemates. He needs more confidence in himself to inspire more confidence from the coaches, in order to get more ice time.

Naslund has good hockey sense in the attacking zone, but he does not play well defensively and tends to shy away from the boards. He needs to work on his game to become more than a one-way winger.

THE PHYSICAL GAME

Naslund is erratic in his physical play. Some nights he will play a little bigger, and make something of a pest out of himself, but other nights he will be invisible. He needs to be involved on a nightly basis.

THE INTANGIBLES

Naslund and Peter Forsberg were born 10 days apart, but they are a world apart in NHL accomplishment. Naslund, a former first-round draft pick (by Pittsburgh in 1991), has never lived up to the hype that surrounded his first few seasons in the NHL.

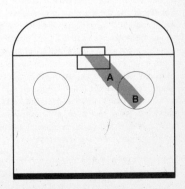

BRIAN NOONAN

Yrs. of NHL service: 8
Born: Boston, Mass.; May 29, 1965
Position: right wing
Height: 6-1
Weight: 200
Uniform no.: 28
Shoots: right

Career statistics:

GP	G	A	TP	PIM
540	106	144	250	456

1993-94 statistics:

GP	G	A	TP	+/-	PIM	PP	SH	GW	GT	S	PCT
76	18	23	41	+7	69	10	0	6	1	160	11.3

1994-95 statistics:

GP	G	A	TP	+/-	PIM	PP	SH	GW	GT	S	PCT
45	14	13	27	-3	26	7	0	1	0	95	14.7

1995-96 statistics:

GP	G	A	TP	+/-	PIM	PP	SH	GW	GT	S	PCT
81	13	22	35	+2	84	3	1	6	0	131	9.9

1996-97 statistics:

GP	G	A	TP	+/-	PIM	PP	SH	GW	GT	S	PCT
73	12	22	34	-3	34	3	1	1	1	100	12.0

LAST SEASON

Acquired from N.Y. Rangers with Sergei Nemchinov for Esa Tikkanen and Russ Courtnall, March 8, 1997.

THE FINESSE GAME

Noonan's strongest attribute is his willingness to go into the corners for the puck, win a battle for it, and come out and do something with it by either finding a man at the point with a pass or taking it to the net himself. He might also draw a penalty.

Noonan has good enough hands and moves to win the blueline almost every time he attacks it with the puck. Defensemen seem to have a difficult time reading him, so they retreat, which buys him an extra 10 feet of ice in which to make a decision. He also varies his attacks to the blueline, which adds an unpredictable element, but he doesn't always identify the best passing option when he gains the line.

No speedster, and often seeming to be moving in slow motion, Noonan doesn't have the world's smallest turning radius. He is reliable defensively, however, and is smart enough to maximize what little speed he has by changing gears a lot. He doesn't always skate at top speed, but can get an extra step by cranking up the pace just at the moment a defenseman has to make the pivot from backskating to frontskating.

Noonan is crafty with his hands, and clever with his shot, which is never overpowering but often unstoppable due to its unpredictability. He also knows his defensive responsibilities and can kill a penalty, though he's no shorthanded scoring threat.

THE PHYSICAL GAME

Noonan is a cruiserweight who uses his skating strength and balance and is difficult to knock down. He favours what might be called a flying hip check, where he throws himself into an onrushing opponent at the sideboards.

He has become more consistent at finishing his checks. He pins his target to the wall and keeps him out of the play. He also plays the gut-check areas on offense. Noonan goes to the front of the net and gives up his body on tips and screens. He is a short-game player who pays the price to be in the right spot. He makes good use of his weight with a quiet strength.

THE INTANGIBLES

Noonan is a third-line player on his best nights. He is a poker-faced guy who doesn't show much emotion and who doesn't really draw a lot of attention to himself. He keeps the game basic, nothing really fancy, but he has a nice amount of smarts and savvy. Noonan is a humble kid from a large family who made it to the NHL on hard work, and he will have to keep at it to have a regular job.

PROJECTION

The Canucks are low on grit up front, so Noonan can earn some playing time. He barely scores in the double digits in goals, but tends to score big ones.

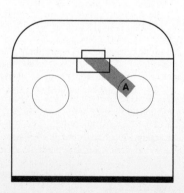

GINO ODJICK

Yrs. of NHL service: 7
Born: Maniwaki, Que.; Sept. 7, 1970
Position: left wing
Height: 6-3
Weight: 210
Uniform no.: 29
Shoots: left

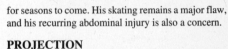

Career statistics:

GP	G	A	TP	PIM
409	43	50	93	1946

1993-94 statistics:

GP	G	A	TP	+/-	PIM	PP	SH	GW	GT	S	PCT
76	16	13	29	+13	271	4	0	5	0	121	13.2

1994-95 statistics:

GP	G	A	TP	+/-	PIM	PP	SH	GW	GT	S	PCT
23	4	5	9	-3	109	0	0	0	0	35	11.4

1995-96 statistics:

GP	G	A	TP	+/-	PIM	PP	SH	GW	GT	S	PCT
55	3	4	7	-16	181	0	0	0	0	59	5.1

1996-97 statistics:

GP	G	A	TP	+/-	PIM	PP	SH	GW	GT	S	PCT
70	5	8	13	-5	371	1	0	0	0	85	5.9

LAST SEASON

Led NHL and team in penalty minutes with career high. Missed five games with groin injury.

THE FINESSE GAME

Odjick is a goon who knows that goons are facing extinction in the NHL. To preserve his job, he has added important elements to become more than a one-dimensional player.

His abdominal/groin injury, which has plagued him for the past three seasons, robbed him of most of the strength and toughness that are his hallmarks. He has improved his skating since dropping some weight, and conditioning must continue to be a priority.

Odjick's scoring chances come from in tight. He works tirelessly around the net for loose pucks, slamming and jamming. He could use a little more patience, since he gets a lot of room for his first move, but his theory seems to be that three whacks at the puck (which he can get easily) are worth one finesse move (which he might not be able to make anyway).

THE PHYSICAL GAME

Odjick takes cheap penalties. He aggravates, hits late and hits from behind, yet is a legitimate tough guy when the gloves come off. He protects his teammates. He is also strong enough to simply run over people en route to the net.

THE INTANGIBLES

Odjick is a huge favourite with the fans in Vancouver, and the coaches can't help but love the effort he puts into his game and his career. If he continues to work at the little parts of his game, he will make a big impact for seasons to come. His skating remains a major flaw, and his recurring abdominal injury is also a concern.

PROJECTION

As long as fighting isn't outlawed, outlaws will remain hockey players.

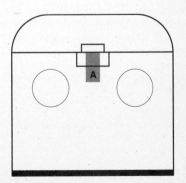

MATTIAS OHLUND

Yrs. of NHL service: 0
Born: Pitea, Sweden; Sept. 9, 1976
Position: defense
Height: 6-3
Weight: 209
Uniform no.: n.a.
Shoots: left

Career statisics (Sweden):

GP	G	A	TP	PIM
119	17	29	46	98

1995-96 statistics (Sweden):

GP	G	A	TP	PIM
38	4	10	14	26

1996-97 statistics (Sweden):

GP	G	A	TP	PIM
47	7	9	16	38

LAST SEASON
Third among team defensemen in scoring for Lulea (Swedish Elite League) with 7-9 — 16 in 47 games.

THE FINESSE GAME
Ohlund has a high skill level and a big body to go with it. Because he is such a wonderful skater, and has a long reach, he is difficult to beat one-on-one. He isn't fooled by dekes, either. He plays the crest and maintains his position.

Ohlund makes a good first pass out of the defensive zone, like Kjell Samuelsson, but his skating and puckhandling skills are better than Samuelsson's. He gets involved in the attack by moving up into the rush, but he won't get caught deep very often.

Ohlund just keeps growing, but unlike many young skaters who experience sudden growth spurts, he has stayed balanced in his skating. He was a regular in the Swedish Elite League at age 19.

THE PHYSICAL GAME
Ohlund is big and powerful, and at least at the international level has played a physical game, clearing out the front of the net and working the boards and corners. The young Swede will probably be more of a finesse defenseman at the NHL level; at least the Canucks aren't expecting him to batter people.

THE INTANGIBLES
Ohlund won't get any better playing in Sweden. The time has come for him to step up into the pros. He might need some seasoning at the minor league level first, but odds are he will be thrown into the mix with the big boys.

PROJECTION
Ohlund can step right into a Canucks lineup that is thin in all areas, but he has dug in his heels on a contract and was the topic of trade rumours.

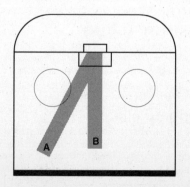

DAVID ROBERTS

Yrs. of NHL service: 3
Born: Alameda, Calif.; May 28, 1970
Position: left wing
Height: 6-0
Weight: 185
Uniform no.: 7
Shoots: left

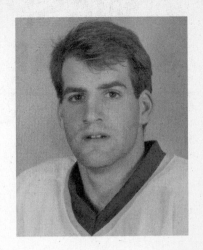

Career statistics:

GP	G	A	TP	PIM
112	19	32	51	79

1993-94 statistics:

GP	G	A	TP	+/-	PIM	PP	SH	GW	GT	S	PCT
1	0	0	0	0	2	0	0	0	0	1	0.0

1994-95 statistics:

GP	G	A	TP	+/-	PIM	PP	SH	GW	GT	S	PCT
19	6	5	11	+2	10	3	0	2	1	41	14.6

1995-96 statistics:

GP	G	A	TP	+/-	PIM	PP	SH	GW	GT	S	PCT
34	3	10	13	-7	18	1	0	1	0	47	6.4

1996-97 statistics:

GP	G	A	TP	+/-	PIM	PP	SH	GW	GT	S	PCT
58	10	17	27	+11	51	1	1	1	0	74	13.5

LAST SEASON

Led team in plus-minus. Missed 24 games with hip flexor/groin strain.

THE FINESSE GAME

Roberts has great skills and skating ability. He is another graduate of the U.S. Olympic program, which has produced some excellent pro players despite having little success in the Games.

Because he has also played defense, and can drop back in a pinch to play that position, Roberts is highly aware defensively and is a complete player. He has good vision and a fine shot from the point. Understandably, he ranks behind Steve Duchesne and Al MacInnis in that department, but give him time and he will be a capable power-play quarterback. He is very creative, and was forced into service as a second-line centre by the Canucks.

Roberts handles the puck at high speed and doesn't get cornered with it. He has the sense to escape and use other players to open up ice.

THE PHYSICAL GAME

Roberts is a finesse player, but has great heart. He will finish his checks. He won't dominate physically and he's not mean, but he's not afraid, either.

THE INTANGIBLES

Roberts has a lot of upside, and was playing well at the time of his initial injury in February.

PROJECTION

Roberts could score 15 to 20 goals in a third-line role.

WASHINGTON CAPITALS

Players' Statistics 1996-97

POS.	NO.	PLAYER	GP	G	A	PTS	+/-	PIM	PP	SH	GW	GT	S	PCT
C	77	ADAM OATES	80	22	60	82	-5	14	3	2	5		160	13.8
R	12	PETER BONDRA	77	46	31	77	7	72	10	4	3	2	314	14.6
C	32	DALE HUNTER	82	14	32	46	-2	125	3		5		110	12.7
L	22	STEVE KONOWALCHUK	78	17	25	42	-3	67	2	1	3	1	155	11.0
C	90	JOE JUNEAU	58	15	27	42	-11	8	9	1	3		124	12.1
R	92	RICK TOCCHET	53	21	19	40	-3	98	4		2	1	157	13.4
D	96	PHIL HOUSLEY	77	11	29	40	-10	24	3	1	2		167	6.6
D	55	SERGEI GONCHAR	57	13	17	30	-11	36	3		3		129	10.1
C	13	ANDREI NIKOLISHIN	71	9	19	28	3	32	1				98	9.2
L	10	KELLY MILLER	77	10	14	24	4	33		1	3		95	10.5
D	3	SYLVAIN COTE	57	6	18	24	11	28	2				131	4.6
C	20	MICHAL PIVONKA	54	7	16	23	-15	22	2		1		83	8.4
L	17	CHRIS SIMON	42	9	13	22	-1	165	3		1		89	10.1
D	6	CALLE JOHANSSON	65	6	11	17	-2	16	2				133	4.5
L	21	TODD KRYGIER	47	5	11	16	-10	37	1		1		121	4.1
L	18	*ANDREW BRUNETTE	23	4	7	11	-3	12	2				23	17.4
D	2	KEN KLEE	80	3	8	11	-5	115			2		108	2.8
L	34	*JAROSLAV SVEJKOVSKY	19	7	3	10	-1	4	2		1		30	23.3
D	29	JOE REEKIE	65	1	8	9	8	107					65	1.5
D	24	MARK TINORDI	56	2	6	8	3	118			1		53	3.8
L	36	MIKE EAGLES	70	1	7	8	-4	42					38	2.6
L	27	CRAIG BERUBE	80	4	3	7	-11	218			1		55	7.3
D	19	BRENDAN WITT	44	3	2	5	-20	88					41	7.3
L	44	*RICHARD ZEDNIK	11	2	1	3	-5	4	1				21	9.5
C	23	KEVIN KAMINSKI	38	1	2	3	0	130					12	8.3
D	28	ERIC CHARRON	25	1	1	2	1	20					11	9.1
G	30	BILL RANFORD	55		1	1	0	7						
D	45	*PATRICK BOILEAU	1				0							
C	14	PAT PEAKE	4				1	4					9	
D	4	STEWART MALGUNAS	6				2	2					3	
L	16	STEFAN USTORF	6				-3	2					7	
G	37	OLAF KOLZIG	29				0	4						

GP = games played; G = goals; A = assists; PTS = points; +/- = goals-for minus goals-against while player is on ice; PIM = penalties in minutes; PP = power-play goals; SH = shorthanded goals; GW = game-winning goals; GT = game-tying goals; S = no. of shots; PCT = percentage of goals to shots; * = rookie

PETER BONDRA

Yrs. of NHL service: 7
Born: Luck, Ukraine; Feb. 7, 1968
Position: right wing
Height: 6-1
Weight: 200
Uniform no.: 12
Shoots: left

Career statistics:

GP	G	A	TP	PIM
468	233	179	412	335

1993-94 statistics:

GP	G	A	TP	+/-	PIM	PP	SH	GW	GT	S	PCT
69	24	19	43	+22	40	4	0	2	0	200	12.0

1994-95 statistics:

GP	G	A	TP	+/-	PIM	PP	SH	GW	GT	S	PCT
47	34	9	43	+9	24	12	6	3	1	177	19.2

1995-96 statistics:

GP	G	A	TP	+/-	PIM	PP	SH	GW	GT	S	PCT
67	52	28	80	+18	40	11	4	7	3	322	16.1

1996-97 statistics:

GP	G	A	TP	+/-	PIM	PP	SH	GW	GT	S	PCT
77	46	31	77	+7	72	10	4	3	2	314	14.6

LAST SEASON

Eighth in NHL and led team in goals (for third consecutive season). Led team in power-play goals and shorthanded goals for third consecutive season. Led team in shots and shooting percentage. Second on team in points. Third on team in plus-minus and assists. Missed three games with groin injury.

THE FINESSE GAME

Bondra is in the category of players you would pay to watch play. His speed is exceptional and he is intelligent on the ice offensively. He accelerates quickly and smoothly and drives defenders back, because they have to play off his speed. If he gets hooked to the ice he doesn't stay down, but jumps back to his skates and gets involved in the play again, often after the defender has forgotten about him. He has excellent balance and quickness.

Bondra cuts in on the off-wing and shoots in stride. He has a very good backhand shot and likes to cut out from behind the net and make things happen in tight. He mixes up his shots. He will fire quickly — not many European players have this good a slap shot — or drive in close and deke and wrist a little shot.

Bondra had never killed penalties until 1994-95, and he has become a real shorthanded threat with 17 shorthanded goals in the past three seasons. He makes other teams' power plays jittery because of his anticipation and breakaway speed, and he follows up his shots to the net and is quick to pounce on rebounds.

Bondra has become a more confident player. Michal Pivonka has long been part of his success, but with Pivonka out with a knee injury, Bondra realized he didn't need to play with Pivonka to be successful, and he should benefit from playing with Adam Oates.

THE PHYSICAL GAME

Bondra isn't strong, but he will lean on people. He has improved his off-ice conditioning and handled a lot of ice time last season. He doesn't seem to tire, and is much more determined in fighting through checks. Other teams keyed on him last year and he responded superbly, carrying the Caps through much of the season.

THE INTANGIBLES

How happy was Bondra with the arrival of Oates? He scored four goals in Oates's first game with the Caps. Oates has always made better use of his right wings than his left, and Bondra will feast; expect more consistency and less streaky scoring from him. The coaching change shouldn't affect him. Ron Wilson usually gets along with his star players.

PROJECTION

Bondra is not only primed to hit 50 goals again, he should rank among the NHL's top two or three goal scorers.

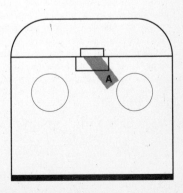

SYLVAIN COTE

Yrs. of NHL service: 12
Born: Quebec City, Que.; Jan. 19, 1966
Position: left defense
Height: 6-0
Weight: 190
Uniform no.: 3
Shoots: right

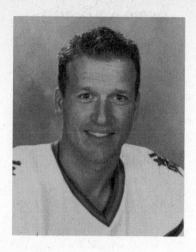

Career statistics:

GP	G	A	TP	PIM
806	95	219	314	399

1993-94 statistics:

GP	G	A	TP	+/-	PIM	PP	SH	GW	GT	S	PCT
84	16	35	51	+30	66	3	2	2	0	212	7.5

1994-95 statistics:

GP	G	A	TP	+/-	PIM	PP	SH	GW	GT	S	PCT
47	5	14	19	+2	53	1	0	2	0	124	4.0

1995-96 statistics:

GP	G	A	TP	+/-	PIM	PP	SH	GW	GT	S	PCT
81	5	33	38	+5	40	3	0	2	0	212	2.4

1996-97 statistics:

GP	G	A	TP	+/-	PIM	PP	SH	GW	GT	S	PCT
57	6	18	24	+11	28	2	0	0	0	131	4.6

LAST SEASON

Led team in plus-minus. Missed 24 games with torn medial collateral ligament in knee.

THE FINESSE GAME

Cote is a solid two-way defenseman. He has good puckhandling skills and can make a pass to his forehand or backhand side with confidence. He overhandles the puck at times, especially in his defensive zone, and when he gets into trouble he seems to struggle with his forehand clearances off the left-wing boards.

Cote can do everything in stride. Carrying the puck does not slow him down and he can rush end to end. He is gifted in all of the skating areas — fine agility, good balance, quick stops and starts. He likes to bring the puck up on the power play. He gets a lot on his shot from the point, which causes rebounds, and it's the source of most of his assists.

His hockey sense has improved. Cote can lead a rush or come into the play as a trailer, but he knows enough not to force and to play more conservatively when the situation dictates.

He still needs to improve his defensive reads, but he is working hard at it and his skating helps cover up for most of his lapses. His instincts lag well behind his skill level. Cote can be beaten one-on-one but it takes a good player to do it.

THE PHYSICAL GAME

Cote is one of the underrated members of the Washington defense corps. He doesn't have great size, but he is a solid hitter who finishes his checks. He isn't mean, however. He will occasionally fall into the trap of playing the puck instead of the man.

THE INTANGIBLES

Because he is such a good skater and an intelligent player, Cote will be able to play at a high level for another six or seven years.

PROJECTION

Cote's numbers have been dwindling. The knee injury was part of it, but he has sufficient skills to score 40 points.

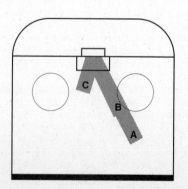

MIKE EAGLES

Yrs. of NHL service: 11
Born: Sussex, N.B.; Mar. 7, 1963
Position: centre/left wing
Height: 5-10
Weight: 190
Uniform no.: 36
Shoots: left

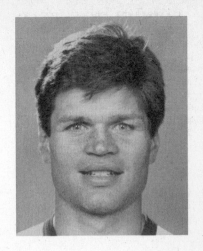

Career statistics:

GP	G	A	TP	PIM
740	67	117	184	847

1993-94 statistics:

GP	G	A	TP	+/-	PIM	PP	SH	GW	GT	S	PCT
73	4	8	12	-20	96	0	1	0	0	53	7.5

1994-95 statistics:

GP	G	A	TP	+/-	PIM	PP	SH	GW	GT	S	PCT
40	3	4	7	-11	48	0	0	0	0	28	10.7

1995-96 statistics:

GP	G	A	TP	+/-	PIM	PP	SH	GW	GT	S	PCT
70	4	7	11	-1	75	0	0	0	0	70	5.7

1996-97 statistics:

GP	G	A	TP	+/-	PIM	PP	SH	GW	GT	S	PCT
70	1	7	8	-4	42	0	0	0	0	38	2.6

LAST SEASON

Games missed were coach's decision.

THE FINESSE GAME

Eagles is the prototypical defensive centre. He is on the puck in a hurry when forechecking, creating turnovers and forcing bad passes. He has never had the touch to convert these chances into scoring attempts, but he can create chaos for the opponents.

Eagles always hustles and hits. He usually concentrates on shutting down the opposing centre on draws. He blocks shots and kills penalties. He can't match up against some of the league's power forwards, but he can keep up with the fleet ones.

THE PHYSICAL GAME

Eagles drives other players to distraction with his dogged pursuit, and he will get the stick up or give a facial massage with his glove. He's no angel. Despite his relatively small size, he never fails to finish his checks.

THE INTANGIBLES

Eagles is a steady, veteran checker, a useful fourth-liner, and a coach knows just what he's getting in terms of effort every night. Unless the Devils acquire Miroslav Satan, Eagles will be the only NHL player whose name matches his team's logo.

PROJECTION

Eagles will always be on the bubble because there is so little offense to complement the rest of his game, but Washington is an organization that prizes intelligence and a strong work ethic.

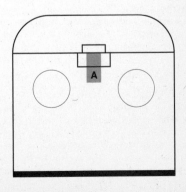

SERGEI GONCHAR

Yrs. of NHL service: 3
Born: Chelyabinsk, USSR; Apr. 13, 1974
Position: left defense
Height: 6-2
Weight: 212
Uniform no.: 55
Shoots: left

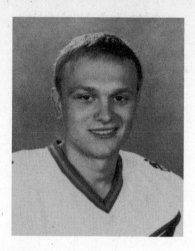

Career statistics:

GP	G	A	TP	PIM
166	30	48	78	118

1994-95 statistics:

GP	G	A	TP	+/-	PIM	PP	SH	GW	GT	S	PCT
31	2	5	7	+4	22	0	0	0	0	38	5.3

1995-96 statistics:

GP	G	A	TP	+/-	PIM	PP	SH	GW	GT	S	PCT
78	15	26	41	+25	60	4	0	4	0	139	10.8

1996-97 statistics:

GP	G	A	TP	+/-	PIM	PP	SH	GW	GT	S	PCT
57	13	17	30	-11	36	3	0	3	0	129	10.1

LAST SEASON

Missed 12 games with knee sprain. Missed eight games with back spasms. Missed two games with bruised knee. Missed one game with flu. Missed one game with hyperextended elbow.

THE FINESSE GAME

It's difficult to believe that Gonchar was known as a defensive defenseman when he played in Russia. He sees the ice well and passes well, but he never put up any big offensive numbers before coming into the NHL. Unlike most young defensemen who have to work in their own end to develop an NHL-calibre game, Gonchar made the quick jump to becoming a complete player by adding offense.

Gonchar jumps up into the play willingly and intelligently. He has a natural feel for the flow of a game, and makes tape-to-tape feeds through people and under pressure. He sees first-unit power-play time on the point, and is maturing into a first-rate quarterback. He plays very heads-up. He doesn't have the blazing speed that elite defensemen have when carrying the puck, but he will gain the zone with some speed. He is an excellent passer.

Gonchar's shot is accurate enough, but it won't terrorize any goalies. He doesn't push the puck forward and step into it like Al MacInnis. Most of the time he is content with getting it on the net, and he is not reluctant to shoot.

THE PHYSICAL GAME

Gonchar is very strong on his skates and has worked hard on his off-ice conditioning. His defense is based more on reads and positional play than on a physical element, but he has a bit of an aggressive streak. He was known as a very aggressive player by Russian standards, but he won't run people. Gonchar will probably become a little more assertive as he gains confidence.

THE INTANGIBLES

Gonchar has a big upside, even given the distance he has already covered since coming to North America. Last season was difficult to judge because he was never in the lineup long due to injuries. He has a lot of tools to be a special defenseman.

PROJECTION

He won't be in the top 10 scorers among defensemen, but he may provide 50 to 55 points backed up by a solid defensive game.

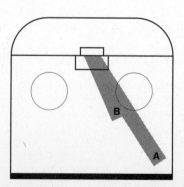

PHIL HOUSLEY

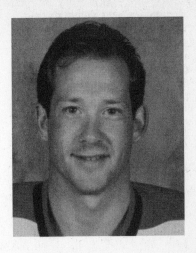

Yrs. of NHL service: 15
Born: St. Paul, Minn.; Mar. 9, 1964
Position: right defense
Height: 5-10
Weight: 185
Uniform no.: 96
Shoots: left

Career statistics:

GP	G	A	TP	PIM
1067	285	705	990	638

1993-94 statistics:

GP	G	A	TP	+/-	PIM	PP	SH	GW	GT	S	PCT
26	7	15	22	-5	12	4	0	1	1	60	11.7

1994-95 statistics:

GP	G	A	TP	+/-	PIM	PP	SH	GW	GT	S	PCT
43	8	35	43	+17	18	3	0	0	0	135	5.9

1995-96 statistics:

GP	G	A	TP	+/-	PIM	PP	SH	GW	GT	S	PCT
81	17	51	68	-6	30	6	0	1	0	205	8.3

1996-97 statistics:

GP	G	A	TP	+/-	PIM	PP	SH	GW	GT	S	PCT
77	11	29	40	-10	24	3	1	2	0	167	6.6

LAST SEASON

Missed five games with groin strain. Led team defensemen in scoring. Lowest point total of career (except for lockout season).

THE FINESSE GAME

Among the best-skating defensemen in the NHL, Housley, like Paul Coffey, takes a lot of heat for his defensive shortcomings, but his offensive skills are extraordinary. He is skilled enough to be used up front, which the Caps did last season because of injuries.

Housley's skating fuels his game. He can accelerate in a heartbeat, and his edges are deep and secure, giving him the ability to avoid checks with gravity-defying moves. Everything he does is at high tempo. He intimidates with his speed and skills, forcing defenders back and opening up more ice for himself and his teammates. Like Mike Gartner, Housley can continue to be an effective offensive weapon because he has barely lost a step over the years.

Housley has an excellent grasp of the ice. On the power play he is a huge threat. His shots are low, quick and heavy, either beating the goalie outright or setting up a rebound for the forwards down deep. He also sets up low on the power play, and he doesn't mind shooting from an impossible angle that can catch a goalie napping on the short side.

Housley has great anticipation and can break up a rush by picking off a pass and turning the play into a counterattack. He is equally adept with a long headman or a short cup-and-saucer pass over a defender's stick.

THE PHYSICAL GAME

Housley is not the least bit physical. Who wants a player as gifted as Housley risking life and limb in routine plays along the boards when there are a dozen less-gifted players who could do it for him? He is not strong enough to shove anyone out of the zone, so his defensive play is based on his pursuit of the puck. He is likely to avoid traffic areas unless he feels he can get in and out with the puck quickly enough.

Success on a rush, even a two-on-one, against Housley is no guarantee, since he is a good enough skater to position himself well and break up the play with his stick.

THE INTANGIBLES

Housley chafed a bit under Jim Schoenfeld's system. New coach Ron Wilson was also the coach of Team USA, likes Housley and should jump-start his confidence.

PROJECTION

The weight of a lucrative new contract, combined with an injury-hobbled lineup, were mere excuses. There is no reason for Housley to be unproductive as he was last season. He can get 65 points again.

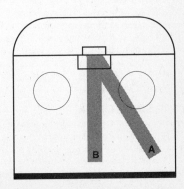

DALE HUNTER

Yrs. of NHL service: 17
Born: Petrolia, Ont.; July 31, 1960
Position: centre
Height: 5-10
Weight: 198
Uniform no.: 32
Shoots: left

Career statistics:

GP	G	A	TP	PIM
1263	313	670	993	3343

1993-94 statistics:

GP	G	A	TP	+/-	PIM	PP	SH	GW	GT	S	PCT
52	9	29	38	-4	131	1	0	1	0	61	14.8

1994-95 statistics:

GP	G	A	TP	+/-	PIM	PP	SH	GW	GT	S	PCT
45	8	15	23	-4	101	3	0	1	0	73	11.0

1995-96 statistics:

GP	G	A	TP	+/-	PIM	PP	SH	GW	GT	S	PCT
82	13	24	37	+5	112	4	0	3	2	128	10.2

1996-97 statistics:

GP	G	A	TP	+/-	PIM	PP	SH	GW	GT	S	PCT
82	14	32	46	-2	125	3	0	5	0	110	12.7

LAST SEASON

Only Capital to appear in all 82 games for second consecutive season. Tied for team lead in game-winning goals. Second on team in assists. Third on team in points. Second to Tiger Williams (3,966) on all-time PIM list.

THE FINESSE GAME

Hunter is a crafty player, especially down low. He doesn't skate well enough to be very effective in open ice, but when the Caps have control of the offensive zone, he digs in deep, setting screens and picks and driving to the net. He is not a big player, but he forces teams to pay attention with his effort.

Hunter is skilled on face-offs. He gets low to the ice, then moves forward and drives back the opposing centre. He never fails to bump his opposite number. He turns his body and grinds it out. He uses his helmet to bump the chin and chest of the opposing centre. And he works at buying time for his linemates by creating time and space with his puck control.

Hunter is a complete player. At this stage of his career he should have settled into a nice role-playing position on the fourth line. Last season, the Caps again needed him full-time due to injuries. He can be more effective by being spotted. His days as a big point earner are over, but he still produces key points.

THE PHYSICAL GAME

Hunter knows only one way to play the game. He gets shots in, hits, harasses and does whatever it takes to win. This has been his hallmark from the first day he pulled on an NHL jersey. Look at the few great moments in the Capitals' history — notably their drive to the Stanley Cup semifinals in 1990 — and Hunter has always been a key player. The size of the opponent doesn't matter to him. He has a low, low centre of gravity that makes it a pain to hit him, and he will take or make a hit to make a play. He is grating.

THE INTANGIBLES

What does it say when the oldest player on the Caps is the only one to answer the bell every night last season? Love him or hate him, you have to respect Hunter for the leadership and work ethic he shows from shift to shift. He might have looked out of place skills-wise at the All-Star game last year, but he earned the trip. He is a fine example for the team's younger players, not for sportsmanship certainly, but for paying the price to be a successful NHL player. The Olympic break will give Hunter a needed breather for the stretch drive.

PROJECTION

This is probably his last season, and Hunter will want to go out with a bang. He can still perform well in a limited role. He is getting older, but he keeps himself in good physical condition, and can contribute 35 points while providing defense.

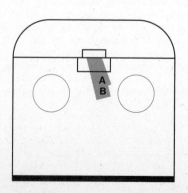

CALLE JOHANSSON

Yrs. of NHL service: 10
Born: Göteborg, Sweden; Feb. 14, 1967
Position: left defense
Height: 5-11
Weight: 200
Uniform no.: 6
Shoots: left

Career statistics:

GP	G	A	TP	PIM
710	77	303	380	387

1993-94 statistics:

GP	G	A	TP	+/-	PIM	PP	SH	GW	GT	S	PCT
84	9	33	42	+3	59	4	0	1	0	141	6.4

1994-95 statistics:

GP	G	A	TP	+/-	PIM	PP	SH	GW	GT	S	PCT
46	5	26	31	-6	35	4	0	2	0	112	4.5

1995-96 statistics:

GP	G	A	TP	+/-	PIM	PP	SH	GW	GT	S	PCT
78	10	25	35	+13	50	4	0	0	0	182	5.5

1996-97 statistics:

GP	G	A	TP	+/-	PIM	PP	SH	GW	GT	S	PCT
65	6	11	17	-2	16	2	0	0	0	133	4.5

LAST SEASON

Missed 16 games with broken jaw. Missed one game with bruised foot.

THE FINESSE GAME

Johansson has tremendous legs, notably big, strong thighs that generate the power for his shot and his explosive skating. He makes every move look easy. He is agile, mobile and great at moving up the ice with the play. Speed, balance and strength allow him to chase a puck behind the net, pick it up without stopping and make an accurate pass. He is confident, even on the backhand, and likes to have the puck in key spots.

He is smart offensively. He moves the puck with a good first pass, then has enough speed and instinct to jump up and be ready for a return pass. He keeps the gap tight as the play enters the attacking zone, which opens up more options: he is available to the forwards if they need him for offense, and closer to the puck if it is turned over to the opposition.

Johansson has a low, accurate shot that can be tipped. He is unselfish to a fault, often looking to pass when he should use his shot.

He has good defensive instincts and reads plays well. His skating gives him the confidence (maybe overconfidence) to gamble and challenge the puck carrier. He has a quick stick for poke- and sweep-checks.

THE PHYSICAL GAME

Johansson is not an aggressive player, but he is strong and knows what he has to do with his body in the defensive zone. This part of the game has not come naturally, but he has worked at it. He is still not an impact player defensively, though he wins his share of the one-on-one battles because he gets so much power from his legs. He stays in good condition and can give a team a lot of minutes.

THE INTANGIBLES

Johansson does so many things well that his position among the team's top four defensemen is secure. He is one of the most underrated defensemen in the league.

PROJECTION

Johansson has taken a back seat to Sergei Gonchar as the team's top offensive defenseman and will probably see his point total decline again slightly to the 30 to 35 range (over a full healthy season).

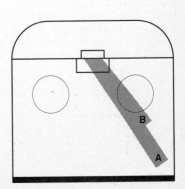

JOE JUNEAU

Yrs. of NHL service: 5
Born: Pont-Rouge, Que.; Jan. 5, 1968
Position: centre/left wing
Height: 6-0
Weight: 195
Uniform no.: 90
Shoots: right

Career statistics:

GP	G	A	TP	PIM
354	90	213	355	124

1993-94 statistics:

GP	G	A	TP	+/-	PIM	PP	SH	GW	GT	S	PCT
74	19	66	85	+11	41	6	0	2	1	164	11.6

1994-95 statistics:

GP	G	A	TP	+/-	PIM	PP	SH	GW	GT	S	PCT
44	5	38	43	-1	8	3	0	0	0	1	7.1

1995-96 statistics:

GP	G	A	TP	+/-	PIM	PP	SH	GW	GT	S	PCT
80	14	50	64	-3	30	7	2	2	2	0	8.0

1996-97 statistics:

GP	G	A	TP	+/-	PIM	PP	SH	GW	GT	S	PCT
58	15	27	42	-11	8	9	1	3	0	124	12.1

LAST SEASON

Second on team in power-play goals. Missed eight games with pulled hamstring. Missed 11 games with back/shoulder injuries. Missed one game with hip strain.

THE FINESSE GAME

Juneau plays at centre, but he seems to gravitate to the left wing and generates most of his scoring chances from there. He varies his play selection. He will take the puck to the net on one rush, then pull up at the top of the circle and hit the trailer late on the next rush.

While the circles are his office, he is not exclusively a perimeter player. Juneau will go into traffic. He is bigger than he looks on the ice. His quick feet and light hands make him seem smaller, because he is so crafty with the puck.

Laterally, Juneau is among the best skaters in the NHL. He has an extra gear that allows him to pull away from people. He does not have breakaway speed, but he has great anticipation and gets the jump on a defender with his first few steps.

Juneau doesn't shoot the puck enough and gets a little intimidated when there is a scramble for a loose puck in front of the net. He is not always willing to sacrifice his body that way. He shoots a tad prematurely. When he could wait and have the goalie down and out, he unloads quickly, because he hears footsteps. His best shot is a one-timer from the left circle.

Defensively Juneau has improved in recent years. He can kill penalties and is excellent on draws.

THE PHYSICAL GAME

Juneau has improved his toughness and willingness to take a hit to make a play — probably dressing room osmosis — but he is still something of a featherweight. He skates in a hunched-over position, like a human letter C, and a hit that would otherwise be clean catches him in the face. He plays with a huge protective shield that doesn't appear to get in his way too much unless the puck is right in his feet.

THE INTANGIBLES

The Capitals' acquisition of Adam Oates could make Juneau a new man, if the pair can recapture some of the magic from Juneau's rookie season in Boston. Expect the Caps to use him as a left wing with Oates on a top line.

PROJECTION

Juneau enjoyed a 100-point year in his first season with Oates in Boston. We don't foresee that kind of outburst here, but after two disappointing seasons, Juneau could redeem himself with 80 points this season.

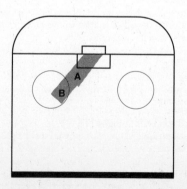

STEVE KONOWALCHUK

Yrs. of NHL service: 5
Born: Salt Lake City, Utah; Nov. 11, 1972
Position: left wing
Height: 6-1
Weight: 195
Uniform no.: 22
Shoots: left

Career statistics:

GP	G	A	TP	PIM
293	67	82	174	252

1993-94 statistics:

GP	G	A	TP	+/-	PIM	PP	SH	GW	GT	S	PCT
62	12	14	26	+9	33	0	0	0	0	63	19.0

1994-95 statistics:

GP	G	A	TP	+/-	PIM	PP	SH	GW	GT	S	PCT
46	11	14	25	+7	44	3	3	3	0	88	12.5

1995-96 statistics:

GP	G	A	TP	+/-	PIM	PP	SH	GW	GT	S	PCT
70	23	22	45	+13	92	7	1	3	0	197	11.7

1996-97 statistics:

GP	G	A	TP	+/-	PIM	PP	SH	GW	GT	S	PCT
78	17	25	42	-3	67	2	1	3	1	155	11.0

LAST SEASON

Fourth on team in points. Missed four games with separated rib cartilage.

THE FINESSE GAME

Konowalchuk is a willing guy who will play any role asked of him. He's a digger who has to work hard for his goals, and an intelligent and earnest player who uses every ounce of energy on every shift.

There is nothing fancy about his offense. He just lets his shot rip and drives to the net. He doesn't have the moves and hand skills to beat a defender one-on-one, but he doesn't care. He'll go right through him. Konowalchuk's release on his shot is improving.

Konowalchuk is reliable and intelligent defensively. On the draw, he ties up the opposing centre if he doesn't win the puck drop outright. He uses his feet along the boards as well as his stick.

THE PHYSICAL GAME

Konowalchuk is very strong. He has some grit in him, too, and will aggravate opponents with his constant effort. He doesn't take bad penalties, but often goads rivals into retaliating. He is very fit and can handle a lot of ice time.

THE INTANGIBLES

Konowalchuk was the number one left wing by default last season, a role that doesn't really suit him. If the Caps successfully shift Joe Juneau to that spot, Konowalchuk can play a more comfortable role on the second line.

PROJECTION

Konowalchuk is a quality person to have, on the ice or in the dressing room, and he can score 20 to 25 goals in a second-line role.

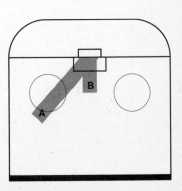

KELLY MILLER

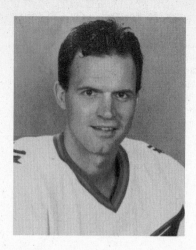

Yrs. of NHL service: 12
Born: Lansing, Mich.; Mar. 3, 1963
Position: left wing/right wing
Height: 5-11
Weight: 197
Uniform no.: 10
Shoots: left

Career statistics:

GP	G	A	TP	PIM
919	172	270	442	442

1993-94 statistics:

GP	G	A	TP	+/-	PIM	PP	SH	GW	GT	S	PCT
84	14	25	39	+8	32	0	1	3	0	138	10.1

1994-95 statistics:

GP	G	A	TP	+/-	PIM	PP	SH	GW	GT	S	PCT
48	10	13	23	+5	6	2	0	1	0	70	14.3

1995-96 statistics:

GP	G	A	TP	+/-	PIM	PP	SH	GW	GT	S	PCT
74	7	13	20	+7	30	0	2	1	0	93	7.5

1996-97 statistics:

GP	G	A	TP	+/-	PIM	PP	SH	GW	GT	S	PCT
77	10	14	24	+4	33	0	1	3	0	95	10.5

LAST SEASON

Missed three games with shoulder sprain. Missed one game with knee sprain.

THE FINESSE GAME

If a team doesn't have complete control of the puck in the zone, Miller will come in hard. If they have control, he backs off to the neutral zone. He's smart enough to know the difference, instead of plunging in with a wild forecheck and expending useless energy. He's one of the top defensive wingers in the game because of his reads.

Miller has never produced the kind of offensive numbers that his skills indicate he could, and now those numbers are dwindling even more. He's never been the same special player he was when he was a teammate with Mike Ridley. He has the skating ability, hockey sense and hands to score maybe 20 goals, but he'll never do it because he's always thinking defense. Miller drives to the net on occasion and has a quick release on his shot.

Defensively, there is no weak part to Miller's game. A complete player, he is always in motion. He creates a lot of scoring chances from turnovers. He reads plays when he forechecks, and either goes to the net or finds a teammate in front with a good short pass. He is one of the best penalty killers around.

THE PHYSICAL GAME

Miller is not very big, but he is strong and durable. Until last year, he had never missed more than four games in a single season since he was a rookie. His stamina allows him to forecheck hard all night, and he drives opponents batty because he is always on them.

There is never a moment's peace when Miller is on the ice.

THE INTANGIBLES

Miller has become more and more a strictly defensive entity, as his diminishing point totals indicate. He remains one of the game's most intelligent penalty-killing and checking forwards, night after night.

PROJECTION

Miller isn't in the lineup because of his points.

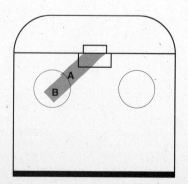

ANDREI NIKOLISHIN

Yrs. of NHL service: 3
Born: Vorkuta, USSR; March 25, 1973
Position: left wing/centre
Height: 5-11
Weight: 180
Uniform no.: 13
Shoots: left

Career statistics:

GP	G	A	TP	PIM
171	31	66	97	76

1994-95 statistics:

GP	G	A	TP	+/-	PIM	PP	SH	GW	GT	S	PCT
39	8	10	18	+7	10	1	1	0	0	57	14.0

1995-96 statistics:

GP	G	A	TP	+/-	PIM	PP	SH	GW	GT	S	PCT
61	14	37	51	-2	34	4	1	3	0	83	16.9

1996-97 statistics:

GP	G	A	TP	+/-	PIM	PP	SH	GW	GT	S	PCT
71	9	19	28	+3	32	1	0	0	0	98	9.2

LAST SEASON

Acquired from Hartford for Curtis Leschyshyn, November 9, 1996. Missed eight games with bulging disc in back.

THE FINESSE GAME

Nikolishin is a strong skater with a powerful stride. He makes some of the tightest turns in the league. His great talent is puckhandling, but like many Europeans he tends to hold onto the puck too long and leaves himself open for hits.

Nikolishin sees the ice well and is a gifted play-maker. He needs to shoot more so that his game will be less predictable. He needs to play with a power winger who can finish off passes and stand up for him a bit. He is eager to learn the game. Nikolishin saw time on the second power-play unit and killed some penalties. He is defensively aware, backchecks and blocks shots.

THE PHYSICAL GAME

Nikolishin is extremely strong on his skates and likes to work in the corners for the puck. He is tough to knock off balance and has a low centre of gravity. He has adapted smoothly to the more physical style of play in the NHL, and while he isn't very big, he will plow into heavy going for the puck.

THE INTANGIBLES

Over the past few seasons, Nikolishin lost valuable playing time due to injuries, and will miss the first half of this season with a knee injury suffered in the World Championships. He was a captain of Moscow Dynamo at age 21, and it wouldn't be a surprise to see him wearing a letter someday for an NHL team. He is very popular with his teammates, both for his personality and his work habits.

PROJECTION

Nikolishin is reaching an age where scorers hit their prime. This season won't be the breakthrough year for him because of the knee injury, but a good second half would set him up well for next year.

ADAM OATES

Yrs. of NHL service: 12
Born: Weston, Ont.; Aug. 27, 1962
Position: centre
Height: 5-11
Weight: 185
Uniform no.: 77
Shoots: right

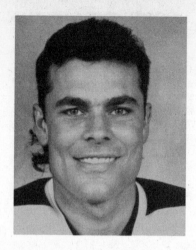

Career statistics:

GP	G	A	TP	PIM
826	258	738	996	263

1993-94 statistics:

GP	G	A	TP	+/-	PIM	PP	SH	GW	GT	S	PCT
77	32	80	112	+10	45	16	2	3	0	197	16.2

1994-95 statistics:

GP	G	A	TP	+/-	PIM	PP	SH	GW	GT	S	PCT
48	12	41	53	-11	8	4	1	2	0	109	11.0

1995-96 statistics:

GP	G	A	TP	+/-	PIM	PP	SH	GW	GT	S	PCT
70	25	67	92	+16	18	7	1	2	0	183	13.7

1996-97 statistics:

GP	G	A	TP	+/-	PIM	PP	SH	GW	GT	S	PCT
80	22	60	82	-5	14	3	2	5	0	160	13.8

LAST SEASON

Acquired from Boston with Bill Ranford and Rick Tocchet for Jim Carey, Anson Carter, Jason Allison, a third-round draft pick in 1997 and a conditional draft pick in 1998, March 1, 1997. Led team in assists and points. Tied for team lead in game-winning goals (four with Boston, one with Washington). Second on team in goals and shooting percentage.

THE FINESSE GAME

Oates remains one of the elite playmakers in the NHL. He uses a shorter-than-average stick and a minimal curve on his blade, the result being exceptional control of the puck. Although Oates is a right-handed shooter, his right wings (Brett Hull, Cam Neely) have always been his preferred receivers, which is good news for Peter Bondra. Oates can pass on the backhand, but also carries the puck deep, shields the puck with his body and turns to make the pass to his right wing.

Use of the backhand gives Oates a tremendous edge against all but the rangiest of NHL defensemen. He forces defenders to reach in and frequently draws penalties when he is hooked or tripped. If defenders don't harrass him, then Oates has carte blanche to work his passing magic.

He is less reluctant to shoot, though passing is still his first instinct. It doesn't matter how hard you shoot the puck when you have the jeweller's precision of Oates. Taking more shots makes him a less predictable player, since the defense can't back off and anticipate the pass. He is one of the best playmakers in the league because of his passing ability and his creativity. He is most effective down low where he can open up more ice, especially on the power play. He has outstanding timing and vision.

Yet, Oates isn't stubborn to a fault. He will also play a dump-and-chase game if he is being shadowed closely, throwing the puck smartly into the opposite corner with just the right velocity to allow his wingers to get in on top of the defense.

He is among the top five players in the league on face-offs, which makes him a natural on penalty killing, because a successful draw eats up 10 to 15 seconds on the clock, minimum.

THE PHYSICAL GAME

Oates is not a physical player but he doesn't avoid contact. He's smart enough at this stage of his career to avoid the garbage, he plays in traffic and he'll take a hit to make the play. He's an intense player and has a wiry strength, but tends to wear down late in the season as his line receives all the checking attention.

THE INTANGIBLES

Oats couldn't get the Caps into the playoffs, which was a disappointment for him as well as the club, but the team wasn't unhappy with his skill level. He's a legitimate superstar, like his former teammate Ray Bouque (Oates switched his number to 77 in honour of Bourque). Unlike Bourque, though, Oates may have a shot at a Stanley Cup before he's through.

PROJECTION

We told you in last year's *HSR* that Oates's demand for a contract renegotiation would be his ticket out of Boston. Washington hadn't settled on a new deal at press time, but Oates is the centrepiece of a team getting ready to move into a new building, so he'll get his dough. He could flirt with the 100-point mark again.

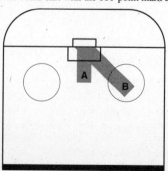

MICHAL PIVONKA

Yrs. of NHL service: 11
Born: Kladno, Czechoslovakia; Jan. 28, 1966
Position: centre
Height: 6-2
Weight: 195
Uniform no.: 20
Shoots: left

Career statistics:

GP	G	A	TP	PIM
756	193	406	599	446

1993-94 statistics:

GP	G	A	TP	+/-	PIM	PP	SH	GW	GT	S	PCT
82	14	36	50	+2	38	5	0	4	0	138	10.1

1994-95 statistics:

GP	G	A	TP	+/-	PIM	PP	SH	GW	GT	S	PCT
46	10	23	33	+3	50	4	2	2	0	80	12.5

1995-96 statistics:

GP	G	A	TP	+/-	PIM	PP	SH	GW	GT	S	PCT
73	16	65	81	+18	36	6	2	5	0	168	9.5

1996-97 statistics:

GP	G	A	TP	+/-	PIM	PP	SH	GW	GT	S	PCT
54	7	16	23	-15	22	2	0	1	0	83	8.4

PROJECTION

The acquisition of Oates will allow Pivonka more freedom, and his alliance with Bondra (assuming the Caps use another right wing with Oates) will result in 80 points in a big rebound season.

LAST SEASON

Missed 20 games with lateral meniscus tear in knee. Missed one game with concussion. Missed one game with flu. Worst plus-minus on team.

THE FINESSE GAME

Pivonka has marvellous skills. On the power play and in four-on-four situations, he takes full advantage of the extra ice. He skates well, with quickness and breakaway speed. He moves the puck quickly and jumps into the play for a give-and-go. His acceleration is outstanding.

He shoots well in stride (a trait of many Europeans), but he is too shy about shooting, usually looking to make the pass first. Since he is usually teamed with Peter Bondra, this works out just fine because Bondra reads well off Pivonka and he loves to shoot. Pivonka's stick is always on the ice. It's a small detail, but it allows him to pick up pucks that bounce off other players' sticks or skates.

Pivonka makes a lot of little dekes in tight, forcing a goalie to move his feet, then he finds the opening.

THE PHYSICAL GAME

Pivonka isn't aggressive enough to physically dominate a game, but when the style is a little more wide-open, he excels because of his elite skills. He is also less likely to be intimidated.

THE INTANGIBLES

Pivonka probably came back from his knee injury too soon, and since skating is such a huge part of his game, his entire season was affected.

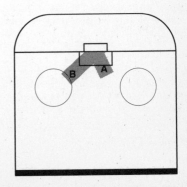

BILL RANFORD

Yrs. of NHL service: 11
Born: Brandon, Man.; Dec. 14, 1966
Position: goaltender
Height: 5-10
Weight: 170
Uniform no.: 30
Catches: left

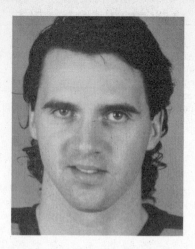

Career statistics:

GP	MIN	GA	SO	GAA	A	PIM
573	32156	1830	14	3.41	23	61

1993-94 statistics:

GP	MIN	GAA	W	L	T	SO	GA	S	SAPCT	PIM
71	4070	3.48	22	34	11	1	236	2325	.898	2

1994-95 statistics:

GP	MIN	GAA	W	L	T	SO	GA	S	SAPCT	PIM
40	2203	3.62	15	20	3	2	133	1134	.883	2

1995-96 statistics:

GP	MIN	GAA	W	L	T	SO	GA	S	SAPCT	PIM
77	4322	3.30	34	30	9	2	237	2054	.885	2

1996-97 statistics:

GP	MIN	GAA	W	L	T	SO	GA	S	SAPCT	PIM
55	3156	3.25	20	23	10	2	171	1514	.887	7

LAST SEASON

Acquired from Boston with Adam Oates and Rick Tocchet for Jim Carey, Anson Carter, Jason Allison, a third-round draft pick in 1997 and a conditional pick in 1998, March 1, 1997. Reached 20-win mark for sixth time in career. Missed 21 games with shoulder injury.

THE PHYSICAL GAME

Ranford is a shining example of a goalie who made it to the NHL on his reflexes and continues there because he added elements of angle play and focus. He comes out of his net and, when he is on his game, he doesn't leave a lot of rebounds. The athletic Ranford is notable for his great first-save capability. He is probably among the top five goalies in the league in that regard.

Ranford hardly ever commits before the shooter does. He has good lateral movement and great confidence in his skating. He moves with the shooter well, keeping the five-hole closed. He doesn't drop down unless he has to; when he does, he bounces back up quickly. He uses his stick aggressively around the net to break up passes. He also stops hard-arounds and whips passes out to his teammates.

Ranford will have to be more patient and relaxed in the nets for Washington, where he will get better defensive support than he's been used to in recent seasons. He won't have to worry as much about second shots.

THE MENTAL GAME

Ranford is a great competitor who will benefit from a little stability, and can be rated among the top 10 goalies in the league even though his numbers wouldn't support that. He has won a Conn Smythe and a Canada Cup, so he should enjoy playing in meaningful games again.

THE INTANGIBLES

Ranford had to adjust to yet another team, and another style. He went from a Bruins team that allows a lot of shots (he faced 1,102 in 37 games) to a more defense-minded Caps team (412 shots in 18 games). But the biggest change will be the off-season surgery that removed a cyst from his shoulder and was the source of his problems last season.

PROJECTION

We've felt for years that Ranford's goaltending was compromised by playing on weaker teams in Edmonton and Boston. Washington will be among the more competitive teams in the East this season, and it will be interesting to see if Ranford still has what it takes.

CHRIS SIMON

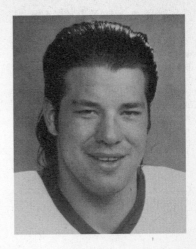

Yrs. of NHL service: 4
Born: Wawa, Ont.; Jan. 30, 1972
Position: left wing
Height: 6-3
Weight: 219
Uniform no.: 17
Shoots: left

Career statistics:

GP	G	A	TP	PIM
188	33	45	78	720

1993-94 statistics:

GP	G	A	TP	+/-	PIM	PP	SH	GW	GT	S	PCT
37	4	4	8	-2	132	0	0	1	0	39	10.3

1994-95 statistics:

GP	G	A	TP	+/-	PIM	PP	SH	GW	GT	S	PCT
29	3	9	12	+14	106	0	0	0	0	33	9.1

1995-96 statistics:

GP	G	A	TP	+/-	PIM	PP	SH	GW	GT	S	PCT
64	16	18	34	+10	250	4	0	1	0	105	15.2

1996-97 statistics:

GP	G	A	TP	+/-	PIM	PP	SH	GW	GT	S	PCT
42	9	13	22	-1	165	3	0	1	0	89	10.1

LAST SEASON

Acquired from Colorado with Curtis Leschyshyn for Keith Jones, November 2, 1996. Second on team in penalty minutes. Missed start of season in contract dispute. Missed 18 games with back injuries. Missed two games with arm injury.

THE FINESSE GAME

Simon enjoyed such a berserk scoring rush in his first six weeks with the Caps that the rest of his season looked like a huge downer by comparison. In many ways, Simon is the prototypical NHL fourth-line winger. He has made his reputation with his toughness, but has shown an added dimension in his ability to make plays that result in points. Whenever he does, jaws drop and observers wonder, "Where did that move came from?" They shouldn't be so dumbfounded. After all, Simon gets a lot of room, which gives a player with modest skills more time to make a play.

With Washington, Simon started to get the kind of ice time he wasn't used to seeing in Colorado, and until a recurrence of his back injury he was on his way to a career year.

Simon has decent hands for a big guy, but all of his successes come in tight. Lack of quickness is a major drawback. If he gets a regular shift, he will answer the questions about his consistency and might produce some surprising numbers, but there are a couple of steps he has to take to reach that level.

THE PHYSICAL GAME

Simon is as tough as they come and has a wide streak of mean. He has already established himself as a player who can throw them when the time comes, and opponents have to keep a wary eye on him because they never know when he's going to snap.

THE INTANGIBLES

The commitment that Simon makes off the ice will tell the difference this season. He planned on working with a back specialist (the same one who has helped Rick Tocchet) during the off-season and may come into training camp in the best shape of his life.

PROJECTION

Simon scored 22 points in just a half-season. Now that he has some confidence, 20 goals and 40 points may be in his range. Few NHL players will be able to combine that kind of production with his brand of toughness.

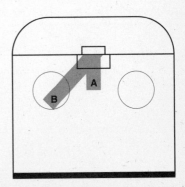

JAROSLAV SVEJKOVSKY

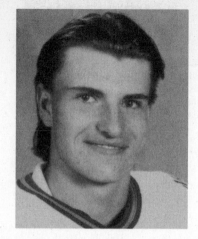

Yrs. of NHL service: 0
Born: Plzen, Czech Republic; Oct. 1, 1976
Position: left wing
Height: 5-11
Weight: 185
Uniform no.: 34
Shoots: right

Career statistics:

GP	G	A	TP	PIM
19	7	3	10	4

1996-97 statistics:

GP	G	A	TP	+/-	PIM	PP	SH	GW	GT	S	PCT
19	7	3	10	-1	4	2	0	1	0	30	23.3

LAST SEASON

Will be entering first NHL season. Second in scoring for Portland (AHL) with 38-28 — 56 in 54 games.

THE FINESSE GAME

Svejkovsky made a dazzling impression in his 19-game stint with the Caps, closing out his season with a four-goal game against Buffalo. That's what he does best. He is a pure goal scorer. He will work to get himself in high-percentage zones and is astoundingly accurate with his shot. He has great hands for tipping pucks.

He is a good skater without real breakout speed, but he has a nose for the net and he pays the price. He wants the puck and knows what to do with it. He is a threat every time he's near the puck.

Svejkovsky is hardly a defensive specialist, but he was the leading plus-minus player for Portland so his game is fairly well developed.

THE PHYSICAL GAME

Svejkovsky is not overly aggressive but he will take hits to make plays. He is an average-sized player and needs to get bigger. He's tenacious and will take a cross-check or a slash to score goals.

Svejkovsky has had a year in junior (Tri-City, WHL) and a year in the minors to acclimate himself to North American life. He seems ready to make the jump and will likely play on one of the Capitals' top two lines.

PROJECTION

If Svejkovsky gets some decent ice time, he could score 20 to 25 goals in his rookie year.

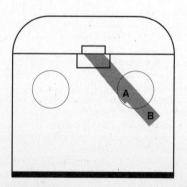

MARK TINORDI

Yrs. of NHL service: 9
Born: Deer River, Alta.; May 9, 1966
Position: left defense
Height: 6-4
Weight: 213
Uniform no.: 24
Shoots: left

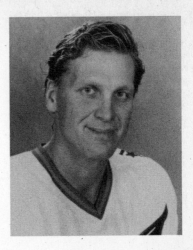

Career statistics:

GP	G	A	TP	PIM
568	44	133	177	1367

1993-94 statistics:

GP	G	A	TP	+/-	PIM	PP	SH	GW	GT	S	PCT
61	6	18	24	+6	143	1	0	0	0	112	5.4

1994-95 statistics:

GP	G	A	TP	+/-	PIM	PP	SH	GW	GT	S	PCT
42	3	9	12	-5	71	2	0	1	0	71	4.2

1995-96 statistics:

GP	G	A	TP	+/-	PIM	PP	SH	GW	GT	S	PCT
71	3	10	13	+26	113	2	0	0	0	82	3.7

1996-97 statistics:

GP	G	A	TP	+/-	PIM	PP	SH	GW	GT	S	PCT
56	2	6	8	+3	118	0	0	1	0	53	3.8

LAST SEASON

Missed 20 games with ankle injury. Missed five games with hip flexor. Missed one game with flu.

THE FINESSE GAME

Tinordi can play both sides and with any partner. He can be the point man on the power play and he can kill penalties. You can use him in the first minute and in the last minute, when you're trying to protect a lead.

Tinordi doesn't have much in the way of finesse skills, but, oh, how he loves to go to the net. He starts out at the point on the power play but doesn't hesitate to crash down low. He is an impact player and a major force on the ice.

Tinordi has an effective point shot: low, hard and accurate. He also sees the play well and moves his passes crisply. He intimidates when he moves low and bulls his way to the net. He is poised with the puck and will use a wrist shot in deep.

An above-average skater, Tinordi is mobile for his large size. He lacks one-step quickness, but once in gear he has a long stride with good balance and mobility. He can use his long reach well around the net or to take the puck away from a defender. He is a strong penalty killer with good hockey sense.

THE PHYSICAL GAME

It's impossible to discuss Tinordi's game without making reference to the injuries that hit him every season. Tinordi plays with the throttle wide open and doesn't recognize any other playing style. One of the reasons why he is so susceptible to getting hurt is that he is more concerned with making the play than with protecting himself, and he ends up in vulnerable situa-

tions. A little less reckless abandon would help keep him in one piece, but we're not sure if Tinordi knows how to play that way. He usually ends up missing a big chunk of playing time each season with some serious ailment.

As honest and tough as they come, Tinordi commands respect on the ice. He has too short a fuse, though in recent years he has done a better job of curbing his temper, realizing he is more important to his team on the ice than in the penalty box. He is competitive and fearless.

THE INTANGIBLES

Tinordi has to work to improve his strength and conditioning, which might help him avoid some of the devastating injuries that come his way every year. He plays a lot on heart. He can extend his career if he plays on more muscle.

PROJECTION

Tinordi could score 25 goals and have a great season, or five goals and still have a great season. He's that useful in that many ways. He is a crunch-time player. Too bad he's the one who so often ends up crunched.

ALEXANDRE VOLCHKOV

Yrs. of NHL service: 0
Born: Moscow, Russia; Sept. 25, 1977
Position: right wing
Height: 6-1
Weight: 194
Uniform no.: n.a.
Shoots: left

Career junior statistics:

GP	G	A	TP	PIM
103	66	80	146	112

1995-96 junior statistics:

GP	G	A	TP	PIM
47	37	27	64	36

1996-97 statistics:

GP	G	A	TP	PIM
56	29	53	82	76

LAST SEASON

Will be entering first NHL season. Third on team in scoring for Barrie (OHL) with 29-53 — 82 in 56 games. Tied for team lead in OHL playoff scoring with 6-9 — 15 in nine games.

THE FINESSE GAME

Volchkov can play all three forward positions with equal skill, and as a left-handed shooter, he could help the Capitals at their weakest position, left wing. He is the kind of player who wants to be on the ice when the game is at a critical juncture; he has the skill to have a say in the outcome.

Volchkov dominated games at the junior level. He is aggressive and confident. He prefers to do the scoring himself, and has a long reach that frustrates defenders. He has very strong hands and wrists for shots in tight and on the backhand.

He is also an intelligent playmaker but is a little bit selfish with the puck, unlike many Russian players. He can kill penalties or work on the power play. Volchkov is a sound skater with mobility, quickness and speed.

Volchkov developed into a more complete two-way player last year, working on his defense and improving his plus-minus by about 30.

THE PHYSICAL GAME

Volchkov is a burly sort who will battle for the puck in the high-traffic areas around the net. He has the strength to bowl people over but isn't a mean hitter. He will absorb a lot of abuse to protect the puck and has a long fuse. Plenty of players will try to intimidate him in his first NHL season, but it's not likely he will be scared off on those nights when he's in the mood to play. Physically, he appears to be ready to compete at the NHL level.

THE INTANGIBLES

Volchkov was considered to be the most NHL-ready of the 1996 draft crop (no one from that draft became an NHL regular last year). He may also prove to be the least predictable of the top dozen choices. Islanders GM Mike Milbury, who bypassed Volchkov in favour of Jean-Pierre Dumont, called the Russian winger, "A wild card. He's a potential 50-goal scorer with a potentially fatal flaw." That flaw is Volchkov's inconsistency.

Scouts liked the fact that Volchkov left Russia to play the last two seasons in the OHL, because that gave him a year to acclimate himself to North American life. His father, Alexander, played for the Soviet Union in the 1972 Summit Series, so Volchkov has the right bloodline.

PROJECTION

Training camp in 1996 was a bit of a shock for Volchkov when he realized how difficult it was to compete at such a high level. The Caps need some size up front, so he will get a shot at a job.

BRENDAN WITT

Yrs. of NHL service: 2
Born: Humboldt, Sask.; Feb. 20, 1975
Position: left defense
Height: 6-1
Weight: 205
Uniform no.: 19
Shoots: left

Career statistics:

GP	G	A	TP	PIM
92	5	5	10	173

1995-96 statistics:

GP	G	A	TP	+/-	PIM	PP	SH	GW	GT	S	PCT
48	2	3	5	-4	85	0	0	1	0	44	4.5

1996-97 statistics:

GP	G	A	TP	+/-	PIM	PP	SH	GW	GT	S	PCT
44	3	2	5	-20	88	0	0	0	0	41	7.3

LAST SEASON

Missed five games with flu. Scored 2-4 — 6 with 56 penalty minutes in 30 games with Portland (AHL).

THE FINESSE GAME

Witt's skill level is very high and he applies his abilities in his own zone. His skating is capable, though he needs to improve his agility and his turning and passing are a little raw. Still, he does not overhandle the puck and by making simple plays he keeps himself out of serious trouble. He skates well backwards and has decent lateral mobility.

Witt gets involved somewhat in the attack, but the extent of his contribution is a hard point shot. He won't gamble low and can't run a power play. He won't ever be an offensive force.

Most of the problems Witt ran into last season stemmed from nervousness and a lack of experience. He can improve greatly with more games under his belt. Over the past few years (he skipped an entire year of junior, and missed most of 1995-96 with a broken wrist), he hasn't played much hockey.

THE PHYSICAL GAME

Witt has a strong physical presence on the ice but he needs to get even stronger. He was beaten by some players in one-on-one battles against bigger players, and a defensive defenseman can't allow that to happen. He blocks shots fearlessly and is naturally aggressive and intimidating.

THE INTANGIBLES

Witt had a poor start to the season and was sent to the minors. Most of his bad habits were ironed out there, and he developed better timing and confidence. He had some big fights down the stretch.

PROJECTION

Witt needs to take a big step this year to become an NHL regular. He won't score many points even if he makes the grade. The Caps consider him a potential Rod Langway.

PLAYER INDEX

Adams, Greg............................127
Albelin, Tommy 55
Alfredsson, Dan......................283
Amonte, Tony..........................89
Andersson, Niklas 248
Andreychuk, Dave..................232
Arnott, Jason..........................162
Aucoin, Adrian 422
Audette, Donald 38

Baker, Jamie 403
Barnaby, Matthew 39
Barnes, Stu 340
Baron, Murray 322
Barrasso, Tom 341
Bassen, Bob............................128
Belanger, Ken........................249
Belfour, Ed............................129
Bellows, Brian..........................4
Berard, Bryan 250
Berezin, Sergei 404
Berg, Aki-Petteri 195
Bertuzzi, Todd......................251
Beukeboom, Jeff....................265
Blake, Rob..............................196
Bodger, Doug 355
Bohonos, Lonny 423
Bondra, Peter..........................439
Bonk, Radek..........................284
Bourque, Ray............................21
Brashear, Donald....................424
Brind'Amour, Rod 302
Brisebois, Patrice..................214
Brodeur, Martin......................233
Brown, Doug 144
Brown, Jeff..............................72
Brunet, Benoit 215
Buchberger, Kelly 163
Bure, Pavel 425

Bure, Valeri 216
Burke, Sean 73
Burr, Shawn 356
Burt, Adam 74
Bylsma, Dan 197

Cairns, Eric 266
Campbell, Jim 371
Carey, Jim................................22
Carney, Keith 90
Carter, Anson 23
Cassels, Andrew 75
Chambers, Shawn 130
Chelios, Chris 91
Chiasson, Steve 76
Chorske, Tom 285
Ciccarelli, Dino 389
Ciccone, Enrico 77
Clark, Wendel........................405
Coffey, Paul............................303
Conroy, Craig 372
Corbet, Rene 108
Corkum, Bob 323
Corson, Shayne 217
Cote, Sylvain 440
Courtnall, Geoff 373
Courtnall, Russ 267
Craig, Mike............................406
Craven, Murray 92
Cross, Cory............................390
Cunneyworth, Randy..............286
Czerkawski, Mariusz..............164

Dackell, Andreas 287
Dahlen, Ulf..............................93
Daigle, Alexandre..................288
Damphousse, Vincent.............218
Daneyko, Ken 234
Dawe, Jason............................40

Daze, Eric................................94
Deadmarsh, Adam..................109
Demitra, Pavol........................374
Desjardins, Eric 304
Doan, Shane 324
Doig, Jason 325
Dollas, Bobby............................5
Domenichelli, Hnat 56
Domi, Tie 407
Donato, Ted..............................24
Donovan, Shean 357
Drake, Dallas..........................326
Draper, Kris............................145
Driver, Bruce..........................268
Drury, Ted................................6
Duchesne, Steve......................289
Dvorak, Radek........................176
Dykhuis, Karl..........................305

Eagles, Mike............................441
Eastwood, Mike......................269
Ellett, Dave..............................25
Emerson, Nelson 78
Eriksson, Anders 146

Falloon, Pat 306
Fedorov, Sergei 147
Ferraro, Ray............................198
Fitzgerald, Tom 177
Fitzpatrick, Rory....................375
Fleury, Theoren 57
Foote, Adam 110
Forsberg, Peter 111
Francis, Ron 342
Friesen, Jeff............................358
Fuhr, Grant............................376

Gagner, Dave..........................178
Galley, Garry..........................199

Gardiner, Bruce 290
Garpenlov, Johan......................179
Gartner, Mike 327
Gavey, Aaron 58
Gelinas, Martin.......................426
Gilchrist, Brent 148
Gill, Todd 359
Gilmour, Doug 235
Gonchar, Sergei 442
Gratton, Chris 391
Graves, Adam..........................270
Green, Travis 252
Gretzky, Wayne.......................271
Grier, Mike 165
Gronman, Tuomas.....................95
Grosek, Michal.........................41
Guerin, Bill.............................236

Hackett, Jeff 96
Hamrlik, Roman 392
Harvey, Todd...........................131
Hasek, Dominik.........................42
Hatcher, Derian 132
Hatcher, Kevin 343
Hebert, Guy 7
Hedican, Bret..........................427
Heinze, Steve............................26
Hendrickson, Darby 408
Hextall, Ron 307
Hicks, Alex.............................344
Hill, Sean 291
Hlushko, Todd 59
Hoglund, Jonas 60
Hogue, Benoit..........................133
Holik, Bobby 237
Holzinger, Brian 43
Houlder, Bill...........................360
Housley, Phil 443
Hrudey, Kelly 361
Hull, Brett...............................377
Hull, Jody 180
Hulse, Cale 61
Hunter, Dale 444

Iafrate, Al 362
Iginla, Jarome 62

Jagr, Jaromir 345
Janney, Craig...........................328
Johansson, Calle 445
Johnson, Mike 409
Jones, Keith 112
Jonsson, Kenny.......................253
Joseph, Curtis 166
Jovanovski, Ed 181
Juneau, Joe 446

Kamensky, Valeri....................113
Kapanen, Sami 79
Kariya, Paul 8
Karpa, Dave 9
Karpov, Valeri..........................10
Karpovtsev, Alexander.............272
Kasparaitis, Darius 346
Keane, Mike 273
Khabibulin, Nikolai.................329
Khristich, Dimitri 200
Kidd, Trevor 63
Kilger, Chad 330
King, Derek 410
King, Kris 411
Klatt, Trent 308
Klemm, Jon 114
Koivu, Saku 219
Konowalchuk, Steve................447
Kovalenko, Andrei 167
Kovalev, Alexei.......................274
Kozlov, Viktor.........................363
Kozlov, Vyacheslav 149
Kravchuk, Igor 378
Krivokrasov, Sergei...................97
Kron, Robert............................80
Krupp, Uwe 115
Kurri, Jari 116

Lachance, Scott 254
Lacroix, Eric............................117
Laflamme, Christian..................98
LaFontaine, Pat.........................44
Langenbrunner, Jamie 134
Langkow, Daymond 393
Laperriere, Ian 201
Lapointe, Claude 255
Lapointe, Martin 150
Larionov, Igor 151
Laus, Paul 182
LeClair, John 309
Leclerc, Mike 11
Leetch, Brian 275
Lefebvre, Sylvain 118
Lehtinen, Jere 135
Lemieux, Claude 119
Leschyshyn, Curtis 81
Lidstrom, Nicklas 152
Linden, Trevor.........................428
Lindgren, Mats 168
Lindros, Eric 310
Lindsay, Bill 183
Lowry, Dave 184
Lumme, Jyrki 429

MacInnis, Al...........................379
MacLean, John 238

Malakhov, Vladimir 220
Malik, Marek............................82
Maltby, Kirk 153
Manson, Dave..........................221
Marchant, Todd 169
Marchment, Bryan...................170
Matteau, Stephane 380
Matvichuk, Richard................136
May, Brad.................................45
McCabe, Bryan........................256
McCarthy, Sandy.......................64
McCarty, Darren 154
McCauley, Alyn 412
McCleary, Trent 27
McEachern, Shawn..................292
McGillis, Daniel 171
McInnis, Marty..........................65
McKay, Randy 239
McKee, Jay...............................46
McKenna, Steve 202
McLaren, Kyle 28
McLean, Kirk 430
McSorley, Marty 364
Mellanby, Scott 185
Messier, Mark..........................431
Miller, Kelly 448
Miller, Kevin 99
Mironov, Boris 172
Mironov, Dmitri 12
Modano, Mike 137
Modin, Fredrik 413
Moger, Sandy 29
Mogilny, Alexander 432
Moreau, Ethan 100
Muller, Kirk 186
Murphy, Gord 187
Murphy, Joe 381
Murphy, Larry 155
Murray, Glen 203

Naslund, Markus 433
Nazarov, Andrei 365
Neckar, Stanislav.....................293
Nedved, Petr 347
Nemchinov, Sergei 257
Niedermayer, Rob 188
Niedermayer, Scott..................240
Nieuwendyk, Joe 138
Niinimaa, Janne 311
Nikolishin, Andrei 449
Nolan, Owen 366
Noonan, Brian 434
Norstrom, Mattias....................204
Norton, Jeff.............................394
Numminen, Teppo...................331
Nylander, Michael.....................66

O'Donnell, Sean 205
O'Neill, Jeff 83
Oates, Adam 450
Odelein, Lyle 241
Odgers, Jeff 30
Odjick, Gino 435
Ohlund, Mattias 436
Oksiuta, Roman 348
Olausson, Fredrik 349
Olczyk, Ed 350
Osgood, Chris 156
Otto, Joel 312
Ozolinsh, Sandis 120

Palffy, Zigmund 258
Peca, Mike 47
Pederson, Denis 242
Pellerin, Scott 382
Peluso, Mike 276
Phillips, Chris 294
Pivonka, Michal 451
Plante, Dan 259
Plante, Derek 48
Podein, Shjon 313
Potvin, Felix 414
Poulin, Patrick 395
Primeau, Keith 84
Probert, Bob 101
Pronger, Chris 383
Pronger, Sean 13
Prospal, Vaclav 314
Puppa, Daren 396

Quint, Deron 332
Quintal, Stephane 222

Ragnarsson, Marcus 367
Ranford, Bill 452
Rathje, Mike 368
Ray, Rob 49
Recchi, Mark 223
Redden, Wade 295
Reichel, Robert 260
Reid, Dave 139
Renberg, Mikael 315
Rhodes, Damian 296
Ricci, Mike 121
Rice, Steven 85
Richardson, Luke 316
Richer, Stephane 224
Richter, Mike 277
Rivers, Jamie 384
Roberts, David 437
Robitaille, Luc 278
Roenick, Jeremy 333
Rohloff, Jon 31

Rolston, Brian 243
Ronning, Cliff 334
Roy, Patrick 122
Rucchin, Steve 14
Rucinsky, Martin 225

Sacco, Joe 15
Sakic, Joe 123
Salei, Ruslan 16
Salo, Tommy 261
Samuelsson, Kjell 317
Samuelsson, Ulf 279
Sanderson, Geoff 86
Sandstrom, Tomas 157
Satan, Miroslav 50
Savage, Brian 226
Schneider, Mathieu 415
Selanne, Teemu 17
Selivanov, Alexander 397
Shanahan, Brendan 158
Shannon, Darrin 335
Shantz, Jeff 102
Sheppard, Ray 189
Shevalier, Jeff 206
Simon, Chris 453
Simpson, Todd 67
Skrudland, Brian 280
Smehlik, Richard 51
Smith, Jason 416
Smolinski, Bryan 262
Smyth, Ryan 173
Stern, Ron 68
Stevens, Kevin 207
Stevens, Scott 244
Stevenson, Turner 227
Stillman, Cory 69
Storr, Jamie 208
Straka, Martin 190
Stumpel, Jozef 32
Sullivan, Mike 33
Sullivan, Steve 417
Sundin, Mats 418
Sundstrom, Niklas 281
Suter, Gary 103
Svehla, Robert 191
Svejkovsky, Jaroslav 454
Svoboda, Petr 318
Sweeney, Don 34
Sydor, Darryl 140
Sykora, Michal 104
Sykora, Petr 245

Tamer, Chris 351
Therien, Chris 319
Thibault, Jocelyn 228
Thomas, Steve 246

Thornton, Joe 35
Thornton, Scott 229
Tinordi, Mark 455
Titov, German 70
Tkachuk, Keith 336
Tocchet, Rick 337
Trebil, Daniel 18
Tsyplakov, Vladimir 209
Turcotte, Darren 385
Turgeon, Pierre 386
Tverdovsky, Oleg 338

Ulanov, Igor 398

Valk, Garry 352
Van Allen, Shaun 297
Vanbiesbrouck, John 192
Van Impe, Darren 19
Vaske, Dennis 263
Verbeek, Pat 141
Volchkov, Alexandre 456
Vopat, Roman 210

Ward, Aaron 159
Warrener, Rhett 193
Warriner, Todd 419
Weight, Doug 174
Weinrich, Eric 105
Wesley, Glen 87
Wiemer, Jason 399
Wilkie, David 230
Wilkinson, Neil 353
Wilson, Landon 36
Wilson, Mike 52
Witt, Brendan 457

Yachmenev, Vitali 211
Yashin, Alexei 298
Yelle, Stephane 124
York, Harry 387
York, Jason 299
Young, Scott 125
Ysebaert, Paul 400
Yushkevich, Dimitri 420
Yzerman, Steve 160

Zamuner, Rob 401
Zhamnov, Alexei 106
Zhitnik, Alexei 53
Zholtok, Sergei 300
Zmolek, Doug 212
Zubov, Sergei 142
Zubrus, Dainius 320
Zyuzin, Andrei 369